EUROPEAN STUDIES SERIES

General Editors   Colin Jones
                Richard Overy
Series Advisers   Joe Bergin
                John Breuilly

This series marks a major initiative in European history publishing aimed primarily, though not exclusively, at an undergraduate audience. It will encompass a wide variety of books on aspects of European history since 1500, with particular emphasis on France and Germany, although no country will be excluded and a special effort will be made to cover previously neglected areas, such as Scandinavia, Eastern Europe and Southern Europe.

The series will include political accounts and broad thematic treatments, both of a comparative kind and studies of a single country, and will lay particular emphasis on social and cultural history where this opens up fruitful new ways of examining the past. The aim of the series is to make available a wide range of titles in areas where there is now an obvious gap or where the existing historical literature is out of date or narrowly focused. The series will also include translations of important books published elsewhere in Europe.

Interest in European affairs and history has never been greater; *European Studies* will help make that European heritage closer, richer and more comprehensible.

EUROPEAN STUDIES SERIES

General Editors: Colin Jones and Richard Overy
Advisory Editors: Joe Bergin and John Breuilly

Published

Religion and Revolution in France, 1780–1804

NIGEL ASTON

First published 2000 by
MACMILLAN PRESS LTD
Houndmills, Basingstoke, Hampshire RG21 6XS
and London
Companies and representatives
throughout the world

ISBN 0–333–58325–6 hardcover
ISBN 0–333–58326–4 paperback

A catalogue record for this book is available
from the British Library.

This book is printed on paper suitable for recycling and
made from fully managed and sustained forest sources.

10   9   8   7   6   5   4   3   2   1
09   08   07   06   05   04   03   02   01   00

Typeset in Great Britain by Aarontype Limited, Easton, Bristol

Printed in China

Contents

List of Maps

Acknowledgements

The author and publishers would like to thank the following for permission to use copyright material:

Oxford University Press for the map of the bishoprics in France, 1789 (pp. 18–19) from *The End of an Elite: The French Bishops and the Coming of the French Revolution, 1786–1790* by Nigel Aston, 1992.

Blackwell Publishers and Ohio State University Press for the maps of numbers of married priests in France (p. 259) and abdicating priests in France (p. 261) from *The Revolution Against the Church: From Reason to the Supreme Being* by Michael Vovelle, 1991.

Princeton University Press for the map of the percentage of jurors by district, Spring–Summer 1791 (p. 211) from *Religion, Revolution and Regional Culture in Eighteenth-Century France* by Timothy Tackett, 1986.

For Jack McManners

Preface

This book has been shaped by the rich and varied scholarship of the last thirty years on the religious history of eighteenth-century Europe and France in particular, not least from its dedicatee. A decade on from the *bicentennaire*, the quality and range of writing on the revolutionary period remains high and the debates as intense as ever; judging by very recent work on Napoleon and his rule, the next few years seem certain to reinvigorate our understanding of the post-1799 era, and the two-hundredth anniversary of the Concordat can be expected to lead to fresh perspectives on that vital event in the formation of modern France.

However, one of the pleasures of writing this book has been the scholarly comradeship it has afforded me. First and foremost stands my debt to Malcolm Crook who has cajoled and encouraged me at every stage, unstintingly passed on the insights of his own research and then performed the thankless task of reading through an early draft chapter by chapter. Colin Jones followed him in going over the entire text, and Jack McManners has also read most of the book in its early stages. I only hope they think the final version has sufficiently registered their constructive comments and suggestions. At the publishers, Vanessa Graham, Simon Winder, Jonathan Reeve, and latterly, Terka Bagley, have been patience itself waiting for the manuscript to arrive. At home, Caroline Aston has patiently put up with my absence upstairs without complaining and, as always, has unknotted some of my most egregious prose lapses; at Luton, several colleagues have patiently allowed me to test out ideas on them and draw on their own expertise, notably Ian Beckett and Larry Butler. Joe Bergin, Jeremy Black, Rodney Dean, Graham Gargett, the late Ralph Gibson, Frances Malino, David Sturdy and Frank Tallett have also read over and improved earlier drafts. I have also benefitted at a late stage from the comments of an anonymous reader for the Catholic University Press of America. I am immensely grateful to them all, and to the British Academy and the staff development fund at Luton for financial assistance towards the research costs of this book. The deficiencies that remain are, of course, firmly my own responsibility.

Introduction

While much has been written about the involvement of the nobility
and the 'middling sort' in the French Revolution, most students of
the subject are less familiar with the place of the clergy and religion
generally in those momentous events. This book aims to correct that
omission by offering an introduction to the history of France
between the reigns of Louis XVI and Napoleon I, one that restores
religious issues to the centre of discussion – exactly where they
belong. In the three decades that ended with Napoleon's coronation
in Notre-Dame Cathedral in 1804, every aspect of the customary
religious life of France was subject to relentless change on a scale
that contributed to and fed on the vivid millenarian currents that
were such a feature of the climate of opinion in France and other
European states in the 1790s as experience of war and revolution
tempered Enlightenment optimism. No one was immune from these
alterations, man or woman, soldier or civilian, Jacobin or royalist,
layman or cleric. For many people, the choice lay between allegiance
to the Revolution or to Christianity and perhaps, on either count,
death as a result of principle; most Frenchmen lost the public services
of an ordained ministry for the first time since the conversion of the
Franks in the sixth century A.D., and women took the lead in keeping
Christianity alive when it was driven underground and persecuted
during the two 'reigns of Terror', those of 1792–4 and 1797–8.

The Revolution had ended the exclusive privileges of the Roman
Catholic Church in the Bourbon monarchy and, temporarily, over-
threw both 'throne' and 'altar'. When they returned, in 1814–15, it
was to a State–Church arrangement that was less of a partnership
than a subordinate relationship; throughout the nineteenth century
the Catholic Church neither expected nor sought much from a state
that was at best disinterested, at worst openly hostile to its pretensions. Faith was moving slowly but irrevocably from the public
sphere to the private, and, in facilitating that transformation, the
French Revolution played a key part in creating and defining
the dynamics of modern religious culture.

The Revolution affected not just Catholic beliefs, practices and structures, but the Protestant Churches (granted limited official toleration in 1787) and the French Jewish communities too. These religious minorities receive full coverage, since any account of France in the 1780s and 1790s that excludes them can have only limited usefulness. But the events of 1789–1804 cannot be understood without reference to the *status quo* before the Revolution, and the first four chapters offer surveys of the organisation and personnel of the Gallican Church, the religious life of the laity, the place of Huguenots and Jews in French religious life, and the impact of the Enlightenment. What strikes most historians writing today is the resilience rather than the weakness of religion in eighteenth-century France. If the Gallican Church was much spoken against, it was also much loved, and criticism originated in concern far more than dislike. Modern scholars would also prefer to see the mid-eighteenth century not as the beginning of modern unbelief but instead as the termination of a long Counter-Reformation in which the Gallican Church at last drew breath from its work of inculcating the faith of the Tridentine Fathers. This was less pastoral enervation than a token of a goal achieved.

On the eve of the Revolution, France remained overwhelmingly a country in which Catholic Christianity, despite its internal stresses and its detractors among the *philosophes*, was both preached and practised. Revolutionary propagandists liked to depict the Roman Catholic Church in eighteenth century France as a top-heavy organisation in which the ordinary parish clergy bore the brunt of the work and were crushed by the burden of the clerical elite – bishops, *abbés*, cathedral canons and monks. It might make a graphic illustration, but it seriously distorts the real picture. The contrast between the income of lower clergy and the corporate wealth of the French Church was striking, if hardly untypical of Churches across Europe. Such discrepancies were everywhere part of the social fabric, and few entertained thoughts of eradicating them before the Revolutionaries attempted as much during the first, heady years of Revolution when consensus politics still prevailed in France.

Chapters 5 to 7 look at the involvement of the Churches in the reform politics of 1789–91, from the summoning of the Estates-General and the 'Fronde of the *curés*' leading down to the momentous passing of the Civil Constitution of the Clergy and its imposition by oath in the winter of 1790–1. The Church was forthwith required to decide whether or not to align itself with the broadly progressive forces directing the Revolution: suddenly discountenanced by the state over the one issue of the Civil Constitution, even moderates among the refractory clergy needed little incentive to discover the virtues of Counter-Revolution, especially after the papal condemnation of the new settlement and the patent discomfort and embarrassment of Louis XVI at being a party to its passing. France was in schism, and the divisions among Christians weakened their influence over politicians whose sympathies for churchmen of any stamp were minimal.

The confessional state had ended; the monarchy followed in 1792, and was replaced by a republic that actively sponsored alternative beliefs to Christianity and Judaism. In Part III the book looks at dechristianisation and the new cults of the 1790s, and examines their impact on French religious life over both the short and medium terms. It also considers how far the mainstream religious organisations coped with state hostility or indifference, and there is particular emphasis on covering the neglected role of the constitutional Church and its leader, Bishop Henri Grégoire. The religious policies of the Directory (1795–9) and the Consulate (1799–1804) are given full coverage in Part IV, with discussion of the negotiations leading up to the Concordat and Organic Articles placing them in their national and international context. The book concludes with a survey of the religious state of France in the early nineteenth century that ties together the recent experience of the Churches with future developments. At every point, *Religion and Revolution in France 1780–1804* aims to assess the success of adapting from privilege to persecution, to consider whether the Revolution merely hastened a decline in Catholicism that had been under way since at least the mid-eighteenth century, and to see how far the expectations of minorities were realised by the Revolution. It argues that the break between the Revolution and Christianity – especially the Catholic Church – was essentially contingent, unintelligible without reference to the specific events and vicissitudes of the Revolution itself. Set within the wider European context, the book emphasises the Churches' capacity for survival, the role of religion in determining political allegiances during the Revolution, the capacity of laymen and women to manage without the services of an ordained ministry, and the turbulence of Church–State relations.

Part I Ancien Régime Religion

1 The Gallican Church: Structures and Personnel

The Roman Catholic Church in France before the Revolution was the most powerful organisation inside the kingdom, with a physical presence to match. Its landed wealth accumulated over centuries enabled the Church to maintain the fabric of innumerable consecrated buildings. The medieval inheritance of cathedrals, great abbeys and convents still dominated the French landscape to underline the institutional supremacy of the First Estate. Despite the unfashionability of Gothic styles for much of the eighteenth century, these edifices remained mostly in good order. The nearer the Gothic approximated to the classical, the more highly it was approved; thus the great theorist of neo-classicism in France, that apostle of architectural primitivism, the Abbé Laugier, singled out Saint-Germain-l'Auxerrois in Paris for praise in his *Observations sur l'architecture* of 1765 for the way 'the Gothic pillars metamorphosed into fluted columns made a grand and agreeable impact'.[1]

Such ideals inspired the design of the numerous new churches commissioned at this time, including work for the religious orders during Louis XV's reign characterised by an elegance and a nobility of style some critics thought more suitable for palaces than places of retreat.[2] Parisians in the 1780s could watch the construction of the church of the Madeleine (started 1764) or, on the other side of the river Seine, Soufflot's masterpiece of Sainte-Geneviève which the Revolution would turn into the Panthéon, the final resting place of national worthies like Voltaire, Rousseau and Mirabeau. It was, reported one young English visitor in 1788, 'the most like of an ancient temple I ever saw ... & it is not yet finished'.[3] Classical rebuilding also occurred in the cathedrals of the French heartlands like Amiens, Bourges, Chartres, Langres, Noyon and Reims, with much whitewashing of the walls and the replacement of coloured glass with plain. Indeed reservations about Gothic 'impurity' were so strong that a classical temple was temporarily erected in the chancel of Notre-Dame Cathedral to mark the wedding of Louis XVI's father in 1745!

3

The cathedrals and larger churches were beginning to be filled with classical monuments by Pigalle, Houdon and their rivals; this was the style favoured for other new fittings and fixtures, such as altarpieces above which were often placed the religious paintings that many prosperous clergy commissioned and installed. As a patron of all the arts, the Church's influence remained pervasive on the eve of the Revolution. Religious art generally remained at the apex of painterly values and the Church continued to support it with commissions that helped to keep numerous artists in work who would never make a name for themselves in the fashionable annual *Salon* in Paris.[4] Musically, the Church was still more important, offering talented musicians posts as organists and choirmasters, and upholding the highest standards of musical excellence in settings for the liturgy. There may have been no successors comparable to Charpentier, Couperin or Lalande in the late eighteenth century, but the inspiration of those composers remained strong without cramping the flair of their successors in the royal chapels and cathedrals. The services held in cathedrals and large city churches in the eighteenth century had a magnificence in ceremony and dignity that has never been surpassed and would not survive the Revolution. Louis XVI's reign witnessed the waning of the fashion for elaborate *grands motets* needing a large orchestra and choir, and much experimentation was underway: in Paris, the well-established *Concert Spirituel* (secular music was also in their repertoire) were attempting musical drama based on Old Testament texts, but it was left to Berlioz's future teacher, Jean-François Le Sueur, to capture the public imagination with his Latin oratorio *Histoire suivie de la Résurrection* (now lost). When first performed on Easter Monday 1787 its touching and poetic treatment of Christ's Passion offered French audiences the multiple pleasure that Handel had given their British counterparts over half a century and more previously.[5]

Le Sueur's masterpiece was given at Notre-Dame Cathedral, Paris, which dominated the capital's skyline. Throughout France cathedrals, parish churches, conventual buildings, seminaries, canons' lodgings and episcopal palaces jostled for space and were an everyday reminder to faithful and critics alike of the Church's importance. In towns from Angers to Metz, Rouen to Aix-en-Provence, and everywhere in between, the clerical presence was pronounced, a major component of the local economy, staffing schools and hospitals as well as churches. Thus in Bayeux, the Norman centre of a large and important bishopric, there was a clerical population of 500 to

600 crammed into a town of 10 000 souls.[6] They formed part of the approximately 170 000 persons ordained into the First Estate or 0.6 per cent of the French population as a whole, a slight decline over-all from a century earlier.[7] These men and women in holy orders were members of the Gallican Church, the most prestigious branch of the Roman Catholic Church in western Europe, surpassing even the Church of Spain or that of the Austrian Empire. Like them, it had remained in full communion with the papacy after the Reforma-tion. Not that its historic ties to Rome in any sense implied a depen-dent relationship on the Holy See. From time to time it suited the Crown to invite the Pope to pronounce authoritatively in a manner that would reinforce royal power, as during the Jansenist disputes earlier in the century, but otherwise his part in the day-to-day life of the Church was strictly formal. His temporal powers were operable only within the terms agreed under the Concordat of Bologna (1516), such as confirming the appointment of bishops to their posts or the creation of cardinals, and even this agreement technically applied to what was within the French kingdom before 1660. The King suppli-cated on behalf of a nominee, and the Pope provided bulls of institu-tion. In theory, the latter could veto nominations, even impose a choice of his own; in practice, he did no more than occasionally block a candidate or impose a delay. The Pope's spiritual supremacy remained intact, but even a doctrinal bull could not be published in France without royal approval, and the expulsion of the Jesuits from the country in 1764 had removed his most reliable followers.

Louis XVI's accession to the throne of St Louis was followed a year later by the election of a new Pope – who took the name of Pius VI – to that of St Peter. Pius stood by the existing conventions, and so did the French King. Indeed, their relationship was a model of cordiality and stability compared with the Pope's difficulties with Joseph II of Austria. At an unofficial level, the signs of renewed interest in papal authority predated 1789. Yet it was only after the Revolution had broken out and the National Assembly ordered the wholesale remodelling of ecclesiastical structures that it became generally expe-dient to discover the uses of the papacy's historic claims to 'fullness of power' (*plenitudo potestatis*). With the King on the defensive in the face of the National Assembly's claim to sovereign power, the bishops, deprived of their monarchical prop, pinned their hopes on Pius VI to bolster what was left of the Gallican Church's institutional power.

Interestingly, even at that late hour, the clerical elite still expected Pius would dance to their tune. It was a sign of the degree to which the French Church remained much less Roman than Gallican, one with a distinctly national character, classically embodied in the Four Gallican Articles of 1682. There were many strands in Gallicanism. The Church saw it as bound up with the preservation of its institutional integrity, though the version that increasingly appealed to the magistrates of the *parlements* and their Jansenist allies insisted that, in the final reckoning, the Church must defer to the State – by which they meant judges like themselves.[8] Bishops and clergy thought more in terms of royal power. To all intents and purposes royal supremacy characterised the French Church as much as it did the contemporary Church of England, for it was less to the descendant of St Peter that Gallican churchmen looked for support than to the heir of St Louis IX. As a corporate institution, the French Church could almost claim equality with the monarchy on the basis of more exalted divine origins and, by virtue of its mediatory role in interpreting the will of God, the Crown could only ignore the injunctions of the Church at its peril.

That was the legal theory though, in practice, the Gallican Church, like most 'national' branches of the Roman Catholic communion, was increasingly dependent on the Crown and thereby vulnerable to diminution of its privileges at the hands of ministers looking to raise extra taxation. Nevertheless, the sovereign in both his public and private capacity could not lightly override the wishes of the Church, especially when the King so conspicuously lived up to his formal title of 'Most Christian King' as did Louis XVI. The son of exceptionally devout parents who had died when he was a boy in the mid-1760s, Louis was one of the most pious monarchs to be found anywhere in eighteenth-century Europe, one 'for whom the poor were as important as the rich and servants as real as court officials'.[9] The King's commitment to his Christian duties was shared by other members of his family. One of his aunts, Louise, took the veil; the other two, Adelaide and Sophie, were notoriously *dévote*, while his young sister, Elisabeth (b. 1764), was even more renowned for her devotions than the king. It was obvious to all his courtiers that their master's regular attendance at the chapel services at Versailles was based on genuine piety before any demands of protocol. Far less anticlerical than contemporary monarchs like Charles III of Spain (1759–88) or Joseph II (1780–90), Louis XVI was eventually prepared to hazard even his throne for the sake of his loyalties to the Gallican Church. Entrusted to such a sovereign's concern, the alliance of 'throne and altar' had a personal as well as a public dimension which makes recent claims by historians for a fatal 'desacralisation' of the monarchy appear questionable.[10] Admittedly, sacral monarchy had been damaged in public eyes by the persistence of the Jansenist dispute for much of the century, yet to some degree Louis XVI successfully 'resacralised' it as an institution and did much to undo the damage inflicted by his grandfather. His own benign temperament, and enjoyment of fatherhood, were appreciated in a country besotted with Rousseau, and did much – despite his wife's unpopularity – to endear the monarchy in his own person to his people until well into the Revolution. For an admiration for Rousseau was not incompatible with a sense that the monarchy was an institution divinely ordained in France and bound up with its destiny.[11] Not necessarily an absolutist model of monarchy, but one operating on constitutional, moderate lines respectful of his subjects' legal priviliges. The debate on that subject was well under way before 1789.

Religion underpinned the claims of both state and Church to authority, leading the late Michel Péronnet, a modern authority on the Gallican Church, to state that 'Catholic religious ideology dominated and animated the monarchical state so that it would not be exaggerating to speak of a theocratic state'.[12] Such a character was most dramatically emphasised at the coronation service, the *sacre*. At Reims in 1775, the twenty-one-year-old Louis XVI swore to uphold and protect the status and privileges of the Gallican Church, while the officiating prelates in return extended God's protection to him through consecration and anointment. The young sovereign's dedication to the service of the state in the *sacre* was, for the episcopate, a chance to rechristianise France in the name of the King, 'the restorer of morals', as the bishop of Senez proposed to call him. It could be a new, unsullied start following the death of his unchaste, unedifying and from the Church's standpoint – unhelpful – grandfather, Louis XV.[13]

The laws of the monarchy accorded the Gallican Church exclusive religious rights. Until 1787 to be a Frenchman was to be by definition a Catholic. At least in legal theory, France could be defined as a confessional state, where membership of the Church conferred rights of access to the life of the state as well. Belief in the veracity of the Christian faith was a given in French society, and the Church saw its mission as teaching the Catholic faith and encouraging its correct practice, rather than stressing any prior need for inner conversion through grace as understood by Protestants. Those who did not belong to the Church were simply non-persons in the eyes of the law. It was the classic embodiment of Bishop Bossuet's famous claim in the 1680s that France possessed 'one faith, one church, one king', but only the last of the three affirmations ever corresponded to the reality.

Despite the legal pretence, religious minorities had resisted every attempt to eradicate them in the half-century after the revocation of the Edict of Nantes in 1685. Protestantism had not withered away – it made up about 2 per cent of the population – and the numbers of Jews remained consistent, especially in eastern France. The corollary of confessionalism was either expulsion or enforced conformity, but neither course of action had succeeded. Persecution had become unacceptable to the educated public by the 1760s as the celebrated cases of the Chevalier de la Barre (the laws against blasphemy and sacrilege) and the Calas family (the role of Protestants in French society) indicated. Church leaders, especially the younger bishops, were in touch with the changing public mood, and were discouraging such repression. But it was not easy to affect practice and prejudice at parish level or to persuade some older prelates that 'heresy' should be left unpunished. It was an embarrassment to these older members of the clerical elite that, despite his coronation oaths, even the King disavowed coercion. He was a willing party to the 1787 Edict allowing non-Catholics the first shreds of toleration, a stance that provoked the remarkable public taunt from Bishop Hercé of Dol in orthodox Brittany that Louis XIV would never have allowed a measure 'that threatened the collapse of the arches of the sanctuary'.[14] Such an unprecedented outburst was indicative of a growing tension between the ecclesiastical elite and the King in the 1780s, seen in other, smaller slights, like the failure to appoint a bishop as his preceptor when the Dauphin's household was formed in 1786.

Any disharmonies between the episcopate and Louis XVI were not directly related to Jansenism, a phenomenon which had originated in the mid-seventeenth century as an austere and intensive Augustinian form of Catholicism but which, very quickly, became politically controversial because of its anti-Jesuit character. The promulgation of the papal Bull *Unigenitus dei filius* in 1713 was intended to silence this articulate, influential minority. In fact it had the opposite effect and, as the work of Dale Van Kley has shown, Jansenism assumed great prominence in late *Ancien Régime* politics.[15] It was an ineradicable part of religious politics for most of Louis XV's reign, usually working against the authority of the Church hierarchy as well as the Crown. Jansenists argued for the supremacy of councils over popes and princes (conciliarism); in other words a constitutional process rather than an absolutist one, whether operated by a monarch in the state or by bishops in the Church. This emphasis was developed further by lawyers like Louis-Adrien Le Paige in the Paris *parlement* (and elsewhere) looking for leverage on royal government and helped destabilise high politics in the 1750s and 1760s just as France resumed hostilities with Britain in the Seven Years War (1756–63).

As religion and politics became hopelessly intertwined, Gallican leaders like Archbishop Christophe de Beaumont of Paris (d. 1781) showed an uncompromising hostility to Jansenism and its clerical sympathisers. He put a ban on clergy giving the sacrament to those who could not produce a certificate testifying to their correct belief while the Paris *parlement* moved legally against priests who complied with his instructions. The refusal of the sacraments controversy strangely anticipated the division between juring and refractory clergy in 1791, and may even have predisposed the Revolution in the direction of such a schism. More immediately, the archbishop's principled but counter-productive policy encouraged moderate opinion to turn against the Church and discover the tactical value of anticlericalism. Only the expulsion of the Jesuits from France in 1764 speedily took the heat out of the issue, leaving behind a disturbing legacy: the breakdown of royal religious policy, a mutual sense of distrust between monarch and episcopacy, and a new bitterness in Church–*parlement* relations. Jansenism had furthered claims that the state had interventionist rights in what might have appeared to be spiritual matters, to the point of denying any fundamental right of the Church to privileges in taxation.[16] Conciliarism played its part in inspiring the resistance of the *parlements* and their allies to Maupeou's onslaught against their constitutional pretensions between 1771 and 1774, explicitly made out in works like Guillaume Saige's *The Citizen's Catechism* (1775). Conciliarist inspiration would again be found informing the 'patriot' cause during the pre-Revolutionary 1780s,[17] while Jansenism encouraged the sense of constitutionalism inside the First Estate by giving a filip to discontented lower clergy, as will be considered later.

If the Church–Crown axis was under strain again after Louis XV's death, it was due more to the actions of ministers rather than to Louis XVI personally.[18] There were the habitual grumblings that the Crown was lax in enforcing censorship, prosecuting non-Catholics, and enforcing the laws closing taverns during Mass, but what particularly alarmed the Church leadership was the way pressure was building for concessions from the First Estate that threatened its ability to administer its own business, especially its finances. Senior clergy were worried that the monarchy no longer appeared much interested in upholding the corporate power and privileges of the Church, and feared that its much vaunted Gallican 'Liberties' were in jeopardy. The government was looking for more direct help from the Church in overhauling state indebtedness than the usual resort of borrowing on favourable terms from the First Estate because its credit was sound with the security derived from its vast land holdings. The quarter of a billion livres of its annual income was looking very tempting to tax-hungry ministers. The reformist plans of Calonne (Controller-General 1783–87) would for the first time entangle the Church in the fiscal networks of the government.

For the time being, its feudal dues (in some dioceses like Angers the main support of all clergy) and its tithes (the most lucrative income of all, worth about 120 million livres annually, especially in the south) appeared safe. Not so its extensive property portfolio. Historically, land ownership was the key to the Church's power and prestige, like the fifth of Paris owned by the regular clergy. It had accumulated land from inheritances and donations over time, so that by the eighteenth century it owned between 6 and 10 per cent of France, up to one-third in the Nord, Picardy and the Brie region, though only about 3 per cent in the Auvergne.[19] Dillon, Archbishop of Narbonne, may have told Louis XVI at the General Assembly of 1785 that 'It is from the munificence of the kings, your august predecessors as well as the pious generosity of the great families of the kingdom that the Church claims the properties that she possesses;'[20] in practice this assumption was under scrutiny. As early as 1749 the Church's right of inheritance and endowment under the archaic feudal survival of mortmain had been restricted by the state. It opened up a debate on the Church's land ownership which was still unfolding when the Revolution started.

Unfavourable notice was thus directed well before 1789 to the First Estate's privileged status, underlined by its continuing immunity from taxation, despite the nobility losing its exemption from direct taxation as long before as 1695. Efforts to break this convention had been tried more than once. In 1725 ministers had come very close to having the Church pay a *cinquantième* levy before the new administration of Cardinal Fleury abandoned it; in 1749, plans were produced by Controller-General Machault d'Arnouville for the clergy to pay the new *vingtième* tax like everyone else, but the Church had thwarted those too. It had thus held on – just – to its right to make instead periodic grants to the Crown called *dons gratuits*, subject to authorisation by the General Assemblies of the Clergy. Between 1715 and 1788 the annual amount of that 'gift' was, on average, approximately 3 600 000 livres, and that was far from a level that would satisfy the Church's critics. By the early 1780s, ministers, casting around for extra revenues after the huge expenses of the American War of Independence, were ready to try again, and their prospects seemed rosier, as indicated by the so-called *foi et hommage* affair – a dispute over requiring ecclesiastical landlords to make declarations of value to the King as their feudal overlord.[21] Most ecclesiastical lands were mortgaged up to the hilt (owing to heavy borrowing), the clerical debt stood at 140 million livres, growing larger with every *don gratuit*, and the Church's scope for financial manoeuvering was correspondingly limited. Government was minded to exploit the vulnerability conferred by clerical indebtedness. Any such move would probably find favour with a public that resented the clergy's appearance of escaping the direct tax burden. The Church was rich, and with national bankruptcy looming thanks to the costs of war, it would have to give more.

French clergy needed only to look to other parts of Europe for an instructive reminder of the growing imbalance in Church–state relations. These were increasingly conducted less on any partnership basis than on governments' assumption of a right to order ecclesiastical affairs so that they conformed to the interests of the monarchy as a whole. The classic case of control was the Holy Roman Empire. The process had been started under Maria-Theresa but, from the moment he became sole ruler in 1780, Joseph II had closed monasteries, confiscated Church lands, and relegated the Pope's powers in the appointment of bishops and other higher clergy almost to a nullity. Such policies were not intended to weaken the faith to which 'national' Catholic churches witnessed, but in practice this assault on the wealth, powers and independent political standing of the Church served over time to loosen public esteem for its creeds, at least among the elite. To a sovereign like Joseph, such a consideration was not a valid objection to his policies: the clergy had to put the national good first, and it was not just in the Austrian Empire that such arguments prevailed. In Spain, Charles III had achieved the sort of *de facto* supremacy over the Catholic Church *vis-à-vis* the papacy that gave him more residual power than anything available to his cousin, the King of France, under the edict of Bologna.

Throughout the Italian peninsula, princes were staking their claims to similar control, and the papacy could do little to stop them. The same was the case in Germany where even the three archiepiscopal Electors of Cologne, Mainz and Trier were subordinating Church to State as part of the policies any good 'enlightened autocrat' would want to adopt.[22] In a sense, the Gallican Church was fortunate to have held out until 1790 before its powers and jurisdiction were altered and curtailed.

Responsibility for defending the Church's temporal privileges lay in the first instance with the General Assembly of the Clergy of France. It met every five years as a matter of course (1775, 1780, 1785), more often if the need arose (1782, 1788), with the bulk of work undertaken by various commissions that drafted reports and proposed legislation. It was the only national and representative forum that the Crown had continuously permitted to convene, with every ecclesiastical province sending elected deputies to Versailles; that invariably meant the higher clergy, particularly the bishops, from whose number the president was always selected. The episcopate took its leadership duties seriously, and used successive General Assemblies to elaborate on its plans for corporate and spiritual renewal. As Archbishop Dulau of Arles stated the position on 12 July 1780, 'the dearer and more precious the glory of the Gallican Church is to us, the more we are called to repair its wounds courageously, in the hope of binding them satisfactorily'.[23] The bishops had the hierarchical authority and experience of public life (or so it was argued) to stand firm against any brow-beating from the government.

It was the General Assembly's most important task to vote a negotiated *don gratuit* in lieu of direct taxation to the King; in return, he was expected to take note of its grievances, for instance, publication of works by the *philosophes*. Deputies reserved the right to apportion their offering as they chose, with clerical contributions known as the *décimes* imposed at diocesan level by the ecclesiastical chambers (sometimes called the diocesan bureaux). The lower clergy had minimal representation in the General Assembly, even in the places reserved for the 'second order', in other words the ordained ministry below the rank of bishop. Between 1755 and 1788, of the 128 'second-order' clergy, 115 were *grands vicaires* (see below) and the others were on the way to that status. Yet the absence of *curé* representation did not prevent the heaviest burden of the *décimes* falling on them. Pressing financial need could result in unscheduled, extraordinary meetings of the General Assembly, as in 1782 at the close of the American War of Independence. On that occasion clerical deputies patriotically obliged with a generous grant to the government, thanks to the diplomatic skills of the president, the Cardinal La Rochefoucauld, Archbishop of Rouen. But cooperation could not be assumed, as the derisory sum offered to Brienne's administration in 1788 indicated. When the General Assembly was not sitting, its powers were delegated to a pair of Agents-General, well-born young men destined for promotion to a bishopric. Talleyrand held one of the posts from 1780 to 1785 and displayed the sort of watchfulness on behalf of the Church's interests that was in direct contrast to his willingness to sacrifice them after the Revolution had begun.[24] He and his colleague, the abbé de Montesquiou, headed a formidable Church bureaucracy, recently judged to be 'without doubt the most effective in the kingdom'.[25]

At a time when in France a strict social hierarchy and neat gradations of rank were unravelling,[26] aristocratic grip on the key offices in the Church was tighter than ever by the 1770s. Family connections, ties of friendship and shared backgrounds still counted for a great deal in the hunt for preferment, and upheld the importance of the patron–client relationship, that cement of *Ancien Régime* politics.[27] The same names – La Rochefoucauld, Colbert, Jarente, Grimaldi, Montmorin – occurred in every generation, a sign of the enduring strength of clerical dynasticism and the power of great families. Birth was thus the main prerequisite for senior office, certainly for a bishopric, and nepotism was tolerated. Familial obligation induced the Archbishop of Reims, Talleyrand-Périgord, to tolerate the scandalous living of his nephew, the future bishop and Napoleonic foreign minister, simply because he wanted his younger kinsman to be assured in time of high office in the Church.[28] Such examples could be multiplied.

It was quite common for uncle to appoint nephew his coadjutor bishop during his lifetime so that a family succession in a bishopric could be guaranteed. The lucky young beneficiary would then become bishop of a diocese *in partibus infidelium*, exotically named after a town in, say, north Africa or the Middle East. This happened, for example, at Albi in 1784, as a royal favour granted to the ambassador to the papacy and absentee archbishop, the Cardinal de Bernis, once the protégé of Madame de Pompadour, foreign minister before the Duc de Choiseul succeeded in 1758. Without patronage ties and rank, talent and Christian virtues were insufficient. Such conventions were not unusual. The higher ranks of most other European churches were increasingly dominated by noblemen and their kinsfolk in the last half of the century, but a proportion of high offices, including the rank of bishop, were usually reserved for men of business and scholars whose connections with the elite might be remote. This situation applied in Catholic regions like Austria and the Netherlands, as well as Anglican England, but not in France.[29] Talented administrators and intellectuals could not expect there to become bishops. It was an inflexible situation, difficult to justify but not to be easily undone because it generated a leadership cadre that had served the Gallican Church competently and sometimes outstandingly since Louis XIII's reign (1610–42).[30] The quality and capacity of that elite in the second half of the century should not be underestimated. As one scholar has well expressed it, 'with a few exceptions, they were active, pious, and of an irreproachable zeal',[31] mostly the old boys of an elite educational institution, the seminary of Saint-Sulpice in Paris.[32]

All this meant that a clergyman could not purchase a bishopric in the same way that a prosperous bourgeois could buy nobility: however dedicated a pastor, skilled an administrator or learned a scholar, a priest's scope for advancement was limited if his father was not a nobleman. Between 1700 and 1748, 9 commoners became bishops but only one, the abbé de Beauvais, between 1743 and 1788. He was the greatest of contemporary preachers, and his interests were endorsed by Louis XV's pious daughters, but the key factor was having as his uncle the lawyer running the office of the Agents-General! The best a non-noble priest could realistically hope for was a senior appointment *below* the rank of bishop. This path marked the pre-Revolutionary progress of Sieyès, author of the most influential pamphlet of 1789 *Qu'est-ce que le Tiers État?*, who was advanced to membership of the cathedral chapter at Chartres and and became secretary to the bishop.[33] Despite this and other late signs that the ice-floes in the Church on the eve of the Revolution might be melting,[34] as an institution it undoubtedly had more than its fair share of frustrated careerists with *rotourier* origins who felt hedged in by parochial duties and wanted to display their talents to better advantage – and be better paid for doing so. For this was a well-educated clergy, the products of Sulpicien, Lazarist and Eudiste seminaries in the dioceses (many were affiliated to local universities by Louis XVI's reign),[35] more capable of responding to the challenge of pastoral service than at any point in the French Church's history. These men were increasingly inclined not to question the existence of the hierarchy, but the opportunities for promotion inside it, and particularly the role of those clergy who held no pastoral office. It was a challenge the ecclesiastical elite was slow in identifying, and perhaps too inclined to dismiss.

The Church was led by those who held the 114 bishoprics and 16 archbishoprics in the Gallican Church, an episcopate active in State as well as Church, a proud, prestigious pastoral elite. As one Auxerre *curé* tersely expressed it in 1789 (and few would have dissented even in that momentous year): 'It is certain that the bishops are the principal citizens of the nation, and that they are born to advise kings ('*conseillers nés*').[36] Some of the sees they held were of great antiquity, dating from the beginnings of Christianity in France. Others, like Nancy and Saint-Dié in Lorraine, were established in Louis XVI's reign and plans to create a new one at Moulins in central France were halted only by the Revolution. The discrepancies of size and wealth between dioceses meant that the most ambitious prelates were alert to promotion possibilities after they had gained their mitre. An average or slightly above-average see, such as Montauban in the Midi, or nearby Castres, was worth about 70 000 livres.[37] No diocese could be accurately described as poor, though the cluster of sees in Languedoc created in the fourteenth century generated little wealth. Thus the diocese of Apt was worth about 20 000 livres, sufficiently meagre for Bishop Eon de Cély to top it up with a pension of 12 000 livres and the rich priory of La Valette in the Toulouse archdiocese.[38] Like many other colleagues on the episcopal bench, the bishop of Apt was titular prior only, and held La Valette *in commendam*. It entitled him to siphon off on average two-thirds of the priory's income. The practice was widespread. Even the more prestigious sees could be made more so by the grant of a rich abbey or priory held *in absentia*. Thus Jérome-Marie Champion de Cicé, Archbishop of Bordeaux from 1781 and, as such, Primate of Aquitaine, enjoyed the abbeys of La Grasse and Ourscamps, to gross what Bordelais opinion estimated to be 150 000 livres annually; Cardinal Rohan of Strasbourg in 1780 secured the Abbey of Saint-Vaast in Arras, perhaps the most lucrative abbatial prize of all, but still not enough to pay his gambling debts, and he had to look for additional funds in the shape of the Abbey of Chaise-Dieu in the Auvergne only five years later.[39] Such uses were coming to seem conspicuous abuses by educated opinion on the eve of the Revolution, to whom it was scandalous that the ecclesiastical aristocracy paid themselves so highly for doing nothing.

The wealthiest dioceses – Sens, Strasbourg, Cambrai and Metz prominent among them – were every junior prelate's hope. But promotion meant gaining royal approval, leaving bishops or would-be bishops no choice but to be courtiers as well as pastors in pre-Revolutionary France. The most spectacular victim of clerical ambition was notoriously the 'prince Louis', alias the Cardinal Rohan, and Grand Almoner of France from 1777, whose office gave him nominal responsibility for the King's religion and religious policy. His court career was terminated in the most public manner following the scandal of the Diamond Necklace. Louis XVI often exercised Crown patronage personally. He sought whenever practicable to promote men of piety and pastoral energy. Thus the first bishop nominated by Louis after his accession was the humble and charitable du Tillet to Orange, followed up by two other imaginative appointments to archbishoprics: Rosset de Fleury to Cambrai and Dulau to Arles, the latter already proving himself to be among the most pastorally talented of his generation. As a rule, names were officially put forward to the King by a prelate who advised him generally on ecclesiastical preferment and held the government office of keeper of the *feuille des bénéfices*; in practice, by 1780, rival court factions like the *dévots*, the Polignacs and the Neckerites (who, ironically, offered their loyalty to a Swiss Protestant, Louis XVI's finance minister from 1776 to 1781) used episcopal candidates as a means of winning or confirming their political dominance at Versailles.

Bishops were free to concentrate on whatever aspects of their office most interested them. Some saw their vocation in purely pastoral terms and were genuinely concerned for the spiritual wellbeing of their clergy and people; others were unstinting in their charity, like Dulau of Arles, who gave away 40 000 livres to the needy in the general visitation of his diocese in 1777,[40] until the changes of the Revolution deprived them of the means to be of much help: 'They [the poor], wrote Bishop Usson de Bonnac of Agen in October 1789, are more our brothers than ever but I cannot be of any use to them'.[41] Such energy was expressed in another direction by the so-called *prélats administrateurs*, whose concern for sound, efficient government of their diocese was often indistinguishable from their involvement in provincial politics. They might, like Duplessis d'Argentré of Limoges, act as a lieutenant to the intendant (in this case, the future minister, Turgot);[42] preside over the meeting of the Provincial (or local) Estates in the *pays d'états*, like Languedoc or Brittany, which retained them; or do the same in the new Provincial Assemblies established in 1778 and 1787. In the complicated patronage networks that enmeshed national and provincial politics and embraced *officiers* and lawyers as well as clergy, bishops were indispensable figures. Some used their prominence at that level as a launchpad to national importance. Many prelates aspired to a place in the central government itself, following the examples of Cardinals Fleury, Dubois and Bernis earlier in the century, and two – Loménie de Brienne and Jérome-Marie Champion de Cicé – achieved the same status in Louis XVI's reign. Men of this eminence were at a vast remove from the parish clergy but as bishops at least held a pastoral office, and that could act as a shield against the persistent grumbling about politically ambitious prelates, reservations that the King was known to share. On the eve of the Revolution there was a distinct line of opinion that was keen for *all* the bishops to give their role as father-in-God their first priority, and stay in their dioceses.

There was a well-trodden route to becoming a bishop. Nobly born clerics invariably trained unofficially for their own diocese by helping an older kinsman or a patron run his as a *grand vicaire* – something akin to a company secretary or a chief of staff; their numbers and duties varied according to the energies of their bishop,[43] but there was a risk that the routine could become dull and make these office-holders anxious that they were languishing away in the provinces, too far from the glance of the king and queen and the courtiers who counted. These frustrations, when combined with inexperience and imperiousness, could infuse higher–lower clergy relations with mistrust.[44] It has been suggested that such posts as that of *grand vicaire* might be included, along with canons, college professors, and the wealthiest *curés*, under the label of 'middle clergy', but that term has not caught on and will not be used here.[45] What the term suggests is a limited or non-existent pastoral element in a post, an exemption that was attracting criticism by the 1780s. It was a muted complaint, most audible in areas of *curé* militancy like the Dauphiné in south-eastern France,[46] and not widely articulated until the public debate over the function and composition of the Estates-General in 1788–9.

Medium-sized cities like Angers, Bourges and Chartres contained chapters of canons in addition to those attached to their cathedral. The wealth of these chapters was often considerable, and they justified their existence on the grounds of tradition, especially the legal rights that could be used as a curb on the power of the bishop. The dignitaries of a chapter often had few duties (many of which could be delegated), but office gave them the leisure and the income

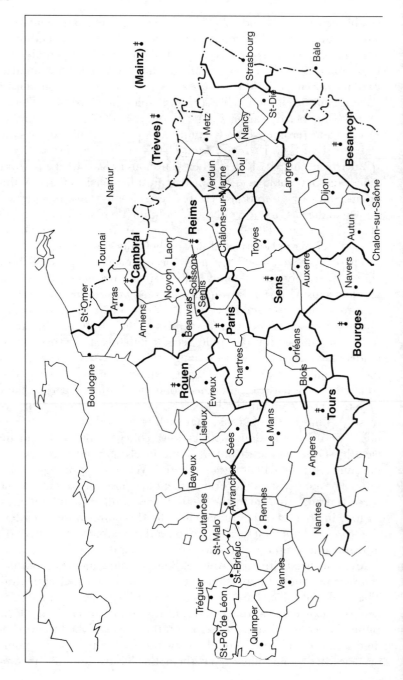

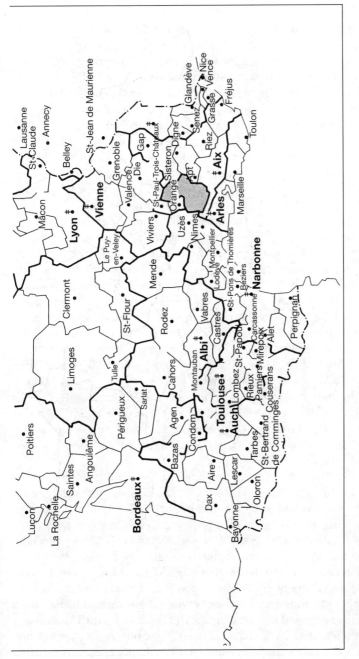

Map 1 Dioceses of France

19

should they want (and most did) to pursue interests in everything from gardening and geology to patristics and philology. Frequently, bishops had limited powers of intervention in capitular affairs and were powerless to influence prestigious communities like the Chapter of Saint-André in Bordeaux, sticklers for upholding their rights.[47] At their best, like the 72 canons resident in Angers or the 62 in Bayeux, these little corporations enriched the life of the local Church; thus the chapter of Saint-Seurin (Bordeaux) was famous for its fine music and Marian devotions. At worst they played into the hands of critics by their nepotistic tendencies, their petty gradations and their reluctance to contemplate minor reforms. A fishwife from the market at Saint-Michel in Bordeaux expressed in dialect the exasperation most ordinary people had for these dignitaries and their easygoing lifestyles: 'These canons, they just drink like princes and have no other worries except singing some horrid sounding litany or other.'[48]

There was a decreasing sympathy in Louis XVI's time for clergy whose primary justification was to say the offices, celebrate the holy mysteries – and live well, 'grazing', as one anonymous author put it, 'in the rich pasturage'.[49] Such 'grazing' could well include illicit sexual activity, despite the risk: 'madames' were under orders to report to the police the names of all clerical visitors to their premises. It was not always easy to tell whether someone was a clergyman or not. Many of the two and half thousand clerics (a conservative estimate) arrested in Paris between 1755 and 1764 for debauchery were tonsured and technically not in holy orders; and of those who were, many were just voyeurs, not themselves seeking the services of a prostitute. But complaints concerning the behaviour of bishops and canons were as nothing compared with those voiced about the regular orders of the clergy.

The 26 500 monks and, to a lesser extent, the 37 000 nuns, were easy targets for Enlightenment writers. They tirelessly rehearsed the salacious stories that sold pamphlets and squibs rather than reported up-to-date news at odds with the mythology, such as the considerable charity of monks during the terrible winter of 1788–9, especially those of the great house of Saint-Germain-des-Près in Paris. The Church was aware that action was essential to remove the sting from the elegant sneers of the *philosophes* and the tavern humour of the multitude. Prompted by Choiseul's administration and feeling itself unable to resist royal wishes, it acted. In 1766 it set up the Commission des Réguliers under the chairmanship of the progressive archbishop of Toulouse, Loménie de Brienne, with a membership composed of clergy and laymen in equal proportions. Buttressed by a combination of royal and episcopal authority, it issued a stream of recommendations until 1780.[50] The commission's work gave the Crown jurisdiction in matters previously reserved for the Church and undoubtedly anticipated the 1790 reforms of the National Assembly in the same area. Among its most important decrees was that of 1768 to the effect that vows could not be taken before the age of twenty-one (eighteen for women). It also abolished several orders outright, and stipulated that smaller monasteries should close and their assets be redistributed among those that remained in an attempt to rejuvenate the religious orders.[51] The work of the commission cut straight across existing monastic traditions like the triennial chapter meetings of the Cluniac Order in France. Its last abbot before the Revolution, Cardinal La Rochefoucauld, Archbishop of Rouen, still presided, but there was little for him and his colleagues to do.[52]

The reform affected recruitment in different ways. Overall numbers fell in the quarter of a century down to 1790[53]: the Benedictines went from 6434 to 4300, the Augustinians from 2599 to 1765, and the Franciscans from 9820 to 6064, and the Cluniacs from 671 in 1768 to 600 in 1785. Yet some orders continued to recruit well, notably a teaching order like the Oratorians, a preaching one such as the Lazarists and the austerely contemplative Cathusians, so there is a case for saying with Bernard Plongeron that, in some areas at least, monasticism took on 'an important new lease of life in the years immediately before the Revolution'.[54] The Brienne commission seems to have strengthened the academic life of the religious orders: Benedictine (who had no less than 400 houses in the eighteenth century) and Oratorian schools were invariably overbooked. The famous Maurist congregation of Benedictines continued to produce scholar-monks and offer an advanced education until dispersal in 1790. Six of the latter's colleges became military schools financed by the State in 1776. One of them – Sorèze – recruited students from across Europe, and there was even an American there in 1789![55] Not the least impact made by the Commission was to induce monks to think again about their *raison d'être*, and there was a lively debate in progress on the eve of the Revolution with one Vannist, Dom Charles Cajot, actually recommending that his fellow Benedictines make teaching the priority and prayer a secondary consideration.[56] It was a sign of just how far the monastic orders were ready to adapt to changed circumstances. And despite the apparent public disdain for monasticism, in large parishes the services of the religious orders still drew in considerable numbers. At the church of the Cordeliers in Paris, for instance, could be found the wife of the porter at the Comédie Française, the receiver-general of the estates and forests of Languedoc, the *chirurgien* of the Duc d'Orléans and the Comte de Fontenoy.[57]

If the gradual decline of academic life in most houses was hard to deny, inside the cloister most individual brothers and sisters kept their vows, still lived out private lives of devotion to God and adhered to the monastic rule of chastity and obedience. The comment of Mme de Genlis, governess to the future king Louis-Philippe I, after a stay in the Benedictine abbey of Origny-Sainte-Benoîte (near Saint Quentin) that she had 'only seen perfect innocence in this abbey, a sincere piety, and virtuous examples of it' was widely echoed.[58] On the eve of the Revolution, there were still serious apologists for the expansion of the regular clergy, like a project of 1786 for the establishment of a corps of canonesses composed of no less than 150 chapters, and justified on the basis that it would give women of ability but reduced circumstances real educational advantages. Bishops were not encouraging: their diocesan government was better consolidated without monastic exemptions. At Toulon, the Bishop wanted to move on the Carmelites and Capuchins to secure land for a new parish church, while the Recollects were under pressure to vacate their premises to make way for a diocesan seminary.[59]

But the student looking for signs of real dynamism in this area must go to the non-monastic religious orders, especially the female congregations dating from the Counter-Reformation who were not living in abbeys, monasteries and convents, in other words *congrégan-istes* rather than *religieuses*. Their growth in the previous century had been phenomenal, despite hierarchical unease over female autonomy. Wealthy widows in several generations had poured money into a variety of institutions and the priority after 1700 was one of consolidation rather than expansion. By the 1770s women outnumbered men in both the active and the contemplative life by three to one. They joined orders like the Visitandines, the Ursulines, the Sisters of Charity and the Daughters of Charity. The congregations and less-formal associations encouraged new devotions, such as those to the Holy Child and to Saint Joseph, and made themselves indispensable as carers, teachers and nurses.

The lives of these devotees dramatically revealed the social philosophy of the Counter-Reformation in action. More than any other group in French society, these congregations bore the burden of caring for the sick and the old in hospitals and other charitable foundations, with an emphasis on prayer, rest, cleanliness and straightforward nourishments for the inmates like beef-tea or rhubarb. Outside the *hôtels Dieu*, the sisters brought supplementary poor relief to the most needy, and were involved in running girls' academies for all social categories; these ranged from boarding schools for the daughters of the elite organised by orders like the Ursulines, where dancing and deportment figured on the curriculum alongside catechism and confession, to rural establishments where the priority was practical skills like sewing, spinning and lacemaking.[60] Although Enlightenment writers could mock the sisters, popular attitudes towards such selfless women were more approving, and the dispersal of their orders during the 1790s was generally regretted.[61]

The female orders had shown a capacity for reform initiatives earlier in the century. In 1727 the Commission des Secours had been created. It lasted until 1788 and was a forerunner of the Brienne Commission.[62] As a result of its initiatives, the gap was narrowed between the minority of well-endowed female monasteries dating back to the early Middle Ages (like the royal abbeys of Fontevrault and Remiremont), and the great majority of the foundations that had existed only since the Catholic Reformation (like the Carmelites, Ursulines and Visitandines). The Commission des Secours still showed a definite favour towards the aristocratic female houses. Thus it agreed to pay no less than 140 000 livres to the Abbey of Remiremont for repairs to lightning damage, about ten times more than the sum normally awarded to monastic institutions. It was no coincidence that the abbess there was the Princesse Christine de Saxe,[63] for nunneries continued to provide a depositary for the surplus daughters of the nobility down to the revolution, including Louis XVI's aunt, Mme Louise de France who, in 1771, had renounced the world and entered the austere Carmelite house at Saint-Denis as a novice, appropriately close to the bodies of her Bourbon ancestors.[64]

By Louis XVI's reign, men who in previous centuries might have entered an enclosed order largely chose the alternative ministry of the parish priest. The term *curé* was used to describe all the parish clergy, though a *curé* was technically the holder of a benefice (in Brittany he was called a *recteur*). He was sometimes aided in his duties by an assistant priest or *vicaire*, whose standard of living was precarious since he depended on a share of the benefice's income, usually the fees collected during services. The holder of an office that could be revoked at will by his *curé*, the humble *vicaire* could not even look

forward to his own independent post as a matter of course.[65]
No wonder that 'as beggarly as a threadbare priest' was a proverbial
phrase across France, and centres like Bayeux all contained their proportion of unemployed ecclesiastics called *habitués*, on the lookout for
a patron and a permanent post; elsewhere, in Brittany, parts of the
Auvergne, the Limousin and the Pyrenees, many of the unbeneficed
joined communities of priests (*communautés des prêtres*) or chantry
priests, though their numbers were declining in proportion to the
number of ordinations after *c.* 1750.[66] Whatever their status and
standard of living most discharged their duties well enough to give
them a strong claim to virtue, so that Rousseau's fictitious but inordi-
nately famous *vicaire Savoyard* could stand for them all, attached as he
was 'less to the spririt of the Church than the spirit of the Gospel, for
whom dogma is simplicity and morality sublime, in whom one sees
less religious practice and more works of charity'.[67] Not every *curé*
could aspire to be a modern paragon. Many were content to get
among their parishoners and live a thoroughly rustic life, pasturing
their cattle and horses, attending the local fairs, and neglecting their
appearance. But there were also hard-drinking, sexually active
would-be sophisticates among the *curés*.[68]

All were better educated than ever before, the beneficiaries of
increasingly high-quality theological courses taught in the seminaries, where much more was on offer by the mid-eighteenth century
than the basic skills of preaching a sermon and taking confession,
with the emphasis increasingly on forming what one recruit called
'an assembly of useful citizens'.[69] Once in their parishes, the products
of these seminaries did not drop their reading. In Normandy *c.* 1700,
only 10 per cent of *curés* built up their own library; by the 1780s most
had a stock of books to rival any held by canons, with an emphasis on
pastoral theology rather than dogmatics.[70] In 1775 the *curé* of Epesses
(La Rochelle diocese) owned 59 books, and only 4 were on non-
religious subjects, indicative of a trend which the influential contemporary historian Jean Delumeau says amounted to the 'creation of a
cultural clerical ghetto; a growing gulf between religious and lay culture'.[71] Delumeau may be too easily discounting other aspects of a
late-eighteenth-century parish priest's life. He may have kept up his
theology but he also wanted a social life. A priest like Paul Robert de
Saint-Amans in Agen, with his ample wardrobe, his jasmine perfume
bought by the packet, and his clothes trimmed with 'silver pieces and
threads, sprigs and little buttons',[72] was exactly the sort one memoir
writer remembered 'who knew how to play the violin brilliantly, and

was adept at dancing, whether minuets, country dances, or the gavotte'.[73] Such a one might well be a freemason, regard his hierarchical superiors with an uneasy mixture of jealousy and toadying, and entertain political pretensions. These worldly *curés* would initially find the revolution had much to offer them.

But young men were holding back from offering themselves for holy orders in the second half of the century.[74] To call it a 'manpower crisis' is excessive – the spectacular increase in ordinations in dioceses like Boulogne and Strasbourg between 1770 and 1790 makes that impossible[75] – but as scholars like Charles Berthelot du Chesnay, Timothy Tackett and Dominique Julia have shown, in some dioceses as far apart as Autun, Aix, Bordeaux and Reims, the number of men coming forward represented a decline that looked ominous in the medium term. Urban vocations fell markedly between 1760 and 1775, then recovered slightly only to fall again in the later 1780s.[76] Patrons were obliged to staff vacancies with men from beyond their region. Thus priests from lower Normandy filled up Parisian vacancies, and men from the Dauphiné spread westwards into the Midi. Above all, it was those originating in the dioceses of Brittany and the Auvergne who made up the shortfall, exactly the areas where resistance to the Civil Constitution from 1791 onwards would be at its most intense.[77] Nevertheless, about 70 per cent of the 40 000 rural priests in 1789 were still local men; 80 out of every 100 in the Lyon archdiocese, 70 in Beauvais and more or less every one in Embrun.[78] Local variations could be considerable. In the Dauphiné, the diocese of Gap called on the surplus of young priests turned out by the seminary in neighbouring Embrun to make good their own vacancies after *c.* 1765.

Aspirants to the priesthood were legally required to possess 150 livres of independent income annually, but recent studies have warned us against any assumption that the *curés* were plebeians. In some northern and western dioceses, the sons of well-to-do peasants were taking the cloth, but this went against a trend visible elsewhere. By 1760 in Strasbourg two *curés* were the sons of noblemen, and the rest predominantly descended from wealthy peasant proprietors and municipal officers.[79] Earlier in the century, 80 per cent of the Reims parish clergy were drawn from the bourgeoisie, 85 per cent in Autun and 78 per cent in Lyon.[80] The rising value of some benefices was undoubtedly attracting a higher social stratum, and these well-connected young men manoeuvred themselves into the best benefices, mostly in the gift of lay patrons, monasteries, chapters and bishops. As one *curé* complained in 1789:

... the government of parishes is often conferred on priests lacking either the talents or the virtues of their status; one commonly sees youngsters from outside the area, lacking in experience, given the best cures in the diocese, while white-haired *vicaires* wait vainly and endlessly for some reward for their heavy and persistent labours.[81]

It seems, however, that peasant ordinands slowly increased from the mid-century as the priesthood became a less attractive option for other sections of society.

Whatever the social origin of the lower clergy, modern scholarship indicates that most benefices generated an ampler income than was once thought. The local variations make any overall assessment hazardous, though it has been calculated that if the average episcopal income *c.* 1750 was 37 000 livres, a *curé* on the *portion congrue* (300 livres; see below) had an annual income of less than 1 per cent of the bishop's.[82] On the other hand, prosperity was increasing, especially for urban clergy. The *curé* of the Saint-Géry parish in Arras virtually doubled his annual income in less than a decade to 9000 livres by 1790,[83] and his comfortable level of income was replicated elsewhere; in the Bas-Maine, for instance, a *curé* could be worth 10 000 livres in rents. By contrast, in rural Norman dioceses like Coutances and Lisieux some benefices stayed vacant because they could not generate enough funds for the holder to live on. In the town of Bayeux the cures were notoriously unremunerative. Parish priests were constantly supplementing a basic income with a second job. It could be teaching in the choir school, acting as a cathedral chaplain or, best of all, attachment to the hospital (*hôtel Dieu*) where payment was in food: fish, beef, duckling, good vegetables and as much cider as one could drink. Such mouth-watering prospects were for the fortunate few.

There were basically two sorts of parish priest: those who were entitled to the tithe rights of their benefice and those who relied on the individual or corporation for subsistence. For those *curés* who drew the tithe themselves, the good harvests of the 1770s brought a new level of prosperity, but increased income was a mixed blessing in pastoral terms, for parishoners resented handing over a slice of their profits to the priest, even more so if collection was in the hands of a contractor from outside the area (that invidious job was sometimes done by a non-tithing *curé*, looking to supplement his income by obtaining the contractor's percentage),[84] insistent on enforcing every last one of the proprietor's rights, and taking the proceeds outside the village rather than putting it into fabric expenses or paying for the services of a *vicaire*.[85] The tithe was defined by one bishop in 1789 as 'a voluntary offering of the faithful', but this, as the *curés décimateurs* well knew, was quite disingenuous. As the parish priest of Vercoiran (Valence) bemoaned, tithe 'banished the good understanding that ought to exist [in a village] and had cost many a pastor the confidence of his flock'.[86] Yet French clergy, like their counterparts everywhere else in eighteeth-century Europe, wanted to live comfortably; conscience took second place, if only on the basis that not to uphold tithing rights was to penalise their successors. Many better-off parish priests with tithe rights tried to plough back – literally – any surplus income, however tiny, into the parish. At Sainte-Pézenne near Niort, the local *curé* was an active farmer, with plenty of jobs for the villagers; only a few miles away, at Chérigné in the Marais Poitevin, *curé* Jallet, who would be the first defector from the first estate to the third in 1789, was the son of a gardener who put his own agricultural expertise at the service of parishoners. This unselfishness was one way of deflecting the criticism that might reduce pastoral effectiveness, though it was seldom enough to overcome the peasant proprietor's sense of grievance.

It by no means follows that priests had to possess tithe entitlement to share in the rise in living standards. For instance in the diocese of Auch, where tithe had been farmed out in almost every parish, three-quarters of the *curés* enjoyed an income of more than 1000 livres in 1790.[87] Apart from tithes, there were other occasional sources of income, particularly the *casuel*, fees payable for special masses, burials, publication of marriage bans, sometimes rental payments due to the parish from legacies. In France as a whole, it was less the beneficed clergy than the humble *vicaires* attached as assistants to their parishes who drew the *casuel*, hoping that an average income of 300 livres would feed, clothe, and house them. While offering a serious income in wealthy, urban parishes, the *casuel* was a notoriously unreliable form of livelihood in impoverished areas. The sliding scale of charges at funerals put any kind of elaborate ceremony beyond the reach of ordinary families, and inspired the ironic phrase to describe a melancholy *curé* – 'he is sad even at funerals'.[88] The diocese laid down the scale of the fees, but they left it to the clergy to collect them and ignored the protests of *curés* who said they dare not levy a high charge because of the anger it would arouse among their parishoners. Necessity could force their hand. The *casuel* was often necessarily drawn on by clerics on the *portion congrue*, which, as a memorandum from the *congruistes* of the Poitiers diocese lamented in 1785 was just not generating enough income to go round.[89] Most clergy everywhere spent a disproportionate amount of time and energy trying to make ends meet. As the *curés* of the Aurillac region complained in 1789:

> Pastoral concern, we must embarrassingly admit, is no longer our exclusive concern. Instead, that of protecting our livelihood takes up a great part of the time that ought to be consecrated to the care of our flocks.[90]

That was uncomfortably the case in parishes where the tithe rights belonged to a wealthy layman (*dîmes inféodées*), a monastery or a bishop (especially in the south-west) where clergy were powerless to prevent these *gros décimateurs* enjoying their rights to the last penny, oblivious of the misery inflicted on tithe-payers strapped for cash.[91] Such *gros décimateurs* were legally required to pay the priest a fixed sum called the *portion congrue*. This had been increased in 1768 (for the first time since 1686) from 300 livres to 500 and finally to 700 livres in 1786, but even the new rates came nowhere near to satisfying material needs at a time when prices were rising steadily. In the Nevers diocese where at least one-third of clergy were *congruistes*, the abbé Cassier, *curé* of the parish of Saint-Sulpice, calculated that after all expenses had been met he was left a yearly sum of one hundred livres from which to find his food, furniture and clothing, or 5 sols 5 deniers a day.[92] In the highlands of the Comminges there was a major distinction between the majority of poverty-stricken *congruiste* clergy and their colleagues who took the tithe. It was the same story in the Le Puy diocese in the Auvergne. The *congrue* was there paid directly by parishioners, and when they refused to meet the new increases there was little the parish clergy could do unless they wanted to render their ministry impossible.[93]

It is arguable that awareness of their corporate rights contributed as much to agitation among the lower clergy in Louis XVI's reign as material impoverishment. They increasingly felt entitled to a partnership with the episcopate rather than receiving insensitive reminders of their subordinate status from prelates whose interest in pastoral affairs could be erratic. Such was not invariably the case. Bishops were as keen as ever in the late eighteenth century to follow the Tridentine recommendations of catechisms, visitations and pastoral letters, and were reactivating dormant diocesan machinery such as rural deaneries (*archiprêtrés*) to be a permanent pastoral link with the parish clergy. Then there were synods and conferences that would bring together the *curés* and higher clergy under episcopal presidency for three or four days.[94] The pastoral concern of bishops like de la Ferronnays of Lisieux or de Jouffroy Gonsans of Le Mans could be counter-productive. Thus when the latter in 1780 introduced ecclesiastical retreats, he did so with the benign intention of bringing together the scattered clergy in seven hundred parishes.[95] But the fact that it was imposed rather than agreed after consultation with those most immediately affected – the *curés* – was an irritant. Similarly, the attempts of François de Bonal of Clermont to impose strict obedience by prohibiting priests from preaching without his authorisation was looked on as intrusive and unnecessary.[96] The ordinary parish clergyman of the 1780s took pride in his pastoral work, but the way the Church worked in practice meant that he was denied promotion while bishoprics and canonries were handed round to those who had never come into contact with ordinary men and women in the parishes. In this way, resentment inside the Church was stoked up, the *curés* and *vicaires* learnt to associate together in defensive solidarity, and the split along hierarchical lines inside the first estate that would be so pronounced when the Revolution erupted developed throughout Louis XVI's reign.

From the mid-century, rather than participate in authorised structures where the scope for their initiatives could be stifled by the bishops and *grands vicaires*, lower clergy often preferred to meet their local colleagues unofficially. 'Ecclesiastical conferences' were popular, especially in areas where Jansenism had been a force, and sociability could assist the formation of group consciousness. Yet, nationwide, the disputes that had riven the Church from the intial registration of the Bull *Unigenitus* in 1713 through to the last years of Louis XV were virtually extinguished. The Jansenists to be found in holy orders by 1780 were the survivors of a generation that had almost vanished. Archbishop Montazet of Lyon (d. 1787) was the last identifiable Jansenist on the bench of bishops, without any younger counterparts; junior prelates or aspirants to a mitre could not afford to alienate court opinion by trying to revive the issue. So, just as Jansenism was becoming *more* entrenched in the higher reaches of the Italian and Austrian hierarchies, it had ceased to impinge on their French counterparts. It was largely confined to lower and middle-ranking clergy in dioceses like Lyon and Auxerre where

Jansenists had earlier benefitted from the patronage of sympathetic prelates but, on the eve of the Revolution, found that episcopal influence was one of the factors helping to marginalise them in Church life.[97] At Poitiers, Bishop Saint-Aulaire overturned expectations after his appointment in 1759 by reducing Jansenist influence in the diocese to a hard-core in the cathedral chapter itself.[98] At Auxerre, traditionally one of their strongholds, the two parties among the clergy were almost equal *c.* 1780, and the Jansenists were the ones on the defensive, if still capable of occasional demonstrations. The death of Salomon, *curé* of Saint-Renobert, regarded locally as a saint, brought them onto the streets as late as April 1788, when they carried the body in procession into the heart of his old parish and on to the cemetery.[99]

Though there was no necessary link between them, Jansenism encouraged the so-called Richerist revival of the later eighteenth century. The embers of controversy were fanned sporadically by the continued publication of the Jansenist weekly and 'house magazine', the *Nouvelles Ecclésiastiques*, founded in 1728 and still going strong fifty years later.[100] It was read by a loyal following of laity and clergy and, apart from an often acute commentary on contemporary issues, offered spicey stories of bishops exceeding their authority or making fools of themselves. It inspired lower clergy to fight still harder for a Church that would relive primitive Christianity and rediscover pastoral care as its overwhelming priority, a compelling vision whose appeal should not be underestimated. At its heart was the bishop as shepherd and, if they flirted with presbyterianism, it was mainly as a reaction to an episcopate which on the surface appeared to under value the appeal of primitive models. As a supplement to the *Nouvelles Ecclésiastiques*, in the last decade of the old régime, ageing Jansenists versed in canon law, like Gabriel-Nicholas Maultrot, also exercised what influence they had on behalf of the parish priests with works like Maultrot's own *Institution divine des curés* [*The Divine Origin of Curés*] (1778) and *La défense des droits du second ordre* [*The Defence of the Rights of the Second Order*] (1788). They gave a deepened intellectual force to Richerism.

This was yet another contemporary exercise in constitutionalism, one which stressed the inherent dignity of the priestly office as heirs to the seventy-two disciples as opposed to the bishops, the descendants of the apostolic twelve. Edmond Richer was an early-seventeenth-century priest and Sorbonne theologian of intensely pro-Gallican views classically expressed in his *De ecclesiastica et politica potestate*

(1611);[101] a century and half after his death, the parochial clergy remained inadequately represented in the machinery of the Church at every level from local synods to the General Assembly, causing them to band together unofficially in the mutual associations mentioned above. Richerism thus considerably enhanced group consciousness among the *curés*, and in some sharply contrasting areas. As early as 1763 a coalition of lower clergy in the Noyonnais had formed to try and extract more money from the diocesan authorities; in 1766, the *curés* of the Rodez diocese insisted on their right to name representatives to the diocesan chamber that distributed the local burden of *décimes*, but had no success; while in 1777 in Périgueux, where – exceptionally – they had no less than sixteen of their number involved in the diocesan bureau, they protested to the Agents-General that their voice often carried mininimal influence in final decisions.[102]

The heartland of this new clerical militancy was the province of the Dauphiné in south-eastern France. While its leaders, like Henri Reymond of Grenoble in his *Droits des curés* [*Rights of the Curés* (1776)], did not question that there should be functional divisions in the Church, they emphasised that the authority of a bishop was not greater in kind than a parish priest's to the point of asserting that 'they *are* bishops each in his own parish'.[103] Lower-clergy notions of acceptable and legitimate leadership were thus changing fast, but they were looking backwards rather than to the future. They hankered for the restoration of what they supposed to be the ways of the primitive Church; it was the counterpart in the 1780s for hopes that the pre-absolutist constitution in the state would be retrieved. And there could be no more important figures within the ministry than the parish clergy with their pastoral commitment. As another contemporary critic summed it up:

> The *curés* therefore compose with the bishops the *pastoral corps* instituted by Jesus Christ, and it is this august and sacred title that constitutes the entire dignity of their state, because the order of pastors is incontestably the first ecclesiastical order . . . [104]

From this it followed that the *curé*'s indispensability to the life and mission of the Church entitled him to far-reaching consultative rights in decision-making. Reymond recommended the creation of a new and permanent body, with a guaranteed majority of *curés*, sitting at Paris, and acting as a clearing house for the concerns of the lower clergy – especially the *congruistes*. It was an ominous sign of how far any expectation that the General Assembly of the Clergy would act on their behalf had collapsed.[105] Above all, Reymond and his allies insisted, the *curés* merited a combination of improved remuneration and a reduction in the heavy burden of clerical taxation (the *décimes*) which fell on this same constituency.

Higher clergy were not unaware of this grassroots unrest. The General Assembly of 1775 had considered a package involving preferment according to merit, an index-linked *portion congrue* and a pension for retired clergy. But this imaginative initiative foundered, and the Church hierarchy fell back on repressing clamorous malcontents.[106] The 1780 General Assembly coincided with the issue of several incendiary publications against 'ecclesiastical despotism', which earned one of their perpetrators, the Abbé Le Senne, a *lettre de cachet* for his *Mémoire des curés* attacking taxes like the *décimes*, the abuse of tithes and the unfair distribution of benefices, and forced him into hiding. Le Senne's prediction, 'That there is not a *curé* in the country who won't buy it and not a bishop who won't proscribe it', was broadly accurate.[107] The hierarchy increasingly had their backs to the wall against their own membership. Unofficial, unauthorised *curé* meetings were prohibited by the Crown at the request of the bishops in 1782, but its implementation was patchy and these gatherings went on regardless.

The lower-clergy leaders would not be deterred either from emphasising their place of honour in the Church or from urging priest colleagues to nurture a spirit of solidarity among themselves. It flourished conspicuously throughout the Midi, and in Lorraine where in 1786 a professor at the seminary Saint-Simon in Metz, Thiébault, published his *Dissertation sur la juridiction respectives des évêques et des curés*. This presented the Church as an egalitarian society founded on the diversity of functions rather than a hierarchy resting on divine right. It sold rapidly, and it was no surprise that Thiébault was elected to the Estates-General in 1789, where he joined another better-known priest prominent in the fight for Jewish as well as lower-clergy rights – Henri Grégoire. Public sympathy for boosting the political importance of the *curés* – the kinsmen and friends of the Third Estate – was in place when Necker and his ministerial colleagues came to draw up the rules for the elections to the Estates-General. Their decision not to guarantee the bishops and higher clergy any seats in that eagerly awaited forum demonstrated just how far Necker – supremely sensitive to the popular mood – was persuaded that the claims of the *curés* to recognition were irresistible. The challenge to the hierarchy was unambiguous. Even the most conservative prelate had been served notice that his sacred office did not confer on him a divine right to exercise power regardless of clerical views. This is not to say that clergy were unwilling to acknowledge the place of the bishop in the hierarchy; it was more a question of how he went about exercising that apostolic power that caused concern. The politic modernisers in the episcopate, like Champion de Cicé at Bordeaux, sensed the new mood, and hammered out a more tactful pastoral approach that would close the gap between prelates and parish clergy; in return for supporting further increases in the *portion congrue*, Champion de Cicé extracted the endorsement (with some reservations) of his Provincial Synod in April 1788 to the edict granting limited toleration to non-Catholics.[108] He was following the lead of another *prélat administrateur*, Brienne of Toulouse, whose synod of 1782 was directly concerned with the precarious situation of *curés congruistes* and *vicaires*.[109] More traditionalist prelates were less flexible, too ready to exaggerate a 'presbyterian' challenge. But there can be no doubting that episcopal absolutism, like any other version of it, was being called into question on an unprecedented scale by the 1780s, as the clergy began to agitate in significant numbers for a new constitutional settlement with fairer terms for all members of the First Estate. Few could have envisaged that within five years from the meeting of the Estates-General in 1789 their Church would end up less reformed than dismantled.

2 Catholicism in Eighteenth-Century France: Varieties of Practice and Belief

The Church's presence was evident at every level in society from the palace to the parish, and one taken for granted. The Church sanctified the average Frenchman's coming into the world, and sustained him with its sacraments thereafter. So long as that regard held, the Church's institutional power was hard to challenge and, as a source of popular allegiance, not least among women, it had no serious competitor even in the 'Age of Enlightenment'. For whatever the criticisms levelled by the *philosophes*, it was the people's sense that the clergy were witnessing on their behalf to God that ensured the majority were inextricably attached to the Church of their ancestors, and kept them loyal to varying degrees throughout the upheavals of the 1790s. Nevertheless, it is hard to deny a slow but perceptible diminution from the mid-century of Church authority over an influential portion of the laity in France. It gave a new twist to that disrespect towards the priesthood that was present in every generation. As will be seen, some historians would go further, and argue that institutional disenchantment followed on from a general dilution of belief *c*.1750, from a change in *mentalités* that suggests a shift away from the priority of winning salvation through faith, good works and obedience to the Church's laws, towards more earthly concerns, where charitable observance and goodwill towards men were valued for their own sake rather than to ease the passage to the next world.

The Gallican Church was a broad Church: it had little alternative if it was to live up to its status as the national Church. The clergy were the first to recognise that they were ministering to every social level. Beyond the common commitment to credal orthodoxy and an essentially sacramental ministry was a willingness to make provision for different expressions of faith according to gender, social status and educational achievement; the result was considerable variation in religious practice at both parish and diocesan level.[1] The general reluctance to abandon local usages in the liturgy was a testimony to the formidable power of custom as well as the regional vitality of

France on the eve of the revolution.[2] Services differed in other respects. So much depended on locality, as well as the taste of the priests and worshippers concerned. Well-crafted sermons were for sophisticated urban congregations; their rural counterparts received homilies that were short and couched in language they could easily grasp. They tended to be based on either a Gospel text or a verse from the Epistle of the day, and emphasised human sinfulness, the need to attend church and pray regularly, and the intercessionary power of the Virgin and the saints.[3]

For most French men, women and children the representative of the Church they were most likely to encounter was the local parish priest. Throughout rural France, not just at baptisms, marriages and funerals, but at festivals and the ordinary Sunday services, the lives of the *curé* and his parishioners would intersect. To him they might bring their tithes, or send their children to be catechised;[4] to him was entrusted the valued responsibility of keeping the living in touch with the deceased by celebrating anniversary masses for the repose of the souls. On a day-to-day basis, across France, the parish priest was the first person to whom ordinary people turned for help and advice on a range of matters. One person might want to borrow money from him, another leaving the village to find seasonal work might seek a reference for a new employee. Some of the wealthiest villagers might even use his decorative schemes in the presbytery for their own homes, and it was not unknown for parishioners to crave his assistance in obtaining a marriage partner![5] At the other end of the scale, bold, down-to-earth young villagers like Jacques-Louis Ménétra could admit their religious doubts in informal conversation with their sympathetic *curé* and be ready to hear him out:

> His one and only response was to say to me: 'All these mysteries must be believed because the Church believes them.' He said to me 'My friend you are enlightened.' It is necessary that for the sake of governments that the people must always live in ignorance.[6]

Ménétra may not have accepted the reply but, as a former altar-boy with the embers of a failed clerical vocation flickering in his memory,[7] he took it seriously because in parochial terms the *curé* spoke with an authority no one else possessed.

The *curé* was the recognised intermediary between the elites of wealth and power and his parishoners, an integral part of the community where he resided. The ordinary villager would expect his priest to act as spokesman for the whole parish, and not become the obsequious follower of the local landowner who may well have appointed him to the living. Modern research suggests considerable variants. *Curés* could be critics of noble families in the district, so much so that at Gissey in Burgundy, the priest was physically threatened among his parishoners while, in complete contrast, not far away at Saint-Germain-le-Rocheux, the *curé*, François Fournier, acted as agent for the Marquis de Ragny, the main landowner.[8] Where a parish priest had upset his community for whatever reason, young men – the *garçons de paroisse* – might congregate at night and set up the kind of din which could turn in to serious public disorder.[9] Yet the majority of clergy exhibited a degree of dispassionate conduct that won respect and, even if many among them aroused indifference or aversion, most villagers could not afford to stay away from church if they wanted to know something about life beyond the parish boundaries.

It was from the *curé's* pulpit that his people would hear announcements about taxation, poor relief, the militia ballot and other items from the wider world that impinged on otherwise humdrum domestic lives. Increasingly, after 1750, the civil authorities had more use for the parish clergy than the habitual administrative duties of keeping the registers of births, marriages and deaths up to date, supplementing those mundane events with great happenings in the history of France – the birth of a dauphin, the death of a king, the signing of a peace treaty. The parish clergy could organise assistance in times of dearth, and ensure that the sick received such primitive medicinal treatments as there were available. Indeed, some clergy even invented their own patent medicines, like Le Joyant in the diocese of Le Mans with his specific against rabies; in October 1789, a parish priest of Poitou wrote to ministers saying he had been 'apostle, judge, surgeon and doctor' to his people for thirty-four years.[10] No wonder that the *curé* was so often trusted to act as the voice of the locality as well as the Church. In the most remote areas of the countryside, parish clergy would, in effect, act as translators, speaking in the *patois* with the locals and in French with officialdom and the educated; in some south-western parts sermons and catechetical classes were all in the vernacular. 'In most of our communities', observed the deputies of the Sélestat district (containing 153 parishes) of Alsace in 1789, 'there are only the *curés* and the councillors [*prévôts*] who know how to read and write, especially the French tongue.'[11]

The parish clergy were not required to decide whether or not they were priests first and citizens later until the Civil Constitution was introduced in 1790–1. The assumption before then was that the two were more than compatible. As early as 1735 one abbé insisted: 'The priests and the *curés* are officers of the state destined to correct manners, that is to say, daily to make citizens just and beneficent so as to please God.'[12] Christianity and civic concern were not then at odds, and the primary religious allegiance of the vast majority of parish clergy has perhaps too readily been downplayed by recent scholars. Here, the resounding affirmation of the *curé* Mollevant speaks for most: 'No worldly interest attaches me to religion; no worldly interest will ever pull it away from my heart; all my desire is to serve it, and I will devote myself to it down to the last drop of my blood.'[13]

Of course, the story is not one of uniformity: there were, as one *curé* insisted to an inquisitive English Catholic, several priests known to him personally 'worthy of apostolic times',[14] but these role-models, secure in the affections of their parishioners, had colleagues with nothing like the awesomely simple virtue of Rousseau's famous *vicaire Savoyard*. On the whole, the picture in 1789 was encouraging. Most parish priests commanded the respect of their people even where affection was absent; in the west of France in particular, historians have noted exceptional acceptance of a 'clericalized' religion, perhaps due to what Professor Timothy Tackett has called 'the superior status of the *curé* and his assistants in the cultural symbolism and the lines of social power'.[15] Here, in the future heartlands of the Counter-Revolution, the priest was for the laity more than anywhere 'their' man, perhaps the one professional they would ever really know, whose life (if he was carrying out his functions properly) touched their own at its most crucial moments. How sensitively he handled such contacts made all the difference to his local standing. In all areas of France, the Gallican Church was not short of priests whose pastoral skills helped to keep attendances at Sunday Mass at an acceptable level, even those in poorly endowed benefices in the Paris region whose occupants tended to attract much less respect than their counterparts in the west. Life in a rural parish was hard, often dispiriting work for men from a bourgeois, urban milieu; they could not live long amid their rural flock without losing a few illusions. The journal of Christophe Sauvageon, *curé* of Sennely in the marshy woodlands of the Sologne south of Orléans, shows us how he knew at first hand how basic his people could be: 'God's commandment to honour your father and mother is completely ignored in these parts,' he noted, but he still went on visiting, trying to satisfy material wants and bring the sacraments to his flock.[16]

For priest and layman alike, the parish church was at the heart of their community's individual and collective existence, a link between the living and the dead, a public meeting place as well as a focus for the worship of God, a primary source of identity for the villagers, whatever their place within its life, its fittings and fixtures – especially the church bells – a matter of proprietorial pride.[17] It was the one building where the community could foregather and in which, at service, all ranks would assemble together. Every sort of idea was bound up in the church building. As Suzanne Desan summarises: 'Public ritual, localized sacred power, the interwoven texture of the sacred and profane, individual or communal prestige and identity, patterns of sociability and festivity, divine aid, strengthening of faith, moral order, salvation.'[18] From this, the most important sacred space in the parish, there were usually other spots known for their holiness to every generation of villager. It might be a wayside chapel, a fountain, or a hermitage, all components of a geography that gave meaning to lives of toil and struggle.

Whatever the nature and extent of a villager's Christian beliefs, there was no ignoring the rhythms of the liturgical year with its rich sacramental life fitting into the wider religious culture with local patron saint(s), the observation of holy days and the engrained belief that the Almighty daily intervened in the ordering of events. Christenings (usually conducted a day or two after birth), weddings and funerals were the legal monopoly of the Gallican Church, the first two legal as well as religious occasions requiring oath taking of the greatest solemnity. Marriage was one of the seven sacraments for Roman Catholics and, as the century progressed, the clergy were becoming more and more fearful at the spread of contraception (especially by *coitus interruptus*), thus placing a sinful limit on fertility.[19] Historians have located signs of it in the major urban centres even before 1700 (Paris particularly), and it spread gradually to smaller centres. After the mid-century the practice had undoubtedly reached many country districts, with rural fairs notorious for encouraging the practice. The extent of contraception should not be exaggerated: it was the upper levels of society who were the major practitioners before the Revolution.[20] Nevertheless, the trend was unsettling enough for the Church, especially when it was combined with a steady rise in bridal pregnancy, illegitimacy and abandoned children.[21]

There are signs that more enlightened priests in Louis XVI's time were handling these awkward moral issues more tactfully, tacitly allowing contraception by finding casuistical precepts to fit the bill, for instance accepting that the man might withdraw from his wife without ejaculating or, at any rate, not intending to ejaculate. But most couples probably experienced a sterner line than this in the confessional. Some women stopped going to it, others blamed their husbands for practising contraception or the other immoderate conjugal acts the Church also deplored and, in this way, young fathers and husbands built up resentment against the clergy for what they supposed was privileged access to the secrets of family life. The perils of confession may have multiplied the attractions of the tavern for men at the expense of the parish church; it undoubtedly played its part in introducing the first signs of sexual dimorphism into religious practice by the mid-century.[22] Ironically, the confession of a male tended to be much more straightforward for both penitent and priest – 'In general, one runs less risk and does more good in confessing men', advised one pastor in 1783[23] – while family problems could result when women who insisted that they could not do without the comforts of the sacraments, were prepared to defy their husbands on the issue. In return for this loyalty, resourceful and realistic directors of conscience appear to have been more than ready to find circumstances when the rule of the Church against contraception would not be enforced. It is unlikely that this concession – additional evidence of the increased moral status granted to women[24] – brought their husbands back securely into the fold.

The clergy could and did exclude those on whom the Church's ban had fallen, for instance ordering the authorities to take action against couples living together outside wedlock, and refusing to have the excommunicated buried in consecrated ground. It required careful strategems to outwit the priests in such circumstances, most notoriously in the rush to return Voltaire's body to, literally, safe ground at home in Ferney after he had died in Paris in 1778.[25] And only those who had confessed their sins and stood in love and charity with their neighbours could receive communion at the Mass, which was, at village level, an essential means of preserving the local peace. This service remained the central focus of the Church's worship at every level. It was at once a sign of heavenly grace and of earthly good-standing, the incentive and the inspiration for the laity to go on to the performance of good works towards their neighbours 'each according to his state'.[26] Witholding access to the sacrament could have national repercussions, as was shown earlier in the century when most bishops as a guard against the Jansenist 'heresy' ordered it not be administered to those who had no *billet de confession* to receive Holy Communion.

Church attendance figures in rural areas were holding steady in the late eighteenth century, though reliable figures are scarce, with episcopal visitation records offering most help to the historian. Should, for instance, we include the man who felt his Sunday obliga-tion satisfied if he crossed the road to catch the sound of the Mass by standing in the church porch while waiting for the *cabaret* (the tavern) to open?[27] Contemporaries would have given these recalcitrants the benefit of the doubt. All the locals would turn out in strength to wit-ness and support the first communion of young people aged twelve to fourteen, and Easter communion was received by the vast majority of the rural population. Services could be lively affairs, with the congre-gation not always paying much attention to the celebrant's conduct of the service. One British visitor expressed her concern at the behav-iour she witnessed in Rouen:[28]

> I went to High Mass at one of the most considerable Churches in the Town, & was astonished at the want of Devotion in the Audi-ence; some were counting their Money, some arguing with the Beggars who interrupt you without ceasing, some receiving Mes-sages and dispatching Answers, some beating time to the Musick, but scarce any one praying except for one moment when the Priest elevated the Host.

As ever, services varied enormously, and in cathedrals and collegiate churches the standard of the music and the liturgical presentation could be very high indeed, as at Saint-Sulpice. One traveller in 1775 found the experience 'far above the force of my imagination – no wonder that the Devotees there kissed the ground at their depar-ture – it was heaven upon earth in miniature'.[29] Saint-Sulpice had an international reputation.

The presence at Sunday services of most men was a crucial distinguishing feature of pre-Revolutionary Catholicism as opposed to its nineteenth-century successor, though they might prefer to attend shorter, less ceremonious Low Masses in their parish church, or at a local convent or chapel. Admittedly, in some parts of the Parisian region, through the Seine Valley to the Champagne, parts of Burgundy, and the Auvergne, there are more definite emergent signs of variations between the sexes in key religious practices such as Lenten confession and Sunday observance. Thus at Mennecy near Gonesse (Seine-et-Oise) in 1780, 91 out of 198 male householders, 28 out of 66 bachelors aged 25 or above, 149 out of 198 married women, and a totality of widows and spinsters performed their Easter duties.[30] Despite these pre-Revolutionary pointers to future variants, the greater part by far of rural France, with a few significant exceptions like some coastal villages in Languedoc[31] and centres like Nîmes or La Rochelle, where illicit Protestant worship went on, can accurately be described on the basis of Sunday Mass attendance as holding firm to the faith. Although there are some telling signs that rural women living above the poverty line were starting to give more to charities and their church than the men, were staying loyal longer to the devotional confraternities and were purchasing religious tracts where they had time and money, we should be wary of making the eighteenth century one characterised by imbalances between the sexes or too readily accept the notion of the 'feminization of Catholicism' during the eighteenth century. As Olwen Hufton has concluded:

> In the century preceding the Revolution in most rural parishes a near totality of men and women observed, however perfunctorily, their religious obligations.[32]

Women found in Catholicism an outlet for their emotions that could not easily find expression elsewhere. For two centuries young women had flocked to join the religious orders, a tendency that was still in evidence prior to the Revolution. The hierarchy preferred the figure of the confined, contemplative nun as a role-model, but the reality was that most women opted for a family life rather than virginity. It was this majority that the Church had been working on since the Counter-Reformation with some success, and a new rhetoric was emerging to counteract the traditional gendered emphasis on female corruptibility and the awful warning of Eve's part in the Fall of Man.

Within the home women were to obey their husbands and go diligently about their tasks; yet outside it there was slowly expanding scope for independent initiative. The clergy encouraged them to take a proactive role in the spiritual life of their parishes through charitable works. They used Marian examples to stress the high calling of married women as well as spinsters, to encourage a spiritual responsiveness finding expression within a well-established tradition of piety. Next to their families, the first loyalty of millions of women was to their church and their priest. No other public body empowered them in a similar way, and when the Revolution came it offered them nothing like the same participatory possibilities. Because women were so tenaciously attached to a religious life and institutions they regarded as distinctively 'theirs', the task of the Revolutionaries in setting up alternative structures and practices was made infinitely harder.

The *curé* and his female parishioners did not always share the same emphasis in living the religious life. The parish priest by his training embodied a disciplined, structured form of the faith and it was his duty to lead his people in the same path − the classic objective of the post-Tridentine Church for over two centuries. Yet the religion of the *curé* and the religion of perhaps the majority of ordinary country people still showed considerable variations even as late as the 1780s. 'Popular Christianity' is a notoriously ambiguous term, and a working definition of it as religion as lived out by the majority of the faithful, poorly off peasants and artisans (as distinct from what was prescribed to them) comes as close as any.[33] In its various forms, it might be no more than a pause in gathering in the harvest for the angelus bell, or a hurried genuflexion as the sacrament went through the village street on its way to comfort a dying person, but it often went deeper than that, to include a vast range of practices that, on the surface, had little to do with the Christian religion according to the catechism.

Though we should beware of a simplistic picture that depicts clergy and people as perpetually at loggerheads over the contents of religion,[34] it is generally the case that the French Church made continuing efforts to prescribe what might almost be called an alternative religion where, in Hufton's memorable phrase, it was trying 'to harden the spirituality of the faithful', to purge it of superstitious abuses, miraculous claims and riotous celebrations such as attended trade guilds' saints' days. This strategy was comparable to manifestations of the Catholic Enlightenment elsewhere in Europe, to be found classically in the religious policies of Joseph II in the 1780s and his brother Leopold in Tuscany.[35]

There were particular reasons for this emphasis in France. The Church was vulnerable to criticism from the *philosophes* over tardiness in eradicating specious cults and observances – new shrines sprang up throughout the century, and many became the destination for pilgrims, inviting Voltaire's mischievous taunt that they were invented by innkeepers! As far as the *philosophes* and most other members of the educated elite were concerned, obscurantist, objectionable practices were an affront to an enlightened century. They were quick to point out any ecclesiastical compromise with 'superstition' as an admission of its embarrassingly close relationship with the Church's own faith, and they exploited the perceived convergence fully. Most clergy worked hard to restrict popular religious excess, and resistance was generally ebbing away by mid-century. Though the upshot was raised standards of public morality, the price in terms of public goodwill towards the Church authorities was always high. The resentment that implementation of a Catholic reform agenda often stirred up at parish level needed careful pastoral handling. It was often Jansenist clergy who insisted on a high standard of behaviour from their parishioners. Not only did they suppress riotous clebrations of saints' days, but they also imposed stiff penances.[36] Such behaviour could be counterproductive in securing affection, just as the moral strictures in the confessional by priests sympathetic to Jansenism might result in gradual detachment of uneducated villagers from the sacramental life of the Church.[37] It offered another justification for individuals so minded to distance themselves from public religious activity or take part in it without inner conviction. After 1789, they would have the chance to concentrate their loyalties within Revolutionary culture, work to cut clerical pretensions down to size and no doubt settle private scores in the process.

Historians have understandably found here components of incipient dechristianisation, but several cautionary points need to be registered before admitting the importance of Jansenism in this area. For a start, it is implausible to construct a putative revolutionary alliance between those who rejected unpopular *jansénisant* policies in the parish and those laity and clergy, partly inspired by Jansenism, who sought to recreate the values of primitive Christianity in the Constitutional Church. And, besides, after *c.* 1750 the number of parish priests (especially in the countryside) who might accurately be identified as Jansenists was declining every year. But then it had never been *just* Jansenists involved in the processes of tightening up parish life and driving a wedge between the sacred and the secular and making them stand in much sharper mutual relief: it was an ineradicable aspect of post-Tridentine pastoralia. To argue that *janséni-sant* practices from the episcopacy had depopularised Christianity in many areas both exaggerates the number of prelates within that category (certainly by the mid-eighteenth century) and makes too small an allowance for the mediatory role of the parish clergy. Pastoral sensitivity to popular observances frequently made *curés* reluctant to enforce episcopal orders and so hampered reform on the ground. This was especially true where Jesuit influences lingered, as in Flanders and Hainault in north-eastern France. Priests here knew that popular Christianity and folklore were more inextricably linked than either the higher clergy or the *philosophes* appreciated, with a resilience that enabled them to survive in tandem throughout the nineteenth century. Popular religious beliefs went too deep to be eliminated except gradually through a carefully directed teaching ministry, which the Church was not always able to provide, not least because its catechism could only be taught orally to illiterate country people, and the classic post-Tridentine linking of literacy and solid religious culture could therefore not be attempted.[38] In such circumstances, it made sense to reconcile indigenous tradition with the best elements of popular religion.

The strictures of the post-Tridentine Church could not prevent recourse by parishioners to any number of the habitual practices their families had used from one generation to another to cope with present problems and guard against future ones. It could be a woman placing a cross on dough left to rise, washing in a local spring associated with an appearance of the Virgin, or invoking the aid of St John the Baptist in pregnancy on the basis that the executed saint would ensure the baby would be born head first. The same concerns for their prosperity in this world led their husbands and sons to take their cattle up the hill to seek the blessing of St Guiral. These people needed their saints. Their intercession was the nearest approximation to an insurance policy they possessed, for, as Judith Devlin has written, 'Saints filled the role nowadays played by doctors, psychiatrists, priests, counsellors and insurance agents.'[39]

So instruction in the doctrines and teaching of the Church had not eliminated rural superstition; instead they coexisted. But then average late-eighteenth-century French Catholic probably knew more about the Christian life than any of his ancestors and to talk, as Roger Chartier has done, that 'mutual incomprehension was unavoidable' between the faithful and their parish priests is misleading.[40] The support given by the monarchy to episcopal efforts to bring the people into the so-called 'little schools' throughout the century helped bridge that gap. A rudimentary education under clerical control was on offer there.[41] Such Catholics were the product of the very high level of 'Christianisation' achieved in French religious life between about 1680 and 1750, for, as such recent studies as that of Philip Hoffman on Lyon have reminded us, the Counter-Reformation was still going on in the eighteenth century and was moving towards a successful climax.[42] It was then, as Harvey Mitchell has written:

> that standard forms of the catechism were introduced, the mystic significance of the sacraments exalted, the practice of easy confession proscribed, and, under the guidance of the Jesuits, priests were trained in seminaries to deal with the practical requirements of the confessional and the sermon.[43]

The impact of this work could be quite varied, even within a well-defined area in western France, as Mitchell has himself shown. Nevertheless, the results of applied catechetical teaching were there for all to see every Sunday in most parish churches, with the laity taking a more active part in the Mass than ever before, sometimes reading the lessons in the vernacular. Outward religious observance had thus been essentially regularised, though it may be that in the process, with the clergy concurrently waging war on religious 'abuses', conformity was achieved at the price of spiritual nourishment.[44] It is a difficult question, especially when one considers the greater availability of the Bible to the laity, so memorably evoked by Restif de la Bretonne in his memoirs recalling his father reading scripture round the fireside to his family. There had been some distinguished Jansenist translations of the New Testament available since the late seventeenth century, and much was, ironically, owed to Louis XIV: the Sun King had ordered the greater provision of Bibles for former Protestants as a means of easing their passage to Catholicism after the Huguenot faith was banned in 1685.

Particularly significant in 'Christianising' the countryside and seconding the work of the hard-pressed *curés*, were the new religious orders for lay women and the parochial missionaries. As befitted organisations designed to instruct little girls and care for the ill and indigent, their practice was to send three or four sisters into villages to form miniscule convents that could fulfil every form of practical task and work closely with the parish priest. Their activities won them the name of 'Houses of Charity'. One group, the Daughters of the Holy Virgin, offered retreats and spiritual renewal for underprivileged women longing for a break in their domestic routines. Their educational work underlined the continuing vitality of the French Church, and these still poorly known institutes of *filles séculières* scattered around the provinces played a vital and neglected part in sustaining women in their faith throughout the Revolution. Their work was phenomenonally popular: the Daughters of Wisdom grew from 118 members in 1759 established in 40 houses to 77 houses and 300 sisters in 1789.

No less important was the *béate*, usually a responsible widow or spinster whose simple dwelling (often provided by the village) acted as a crèche and school by day and at night afforded a hearth for mothers to make lace, share soup, sing hymns and recite the rosary together. The *béates* had their origin around Le Puy and the Velay district on the edge of the Auvergne in 1665, but a century later they were active on a much more extended scale with just enough education themselves to teach lace-making to the village girls while they recited their catechism.[45] The real importance lay in fortifying the faith of female villagers. There were increasing numbers of aids to facilitate the progress of young girls in learning the faith, like Catherine de Billy's *Instructions historiques, dogmatiques et morales en faveur des laboureurs et autres habitants de la campagne* (1746) [*Historic, Dogmatic and Moral Instructions Intended for Labourers and Other Rural Inhabitants*]. Despite the forbidding title, it used simple language of immediate usefulness to catechiser and catechised alike.[46] So the *béates* helped the village economy, gave wives and mothers a focus for their lives outside the home, and renewed and confirmed their faithfulness.

Missionary priests were also at work across France, with Lazarists in Anjou, the Fathers of Christian Doctrine in Gascony and the Pyrenees, and completely new companies of priests – the Mulotins – sprang up to work alongside the existing orders. Charismatic figures like Grignion de Montfort (1673–1716, canonised 1947) left a lasting mark on those who heard him preach in accessible, even emotionally charged ways during his missions across western France. It has been calculated that about 20 per cent of the total population of the Angers diocese were exposed to missionary preaching between 1710 and 1720 and, though there is still much further work to be done, preliminary indications suggest that areas visited by parochial missionaries in the eighteenth century were less likely to experience the radical dechristianisation imposed from the 1790s onwards.[47]

These missioners stayed in their selected parish for three to six weeks. They urged local people to follow new paths of piety and renew their practice of Christian observances, propagated Marian devotions, and staged highly dramatic presentations: processions would be led into church with the faithful carrying in their hands the crosses that would rest on their own graves, while in Lorraine one *curé* was so inspired that he ordered the whole interior of his church to be draped in black. Though there could be suspicions that the missions were encouraging the faithful to loosen the bonds that bound them to the parochial clergy, they were mostly welcolmed by the majority of parish priests (except for those of a Jansenist persuasion), who were encouraged to carry on the good work after the missioners had left.

This Catholic offensive, this 'golden age of the mission in Europe' was scaled down after 1750, with the countryside apparently christianised.[48] Scholars differ in their explanations as to why this occured. To some it represents a waning energy, 'a diminution of clerical vitality'.[49] Others point to business accomplished: the great reforming work of Counter-Reformation Catholicism was all but over, with episcopal visitations reduced to cross-country progress in confidence that there would be little to remedy later. Three points further might be added to the discussion. First, in dioceses across France (including some of those studied by Mitchell in the west), there was no slackening in the pace of pastoral energies whether exercised by bishop, parish priest or non-beneficed clergy building on the missionary work of their predecessors. Thus in Lorraine immediately before the Revolution, Father Jean Martin Moyë, assisted by the Sisters of Providence and working in conjunction with the *curés*, attempted to visit the most remote parishes in the diocese of Metz and undertake wide-ranging catechetical instruction.[50] Second, the extent to which Christianity with all its popularist accretions had won the loyalty of country people was shown by the willingness of so many to die for their faith in the 1790s. We cannot easily dispute such affirmations as the one made by a *curé* in 1788 assuring an English Catholic that he was touched with the decency, the attention, and the piety of by far the greatest number of those who frequent it [the church]. I often groan about the sinful conduct of some of my parishoners, but many good folk still remain to me for consolation.[51]

Lastly, geography is crucial. Some regions were more fervent than others, and had been from well before the Revolution. People from the Paris hinterland (especially to the south-east) were reluctant Mass-goers. They were also sluggards at sending their children to be catechised, and did little to encourage their sons to enter the priest-hood. In this area, Jansenism was historically more influential among the clergy than any other region of France, but it had not endeared itself to the laity in the same way. The eastern Champagne, the Mediterranean Languedoc and Provence had resisted 'clericali-sation' more noticeably than their counterparts towards the west (with some exceptions like parts of Poitou), and relations between clergy and laity were often openly hostile and it seems likely that for hundreds of people in these regions – men especially – the Revolu-tion would offer a more satisfying alternative ideology and a welcome means of subordinating the Catholic Church. Yet even within a small area, the variations could be striking. In the future Sarthe *département* (around Le Mans), the east was irreligious while piety flourished in the west.

How were French men and women spirirtually nourished? The pre-Revolutionary Church may have felt no overwhelming need for saints to act as inspirational models for the faithful, but the quality of spiritual life was still rich enough to produce more than the occa-sional candidate for canonisation, men such as the Jesuit Nicolas Grou (d. 1804) and the Capuchin Ambroise de Lombez who, in their lifetimes, had been renowned for their gifts of humility and grace.[52] For the literate majority, who drew their inspiration from reading and meditation, there was an endless supply of devotional books. Some of them, like Jacques Emery's *Spirit of Saint Theresa*, give the lie to the common assumption that the eighteenth-century Catholic Church had a rational, high-and-dry theology. Emery's book – known as 'the angel of the Church of France', he combined mysticism with a this-worldly political sense[53] – showed that any-one dedicated enough could lead a rich interior life.

The *Spirit of Saint Theresa* sold well and joined a backlist of titles from lesser-known authors. Wherever the 'clericalised' principles of

Catholic reform had taken firm root – as in Brittany, Lorraine, Franche-Comté – religious books dominated circulation and even in 1789 titles like *L'ange conducteur en la dévotion chrétienne* [*The Angelic Conductor in Christian Devotion*] and *Faut mourir* [*We All Have To Die*] were best-sellers. There were numerous books on the subject available, most of them best-sellers from the previous century.[54] Readers were not easily frightened by the morbid or the macabre, and most people wanted help in making the best spiritual preparations for dying. Devotional works – with well-known psalms and prayers written in French – retained their appeal for private use to supplement, as the liturgical season indicated, the public observances of the Church. They played a crucial part in spreading interest in the active practice of piety on an unprecedented scale, albeit commending a restrained devotion, truly the devotion of the Enlightenment.[55] These texts could stand in large number and without any sense of mismatch on the shelf next to Enlightenment works on secular topics, but there were changes of some importance going on slowly in purchasing patterns and reading habits. The researches of Jean Quéniart on private libraries in the west of France have shown a dramatic fall-off in the purchase by the urban elite of books of devotion in the 1770s and 1780s, and this trend should be set against a continuing and increasing purchase of books on broadly Enlightenment themes in the sciences and the arts among consumers in this category.[56] Quéniart's work stands in need of supplementation from other regions before the picture can be admitted nationally. Yet overall, if there was a relative decline in the numbers of religious books published in the capital (especially books of devotion), libraries public and private could and did purchase lives of the saints in confidence that they would be heavily used, especially by the great mass of country-dwellers. In the 1780s, over 60 per cent of the books sold in provincial France were still religious works.[57] On this evidence, it has been well said that 'Intelligent scepticism was increasing in France, and so too, it would seem, was highly individual personal piety'.[58]

In line with this trend towards continuing religiosity at most levels of society, the cult of the Virgin continued to flourish.[59] It included a new commendation of her status as a wife and mother, as well as a woman standing apart, the Mother of God. The entire Holy Family became a pattern that the Confraternity of Christian doctrine recommended lay people to copy in all their doings, with parents encouraged to transmit the faith to their children who, in their turn, should submit to their parents' loving correction. Clergy, especially those influenced by Jesuit teachings, took up the theme.[60] The most important cultic innovation was the widespread adoption of the Sacred Heart of Jesus. It had its origins in seventeenth-century Normandy, was adopted by the bishops of Provence during the great plague of 1720, and was formally commended to the whole French faithful by the General Assembly of the Clergy of 1765, when the Vatican authorised the clebration of a feast day; it thereafter spread rapidly thanks to the writings of devout prelates like J-F-H. de Fumel, Bishop of Lodève, and Partz de Pressy, Bishop of Boulogne, both enemies of the *philosophes*.[61] It was aimed particularly at the less well educated. As the Bishop of Amiens put it in a *mandement* of October 1767: 'Because most of the faithful are not able to read learned works, we believed we should offer them a simple, solid and sensible devotion like this.'[62] Despite the coolness of Jansenist sympathisers towards the Sacred Heart on grounds of idolatry — the parlement of Paris rejected a festival in its honour in 1764 as 'impious and extravagant' — it was unstoppable, the latest testimony to the popularity of the devotional life, spreading 'like a fertilising wave' as Jean de Viguerie recently put it.[63]

These phenomena have to be taken into account in any assessment of the religious climate on the eve of the Revolution, and put into the balance alongside arguments based on the impact made by vulgarised versions of the writings of the *philosophes* or calculations founded on declining male membership of the confraternities.[64] Venal office-holders and rentiers in some areas like Provence might have been increasingly reluctant to serve as rectors or vice-rectors of confraternities in preference for membership of the Masonic lodges,[65] but much depended on locality. There were well-established Marian congregations of laymen in much of Alsace, significantly an area where both Lutheranism and Jesuit influences were equally strong. The suppression of the latter order made little difference. In Molsheim alone membership passed the 400 mark just before the Revolution. In another district — Gascony —marked by a non-Catholic presence (in that case, the Sephardi Jews) there were no less than 26 new confraternities founded in the Bordeaux archdiocese between 1770 and 1789; the Toulouse archdiocese in 1789 had 215 parishes, for example, but 228 confraternities.[66] Eighteenth-century women were joining in new confraternities and charitable organizations, taking full if belated advantage of the opportunities for public expression of their faith created by the Catholic Reformation.[67] Confraternities such as those dedicated to the Rosary, the Sacred Heart and St Catherine were a bedrock of female piety before the Revolution, trusted by most clergy to uphold the authority of the Church's ministry. And even those women – the majority – who were not admitted could club together to present statues of the Blessed Virgin and her mother, St Anne to their village churches. Wherever one looks, there is a complex network of relationships centred on the Church, with females playing a full part, sufficient to ensure that women were ready to play a key, independent role in ensuring the survival of Catholicism during the 1790s.[68]

Confraternities were mainly urban phenomena, and historians are starting to reconsider the traditional claim that large towns and cities were losing their commitment to Catholicism in the course of the century, eloquently stated as recently as 1976 by Emmanuel Le Roy-Ladurie: 'The city had become abandoned terrain, a dechristianised zone in the heart of a countryside thoroughly christianised according to the reformers' definitions.'[69] Recent scholarship has clearly shown the persistence of Catholic reform energies in an urban context and the capacity of the Church to adapt its ministry in areas where Enlightenment values potentially inimical to its pastoral work had been disseminated.[70] The Catholicism of cities like Strasbourg or Toulouse was still vigorous. The latter was home to the four penitential companies of laymen and clergy that had their origins in the religious wars of the sixteenth century; it was the city that tried and executed Jean Calas, and found itself called an outpost of fanaticism by Voltaire.[71] Paris, as usual, followed its own course, and we are fortunate to have some outstanding modern work on the capital, notably Bernard Plongeron's, David Garrioch's and Jeffrey Kaplow's,[72] which is much more nuanced than the older accounts. Nevertheless, while noting the considerable religious fervour that existed among Parisians (especially to the Virgin, as the numerous statues placed in niches at street corners or above doorways indicated), in a city with 53 parish churches and 47 monasteries and 60 convents serviced by an estimated clerical population of about 8000 in 1768,[73] these historians tentatively caution against exaggerating the importance of the institutional church to many Parisians. They made the most of the opportunities for recreation on the 29 obligatory feast days, especially the great Feast of Sainte Geneviève, the patron of the city, on 3 January, but that must be set against the decline in fasting in general, including Lent.[74]

Evidence currently available points towards a slow but discernable decline in Easter observance during the 1770s and 1780s, and suggests both increased religious indifference in some sections of the urban population and the distinct likelihood that such patterns were spreading over into the adjacent countryside. There were complaints that only a small minority made its Easter communion in the parish of Saint-Sulpice, Paris, and less than a half in the city of Bordeaux did so in a survey authorised by the archbishop in 1772.[75] There is much to be discovered yet, especially as regards the smaller country towns.[76] One contemporary, writing in 1768 about the popular spa-town of Montpellier in Languedoc, commented on the decline of religious enmities:

> No one quarrels any more over Calvinism, Molinism and Jansenism. All that has been replaced by the reading of philosophical books, which has now become so prevalent, especially among the young, that there are more deists than anyone has ever seen.[77]

Such a gloomy assessment only partially chimes in with an Easter abstention rate of 11.4 per cent in a sample of 57 parishes across the diocese in the 1770s. At Auxerre in upper Burgundy, half the population stayed away, while in the parish of Saint-Savine at nearby Troyes 228 out of 600 people of communicant age failed to attend Easter Mass.[78]

Thus participation rates in Church services in some towns and their hinterland were faltering. This may be read as a sign of 'dechristianisation', to use a term which would have meant nothing to contemporaries. For them, people were either Christians or infidels and even those whose interest in religion was tepid would not have cared to be placed in the second category. Non-attendance in urban centres may well have owed more to an increased range of leisure opportunities and weaker family networks than to dislike for organised Christianity; it was more likely to imply temporary indifference and other preoccupations than serious anticlericalism. It is also clear that contemporaries were happy to measure religious sensitivities by other criteria than a dutiful but unmotivated involvement in sacramental life.

We also need to take into account the role of the urban parish as a major employer and consumer, whether in terms of church maintenance, new building, or the trade for tapers, tapestries and flowers generated by major festivals such as Corpus Christi when the whole city came into contact, as Professor Garrioch has written:

> The Fête Dieu brought the whole city into physical and symbolic unity: those who did not participate watched from the street or from the window. The processions penetrated every part of the city, and no one could remain unaware of the celebration.[79]

Similarly, in Toulouse right down to 1789 peasants, tourists, townsfolk mingled every year on the 17 May procession to celebrate the expulsion of the Huguenots from the city in 1562. In that great southern city, ceremonies for canonisations of saints, jubilees celebrated by order of the Pope every few years,[80] or parading the Black Virgin of the church of the Daraude to function as an intercessor against fire, drought or sickness, acted as showpieces for collective Catholic devotions, the highlight of those countless routine rites that filled the individual lives of the faithful.[81] As one British traveller noted at the end of 1788, 'you do not walk ten yards in the street but you are stopped by some Procession or other.'[82] Such processions were the means whereby the Church 'conquered' urban space and reaffirmed its presence colourfully and dramatically in regional centres, nowhere more so than in the splendid Corpus Christi celebrations in Anjou, the 'sacre d'Angers' as it was called.[83] These processions were probably attracting a more committed, genuinely religious following than at any point since the Middle Ages.

Even if the majority of urban populations can be described as 'settled', encased in its *quartiers*, there could be sizable influxes from outside. In the countryside, unbelief or heterodoxy had made minimal impact, except perhaps on seasonal migrants or those whose occupations – as carriers, muleteeers, soldiers, servants, men connected with the drinks trade – took them away from home and concurrently diminished their opportunities to fulfil their religious duties;[84] much the same could be said of the numerous bands of vagrants roaming the woods and fields of France, habitually on the move, looking for relief in the towns when harvest yields were low and bread prices correspondingly high.[85] These people gravitated towards the towns, intermingled with the urban lower orders and found plenty to arouse their disdain for the culture of Catholicism in broadsheets, popular pamphlets and tavern talk. The varying, fragmented pattern of urban settlement made it harder for incumbents to keep an eye on individual members of their flock, especially as town parishes tended to have higher numbers ordinarily resident than their rural counterparts. Mercier for one was in no doubt that people could and did avoid priestly ministrations in Paris, except on family occasions like baptisms: 'You can live here thirty years without ever putting foot inside the church and without knowing the face of your *curé*.'[86]

Moreover, the social pressure to conform to the norm for urban artisans and seasonal labourers in, for instance, the silk industry of Lyon by attending service was minimal; likewise, in the town of Clermont-de-Lodève, textile workers before the Revolution were notorious for their impiety and irregular Sunday attendance.[87] Higher up the social scale, shopkeepers, merchants, *avocats*, notaries, members of municipal corporations and minor office holders – people of the middling sort – were more exposed to Enlightenment hostility to the Catholic Church, but paradoxically would be more inclined to attend services regularly, since their careers and social standing stood to benefit from the respectability it conferred. In Paris such worshippers valued the chance to obtain leadership roles like churchwardenships, to join the vestry or the *compagnies de charité* with responsibility for poor relief shared with the *curé*. These posts brought them the peer prestige of participation in parish management and, as David Garrioch has indicated, could limit their priest's authority for independent action: such parochially prominent laymen were often attracted to Jansenism precisely because it stressed a place for lay decision-making in the parish vestries.[88] As yet, research on urban parish life is insufficiently advanced to indicate the scale and nature of middle-class assertiveness in those constituencies, and to presume a clash between laity and clergy is unwarranted. In most cases, the parish priest had similar social origins, and fellow feeling might have constituted an incentive to mutual cooperation. In provincial France, where local candidates for holy orders trained at their local seminary, there was every chance that their pastoral duties would anyway take them into an urban world with which they and their families were already familiar.

Yet if we are, like some of the most eminent historians of their generation such as Michel Vovelle and Philippe Ariès, to seek out evidences of incipient revolutionary dechristianisation from the mid-century onwards it is to the 'middling sort' of urban France that we should look. In a seminal work on Provence, *Piété baroque et dechristianisation en Provence au xviii siècle* (Paris, 1973), Vovelle drew attention to the disappearing language of piety in the wills and testaments of the professional male bourgeoisie drawn up in the century before 1750. He found the decline of invocations to the Virgin and tutelary Saints for the salvation of the testator's soul, a fall in the making of bequests towards religious institutions like monastic orders or lay confraternities, and evidence that in 60 to 80 per cent of last testaments there was no specific profession of Christian faith. Vovelle's findings were reinforced by Chaunu's work on Paris,[89] while Ariès, in his monumental study of attitudes towards death and dying in eighteenth-century France, *L'Homme devant la Mort* (Paris, 1977) adduced evidence that seemed to show that the 'pious death-bed' was much less popular than it had been a century earlier. How should this work be viewed a quarter of a century on? To say it reveals dechristianisation is slightly misleading. Rather than indifference, it suggests a late *Ancien Régime* change in attitude towards piety and its profession in French society that was both positive and new.[90] We are not looking at the birth of modern secularism, but at new modes of spirituality and perhaps the emergence of what Lebrun in his work on Anjou claimed was the progressive laicisation of society.

In recent years, the significance of such work has indeed been warmly debated. It is generally agreed that Vovelle in particular, in examining the decline of Baroque piety, was giving his evidence an interpretetive weight it could not properly carry. Even within Provence, variations in the pattern of testamentary forms and bequests give generalisations on a wider scale only limited persuasive force: the clergy and educated were dropping pious rigmarole as a preface to wills because of the developing sense that it was quite inappropriate in that context. Insufficient work has been done on confraternities, especially in northern France, on which to base adequately notions of 'decline', and the impression elsewhere is that they held their ground remarkably well against more recent, competing forms of sociability.

The findings of Vovelle, Ariès and Chaunu arguably point towards the emergence of what one might call 'enlightened piety', in which testators were more confident about abandoning themselves to God's mercy and sought worthier objects for their generosity such as destitute children and foundling hospitals. Even *curés* were affected by changing taste in this area, with those in the Périgord cutting back on the amount they bequeathed for their own souls.[91] Perhaps

Vovelle's findings may best be considered less as evidence of the decline of religious belief than as the retreat of fears about eternity among more sophisticated and literate Catholics, the reduction of social and legal constraints in religious practice, and the diversion of spiritual life into fresh channels.

The available indicators suggest that the 'middling sort' in late-eighteenth-century France remained overwhelmingly attached to the Catholic faith and practice, to those ceremonies and processions that characterised urban life and symbolised social unity under the crook of the Church. There is much to be said for Jacques Solé's reference to that 'simple, unaffected piety, attentive to civic duties of the kingdom, one nourished by holy scripture, concerned for the inner life of the layman' that was so much the norm, *despite* the Enlightenment.[92] Of course, generalisations are hazardous, and comparisons of religious practice between towns often reveal interesting variants, but it would be rash to underestimate the depths of Catholic fervour among the bourgeoisie, who flocked to hear good preachers, threw themselves into making the Jubilee of 1775 proclaimed by Pius VI a triumph of piety, generally supported parochial missions and responded eagerly to the evangelical and sacramental involvement of the religious orders in the renewal of urban congregations by sponsoring particular devotions and championing the cults of saints and relics. We should not underestimate the piety of this group on the eve of the Revolution. As Robert A. Schneider has written of Toulouse, 'The penitents' regime of processions demonstrates that the crusading zeal so evident during the religious wars − still lived in the eighteenth century',[93] and must be set against the evidence from Provence. Such high levels of involvement among the bourgeoisie − and by no means only at Toulouse − suggest a dynamic, national, even militant piety that was showing no sign of tailing off as 1789 approached, and would offer to the Counter-Revolution a bedrock of support its enemies might have envied.

Signs of religious fervour are less evident as one ascends the social scale, and there are several pointers towards elite uninterest in intensive versions of Catholicism. Mercier remarked on 'the general insousiance which characterises today all those men in the capital who can't be described as belonging to the populace'.[94] Foreign observers also detected unmistakeable signs of religious indifference at this level: John St John, travelling in Burgundy in 1787, found 'the generality of their [the French] genteel people make a scoff of the faith, and think it ridiculous to be a Christian,' and John Villiers noticed card games going on during intervals in the Mass.[95] Yet once again caution is necessary, for the divergences between courtiers and magistrates, Paris and the provinces were marked within the Second Estate. Someone like *président* Claris of the *cour des aides* of Montpellier went on making pious purchases to add to the theological works (many of them Jansenist) in the library he inherited from his father, but this was not a buying pattern likely to be encountered among wealthy courtiers and ministers, creators and consumers, as they were of Enlightenment culture.[96] To judge by the libraries of the nobility, religious devotion and enquiry were playing second fiddle to entertainment and instruction and, in the learned culture of the provincial academies they joined in some number, religious matters were peripheral. As for the wealthy professional classes and *rentiers*, those in or on the fringes of the nobility, they largely followed the example of the king himself by attending services regularly in their parish church or proprietary chapel; however, this was increasingly a form of Catholic commitment where the external practices could count for everything, and the value placed upon them was slowly declining after *c.* 1760. Church services *inter alia* offered the opportunity, as they always had done, for fashionable display, ogling women, or asserting one's rank in a world where precedence was fundamental to etiquette.

At the close of the eighteenth century, the model of the courtier as devout layman in the best tradition of the Counter-Reformation was hard to find. 'Among the great and the rich, who can count today those who observe the practice of Lent?' bemoaned the Archbishop of Lyon in 1789, and it has been well said recently that 'in France the figure of the *dévot* under Louis XIII gave way to that of the libertine under Louis XV'.[98] The latter's grandson had ministers who were largely inconspicuous for their piety: Maurepas, the most senior of them until his death in 1781, was neither Christian nor religious; Turgot, like Malesherbes, was a minor *philosophe*. He favoured a state-sponsored church and cult to keep the populace in check, but had no sympathies for the inflexible dogmas he identified with the Roman Catholic Church;[99] Necker's Protestantism tended to a rational deism and relatively few religious books were found in Breteuil's library when it was subsequently confiscated during the Terror.[100] Vergennes, Foreign Minister from 1774 until his death in 1787, was a fervent Catholic believer who lodged the *anti-philosophe*

Antoine Sabatier in his apartment at Versailles and secured him four pensions. His involvement in financing anti-Enlightenment literary outpourings helped win him one journalist's stinging condemnation as that 'cordonned Tartuffe'.[101] Vergennes acted as a rallying point for what remained of the *dévot* party and the man who had secured the see of Paris for his like-minded relative and friend Juigné in 1781, rather than have Brienne imposed on the King.[102] His successor as Foreign Minister, Montmorin (educated alongside the King), had an aunt who had been Abbess of Fontevrault and an uncle as Bishop of Langres. Otherwise there was just Louis XVI himself, educated by his governor, the Duc de La Vaugyon (d. 1771), in a manner befitting the son of a Dauphin famous for his piety and protection of the Church, the King who resumed the ritual of touching the victims of scofula for the first time since 1738 though only after he had first confessed and communicated.

It was among some of the wives and widows of the nobility, *dévote* ladies such as the Maréchale de Noailles, sponsor of anti-*philosophe* authors, that the spirit of piety lived on in high society. Such a location was not in itself surprising. Religious practice and instruction was fundamental to female education throughout the century, and noble women went on buying books of a devotional nature in a higher proportion than their husbands, fathers, and brothers;[103] leaders of society like Mme de Genlis and Mme Necker even published in defence of religion.[104] A high proportion of elite women maintained ties with the convents in which they had been taught well into adult life, though such associations were no guarantee of avoiding the dissipation that marked many aristocratic circles, as Choderlos de Laclos's racy novel of 1783, *Les Liaisons dangereuses*, notoriously revealed to a scandalised but fascinated readership.

Yet cases of young nobles like Chevalier de la Barre becoming mixed up in sacrilege were isolated; the scandal in Rouen in 1770 when a trainee lawyer leaned half-dressed from his window just as the sacrament was passing in procession was an exceptional occasion.[105] Open commitment to unbelief remained rare, and funerals could offer occasions for ostentatious displays of wealth and religion. Take the procession of one member of the *petite noblesse* with its 'one hundred and fifty priests ... a cortège of more than four hundred people ... 25 000 vases filled with flowers, six halts for prayers ... a wake for eight hundred guests ... more than five hundred carriages came out from Paris'.[106] Salons like the Baron d'Holbach's had in the 1760s been well known for the presence of avowed atheists, to the consternation even of extreme religious sceptics like the philosopher David Hume. Twenty years later, the habitués of those that remained – like Mesdames Helvétius and Necker – could best be characterised as passive believers, indifferent to confessional bickering, and sympathetic to those arguing for removal of religious disabilities still incurred by Protestants and Jews. They might attend Catholic services, but the fulfilment of this duty, as much social as religious, in itself signified little, though in the mid-1770s, in the immediate aftermath of the coronation, a revival of noble interest in Catholic piety flickered into life.

The flame soon died. It turned out to be 'a style, a craze, competitive with high hairdos and dangling earrings',[107] as fashionable interest became absorbed in the arrival of Benjamin Franklin in Paris and France's participation in the American colonists' side against Britain from 1778. To a considerable degree, revealed religion had been marginalised, especially in the highest levels of the court aristocracy. They left heavy theological tomes in their country chateaux and filled the libraries of their Paris town houses in the *quartiers* Saint-Germain and Palais-Royal with the latest volumes on science and philosophy. Yet to talk without qualification of elite alienation is too strong: more than lip-service was paid to the forms of Catholicism, and in the masonic lodges and the provincial academies, to quote Daniel Roche, 'there was no manifestation of a crisis of the "sacred", but on the contrary, everywhere an attachment to external practice, and denunciation of atheism and libertinism.'[108] A mystical form of Christianity was unfashionable, by stark contrast with the fascination of the elite in the 1780s for the occult arts of such as Cagliostro and Mesmer.[109]

In Paris and the provincial capitals, fashionable society was still well represented at services. On the outer circle of the royal family, Philippe-Egalité's father-in-law, the duc de Penthièvre, noted his communions in his journal, and great noble families like the Aguesseau, Aiguillon and Montyon stayed Christian.[110] But piety was not modish. Even among fellow members of the nobility at the Estates-General, the Marquis de Guilhem-Clermont-Lodève appears to have been in a minority in openly professing, 'Without religion, all the bonds of society are broken; without religion I could scarcely master my own life. Without religion, in a word ... we would be the playthings of mere chance.'[111] By Louis XVI's reign, younger nobles

were generally more interested in social amelioration than in sacraments, and expressed their humanitarian interests by working for the
abolition of torture, the freeing of slaves and granting religious toleration to Protestants. As these were causes that either aroused minimal
notice or outright opposition in the Gallican Church, an opportunity
for the clergy to reach out to the young and powerful was passed over.
While the number of aristocratic vocations for holy orders remained
steady, the hierarchy could not rely on any more than a small minority of the lay elite in Paris wanting to associate openly in the defence of
the Church's faith and structures. Even taking into account the aristocracy's traditional worldliness, it was a sign that the Church's pastoral ministry at this level lacked a cutting edge. It was all very well to
have the continuing loyalties of the numerous small nobility across
a province like Brittany, but the inability of any of the versions of
Catholic practice on offer in the late eighteenth century to commend themselves to the elites of Paris and Versailles was a serious
strategic weakness which would not escape the notice of many post-
Revolutionary commentators trying to explain the collapse of the
established order. The fact was that the younger noblemen, like
others below them on the social scale, had found in the debates of
the French Enlightenment compelling intellectual and moral alternatives to judge in the scale alongside those associated with Christian orthodoxy.

3 Other Denominations

Late eighteenth-century France was also home to two distinctive religious minorities, the Protestants and the Jews. Protestants were the most numerous on the eve of the Revolution, despite the legal fiction that the majority Calvinists among them did not exist.[1] That was as stated in the decree revoking the Edict of Nantes in 1685, and their 'non-existence' had been confirmed as recently as 1724 by a royal declaration.[2] Estimates of numbers vary, but most authorities suggest about 700000 or about 2 per cent of the population, much less than claimed by their contemporary Catholic detractors. French Protestants were adherents of the two major continental versions of their religion, with Calvinists concentrated in the Midi, and the second major grouping, the 200000 or so Lutherans, in Alsace; the latter exclusively enjoyed toleration as a result of the 1648 Treaty of Westphalia, which still governed their status on France's contested eastern frontier. Thus Marshal Saxe, France's outstanding general of the War of the Austrian Succession (1740–8), had been accorded a Lutheran funeral in 1751, with Louis XV himself paying the costs of a memorial to his memory erected in the Lutheran 'temple' at Strasbourg.[3]

In social terms, eighteenth-century French Protestantism had long ceased to be a religion for the elite. It was predominantly a rural phenomenon, whose followers tended to be no higher in rank than small-scale farmers. It was often the physical isolation of such people from village communities and their parish structures that enabled them to evade ecclesiastical surveillance. Urban Protestants were, by contrast, a distinct minority. In La Rochelle, the same thirty to forty families dominated the life of the consistory (the primary agency for controlling Huguenot affairs at local level) throughout the second half of the eighteenth century; this out of a total community of 1100 in 1787, a large fall from the 7500 recorded after the revocation of the Edict of Nantes, but probably better explained by artisan emigration to the colonies than by conversion to

Catholicism.[4] Nîmes, the capital of Protestant France and a centre of the silk industry second only to Lyon, had a population of 43 000 in 1787–9, of whom about 13 000 adhered to the Reformed faith.[5] Whether resident in town or country, Protestants shared the same pride in their indomitable resistance over the century to Catholic persecution, and their distinctive cultural and economic achievements.

Stringent legal disabilities attached to the practice of Protestantism in France before 1787. In areas where they were a minority and took steps to conceal their allegiance, most of their marriages took place in the parish church in order to obtain what the state deemed the only legal form of matrimony. Such proceedings were risky. The law laid down that Huguenots were forbidden to be married as Catholics unless they subsequently presented a written renunciation of their faith. No wonder then that from early in the century most Protestants who wanted to wed resorted to the nocturnal services of a minister of one of the 'Churches of the Desert', as the Protestants liked to call their clandestine meetings in the countryside. The custom was to make a contract of marriage before a notary, with the safeguarding clause that they would procede to the rites of the Roman Church 'whenever either party might desire it' – then they waited for a 'desert' assembly! Any children born to such technically felonious unions were by definition bastards and could not legally inherit, though many law courts by c.1760 had found devices to prevent collateral Catholic heirs from appropriating inheritances from the wives and children of deceased Protestants. Despite clerical complaints, the judges were intimating that public recognition of a marriage over a period meant there was no need to produce a certificate to say there had been one.[6] Most baptisms, on the other hand, continued to be performed by the *curé*. In the mid-century there was a royal edict ordering the forcible christening of children who had not been brought to the parish font and, in Languedoc, the *maréchaussées* (or town councils) went around supervising the baptisms. Protestant parents then faced the agonising choice of whether to put their child's inheritance prospects before their religious principles.

Such sacrifices by members of the Reformed faith were not enough to satisfy the more elderly members of the Catholic hierarchy that there was a genuine 'spiritual unity' in France. These bishops and priests regarded the continued existence of Protestantism after nearly a century's official prohibition as both a scandal and an embarrassing token of the Church's failure to cajole or coerce non-Catholics into the Gallican fold. At General Assemblies of the Clergy well into Louis XVI's reign, these conservatives insisted that the government make more effort to enforce the penal laws. The realists were located among younger members of the clerical elite and prelates actually resident in Protestant strongholds, like Champion de Cicé, Archbishop of Bordeaux, who justified his tolerant attitude by 'the precepts of the Divine Legislator'.[7] Such progressive figures as the Archbishop sensed that in the changed climate of public opinion, the Catholic Church stood to gain from some show of fraternal acceptance of the Huguenots rather than denouncing the continuing scandal of heresy in its midst.

In any event, the Crown was not listening to the General Assembly on this point. The attempts of the French government to impose Catholicism on the King's Huguenot subjects had been discarded in favour of a grudging acceptance of them just before the accession of Louis XVI. Policy under the long-serving minister for the *Maison du roi* (which included responsibility for the affairs of 'the so-called Reformed Religion'), the Comte de Saint-Florentin (1725–75), evolved from one of severity to one of cautious containment. Instead of the mass arrests and *dragonnades* that had immediately preceded and followed the revocation of the Edict of Nantes, domestic worshippers were rarely disturbed. In wartime there was still a tendency to regard Protestants as fifth-columnists, especially in coastal regions where there were fears of a British landing. Repression could be severe in those areas even as late as the War of the Austrian Succession in the 1740s; one young British traveller, Henry Lyte, told his friend at home in 1754 of how the Calvinists in the Cévennes were harassed by the soldiers quartered on them.[8] There, and on the coastal plains around Nîmes, members of illegal congregations were still packed off to the galleys; rewards of 3000 livres for handing over pastors were on offer when the next European conflict opened in 1756. Such forceful precautions were not groundless, for a few pastors were prepared to contemplate fighting against Louis XV at the beginning of the Seven Years War. This stance was tied up with a conspiracy centred on the King's cousin, the Prince de Conti, and an expectation that he would inaugurate civil rights and public worship. Even the British government was banking on a strong Huguenot response to a landing on the French coast, but these hopes were disappointed when it was attempted at Rochefort in 1757.[9] Protestants prepared to look favourably on any British rescue from their state of subordination were in a definite minority, by comparison with those ready to defend La Rochelle against attack from the sea.

The experience of defeat at the hands of Britain and Prussia in the Seven Years War kept religious tensions alive, and fuelled an atmosphere in the south that occasionally veered on religious hysteria, and which Saint-Florentin did little to discourage.[10] Protestant leaders could take nothing for granted, especially where numbers were thinnest and Catholic suspicions high: when troops were available, the authorities could still crack down harshly. The last Huguenot to be sentenced to the galleys received his penalty in 1762, the same year as the Protestant pastor Rochette was hung; Rochette went to the scaffold only twenty days before Calas – as the whole of Europe knew, thanks to Voltaire – was broken on the wheel.[11] And that was not yet the end of it. Other Protestants were arrested into the 1770s, cavalry dispersed an assembly at Brie east of Paris in 1771, and the last 'galley-slaves for the faith' were only freed from the prison hulks at Toulon as late as 1775.[12]

But the 'martyrdom' of such as Calas had the effect of advancing the cause of toleration[13] and, for the most part, the government's coercion became limited to the levy of collective fines against entire Protestant communities. It was a realistic (and profitable) concession to the tolerant spirit of the Enlightenment, but more a recognition that the Huguenots simply did not constitute a threat to the French monarchical state. Intendants were commonly unwilling to follow up cases as Saint-Florentin still requested, and the *philosophe* Prince de Beauvau, military governor of Languedoc in the 1760s, deliberately defied the Crown, confident that it would not harm his service record. The Prince let Huguenot prisoners slip out of gaols in his jurisdiction and released galley-slaves; in the *généralité* of Montpellier, 'desert' assemblies were even sanctioned, so long as there was advance notice to the local authorities.[14] The Scottish traveller Humphrey Smollett noted how the changes could operate in practice in the neighbourhood of Montpellier and Nîmes by the early 1760s:

> There are many protestants in this place, as well as at Nismes, and they are no longer molested on the score of religion. They have their conventicles in the country, where they assemble privately for worship. These are well known, and detachments are sent out every Sunday to intercept them; but the officer always has private directions to take another route.[15]

Proven loyalty was the key to the authorities' restraint. Far from being republican in their politics as, officially, Saint-Florentin and the General Assembly of the Clergy – as late as 1780[16] – liked to claim (so, incidentally, did Montesquieu's massively influential *L'Esprit des lois*, first published in 1748), Protestants emphasised their unconditional allegiance to the throne,[17] and their national synod of 1756 had categorically condemned rebellion just as the Prince de Conti's conspiracy was being hatched: thereafter even additional visits from the taxman could not deflect their pastors from emphasising their loyalty as part of a bid to show that their faith stood for order, not for anarchy.

The dropping of harassment by government was the prize obtained by an astute Protestant leadership abandoning the old Calvinist claim to a right of resistance to ungodly authorities, and reconstructing the different levels of Church government. Antoine Court was the first man to try and restore a degree of organisation and leadership to the scattered congregations. He succeeded brilliantly, and ordained ministers trained at Lausanne in Switzerland. They were then infiltrated into France to strengthen and lead the Churches of the Desert. In some areas like the province of Guyenne in the south-west, entire populations of Catholic 'converts' were won back to their former religion by the increased profile of their old Church, as its influence in regional life rose steadily. By mid-century, church structures were largely once again in place right down to congregational level, with a matching emphasis on spiritual discipline, but with a flexibility that made for long-term survival.[18] Court built up a leadership cadre from the Protestant urban elites well placed to continue his mission of guiding the Church out of the 'desert' when he finally retired after 1760. By Louis XVI's reign, leadership had passed to men in early middle age or younger, like Jean Paul Rabaut de Saint-Etienne of Nîmes (himself the son of Paul Rabaut), products of a broad Enlightenment culture, insistent on their rights but patient and flexible in having them recognised.[19] No national synods were held after 1763, so the authority of the pastors like him was extensive.

Intelligent pastoral work went hand in hand with putting the case for toleration before the educated public. This went to the heart of Enlightenment values, and Huguenot leaders were able to rely on most of the leading *philosophes* arguing in favour of religious toleration without having to involve themselves directly. Publications like the great *Encyclopédie*, Voltaire's *Traité sur la tolérance* (1762), his notorious *Dictionnaire philosophique portatif* (1764) and Marmontel's novel *Bélisaire* (1767) were decisive in forming a climate of public opinion in which a right to toleration was put beyond question.[20] Nevertheless, this working alliance between *philosophes* and Protestants was considered a high price to pay for toleration by the more conservative Huguenot congregations, especially as an anti-Christian theme became a marked character of *philosophe* texts of the 1760s. Even the theologically progressive Paul Rabaut, who discarded doctrinal Calvinism in favour of a simplified religion which could include elements of Catholicism, Protestantism, Judaism and rational philosophy, felt that the contents of Voltaire's *Dictionnaire philosophique* were so subversive of belief that they merited refutation.

Calvinists were under the same pressures to abandon orthodox Trinitarian beliefs as other groups of Christians, as the controversial article 'Messiah' written by Voltaire's pastor friend Polier de Bottens (he was director of the French seminary of Lausanne), for the *Encyclopédie* indicated. Bottens's piece reinforced D'Alembert's claim in his article on 'Geneva' that 'Respect for Jesus Christ and for the Scriptures is perhaps the only thing which distinguishes the Christianity of Geneva from pure deism'.[21] Certainly, 'philosophic' ideas were in wide circulation among young men who trained for the ministry at Lausanne, then came back to serve their people in France.[22] Many surviving sermons, for instance, indicate that a large number of pastors were opting to call Christians to the practice of virtue rather than holiness.[23] This thinking can be seen as the latest manifestation of a culture gap between pastors and people in evidence from at least the time of the Revocation. Other French ministers, still a majority, refused to imitate the example of Jacob Vernet, leader of the Genevan Church and the most distinguished pastor of his time. They stayed loyal to the historic tenets of the faith and resisted the appeal of Socinianism (a form of unitarianism, which denied the divinity of Christ). Indeed, recent work on Protestant literature in the Vivarais indicates that sixteenth-century apologetics and apocalyptic insights still fortified the spiritual lives of ordinary worshippers who had cast themselves as the people of Israel living in captivity in Egypt, just as their ancestors in the Wars of Religion might have done.[24]

Doctrinal debate mattered little to the average rural French Calvinist. By the 1770s in Aunis, Saintonge, Poitou and Montauban, semi-private worship by Huguenots in a 'house of prayer' went on

undisturbed however much Catholics grumbled[25] while, in Languedoc, Protestant assemblies were seldom intimidated and were often
held close to towns. Numbers meeting for worship could be prodi-
gious: the English traveller, Philip Thicknesse, reported no less than
18 000 coming together, unmolested, outside Nîmes in 1775.[26]
Indeed, it became fashionable for Catholics to attend them, almost
as if they were tourist attractions. On Christmas Day 1768, when
a Protestant assembly near Marsillargues in Languedoc attracted a
large congregation, several seigneurs and barons of the local Estates
along with a few bishops acted as hosts to the Marquis de Calvisson,
one of the few Calvinist nobles left in France. They were all at one
in 'agreeing that the Protestants were worthy of the government's
protection'.[27] In the mid-1780s, another British visitor was very
impressed by improving Protestant-Catholic relations at Nîmes:

> The protestants here are a quiet people & neither give or receive
> any molestation. They have applied to government for leave to
> build a church, & their prayer [petition] has been seconded
> by the archbishop of Narbonne [Arthur de Dillon, himself of Irish
> descent].[28]

There was thus something like a *de facto* toleration, but little to stop
covert persecution, or over-zealous officials and clerics from trying
to enforce the strict letter of the 1685 laws when they saw fit. The
pastor Olivier Desmonts of Bordeaux perceptively pointed out that if
the King's 'confessor or his ministers were ambitious or fanatics,
everything could change in a moment'.[29] Meanwhile, Protestants
were less fearful of coming out into the open. The number of pastors
in the Vivarais rose from 5 to 9 between 1776 and 1789, with most
curés turning a blind eye to their advent.[30] But we should be cautious
about exaggerating the universality of such slow trends. As Timothy
Tackett (following the earlier study of Burdette Poland) has insisted
with reference to the Dauphiné, there was no greater obstacle to the
policy of *de facto* toleration preferred by the government after the mid-
century than the continuing belligerence of so many parish clergy.[31]
The attitude of the local bishop was crucial. At Dax, in the south-
west, the Bishop in 1777 complained to Amelot (the Minister for
the *Maison du Roi* in charge of supervising reformed religionists)
of 'the scandalous style' in which Protestants openly worshipped,
but the Minister's muted response was to order the intendant to do

nothing that might upset public tranquillity.[32] This stood in sharp relief to Saint-Florentin's uncompromising stance.

A change of bishop could make a difference. Despite the publication of about a hundred *mémoires* recommending the granting of a civil status to Protestants between 1750 and 1774, the struggle for official recognition was still not won when Louis XVI became King. There might be 'tacit tolerance' of Protestants in Languedoc (as Breteuil, by then Minister for the *Maison du Roi*, called it in 1785), but life for members of the reformed church in the provinces could still be hazardous, and even in Languedoc there were limits to what ministers would permit. The Protestants of Orthez were told bluntly in 1778 there was no chance of opening an expensive new chapel with an elaborate public ceremonial.[33]

Concessions remained elusive though significant. Thus, during the so-called 'Flour War' of 1775, the Controller-General, Turgot, insisted that the pastors of Languedoc be permitted to warn their people about the effects of disturbances on the same basis as local priests, so that, as Norman Ravitch has said, 'in effect, the outlawed ministers were being treated like unofficial civil servants'.[34] Turgot was a celebrated *philosophe* turned minister, but such progressive thinking was not unusual. The well-placed magistrate Gilbert de Voisins had written two reports for the King in 1767, recommending that a form of civil marriage be allowed for Protestants (a sign of the legal problems caused by Protestant inheritance battles), and this was discussed no less than four times in the Council before it was put aside.[35] It was a token of the new *realpolitik* in government circles.[36] But though the veteran Protestant leader Paul Rabaut may have persuaded the opinion-formers, the public at large remained generally indifferent.

Unperturbed, Rabaut and his son quietly lobbied the government and those on the fringes of power, and this was decisive in securing the grant of the Edict on Non-Catholics in 1787. It came only after thirteen frustrating years in which Louis XVI, essentially tolerant, but respectful of the Church and the weight of tradition, had heeded the cautionary advice of his chief minister, the elderly pragmatist Maurepas (d. 1781), and done nothing in a hurry. Other ministers, first Turgot, then Malesherbes, were more inclined to act; both in 1775 urged the deletion from the King's coronation oath of the pledge to extirpate heresy. They failed, but it was a sign of the government's basic tolerance that the Swiss Protestant, Jacques Necker, himself married to the daughter of a pastor, was appointed Director-General of Finances two years later. In fact, Necker proved more anxious to gain allies among the Catholic higher clergy than ease conditions for his co-religionists. The wartime alliance with America kept up the pressure for change despite the conservatives; Huguenots were permitted to buy and sell property without restriction after 1781, and in a decree of May 1782 concerning the baptism of suspected Calvinist children, the priest was directed to enter details in accordance with the statements of those who presented the infant for baptism and not to volunteer his own written comments. Its effect was to make churchmen furious and Protestants refrain more than ever from presenting their children at Catholic fonts.[37] The Archbishop of Arles complained that it made parish priests the blind instruments of state policy, but it was a sign of how irresistible the pressure for change on government was becoming despite complaints from the 1780 General Assembly of the Clergy about the new-found provincial prominence of Protestants. The bishops warned darkly that 'A first victory for Calvinism would prepare the road for still more terrible revolutions', but Louis XVI was not particularly sympathetic.[38]

Events came to a head after the appointment of the Baron de Breteuil to the royal council in 1783. The historian Rulhière was commissioned to prepare a study of the Huguenot question. He liaised with Malesherbes and the hero of the American War, Lafayette who, as much as anybody, made the cause of ending what he called the 'intolerable despotism' to which the Huguenots were technically subject, his own.[39] Lafayette spent two weeks in Nîmes during June 1785 with Rabaut de Saint-Etienne to obtain a first-hand view of how the Calvinists viewed the situation, while Malesherbes drew up two important memoranda for the King, with the goal of persuading him that civil status for Catholics somehow accorded with the real intentions of Louis XIV.[40] Breteuil then took up the issue again in 1786, and it was raised by Lafayette and others when the first Assembly of Notables gathered in February 1787(see Chapter 5).[41] Yet with traditionalists in the administration like Miromesnil, the Keeper of the Seals, holding out against change, it took the diplomatic crisis of that summer caused by the defeat of France's traditional allies in the Netherlands (the largely Calvinist Patriot party) to achieve the longed-for concession.[42] The pressure from would-be refugees fleeing from Amsterdam forced the hand of the new administration, headed by Archbishop of Toulouse, Loménie de Brienne,[43] and the 'Edict Concerning Those Who Do Not Profess the Catholic Religion' was published in November 1787. After the acceptance of some conservative amendments from the Paris *parlement*, it was ready for promulgation in February 1788.[44]

Concessions under the Edict were modest; they bore little resemblance to the Austrian Emperor's Patent of Toleration (1781).[45] Members of the Reformed Churches could marry before a royal judge or a *curé* (acting only as a civil officer), register the births of their children and die knowing they could bequeath their estates to fellow Protestants. The limitations of the Edict were all too clear. Thus the word 'Protestant' appeared only once, in the preface, and the monopoly of the Catholic Church in public worship was affirmed. There were real problems of application in such areas as mixed marriages.[46] Protestants became citizens, but second-class ones, and stayed ineligible for public office. Yet, however mutedly, the Edict made clear that the traditional identification of citizenship with religious orthodoxy no longer held good – 'The entanglements of the confessional state were here rapidly coming apart.'[47]

There was a mixed reaction to the Edict inside the First Estate. At the end of the 1788 General Assembly, Archbishop Brienne reminded members that it removed from their altars 'the danger of deception and perjury and had re-established the harmony that ought always to reign between the law and the rights of nature',[48] but he could no more prevent his colleagues from issuing remonstrances against it than have them grant him a large *don gratuit*. The mass of parish clergy were uneasy about the whole business, puzzled at elite readiness to concede the argument to their adversaries, and feeling let down by the government's readiness to dilute the confessional state. Clergy saw how the Protestants tended to assume a greater grant of rights than the narrow language of the Edict really authorised, with 'heretics' ready to extend its terms by gathering without any attempt at secrecy. In Bordeaux (a city with a limited Protestant population), the clerical provincial assembly meeting the next spring was one of the few to welcome the new law. Its only concern was that the Edict might, 'against the king's intention, tend to favour error or even indifference in religion, and enfeeble the essential principles bound up with the constitution of the monarchy'.[49] Catholic hardliners were in doubt that such would be the case. The Bishop of La Rochelle in February 1788 issued such a hostile pastoral letter (*Mandement*) that it was referred by the presidial court in the town to the *parlement*, which promptly ordered its suppression.[50] Other parlements also had their doubts about the limited concessions, as seen in the refusal of three – Besançon, Bordeaux and Douai – to register the Edict at all.[51]

Once the measure passed, concern among Catholic clergy and the more pious laity only slowly ebbed. They looked on uneasily while Crown officials went about their business over the next twelve months as the Edict required, and information about previously contracted marriages not recognised in law was made public. Fresh demands were made by Protestant laymen in their *cahiers* before the meeting of the Estates-General in the spring of 1789. If only three clerical *cahiers* (Metz, Le Puy, Bordeaux) asked for complete withdrawal of the Edict of toleration, the rest wanted the extension of civil rights to Protestants halted and perhaps some concessions cancelled. There were some calls for its revision by the Estates-General to clarify the legal position in the light of what the clergy of Paris admitted were 'the lively alarms which this edict inspires in us.'[52] Here are the clergy of Dourdan in the Orléannais who wanted deputies: 'To consider the representations made by the last assembly of clergy with respect to the edict concerning non-Catholics, and not to permit any religion, other than the Catholic religion, to engage in public worship or instruction'.[53] More generously worded references like those proclaimed by the clergy of the *sénéchaussée* of Saintes were exceptional:

> We consider the protestants like brothers whom we must cherish. We will not cease to call for moderation, and even demand the complete abolition of the penal laws enacted during the last two reigns.[54]

Among laymen as a whole, there were few signs of overt resentment at recognising the existence of Protestantism (the *cahiers of* the Third Estate said very little on the issue) and a general reticence on the whole issue,[55] perhaps a sign both of declining interest in dogmatic controversy and the Protestants' peaceable behaviour as long as anyone could remember. But in areas of the south-east where the two confessions uneasily coexisted, the tensions remained high at the beginning of the Revolution, and the reduction of theological disputes had done nothing to dampen them down. Daniel Ligou, in a recent study of the town of Montauban, has persuasively argued that historians may have underestimated the extent of opposition to the 1787 Edict in such centres.[56] Certainly, Catholics in Nîmes and other towns densely populated by Protestants were angry and defensive about the threat to their material supremacy posed by the Edict of 1787, and kept their religious rivals out of the mayoralty and some other municipal posts.[57] Huguenots were bent on building on the concessions it had given them to extract more from a sympathetic Estates-General. Confident in the state's official adoption of religious toleration, they assumed much too easily that their Catholic neighbours would stand by and see their privileges and social standing eroded completely without resistance.

II

Jews in 1789 had made a few precarious steps towards limited legal recognition (thus forced conversions of legitimate children had been banned throughout France for over half a century), but their lives were still hedged around with restrictions, and antisemitism remained endemic. In a controversial book published in 1968, *The French Enlightenment and the Jews*, Rabbi Hertzberg even argued that 'Modern, secular anti-Semitism was fashioned not as a reaction to the Enlightenment and the [1789] Revolution, but within the Enlightenment and Revolution themselves.' It is an extreme interpretation,[58] which dismisses too easily the passionate commitment of the *philosophes* and their followers at the mid-century to toleration in general though, admittedly, few of the Encyclopedists had much to say specifically in favour of Jewish toleration and regarded the survival of Hebrew religion and customs down to the eighteenth century as quaint and obscurantist. They did little to temper the prevailing climate of popular anti-semitism. Voltaire and his disciples, in the name of reason and tolerance, presented the Jews as religious fanatics; Montesquieu proposed the more systematic segregation of the Jews and the creation of a Jewish town on the frontier with Spain.[59] Nevertheless, by Louis XVI's reign most committed reformers accepted that there had to be improvements in the status of the Jews, but were able to obtain only limited concessions from government before the Revolution. The reformers, whatever their own Christian faith or lack of it, still insisted that tolerating Judaism would be the most likely method of inducing Jews to abandon faith and family ties in favour of Christianity.

Most members of the elite – when they bothered at all – continued to think of the Jews as aliens rather than *bona fide* French subjects. This stereotyped inferiority as the sinister 'Other' was reinforced by conventional Christian apologetics, as in the widely used abbé Fleury's catechism, which justified their dispersion and suffering on the basis of 'deicide'. They were a miniscule fraction of French society, much fewer in number than Protestants, with a population estimated at 40 000 to 50 000.[60] The main communities were in Bordeaux (3500 approximately), Marseille, Alsace, Lorraine, the Three Bishoprics (principally Metz) and in the papal provinces of Avignon and the Comtat Venaissin (about 2500 in 1770), with others in Nîmes, Montpellier and Lyon. In Paris the Jews (just over 500) did not officially exist and were treated only as persons passing through the capital; they found it easy in practice to elude the prohibitions that their provincial brethren frequently faced. The precarious legal status of the Jews left them vulnerable to prejudicial interpretations of the law rather than outright persecution, 'Jew hunts' spontaneously staged by suspicious neighbours rather than pogroms initiated by the state. Nevertheless, French Jews indeed possessed some very limited rights to worship. Three public synagogues were recognised for the 8000 Jews of Upper Alsace. All the others were barely tolerated conventicles, and hedged around with restrictions. When the Jews of Horburg applied in 1773 to build a synagogue it was allowed only on condition that it be called a *'maison pour prier'*. Yet, compared with the Protestants, the Jewish communities of pre-1789 France (especially the Sephardim) enjoyed a greater degree of concessions from the state, as one of the finest synagogues in France, built during the eighteenth century in the 'Avignonese' town of Carpentras (geographically part of France, but a papal territory) still testifies. Thus Jewish laws pertaining to property rights in marriage were recognised by the French authorities. Marriage contracts drawn up by rabbis had to be registered with the authorities, but this was only done to protect Christian creditors.

Despite their existence on the margins, the two distinct groups of Sephardi and Ashkenazi Jews felt mutual distrust rather than any sense of solidarity. Links were few, since the Sephardim viewed the Ashkenazim with their Yiddish culture, distinctive dress and prayer curls as socially inferior to themselves.[61] The Sephardim were in the minority, with numbers around 3500, concentrated in the Bordeaux area. Their internal affairs were conducted by 'the Nation', composed

of a syndic and his deputies, drawn from the leading families. Its auto-
cratic character, especially in tax-raising, was much disliked by the
less wealthy and influential, but it survived until the Revolution.
Respectful of the ordinary law courts, commonly with gentile friends
and mistresses, the Sephardi Jews of Bordeaux were heavily involved
in commerce and industry (even the slave trade).[62] They were effectively barred from other occupations and were not eligible for the Bordeaux Chamber of Commerce. Despite the odds, social acceptance
was slowly coming, assisted by such patriotic gestures as the gift of
60 000 livres from the 'Portuguese nation' of Bordeaux in 1782 to
defray the costs of fitting out a warship. One of the Bordelais Jews,
Joseph Niemes Pereyre, had indeed bought feudal properties in
1720, becoming both vicomte and baron in the process, while Abra-
ham Gradis, head of a family that had helped provision Quebec
during the Seven Years War, died worth 10 million livres and
attracted some of the princes of the blood to his funeral.[63]

Ministers treated them more advantageously than the Ashkenazim. In 1776 Louis XVI by Letters Patent renewed the old privileges
that had been granted since 1550 to the *marranos* or 'New Christians'
originating from Spain and Portugal[64] and who, since 1723, had
lived openly as Sephardi Jews where they had not converted to
Christianity. To serve them, seven private houses in Bordeaux by
1752 discretely served as synagogues. They were, in effect, another
corporate body within the monarchy. Renewal of these privileges
was not cheap: in 1723 the right to stay in France cost 100 000 livres.
There was a considerable contrast between Bordeaux and Bayonne,
where the Jews were excluded from the city itself and forced to live in
the suburb of Saint-Esprit-les-Bayonne. The relatively generous
terms of the 1776 Letters Patent lifted the restriction on right of
residence to embrace all the territory within the jurisdiction of the
Bordeaux *parlement*, though movement hardly occurred. In more
northerly cities like Rouen and Nantes, Jews were still liable to persecution; two from Bordeaux were arrested in Orléans and Rouen in
1781. Nevertheless, this precedent was used by other communities
which tried unsuccessfully to gain legal status by registering the
Letters Patent with their local *parlement*: early efforts in 1776 and
1783–85 to have the privileges of 1776 recognised by the Paris
parlement failed.

For the most part, the Jews of eastern France also lived in their
own communities with corporations or *Kehillots* to distribute charity,

support schools and rabbis, and divide up the tax burden.[65] Under
the control of syndics, such organization facilitated the royal protection required to keep local anti-Semitic outbursts in check, but also
ensured that the Jews continued to be seen as a people apart from the
mainstream of the French population. Their 'otherness' was confirmed for the majority of gentiles by their long beards, kosher diet,
Judeo-Alsatian dialect, and use of Hebrew characters in writing.[66]
The price of toleration – and limited protection – was the payment
of special additional taxes. In 1785–9 the 3000 Jewish inhabitants of
the Metz *quartier* paid no less than 360 livres each year to the Crown,
the Kings of France having inherited rights regarding the Ashkenazi
Jews in Alsace, with corresponding privileges for the municipalities,
principally levying the 'body-toll'. Not satisfied with the proceeds,
royal officials were keen to extract additional impositions from these
marginal subjects whose alleged wealth and precarious legal status
made it tempting to consider levying the *droit d'aubaine* (a tax placed
on the property of aliens).[67] Yet none of these burdens could deter the
Jews of Metz from publishing loyal addresses to the Crown whenever
there was occasion.

Jews were permitted to live in 182 Alsatian towns and villages on
the eve of the Revolution, and constituted 70 per cent of the total
Jewish population of France; in neighbouring Lorraine there were
by comparison only 180 Jewish families and a single rabbi in a total
of 52 communities. The earliest census for the Alsatian Jews dates
from 1784 and gives the figure of 19 707, though it cannot be assumed
that everyone registered; a total of nearer 30 000 would be more
accurate.[68] Many lived on the breadline. The *bailli* of Molsheim
reported that some lived all day 'on a piece of bread or some apples,
pears or other fruits depending on what's in season'.[67] While some
dealt in second-hand clothes, grain or horses, many others were loan
merchants, as much from necessity as choice, because they were by
long custom prohibited from working in other trades, including agriculture. Very frequently they were the intermediaries between gentile creditors and debtors, or were transferrees (*cessionnaires*) who
bought the rights to debts from non-Jewish creditors or were repaid
for debts owed by gentiles. They were like private bank institutions
with a large number of customers. The Jewish creditor lived in
consstant fear that gentile debtors would refuse to pay back loan or
interest or both. He dreaded the severe winters, heavy rains or bad
crops which often produced new decrees legalizing the peasant's

repudiation of payment. Jews themselves decried usury, but even honest Jewish creditors could be persecuted by unscrupulous debtors as money lenders. And in lawsuits between Jews and gentiles the term 'Jew' was used as frequently as possible. It was an almost universal belief that the Talmud allowed, and even ordered, Jews to charge exorbitant rates of interest on loans to non-Jews.

A few enterprising spirits established themselves outside the banking field, like Théodore Cerf-Berr of Nancy, who operated a cloth factory in Pont-Saint-Vincent in 1787, where between thirty and forty children were employed. During the winter of 1788-9 the municipality of Nancy a loan of 50 000 livres to buy wheat, and he also promised to make another purchase for the city himself. This gesture was quite counterproductive. When the wheat did not arrive in time, he was accused of hiding it for speculation and his storehouses were attacked.

Such an anti-Semitic outburst was one of the hazards of daily life for the Jews in Alsace. The most notorious incident occured after the province was inundated by a mass of counterfeit receipts signed in Hebrew in 1777. When Jewish financiers requested payment for credit given in good faith they were presented with these falsified receipts for sums allegedly paid them in part or full payment of the debts. The counterfeiting of the receipts was accompanied by riots in August 1778. These formed part of a conspiracy in which the bailiff of Landser, the appropriately named Jean-François Hell, was heavily implicated. A settlement took several years.[70] In November 1786 the government recommended that the Jewish creditors be allowed to request only one-fifth of their debts, meaning in effect the dispossession of four-fifths of their properties. This decision was modified later in the year, but the debts had still not been paid off when the Revolution broke out.

Over the medium term, the case of the counterfeit receipts indirectly benefited the status of the Jewish community in Alsace, as it made local citizens of goodwill far more aware of their downtrodden Jewish neighbours. The Enlightenment case for toleration was at last made in Alsace in the 1780s. The 'body-toll' was abolished despite resistance from the conservative city authorities in Strasbourg; there was the publication in 1782 in French translation of the German writer Charles Dohm's book on the amelioration of the status of the Jews (*De la Réforme politique des juifs*), and the issue of royal Letters Patent on 10 July 1784, a concession which owed much to lobbying by Cerf-Berr.[71] By its terms, the Jews were freed from the seigneurial poll tax and allowed to embark on agriculture and manufacturing, and to lease land if not to own it outright. A census was ordered at the end of the year to establish and legalize the number of Jews in each community, and detect illegal immigrants.

If less generous than the terms accorded the Sephardim in 1776, the Letters Patent of 1784 remained a significant concession, albeit difficult to enforce. Practical considerations had motivated ministers, above all lessening tensions in Alsace, by giving the Jews an opportunity not to be so identified with the practice of usury. They were determined local authorities should not impede the process. In Strasbourg, the King's representatives forced the city to grant Cerf-Berr permission for temporary residence within its boundaries because of his importance as an army contractor. The case became a legal *cause célèbre*, with the new Provincial Assembly of Alsace allying with the city against the grant of special status to Cerf-Berr owing to the fear that it would establish a precedent. The 1787 Edict on non-Catholics did little to help the Jews directly. They could notify the authorities of their existence under its terms, as was done in Nîmes where Jewish births, marriages and deaths were entered in the registry opened to Protestants; in Paris, many Jews stated their religion in registrations at the Office of Properties (*Bureau des Domaines*). And there was another small gain in February 1788 when the Jews of Marseille finally had the Letters Patent of 1776 registered with the *parlement* of Provence, though the price was a legal subterfuge declaring a mixed community to be wholly Sephardim. The latter group in Bordeaux meanwhile made it clear they were not interested in assisting their co-religionists in the east. In a memoir of June 1788 they told the government not to allow poor, uneducated Jews from Alsace to infiltrate the prosperous communities of the south-west where, uniquely, Jews who were first and foremost Frenchmen could be found.[72]

Small in scale the adjustments might be, but the commitment of French ministers to a pragmatic toleration for the Jews did not go unnoticed elsewhere in Europe. As with the Protestants, it was Malesherbes (a minister in 1774–5, and again in 1787–8) who led the way. He was put in charge of a special commission to study the Jewish question in the whole of France, which argued that toleration would contribute to their conversion or, at least, the reform and refinement of Talmudic Judaism. The progressive means thus justified the traditional end. The abbé Grégoire's hopes were much the same, but a shade more liberal. He produced a prize-winning essay for the Academy of Metz in 1788 which received notice nation-wide; that he was a clergyman, but one who had been reading the Talmud in Hebrew since 1770 and was speaking from personal knowledge of conditions in Alsace, gave zest to his literary fluency, but his vision of toleration was inseparable from eschatological con-siderations and the bright future of Jews embracing a purified and enlightened Catholicism: 'The Jews are members of that universal family that must establish brotherhood among all peoples'.[73] The practical combat on behalf of the Jews in the region was initiated by Pierre-Louis Roederer, the attorney of the *parlement* of Metz. He argued that the Jews should be assimilated in all civil matters, and should be allowed to congregate for religious purposes, although only under the eye of French officials. It was a limited move, but daring in its way given that the Metz *parlement* had delayed registration of the Edict on non-Catholics until March 1788 fearing the city would become 'a second Jerusalem'.

The hopes of these reformers were not widely shared. On the eve of the Revolution, anti-Jewish sentiments were still held at every level of French society. There was an interesting difference of views among French Protestants. Whereas Calvinists, who knew at first hand the pains of discrimination and persecution, were sel-dom overtly hostile to Jews, the Lutherans of Alsace, blessed with significant privileges themselves before the Edict of 1787, were averse to Jewish civil claims. Alsatian politicians in the new Provin-cial Assembly of 1787 had deplored the willingness of central gov-ernment to make concessions to the minority community. That Hell was president of the Alsatian Intermediary Commission in 1788–9, was an indication of the strength of anti-Jewish senti-ment in the province. Indeed, Lutheran Protestants joined locally with Catholics in a common fight against Jewish emancipation. Their leader, Christian-Guillaume Koch, a deputy at the National Assembly, expressed his views in an unpublished memorandum of June 1790, reiterating the demand that the Jews should be denied full citizenship, and it was popular with the majority of revolution-aries in Alsace. Even Reubell, a future Director, shared these prejudices, and would argue in the National Assembly in August 1789 that far from being excluded from national life, 'they exclude themselves'.

In the face of this hostility, the Ashkenazi Jews came tentatively together. Having been left out of the electoral plans for the convocation of the Estates-General, the Jews of Alsace, Lorraine and the Three Bishoprics petitioned Necker for concessions and were authorised to elect six deputies (two per province) to meet together in Paris in August to draw up a *cahier de doléances*. They wanted to preserve their autonomy, but concurrently demanded access to whatever professions they wanted. They maintained minimal political contacts with their Sephardi brethren who had participated like other Frenchmen in the primary assemblies of spring of 1789 and in some cases had voted for the election of deputies with everyone else.[74] They still fought projects favouring equally all the Jews of France, and insisted on retention of their privileges as a corporate body. At the same time, they welcomed Malesherbes's hopes after the Edict on non-Catholics was passed of bringing them as Frenchmen into the mainstream of national life. On the face of it, that seemed feasible for the Sephardim, whom the electoral rules had designated 'Frenchmen', but much less likely for the Ashkenazim, whom the same process had marginalized as 'Jews'.

Though sympathy for emancipation was growing among educated Catholics in Alsace and Lorraine, the pressure on the hierarchy to procede cautiously was unrelenting. Bishop La Fare, newly appointed Bishop of Nancy, was told by his Provincial Assembly in 1787 that 'Should we lose you, a Jew will take your place and become our bishop.' He was too recently in post to distance himself from such inflammatory nonsense. Not that his own sentiments were generous; he later spoke against active citizenship for Jews in the National Assembly debate of December 1789.[75] Other members of the First Estate were less cautious. Completely divided though they might be in their response to the Revolution, Grégoire and Cardinal Rohan, bishop of Strasbourg (the disgraced prelate of the famous Affair of the Diamond Necklace of 1785–6), could both agree that the Jews deserved better. Rohan advocated stringent yet 'honourable' regulations for the Jews. He frequently came into contact with them and was by no means unpopular. Indeed in 1798, post-Emancipation, a Jewish congregation chanted a special ode in his honour in the synagogue. By then, Rohan and a large proportion of Catholic clergy had experienced the full force of state intolerance for themselves while Protestants and Jews, after having initially benefited from the tolerant religious policies of the National Assembly

(1789–91), were also under pressure from Jacobin politicians in the Republic to abandon the active practice of their faith. But, as at spring 1789, minority religionists, like the French population as a whole, looked to the future with optimism unparalled in the national memory. They wanted their status improved and recognised, so that, at last, they would be accepted as Frenchmen.

4 The Church and the Enlightenment

Eighteenth-century France retains to this day its supremacy as the most celebrated example of an 'Enlightenment' culture, notwithstanding current scholarly suspicions about seeing the Enlightenment as a monolithic movement. Recent historians emphasise the sheer variety of the Enlightenment experience, with Roger Chartier even advancing the proposition that the Revolution, to a significant degree, 'invented' or 'constructed' the Enlightenment and reduced to a false unity an extreme diversity of thought.[1] Whatever one's views on this interpretation, it is clear that opinion-formers and the educated public in eighteenth-century France (as elsewhere in Europe) wanted institutions to function along more rational lines, believed in the rule of law, the supremacy of empirical methodology in the experimental and the social sciences, and were turning their faces against religious intolerance. These were central tenets of what most scholars are willing to call – if only for convenience – the Enlightenment, with reason, liberty, happiness and nature the keywords denoting its presence.[2]

Yet the French experience of this transformation in ideas and outlooks, in one central aspect at least, was not at one with the general European trend for Enlightenment to have its roots firmly in reformist-minded Christianity, whether Catholic or Protestant. That was very much the case in Germany or Scotland, rather less so in France.[3] Admittedly, French Jansenism had, in its strictly religious manifestations between *c.* 1670 and 1740, given rise to a critical attitude towards the Church authorities, but the relationship of Jansenism and the French eighteenth-century Enlightenment remains problematic and insufficiently explored. Dale Van Kley's justifiably influential writings suggest that as Jansenism expired in theological terms, its mission accomplished with the expulsion of the Jesuits, so it found expression in alternative guises. Thus the magistrates of the *parlement* of Paris, attacking what they deemed excessive clerical influence in strictly juridical concerns in the 1750s, were articulating a 'judicial Jansenism' which emphasised the need for curbs on excessive powers concentrated in one institution, be it monarchy, papacy or episcopacy, and which manifested itself further in protests at the Maupeou coup of 1771 and the May Edicts of 1788 (see below). Hence the Jansenist theological locker was plundered for secular political purposes. Van Kley makes a powerful case, but his latter-day Jansenism is one with the theology either discarded or put aside, and this is troublesome if one defines it as a version of Catholicism concerned primarily with the economy of salvation.

As has already been argued, Jansenists in that religious sense – like Archbishop Montazet of Lyon – were apparently few and far between by Louis XVI's reign, even if one concedes them an influence disproportionate to their numbers. Far more common, following Van Kley, is a *jansénisant* state of mind, spilling over from theology and ecclesiology into other areas of public and private life, encouraging a critical view of monolithic institutions like the Church that could so readily be accused of oppressive behaviour. This critical bent, suspicious of (recently invented) tradition as a pretext for institutional power, clearly links Jansenism with the Enlightenment, at least in its early stages; it nurtures a critical, even captious, mentality among the reading public and helps fashion an audience likely to respond positively to the writings of the high Enlightenment of *c.* 1745–65. But to move from there to argue that Jansenism is transmuted into the infidelity and unbelief of the *philosophes* and their imitators later in the century goes too far: Jansenism is selectively anticlericalist, ever alert to hierarchical pretensions and bent on puncturing them, but in essence it is not irreligious, let alone anti-Catholic. Many Jansenists, their victory won in 1764, may well have worked with the Church and been ready to engage *for* the Church rather than against it. That may not have been the case in Paris, as we know from the 1770s, but our knowledge of other areas is simply too flimsy to rule out the likelihood of the capital being the exception rather than the rule. Late Jansenists proper had an alternative ecclesiological vision for the Church based on primitive Christian practices as opposed to latter-day 'corruptions', and the Revolution would give them the opportunity to try them out. But in terms of belief, their Catholicism was that of the Church Fathers, an Augustinianism that had little of the optimism to be found among the lay contributors to the great *Encyclopédie* and was, as far as we know, of little interest to all but a few ageing clerics and canon lawyers.

By contrast, the French *philosophes* and their numerous supporters were as critical of dogmas as they were of the hierarchy, so that the Enlightenment in France was associated with religious heterodoxy and indifference to a degree rarely found elsewhere. On the other hand, Catholic apologists never ceased to insist that reason and the revelation of the Gospels were wholly compatible. The number of moderate voices in the French higher clergy should not be underestimated, nor the appeal of the middle ground on which they stood to public opinion. As was suggested in the first chapter, Church leaders were willing to consider practical reform of their own structures and procedures (not to mention dubious popular beliefs) in the interests of rational progress. This was the 'Catholic Enlightenment', a tendency historians recognise in Spain, Austria and Italy, but which was no less present in eighteenth-century France and which, as Bernard Plongeron has famously shown, would decisively affect clerical attitudes towards the Revolution.[4]

But the 'Catholic Enlightenment' was a side-current in the main channel of ideas flowing across the nation. By the 1780s, the French Church had long experience of 'enlightened' criticism: well before the end of the Sun King's reign in 1715 scepticism about the claims of Christianity had begun to influence intellectual opinion and, from mid-century, the Church's critics gained more converts as Voltaire adopted a position of open hostility to the faith as the enemy of progress.[5] The public listened readily to this masterful onslaught and the host of imitators who, less elegantly, chorused the same theme. Yet the Church stood up to this kind of castigation and − at least to outward appearance − survived with its institutional vigour intact. But in the process the public had been taught by the *philosophes* not to take for granted the claims to power of any organ of authority in the State, however venerable or sacrosanct, including the Church. Everything was open to assessment on the basis of usefulness and its contribution to human happiness. The Enlightenment thus made an enquiring, critical outlook the norm in French society by the 1760s and in that sense at least prepared the way for Revolution.

The criticism the *philosophes* directed against the Church had several aspects. These included their strident anticlericalism, a phenomenon hardly unique to the eighteenth century but given a new impetus by the *billets de confession* controversy in Louis XV's reign (when most clergy were under orders from their diocesan bishop to withold the last rites from anyone who could not show they were not a Jansenist) against the power and status of the Gallican clergy in the French polity.[6] Anticlericalist sentiments received an indirect impetus from Jansenist attacks in the *Nouvelles Ecclésiastiques*, but whereas Jansenists genuinely had the good of the Church at heart, those who advanced under their cover were firmly, even dogmatically against 'priestcraft' in any of its manifestations. There is a view that the divisions within Gallicanism on the Jansenist question had made it more susceptible to anticlerical attack. Up to a point no doubt, but anticlericalism had an independent vitality in France as in most European countries, and its propagandists took advantage of any opportunity to advance their antisacerdotal cause: whatever his theology, as far as they were concerned, a priest was still a priest. More importantly, the Jansenist wrangling had made many clerical controversialists inward-looking, more concerned to turn their fire on each other rather than to stand together against an external threat.

The theological corollary of anticlericalism was the deism associated in a variety of forms with the leading *philosophes*, notably Voltaire, Rousseau, and their imitators and apologists. It rejected the framework of traditional Christian theology, especially the claims to divinity of Jesus Christ, for a faith that found evidence of the Creator exclusively in nature. But this was a creator who did not intervene in the world, and to whom human beings had no obligations. Some deists believed that God had instituted a system of rewards and punishments, but they were a minority. More controversial still were the radical alternatives to any recognizable religious belief, such as atomism or systematic materialism, identified with thinkers such as Diderot, d'Holbach, Helvétius and La Mettrie. Their writings fascinated the public, and by the 1770s the easy availability of cheap editions of atheistic works enabled readers to acquire them as soon as they appeared; Helvétius's notorious *De l'Esprit* sold extraordinarily well for thirty years after its first printing in 1758.[7]

Deism seems to have had remarkably little appeal for the clergy as a body. Most Parisian hostesses knew an unbelieving abbé or two, like the abbé Raynal whose *Histoire des deux Indes* (1770) sold something like 25 000 copies before it was condemned and burnt for its antireligious audacity in 1781;[8] and there was the odd bishop like La Font de Savine of Viviers, who was a disciple of Rousseau rather than of Jesus. Clerics of this persuasion were the exception.[9] What is most striking about the Gallican Church in the 1780s is that it retained its commitment to orthodoxy largely intact at every level. Evidence of heretical beliefs like Socinianism infiltrating the clergy is rare. Clerical imitators of Rousseau's fictional *vicaire* from Savoy, founding his belief in the God of Nature, were hard to find.

The ideal of a learned clergy was still embodied in the First Estate on the eve of the Revolution, a clergy interested in every kind of academic discipline, old and new, contemporary or pre-Enlightenment. Among the most internationally celebrated was Jean-René Asseline, Professor of Hebrew and Director of the Sorbonne, whose prominence was reflected in his nomination to the see of Boulogne in 1789, the last prelate appointed before the Civil Constitution and, appropriately, the first commoner to break the noble stranglehold on bishoprics since Louis XV's reign.[10] He joined some distinguished intellectual company on the episcopal bench with Archbishop Le Franc de Pompignan of Vienne in the vanguard. He had been a tireless campaigner for orthodoxy since the mid-century in sermons, pastoral letters, and pamphlets, while his combination of mental agility, pastoral concern and personal charm made it hard for the *philosophes* to asperge his character as they had done his colleague, Christophe de Beaumont, Archbishop of Paris, an uncompromising anti-Jansenist and stickler for clerical discipline. The monastic orders also maintained an intellectual tradition. Among their leading lights were Dom Joseph Pernetty, a Benedictine Maurist and author of a Newtonian mathematical course, who accompanied the explorer Bougainville on some of his Pacific voyages and saw all learning as part of God's great canvas of universal knowledge. His fellow Benedictine, Dom Pierre Deforis, clashed with Rousseau over some of the educational views contained in *Émile*,[11] while Dom Deschamps, Prior of Montreuil-Bellay (diocese of Poitiers), invented a philosophy that anticipated some of the essential ideas of Hegel about the nature of God – and sought to make converts among his colleagues.[12]

With the Church's creeds battered but intact, French theologians like the Maurist Dom Nicolas Jamin (*Theological Thoughts on the Errors of the Time* – 1769), the confuter of Voltaire, the abbé Nonnotte with his *Anti-Dictionnaire philosophique*, and the abbé Nicolas-Sylvestre Bergier (*Deism Refuted by itself* – 1765, and *Dictionary of Theology* – 1788–90)[13] were ready to carry the fight to the *philosophes*; the abbé Barruel, who would in the 1790s present the Revolution as a deliberate conspiracy, was already pointing the finger at the *philosophes* and the impious for the political crisis in his *Helvétiana or Provincial and Philosophical Letters* (1781).[14] Several displaced Jesuits like Julien-Louis Geoffroy and Thomas Royou lent their services to the widely read anti-*philosophe* organ, the *Année littéraire*, edited by Elie-Cathérine Fréron. Fréron was constantly on the look-out for new recruits to join his stable of writers calling the new philosophical orthodoxies (and their authors) to account[15] and, as has recently been argued, there was no shortage of literary hacks to seek their bread from his hands: men like Nicolas-Joseph-Laurent Gilbert (1750–80), Antoine Sabatier (1742–1817), once spurned by his hero Voltaire, thereafter his vituperative pursuer, and Jean-Marie-Bernard Clément (1742–1812), another tireless critic of Voltaire and the 'contagious licence' of the *philosophes*. Church patronage was available in limited quantities to some of these men. Thus the abbé Jean-Baptiste Grosier (1743–1823), founder of the pro-Catholic *Journal de littérature, des sciences et des arts* in 1779, acted as private secretary to Archbishop Beaumont. Funds were also made available to some of the more fortunate lay anti-*philosophes*. Caution should not be mistaken for parsimoniousness: the orthodoxy of some of these pamphleteers was not beyond reproach.[16]

The enemies of Gallican power did not fail to exploit their victory over the Order of Jesus, probing the defences of the Church to strike at the wounded giant, with the 'Sage of Ferney' leading the way; ironically, one of the Jesuits' most illustrious pupils, in the final two decades before his death in 1778, Voltaire continued to produce the spicy anticlerical tracts he called his *petits pâtés*.[17] He, like the majority of *philosophes*, was the uncompromising enemy not of the ordinary parish priest but rather of the Catholic hierarchy: cathedral canons, monks, bishops, ecclesiastical lawyers, those who held power in the First Estate and were determined to hang on to it, the beneficiaries and proponents of 'priestcraft', with minimal concern for social utility or the public good.[18]

But if superstition-trading-as-religion had been the only constituant of what the Sage of Ferney meant by '*l'infâme*' then churchmen and *philosophes* might have sat down together. The fact was that Enlightenment luminaries like Voltaire and their popularizers extended that deliciously vague term to embrace a general assault on all revealed religion. Voltaire deployed his considerable Biblical scholarship to undermine the ethics and the historicity of the Old Testament; Rousseau stripped Christ of his divinity and presented him as a virtuous prophet unsung in his own time (much like himself),[19] and there were several devastating attacks on miracles as a viable foundation for faith in the incessant polemic of Parisian atheists like d'Holbach, Boulanger and Damilaville.

For all that, the Church itself, like other constituents of the French establishment, had by Louis XVI's reign absorbed some mainstream Enlightenment values. As Peter Jones has well said, 'No other estate responded more thoroughly to the varied stimuli of the Enlightenment'.[20] Even the Sorbonne, headquarters in the defence of theological orthodoxy, was producing modernizing theologians like Luke Joseph Hooke, one of the leading products of the Catholic Enlightenment in France, well able to use reason and natural law theory in the service of the faith.[21] The influence of such teachers and apologists on elite middle-aged and younger clergy of 1789, those who had grown to maturity in a world penetrated by the perspectives and publicity of the *philosophes*, is only just being calculated. For many of these men, fashionable Enlightenment phrases had passed almost unconsciously into their everyday parlance. Gay-Vernon, for example, future Constitutional bishop of the Haute-Vienne, at a meeting of priests and laymen in a Limoges parish in 1788 spoke of how 'Reason alone ought to be our sovereign guide. We ought only to progress in the light of its torch.'[22] Not just language but concepts: the *curés* of the Lille *bailliage* in 1789 referred unselfconsciously to the 'Supreme Being' with no hint that they had any intention of thereby disavowing their Christian beliefs.[23]

The Church had fought against infidelity throughout the century, yet its ranks included many tolerant men, who, thoroughly familiar with the intellectual issues of the day, were willing to read the *philosophes* before condemning them. Indeed, the better educated the priest or prelate, the more likely he was to admire the critical insights of a work like Montesquieu's *The Spirit of the Laws* (1748) or the great *Encyclopédie*. Even as a court preacher and vicar-general of the Archbishop of Bourges before the Revolution, the abbé Claude Fauchet, author of the influential *Religion nationale* of 1789, rejoiced that philosophy had recalled mankind to the principles of true religion; by 1790 he was calling the Gospel the philosophy of Heaven.[24] Fauchet mixed a tinge of mysticism with his admiration for philosophy that brought him back to the Scriptures as a key that Christian philosophers could use to decode the future, and this had a wide appeal in the early stages of the Revolution when, as Fauchet wrote, 'We're at the close of decadence [*des excès*]. Regeneration is approaching'.[25] One finds it, for instance, having an impact on the Carthusian Dom Gerle (one of the foreground figures in David's print of the *Tennis Court Oath*), and on others such as Lamourette and Pontard, who would, like Fauchet, become bishops of the Constitutional Church.

Fauchet, like far more priests then than at any other stage in the Church's history, was exceptionally well read. Lower clergy were discriminating as well as eclectic in their reading, by no means shunning an author because one or more of his books was adjudged unacceptable by their hierarchical superiors. Thus in the diocese of Verdun in 1789, priests met regularly at each other's houses to study and, along with the Bible and the history of Church Councils, also attempted to digest Rousseau's *Contrat Social*.[26] Across France the more prosperous clergy, not excluding *curés*, do not seem to have hesitated before joining either provincial academies[27] or that archetypal Enlightenment expression of male sociability, the Masonic lodge. In Bordeaux, for example, the Archbishop's secretary, the abbé Jolly, was only one of numerous local clergy with Masonic links; the abbé Lapauze was designated in 1782 to preside over the General Lodge of the Grand Orient. Even Regular clergy participated. The Benedictine congregation of Saint-Vanne had some masons among them, but stayed largely faithful to their vows, while nine monks at the great abbey of Fécamp in 1778 founded the lodge of the Triple Unity on their premises.[29] The Enlightenment in France thus had a Christian dimension too readily overlooked, and its distinctive agenda would, in time, be emphasised in the pastoral instructions of the Constitutional bishops taking up post in 1790–1, many of whom before the Revolution had been parish priests or members of the ecclesiastical teaching orders like the Oratorians.[30]

Oratorians had been drawn into the Jansenist dispute, at least in terms of religious controversy, which had been reduced to its embers by the reign of Louis XVI. Officially, orthodoxy had triumphed, but the debate had revived conciliarist theories. These stressed the rights of subjects and questioned those of absolute authority, whether wielded by bishop or king, and influenced the subsequent political thinking of both upper and lower clergy. Preaching the Coronation sermon of 1775, Archbishop Boisgelin of Aix even dared commend the objective of limited monarchy to the young Louis XVI, and his words twice drew applause from the congregation despite the hallowed occasion.[31] It was an opportunity to get across the message that any *philosophe* would have relished; Boisgelin did the job verbally as effectively as any of them could have managed in print, and he went on to complete twelve hundred pages of unpublished manuscript notes called 'Reflections on the Spirit of the Laws'.[32] Throughout his reign, Louis was regularly reminded from the pulpit of the Church's interest in reformist politics, often elaborately expounded, sometimes very tersely like Fauchet's words in 1786: 'There should be kings, not tyrants; subjects, and not slaves.'[33] Many higher clergy avidly followed events in the American War of Independence, and letters of the future bishop of Nancy, La Fare, make plain his desire that the cause of liberty – and republicanism – should prevail.[34]

A perspective on French politics derived from Montesquieu was unexceptionable by the 1770s, but the writings of other *philosophes* hostile to religious orthodoxy continued to provoke passionate complaints from a wide cross-section of the clergy and laity, alarmed by the apparent popularity of such works among the larger reading public. As one petition to the General Assembly noted:

> We speak of irreligion, which for some years now has spread in all directions like a torrent, and does the gravest damage among us. This terrible fire consumes everything and if we don't hurry to stop its progress, the malady will be beyond all remedies.[35]

The petitioners had in mind every sort of text produced by those authors great and small who had joined forces in the 'philosophic confederation', whether it was the mocking irony of a Voltaire in a work like the *Dictionnaire philosophique portatif*, the rhapsodic acclaim of the divinity in Nature evident in Rousseau's *Émile*, or the vituperative anti-dogmatism of d'Holbach's *Le Christianisme dévoilé*. Churchmen had long seen the need to reaffirm the tenets of the faith in response to earlier philosophical systems like Cartesianism; but in the eighteenth century Gallican Christians were almost constantly on the defensive against every sort of heterodoxy and unbelief. They had never been able to seize the initiative from their opponents, write the kind of ripostes which would capture the whole nation's attention. As the conservative Dominican, Charles-Louis Richard, regretted in 1785, most eighteenth-century apologists had 'by and large touched only a certain number of people for whom they [were] the least necessary', in other words theologians.[36] This was arguably excessively pessimistic, but it reveals how much clerical morale had been undermined.

At every General Assembly of the Clergy held between 1765 and 1788, the Church at least attempted to go on the counter-attack against its detractors.[47] In 1770 the Assembly appealed directly to the laity (in a manner which would be very influential for secular politicians) with a pamphlet called 'Warning on the Dangers of Incredulity', and followed it five years later with a tract on the 'Advantages of the Christian Religion'. Individual prelates like Montazet of Lyon and Dulau of Arles backed up these initiatives in the Assembly by action at diocesan level, 'guarding their faithful against philosophical propaganda' as the latter called it.[38] Concurrently, there were demands from the majority of delegates that the government must impose an effective ban on the most offensive writings of the *philosophes*. The bishops had no hesitation in linking sedition with anti-christian sentiments, and they wanted ministers to prevent anti-Christian tracts from circulating: 'It is time, sire, to put a stop to this frightful, deplorable government lethargy. A few more years of silence and this commotion will become universal leaving only debris and ruin [in the state].'[39]

Such jeremiads were only patchily effective in influencing opinions (the government, for one, offered no reply), for this determined opposition to the influence of Voltaire and Rousseau came when many of the younger clergy, like their secular counterparts, had succumbed to the cult of both. In some celebrated cases, like Archbishop Loménie de Brienne's, there was a personal friendship with *philosophes* Turgot and d'Alembert dating back to student days in the early 1750s when his interest in philosophy first awoke; it was a lifelong passion, so that Louis XVI is notoriously supposed to have remarked in 1781 when Brienne's name was under consideration for promotion, 'that it was necessary that an Archbishop of Paris should at least believe in God'. Few of Brienne's contemporaries were so compromised, but their admiration for philosophical writings, however discretely and conditionally held (few were ever found *in flagrante* with 'forbidden books'), made them pay just lip-service to the protests. Thus the effectiveness of the actions sponsored by more conservatively minded colleagues in the General Assembly of the Clergy was undoubtedly reduced. It also reflected the diminished influence of the official censors, for despite the growth in their numbers over the course of the century, success in enforcing the censor's ban was in inverse proportion to their recruitment level. After some hard-won battles against the proponents of Enlightenment in the 1760s, the Church's own machinery of censorship (based in the Sorbonne) itself attracted unfavourable notice and ceased to function effectively. Everyone had their own justification for rushing out to obtain prohibited literature, not least the clergy, no doubt often justifying it on the basis that refutation was impossible unless the poisonous draught was first drained.[40] Certainly, the Church's ban could not even prevent theological students from reading prohibited works; one seminarist at Toul was discovered reading Helvétius's *De l'esprit* in a religious procession, and at the Collège Louis-le-Grand 'mauvais livres' were apparently smuggled in by barbers and lavatory attendants![41] The most that could be expected by Louis XVI's reign was the occasional token victory, as occurred in the 1782 General Assembly when deputies were named to confer with the Keeper of the Seals, Miromesnil, about a law against 'mauvais livres'. Three years later a royal decree condemned the collected Kehl edition of Voltaire's works (being published on the German side of the Rhine a few hundred yards from the jurisdiction of the French Crown) for tending to destroy religion and morality as well as shaking the fundamental principles of social order and legitimate authority, but this stern-sounding notice was partly designed to extract taxes from the clergy.

The Church was particularly alarmed at the dissemination and popularisation of anti-clerical and anti-Christian 'forbidden books' among a wide cross-section of the urban community written, as Robert Darnton has made clear, not by the most famous hands, but by authors largely forgotten in literary history; they probably outnumbered (but by how much remains unclear) their enemies among the Grub Street hacks latterly identified as precursors of the Counter-Revolution.[42] It was bad enough when an educated, influential readership had direct access to the writings of the leading *philosophes*, but the vulgarisation of their output (often in a vitriolic and salacious mode, the classic libertine combination)[43] fortified resentment at the Church's status, its income from tithe, and further undermined its call on the loyalties of literate artisans, clerks and shopkeepers in town parishes. To quote Darnton again: 'Freethinking was not free, but by 1770 it had come within the purchasing power of the middle classes and the upper ranks of artisans and shopkeepers.'[44]

Taking their lead from the high priests of the Enlightenment – Voltaire, Helvétius, Diderot, d'Holbach – it became a commonplace for every hack pamphleteer to play on the discrepancies of income between higher and lower clergy and the drone-like existence of bishops at court scrambling for preferment.

Other targets included cathedral canons idling away their hours without pastoral responsibilities, and monks and nuns shut away in 'unnatural' confinement contributing nothing to the good of their fellow human beings, but finding plenty of opportunities to develop their taste for buggery, lesbianism and lascivious enjoyments of every kind. As well as lacking any sense of spiritual vocation, the religious orders were condemned for failing to satisfy the supreme test of eighteenth-century ethics – usefulness – and their life behind monastic walls was luridly portrayed as an exercise in tyranny, superstition and perversion: 'Oh, Sir,' exclaimed Diderot's unwilling and vocationless novice Suzanne in his novel *La Religieuse* [*The Nun*], 'you have no conception of the deceitful wiles of these Superiors of convents'.[45] Tyranny and sex were indispensable components of the popular demand for irreligious and pornographic works on the eve of the Revolution; the best-sellers combined both dimensions, like *Thérèse Philosophe*, which featured Father Dirrag and his famous 'cord'.[46] Voltaire himself satisfied the public's craving fairly politely in *La Pucelle*, and he had innumerable, more salacious rivals in the same genre, like the unknown author of one of the century's best-sellers, *Histoire de Dom B . . ., portier des Chartreux* (1741), or the no less lubricious *Histoire galante de la tourière des Carmélites* (1743), both frequently reprinted.[47]

However exaggerated or distorted the charges made against it, the Church was slow to use the talent in its own ranks to produce a convincing defence. The pamphleteer Rivarol wrote truly when he commented that 'at the approach of the Revolution, the intelligence of the clergy was the equal of the *philosophes*', but it was clearly the latter who had the flair for publicity, for popularising their opinions, and for appealing to the public imagination. Clerical silences could not be blamed on lack of training in updated apologetics: scholastic professors had produced a treatise – *De religione* – designed to combat incredulity, and from 1786 students were tested on their familiarity with the text in the oral examination for the baccalaureate.[48] Nevertheless, seminarians – like those in Cambrai – were tardy to recognise the peril, possibly wanting to close their eyes to its existence.[49] No amount of instruction could contain the dissemination of increasingly bitter anticlerical commonplaces on the eve of the

Revolution. Up to a point they demonstrated the growth of a healthy political culture in which institutions like the Church were adjudged capable of absorbing criticism from a variety of quarters. The scurrilous attacks made on the royal family and life at Versailles provide perhaps an institutional parallel: desacralisation of the monarchy as the counterpart to demoralising attacks on the higher and regular clergy.[50] But the term 'desacralisation' has not met with universal acceptance, and one of the strongest objections to it is how much it underestimates the pervasive influence of Christianity and persistent popular reverence for the person of the King in French society up to and beyond the Revolution. It is therefore perhaps more accurate to think in terms of a corrosion of respect for established authority as embodied in the organs of Church and State, the precise extent of which remains elusively hard to chart.

The majority of critics exempted the parish priests from their animadversions against the Gallican Church and depicted them in a positive light. Writers significantly said little about the steady attachment of the *bons curés* to preaching and living the Catholic faith. Critics concentrated on the *curé*'s social utility, his pastoral toil in educating children, marrying young people, visiting the sick, relieving the destitute and comforting the dying. Voltaire, for instance, in his *Carnets* [*Notebooks*], contrasted the parish priest's concern for the public good with that of the cardinal's: 'Nothing is more useful than the *curé* who keeps the register of births, who can double for the magistrate, who looks after poor folk, and brings peace into the midst of warring families.'[51] The *philosophes* presented these labours as evidence not of a continuing commitment to the injunctions of the Counter-Reformation but of a disinterested benevolence that could be disconnected from a specifically Christian moral teaching, a short step to the Revolutionary ideal of the 'citizen-priest'.[52] The most notorious articulation of this position was included in Rousseau's *Émile* (1762), where through the 'Profession de foi du Vicaire Savoyard', Rousseau pens a rhapsodic apostrophe to the God revealed in Nature as the inspiration for all the *vicaire*'s good works. However atypical of the average French *curé*'s beliefs, Rousseau's priest excited a whole generation, and confirmed the parish priest as the archetypal man of virtue. As such he was held up as a model of usefulness to inspire other sections of society and, simultaneously, provide a clerical role-model against which to show up the alleged laxness of clerics further up the hierarchy.

II

Pre-Revolutionary society remained at its close as much legitimated by its religion as ever. In the 1780s, the life of the royal court still revolved around religious observances, if anything more so than for several generations. Such practices were still adjudged essential to social cohesion, even after the forced removal of the royal family to the Tuileries palace in October 1789.[53] And whether from the pulpit in the chapel of Versailles palace, the churches in the capital and the great provincial cities frequented by leading laymen, or the 131 cathedrals of France, preachers responded eloquently and intelligently to the challenge of sustaining the historic faith of the kingdom, and could draw fashionable crowds to hear them. Some churches had a particular reputation for pulpit oratory, like Saint-Nicolas-des-Champs in Paris, where the police were instructed to keep order and eject women whose dress was more appropriate for an evening assembly than a church service.[54] High society followed individual preachers. None was more distinguished than the abbé Beauvais, later Bishop of Senez, Canon of Notre-Dame, deputy to the Estates-General, and founder of a school for preachers. He shared publicly his gift of exploring the expanding mental world of his age in an intelligibly Christian context. He suffered from no illusions about the burden faced by those in the Church who would preach convincingly to a generation schooled in the Enlightenment's proselytising:

> The eloquent men who instructed your fathers would in vain reappear among you; because of the century's impiety, how would they undertake to make themselves heard on matters that now appear no more than popular prejudices?[55]

If there was this tendency – especially after the expulsion of the Jesuits in 1764 – for leading preachers to stress moral conduct rather than the fundamental dogmas of Christianity, to neglect the Trinitarian unity of the Godhead and the mystery of the Incarnation, and to deliver a sermon which 'could be preached equally well in Paris, London or Constantinople',[56] it perhaps showed less a crisis of confidence in their creeds than an urge to speak to men and women in the language of their time rather than Bishop Bossuet's.[57] As the abbé Trublet unashamedly put it:

We ought to preach more than we do on the duties of the citizen since one cannot be a good Christian without being a good citizen. And one cannot object that this would be to preach a purely human morality ... since that has its own place in the Christian moral sphere.[58]

Other themes were seamlessly stitched on to the dominant one of religion's social utility, and they included popular sovereignty, the universality of the Christian family, and the need for loving correction of those who had offended against society's well-being. Such topics accorded with the preoccupations of privileged, urban Catholics, but there is little sign that they were displacing the catechetical emphasis on sin and the need for repentance to be heard week by week from the pulpits of rural *curés*. These classic preoccupations of post-Tridentine Catholicism remained the stock-in-trade of the clergy as they urged their flocks to despise worldly comforts and pleasures. As Fr Yves-Michel Marchais told his people:

Let us all remember together that soon our career will be ended, that our last hour is ready to strike, and that the longer we have lived the less time we have left to live, that we are hanging by a thread, that our grave is already open beneath our feet, and that at the first shock we shall be precipitated into it.[59]

So there were striking homilectic variations within Gallicanism, Enlightenment emphases less displacing the older, gloomier ones on Man's fallen nature than supplementing them, so much depending on the social and intellectual formation of the clergy and that of the people gathered for worship below their pulpit.

Aware of its vulnerability to the criticisms of the *philosophes*, the Church significantly limited its acknowledgement of miracles to those reported in scripture and was not disposed to credit current evidences of those breaches of the natural order so readily reported by humbler members of the flock. Though there were no concessions to the view that the Apostles were unreliable witnesses of the Gospel accounts, theologians preferred to ground their defence of the faith elsewhere – namely, on the validation of the scriptural accounts of Christ's life from independent contemporary sources, and increasingly not in the area of revelation at all, but in that of natural religion. Nevertheless, because of the centrality of transubstantiation in eucharistic teaching, there were limits to clerical defensiveness on the miraculous. As the abbé Molinier told his parishioners: 'the mere mention of a miracle must provoke mocking among worldly people, and they must feel sorry for people like ourselves, who believe in miracles when they are obvious.' The final stress was intended, for churchmen and *philosophes* alike strove to make Frenchmen less credulous, though neither group had much success. Fascinated by the workings of the universe revealed through the popularisation of Newtonian science, even the wealthy bourgeoisie were ready to look at Christian mysteries in the context of new ones such as mesmerism and 'dephlogisticated air'. Higher still up the social ladder, Swendenborgian mysticism revealed the secrets of the future and the government of the universe to the Duchesse de Bourbon and other noblewomen, while servants, peasants and artisans reckoned contemporary prophetesses like Suzette Labrousse and Cathérine Théot the equivalent of the saints.[60] This mixture of classicism, pragmatism and utopianism one finds gathering pace from *c.* 1770 has been dubbed the generation of the 'Secondes Lumières' by some French scholars.[61] However one looks at it, Enlightenment was nothing if not eclectic on the eve of the Revolution.

Increasingly, it was the ethical dimension to Christianity that appealed to educated Frenchmen. Yet we should be wary of concluding that the laity, however sympathetic to the human Jesus, were incapable of integrating their appreciation with a continuing subscription to the teachings of the Gallican Church. By 1789, few of the scores of thousands of French men and women reading Rousseau's best-selling books like *Émile* or *La Nouvelle Heloïse* would have deemed them to be in any sense at odds with their Christian beliefs. The majority of Rousseau's readers were and remained Catholics who finished such works as *Émile* with their faith still intact, and took so much delight in the way he spoke from the heart that the author was inundated with 'fan-mail'.[63] His writings contributed to an enrichment of their spiritual lives, arguably of their Christian heritage, and a few of them ended up as disciples so committed to Jean-Jacques that they had come to share his personal rejection of revelation or replaced it with a version of 'natural religion'.

This was a public that, without blaspheming, tended to regard Rousseau as someone genuinely following in the footsteps of Jesus Christ. His works may have been condemned by the Sorbonne in the 1760s, but it did nothing to undercut his popularity: reading

Rousseau helped Lucile Laridon-Duplessis, future wife of the Revolutionary leader Camille Desmoulins, to overcome her early anticlericalism and come to a recognisable form of Christian faith. She was typical of thousands of educated young people in the 1780s.[64] Even that distinguished Catholic apologist Archbishop Lefranc de Pompignan conceded, in a pastoral letter of 1781, which prohibited the sale and reading of Voltaire, Raynal and Rousseau in his diocese, that the last's books 'were less depraved than [those of] other unbelievers'.[65] Indeed, the personal piety of the French on the eve of the Revolution may well have been enhanced rather than diluted by such best-selling authors as Rousseau. Christian pilgrimages may have become unfashionable in elite circles, but plenty of good Catholics flocked to Rousseau's tomb at Ermenonville north of Paris after the sage's death in 1778, even the queen and her entourage paying their respects in June 1780.[66]

Few of Rousseau's readers before 1789 appear to have read *Du Contrat Social* [the *Social Contract*] with its interest in a state religion. Instead they concentrated on their favourite author's emphasis on ethical integrity and the educational discussion provoked by *Émile*. Some churchmen tapped into the new market, like Antoine-Hubert Wandelaincourt, administrator of a royal military school at Paris, who in 1782 published a book on logic aimed at young women, a follow-up to the courses he offered them on the help the Christian virtues could give them in their newly important roles as wives and mothers. He saw how Rousseau had his uses for Catholicism.[67] Above all, Rousseau's cultivation of personal sentiment and emphasis on the 'inner light' (which anyway owed much to the Quietist mystical tradition of Fénelon, as popularised by his disciple Mme Guyon) encouraged the educated lay men and women who read him to seek the recreation of Catholic Christianity according to a more primitive (a fashionable mid-century concept) model, in which worldly considerations of preserving institutional power and status no longer obscured the simple and accessible teachings of the Church's founder. This lay interest in reforming the Church so that it could better perform its evangelical task is, arguably, the result of the widespread dissemination of Enlightenment texts among the middling sort of readers.

The moral emphasis of Rousseau's writings seemed fresh and relevant to the public, a rejuvenating supplement to the Church's catechetical restraints but also one hard to control by the priest from his confessional. Rousseau had little time for sacraments as an out-ward sign of grace when the whole of nature stood witness to divine beneficence towards the created order. As a result, the Tridentine code of pains and penalties lost credibility among the educated and half-educated. Sin considered as an offence against divine command-ments propounded and upheld by the Church was, under the influ-ence of the sentimental moralising of the pre-Revolutionary era, increasingly seen as mere anti-social conduct towards one's fellow men. If the Church condemned what was *natural*, then the Church was simply wrong and could be disregarded. Thus where there was a discrepancy between the ethics of the leading *philosophes* and Chris-tianity, it was the latter's teachings that tended to be ignored.

As a species of morality that stressed man's inherently uncorrupted nature and capacity for improvement without grace – whether sacramental or otherwise – a Rousseauian philosophy unavoidably came into conflict with Catholic teaching, though most churchmen after the 1750s were willing to tolerate the theory if it contributed to responsible and neighbourly conduct within the parish. Such a loose moral code, based on man's goodness of heart and the cultivation of feeling, incidentally marked the final collapse of interest among the middle classes in the sterner rigours of a Jansenist programme for reli-gious invigoration. Instead, as suggested above, the public found the more humane teachings of Jean-Jacques increasingly to its taste, and in the quarter century before 1789 Rousseauian-style moralising became fashionable among the urban elites. Its influence undoubt-edly encouraged some to a new, critical awareness of the Church's institutional shortcomings as originating from its place in a corrupt-ing social order.

Public opinion was, in the second half of the century, discriminat-ing enough to overlook the various degrees of unbelief favoured by Voltaire, Helvétius or Raynal while using their critical insights into the alleged ills of the French Church to produce moderate reform proposals. To suggest, as some historians have done, that the ground for the Revolutionary dechristianisation of the 1790s was well pre-pared in the two preceding generations is overstated. What one sees is a spiritual reawakening that drew on the fashionability of senti-ment Rousseau had helped to popularise as well as 'the religion of feeling which had been spread so widely in the country districts, all through the eighteenth century'.[68] These played a part in revivifying strictly Christocentric devotions such as the cult of the Sacred Heart, all helping to create what the Bishop of Amiens in 1767 called 'a simple, solid, and sensitive devotion'.[69] It constituted a change of direction away from the aridities of Jesuit and Jansenist preferences towards renewal in a society that remained recognisably Christian. And meanwhile, despite the Enlightenment, popular religious observances continued, a mixture of superstition and pity, deprecated by *philosophes* and abbés alike, but resistant to the strictures of both. They would play an unacknowledged part in creating a popular sense of boundless expectation that the Estates-General, finally summoned for May 1789, would create a harmonious new order in France blessed by God, the Blessed Virgin, and the Saints.

Part II The Impact of Revolution

5 The Gallican Church and the Crisis of the Monarchy, 1786–89

In the mid-1780s, with royal power faltering before the menace of state bankruptcy, the Crown and its servants contemplated the introduction of fiscal and administrative structural reforms on an unprecedented scale.[1] The exercise was likely to test the capacity and the stability of the French polity to the limits, as the institutions of government, local and national, and, above all, the taxation system, were candidates alike for modernisation. The clergy could not stay aloof from the interest these issues generated among their parishioners, and their own opinions mirrored the range to be found in the nation at large. Few prominent clerics doubted the desirability of overhauling existing institutions and, where necessary, creating new ones in a way that would both widen the chance for elite participation in affairs of state and recognise the influence wielded after *c.* 1750 by the force of public opinion – 'an implicit new system of authority', as Baker has called it.[2]

Any such modernisation would extend the elective and representative elements in French public affairs, but there was no sense that ambitious, politically-minded clergy were disadvantaged. So much still depended on patron–client ties at Versailles. Thus when Jacques Necker set up the first Provincial Assemblies in 1778, two bishops, Jérome Champion de Cicé of Rodez (later Archbishop of Bordeaux) and the Archbishop of Bourges, Phélypeaux de La Vrillière, were appointed presidents of the initial two bodies established, in the Haute-Guyenne and Berry.[3] It was a gesture that caused a future Controller-General, Calonne, to reflect – somewhat cynically – that Necker's Protestantism mattered little to these ambitious prelates – 'the clergy was sold to anyone who increased their power.'[4] In fact, the way prelates managed these first assemblies gave the impression that reformist-minded clergy were genuinely willing to shoulder a greater share of the tax burden alongside their fellow citizens. In the Haute-Guyenne, for instance, Seignelay-Colbert

(Champion de Cicé's successor as Bishop of Rodez) in 1784 made it clear the clergy would pay their slice of the new tax replacing the hated *corvée* (the tax on roads).[5]

Reform in the state was one thing, but would the Church consent to put its own house in order, or must the government compel it? The more imaginative leaders of the Gallican Church, especially those close to Necker, were aware that it could be no more exempt than any other institution in a climate favourable to reform root-and-branch than at any point since the Bourbon family had inherited the monarchy in 1589. With its landed wealth and its extensive debt, the Church was likely to figure prominently in ministerial reform plans. The onus was on the hierarchy to contemplate changes on a scale previously unthinkable, if only to ward off drastic solutions like that advocated in *The Rights of the Sovereign over the Property of the Clergy and Monks* (1770): the nationalisation of all ecclesiastical property to solve the state's fiscal problems, a solution that anticipated the radical surgery of the 1790 Civil Constitution.[6]

Churchmen were caught in a double bind: they were brought up to regard Gallican liberties, privileges and immunities as protection for their order against a monarchy with extensive reserve powers. In 'patriotic' rhetoric, that threat was presented as being as formidable as ever after the Maupeou changes imposed on the *parlements* between 1771 and 1774. Thus to dismantle those privileges risked opening the door for ministerial 'despotism'; conversely, to use the royal 'threat' as an excuse for attempting minimal internal reorganisation was increasingly unacceptable to informed opinion. In some areas like the overhaul of the regular orders, Church and State in partnership had long been at work; elsewhere the will to introduce and implement change was less apparent. The risk for the hierarchy by the 1780s was that if First Estate leaders did not produce plans for new-style clerical taxation and reduce the glaring income discrepancies among the clergy, then the King's ministers were likely to impose their own blueprint for change on the Church. Whatever the risks, the episcopate preferred inaction to drawing up its own corporate reform agenda in the General Assembly and left it to individual prelates to make the existing machinery function more effectively – should they be so disposed.

Virtually nothing was done to appease lower clergy demands for a more equitable redistribution of income within the ordained ministry. It was a demand to which *curés'* criticisms of their hierarchical superiors returned repeatedly, and was prominent in a pamphlet of 1787, *L'ecclésiastique Citoyen* [*The Citizen Ecclesiastic*], as part of a comprehensive, basically Jansenist programme to end a situation in which 'all the honours and revenues [are] on the one side, all the work and responsibility [are] on the other.'[7] It was offensive to large swathes of lay opinion that the parish clergy – the most 'useful' members of the priesthood – were relatively badly off by comparison with colleagues higher up the hierarchy because they were tithe-deprived; it was downright scandalous to tithe-payers that Church wealth was siphoned off into the pockets of the major tithe owners (*gros décimateurs*) where it could only dilute their sense of apostolic mission and increase their worldliness. In twelve parishes on the estates of the cathedral chapter of Beauvais, for instance, total tithe payments with extras took no less than 18 per cent of the peasants' crops, and the resentment this caused was very much in evidence in the Third Estate's *cahiers* from this area.[8] As agricultural prices rose, so did the income of tithe owners in proportion – and their own unpopularity with payers. That took the form of a tithe-paying revolt in some parts of France, one that clogged the law courts with litigants, part of 'an envious alliance of magistrates and cultivators' that had formed against the *décimateurs*.[9]

There was little sign that the principal beneficiaries of the *status quo* – the episcopate and higher clergy generally – were prepared to preside over the dismantling of these inegalitarian ways. The most that could be extracted from them was raising the minimum income payable on the *portion congrue*, increased in 1786 for the second time in two decades. The lower clergy could take or leave what was on the table. Beyond that, the fundamental issue of opportunities above and beyond the parish for the humbly born priest remained unaddressed. These few extra crumbs were far from enough to satisfy those who actually had to live on them, let alone the thousands of *vicaires* who did not even possess a benefice. So the concession did nothing to damp down the flames of Richerism spreading out from the Dauphiné, Provence and Normandy, and amounting to what some historians have argued constituted a 'revolt of the *curés*' between 1786 and 1789.[10] There were many obscure priests like the abbé Le Senne with their clandestine pamphlets pouring out bile at the power and pretensions of their superiors in the Church. To quote Robert Darnton: 'They represented an ideology that had gone beyond Richerism to Voltairianism, and they spoke for an alienated intelligentsia of poor devils within the ranks of the Church itself.'[11]

Money was not the only cause of complaint. The grip of the aristocracy on offices in the Church was getting no looser by the 1780s – quite the opposite in fact. Of course, the association between nobility and political leadership remained entrenched across Europe in the eighteenth-century; there was an ineradicable dynastic element to public life. On the other hand, the practical consequences for the First Estate of denying access to its upper ranks for some of its most talented clergy on the basis of their non-noble origins were serious. Those blessed with learning, pastoral skills and administrative competence were compelled to function at lower levels in the hierarchy than their less gifted but bluer-blooded counterparts. In reserving its choicest bishoprics and canonries exclusively for the aristocracy, the First Estate was both reducing the quality of its leadership and increasing its vulnerability to external manipulation. And rewarding the privileged with additional wealth to maintain their status through such devices as the *commende* was just adding insult to injury, as it conflicted with the rising demand for equality and the emergence in other areas of French public life of a society of 'notables' rather than nobles.

It was to these highest echelons of Church and State that the monarchy turned when it embarked on a series of hazardous reform initiatives summoning (the first) Assembly of Notables to advise the King and Calonne, the Controller-General, on major fiscal reforms.[12] It eventually convened in February 1787. All sixteen members of the First Estate were drawn from the higher clergy, the majority of them prelates, men like Boisgelin of Aix, Brienne of Toulouse, Champion de Cicé of Bordeaux and Dillon of Narbonne, whose familiarity with the work of government in the provinces and inside the Church made them obvious choices. Any hopes that Calonne may have entertained that the Notables would act as, in the words of one critic, 'docile instruments',[13] were soon corrected. From the outset, the episcopal deputies took the lead in attacking both Calonne's tax proposals and the minister personally: the first were unworkable and the second was corrupt. It must be stressed that throughout the so-called 'Pre-Revolution' of 1787–9, bishops accepted the need for a reformed fiscal system and Church participation in it, but they were adamant that consent to new taxes must be freely given rather than exacted as a right by government. This was not fiscal evasion, but reflected a concern for constitutional guarantees that was widespread throughout French society.

They were threatened by Calonne on two related fronts. First was the scheme of direct taxation, which would require a land registry. Second was the proposal to make the First Estate redeem its corporate debt through the sale of property and feudal rights; that way, the Church would no longer be able to justify its tax exemption with the excuse that it helped the monarchy by borrowing on its behalf. Neither proposal was acceptable unmodified. Senior churchmen realised that retaining financial autonomy was essential if the First Estate's political power was to be preserved, but beyond that was the important principle that existing rights and privileges, whether corporate or individual, should not be violated by the Crown. In defending this position, churchmen stood shoulder to shoulder with other constitutionalists in 1787 who were not prepared to rubber-stamp the streamlined absolutist monarchy that might emerge from an improved fiscal base. The Notables had forced Calonne out of office by the end of April. This followed a contest of political wills that had an unprecedented public dimension (Calonne even made a direct appeal to public opinion over the heads of the Notables in an *Avertissement* that the Parisian clergy were supposed to read from their pulpits) and was more redolent of British parliamentary politics than Bourbon administrative monarchy.

Louis XVI's reluctant acceptance of Loménie de Brienne as Calonne's eventual successor in May 1787 appeared a triumph for reformers and recognition of the Gallican Church's formidable influence within the monarchy.[14] Brienne was given official exceptional status as Principal Minister with a Controller-General [Laurent de Villedeuil] subordinate to him. But Brienne's tenure of power (until August 1788) was far from the success his supporters in the Notables had hoped. He inherited Calonne's planned expansion of the network of Provincial Assemblies, and made it more attractive to the Notables by slightly increasing the powers of its members, as well as offering key presidencies to several fellow bishops. None of these concessions was enough to offset disappointment that he was persisting with Calonne's original scheme for a *subvention nationale* (or land tax) virtually unchanged. The Edict of toleration for non-Catholics (November 1787) was another cause for concern. It aroused resentment among First Estate leaders less for its passing than for Brienne's failure to consult them, and his unimaginative use of Church patronage did little to heal the wounds; his administration was popular only with a minority in the Church, leaving higher and lower clergy disposed to play the patriot game against him.

These clerical malcontents during the winter of 1787–8 aligned themselves with the magistrates, lawyers and noblemen who deplored the government's apparent resolve to stifle opposition to its policies. They were insistent that the ancient laws of France should be respected and institutions put in place to ensure that they were, especially the revived or new Provincial Estates, generally regarded as far more independent of the ministry than the Provincial Assemblies. Throughout France, in Provence, Brittany, Artois and Navarre, and above all in the Dauphiné, clergy were caught up in the demand for national and provincial rights to be reaffirmed and upheld. It was a cause as popular with *curés* as it was with canons, as parish clergy of all descriptions came to identify with their counterparts in secular life, busily attacking alleged manifestations of 'despotism'.

In these circumstances, any sense of collegial loyalty towards Archbishop Brienne from fellow prelates became very frayed and, with the notable exception of the venerable Archbishop Le Franc de Pompignan of Vienne, pastoral instructions advising submission to the monarchy and its servants were conspicuous by their absence. Nowhere was this turning away of the Gallican elite from the Principal Minister more dramatically demonstrated than in the summer of 1788 when the General Assembly of the Clergy offered only the most derisory percentage of the 8 million livres' *don gratuit* requested by ministers.[15] The May Edicts, permanently reducing the status of the *parlements* and establishing a nominated Plenary Court, were also condemned in the Remonstrances issued by the General Assembly on 15 June. These were rebuffs that Brienne had feared, so much so that he had postponed the Assembly by a year, but that tactic did him no good. The session was an embarrassing display of ministerial mismanagement; Brienne had simply not prepared the ground, lobbied the delegates or offered enough sweeteners to achieve his end.

A feature of the proceedings was the sense that the clergy were speaking for a much wider constituency than the Church alone. The episcopate and higher clergy saw themselves as spokesmen for the nation as a whole, uniquely well placed to lay their countrymen's grievances before the King: institutional upheaval to secure dubious reform schemes was not just a heavy-handed infringement of their own corporate rights, but by implication imperilled every Frenchman who valued his liberties:

> When the first Order of the state finds itself the only one able to speak; when a public outcry urges it to carry the will of all the others to the foot of your throne; when the national interest and its own zeal for your service require it, ... it is shameful to be quiet. Our silence would be one of those crimes for which the nation and posterity would never forgive us.[16]

Here was an explicit acknowledgement by the clerical elite of the nation as the supreme arbiter in public life: traditional Gallican emphases on liberties were merging with a modern 'patriotism' that stressed the involvement of the clergy in the life of the state; not merely because effective pastoral responsibility demanded it but from the belief that it was a mark of good and therefore active citizenship. Given this enlightened rationale, for the Church at the same time to insist on retaining its corporate rights unimpaired sounded less convincing to the wider nation by the late 1780s. The inconsistency could not prevent the First Estate from acting the 'patriotic' part, and their remonstrances in the General Assembly were given maximum publicity by appearing in the widely distributed journal the *Gazette de Leyde*. The public response to this very Montesquieuian politics was disappointing, with some commentators, especially those sympathetic to a Jansenist agenda, wanting much more.[17]

In the provinces, higher clergy were frequently active in support of the exiled *parlementaires*, nowhere more so than at Troyes. To this town the Paris magistrates were sent in disgrace, but found themselves hosted and applauded by the cathedral chapter, whose *grand chantre* even proposed to erect a public monument to thank them for their efforts 'for the general cause and for us: *la patrie* and religion together demand it as an immortal interpreter of the sentiment that now animates us'.[18] Such gestures dramatically depicted the collapse of elite confidence in Brienne's government just as much as the protests of the Vizille assembly in the Dauphiné (which included 150 clergy) or the exile of the aggrieved Paris *parlementaires*.[19] The provincial revolt helped to extract concessions from Brienne and his much reviled colleague, Lamoignon, the acting head of the judiciary, notably the decree of the royal council on 8 August 1788 that the

Estates-General should meet for the first time since 1614 on 1 May
the following year. That surrender to the power of opinion in the
French state was insufficient to deflect suspicion of Brienne's conduct
or save his ministry. He was finally forced out of office by the combination of bankruptcy and credit crisis. On 25 August he resigned his
post as Principal Minister, recompensed by the twin consolation
prizes of a cardinal's red hat and translation to Sens, the richest see
in France.

Most clergy did not regret his departure. Attention had shifted to
his successor, Jacques Necker, universally assumed (Louis XVI was a
rare exception) to be the financial saviour of France. Necker's Protestantism was no obstacle to clerical acclaim at his return to government, and there was much inaccurate speculation in the autumn of
1788 that he would name a bishop – Champion de Cicé of Bordeaux
and Louis de Conzié of Arras were both mentioned – to a ministerial
post. Not that Necker saw much for ministers to do before the Estates-
General met for the first time in the spring of 1789. Before that
longed-for event could take place, a national debate was opened on
the composition and procedure of the Estates-General, a debate that
both fractured the loose 'patriotic' alliance of 1787–8 and intensified
internal clerical divisions by challenging the right of the hierarchy to
speak for the whole Gallican Church.

In the end, Necker's overriding desire to preserve his popularity
and power narrowly persuaded a majority of government members
on 27 December 1788 to opt for doubling the numbers of the Third
Estate to give them 50 per cent of the membership.[20] The decision
delighted lay reformers, not to mention the parish clergy who spent
the first month of 1789 writing collective letters demanding that ministers should not overlook the fact that they, as the majority of the
First Estate, were fully entitled to a proportionate share of the
Church's seats in the Estates-General.[21]

It was a decisive stage in the 'revolt of the *curés*' against the universal application of the hierarchical principle; the assumption that the
higher clergy, particularly the bishops, should speak for the Church
on all matters that concerned it, irrespective of whether they related
to its pastoral and spiritual role in which the first-hand experience of
the lower clergy was abundant but discounted. The *curés* sought the
general, unconditional acknowledgement that they themselves were
entitled, by virtue of their priesthood, their useful pastoral work and
their contact with the mass of the population, to have their rights

confirmed in a manner comparable to the Third Estate's.[22] They found that ministers were ready to listen sympathetically. On 25 January 1789 a ruling was published laying down the framework for clerical elections to the Estates-General, which, as for the other two Orders, would take place on the basis of *sénéchaussées* and *bailliages*, archaic judicial areas. *Curés* and bishops were treated on a basis of pastoral equality: each would have one vote, with no further rights extended to prelates. Monasteries received a single vote for each house; canons from cathedrals and other chapters would have only 1 vote per 10 persons if they held no other benefice giving them voting rights. Unbeneficed priests were also denied a vote in person; in towns they had 1 vote for each 20, and the same applied to minor ecclesiastics employed by the chapters. Hospitals, colleges and mendicant houses had no vote. The schedule entitled *curés* like Derne, from the parish of Charly in the Lyon archdiocese, to make a triumphalist noise: 'Who are you, messieurs the *grands vicaires*? Nothing. But me, I am a *curé*: nothing can take away my title [to vote]!'[23]

Eighteen months before the Civil Constitution of the Clergy we therefore see the traditional, monarchical state imposing its will on the First Estate. The government knew that the electoral provision overturned the age-old precedent of the leaders of the hierarchy speaking for the entire Church: if the monarchy was making itself vulnerable to major institutional change by calling the Estates-General there was no good reason why the Church should not do likewise. The decree of 25 January, coupled with others like limited freedom of worship for non-Catholics in 1787, emphasised the extent to which the government had finally gained the whip hand in its dealings with the Gallican Church. The French bishops were coming to terms with the status of junior partner in a relationship where neither side quite trusted the other, one which was more about subordination than mutual support. The awareness was dawning of how vulnerable the Church was to reforms proposed in the national interest, and resistance on behalf of a sectional interest was becoming unsustainable against the weight of public opinion.

While the *curés* rejoiced over this official recognition of their status (especially those from rural areas who were guaranteed a preponderant influence), chapters the length of France bombarded Necker with letters of protest, the general tenor of which echoed the Auch complaint that such a form of convocation gave 'to the inferiors an entirely destructive influence over that of their superiors'.[24] However, these capitular bodies otherwise found few allies to put in a word for them: the bishops at least had a vote individually, and they knew that the first minister enjoyed a degree of power based upon a popular mandate that could not realistically be challenged. Younger prelates paid court to Necker when they could, and left older malcontents like the Bishop of Rieux to grumble about 'the spirit of vertigo and error, of anarchy and republicanism which seems to manifest itself everywhere'.[25] Necker predictably ignored the higher clergy's grievances, and the lower clergy were inspired afresh to keep members of proud, independent chapters like Saint-Etienne at Bourges, and Saint-Sernin and Saint-Etienne at Toulouse, from election as deputies. When the electoral assemblies met, some canons were desperate enough to try to halt proceedings. Thus, at Rouen, the chapter began to read from the memorandum against the *règlement* at the start of the assembly, but this ploy collapsed when the *curés* drew up a counter-protest.

As for the bishops, they were left to reflect that in the campaign for seats in the Estates-General they would receive no special favours, especially as there were 130 of them as against 176 *bailliages*; 57 of 130 episcopal towns were not given status as principal constituency centres and the electoral units themselves cut across diocesan boundaries so as to fox the ambitions of many would-be legislators right from the start: Chartres and Sens, for instance, took in no less than six *bailliages*, while in Béziers the bishop of the town was competition with his brother prelates of Agde and Saint-Pons for a seat.[26] It was a far cry from only a few months earlier when they had posed as spokesmen for the whole nation in the General Assembly of the Clergy. Since then, that stance had been called into doubt. They had paid a high price for tardiness in recognising the changing public mood, not least through their general support in the second Assembly of Notables and elsewhere for the Second Estate's unwillingness to make concessions to the Third. National feeling had turned suddenly against privilege when it was perceived to be no longer a weapon against a powerful monarchy, but rather a device to protect vested interests from painful sacrifice and reform.

Pamphleteers left voters in no doubt that the higher clergy and nobility could not be allowed to stop the momentum of change through their own special pleading, with Emmanuel Joseph Sieyès, Bishop's secretary and canon of Chartres, producing his masterpiece

Qu'est-ce que le Tiers État? to define the new patriotism on the eve of the Estates-General. The clergy read it like everyone else and found themselves defined as part of the 5 per cent of France that could not properly be called part of the nation. Lower clergy were encouraged to distance themselves from their hierarchical superiors. Aristocracy was now an emotive issue in itself, with the episcopal corps encountering hostile publicity that centred on their exclusive composition and 'the revolting pride with which they treat the *curés*'. Charges based on social origins were not capable of rebuttal; it would be up to them to demonstrate in the face of adverse publicity from Sièyes and his numerous imitators that blue blood and patriotism were not after all incompatible.

The final returns indicated a clear majority of clerical deputies who were parish priests – over two hundred of them. That was not in itself surprising, since Necker's electoral *règlement* of 25 January had been intended to achieve that end; the ruling coincided with the first printing and wide distribution of pamphlets putting the case for the lower order of the clergy by their own members to the public at large and, no less importantly, appealing to colleagues in distant parts of France for solidarity. Predictably, the Dauphiné was the cockpit of agitation with an influential tract addressed to the Breton *recteurs* urging them to stand up for their rights and to resist browbeating by the nobility and *parlement* of Rennes.[27] Such tactics were widely imitated. Thus the memorandum issued by the *curés* of the Angers diocese in December 1788 was circulated by their colleagues in Bourges around the whole province of Berry with an appeal to join in the common cause and secure a monopoly of the seats in their constituencies.[28] Pamphlets could also be destined simply for use within a diocese like the *Letter of a curé from the Le Mans diocese to MM. his brothers on the occasion of the next holding of the Estates-General*.[29]

In terms of their contents, these pamphlets largely had the telling combination of concrete demands with appeals to the heart, as in F.X. Laurent's *Essai sur la réforme du clergé par un vicaire de campagne*, calling for an end to pluralism and a system of inequitable benefice holding that, the author complained, ensured that 'some die of hunger while the others gorge themselves in abundance'.[30] In Lorraine, it was the abbé Grégoire who mobilised his fellow *curés* in a campaign that began in Nancy and spread out across the province.[31] It was a moment of electrifying excitement:

We are citizens, first; . . . but as *curés* we have rights. For twelve centuries perhaps there has never been such a favourable opportunity to make these rights worth something, and to develop patriotic sentiments, and to honour the sacred ministry of which we are an essential constitutive part. Let us therefore seize our opportunity so that our successors may never reproach us for having neglected their cause and ours.[32]

Taking comfort from their belief that the rank of *curé* was of divine origins, the Lorraine lower clergy hardly bothered to disguise their support for the Third Estate in its struggle for recognition and fair treatment. Such sentiments were commonplace. As the Dauphiné *curés* put it:

The interest of the people and your own are inseparable. If the people emerge from oppression, you will emerge from the humiliation into which the higher clergy have plunged you and you have endured for so long.[33]

When the electoral assemblies opened, it was the pattern for the Clergy to assure the Third Estate of their lively sympathies, which were usually accompanied (as at Le Mans) by a gesture such as affirming commitment to equality of taxation.[34] These patriotic words and demonstrations caught the national mood brilliantly. Despite their previous political marginality, many *curés* exhibited impressive organisational skills, often meeting informally before the assembly opened to co-ordinate tactics. It was commonly the more prosperous beneficed priests, untroubled by making ends meet, who were the strongest candidates, ready and willing to stand up to higher clergy blandishments or bullying. *Curés* were often elected (as, for instance, at Mâcon in Burgundy) because it was (with good reason) believed that they would represent the material and political grievances of their colleagues more adequately than a prelate who had not endured them. There was particular bad feeling towards the non-episcopal sections of the higher clergy in debate. At Le Mans every time a canon or a member of a religious order rose, there were cries of 'Sit down, sit down! Silence! Silence!'[36]

Where *curés* were set on excluding bishops from election they generally had their way, as in the *sénéchaussée* of the Landes in the south-west, where the Bishops of Aire and Dax were kept out. (One priest,

Laborde of Ossages, was viewed as suspect simply because he had eaten at the palace!) In Angers, Pierre Chatizel, *curé* of Soulaines since 1771, acted as whip for his colleagues and gave them blunt instructions: 'no bishop, no canons, no regular clergy, only *curés*'.[37] Despite the *règlement*, lower clergy success was by no means assured: the parish priests were not a homogeneous party, and divisions between urban and rural clergy, the well-off and the impoverished, were marked. Indeed, one of the most interesting features of the electoral contest involving the First Estate that spring of 1789 was the victory against the odds of one-third of the episcopate to make a final total of 51 places gained,[38] and there would have been more had not a dozen been absent from the elections for official or family reasons; others ruled themselves out in advance for election through ill-health, or the realisation that they could not hope to succeed, and the Breton bishops boycotted the elections because Necker's *règlement* deliberately by-passed the local Estates, the focus of elite power.[39] Otherwise, the relative success of the bishops underlined the inability of many priests to break the habit of deference towards their superiors in the hierarchy when they had the chance to do so.

There were those, like Bishop Clermont-Tonnerre of Châlons-sur-Marne, who shrewdly rode the political tide. His speech, on 13 March 1789, hit exactly the right note. He appealed to the clergy that when it came to the Church, they should 'conserve all essential constitutional elements, correct abuses by appropriate reforms that do not enfeeble its jurisdiction or shake its foundations'.[40] Less committed patriots among the prelates had to adapt hastily if they were to gratify their ambitions, and that often in the face of militant *curés* hell-bent on excluding them from the representation. One tactic, tried in more than one constituency, was for bishops to deflect parish priests' animus from themselves to the unpopular chapters. This – along with a patriotic speech bemoaning the predicament of the 'least leisured classes, groaning under the weight of taxation' – helped Jean-Baptiste-Marie Champion de Cicé, Bishop of Auxerre (brother of the archbishop of Bordeaux), to scrape home in the town;[41] in the *sénéchaussée* of Draguignan, Bishop de Bausset-Roquefort of Fréjus had no problems in contrasting his readiness to embrace the new order of things with the Fréjus chapter's exasperation at the terms of the electoral *réglement*. By contrast, in Caen, Bishop Cheylus of Bayeux threw away his hopes of election by solidarity with the chapter.

Feelings could run so high that violence sometimes marred the election campaign. At Toulon a mob ransacked the bishop's palace, while Bishop Chilleau of Chalon-sur-Saône was attacked with stones en route to the assembly of his *bailliage*. Neither prelate was elected, but most of the *prélats administratifs* – Boisgelin, Champion de Cicé of Bordeaux, La Rochefoucauld of Rouen, Seignelay–Colbert of Castlehill – were. Brienne was abroad, frightened to show his face, and impending bankruptcy was instrumental in deterring Dillon from a contest. Cardinal Rohan, the disgraced intriguer of the Necklace Affair, was returned in Alsace by clergy in the *bailliage* of Haguenau who found his status as an anti-courtier quite irresistible. His successor as Grand Almoner, Montmorency-Laval of Metz, cancelled a trip to Rome to receive his new cardinal's hat from the hands of Pius VI rather than imperil his electoral prospects. He was not chosen, despite the sacrificial gesture.

Montmorency-Laval's defeat owed much to his neglect of diocesan duties in favour of attendance at court. Prelates like Lauzières de Thémines of Blois, and de Gain-Montaignac of Tarbes, were other casualties. Having correctly gauged their lack of local popularity, neither even contested a seat. Godart de Belbeuf of Avranches reached his electoral assembly in full episcopal trappings, but pomp and splendour could not browbeat the *curés* of the Cotentin region of Normandy. They preferred the low-key, conciliatory stance of Bishop Talaru of Coutances, and were glad to see the back of his colleague from Avranches, who left the assembly in disgust after failing to gain a clear majority on the first ballot. Any attempt at blustering intimidation was usually counter-productive. The Bishop of Mende had reckoned that his presence in the galleries with supporters would pressurise the lower clergy below into deferring to him, but nailing up the entrance to them with planks scotched his expectations.[42] In general, respected unworldly prelates such as Royère of Castres or du Tillet of Orange were elected to acclamation, for all their diffidence about going to Versailles. More controversial characters had to fight hard to overcome resistance. At Nîmes, the Bishops of Nîmes and Uzès managed it, 'despite the caballing of a number of the *curés*, who believed they could have these prelates excluded [from representing the clergy]'. For all their lingering sense of deference, these electors insisted, however, on two *curés* completing the delegation, and it was the same story at Carcassonne where Cardinal Bernis's nephew, the Coadjutor-Archbishop of Albi, was sent to Versailles with the *curé* of Saint-Nazaire (Carcassonne) for company.[43]

The clergy, like the other two Orders, had also assembled to decide on the final list of grievances and recommendations to be extracted from the *cahiers particuliers* they had brought with them from the primary assemblies. As the *règlement* of 24 January stipulated, they were to indicate abuses and suggest remedies.[44] This remarkable exercise in consultation revealed the essential moderation of most Frenchmen from a range of social backgrounds. They sought the renewal and updating of the monarchy and the Gallican Church, not the destruction and spoliation of these institutions. For instance, there was little interest anywhere in the abolition of either monasticism or tithes.[45] About one-third were silent on these questions. The others spoke in terms of restoring the tithes to the uses of the parish priest, and cancelling the claims of the *gros décimateurs*. Property rights were, generally, to be safeguarded and, though the universal cry was for equality in all matters of taxation, the charges were to be distributed through the Church's own administrative apparatus, not by the state.[46]

Clerical *cahiers* reveal an expectation that the state would – and perhaps should – order matters thought formerly to be the preserve of the Church, and there were long lists of recommendations for legislation on ecclesiastical subjects. The *cahiers* were the responsibility of the whole assembly, and delegates were watchful for any form of episcopal interference or intimidation. Where, for instance, a bishop nominated all the commissioners to write the *cahier* – a tactic of Bishop d'Agoult's at Pamiers – lower clergy were quick to appeal to Necker to have the proceedings quashed. Prelates respected by their *curés* in practice found little difficulty in influencing the contents of their order's *cahier*, as at Boulogne where the venerable Partz de Pressy had been Bishop since 1743. All his preferences – restrictions on the press, penalties against Sunday working, and the condemnation of luxurious living – were to be found in the final version. But then this moral emphasis was popular with the clergy in most places, for they could not easily separate the political reconstruction of France from its ethical renewal. Only thirty-six *cahiers* did not stipulate that there should be respect for the Sabbath, and it was no coincidence that they were virtually the same ones that did not attack the circulation of '*les mauvais livres*'. This is a fascinating and neglected side of the 'revolt of the *curés*', a sign of a desire to couple institutional with moral reform in line with a tradition of Tridentine Catholicism over two centuries old.

The commitment to constitutionalism was emphatic, alongside the determination to curb the excessive powers of the Crown in favour of reinvigorated provincial liberties; in future, it was urged, local Estates should supplement the watchfulness of the Estates-General at the centre, the primary forum of the nation. It must freely consent to all laws proposed by the government, and the principle of ministerial accountability to the Estates-General (or a tribunal chose by it) was also a popular stipulation.[47] There was a universal empha-sis on setting new standards in public life and, to that end, venal office-holding should be abolished, along with unjust indirect taxes like the *gabelle* and the *aides*. Interestingly, there was a reminder from many constituencies that, for all the *curés'* identification over the previous winter with the Third Estate, the Estates-General should be required to respect what the clergy of Bordeaux called the distinction '*inviolable et constitutionnel*' of the three Orders. A minority, like Nîmes, even requested voting by Order, but most were content to leave the matter to the King and the Estates-General to decide jointly after opening.[48]

As regards the Church itself, while the lower clergy evinced no desire to subvert the concept of hierarchy, the majority of them articulated moderate Richerist sentiments: the recovery of national rights was to have as its counterpart the *curés* restoring their own. Thirty-four *cahiers* asked that all posts in the Church should be awarded on the basis of merit.[49] Typically, the *curés* of Limoges wanted frequent diocesan synods and the right to appoint a syndic to look after their interests. They also recommended that no priest should receive a cure of souls until he had been a *vicaire* or had taught in a colleges for a minimum of seven or eight years.[50] Not that monks and nuns were seen as incubuses on the Church. Far from it. The majority of *cahiers* wanted reforms in the regular orders to continue. Two particularly singled out were abolition of the last surviving honorific privileges they were imposing on the parish clergy on the basis that they were acting as '*curés primitifs*', together with the bishops receiving abbeys *in commendam*.[51] There should also be closer diocesan supervision of their revenues, and some redistribu-tion in favour of the *curés*.[52] Most also wanted a reduction in the status of abbés and canons (not the abolition of these ranks), the opening up of noble chapters to clergy of humbler origin,[53] and at Troyes the *curés* asked outright for precedence in assemblies immediately below the bishop.

No one disputed the principle of episcopal supremacy, but there were complaints against the excessive wealth both of ecclesiastical corporations (such as the chapters of Saint-Etienne and Saint-Sernin in Toulouse) and individuals (the Archbishop of Narbonne was a favoured target), with lower clergy deploring 'the multiple gratifications for prelates who rarely take a service, the fortunes that insult their own destitution'.[54] Such *cahiers* commonly went on to recall the bishops to their own apostolic mission, to the duties of residence,[55] and the good sense of leadership by consultation rather than imposition. The re-establishment of national and provincial councils was designed to achieve a measure of collegiality within the Gallican Church that should ensure its more effective impact on the whole nation. And lower clergy persuasively argued that they could concentrate wholeheartedly on their work if glaring inequalities in income were levelled out, the *casuel* suppressed and the *portion congrue* raised to a minimum of 1500 livres. Twenty *cahiers* asked for a better sharing out of clerical possessions; that relatively low figure, coupled with the fact that nowhere was the abolition of tithe prescribed[56] and that only a minority recommended the outright abolition of the *portion congue*, is powerful evidence of clerical moderation on the eve of the Revolution.

With the elections over, and the clerical deputies converging on Versailles from all corners of the kingdom and hunting for lodgings, there was not much that those left behind could do but wait, and fulfil the official duty of praying publicly for the success of the Estates-General. Winners and losers alike among the bishops performed this task with the varying degrees of grace at their disposal, none more thoughtfully than Raymond de Durfort, Archbishop of Besanéon, who held himself above the electoral struggle. In ordering prayers on 13 May for the work of the deputies, he conceived it as a matter of

> maintaining the splendour of the throne, without oppressing the people; of irrevocably fixing the constitution of the state without changing it, of anticipating the conflict of powers without subduing them, of assuring the liberty of the citizen, without giving a hand to licentiousness, of favouring the progress of enlightenment, without giving a free run to error.[57]

Other colleagues used the opportunity in the *mandements* they prepared to warn against what Cortois de Balore, Bishop of Nîmes,
dubbed 'the senseless and frivolous crowd', presumably meaning
those who wanted to substitute what Bishop Partz de Pressy called
the 'chimera of equality' for measured monarchical government.
It struck an appropriately Lenten mood, but it was not one that corresponded to majority feeling in the country. The Bishop of Saintes
was also glum. He feared that the craze for equality had won over
most parts of the country and was causing the 'forgetting of principles
and the contempt of duties'.[58] The way in which the summoning of
the Estates-General had given a fresh impetus to anticlericalist dia-
tribes could not easily be ignored, tirades that were often obscene as
well as insulting and tended to focus exclusively on the higher clergy.
The Gallican Church was on the defensive and, amid the cacophony
of voices of voices competing for public attention in 1788-9, its enemies were ready to take full advantage of its predicament.

No wonder that the Archbishop of Paris found his platitudes about
'the safety of the people is the supreme law' of little personal comfort,
and more honestly admitted that 'when one considers the efferves-
cent feelings, the storms on all sides, we cannot help ourselves from
being alarmed!'[59] His senior primatial colleague, Marbeuf of Lyon,
was no less gloomy, seeing in the heady optimism sweeping France a
cause for despair rather than excitement:

> New ideas, abruptly substituted for ancient maxims, have sown
> discord and defiance among my fellow citizens; a general subver-
> sion seems to menace all our institutions political, civil and reli-
> gious. The kingdom is experiencing a fearful crisis.[60]

From his angle – and as Minister for the *feuille des bénéfices* he had
been privy to discussion and gossip at the highest level – there was
undoubtedly room for anxiety. Pamphlets like *Le Gouvernement-
sénati-clerico-aristocratique* (1788), which had spoken of the Church as
'one of those ancient Gothic monuments just waiting to collapse, and
for which you ought to have no respect',[61] had been followed by a
wave of others even more emotive insisting that the Church had
usurped rights properly belonging to the nation. Moderate opinion
was moving towards a position that would restrict the involvement
of priests in temporal affairs, and would go on from there to deny
the Church's right to constitute an Order.[62]

Though it had come under severe strain during the electoral proceedings, the unity of the First Estate was just about intact on the eve of the Estates-General. For all the brave and bold words about the clergy as citizens, and the identification of numerous *curés* with the aspirations of the Third Estate, these generous sympathies were not necessarily at odds with the desired good of the Gallican Church. These were, after all, in the words of one recent authority, 'a mature and highly respectable group of men',[63] and bishops and priests retained the basic solidarity that came from their cloth. The task of episcopal deputies would be to persuade rather than expect obedience from fellow clergy as a right and to overcome the suspions that had allowed higher – lower clergy tensions to fester in recent years. That should not have been beyond their political and pastoral skills. Most *curés* going to Versailles, while brimful of hope and proud custodians of their Order's *cahiers*, were awed by this wholly new status and, for the most part, looked instinctively to the episcopate for guidance in an unfamiliar world. Indeed, 11 bishops going to the Estates-General had been members of the 1788 General Assembly of the Clergy, and 10 were ex-Notables from the first Assembly of 1787. Such experience was not to be despised. In Cardinal La Rochefoucauld, Archbishop of Rouen, the First Estate had a president who was widely trusted by both higher and lower clergy. In a new political arena, he would require all his powers of leadership to contain and guide the *curés* sitting on the benches behind him who, largely because they were political novices at a national level, too confidently expected the work of regeneration to start without delay.

In that, they were of one mind with the majority of the French population, where the mood of expaction was hard to contain. Belief in the new political process as an alternative 'creed', more modern and relevant than anything organised Christianity could offer, was thus present in embryo in 1789 even before the Revolution took recognisable form.

6 The Collapse of the Historic Ecclesiastical Order, 1789–1790

On 4 May 1789, deputies of the newly elected Estates-General walked in procession to the church of Saint-Louis in the town of Versailles. It was one of the last occasions on which the ceremonial splendours of the monarchical order would be on colourful display, the working alliance of Church and Crown vividly brought to life on the grand scale. The crowds had to wait to see the Church's representatives. These, higher and lower clergy together, were placed at the rear of the column, closest to the King himself, so underlying the First Estate's symbolic place at the apex of French society. In the front rank of the clergy were the *curés*, each carrying a candle, wearing their cassocks and bands, a dress code that was at least familiar to all parties, unlike the nobility in their white-plumed hats and early seventeenth-century court dress, and the mass of Third Estate deputies in staid black and white. Behind the lower clergy, cardinals, archbishops, and bishops processed in full canonical robes; finally, immediately before the King, Archbishop Juigné carried the Blessed Sacrament in a monstrance protected by a cloth-of-gold canopy. Religious worship preceded political debate. In church, the Mass of the Holy Spirit was celebrated by the Archbishop of Paris, while deputies joined in the singing of the *Te Deum* and heard the Bishop of Nancy, La Fare, preach a sermon of impeccable but unspecific reformist sentiments. With its range of historical references, criticism of court luxury, and the exactions of tax collectors on the rural poor, it caught the national mood well enough.[1] Next day, the real business began, with the formal opening of the Estates-General in the Salle des Menus-Plaisirs at the palace of Versailles and some inaudible speeches from ministers before the three Orders adjourned to their own chambers for debate, the clergy to the Salle des Cent-Suisses. It was from there, for the moment on the sidelines, that the clergy watched as the other two Orders initiated a contest of wills over whether their deliberations should be conducted separately or together. The decision on that one procedural question would determine whether or not there would be a clear path to the implementation of major reform.

The Third Estate signalled its resolve to introduce voting in common by declaring that it would only verify its election returns meeting together with the other Orders, and would transact no other business until its wishes had been met. The nobility on 7 May took the opposite tack. It voted for separate verification by no less than 188 votes to 46, but there was no such unanimity in the clergy. Any comparable vote risked exposure of its fragile unity as a single Estate, and either the humiliation of the higher clergy or the calling into question of the patriotic credentials of the *curés*. Nevertheless, the issue could not be indefinitely deferred, and the narrow majority of nineteen votes for separate verification made plain the tenuous episcopal influence over debates. The Church threw its weight behind a series of conciliatory talks – but not hard enough. In the chamber the diminished deference that the electoral politics had revealed carried over into the proceedings. The Bishop of Nîmes reproved a *curé* for daring to interrupt Cardinal La Rochefoucauld, but received no apology. Abuse flowed between higher and lower clergy: the *curés* were branded 'peasants' sons' while prelates were denied the title of 'Monseigneur' and called 'mercenaries' by the disgruntled.[2] Disillusionment spread fast among clergy who had hoped for more than aristocratic aloofness from their bishops. As one clerical deputy lamented, 'they are nothing but mercenary, almost Machiavellian politicians, who mind only their own interests and are ready to fleece – perhaps even devour – their own flocks rather than pasture them.'[3]

At the end of May the issue was no nearer resolution, not least because the divergent views within the clergy made it impossible to define a distinctive negotiating stance. Meanwhile, the Third Estate raised the stakes, first by fresh appeals to the clergy (especially the *lower* clergy) to join them in common verification. It was an invitation that many priests found impossible to resist. In a conflict of loyalties between their character as *curés* and as citizens, the latter tended to prevail and, in the ten days after 10 June, the first defections from the First Estate occurred. On 13 June, three *curés* from the *sénéchaussée* of Poitou – Jallet, Ballard and Le Cesve – made the short but dramatically symbolic walk from their own chamber to join the Third Estate in the Menu-Plaisirs, after last-minute alarmist interventions from the higher clergy – one bishop was reported to have called the assembly of the Third 'a den of thieves' – failed to deflect them from their purpose.[4] Jallet, their leader, in his own person, symbolised everything the opinion-formers associated with the 'virtuous' lower clergy: the son of a gardener but himself an educated man, his ambition for thirty years had been limited until 1789 to performing his duties as *curé* of the marshy village of Chérigné, a man at home among his very unexceptional flock. Suddenly, the whole of France was watching him, the catalyst of Revolution, his loyalties committed to the Third not the First Estate. Jallet's example was contagious. Day by day, the defections continued, and they played no small part in prompting Sieyès to proclaim the existence of the National Assembly on 17 June. And it was not the lower clergy alone who were susceptible to the entreaties of the 'Commons' of France: as in the Second Estate, an influential number of the clerical elite warmed to the ideal of national unity and did not feel their own pre-eminence imperilled by it. This diverse coalition of prelates (it included Champion de Cicé of Bordeaux, Lefranc de Pompignan of Vienne and Lubersac of Chartres) distanced themselves from other colleagues and, in so doing, only encouraged further defections among the *curés* to the Third Estate.

On 19 June, in a sharply contested vote, a majority of the First Estate opted to join the National Assembly. Several conservative bishops led by Cardinal La Rochefoucauld, unable to cope with the twin pressures of insubordination in their own Order and intimidation outside it, met the King secretly at the palace of Marly and begged him 'to protect his clergy and save religion.'[5] These emotive entreaties were one of the pressures behind the royal policy statement of 23 June. Though scheduling an imaginative list of reform proposals, Louis XVI's 'Royal Session' of that day also insisted on the fundamental integrity of the historic Orders, and the right of clergy and nobility to a veto on all that concerned their particular rights and interests. At the end of the session, the three Orders were commanded to resume their individual meeting places on the next day. Not all agreed. The majority of clerics trooped away with Cardinal La Rochefoucauld, but those who had already joined the Third Estate remained in their places. Encouraged by Necker's pointed absence from the 'Royal Session', by rumours of military disaffection in the armed forces (the Gardes Françaises in particular) and by demonstrations of popular support, they gambled on royal capitulation.

It came only four days later, when Louis wrote to the presidents of the clerical and noble Orders requesting them to join the Third Estate. The injunction was academic as far as many clergy were concerned. By 24 June, just twenty-four hours after the King had spoken to the assembled deputies, a total of 150 priests had accepted the logic of events and crossed over to the self-styled National Assembly, and they were soon followed by the duc d'Orléans and an influential minority of the Nobility.

Just as the General Assembly of the Clergy the previous summer had won some acclaim for refusing to accede to ministerial wishes, so the majority of clerical deputies in June 1789 found their resolute behaviour reflected the public's overwhelming desire for harmony and unity to reign among *all* its elected delegates at Versailles, however much this conflicted with the insistence from an alarmed Marie-Antoinette and the King's anti-Necker advisors that Louis stand firm, perhaps even use repressive tactics. But the King gave way and abandoned the noble and episcopal loyalists when on 27 June he ordered them to join the 'Commons'. Confronted with a straight choice between loyalty and patriotism, the clergy had found the latter irresistible. Its attitude during the Estates-General can be well summarised in one acute female contemporary's judgment:

It behaved with effervescence, a mood which, without wanting the Order's destruction, led the Clergy to be dragged along in the current, in the wake of so many new things. Feted at all events by members of the Third Estate, it found itself disposed to support their cause.[6]

It remained for the leaders of the First Estate to come to terms with the implications of verification of powers in common. Any hopes that the right of voting as an Order even on a limited range of issues had survived the junction of 27 June were dispelled during debates on 6 and 7 July. The clergy were expected by the majority of the National Assembly (not least a majority of the *curés*) to put aside their cloth and their interests as an Order in the name of national regeneration. Any alternative was simply too 'unpatriotic' to be acceptable, even if this left the Church vulnerable to the imposition of reforms without its corporate consent being obtained. The logic of political events was therefore to nullify the privileged status of the First Estate well before formal juridical abolition. In a strictly political sense, it ceased to count collectively from July 1789, though it should be emphasised that the politics of deference were far from defunct. Indeed, a forceful reminder of how much the former Third Estate still looked to the elite for leadership came when Archbishop Le Franc de Pompignan became the first President of the National Assembly after a royal prince of the blood, the duc d'Orléans, had refused the honour. It was a sign that a reputation for 'patriotism' could, by careful leadership, be the soundest means of protecting the influence of the Gallican Church over the coming months.

II

The Bastille fell on 14 July: the military threat to the Revolution was over. Churchmen had not been directly involved in events leading up to it, but knew of the risk of reaction – in the dismissal of Necker as chief minister on 11 July and the imposition of the 'One Hundred Hours' government of the duc de Broglie.[7] The presence of clerical deputies among those accompanying Louis XVI on his historic trip to the Hôtel de Ville in Paris was welcomed, especially the 'three curés of Poitou', who were enjoying unprecedented acclamation for their role in achieving the creation of the National Assembly. The three priests also had their legislative duties to attend to, for churchmen could hope to share in the National Assembly's constitution-making. As early as 15 July the clergy made it plain that they would participate in the debates of the Assembly, and their involvement in all forms of legislative work was soon apparent. Members of the reformist elite dominated the first committee entrusted with drafting constitutional proposals (among clergy members were the Archbishop of Bordeaux, the Bishop of Clermont and the abbé Sieyès).[8]

Their progress was slow until after the famous night of the 4 August, when the Church volunteered the kind of concessions that would fundamentally affect its power and status. The curés agreed to relinquish their casuel, and even more momentously, to the Church's abandonment of its principal revenue – tithe. They spoke merely of its commutation, but most deputies thought of outright abolition as latent anticlericalist sentiments impelled some among them to look on confiscation of the Church's landed wealth as a remedy for the nation's perilous public finances; one noble deputy, the marquis de la Coste, specifically proposed such a plan on 8 August. Tithe payments would be an obvious casualty of any such upheaval.

Yet their hasty abandonment would jeopardise hopes of paying the parish clergy more money, and went against the overwhelming demand in the *cahiers* for reform rather than outright abolition. The patriotic intoxication of 4–5 August 1789 may have led clerical deputies to overlook this possibility, but it proceeded less from disinterestedness than apprehension. The 'Great Fear' (a form of social breakdown in the countryside fanned by rumour and counter-rumour) was sweeping across several provinces, and a high proportion of the rural population had simply stopped paying the tithe along with more notorious forms of 'feudal' income. With the inaction or complete collapse of the customary agencies of authority in the provinces, the Church was powerless to coerce recalcitrant parishoners.

On 11 August another decree insisted that the financial support of the clergy would be undertaken by alternative means, but nobody for the moment knew how much the salary would be or who would pay for it; the decree was predicated on the clergy having the new status of salaried officials and giving up claims to be independent property-holders. Tithe abolition had introduced a note of uncertainty into the life of every clergyman whatever his status, *décimateur* or *congruiste*. All were affected; their consent had not been directly obtained. 'The abolition of tithes is also that of our revenues, signed with one pen', complained seven *curés* from the Châlons diocese on 4 December 1789 who were paid the *portion congrue*. They and others might have to abandon their parishes if money did not come in soon. There was smouldering resentment at the conduct of the clerical deputies for having forgotten the reality of the situation in the parishes, for making the charitable role of the *curé* next to impossible. 'Why don't those gentlemen, your orators, come here to find out what is going on?' asked the abbé Coulomber, *curé* of Saint-Denis-sur-Sarthon near Alençon:[9]

> They would soon find out the consequences of their wonderful speculative projects ... Yes, there were abuses in the distribution of tithes because it was unjust that the *décimateurs* without pastoral responsibilities carried off the greatest share without doing anything for them. But it was that which should have been reformed and nothing further ...

In fact this frustration was shared by clergy inside the chamber. 'They treat us as though we came from another planet', one canon wrote home, part of a general chorus denouncing the sacrifices an irresistible pressure was compelling them to make. Here is another *curé* writing on 14 August:

> It's done. The Clergy of France has lost all its lustre ... that the whole Clergy becomes salaried officials, consequently outside all political business, that's not what we wanted, and we've strongly contested the fact, but that's just what has been done.[10]

The gesture of renunciation may be attributed to a nostalgia for apostolic poverty in uneasy conjunction with Enlightenment idealism, to patriotic panic or to an uncomfortable sense that the game was up; the fact remains that the Church was in no position to veto any proposal to abolish tithes or other customary forms of income like vestry fees, a decision which was made for it by the huge lay majority in the Assembly, led by young and wealthy noblemen. It was just as the abbé Barbotin, himself a deputy, appreciated – 'They're going to put us all on the *portion congrue*, everybody, archbishops, bishops, all the clergy.'[11] Yet, for the moment, *curé* deputies were ready to underpin their commitment to the national good by abandoning a basic income without any hint yet of what would replace it.

As the debates on tithe suggested, there were no longer any specifically clerical issues, and this was in line with Article 3 of the Declaration of the Rights of Man and the Citizen (adopted on 26 August), which stated that all authority in France originated from the nation, and that included the Church's. Clerics could take some comfort from Article 16, urging respect for religion for the good order of society, and Article 17 on the need for public worship. Article 18 caused much debate with interventions from Talleyrand and Mirabeau, but the Church had to content itself with the wording, 'No-one can be disturbed for his opinions, even religious ones, provided that their expression does not infringe the public order declared by the law' (the formula was invented by a *curé*). If this was not quite full-blooded enough for clerical opinion, some compensation could be derived from the exclusion of '*mauvais livres*' from the article establishing press freedom.[12] Explicit recognition of the Roman Catholic Church in the new France was unacceptable to a majority in the Assembly; the only concession to Catholic sentiment was the refusal to include in the Declaration of the Rights of Man the liberty and equality of denominations (*'cultes'*), as Mirabeau and Rabaut de Saint-Etienne had requested in the discussion of Article 10. This did not stop some clergy from trying unsuccessfully to urge reconsideration: on 28 August the abbé d'Eymar's motion to declare the Catholic religion the religion of State in the first article of the new constitution was rejected on a procedural basis.[13] The nation via its elected representatives was determined to have the last word on what had once been the specifically sacerdotal. Such logic ominously anticipated the rationale behind the Civil Constitution of the Clergy.

Less than six weeks after the Gallican Church had abandoned its exclusive status as the premier Order of France, it found itself suddenly, unpredictably, minus the financial rights that were fundamental to the maintenance of its power and prestige, though its estates remained for the moment in its hands. Talk of compensation had not found favour against the background of continuing financial crisis, and the sacrifice of ecclesiastical silverware (retaining only what was required for the conduct of divine service) to the national coffers ordered by the bishops in late September only briefly delayed more radical measures. The Church lay vulnerable to further assaults, with minimal constitutional safeguards to protect itself, the Declaration of the Rights of Man notwithstanding. None of the clergy had anticipated that when the nation's sovereignty was affirmed in 1789, it would soon view the political independence of the Church as a threat to its own, and seek to dismantle it so quickly. Religious reform would go ahead faster than expected, with plans prepared initially by an ecclesiastical committee of fifteen deputies set up on 12 August. Though its membership was exclusively confined to Catholics and included two bishops – Clermont and Luçon – the driving force was the Jansenist canon lawyer, Durand de Maillane.

The Church was being pushed to the margins without any real idea of how to make its presence felt either in determining national policy or its own fate. Its diminution of power was emphasised again in decisions taken on some of the basic features of the new settlement, ordered in the face of advice from the constitutional committee. Senior clerics were keen on giving the Assembly an upper house for revising legislation. A bicameral legislature would have introduced a series of checks and balances in the working of the Assembly that would have aligned French constitutionalism on a loosely British model. It appealed to the Anglophiles among the elite, not least Bishop La Luzerne of Langres, whose published proposals attracted a lot of interest. He and his supporters wanted to bring nobles and bishops together in something resembling a British House of Lords, but failed to command the support of a majority in the Assembly. Proponents of bicameralism offered schemes that were incompatible; some clergy were unhappy at being divided from their brethren for parliamentary purposes; while lesser noblemen feared there would be no place for them in any Senate. But what principally doomed the scheme was the suspicion that creating an upper house in the Assembly with delaying powers would recreate the opportunities for obstructionism, revive aristocratic power and hinder the implementation of reforms that the Assembly believed the nation wanted. The proposal was rejected by 490 votes to 89 on 10 September.[14]

If there was to be no Senate to curb the revolutionary zeal of deputies, the reasons for granting the Crown substantive rights of veto over legislation became more compelling. This, at least, was the basic case propounded by numerous moderates, including several prelates, for whom – if the papacy was for the moment left to one side – the monarchy had almost overnight become the one institution in any position to defend the integrity of the former First Estate. Their problem was that Louis XVI's reluctance to register the decrees stemming from 4 August had underlined for patriots the capacity of the King for delaying tactics. Advocacy of an absolute veto was therefore disadvantaged by the current legislative impasse, and the initiative passed to the eloquent supporters of a suspensive veto. Necker's intimation that both he and the King were happy with that proposal was decisive, and it was agreed by 673 votes to 352 on 15 September.[15]

The respectable number of votes cast for the defeated option was a reminder of the sizeable scale of conservative opinion inside the National Assembly by the autumn of 1789. But with the national mood still overwhelmingly optimistic about France's constitutional future, it was hard for voices urging caution to find much of a hearing, even among moderates. The autumnal mood was brilliantly captured in a letter from Sieyès' old patron, Bishop Lubersac of Chartres, to his English friend, the Marquess of Lansdowne:

I find myself in the way, without having sought it, of playing a role myself [in the Revolution] ... At present therefore, the torrent pulls me along like everyone else because it would be too dangerous to oppose it. But I give way with repugnance and with a disquiet too well founded that all this excess may force us back to the other extreme.[16]

In the country at large, the Church was one of the few institutions that had neither imploded nor lapsed in 1789. Putting aside their own precarious future, its personnel were generally doing what they could to allay public anxieties in areas affected by the 'Great Fear' or the failure of the wine harvest; the remedies were the time-honoured ones of charitable relief and public prayer, like the general procession of secular and religious clergy to the church of Saint-Europe in Saintes on 20 September followed by benediction at the cathedral.[17] Parish priests were heavily involved in staffing the *ad hoc* local government units hurriedly put in place over the summer months. They could be found at every tier of authority, even in rural areas like what would, from 1790, be the *département* of the Morbihan, where no less than 18 per cent of 232 mayors were clergymen. Clergy also encouraged the formation by property holders of National Guard units in the provinces. Blessing the new flags was a local occasion that autumn, as at Besançon where Archbishop Durfort himself turned out to do the job in November.[18]

Clerical deputies, including several prominent *curés*, appreciated that with inter-Order distinctions now merely honorific, their best hope was to form working alliances with other cautious constitutionalists. Clergy were prominent in some of the new clubs founded that autumn like the *Impartiaux*, one of whose articles (number eight) insisted that the 'tranquillity and interest of the state require that the Catholic religion continues to enjoy uniquely in the kingdom the title of national religion and the solemnity of public worship'.[19] Several were linked with the grouping known as the *Monarchiens*, led by liberal nobles like Clermont-Tonnerre and Lally-Tollendal, and supported by Mounier, the hero of the Dauphiné revolt. They emerged as the principal backers of bicameralism and an absolute veto, and their defeats on both issues were a reminder of how much organisational skills were the key to making an impact.

But the possibilities of the moderate Right increasing their influence were not assisted by the forced removal of the National Assembly from Versailles to Paris on 6 October. The anarchy, disorder, and intimidation of the 'October Days' were profoundly disturbing for all sections of opinion among clerical deputies, as they heard the abuse hurled on them by the crowds – 'down with the skull-caps!' The Assembly was violated no less than the palace, with its President, Bishop La Luzerne, mocked and pushed from his chair. However much they deplored the King's delayed acceptance of the August decrees, the direct action of the crowd was repellent to the majority and contrary to the respect for the rule of law that was central to the Assembly's task.

The intimidation of royal family and National Assembly was too much for some of the *Monarchiens*, who decided to return to the provinces rather than sit under the glare of revolutionary activists in the capital. Mounier was among those who left, and the Archbishop of Paris another. His nerve already broken by a crowd pelting his carriage with stones on 23 June, Juigné slipped away to take the waters at Aix-les-Bains in Savoy and never returned. But most constitutionalists (including virtually all the clergy) stayed on, hopeful of yet influencing events. More immediately, the question of what would replace the tithe as the basis of clerical remuneration remained to be settled, and for episcopal deputies to join the small wave of royalist emigration that followed the 'October Days' would have amounted to a breach of pastoral responsibility for the priesthood that few were prepared to contemplate.

This issue became bound up in the wider question of a national financial settlement to resolve the state's soaring short-term debt. As a crisis mood developed, the King expressed a wish that there should be public prayers calling for calm, and a pastoral instruction to that effect was published by his *grand aumônier*, the Bishop of Metz, on 19 September.[20] This was, indirectly, a chance for the higher clergy to voice their response to the Revolution to date (some had not even waited for the formal invitation), and most took care to be discrete, while warning that France was perilously close to anarchy. Archbishop Puységur of Bourges blamed not the Revolution, but 'this audacious and culpable philosophy which, in its fury, has attacked heaven only to see things on earth overthrown'.[21] This sort of rhetoric from senior churchmen was too familiar to concern the authorities unduly, but the *mandement* of the conservative Breton bishop, Le Mintier de Saint-André of Tréguier, dated 14 September, struck a more extreme note. It was not just his inveighing against religious toleration, or the way 'religion was annihilated, its ministers reduced to the deplored condition of agents appointed by brigands', but his blatant warning to the Assembly against any sale of Church possessions that offended. The letter was judged inflammatory enough to land him before the criminal judges at the Châtelet on a charge of '*lèse-nation*'.[22]

The bishop's forebodings were well-founded. The key to financial stability, as patriotic opinion-formers in the Assembly saw it, was the state ownership of Church lands, and their rapid sale thereafter to the highest bidder. On 10 October, just five days after the ignominious removal of the legislature from Versailles to the Salle du Manège in the Tuileries palace, confiscation and sale was formally proposed by Talleyrand, Bishop of Autun, who, as Agent-General of the clergy as recently as 1785, knew as much about the extent and running of Church properties as anyone. For him, it was an initiative that confirmed his standing as a patriotic leader, but for his episcopal colleagues, it was the supreme betrayal of his cloth and his Order, one, it was said, that fell not far short of Judas Iscariot's. They despised as disingenuous his insinuating presentation of a Church recalled to its evangelical purpose and, concurrently, playing a vital role in stabilising the new French State. No less astutely, Talleyrand courted popularity with the *curés*, by arguing that two-thirds of revenues generated should be used to pay them a respectable salary with the rest reserved for the state; but the debates, which lasted for the rest of the month, revealed the majority of deputies as favouring unconditional appropriation. On 2 November, 510 of them to 346 declared that all the property of the Church should 'be placed at the disposal of the Nation'. The wording was ambiguous, a reflection of uncertain motivation, as one foreign onlooker in the galleries shrewdly opined: 'Whether the assembly has acted in that circumstance entirely through patriotism or from a great desire of lowering the clergy I will not pretend to say'. In December 1789 a massive sale of Church lands was authorised by the Assembly.[23]

But the confiscation of the Church's vast estates has another dimension that can hardly be exaggerated: the continuing vitality of the anticlericalism that had been such a dominant note of the Enlightenment. Priestly 'privileges' were an emotive subject for anyone who had read Voltaire, or indeed any hack author who had railed at the baleful influence of 'priestcraft' in French life. Confiscation was further evidence that the Assembly was intent on confining and recalling the former First Estate to its pastoral task, and it would be denied the political power base (its land) from which it had so recently had such an impact on affairs of state. Comparisons with Henry VIII's nationalisation of Church lands in England during the 1530s are misleading, for Henrician confiscations were confined to monastic lands, leaving the property of chapters, cathedrals, and colleges, largely alone. In France in 1789, the Assembly knew no such restraint: the Church's title to all its possessions had passed not to the Crown but to the nation.

Despite the spoliation and massive loss of status that the Gallican Church had incurred, most of its representatives continued to attend the National Assembly through the winter of 1789–90, still clinging to what remained of the euphoric expectations of a few months earlier that all would come good, and using the clubs frequented by the moderate Right to formulate their tactics more effectively.[24] This was capable of bringing results, like securing the election of the *Monarchien* Boisgelin, Archbishop of Aix, to the presidency of the Assembly in late November, who expressed himself pleased he had stayed in post and not 'listened to the advice everyone was giving me'.[25] Churchmen were prominent in putting the case for caution in pursuing the Assembly's constitutional programme. There was Boisgelin himself, suave and sharp in debate, the abbé de Montesquiou, 'like an angel with eyes of sapphire and golden hair', and the abbé Maury, truculent, hard to silence, as stout as Mirabeau and having no less a flair for oratory. 'One would have taken him', said one observer, 'for a grenadier disguised as a seminarian'.[26]

But there was no let-up in the changes imposed by the Assembly on the Church. The monastic orders only just survived into 1790. They were an obvious target for legislators convinced that monks and nuns would be a useless and expensive incubus in a reformed Church, and a decree for suppressing the religious orders existing under solemn vows had actually been proposed as early as 17 December by Treilhard, a member of the Ecclesiastical Committee. He was immediately criticised for his plan in the full Assembly by a fellow member of the Committee, Bishop Bonal of Clermont, and it was temporarily shelved.[27] The respite lasted only until 13 February, when all monasteries and convents containing regular clergy, except those dedicated to educational and charitable work, were declared dissolved. No new novices were to be accepted; members of religious communities were relieved of their vows by the State, and could leave at once with the promise of a pension varying from 700 to 1200 livres; those who refused would be dispersed, irrespective of their particular order, and packed off to specified monasteries and an uncertain future. Congregations of secular clergy like the Oratorians (who had a reputation for political progressiveness) were unaffected by the new law.[28]

The Assembly had taken no interest in the addresses received from many religious houses asking it to hold back, like the one from the four Carmelite houses in the archdiocese of Paris:

> People in the world love to say that monasteries only contain victims slowly consumed by regrets; but we protest before God that, if there is true happiness on earth, we enjoy it here in the shadow of the sanctuary, and that, if we're forced to decide between the century [i.e. the outside world] and the cloister, there isn't one among us who would not ratify, with still more joy, her first choice.[29]

In the Assembly itself, Bishop Bonal led the protestors making, on 11 February, what one critic called 'a discourse worthy of the 11th century'; he was appalled that the legislation amounted to a claim by the revolutionary state that there was no limit to its competence, certainly nothing posed by the Church.[30] He had no success, and neither did La Fare of Nancy in the demand that the Assembly conform to the preferences expressed in the *cahiers* on the question, which left Clermont-Tonnerre of Châlons to ask openly if the Assembly wished to undertake the outright destruction of the Church.[31] Yet deputies – including churchmen – were perfectly aware of the changes imposed on the religious orders by the state throughout the course of the century. What was proposed in 1790 could be dressed up as the logical culmination to that process – the final suppression of such communities. The measure passed, with the reasoning of Barnave much more to majority taste:

> I do not believe it is necessary to demonstrate that the religious orders are incompatible with the rights of man. A profession that deprives men of the rights you have recognised is incompatible with those rights. Obliged to undertake duties that are not prescribed by Nature, which Nature reproves, are they not by Nature herself condemned to violate them?[32]

Cardinal La Rochefoucauld thereupon immediately asked Pius VI to ensure its operation, and his Holiness diplomatically issued a consistorial decree on 31 March granting permission for bishops to

dispense regular clergy from their vows.[33] That was an essential preliminary, but the Assembly wanted more: it expected the diocesan
authorities to join with local government to supervise the dispersal of
the regular congregations. Most bishops cooperated to make this
painful operation as easy as it could be for the departing regulars and
to forestall the breakdown of public order. The majority in the male
religious orders in fact offered no concerted opposition to the legislation. Submission to authority was ingrained among them, so that it
was left to a minority of communities and isolated individuals either
to make their protests, like the collective letter of the Prior and monks
of Corbie asking for the maintenance of the congregation of Saint-
Maur because of its record in literary and scientific research, or
simply to stay on, like a high proportion of Capuchins in Normandy.[34]
Others, with no real sense of vocation, were anxious to leave. Shortly
after the vote in the Assembly on 13 February, a deputy was accosted
outside by a Capuchin eager to know how the decision had gone:
'Saint Francis, is he up the creek?' he asked. 'Far more than that,'
came the response. 'Excellent!' said the Capuchin, 'so long live Jesus,
the King, and the Revolution!'[35] Barbers and outfitters did good business that spring as members of the religious orders rushed to equip
themselves for life in the outside world.

As the decrees were enacted over the next few months, and the
municipal officers made their inventories, monks were often only too
eager to demonstrate goodwill towards the new order, whatever their
individual decisions. In Bordeaux, Dominicans not only called at the
town hall but even at the Society of the Friends of the Constitution to
affirm their adhesion to all the Assembly's laws.[36] It was local lay
people, worried about the impact of monastic closures on their livelihoods, like the people of Ribeauvillé and Colmar in Alsace, who protested to officials while the Augustinians concerned quietly packed
up. At Castillonnès in the Lot-et-Garonne, the municipal council
petitioned for the retention of the monks 'because of the great services
that they have always rendered and that they continue to render to
the people.'[37]

The first enquiry of the spring of 1790 showed the male orders
roughly split equally between those who intended to abandon
the monastic life and those who intended to stay on and try and
adjust to the changed conditions; in some great houses – Saint-
Riquier (Picardy), Saint-Vincent de Besançon, Faverney (Franche-
Comté) – there was a clear majority for staying on, with 37 monks

of 47 at Saint-Germain-des-Près deciding likewise. Only when the Assembly in October made it mandatory for each *département* to assemble the religious together irrespective of order in houses containing a minimum of twenty did many of those who had first hoped to persist with their vows reconsider and, from spring 1791, their temporarary homes started to empty rapidly: the unsatisfactory nature of trying to lead a monastic life with those from other traditions in a 'common house' was often more instrumental in making them opt to return to their families than any new law could have been. Overcrowding could be rife. One Augustin monastery in Flanders, warned to expect about 50 refusers of 'liberation' had to take no less than 116.[38] A minority of monks managed, despite new premises, to stay together. The Benedictines of Saint-Bertin and those of Maroilles continued their common life until June 1792, after a compulsory move to other sites.[39] By contrast with the men, a majority of female congregations opted to try and continue a conventual life, despite the likelihood of having to move elsewhere to do so, so evincing what two recent historians have declared to be 'a dogged loyalty towards the Church as they knew it.'[40] As some Visitandines unavailingly lamented: 'We ask to live and die in the holy and blissful state that we have freely embraced, that we zealously observe and that constitutes the sole happiness of our days.' Yet they too had to move on if they wanted to preserve any shred of a common life.[41]

III

There was little the constitutionalist Right could do to counter the enactments against the religious orders, but as a political force it remained far from finished on religious issues: demands that Maundy Thursday and Good Friday be observed were conceded by deputies, and the resilient Bishop Bonal was even applauded when he insisted that the best Christians would always be the best citizens.[42] Easter 1790 was the prelude to a forceful counter-attack by Bonal, Boisgelin and their allies when the Carthusian monk, Dom Gerle, proposed that Catholicism should be declared the national religion. Much planning went into the preparation of this motion among the several factions of the Right, and there was a sense that, with the abbé de Montesquiou enjoying the presidency of the Assembly, the time was right to test opinion. Dom Gerle himself had an unimpeachable patriotic reputation as one of the first clerics to go over to the Third Estate in June 1789; if he could not sway the votes of the uncommitted, then the Right had little hope. His motion asked deputies to recognise publicly that the events of the last twelve months had done nothing to alter the fact that Frenchmen and women remained overwhelmingly Roman Catholic in their religious allegiance, and the Assembly should be honest enough to admit and respect it.

It would not. Mirabeau talked wildly about a new St Batholomew's Day massacre in what turned out to be 'the most acrimonious confrontation between the clergy and the Left since the beginning of the Revolution'.[43] Fears that if accepted, it might threaten the recently declared civil rights of Protestants and Sephardi Jews, or cast a shadow on the Declaration of the Rights of Man, were undoubtedly persuasive. The most the majority would concede was a declaration of the Assembly's continuing 'attachment' to the faith. Seeing defeat as imminent and unwilling to submit to intimidation from crowds gathered outside, many deputies abstained on the vote. But they registered their feelings all the same when, on 19 April, over three hundred of them met privately and published a dissenting opinion in favour of Dom Gerle's original motion.

The fact that the latter had been sponsored by one of the 'patriot' lower clergy (in this case, a monk) indicated that internal divisions within the Church were decreasing. The impact of unprecedented change was knitting together the different ranks of the hierarchy after the tensions and fissures of the 1780s, especially the wrangling and litigation that had marred relations between bishops and chapters. Now they had a common interest in mere survival. No clerical deputy had denied outright the obligations owed to their episcopal superiors except in a strictly political sphere, and with reduced inequalities in income decreed, the way was clear for the re-establishment of mutual hierarchical respect.

Amid the uncertainty about the Church's future, bishops and priests impressed on their people the need to remain calm and law-abiding, to take comfort from the National Assembly's decision to adjourn for Holy Week and from the orders of the municipal authority in Paris for citizens to respect Corpus Christi Day as usual. Prelates displayed their patriotic credentials in such innovative rituals as taking the new civic oath ordered on 4 February in public before the municipal officials,[44] blessing the standards of National Guard battalions, as at Verdun on 25 April where Bishop Desnos's speech was 'generally applauded;'[45] several, like the Bishop of Bayeux, took office as mayors. Their presence was testimony to the continuing pre-eminence of the clergy in the life of the provinces, and the population's inclination to look to them for a lead. The introduction of the new local government legislation later in 1790 actually diminished scope for a clerical presence within it. The Assembly was generally keen to reduce the opportunities available to clergy to assume public office and confine them to a primary pastoral role, in line with what most revolutionaries felt was their sole function. As one pamphleteer put it: 'public affairs are not the business of priests; exclusively concerned with God's cause and the salvation of their people, they ought to spend their lives kneeling in front of altars'.[46]

Events suggested the clergy might have little choice: after long, bitter debate on 14 April, the Assembly voted for the complete dis-possession of the clergy, and turned its face against some powerfully argued last-minute speeches by those advocating leaving the former First Estate with some property. Indeed, the debate merely con-firmed a process already under way, because on 9 April the civil authorities had taken over the administration of all ecclesiastical pos-sessions, and made arrangements for the payment of salaries. It was a symbolically appropriate finale to twelve months in which the Gallican Church had suffered a more pronounced diminution of its institutional integrity and power even than that undergone by the monarchy. The insuperable problem for the Church was that after the Revolution the threat to it came no longer from the monarchy but from a state reconstituted on the basis of a much-reduced recog-nition of the Church's proper jurisdiction. In the transformed politi-cal landscape of 1790, the validation of sovereignty proceeded directly from the nation rather than from God. Assembly members wanted the Revolution validated by Catholic Christianity, but on their own terms, and this often insensitive insistence was to cause a decisive rupture before the end of 1790. It was ironic that just as many lower clergy, anxious to preserve the alliance between the Revolution and Catholicism, began to see the merits of summoning a national council to advise on legislation affecting ecclesiastics, deputies in the Assembly (including the Jansenist sympathisers who might once have been natural supporters of this plan) turned their faces against it. The consequences of that decision would be funda-mental to subsequent French history and to Catholicism generally.

7 The Civil Constitution

I

The passing of the Civil Constitution of the Clergy followed logically upon the measures already adopted by the National Assembly in its religious policies. With sovereign power exercised on behalf of the nation by a legislature that, in the spring of 1790, was in no doubt about its popular mandate,[1] the Church was juridically relegated to the ill-defined status of just another sectional interest in France, albeit an extremely important one: it might make representations to deputies about proposed laws, but could not exercise a veto over them, let alone legislate for itself through an agency like the General Assembly of the Clergy (which had effectively lapsed since 1789). To do either would amount to the usurpation of powers abrogated to itself by the National Assembly, and no one, including most churchmen, felt easy about having their patriotism called into question, even as the Civil Constitution was debated and clerical deputies one by one expressed their doubts about its contents. After all, the Gallican Church had long prided itself on being the *Ecclesia Francorum*, the Church of all the French people, and well-meaning lay reformers on the Ecclesiastical Committee of the Assembly (reconstituted and enlarged on 7 February 1790, when two bishops withdrew so that initiative passed to former *parlementaires* sympathetic to a Jansenist constitutionalist stance)[2] like Durand de Maillane and Jacques de Cazalès intended merely to bring that tradition to its culmination. What had changed since the Revolution was the nature of the Church–State nexus. It was no longer a partnership, a relationship of legal equality, and one of mutual benefit to both. After 1789, the separate spheres of *imperium* and *sacerdotium* were gone past recall. The Gallican Church had become a subordinate institution, whose government and functions were unreservedly determined by and subject to lay politicians. If anyone still doubted this diminution in early 1790, the terms of the Civil Constitution of the Clergy would offer a stark reminder.

Those like Martineau, Lanjuinais, Durand de Maillane and Treilhard who drafted the legislation believed themselves to be friends of
the Church and proceeded on the assumption that Christianity per-
fected the social order.[3] They wanted reforms designed to eliminate
or minimise what they saw as the 'abuses' that hindered the clergy
from carrying out pastoral work, namely wealth, contemplation,
administration, scholarship, politics. It was a case not of dechristianisation, but of rechristianisation; Treilhard had fondly hoped
that 'Your decrees will not carry any attack on this holy religion:
they will only return it to its primitive purity, and you will truly be
the Christians of the Gospel.'[4] Clerical deputies for a time went along
with this rhetoric. It was an aim that the Ecclesiastical Committee
believed the country at large shared, if the unsolicited individual
requests and advice received were anything to judge by.[5] The Civil
Constitution of the clergy would work in accordance with the same
Revolutionary principles that operated in the recast local government and judiciary.

The Ecclesiastical Committee presented the Civil Constitution to
the Assembly on 29 May, and debate on it lasted over six weeks until
it was agreed without a vote on 12 July.[6] Its provisions were far-
reaching. The episcopate was greatly affected. 52 sees were suppressed outright. There was to be a rationalisation and realignment
of diocesan boundaries so that each of the 83 new *départements* would
have its own bishop;[7] none of them would be accorded archiepiscopal
rank, and the 10 most senior would have to rest content with the
honorific status of 'metropolitan'. All, however, could glory in their
new official designation as 'public officials'. Parishes would also correspond more accurately to density of population, and clergy who
had no cure of souls – principally cathedral chapters – would lose
their places. Instead of argumentative canons and ambitious *grands
vicaires*, bishops would consult on all policy matters with a permanent
diocesan council in a relationship that stressed fraternity within the
hierarchy; without its consent, any episcopal act would have no legal
force. So 'proud prelates' would be creatures of the past if the Assembly had its way, with the emphasis on the common ministerial status
of bishops and *curés* underlined by the stipulation that every bishop
should have previously served fifteen years in a parish, and each *curé*
five years as a *vicaire*. Cumulatively, it symbolised the rejection
of a Tridentine or Counter-Reformation ecclesiology in favour of
new structures impregnated with some Jansenist, even presbyterian

elements (like the episcopal councils), although the place accorded the lower clergy in synodical government of their diocese was no improvement on the pre-1789 situation. The purest disciples of Richer would be among those who with older canon lawyers and theologians of Jansenist persuasion would subsequently refuse the oath to the Civil Constitution.[8]

A Richerist bias (another nod in the direction of recreating what was assumed to be primitive Christianity) was seen elsewhere in the legislation: existing patronage rights within the Gallican Church were nullified. In future all clergy were to be elected by the laity – bishops by departmental assemblies, *curés* by district ones. It was a proposal which, according to Timothy Tackett, 'probably took most Frenchmen utterly by surprise'. That said, it was a feature of much other legislation brought in by the Assembly, a testimony to the future electoral power of the bourgeoisie.[9] Non-Catholic affiliation was no barrier to casting a vote, for, in the new France, the duties of common citizenship were deemed to override the privileges conferred by baptismal vows. As Mirabeau said, 'religion belonged to everyone', and for the majority of deputies the civic character of the parish clergy counted for more than their priesthood. No formal consultation of ordinary clergy took place before the Committee made its recommendation. Their moderate pro-Revolutionary enthusiasm over the last year was assumed to indicate their basic sympathies as *curés-citoyens* for the new order, and for there to have occurred a corresponding diminution of their sense of sacerdotal identity. Any hesitation over the electoral provision was expected to be overlain for the majority of priests by increased remuneration on a graduated scale (a basic salary of 1200 livres as opposed to the *portion congrue* of 700 livres), a pension, and a place of respect in civic society.

All of this was proposed without any reference back to Pius VI – to his growing consternation. The events of 1789–90 unavoidably imperilled Franco-papal equilibrium, as it forced Rome to respond to events and to turn Pius's honorific status *vis-à-vis* the Gallican Church into a more active role. That Church's major reduction in power and status, the refusal of the National Assembly to offer it the official if often uneasy protection it had enjoyed under Louis XVI and his grandfather, and the King's powerlessness to defend it against the imposition of change, all combined to give the Pope a potential scope for involvement in the French Church's affairs that none of his predecessors had enjoyed for centuries. With Gallicanism recast to fit a revolutionary

mould, many of the Church's leaders from 1790 onwards found themselves in the unfamiliar situation of looking across the Alps to see what
sort of defensive shield Pius VI could offer them.

The precedents were not encouraging. Not even a personal visit by
the Pope to Vienna in 1782 had deterred Joseph II from undertaking
a comprehensive rationalisation of the Austrian Church, the episode
highlighting for contemporaries the institutional weakness of the
modern papacy. Anyway, if the renewed but revised Gallican polity
inaugurated by the French Revolution showed itself defiant towards
Rome, that hardly amounted to a break with tradition: as early as
August 1789 the National Assembly had abolished the payment of
Peter's Pence for the upkeep of the Holy See, the famous Annates
which Luther had deplored and which had marked the beginning of
the Reformation in sixteenth-century Europe. It had done so without
any protests from clerical deputies. Then, in the months before
debate began on the Civil Constitution, the Assembly and Pius VI
clashed over the enclaves of Avignon and the Comtat Venaissin
inside France, with a majority of deputies willing to see papal jurisdiction overthrown by popular pressure. The annexationists who had
gained control of Avignon city council declared that their laws would
in future be governed by the French constitution, which they proceeded to adopt. The Pope refused to countenance their plans, and
his supporters instigated a day of rioting in Avignon on 10 June
1790. Without further delay, the pro-revolutionary party in Avignon unilaterally declared the enclave annexed to France, and several
parts of the Comtat followed suit, a decision that provoked civil war
in the territory for the next twelve months.

Pius VI had, by then, seen enough of the Revolution's impact on
the Gallican Church to make him anxious about developments, but
not enough to cause him to declare himself openly against the new
regime. For the moment, there seemed more to be gained by diplomacy; hence his condemnation before a Roman consistory of the
Assembly's anti-Catholic religious policies and of the Declaration of
the Rights of Man on 29 March 1790 was discretely done in camera.
Nevertheless, his words were ominous, bleakly predicting religious
schism and possibly civil war if Louis XVI approved further decrees
that would inevitably trespass on the doctrine and discipline of the
Church.[10] Such a veiled approach could not survive publication of
the Assembly's plans for the wholesale reorganisation of the Church.
The start of debate on the Civil Constitution two months later

showed that deputies were set on a course of confrontation with the Vatican that would terminate the Pope's residual temporal oversight of the French Church. The Concordat of 1516 would be ended, bishops would no longer require his formal confirmation, and he would be expected to sanction the Civil Constitution in its entirety. Failure to do so might result in the Assembly accepting the proffered annexation of the papal enclaves in France.

As Pius took stock of events in France, the stage was set for the prolonged debate in the Assembly on a very radical set of proposals during June 1790. After previous setbacks in the division lobbies, it was unrealistic for the Centre Right to imagine it could defeat the scheme out of hand, and its best chance lay in revising it, perhaps by winning for the ecclesiastical authorities an independent voice (not necessarily a veto) on spiritual matters and canon law. When general discussion on the Civil Constitution opened on 29 May, deputies with reservations about the Civil Constitution therefore took their stand less on its contents or by denying the Assembly's right to legislate than on the means of its implementation and the refusal of the Ecclesiastical Committee to admit the existence of 'spiritual matters', in other words that part of the Church's life that was no business of the politicians. Archbishop Boisgelin for one was ready to accept substantial change, but the main point that underpinned his speech was that no human power was entitled to reorganise the Church without its consent, 'without recourse to the intervention of a national council or the head of the universal Church'. Clerical deputies rose to express adherence to Bonal of Clermont's declaration that, without such a gathering, he could not submit to any of the decrees the Assembly was about to enact.[11] In reply the veteran Jansenist lawyers Camus and Treilhard were adamant: 'The Church is part of the State. The State is not part of the Church', and the state could even change the religion of the French nation if that corresponded to the wishes of the majority. Such a rebuff to the clerical party did not succeed in silencing them, though debate turned out to be dominated by lay deputies, Camus above all, erudite and eloquent, appealing to 'the faithful witness of the Church's most glorious days'.[12] Only minor modifications were accepted, such as Martineau's recommendation for a cut in the scheduled number of seminaries.

The Bishop of Clermont was, by early June, emerging as the leader in the Assembly of clergy implacably opposed to elections as contrary to the decrees of the Council of Trent, and he led like-minded followers of the moderate Right out of the chamber in protest at the scheme. This approach played into the hands of the majority. Other, more tactically minded clergy opted to question less the principle of election than the qualification of the electors. Martineau fell back on the precedent of the primitive Church, and recommended that the laity should be the electors; a riposte from the abbé Jacquemart that this overlooked the practical point that laymen (especially Protestant laymen) were likely to select poorly qualified candidates caught the attention of uncommitted members of the Assembly, and the debate moved on to consider the possibility of a veto over the popular will as expressed in elections. Camus eventually persuaded a majority that the bishops could have a veto, but hedged around with restrictions to guard against abuse: it could only be on the grounds of doctrine and morals, and the rejected candidate had the right of appeal.

The lay proponents of reform were relying on the goodwill of these citizen-*curés*, trusting that the thrust of two related principles had become acceptable to all but the most reactionary clergymen: the irresistibility of the general will of France as expressed in the National Assembly and the inadmissibility of sectional interests. If these were not enough in themselves, there was always the appeal to self-interest, and pressure at parish level. Encouraged by the minimal public opposition to the earlier removal of the Church's landed and financial power, the assumption was that lay people at large would welcome a measure enacted in its name and in its supposed interest. This was seriously to misjudge the religious sympathies of the majority of French people, to confuse their habitual and often heart-felt allegiance to Catholicism with the undogmatic faith and anticlericalism of most deputies, often educated men with urban backgrounds who accepted at face value the Enlightenment commonplace that popular belief afforded excellent cover for unsavoury clerical manipulation. Quite apart from its arrant disrespect for majority feeling towards the French Catholic Church, this misreading of public opinion was to have terrible consequences in shattering the national consensus in favour of the Revolution.

A national council would once have attracted support from several vociferous lay Gallicans in the Assembly but, in the changed revolutionary world of 1790, they and the majority of deputies would not tolerate summoning an agency that would in effect constitute one of those corporate bodies abolished only a few months earlier, one possessing a veto over the legislature's wishes: the only genuine national council to their minds was the National Assembly itself. Besides which, the last national council had not been summoned since the days of the Valois monarchs, and argument on its composition could act as a drag-anchor on expediting implementation of the Civil Constitution. There was never any question of compromise in the interests of expediency, and lay deputies were encouraged in their intransigence by the hesitancy of some parish priests, who feared that a national council would be another General Assembly of the Clergy in all but name, one that would revive episcopal influence to an unacceptable degree, and would not speak for them.

Yet, having hitherto submitted to the changes imposed on their Order, the patriotic commitment of most clerical deputies had now reached breaking-point. The basic episcopal and parochial structures of the Church might survive the Civil Constitution, but what stunned a high proportion of the clergy was how emphatic the legal subordination of Church to State was turning out to be: the refusal of the Assembly to take soundings, let alone obtain the Church's formal consent to the edict, was a form of advance notice that the Church's voice would count for little in national decision-making. Put simply, without a national council, reformist-minded clerics with staunch Gallican credentials, ready to put aside their reservations and contemplate the implementation of the Civil Constitution, would have no alternative but to look to the papacy as a defence of last resort. It was a challenge the lay majority of the National Assembly were prepared to ignore when they approved the Civil Constitution on 12 July 1790.

II

Whatever its threat to the spititual independence of the Gallican Church, the passage of the Civil Constitution through the National Assembly did not prevent the Church from full involvement in the first anniversary celebrations of the Revolution, the so-called *Fête de la Fédération* of 14 July 1790, aptly described by William Doyle as 'perhaps the high-point of national consensus'.[13] In towns and cities throughout France that summer the clergy (including most of the bishops) celebrated masses, blessed flags, sang *Te Deums* and preached sermons saluting the achievements of the first year of the new order. Even a right-wing bishop like Louis de Conzié talked approvingly to the revolutionaries who had come to the service in Arras that 'religion recognises in you its worthy children':[14] he, like the rest, subscribed to a new solemn oath of allegiance, and kept quiet about the reservations he possessed about the revolutionary project. 'Our bishop is getting too involved in all this', grumbled some malcontents about the unashamedly patriotic La Font de Savine of Viviers,[15] but it was not a day for misgivings. At Sens, Archbishop Brienne and his nephew had arrived back from an extended stay in Italy in plenty of time to lead the celebrations on a day of concord.[16] Everywhere, there were diverting and impressive spectacles, often with a military as well as a religious character, well attended by the National Guard, bands playing and with altars made out of drums set up in the open air. The main national commemoration, in Paris, was led by Bishop Talleyrand of Autun, the revolutionaries' favourite prelate and the one most publicly committed to the work of the Assembly, his vestments an uncanonical medley of blue, red and white, but a powerful patriotic symbol of a union between Church and Revolution that the majority of French people still hoped for despite the Civil Constitution. He celebrated the divine mysteries in the pouring rain on the 'Altar of the Fatherland', where the iconographic symbols were more constitutional than Catholic, a relegation that reflected the underlying rationale of the occasion: revolutionary renewal in oath-taking led by the King and Lafayette rather than a conventional ceremony of state with the celebration of the Mass as its centrepiece. Nevertheless, the deluge could not dispell the patriotic fervour of the crowds packing the Champ de Mars, who were told by the Bishop to 'Sing and weep tears of joy, for on this day France has been made anew.'

The revolutionaries preferred to suppose that the approval of a calculating maverick like Talleyrand was tantamount to endorsement by the entire Church of all that had happened over the last year. That was far from the case. Distrust of the revolutionary authorities was rising at every level in the Church by midsummer, though it was not appreciable enough to dent the trust of most of the *curés* in the work of the Assembly. Those in the sacred ministry who held secular office in local government worked hard at conciliation among their fellow citizens; at La Rochelle, on 20 June 1790, Bishop Coucy, an elector himself, who had been asked 'to thank the Supreme

Being' for the settling of a dispute over local representation, celebrated a Mass at which not just the *Te Deum* was sung but the appropriate motet, '*Ecce quam bonum et quam jucundum habitare fratres in
unum*'.[18] [Behold, how good and how pleasant it is to live in unity
with our brothers].

Those higher clergy without any such responsibilities were under
no patriotic constraints. 'What is there', demanded the Bishop of
Toulon, 'of this regeneration you have been solemnly promised?
Instead of the happiness you want to enjoy, I can only see confusion,
disorder, and anarchy everywhere.'[19] This sourness verging on despair was spreading. Among other members of the episcopate, there
were such as Godart de Belbeuf, who in his cathedral at Avranches
made clear that he could not tolerate any circumscription of the
Church's spiritual authority while, not far away, in Lisieux, Bishop
de la Ferronnays, whose pastoral energies in 1790 were in evidence
across his diocese, was ordered to appear before a tribunal with his
secretary to face accusations of inciting his flock to rebellion through
his words and actions; in Bourges the authorities reported talk among
the *curés* of how religion was '*perdue*', and their growing readiness to
fight the religious work of the National Assembly.[20] The mood intensified and spread in early autumn once the euphoria of the patriotic
fête had ended. Clergy had time to contemplate the future order of
the French Church that politicians would impose on them. Lay deputies had noted the long faces of the bishops even before the Civil
Constitution passed, and Boisgelin told his former mistress how much
he stood to lose: 'All is lost. I will have 30 000 livres annually, and
nothing more. Nothing for all my abbeys, nothing unless I reside in
my diocese, nothing but dependency on the municipal government.'[21] The changes would have huge logistical implications, and
throw many in the Church out of work. For many of them – canons,
monks, nuns and nearly fifty bishops – there would be minimal
future in the streamlined hierarchical scheme, and they were faced
with the straight choice of resistance or acceptance. Including the
women members, nearly three-fifths of the entire religious corps
would find themselves pushed out of their former positions, a massive
reduction in personnel that in itself could be expected to curtail clerical influence in national life.

Much still depended on how the Civil Constitution was enacted:
the likelihood in July 1790 was that even without a national council
all bishops and clergy would have little alternative except to go

along with the changes, with the best hope for concessions lying in pressure exerted on the Assembly as a condition of acceptance by Louis XVI and the Pope. One consideration working towards acceptance of the Civil Constitution was the strong possibility that rejection or non-cooperation by the clergy might lead the French Church into schism, for it was still assumed that Pius VI would accept legislation passed by the Assembly and approved by the King.

Though Cardinal Bernis, the ambassador in Rome, made comforting suggestions that 'The Pope asks nothing better than for wisdom and moderation to prevail in what happens in France',[22] the reality was that Pius was making last-minute private efforts to hold up the passing of the Civil Constitution, in which he saw a renewal of the Jansenist challenge.[23] He warned Louis in a private letter of 10 July that acceptance would 'lead the entire nation into error, the kingdom into schism, and perhaps be the cause of a cruel civil war'. The despatch reached the King too late to influence his conduct. Anxious not to strike a discordant note during the festival month of July, Louis had accepted the advice of bishops close to the court (especially the two episcopal ministers, Archbishops Champion de Cicé and Le Franc de Pompignan), and granted his preliminary sanction to the measures contained in the Civil Constitution on 22 July. He included a memorandum from them in his private letter to the Pope of 20 July 1790 announcing his intention of accepting the decree, though refusing formal promulgation until 'necessary measures' had been taken, a clear hint at the need for the papacy's consent. Three days later, to their mutual embarrassment, Louis received Pius's uncompromising letter of 10 July, in which he warned the king and his ministers that approval would lead the kingdom into schism and error, and probably cause a civil war. Ineffective diplomatic liaison between the two powers, for which the papal nuncio in Paris (who hoped Pius would agree to the proposals) and the French ambassador in Rome, Cardinal Bernis (a barely concealed opponent of the changes) must bear some responsibility,[24] now caused a serious misreading of each other's approaches. Thus the uncompromising firmness of Pius VI surprised the king and his advisers, and had the unexpected and unintentional effect of – officially, at least – aligning the monarchy alongside the National Assembly against the pope.

The chances were that even if Pius rejected the Civil Constitution it would still be imposed on the Church, but nonetheless the new legislation had increased his consultative importance, certainly for those (still a minority) who hoped the papacy would lead the fight against it, and rally those Gallicans who in the last analysis would prefer cooperation with the Holy See rather than with the National Assembly. Throughout July and August the Vatican received much unsolicited advice from senior French churchmen like Archbishop Boisgelin (who was ready to travel personally to Rome)[25] to the effect that there was more to be gained by working with the new order than lost by rebelling against it. Adoption by the Pope of the Civil Constitution would be a magnanimous gesture of conciliation and one advocated by the Archbishop of Auch in a letter for his whole province.[26] The Keeper of the Seals, Archbishop Champion de Cicé, received daily delegations from the Assembly in his office demanding promulgation of the Civil Constitution, and reluctantly advised colleagues in government that the King was in no position to reject it outright, so that the most practical policy was for Pius to go back on the private letter of 10 July; his colleague, Le Franc de Pompignan, mortally ill, demurred. But the Pope was anyway not inclined to retract. The most he was prepared to do at this stage was, as he made clear to the French administration, to ask for an official report on events from the assembled cardinalate in Rome, and make no pronouncement until they had made their recommendations.

In Paris, under the pressure from the constitution-makers in the Assembly and the impatience of revolutionary sympathisers every-where, Louis XVI was permitted no such interlude for reflection and deferment. As a monarch whose reign indicated the high serious-ness with which he took his consecrated role as most Christian king, the upholder of the one apostolic faith in France, signalling his assent to the document caused him the gravest misgivings. But undue delay might imperil his tenure of the throne in favour of a Regency in the name of either his six-year-old son, his brother Provence or his cousin Orléans. On 24 August 1790 he formally promulgated the Civil Con-stitution, and it was widely – and wrongly – assumed the papacy must have endorsed his action. By that date, Bernis had increased the Holy Father's appreciation of the French King's distress at the pace of events (Louis had himself pointedly told the Pope on 28 July that 'Your Holiness knows better than anyone how important it is to conserve the cords which unite France to the holy see.')[27] On 22 Sep-tember Pius sent a papal brief to Louis which still condemned the

Civil Constitution, but couched his words in a concerned, paternal tone, and made it clear he reserved his final verdict until the judgment of Congregation, expected in November.

III

Many committed churchmen outside the Assembly, and the articulate conservatives within it, notably Archbishop Boisgelin and the abbé Maury, were dismayed by the King's precipitance. While they appreciated the pressures on Louis, they had still hoped for more of a breathing space between the Civil Constitutions's passage through the Assembly and its receiving the royal assent, time they could have used in a last-minute bid to extract concessions from the majority of deputies. Suddenly, the measure was law, and while the more *politique* clerics in the Assembly clung to the fading hope that moderation might achieve some acknowledgement from the politicians, the new law soon became a cause to unite the Right together. In newspapers and pamphlets they denounced the Assembly's Civil Constitution as an unwarranted intrusion into the spiritual sphere amounting to an annexation of the Catholic faith. 'What they call the Civil Constitution of the Clergy', stormed the leading royalist journalist the abbé Royou in his paper the *Ami du Roi* in November 1790, 'is really just the complete overthrow of the hierarchy and the spiritual discipline of the Church.'[28] Nothing caused more consternation than the electoral stipulation. There were precedents for popular election in the early Church – the legislation even contained a scriptural reference to the Acts of the Apostles – but times had changed, as one clerical deputy from Anjou expostulated:

> Where the name of Christian was synonomous with saint, when the faithful, united by charity, formed one single family of brothers, when their ambitions rose no higher than their yearning for a martyr's crown – then you could have confided to the people the duty of choosing their Pastors.[29]

Such writings and speeches gave voice to widespread misgivings and swelled the numbers of those who could, with increasing accuracy, be labelled as counter-revolutionaries. Conversely, the proponents of the Civil Constitution were increasingly inclined to treat it as a test of loyalty to the Revolution as a whole. They were vexed by the tendency of most bishops and clergy in the early autumn of 1790 to carry on their work as if the legislation had no bearing on their pastoral and administrative lives, seeking the false security of voluntary marginalisation.

Not all the hierarchy omitted to address the issue. The Bishop of Quimper had publicly stated his opposition to the Civil Constitution – and indeed everything recently overthrown that the 'wisdom of the centuries had established' – as early as 18 June (with his Breton colleague at St Pol-de-Léon he also begged the Pope for advice);[30] the Bishop of Toulon followed in July, then other colleagues in August including d'Aviau of Vienne and Machault of Amiens. On 22 September that embodiment of episcopal pomp and worldliness in the pre-revolutionary Church, Archbishop Dillon, protested in 'honour and conscience' to Louis XVI that it was 'impossible to acquiesce in the archiepiscopal and primatial see of Narbonne becoming, without any canonical form, the suffragan bishopric of another see'.[31] Another thorn in the side of the revolutionaries, Bishop Le Mintier of Tréguier, produced a pastoral letter on 14 September that took the blackest view of things, speaking of:

> The most illustrious throne in the world shaken to its foundations ... laws without strength and vigour, authority in the hands of the multitude ... the Church fallen into degradation and servitude, its ministers threatened with reduction to the condition of appointed officials [commis] ...[32]

If this militancy and despondency was still a minority option, so was episcopal willingness to prepare dioceses for the implementation of the legislation. It happened at Auch and Béziers, but these were rare instances. More in keeping with majority prelatical opinion was the 'Pastoral Instruction on the Spiritual Authority' letter drawn up by Jean-René Asseline of Boulogne in conjunction with about forty colleagues and published on 23 October inviting the laity to respect all the Assembly had decreed in the temporal sphere, but declaring that the Civil Constitution was trespassing on the spiritual domain. The letter was widely circulated. Encouraged by this manifesto of their colleagues in the dioceses, clerical leaders in the Assembly decided on action.

On 30 October 1790, thirty bishops from the Assembly produced an *Exposition of Principles* drawn up substantially by Boisgelin which explained why they (and 98 other clerical deputies who also signed) had voted against the Civil Constitution. It was a moderately worded document, but insistent that the Church must be consulted through either a council or the Pope. Without these provisions, talk of dismissing bishops whose dioceses had been abolished was meaningless:

> A bishop contracts with his church an alliance constituted by God Himself; it is not human force, but the divine authority conferred on the Church that can shatter the bonds of this irrevocable link, for the greater good of religion.[33]

If the Assembly ignored this reality, the authors of the *Exposition* insisted, then the election of bishops and priests would have no canonical validity, and those who collaborated in such proceedings risked excommunication. Passive resistance was recommended to parish clergy.

The *Exposition* was an exercise in pastoral leadership that played an important part in making lower clergy think hard about their response, especially as the bishops tantalisingly offered the parish clergy a direct say in filling benefices themselves instead of leaving it to the vagaries of a lay electorate.[34] With 119 prelates adhering to it, it may be seen as a final flourish of traditional Gallican leadership, uncompromising in its assertion of episcopal power (the new councils to advise bishops were strongly resisted),[35] one that drew much praise from the lower clergy like those in Saintes, who gave thanks for their bishop's unbending conduct and talked 'of doing ourselves the glory of imitating you as our model, and of following you as our guide in the current crisis ...'.[36] The *Exposition* was also intended to pre-empt papal intervention to ensure that the controversy aroused by the Civil Constitution could be settled internally. Failing that, it had the effect of an authoritative pronouncement in lieu of the Pope – and could hurry him into breaking his ostentatious public silence.

The absence of clerical cooperation ensured that there would be no peaceful transition to a new order, and with ministers holding back as long as they dared in sending the decree down to the districts, in many *départements* the new law was not even published before

September or October. The *Exposition* was treated by local authorities as a seditious, unpatriotic tract, one which actually provoked them to begin enforcing the Civil Constitution. Typical was the administration in the Bouches-du-Rhône *département*, which on 10 November decreed that 'no one could doubt any longer that most bishops have formed a seditious league in order to light up the torch of fanaticism everywhere and attempt a counter-revolution by this means'.[37] Cathedral chapters were forcibly dissolved, Notre-Dame de Paris in November, but others like Bourges, Sées and Troyes held out under pressure from the local authorities until January 1791. Vociferous protests as at Lyon, Arras, Rouen, Saint-Omer and Tours went unheard. Intimidation, even the use of force, was always a possibility as clergy provoked clashes with officialdom backed by the National Guard, those custodians of the revolutionary settlement who saw their task as upholding national sovereignty against 'officials' – in this case, priests – who would hold 'the general will in bondage'.[38] In October and early November 1790 the first departmental bishops were elected to vacancies caused by deaths. Expilly, a radical *curé*, deputy and member of the Ecclesiastical Committee that had drafted the Civil Constitution, was elected to the vacant see of Quimper in the Finistère on 1 November: a plea by a neighbouring bishop for deferral until the Pope had pronounced was ignored, though Archbishop Champion de Cicé, desperate for an accommodation, even offered to act as an intermediary with Rome to achieve papal sanction.[39] His offer had little relevance to the situation on the ground, where the Bishop of Rennes, Bareau de Girac (Expilly's metropolitan according to the Civil Constitution) both refused to confirm the intruder, and infuriated the new local authority by insisting they were altering parish boundaries without consulting the bishops, as legislation of 14–15 November 1790 allegedly provided.[40] Feeling its authority insulted, the Assembly decreed that any prelate could in future undertake canonical confirmation.[41]

Only exceptionally were there signs of voluntary cooperation. The Archbishop of Besançon and the Bishops of Vannes, Perpignan, Langres, Blois, Chartres, Rodez and Saint-Malo took the first tentative steps towards organising their dioceses along the lines stipulated in the Civil Constitution, as at Orléans, where Bishop Jarente the younger (a future juror) had named fourteen vicars-general as his new episcopal council, or at Sens.[42] Otherwise, local pressure on the clergy to conform could only be screwed up more tightly still. Bonal,

Bishop of Clermont, used the language of patriotism to express his unhappiness at the coercion experienced by the Church:

> There is no citizen more decided than myself in setting an example of fidelity to the nation, the law, and the King, but there is also no bishop convinced than me that it would be to betray the sacred responsibility of the Church if we anticipate its judgment on the reorganisation of the Church according to the Constitution.[43]

Few of the higher clergy were prepared to articulate such conciliatory sentiments. Persuaded by the *Exposition* after earlier wavering, Archbishop La Tour du Pin of Auch professed himself, like most colleagues, willing to respect temporal power in its legitimate sphere, but excoriated its abuse in the Civil Constitution, which was schismatic and heretical in its entirety: 'I could not even provisionally admit the least part of it, however innocent it may be in appearance, because one cannot compromise with error.'[44] Clermont-Tonnerre of Châlons-sur-Marne was determined to let his clergy know in no uncertain terms, even to a second edition of a pastoral letter published on 23 December. He denounced the whole heretical enterprise as one that 'denatures ecclesiastical government and transports a form of of republican government to it', so that 'episcopal authority and teaching will be concentrated in a presbyterian assembly', while to that error the Bishop of Angoulême added Lutheranism and Richerism.[45]

Many deputies in the National Assembly were as impatient with the resistance of the clergy as they were with the delays and silence of Pius VI. To force the issue, Voidel on 26 November 1790 proposed that all clergy exercising public functions be made to swear an oath of undivided loyalty to the Constitution within eight days, or risk dismissal with attendant of loss of pension and civic rights. Deputies applauded this tough stance as a means of showing the need for all sections of the population to respect the law, but some members of the Ecclesiastical Committee (as opposed to the more radical Committees for Research and Reports, which had taken this initiative) sounded a cautionary note. Cazalès, for instance, warned of the emerging threat to public order from the unrest provoked in the provinces by promulgation of the Civil Constitution; Bonal, made another plea for a national council, insisting that the Constititution might be called 'civil' but that it was really concerned with spiritual matters. His pleas brought like-minded deputies to their feet in applause, but this last-minute bid was no more successful than earlier ones. It sounded to many of his hearers too much like special pleading on behalf of an episcopal elite compromised by its association with the monarchy and unable to adjust to the new order.

Louis XVI did nothing precipitant for another month. Well aware of the widespread clerical discontent at having the Civil Constitution foisted upon them, the King was loathe to make himself the instrument for ensuring that there would be by oath no escape from the measure. His determination was reinforced by the guilt he felt for his promulgation of the Civil Constitution the previous August.[46] And from the countryside, the uncompromising pronouncements of the hierarchy testified to their unhappiness over the oath decreed on 27 November. On 21 December, Bishop Polignac of Meaux drew up a formal declaration refusing the oaths, though he for the time being deferred publication, hoping the crisis would pass. Six days earlier, at Sées in Normandy, the *département* of the Orne had received the negative response of Bishop du Plessis d'Argentré. They were so desperate to obtain his consent that they were ready to admit all the restrictions he adjudged necessary on the oath, but that was still not enough to win him over.[47]

So much hinged on whether Pius VI would or would not 'baptise' the Civil Constitution, but there was little chance of that happening in the light of the Congregation's unanimous recommendation of 27 October that the pope should not disguise to the King the extent to which the new decree contradicted the principles of the Catholic religion. It was not quite the end to hopes of a compromise. A commission of Cardinals had begun to meet in September to advise the Holy Father on an authoritative pronouncement, but their report was not expected before the spring,[48] and Pius was not in the interim prepared to act on the unofficial advice still coming from Archbishop Boisgelin, who, in a memorandum of early December, pressed Pius to accept the reforms and counsel Louis to make a provisional acceptance of the Civil Constitution or risk imminent schism. With the Pope disinclined to hurry and the diplomatic correspondence leaving little room for doubt about his inclinations, Louis again risked his patriotic credibility by resort to delaying tactics, so that on 23 December Camus asked in the Assembly why Louis had not promulgated the decree requiring the oath to be taken. Camus tried to frighten the king with talk of the damage that would be inflicted on royal authority if the Assembly was obliged to disregard Louis's inaction. The king sensed he could hold out no longer against the Assembly's pressure, and he fatalistically submitted on 26 December, believing that events would soon come to a head irrespective of his part: 'I had much rather be king of Metz than stay the king of France in this position, but it will all finish soon.'[49]

Debate on the oath started the next day, when the abbés Grégoire and Gouttes and sixty other clerical deputies took the oath. It was a disappointingly low figure for proponents of the Civil Constitution, an indicator that the number prepared to sign up was less than anticipated. Cazalès's request that clergy in the Assembly be given more time to make up their minds was only partly heeded, and Bishop Bonal's plea on 2 January 1791 that a rider be added to the oath 'excepting formally those matters which essentially depend on spiritual authority' was dismissed without hearing the full contents of the speech he had prepared. His protestations that he would adhere to all strictly civil decrees and the other bishops rising in their places to show their support of his principles was a dramatic highpoint of the proceedings:

> You have declared that all power comes from the nation; from that, you have concluded that the title of the public functionaries of the Church comes from the same source. If it was thus, we would be left only with a human religion, a religion of circumstances, a religion for *politiques*.[50]

This frustrated eloquence achieved nothing. On the afternoon of 4 January the clerical deputies were finally called upon to subscribe individually to the new law by taking the oath to the Civil Constitution of the Clergy without any qualifications. With these ruled out, oath-taking had been turned into a deceptively simple public test of acceptance or non-acceptance of the Assembly's sovereignty and thereby of the Revolution as a whole. Undeterred by the crowds outside roaring for the heads of non-jurors, the majority of higher clergy adhered to the position they had stated two months earlier in the *Exposition*: without independent sanction by a national council or the papacy, the Civil Constitution could have no validity. One by one, pointedly called in order of surname rather than diocese, each of the 44 prelates in the Assembly refused to take the oath, with the conspicuous exception of Talleyrand of Autun, casting himself as episcopal chaplain to the Revolution,[51] and Gobel, the coadjutor Bishop of Basle. The refusal of the majority was undeniably principled, and though it consigned them to political insignificance and material impoverishment, it was a sign of moral leadership, one to which many lower clergy were responsive.

If the rejection of the oath by the bishops and other higher clergy remaining in the Assembly was predictable, somewhat less foreseeable were the numerous non-jurors among the parish priests. No group suffered greater agonising over the issue than them. Enthusiasts for the Revolution from the start, as instrumental as any in breaking the impasse of June 1789 over verification of powers, the unwillingness of the Assembly in 1790 to respect the integrity of the Catholic heritage in France had for them irrevocably tarnished the appeal of the role of citizen-*curé*. The issue of the oath put them on the spot about the priority of their allegiance to Church and State. Only 109 in the National Assembly were ready to fall into line and continue 'loyal' to the Revolution, which left about 40 per cent as a very appreciable minority of non-jurors, in the end unswayed by the pleas of the Feuillant leader, Barnave. They felt that to take the oath without amendment would be an unacceptable denial of their sacerdotal standing, and they were ready to follow the episcopal example. As the abbé Fournés put it, 'I will say with the simplicity of the first Christians: I do myself honour and glory by following my bishop, just like the deacon Laurence followed his pastor.'[52] So many stood up and made these little speeches that left-wing deputies insisted they should simply stick to either 'I swear' or 'I refuse'. Far too many chose the latter for the Left's liking, effectively disowning the revolutionary achievement to date because they found the imposition of the Civil Constitution on a reluctant Church intolerable. There was a sense that this commitment to principle had restored self-respect. According to Jacques Emery of Saint-Sulpice, 'This sitting is the triumph of the Church of of France; we must conserve its memory and celebrate its anniversary.'[53]

The total number of clergy in the National Assembly accepting the oath amounted to just over one-third.[54] The initial response of the revolutionaries was one of anger and frustration. Thomas Lindet, a future member of the Committee of Public Safety, insisted 4 January ought to be called 'The Day of Dupes', with 'the Clergy in general the dupe of the nobility; many poor *curés* the dupes of the bishops, and the bishops the dupes of their vanity'.[55] Yet soon the practical

implications of this degree of non-cooperation caused the most strident advocates of the oath to pause. Barnave put and carried the
motion that non-juring clergy were to be deprived of office, but then
the Ecclesiastical Committee went to work to produce a gloss
on the oath in line with Mirabeau's emollient speech of 14 January
(some suspected he was selling out to the Right) distinguishing the
private expression of religion, which was no concern of the Assembly's, from the public worship that was within the law's reach.
A week earlier he had proposed that bishops need have only five years
of pastoral experience, not fifteen, that the episcopate be open to
clergy with any sort of public ministerial experience rather than just
the pastoral, and had even lured former monks to become secular
priests with the bait of retaining half their pension! The Assembly
was becoming desperate.

Other members insisted that Roman Catholicism was a faith
established by God, that the Assembly was not trying to interfere
in spiritual matters and that its only concern was the public good.
Such an explanation did not survive close scrutiny, or change attitudes on either side towards the oath. Unwilling to offend the clear
majority of laymen in favour of the measure, on 26 January the
Ecclesiastical Committee moved to replace the non-juring clergy.
Cazalès intervened yet again with a plea to suspend the decree and
made dire predictions of what could lie ahead if the Pope finally condemned the Civil Constitution and most Catholics obeyed him: these
refractories would wage war on their excommunicated successors,
and the cause of the faith would become a rallying point for counter-
revolutionaries throughout France. He warned 'If your laws can only
be executed by force, beware of the convulsions that will drown
France in blood.'[56] Such talk was readily dismissed as extremist by
majority opinion, unwilling to accept the extent to which religion
was shattering the national consensus and making opposition to
the Revolution popular for the first time. The right-wing champion Maury wanted to bring issues to a head. 'We need your decree,'
he wrote sardonically, 'we love your decrees, give us two or three
more of them.'

The crisis of the Revolution – centred around religion – was at
hand, and was finally precipitated by the consecration of the first
Constitutional bishops on 24 February 1791 in the Parisian church
of the Oratory in the rue Saint-Honoré – Mgrs Expilly and Marolle
for the *départements* of the Finistère and the Aisne respectively. Despite

the fact that he had resigned his see of Autun a month earlier, Talleyrand offered his episcopal services when no other diocesan bishop would agree to consecrate prelates committed to the new Church order. Assisted by two coadjutor bishops, Talleyrand followed the correct rite to the letter, except for the reading of the pontifical bulls and the taking of the oath of fidelity to the Pope.[57] Had he not volunteered to act and do so in accordance with protocol, the Constitutional Church either could not have started or else could have done so only having shown to its adversaries that it cared nothing for the Catholic doctrine of apostolic succession within the episcopate. Talleyrand was villified for putting his office as bishop at the service of the new regime, a display of energy that further confirmed his reputation as a figure capable of Judas-like treacheries, but the non-jurors had to accept that their dispossession was only a matter of time, with about sixty new bishops installed and at work by the end of April. As much as any other development, this one obliged the Pope to break his public silence.[58]

'Take care, gentlemen,' Maury had warned the National Assembly back in November 1790, 'it is dangerous to make martyrs', but the advice was not heeded as the fault lines among French Catholics widened every day, and some influential right-wing journalists like Royou positively welcomed them, acclaiming 4 January as one on which the Gallican Church had shown itself 'triumphant and covered in an immortal glory'.[59] The split among the deputies of the former First Estate in the National Assembly would be mirrored across France, and bears out Timothy Tackett's proposition that the oath turned a crisis into a disaster. The bishops and a sizable proportion of priest deputies had been eager, even desperate for compromise, but that word was not a favoured one in the patriotic vocabulary in the winter of 1790-1. Even the Protestant Rabaut de Saint-Etienne had his misgivings about the way the Civil Constitution threatened concord, writing in late 1790:

> The National Assembly would have done better not to have concerned itself so much, because every profession should organise itself as it wishes, subject to government inspection. It has exposed itself to the danger of recreating in another form the corps that it destroyed under another.[60]

Rabaut's perceptiveness was lost on most deputies. As spokesman for a sovereign nation, the Assembly felt itself unable to compromise its standing by acknowledging that the Roman Catholic Church too (even its Gallican branch) had a supranational dimension and a claim to universal sovereignty based on its divine commission. The compulsory imposition of the oath on a reluctant clergy completed the collapse of the historic Gallican Church by the creation of a state Church to replace a Church-state partnership; under the new, militantly Erastian arrangement, the reconstructed state was not defending the Church, but annexing it and opting for a 'brusque and busybodying interference in the pastoral life of the Church'.[61] Those who mourned its loss would have to look outside France for allies in any work of restoration, above all to the papacy, raising the distinct possibility that Pius VI might have the chance to regain a degree of influence in Gallican affairs that had not been known for centuries. The Roman Catholic Church and the Revolution were beginning to pull in separate directions, and in those circumstances the presentation of the Revolution as a virtual 'civil religion' with its own allegiances would develop apace.[62]

Disputes over religion had thus destroyed the revolutionary consensus of 1789, but the responsibility for that divergence lay squarely at the door of the politicians in the National Assembly responsible for policy choices. The *cahiers* had made clear the hopes the French public held out for religious reform and renewal. That is incontestable. Such prospects were seen as part of revolution, not at odds with it, and, had the two remained in alliance beyond the first eighteen months, events would have taken a more moderate course and scores of thousands of lives would have been saved. Instead, influenced by anticlericalist commonplaces and the new Rousseauist antipathy to any form of corporate survival, the National Assembly had imposed a unilateral reform on the Gallican Church in the shape of the Civil Constitution. The irony is that, instead of splitting down the middle on the issue, the Church might have assented to the Civil Constitution had it been permitted a *collective* response. Instead, the Assembly insisted on *individual* affirmations through the oath stipulated in November 1790, and it was, at least initially, as much this denial of the Church's continuing corporate character as the legislation itself that was unacceptable to nearly half the ordained ministry. Thus the Civil Constitution, because of the way it was passed, promulgated and imposed, performed the minor miracle of splitting residual Jansenist opinion, Gallican opinion (as between royal and parlementary Gallicanism and ecclesiastical or conciliar

Gallicanism), and, thereby, even 'enlightened' Catholic opnion. As Langlois has argued, the policies of the National Assembly were based in two contradictory logics: the logic of laicisation and the logic of total inclusion. Both could not coherently be supported as the Church could not be both excluded and included in the new nation.[64]

Gallicanism foundered on the rock of the Civil Constitution and so did the nationwide endorsement of the Revolution in 1789–90.[63] Deputies were already sufficiently remote from the people whose sovereignty they exercised not to see how deeply popular attachments continued to the Catholic religion; half the nation, when in practical terms presented with the choice between the preference of the National Assembly for a subordinate Church, and the preference of the clergy for an arrangement negotiated with Assembly and papacy that preserved their integrity, opted for the latter. Faced with what was crudely reduced to a stark choice between religion and revolution, half the adult population (and the great majority of women) rejected revolution. It was a contingent parting of the ways, but one freighted with significance.

Part III From Schism to Terror, 1791–5

8 Church, State and Revolution, 1791–5

The 1791 Constitution reserved for the Constitutional Church an honorary supremacy, and insisted that France remained officially a Christian state. That presumption was placed under intolerable strain after the abolition of the monarchy in August 1792 and the execution of the King five months later. Instead of upholding what in effect was the rump of the Gallican Church that had remained loyal to the Revolution, the new republic, in a dramatic display of the assertive authority constantly displayed towards the sacerdotal order since beginning of the Revolution, turned against its creature. In 1793 the state completely severed its ties with the historic faith. It subjected the Constitutional Church as well as non-jurors, Protestants and Jews to persecution, while encouraging dechristianisation and working to stir up popular interest in revolutionary cults. This overt hostility to the Judaeo-Christian heritage in France lasted for two years until the post-Thermidorian regime declared its religious neutrality and affirmed the principle of religious toleration in 1795. This chapter looks in outline at those four middle years of the Revolution (1791–5), and the background to changes that led the state from supporting the new, streamlined Constitutional Church to outright hostility to all forms of Christianity. The four subsequent chapters deal with the extent to which the religious groupings accommodated themselves to the rapidly changing character of the Revolution in the same period.

I

From 1791 French Roman Catholics – notably the 80 per cent of the population resident in the countryside – had a choice of two Churches: either the Constitutional one imposed by the National Assembly, or the refractory alternative clandestinely organised and subject to bouts of prosecution from the authorities. Faced with this unprecedented level of religious change that went far beyond their

165

preferences as expressed in the *cahiers* of 1789, it is not surprising if the reaction of the laity was predominantly one of bewilderment and anxiety. Yet scholars have tended to write about the religious history of the early 1790s as if the options for the people in the parishes were clear-cut. One can indeed point to areas like the Vendée or the Dauphiné where preferences at local level were immediately obvious. Such regions were in fact exceptional. In general, the business of opting for one allegiance or another became an embarrassing imposition for all but the most politically committed Catholics; evidence suggests that in most regions of France a sizeable number turned up at *both* juring and non-juring services in 1791-2, possibly as a response to pressure from inside their families. It was in some respects the lay equivalent of the obfuscatory expedients to the oath found among the clergy. The situation remained volatile throughout the next four years, with loyalties varying, unstable and unpredictable. Three significant changes were apparent over this period. First, it became increasingly dangerous to attend worship conducted by refractory priests, let alone shelter them; second, the Constitutional Church tended to implode as the First Republic disinherited this revolutionary creation and its leaders abandoned it for non-Christian alternatives; and, third, communities learnt to organise and express their faith without priests of any sort, drawing on the continuing vitality of a religious culture that neither the Counter-Reformation nor the Revolution had succeeded in standardising.

These developments were barely discernible in the early part of 1791, as local authorities began the task of ordering bishops and priests to take the oath to the Civil Constitution – or face the consequences of dismissal from office and eviction from their homes. Clerics' futures depended on the choice they made, and parishioners could decisively influence priestly decisions: where the final outcome was unacceptable to the parish – as it was in thousands of cases – the repercussions for religious stability were enormous. For most people, certainly those living in the remote countryside, nothing brought home the intrusive power of the revolutionary state more than the departure of one parish priest and the arrival of his successor: local circumstances dictated whether or not there would be a welcome.

Modern historians are in no doubt that this whole process marks both a crucial rending of the Catholic fabric of France and a watershed in the experience of Revolution. Claude Langlois can write of the oath as the 'sacrament' of the Revolution, a vital stage in tranferring notions of sacredness from Church to the revolutionary state. William Doyle, in declaring the oath of the clergy to be 'if not the greatest [turning-point], unquestionably one of them,'[1] is one among many writers who look upon the process as a divisive mistake, an end product in church legislation passed by the Assembly that, in Gwynne Lewis's words, 'produced a seismic fault in the political geology of the French Revolution',[2] where the divisions within the National Assembly were reflected across the whole of France.

There is much to be said for this reading of the Civil Constitution as an unhappy and avoidable blunder, but caution is required. It tends to underestimate the extent to which revolutionaries had by 1791 developed their own distinctive programme and built on loyalties that, fuelled by conventional Enlightenment common places, looked upon the Catholic Church as a formidable rival whose influence in the state would inevitably have to be confronted. Yet whatever the hopes of the Constitutional clergy for a convergence of revolutionary and Christian values, the fact is that in promulgating the Civil Constitution, the Assembly seriously underestimated the continuing power of the French Catholic Church, two years into the Revolution. It still commanded the affections of the vast majority of the population, and nourished them with a scheme of salvation that overlay the rhetoric of Revolution. The sympathies of his flock could not easily be ignored by their priest when he decided whether or not to swear. Oath-taking became, in effect, a referendum on whether one's first loyalties were to Catholicism or to the Revolution. The result was a body of clerical opposition to the oath (and, by extension, the Revolution) sufficiently representative of the clergy as a whole as to make the entire order vulnerable sooner or later as symbols of Counter-Revolution.

As early as 23 February, in a letter reproaching Archbishop Brienne for taking the oath, the Supreme Pontiff had signalled his condemnation of the Revolution in its approach to religion: 'Who cannot see that along with the other novelties it [the Civil Constitution] introduces, it overthrows absolutely the authority of the Church and annihilates all its rights?'[3] Then, on 10 March, Pius VI despatched a Brief, *Quod aliquantum*, to the bishops who had signed the *Exposition of Principles*. While it did not contain a formal condemnation of the Civil Constitution – indeed he called on the French episcopate to suggest to him a means of conciliation that would infringe neither dogma nor discipline – there was much swingeing criticism both of that enactment and of the revolutionary principles articulated in the Declaration of the Rights of Man, 'establishing among men this liberty and equality which appears to stifle reason' and which destroyed the subordination needed for social harmony.[4] The breach of the 1516 Concordat elicited the Pope's robust protest, as did the abolition of monastic orders, while the election of new bishops was bluntly labelled 'sacrilege'.[5] Pius followed this up on 13 April with a formal request to the episcopate not to take the oath, a fairly redundant exercise in itself since, denied a consultative role by the Assembly, most had no intention of doing so; clergy who had taken the oath were allowed a fortnight's grace in which to retract or be excommunicated. All the papal texts were not published or available for the wider public until issued in the Brief *Caritas quae* on 4 May, by which date positions on both sides were becoming entrenched. That document gave juring priests forty days to recant or lose the Roman Church's recognition. Any possibility that Papal hostility could prompt moderation in official policy was soon shown to be unrealistic when the supporters of the Civil Constitution ran together two inconsistent responses: insisting, on the one hand, that the briefs were forgeries, and, on the other, working hard to prevent their distribution.[6] Meanwhile, the National Assembly reopened the issue of annexing Avignon, and turned a blind eye to the Parisian crowds burning Pius in effigy as the 'ogre of the Tiber' with 'Fanaticism, Civil War' inscribed around the guy's neck. Renegotiation of the Civil Constitution was out of the question: the new French envoy to the papacy, the comte de Ségur, was not recognised by Pius, who also ordered the withdrawal of the Nuncio, Mgr Dugnani, from France in late May. The rupture was complete.

The Assembly's firm anti-papal line contrasted with softer tendencies in its religious policies in the first half of 1791. If there was no intention of altering the stipulation of the previous November 1790, that all clergy must take the oath to the Civil Constitution, some deputies were unhappy that the intolerant denial of rights to freedom of worship to non-jurors might conflict with Article 4 of the Declaration of the Rights of Man and so cause the Assembly to be in breach of the law as well as its principles. Others had grown irresolute in the face of opposition to the oath, and began to contemplate concessions. There had been some earlier tokens of this trend. On 21 January the National Assembly published an *instruction* on the Civil Constitution which, while reiterating its right to make the law on the civil organisation of the clergy and determining their relationship with the political order, nevertheless insisted that the representatives of the French people were attached to the Catholic Church and that it was not in the Assembly's power to limit its spiritual authority. Such a declaration still sounded hollow to those non-jurors who, on 27 January, were automatically deprived of their posts. Despite the provocation, episcopal deputies opted to stay on in the National Assembly, as pressures on all the bishops to conform to the Civil Constitution mounted. Moderate supporters of the Civil Constitution moved to contain the ardour of 'Patriots' and thereby hoped to mollify the dwindling number of ex-First Estate deputies still carrying out their legislative duties. Thus no action was taken when Cardinal La Rochefoucauld prohibited two Constitutional priests from preaching and hearing confessions. On 11 April 1791 the municipality of Paris conditionally lifted restrictions on exclusive use of the city's churches for the Constitutional clergy. Prompted by Bailly and Lafayette, they permitted the hire of buildings for worship by any sect, so long as the hirers attached a notice to the premises declaring their authorised presence and abstained from attacking the Constitution.

There were other signs of a new restraint, perhaps even a new constructiveness on both sides. Episcopal deputies defended their work on the new Constitution and the principles of public liberty against implied papal criticism in a collective letter of 3 May, which insisted that their vision of liberty was not incompatible with *Quod aliquantum*:

> We have followed, in the ordering of the civil government, the principles that have appeared to us most conformable to the public interest in an established monarchy, whose foundations we have never wished to overthrow .... The questions of the extent and limits of social equality, on the principles and effects of a well-ordered liberty... have become, particularly in the present state of France, worthy of exercising the minds of all men capable of thinking.[8]

This proclamation of Gallican independence of mind with a determination to distinguish between their duties as bishops and their duties as deputies was a brave gesture that was appreciated more by many lay deputies than clerics in the countryside, not to mention

Pius VI. So long as the National Assembly continued in existence, episcopal members who had denounced the oath to the Civil Constitution sat in it. They made up an unofficial working committee that would not accept the preferences of Rome uncritically as, for instance, in their holding up the condemnation of Pius's condemnatory Briefs.[9]

On 7 May, it was agreed that refractory clergy across the whole of France could hire church buildings for their own ceremonies and, with prior authorisation, be allowed to celebrate the sacrament in Constitutional churches; significantly, preaching was not permitted.[10] Talleyrand and Sièyes had struck an important blow for the principle of religious liberty, while disavowing any ambition of instituting general toleration or state neutrality. It was subsequently decided that non-jurors were to be allowed pensions, and local authorities were ordered to relax their drive against them: non-compliance with the oath would be viewed as a religious decision which merely debarred a priest from continuing to act as a public official. In the last months of its existence, the National Assembly had been forced to see that there was nothing irresistibly popular about the legislation it published in the name of the sovereign nation. It was a hard lesson for revolutionaries to learn, but some of them, if only for reasons of personal survival, were capable of so doing. Thus if, as Norman Hampson writes with reference to the Civil Constitution, 'the Assembly made the worst of all worlds and played into the hands of its enemies, [and] much of the responsibility lay in its own arrogance and insensitivity',[11] one might suggest limiting its applicability mainly to 1790. A year on, some of its members were offering more pragmatic counsels in the light of public reaction to the oath.

There were still Church leaders like Bishop Bausset of Alais who deplored the 'fanaticism that agitates hearts and minds, and which makes people find I don't know what sort of pleasure in paying back evil for evil'.[12] Few listened. At Verdun, many young men took to the streets and attacked religious houses, smashing stained glass, in indignant response to Bishop Desnos's *mandement* against the Civil Constitution published in February.[13] In north-eastern France high local grain prices and the election of a Constitutional bishop combined to cause a riot in Douai in which two men were lynched in March 1791. At Sisteron, in Provence, refractory priests in August 'went from house to house abusing the law, the deputies and the priests who had taken the oath', but failed to raise the town for their cause.[14] Breton peasant critics of the Civil Constitution directed their anger at local government offices. The town of Vannes in the Morbihan was attacked by armed peasants seeking out officials and National Guards from the naval base at Lorient nearby had to be despatched to save them.[15]

The capital, as always, provided the flashpoint. There had been allegations from at least January 1791 that the non-juring clergy had built up a city-wide subversive movement, and the discovery by a senior police officer of small crosses for sale was taken as a sign of an impending rising or the flight of the royal family – or both. When arrested, pamphlet distributors, often women, were found to be hawking pastoral letters from refractory bishops, and after the occupants of convents had been beaten up on more than one occasion, the city authorities were obliged to lay on armed guards to protect them. Further trouble soon erupted. On 17 April angry crowds prevented Pancemont, the non-juring former *curé* of Saint-Sulpice, from holding a service in the church of the Théatins in Paris, as the *arrêté* of the 11th technically permitted, despite the fact that there was a notice outside declaring 'Church consecrated to religious worship by a particular Society. Peace and liberty'; efforts by the authorities to reopen the church six weeks later were abandoned in the face of mob violence.

It was a very similar tale in provincial towns up and down France, where non-juring congregations trying to take advantage of the law of 7 May had their efforts frustrated by the municipalities; there were very few centres like Amiens where the authorities confronted Jacobin-led riots against churches used by non-juring congregations and refused to bow to pressure to shut them down.[16] Quarrels in Brittany (*département* of Deux-Sèvres) between the partisans of both sides were so lively that the Ministry of Justice sent down two commissioners to hold an enquiry and re-establish order; in April the directory of the Finistère (with the backing of Bishop Expilly) technically exceeded its powers when it ordered all refractory priests to move a minimum distance of 5 miles from their former parishes.[17] The disquiet of deputies was well captured by Ménard de la Groye, whose comment, on hearing what was going on back home in Le Mans, was 'the zeal of our administrators has carried them away, and they would have done better not to abolish such a large number of parishes'.[18] These various incidents highlight the emerging differences on religious issues between the legislature and both metropolitan and provincial radicals by mid-1791 that have their counterparts in wholly secular politics, especially the growing popularity of republicanism after the King's abortive flight to Varennes in June 1791. Historians have often noted the Revolution's Rousseauist emphasis on the general will and the way those who were deemed in conflict with it were placed outside the nation. Here, briefly, in the spring and early summer of 1791 was an important and neglected effort by the new regime to operate a polity that permitted minorities the expression of their views.

The effort had very limited success. As has been seen, it encountered the unwillingness of a wide cross-section of revolutionary opinion to view refractories as deserving any legal protection. Frenchmen could still not think in terms of either a lay state or religious pluralism. Most deputies could not admit that there could be *two* legitimate expressions of Catholicism in the state. They regarded such a practice as introducing schism and making the nation itself schismatic, as Treilhard complained in the debate on 7 May. In some parts of France, the automatic assumption was made that any absentee from church must be a supporter of the refractories.[19]

II

By early summer, a national pattern of clerical responses to the oath was already discernible, one mapped out at regional level by the researches of Timothy Tackett. The striking geographical differences in the incidence of acceptance and non-acceptance tell us much about the extent of religious practice in the regions, with the figures broadly confirming pre-existing patterns of religious fervour. By and large, where devotion was intense, the churches full, and the number of ordinands steady, the number of non-jurors would be high. Where such conditions did not exist, those taking the oath were numerous, as in the capital and the central zone of France, the latter extending well beyond the Paris basin to encompass most of Picardy, the Champagne, the Berry and into Poitou. The related question of clerical wealth was influential in deciding some priests to swear, as in the Pyrenees, heavily populated by badly off parish clergy. Where income was higher, material considerations played little part in a final decision. Thus in the district of Compiègne, 48 out of 70 priests earned 1200 to 1500 livres annually, and they were evenly split on the Civil Constitution.[20]

In the south-east, Provence and the Dauphiné, early commitment to the Revolutionary cause kept fervour high. Elsewhere in the south it could be a different tale. In the huge province of Languedoc most clergy refused to subscribe, affronted by the new social and political prominence of Protestants. Indeed, wherever the latter were thick on the ground, the number of oath-takers was among the lowest in the kingdom. In Flanders and Artois refusal levels ran at over 75 per cent, and there were high levels of non-subscription in Alsace and Lorraine. It was above all in western France – Lower Normandy,[21] the whole of Brittany, Anjou, much of Poitou, and down the coast to La Rochelle – that the number of jurors was smallest, less than 10 per cent in some places.[22] In such areas, especially Brittany, most beneficed priests were too comfortably off, with the tithe in their hands already, to benefit from the Civil Constitution, and their contentment reinforced political distaste for the humiliation of Church and Crown at the hands of the revolutionaries. Yet this clerical prosperity in the west had not curtailed a dedication to preaching the faith that now helped create and sustain a wide degree of solidarity against the oath at every level – not just in diocesan centres like Nantes and Angers, but in the smaller towns of the west too. Indeed, rates of refusal generally were often higher in the towns than in the countryside, with Tackett suggesting that (leaving Paris aside) the larger the town the less likelihood of a majority of clergy taking the oath: where the population was more than 50 000 the average number of juring priests comes out at approximately 25 per cent, a sign of the persuasive influence that a dense clerical network could exert. These factors resulted in a slightly greater readiness to refuse the oath among urban clergy than with their rural counterparts.[23] Even in areas like Provence, where acceptance overall could run to 80 per cent, towns like Arles were important bastions of Catholic royalism, ready to offer support and shelter to the enemies of the Revolution beyond the town walls.

For most of the clergy, taking a final decision on the oath to the Civil Constitution was agonisingly difficult as they weighed up the relative claims of conscience and conviction, patriotism and obedience. As the *curé* of Bonnétable in the Sarthe movingly reported, 'They [the uncertainties] don't give me a moment's rest day or night; sleep has fled, my health has worsened, and I could collapse completely'.[24] Rural isolation made matters no easier. In Anjou, for every *curé* like Bassereau of Lion – who passed for something of a *philosophe* locally and insisted 'In order to live, I'd gladly take as many oaths as there are threads in my wig'[25] – there were a dozen others who agonised over their conduct. Many travelled to Angers to take their lead from the city clergy, only to come home no less bewildered. With compelling reasons for acceptance or refusal on both sides of the question, there were many pathetic efforts by clergy either to hide the legal formula inside a rambling discourse or else to devise a restrictive formula of acceptance turning them into the hybrid state of 'demi-jurors'.

This was also a sign of how hard it was for ingrained loyalties to the state to wither among the non-juring clergy. Even after midnight had struck, hopes that a compromise could be worked out in the interests of peace would not evaporate in the hearts of those who protested, like a *curé* from the Somme, that patriotism 'flows like blood in our veins'.[26] This sentiment was classically expressed in the pastoral instruction of Bishop La Luzerne of Langres (15 March 1791), the champion of political reforms and civic rights for religious minorities, who tried to distinguish between jurors as a whole and priests 'intruded' into parishes. He advised the faithful to deal respectfully with civic officers much as they had formerly dealt with the clergy, but also defiantly restated the underlying objections of nonjurors to the Civil Constitution.[27] These tactics left the local authorities confused: officials imposing the oath could vary considerably in how much leeway they permitted dissentients.

For clergy preparing to take a momentous decision, so much depended on local circumstances, the wider feeling in the parish, the attitudes of neighbouring priests and the stronger personalities among them. And, while the directives of the bishops appear to have been less than decisive, the influence of lay men and women – going against the preference of pious spinsters and widows was not lightly to be undertaken[28] – was commonly a vital determinant. At Sommières in the Gard, angry women vociferously defended their priests from the officials who had come to pressurise them, and defied the latter to remove them: 'It's not just the business of men but women too, and we have nothing to fear.' Only occasionally did women lobby for the Civil Constitution. At Rouen between May and September 1791, fourteen delegations were sent to the council

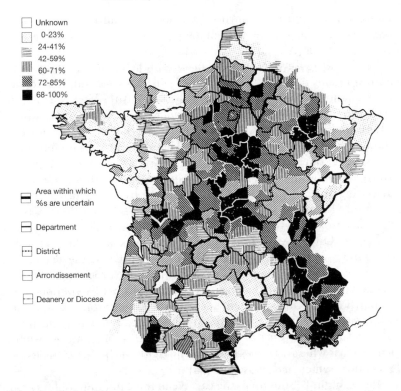

☐ Unknown
▨ 0-23%
▤ 24-41%
▥ 42-59%
▥ 60-71%
▨ 72-85%
■ 68-100%

▬ Area within which
%s are uncertain

⊟ Department

⋯ District

⋯ Arrondissement

⋯ Deanery or Diocese

Map 2   Oath-taking

requesting votive Masses for the completion of the new Constitution and declaring refractory priests to be the 'enemy of the public good'.[29] So while local authorities and left-wing clubs sedulously urged the oath on local clerics, such pressures had to be set against those exerted in the parish, the diocese, even an entire ecclesiastical province: disobedience to episcopal injunctions was not something most French *curés* were used to undertaking lightly. The evidence suggests that the Pope's belated but unambiguous intervention in May 1791 had a considerable impact on clerical attitudes. As many as between 6 and 10 per cent of clerics who had taken the oath retracted their consent after 4 May, so that the final total of jurors amounted to between 52 and 55 per cent of the parish clergy, with *curés* (57 per cent) more inclined to swear than *vicaires* (47.8).

However, the number of jurors retracting continued to mount up, reducing the percentage of their numbers to no more than 45 per cent by September 1792.[30]

While the significance of the oath for millions of observant lay men and women is too easily overlooked, Louis XVI's personal distaste for a measure he had sanctioned is well known. After Mass celebrated on Palm Sunday by his Grand Almoner, the refractory Cardinal Montmorency-Laval, Bishop of Metz,[31] he decided to leave for his summer palace. His plans were foiled. He suffered public humiliation when he set out with his family for Saint-Cloud next day (Monday, 18 April), an excursion that was widely expected to culminate in his attending an Easter Day service there taken by a non-juring priest. Certainly Lafayette's National Guard thought so, since they refused to clear away the crowds blocking the royal coach's way out of the Tuileries. On 20 April Louis protested in person at the National Assembly over events, but received scant sympathy: the President characterised the incident as inseparable from the progress of liberty. Whatever their private feelings, deputies could hardly condone the inspiration the King's recalcitrance afforded non-jurors – and those who were still hesitating – across his kingdom. Meanwhile, the incident ensured that, on Easter Day, there were more confrontations across Paris where churches had been hired for use by clergy and congregations which had refused the oath.

Louis might be shut up as the captive in the Tuileries; other members of his family less vital to the life of the state quietly crossed the borders, unable to tolerate the new religious order. He connived at the departure of his pious aunts, Adélaide and Victoire, for Italy in February 1791, followed five months later by his brother, the Comte de Provence. 'Monsieur' had long been a conspicuous constitutionalist, even a monarch-in-waiting, should his elder sibling prove impossibly uncooperative with the new establishment, and his departure formed part of the most important wave of emigration since the outbreak of the Revolution. It was provoked far more by the Civil Constitution than any secular measure passed in the National Assembly. The combination of a humiliated Church and Crown in 1791 was too much for those noble families (and there were plenty of them) who resented their loss of influence over the nature and pace of change in French politics, and had no faith in the possibility of peaceful transition to a constitutional regime. On the same night in June 1791 that Provence and his family crossed into the Austrian Netherlands,

Louis XVI himself, Marie-Antoinette, their children and his sister, Madame Elisabeth, found their flight east towards the river Meuse cut short after recognition by the postmaster at Varennes in Lorraine.[32] Their humiliating return to the capital under armed guard plunged the revolutionary state into crisis on the eve of the Constitution's completion. But this failure did not deter other members of the elite from leaving France, especially Bishops and army officers, both categories who could not take oaths of subscription to a polity that had reduced their status while declining to register their views. Many prelates had stayed on in the face of intimidation as long as practicable. Their protest made, most reluctantly left France, hoping it would be easier to have a hand in directing refractory operations from a distance without having to make personal survival and concealment the priority if they stayed on French soil. But most French men and women, whatever their opinion about the Civil Constitution, had no choice but to stay in their neighbourhood.

The aftermath of Varennes increased the pressure on politicians to calm the provinces by coming to terms with the fact that between a third and a half of clergy were never going to accept the Civil Constitution. They had already shown a formidable capacity for attracting support and the Feuillants, the dominant grouping in the Assembly, were beginning to view them as a useful counterbalance to their own, increasingly republican, enemies on the Left. Thus ignoring furious Jacobin allegations about the extent of clerical plotting, the 'Triumvirs' – Charles de Lameth, Duport and Barnarve – inspired attempts at conciliation on ecclesiastical issues between July and September 1791, further if belated recognition on the part of moderates in the last months of the National Assembly of how divisive the Civil Constitution of the Clergy had turned out to be.

Yet to talk in terms of a consistent ecclesiastical policy from the National Assembly at any point in the period between February and September 1791 remains dubious. The deputies had created the Civil Constitution, then imposed it, and cancelling it in the face of massive opposition was politically unthinkable. The best the Feuillants could do was urge moderation on local authorities and the militants in the clubs. Sometimes this policy – if one can call it that – chimed in with the situation on the ground. Thus, in the Maine-et-Loire, the departmental authorities had actually asked refractory priests to stay in their parishes if they could not be replaced, a policy more than acceptable to the 'Triumvirs'. But such

moderation was not to everyone's taste as, once again, local politicians savouring power for the first time baulked at the Assembly's
new caution. During the summer one-quarter of *départements* had
called for new legislation to permit closer supervision of known
refractories, while in Brittany *départements* were following their own
policy of exiling or imprisoning them irrespective of preferences in
the Assembly or the government. On the whole, deputies were in too
much of a hurry to complete the Constitution of 1791 to insist that
local authorities adopt a uniformly conciliatory manner towards the
non-jurors and, a year after the Civil Constitution had become law,
the chasm between the revolutionary politicians and the refractory
clergy was almost too great to bridge anyway.

The Assembly marked the end of its work on the 1791 Constitution
by proclaiming a general amnesty for prisoners, which, of course,
benefited many refractories. But the Constituents would go no
further: the political price it would entail of losing the active goodwill
of the revolutionary activists in the provinces was unacceptably high.
Already, the Assembly's temporising line – restated by the constitutional article of 9 August guaranteeing 'liberty to all to practise the
creed to which they are attached' – flew in the face of petitions from
numerous *départements* after Varennes demanding a law that would
exile refractory priests automatically.

The contradictions in the Assembly's religious policies remained
right up to its dissolution on 30 September 1791, and reflected the
emerging divisions between Feuillants at the centre and Jacobins in
the provinces. Significantly, the Civil Constitution of the Clergy
was even excluded from the constitution accepted and signed by the
King on 13 September 1791 in an atmosphere of national rejoicing
tempered by relief, with Masses and *Te Deums* across the country celebrated by the constitutional clergy. The omission of the Civil Constitution thus severed the disastrous assumption made in November
1790 that loyalties to the new order in both Church and state were
one and the same. It was also decreed that the Civil Constitution
might be amended or replaced as an ordinary law by any future legislature without going through the ten-year process laid down for changing the constitution itself. Yet, and this was typical of policy
inconsistencies, nothing was done to mend fences with the papacy,
whose role in French Church life had become more important than
at any time since the passing of the Bull *Unigenitus* in 1713. Indeed
further papal territory inside France was seized only days before

the final closure of the National Assembly on 30 September, to give
Pius VI more incentive than ever to head a counter-revolutionary
movement that looked primarily to the Church for leadership and
inspiration.

III

The new Legislative Assembly convened on 1 October; it coincided
with Parisian theatre audiences flocking to see a tragedy called *Jean
Calas,* and then listen to the anticlerical tirades of the actors echoing
those heard on the streets.[35] The Assembly was made up in large part
of politicians who had cut their teeth in clubs and local government over the previous two years, precisely those who knew at first
hand how destabilising clerical resistance to the Civil Constitution
could be, and from whom refractories might expect few concessions;
clerical membership was minimal, with only a handful of constitutional bishops like Lamourette of Lyon and Fauchet of Caen winning
seats. For politicians tempted by republicanism, Louis XVI's distaste
for the Civil Constitution was an ever present disincentive to uphold
the new monarchy while, on the other side of the political divide, the
flood of clerical and noble *émigrés* were busy shocking their host
countries with stories of the outrages being perpetrated against the
Church at home in the name of the Revolution.

Despite the more conciliatory approach towards non-jurors that it
inherited from its predecessor, the Legislative Assembly had no intention of ceasing to uphold the claims of the Constitutional Church, for
all the evidence of widespread clerical refusal to participate in it: obedience to the law and submission to the official religion of state went
together as far as most deputies were concerned. And, as the threat of
war with the Habsburgs intensified after the Declaration of Pilnitz
(July 1791), refractory priests seemed a counter-revolutionary fifth
column that could be a threat to France's internal security should hostilities break out. The role of clergy in aggravating the turmoil in
southern and south-eastern France could not be ignored. Arles, for
example, had fallen into the hands of Catholic royalists who urged
local people to reject the Constitution and all its works. Clubs up and
down France were clamouring for more repressive measures against
these enemies of the state.[34]

It had thus become a political imperative for the new legislature to move against the refractories without completely denying the principle of toleration. In further debate on the subject during the autumn, it became apparent that cancelling the special oath granted to the refractories on 7 May and exiling the principal troublemakers among them was the preferred majority option of deputies. A way had to be found of preventing them working against the new constitutional regime. The fiery deputy Maxim Isnard, from the *département* of the Var, associated with those like Brissot, Vergniaud and Guadet, articulated his friends' anti-Christian sentiments on 15 November. His denunciation of the 'factious' and 'pestiferous' priests won much applause in both the Assembly and the galleries as he theatrically insisted 'Don't you know that just a single priest can do you more harm than all your other enemies?'[35] Reports from the Maine-et-Loire appeared to lend credence to this; several thousand armed men gathered in support of the refractories using pilgrimages and religious processions as a pretext.[36]

Eventually, on 29 November 1791, the Assembly decreed that all non-jurors should take a new civic oath inside eight days, with those who refused to do so declared 'suspected of sedition' and thereby deprived of their pension rights as well as liable to removal from their ordinary domicile. They thus stood to become refractories twice over, in conspiracy against the *patrie*, and to be placed under official surveillance for their disobedience. The parish church was reserved for the exclusive religious use of the Constitutional clergy, with unsworn priests legally incapable of taking any service; true, the 7 May law still stood, but the new insistence that non-juring clergy hiring premises must have taken the civic oath effectively made it a dead letter. Barnave orchestrated a petition from the refractory clergy of Paris to Louis on the grounds of liberty of conscience. It was enough of a feint to give some credibility to the King's refusal to accept what he judged to be punitive provisions and the overthrow of the law of 7 May, and he vetoed the latest decree on 19 December.[37] Demonstrations in Paris and other anticlerical centres like Lyon and Marseille were not enough to deflect him. Forty-two *départements* went ahead anyway and, under pressure from patriots in the Clubs, applied the decree as if it was law: 'The maintenance of order must take precedence before freedom of worship' was how the administrators of the *département* of the Vienne excused themselves.[38] It all exacerbated a growing crisis caused by the monarch's similar behaviour over a measure against the *émigrés*: to ardent revolutionaries, the latter with the refractories seemed to be twin forks of a common threat to France, whose collusion imperilled the state itself.

The publication of a third Brief (*Hae litterae*) from Pius VI on 19 March 1792 condemning the Civil Constitution as both schismatic and to a large degree heretical, together with the outbreak of war against Austria in April, cast the non-juring clergy in the role of traitors still more forcibly. The vast majority of such clergy were not counter-revolutionaries in cassocks; their first priority was pastoral ministry, but such protestations did nothing to eliminate 'patriot' suspicions that priests were behind the setbacks on the battlefields experienced by the French armies that summer and were biding their time until Austrian and Prussian troops arrived in Paris to restore the old order in Church and State. As that prospect appeared far from unlikely, so the suspicion of 'priestcraft' in revolutionary circles became uncontainable. Legislation articulated this new toughness. On 27 May 1792 decrees were passed by the Legislative Assembly providing for the deportation of stubborn refractories, in other words clergy whose activities were denounced by a minimum of twenty active citizens. Not all local authorities were in any hurry to enforce it. In parts of the rural Rhône-et-Loire *département*, administrators gave tacit support to non-jurors in the name of freedom of speech, while in some areas of Lyon, the municipality offered non-juring priests two months to reconsider before being replaced, but this was exceptional.

Elsewhere, mob violence often took the law into its own hands, as when in Bordeaux on Bastille Day 1792 a refractory priest was seized, beheaded, and his head carried round on a pole to cries of 'Long live the Constitution! Death to the priests! Down with the refractories!'[39] National Guards were also given powers to search private property to hunt out priests. Should one be caught, he was liable to 10 years' imprisonment, and those concealing him would be called on to pay the wages and expenses of those performing the search. Despite his own precarious prospects of survival, Louis XVI was ready to veto this last proposal, and defended the Church's interest as best he could until the collapse of the monarchy in August. Ominously for the Constitutional clergy, the attack on the refractories barely concealed a growing disdain within the Assembly for *all* manifestations of Catholicism: the refusal to allow any official participation by deputies in the Paris Corpus Christi procession of 1792 was a surer indicator of opinion than the Mass celebrated at the funeral service on 10 May of General Dillon, killed in the unsuccessful opening campaign of the Austrian War. By that date only one-fifth of communes in Provence preceded oath-taking ceremonies with a Mass, as opposed to three-quarters in 1790, while in Bordeaux festivals had a scaled-down Christian component and were centred less on the Cathedral of Saint-André than on the city's streets and squares.[40]

From 11 August onwards, following the collapse of the monarchy, the Legislative Assembly, impelled by the revolutionary Paris Commune, introduced a string of fresh anticlerical measures, including the suppression of teaching and hospital orders along with the sale of conventual buildings. It meant the final loss of the female religious orders, despite their popularity with the public at large. As one visitor reported:

> I have met with no person who could conceive the necessity of expelling the female religious from their convents. It was, however, done, and that with a mixture of meanness and barbarity that at once excites contempt and detestation.[43]

The Convention did not stop there. Confraternities were also banned, along with the wearing of clerical dress, though Grégoire, sitting with the Montagnards, defiantly retained his episcopal purple.[42] To pay for the costs of war, treasures and funds not yet confiscated from the churches were rapidly acquired. On 14 August the oath of 'liberty and equality' was imposed on all priests without exception: 'I swear to be faithful to the Nation, to maintain with all my power liberty, equality, the security of persons and property, and to die if necessary for the execution of the laws.' The penalties for refractories became still more draconian. On 26 August, declaring open season for 'priest hunts', the Assembly ordered non-jurors to quit the country within a fortnight on pains of deportation to Guiana. The atmosphere was one of paranoia generated by military defeat and impending invasion (news of the reported fall of Verdun reached the capital on 2 September), and it notoriously culminated in the singling out of priests for summary execution during the September Massacres in Paris.

For the most part, clergy had continued with their ministry despite state repression. The prisons had filled up steadily over the summer

and, in the cities, priestly prisoners were an obvious target for Revolutionary taunting and petty violence. But the September Massacres
were an act of butchery perpetrated by mobs looking for those internal 'enemies' who were undoing the work of the armies in the field.
In three days (2–4 September), 3 prelates and approximately
230 priests were savagely murdered by anti-clerical fanatics among
the total of 1300 prisoners executed in Parisian gaols; they found
150 priests in the Carmelite convent, and about 115 of them
died under 'the axe of vengeance', including the Archbishop of
Arles and the Bishops of Saintes and Beauvais. Approximately 80
to 120 perished in other holding centres.[43] At the inauguration of
the Republic, the non-jurors were unequivocally the enemies of the
state. Soon, it would be the turn of the Constitutional clergy to be
treated similarly.

IV

In the new republic, sovereign power was vested in the Convention,
and it had initially a Girondin (or Brissotin) majority. Girondin
attitudes towards the Church in 1792–3 were not remarkable overall
for their tolerance, and any lingering hope that the Revolution and
Christianity could be syncretically combined was soon thrown into
doubt. Admittedly, when faced with unrest in the Vendée in March
1793, the representatives on mission, Carra and Auguis, stated in
the name of the Convention that the republic was founded on the
moral precepts of the Gospel, but such a claim did not persuade the
insurgents. For the time being, the Convention let the Constitutionalists get on with their work and services, making full use of the
state Church's bishops and priests to justify legislative measures from
their pulpits when appropriate: a proposal by Cambon speaking
for the *Comité des Finances* on 13 November to abolish the fund used to
support the Constitutional Church was not acceptable to the majority in the Convention.[44]

Not that deputies were inclined to offer much positive support for
their clergy. By the time the Legislative Assembly closed on 20 September 1792, the state had been laicised to an unparalleled degree,
with the clergy stripped of responsibility for maintaining the parish
registers of births, marriages and deaths. Records had been imper-
fectly kept since the Civil Constitution, and the Convention saw

mayors as more reliable servants than priests for this task. The change of marriage into a purely civil ceremony dealt a massive blow to ecclesiastical authority. It fell just as local authorities were banning the public processions of the Constitutional Church and melting down precious objects like crucifixes still kept in the parish churches. On Christmas eve, the Paris *commune* even tried to close down the city churches, only to find the faithful forcing *curés* to celebrate midnight Mass.

Those involved were members of the Constitutional Church, for the Convention owed nothing to the refractories. The open association of the non-jurors with the Catholic and royal armies of the counter-revolution in the Vendée gave the state additional justification for repressive measures in 1793: on 13 March priests sentenced to deportation and subsequently found in France were liable to trial by a military jury and execution within twenty-four hours; in April it was decreed that priests who had not taken the oath of liberty and equality were liable to immediate deportation to Guiana. This fearsome legislation culminated in the laws of 29 and 30 *Vendémiaire* Year II (20 and 21 October 1793) by which any non-juror was liable to the judgment of a military commission and could be executed within twenty-four hours if two witnesses vouched for his status. As far as the militants were concerned, to be less harsh risked allowing the domestic enemies of the Revolution a freer hand than was compatible with the state's survival. Pressure on clerics mounted further with the dispatch of the representatives on mission and the establishment of watch committees (*comités de surveillance*) to scrutinise the activities of foreigners and suspects (21 March 1793). It did not ease for the rest of 1793, especially after the fall of the Brissotins in June gave the *Enragés* the initiative in Paris for the rest of the year. Across France the willingness of republican authorities to equate the profession of Christianity with hostility to the Revolution mounted, and in October the Convention abandoned the Gregorian calendar and proclaimed a new republican one that showed its resolve to distance the state culturally from Christianity.

The Committee of Public Safety (established in April 1793) openly encouraged attacks on every manifestation of Christianity, not least on its iconography, including the cross and Christ Himself. Christianity was presented as a rival cultural system to the Revolution whose existance could no longer be tolerated. As Frank Tallett has succinctly expressed it, the ambitious aims of the active dechristianisers were nothing less than 'the eradication of Catholic religious practice, and Catholicism itself'.[45] Republican agents acted as midwives to a varied and discursive range of beliefs resting on a notional rationality that would act as a new kind of non-Christian public culture. In place of the historic faith, the state looked to sponsor religious alternatives, loosely based on deism now decked out in republican emblems, with a rhetoric to match drawn from the classical past. In this way might be created a new man for the new world:

Cults

> Release the sons of the Republic from the yoke of theocracy that still burdens them .... If you are free of prejudice and worthy to represent the French nation, you can found the single universal religion on the debris of dethroned superstition.[46]

Prosecution of this offensive, as ever, depended on local circumstances. Many municipal officials, like those in Dijon, welcomed the new emphasis. It was especially appealing to those who had grown cynical about the capacity of the Constitutional Church to communicate its message and attract followers, or had come to associate its clergy as compromised by the 'federalist' politics adopted by great cities like Lyon and Bordeaux (which rejected the Parisian overthrow of the Brissotins on 31 May and 1 June 1793). Such committed Jacobins were eager for strong measures, like this one from the Mâconnais:

> Since the beginning of the Revolution, the Catholic cult has been the cause of many troubles. Under the cloak of religion, the progress of civic-mindedness has been much hampered. Disastrous wars have taken place. Would it not be appropriate to authorize only the cult of the Revolution?[47]

Good acts

Republicans knew that weaning the nation from the old one would take time, but with the Catholic Church's grip on education broken, zealots placed their hopes on the secular, state-paid instructors (*instituteurs publiques*) who, though never very numerous because of inadequate funding, had the young learn 'republican catechisms'. Clerics on all sides echoed Grégoire's denunciation of the institutions involved as 'schools of the devil'.[48] For every official keen to do his best to create a new religious order, there were others reluctant to deal harshly with practising Christians personally known to them.

Such recalcitrants soon had their scope restricted, as initiative passed to the militant republican clubs, which, as in the rural Pays de Caux of Normandy, 'sent out apostles' from towns like Fécamp and Dieppe to counteract surviving clerical influences.[49] Crosses in the towns and villages must go; the patriots of Dreux wanted them replaced by 'columns dedicated to liberty and equality'. Church bells, too, had their critics – 'the lugubrious din of these agonising bells just frightens the living without being useful to the dead'.[50] The most fanatical wanted to cut off the contamination at source. The head of the Beauvais detachment of the revolutionary army, Mazuel, stated the aims of the popular Dechristianisers starkly enough: 'We're going to fight fanaticism and supersition; the murdering priests whose dogma is only imposture, and whose empire only rests on credulous women'.[51]

The battle was led by the representatives on mission, whose very lack of association with the districts they were supervising was designed to encourage ruthlessness against counter-revolutionary suspects. More than most, they tried to make the new pseudo-religious practices visible at every level of the community. In practice, such initiatives often took the crude form of a sudden and violent offensive unleashed against every manifestation of Catholic Christianity.[52] While one should be cautious about assuming uniformity in attitudes among the representatives on mission, their underlying dislike of Christianity proclaimed their absorption of popularised Enlightenment propaganda: revealed religion (including Protestantism) and superstition were synonomous. With France at war with most of Europe, these beliefs were not merely laughable relics of darkness but also a threat to the Revolution, and had to be replaced by forms of observance that reinforced rather than undermined the regime they served. Of course, a high proportion of the representatives had their anti-Christian fervour sharpened by an awareness that eliminating the symbols and supporters of the Old Regime was the key to advancement, but others had a single-minded dedication to the task of ideological purification of the republic as the highest form of calling, seeing Revolution as the new revelation, or what the nineteenth-century historian Jules Michelet viewed as the cult of itself.[53]

In the Nièvre the representative Joseph Fouché (an ex-Oratorian priest and one of the original authors of the official policy of dechristianisation)[54] believed without qualification that Christianity and the Revolution were irreconcilable. Instead, he inaugurated his own civic religion in the church of Saint-Cyr at Nevers with a 'Feast of Brutus' on 22 September 1793. He followed it up with a manifesto in which he proclaimed that he had come 'to substitute for superstitious and hypocritical worship ... that of the Republic and of a natural morality'. In the Somme and then the Oise, the young *conventionnel* [member of the Convention], André Dumont, looked to Fouché for inspiration.[55] He was one of the pioneer dechristianisers, who personally favoured public abjuration of holy orders; in Reims, Ruhl oversaw the destruction of the phial holding the sacred oil of Clovis. Whatever their motivation, these servants of centralised power, many of them former clergy,[56] aided and abetted by the local revolutionary committees and popular societies, were hard to thwart. Another classic agency of dechristianisation was the revolutionary Army of Paris *en route* to Lyon; troops encouraged the renunciation of the faith on a grand scale by a combination of ridicule, intimidation and violence.

This phase of intensified severity against the Churches was further underlined by of the Law of Suspects in September 1793, which made the carrying of certificates of *civisme* obligatory, with arrest and imprisonment the penalties for offenders; under a supplementary law of 20 October, any priest lacking appropriate certification could be denounced by six citizens, and then deported. At the same time, the Convention made it clear that those 'criminals' previously sentenced but still resident in France became liable to execution. It was, in effect, another invitation to the refractories to escape across the frontiers, but by this date those who were going to flee had mostly departed (see Chapter 9(ii)). Imprisonment and execution were commonplace for priests during the winter of 1793–4, often after personal humiliation and degradation. At Saint-Chinian, in the Hérault, five were murdered in 1793 by local desperadoes who won the local nickname of 'the eaters of priests' ears'.[57] Yet the majority of clergy who stayed in France and remained loyal to their calling survived: only about 7 per cent of those executed in the Terror were clergy,[58] and a high proportion of them fell victim immediately before Robespierre's overthrow at *Thermidor*. The Law of 22 *Prairial* Year II (10 June 1794) speeded up and simplified the procedure of the Tribunal, and over 26 per cent of clerical victims of the Terror incurred the supreme penalty over the next few weeks. That gives an approximate total (including the post-*Fructidor* repression of the

Directory in the 'second Terror') of somewhere between 2000 and 3000 clerical deaths, or about 2 per cent of the total ordained ministry. The figure takes no account of marked regional variants.

The previous winter had seen the further winding down of state backing for the Constitutional Church from the politicians in the Convention and the *commune* in Paris. Christian symbols were abandoned, and religious ceremonies no longer marked the celebration of revolutionary achievements. The unhindered Corpus Christi Day processions in the capital on 30 May 1793 would prove to be one of the Church's last high-profile activities before the campaign of 'dechristianisation' began in earnest; it had its material counterpart in the decree of 18 September enacting a major reduction in state funding for the Constitutional Church, and thereby anticipated the formal separation of Church and State.[59] Cutting off payments to bishops and clergy put them under pressure from republicans to show their attachment to the revolutionary state by renouncing Christianity and the ordained ministry, and there was widespread approval among Jacobins of Bishop Gobel's public resignation of the see of Paris in November 1793 when, in his red bonnet, he declared 'there should be no more public and national worship but that of Liberty and Holy Equality'. It had been only after hours of heart-searching – and intimidation –that he finally persuaded himself to act. Those priests and bishops who declined to follow his example and stayed in the ministry were given legal inducements by the Convention to marry. Where they followed neither course of action, they risked denunciation by a popular society. In July 1793 the Convention, having decided that wedlock was a civil duty, voted that bishops who tried to stop their clergy from undertaking it should be deported and replaced for 'blasphemy against the sovereignty of the people'.[60]

The Parisian sections were meanwhile busy passing anti-Christian motions and shutting down all the churches in the capital. Other local authorities followed suit and often used the redundant buildings for alternative 'services': the cathedral of Notre-Dame was not alone in staging a great public ceremony to celebrate the blessings of Liberty and the Triumph of Reason.[61] Elsewhere, closure of the parish churches (most were shut by the following spring except in remote districts)[62] largely satisfied revolutionary activists, though it did nothing but increase the number of their local enemies. With only a few hundred of the 40 000 parishes of pre-1789 France still offering Catholic services, the transformation could not have been more dramatic. In a space of only five years, the French government had utterly distanced itself from sustaining Christianity. Religion was relegated to the private sphere, worship was to be practised exclusively behind closed doors.

The wave of anticlerical and anti-Christian militancy sweeping through France in the autumn of 1793 had a spontaneous element at the same time as it was stirred up from above. And, once unleashed, dechristianisation developed its own momentum. The phenomenon brought its own attendant problems for the new elite. Many members of the Convention were disturbed that it might disrupt their control of the Revolution. The inauguration of 'Revolutionary Government' in October 1793 (confirmed by the Law of 14 *Frimaire* Year II − 4 December) and the centralisation associated with it did something to lessen the possibilities for anarchy and anti-religious demonstrations, but it only became operative gradually after Hébert and his *Enragé* supporters had been executed. Danton called for an end to the anti-religious masquerades and mock ceremonies going on in many places, and his views reflected an unease among Jacobin politicians like Robespierre who were, by philosophy and temperament, fearful of disassociating popular morality from religious observance and efforts to spread unbelief among the population at large: atheism, Robespierre said, was aristocratic because the rich needed no hope of compensation in another world for their experience in this one.[63] On 21 November 1793 he had denounced anti-religious excesses (with his eye on the Hébertistes) at the Jacobin Club in Paris; he was instrumental in securing the reiteration by the Convention in the law of 16 December 1793 [12 *Frimaire*] of the principle of religious freedom in a decree which formally prohibited all violence or threats against the 'liberty of cults'. It counteracted Barère's decree of 6 November 1793 effectively giving communes the right to close churches, but came too late to stop the repressive measures taken against Christians of all persuasions (including Protestants) and the buildings they had − sometimes over many centuries − used for worship. Despairing and desperate locals misread the law of 12 *Frimaire* as an invitation to reopen the churches and petitioned the Convention accordingly.[64] When the authorities did nothing, there could be some very ugly scenes. In December 1793, in the Brie, crowds of peasants sacked the local Jacobin club to cries of 'Long live the Catholic Religion, we want our priests, we want the Mass on Sundays and Holy Days.' It took thousands of National Guardsmen and sansculottes from the Revolutionary Army to restore order. Others resorted to petitioning, like the mayor of the commune of Igé in the Perche:

> We are French republicans, we accept the Constitution, we abhor royalism, but we will never renounce our holy religion and we will uphold it with all our power, a holy religion taught to us for more than 1700 years, and we are absolutely insistent that we will not take any other.[65]

If the laity wanted to practice the Christian religion in 1793–4 – and surprisingly large numbers did – it had to be done despite official sanctions and the lack of priests, unless they were lucky enough to secure the occasional services of a refractory on the run and risking death by celebrating the Eucharist. Otherwise they began to do for themselves what had once been the exclusive concern of the priest, and this applied to adherents of both the refractory *and* the Constitutional clergy. Laymen started burying the dead, marrying couples, even taking Masses, so-called 'White Masses' where the bread and wine were venerated rather than consecrated. Continuing research has revealed just how widespread such practices became, with village 'notables' like the schoolmaster or sacristan taking the service in a reverential manner that was far removed from the parody of Christian worship preferred by the dechristianisers.

This constituency was firm in its repudiation of a non-Christian France, but their furtive persistence in the old ways had little impact on public policy. Militant republicans disseminated their message of popular atheism well into the spring of 1794, until there was a decisive move against dechristianisation with the cult of the Supreme Being launched by Robespierre on 7 May and endorsed by the Committee of Public Safety. Robespierre determined to use all his influence against his political rivals and their rejection of religion. After Robespierre had led the Convention to worship on 8 June on a specially built artificial mountain, his growing number of critics were convinced that he was trying to match his political ascendancy with the spiritual leadership of France, and alarm at this accumulation of power hastened his overthrow a few weeks later; with it ended this outlandish revival of officially authorised observances.

The hard-headed Thermidorian realists who replaced Robespierre had no intention of worshipping the Supreme Being. The regime of 1794–5 was characterised by a scarcely concealed disdain for religion as the engine of superstition and priestcraft, and a pronounced anti-clericalism. Nevertheless, the Thermidorian policy was based on a sharpened sense of what the public wanted, and registered the inescapable fact that, despite all the official sanctions and disincentives, Christianity had not vanished from France. It was the inability of republican principles to arouse and sustain excitement let alone devotion in the majority population that was critical in easing restrictions on the practice of Catholicism in 1795 and led, eventually, to the Concordat of 1802. A policy of religious neutrality was introduced, more pronounced than at any point in the Revolution and dramatically set forth on 18 September 1794, when state links with the Constitutional Church were renounced with the end of subsidies. There was no formal guarantee of religious liberty; Grégoire requested one from the Convention before Christmas 1794, but was bluntly told that republican morality was enough for the citizens of France. Nevertheless, the official line was moving perceptibly towards relocating religion strictly within the private sphere. Accordingly, on 21 February 1795 [3 *Ventôse*], the freedom of all cults to worship *privately* was announced, but they would receive no support of any kind from either national or local government, and would have to take the so-called 'little oath' of loyalty to the republic. The gaols were opened, non-juring clergy not subject to the former laws on deportation were freed, and so were the nuns. On 11 *Prairial* Year III (29 May 1795) the Convention made further concessions by allowing parishioners to reclaim unsold parish churches, but Catholic symbols stayed banned.

Those who flocked to the Easter 1795 services, whether from piety, thankfulness or just curiosity, commonly found their churches (where they still existed) either deliberately damaged or in a state of accidental disrepair that followed on from years of enforced neglect or alternative uses as military hospitals, grainstores, prisons or 'temples of reason'. During 1792–5 the state had sanctioned or connived at the physical destruction of France's Catholic heritage on a scale that far surpassed anything seen during the Wars of Religion in the sixteenth century.[66] Visible signs of Catholicism – crosses, pulpits, altars, confessionals, statues – were burnt or broken up to the singing of the *Ça ira!*, and where possible used in the war effort. They joined the church bells and plate confiscated earlier and melted down to form the precious metals needed to finance France's armies. 3300 kilos of silver and 276 tons of bronze were forwarded to Paris from churches in the diocese of Châlons-sur-Marne alone. In the Puy-de-Dôme, where dechristianisers worked hard, a former *curé* wrote in the Year III that 'All the steeples have been damaged or destroyed. A great number of parish churches no longer exist, and you have to look hard for any external signs of Christianity.'[67]

The destruction extended well beyond the closure of the monasteries (as in England during the Henrician Reformation of the 1530s) to include colleges, cathedrals, and parish churches. Virtually every town in France has its list of buildings destroyed: Arras and Avranches had their cathedrals demolished, Toulouse and Angers suffered through the loss of several splendid parish churches, and monasteries that had a European fame were either like Cluny (Burgundy) smashed beyond repair or razed to the ground like Notre-Dame de Montmartre, Royaumont, Longjumeau and Jumièges. At Laon in 1793 all statues of Christ and the angels were taken down and there was talk of removing the towers of the cathedral because they were a reminder of 'feudalism'. In Paris, Notre-Dame Cathedral itself had the kings of Judea and Israel from the Old Testament on its façade grievously mutilated, and those at Amiens and Chartres were similarly vandalised.[68] The artist David thus justified the loss to the Convention on 7 November 1793 as utterly appropriate in the new France:

> Unable to usurp God's place in the churches, the kings took possession of their portals . . . accustomed to laying their hands on everything, they had the presumption of competing with God Himself for the incense that men offered Him. You have overthrown these insolent usurpers; laughed to scorn, they now litter the soil that is stained with their crimes.[69]

And it was not just the buildings that suffered in this state-sponsored vandalism, this turning by a minority against their country's rich Christian inheritance. Monuments, organs, stained glass, heraldic trophies, and communion plate inside the churches were lost on an appreciable scale.

The royal tombs at Saint-Denis were looted and destroyed, and the bones thrown ignominiously into paupers' graves. In only three days, fifty-one monuments, the work of twelve centuries, were destroyed. The Parisian example was imitated all over the country. At Angers, for instance, in the former church of the Cordeliers, the casket holding the remains of the good Duke René of Anjou was used as a football by workmen.[70] Belatedly, the Convention attempted to halt this destruction of the patrimony by an order of 24 October 1793 prohibiting the unauthorised destruction of works of art, but it tempered rather than stopped the pace of iconoclasm in the months down to the overthrow of the Jacobins in July 1794. Thus at Brest in December 1793, Dagorne, agent for the national domain in the *département* of Finistère, deliberately had churches looted, images smashed, and holy vessels profaned in the market place when peasants could be expected in large numbers; at Tours, that same festive season, relics were pillaged and burned to coincide with what would have been Christmas midnight Mass.[71] The famous 'Black Virgin' of Le Puy was blindfolded, put in a cart, and guillotined on the central square before burning in a stylish iconoclastic ceremony. Relics were the object of particular scorn. Jacobins at Epernon on 4 *Frimaire* in an address to the Convention reported how they had found 'amongst these relics of stupidity the hair of that well-known prostitute called Magdalene'.[72] Grégoire, who saw much destruction at first hand, summed it up appropriately for his own and succeeding generations: 'The loss of so many works of art is enough to draw tears of blood.'[73]

These great buildings had become disposable in the interests of a state that decided on limited ideological neutrality only belatedly in 1795. Before then, the republic had been content to wage war not just on Christians, but also on their churches and all that they contained. It marked a short but violent interlude in the commitment to religious toleration that had distinguished the early part of the Revolution, but it left a legacy of anger and resentment on every side that weakened the internal cohesion of the French polity and, as much as anything, kept Church and State from lasting reconciliation for upwards of a century.

V

Only one French regime of the 1790s, briefly in 1791–2, was interested to any extent in recreating a primitive Christian ideal of the sort that had appealed to Joseph II and other eighteenth-century rulers, one that allowed for the modernisation of the institutional Church in the guise of 'restoration'. Thereafter, the republican order in the state was at best officially neutral in matters of religion and, during the crucial period of 1793–4, openly hostile to the faith with an aggression unprecedented in eighteenth-century Europe. France in those eighteen months was more than anti-Catholic, it was anti-Christian. To contemporaries bewildered by the pace of events, there had been no equivalent since the Barbarians overran Rome in the fifth century AD: actions like the September Massacres did much to convince other governments that France was a pariah among nations, an offensive presence within a European order that remained predominantly Christian in character and morality. That the vast majority of Frenchmen – and French women in particular – had no wish to abandon the faith that moulded their existence from cradle to grave compounded the outrage for foreigners, as they welcomed religious refugees from France and heard at first hand about the murder of priests and the conversion of Churches into stables – or 'temples of reason'.

Most native French had no choice but to put up with the changes imposed by urban-based politicians; the non-compliant risked death by their determination not to abandon their Christian faith. But notables and priests left in droves, preferring penury to apostacy, physical discomfort to spiritual denial. They made up a sizeable French Roman Catholic diaspora scattered around Europe by 1795, pushed out of France, as they never hesitated to aver, by a hostile republican state. Their pathetically reduced status spoke as loudly as any preaching about what was going on in France and played a neglected part in affecting the response of governments to an 'atheist' regime. Yet they were not welcome everywhere. Most German states would not admit them, including the conservative young emperor Francis II of Austria who feared their very identity as Frenchmen would involuntarily transmit the revolutionary contagion through his Empire. The Italian principalities and republics were too terrified of retaliation from the French Republic to grant entry to the refugees (except bishops and higher clergy in the kingdom of Naples), and even Pius VI, who allowed in 5000 and created a charitable fund for them, insisted on an anti-Gallican and anti-Jansenist oath as well as requiring a retraction from Constitutional priests. Thus, caught between unsympathetic European rulers and French armies pressing ever further beyond their frontiers during the wars of the 1790s, the French exiled clergy were often forced to keep on the move. They did what they could to inspire the member governments of the First

Coalition to fight on until Jacobinism and all its works should be overthrown. If leading architects of resistance like Baron Thugut in Vienna made strategic decisions on far more pragmatic grounds,[74] there were always highly placed politicians willing to listen to *émigré* animadversions against the devilish regicides of Paris, like the British politician Edmund Burke, who had influential backers at the heart of Pitt's government, notably the Foreign Secretary, Lord Grenville.[75] The cries of the *émigrés* for help in restoring Church and state were taken up by politicians like Burke, and ensured that even resolutely Protestant polities like Britain welcomed religious refugees and stopped assuming that 'popery' and Frenchness went together.

Arguably, more than any single event, even the execution of Louis XVI, it was the insults offered to the Christian religion by the French republic that stirred up European public feeling against France, and kept it at this intense level. No one in living memory could recall any western European state using the apparatus of a centralised government in such a draconian manner against the majority creed. Determinedly using all the weapons of coercion at their disposal, French politicians in the period 1791–5 were intent on exercising control over the public expression of the Christian religion. In 1793 and 1794 repression was severe in the extreme, though this in part reflected the desperate struggle of the Jacobin regime for survival against external enemies. Caught up in a relationship of manifest imbalance with the state, churchmen and parishes were first required to accept the Constitutional Church and then to give up Christian religious practice altogether or face severe legal penalties, frequently death. It is time to consider in more detail the mixed fortunes of the Catholic churches – and those of Protestant and Jewish congregations – in France during the years 1791–5.

9(i) The Survival of the Religious Groups: The Constitutional Church

Most books on the Revolution still hardly give the Constitutional Church more than a paragraph or two after describing its formation, so balanced evaluation is hard to come by, and it remains for many students the Cinderella of late-eighteenth-century religious history. Such marginalisation would have seemed strange to revolutionary Christians, for whom this Church was not, in an important sense, a new creation at all, but one that more authentically corresponded to the ideals of the New Testament than its non-juring rival. Their expectation was that the Gospel and the Declaration of the Rights of Man could harmoniously coexist: the Gospel was fraternity itself claimed the future bishop, Claude Fauchet, and he appealed to Montesquieu for verification.[1] Fauchet's writings, like his *Sermon sur l'accord de la religion et de la liberté* (1791), have even led Bernard Plongeron, the leading modern authority on the Constitutional Church, to see in them an anticipation of 1960s-style 'liberation theology', with Christ presented as 'the God of liberty, tolerance and fraternity'.[2] Certainly Fauchet, like his colleagues, looked to promote a this-worldly happiness, and therefore they unashamedly paid tribute to those progressive *philosophes* who had praised the spirit of the Gospel – such as 'the sublime Rousseau'[3] – while taking care to avoid reference to those like Helvétius and d'Holbach whom the Church had earlier condemned. The future seemed a promising one, in which the hand of providence could be discerned. As the bishop of the new diocese of Versailles put it:

> In this great Revolution, can we not see the work of the most High, the natural conclusion to the neglect the old clergy have for eighty years made of the most precious dogmas, of evangelical morality, of holy discipline and everything in France that there was of virtue, enlightenment and useful establishments?[4]

Though figures for lay adherence to the Civil Constitution remain problematic, it seems the Constitutional Church was, narrowly, the preference of the majority of the French in 1791. They were used to a state-backed Church, the one officially recognised by the monarchy or by the National Assembly after 1790. So the numbers of those refusing to go down this road becomes still more striking. Nevertheless, it would have been a reasonable assumption at the Constitutional Church's formation that its adherents were likely to rise over time at the expense of the refractories. If this increase was not forthcoming, it was hardly the fault of the abundant clerical talent that the Constitutional Church initially succeeded in recruiting. Despite the opprobium heaped on the heads of their successors by displaced bishops and *cures*, and their allies – 'men chosen from bars' lured by the salary, scoffed the royalist journal *The Acts of the Apostles*[5] – they were, for the most part, well-intentioned. The majority had a strong Christian faith, but were keen to see Catholicism work in partnership with a progressive political cause rather than to obstruct it, and so give the lie to Enlightenment writers who would have viewed any such creative synthesis as a contradiction in terms.

Jurors, typically, were often ambitious priests in their thirties and forties, making their way unspectacularly in the parish ministry, who at a stroke found their chances of promotion, even to the point of reaching episcopal rank, had dramatically increased. Many others were former monks who would receive a salary far better than the small pension granted to their former brothers who abandoned holy orders completely. For all of them, the alternative to the oath could be destitution, so that the logic of patriotism was supplemented by the prospect of a decent standard of living; one Angevin *cure*, Maupoint of Cantenay, by habit and inclination an 'aristocrat', shocked his friends by the honest admission that '*il faut vivre*'.[6] Blatant careerists and opportunists were a minority among the Constitutional clergy. Their style was rational and severe rather than devotional, and was reflected in a preference for less elaborate forms of worship that owed much to the Jansenist heritage. With their favoured ethical emphasis on categories like 'utility' and 'happiness' in a manner that developed seamlessly from the pre-Revolutionary cross-fertilisation of Tridentine and Enlightenment influences, they could only welcome a settlement which, in theory, moved towards Rousseauian egalitarianism.

Though the Revolution and its Church existed in such initial harmony, the latter had a life of only ten years, and was disowned by the state after less than three. In any assessment of its work and purpose, the historian soon appreciates that its enemies have always been more numerous than its supporters. From its controversial origins with the oath to the Civil Constitution of 1790, few commentators have had a favourable word to say for it, caught and compromised as it has been between the anathemas of the refractory clergy on one hand, and the dechristianising radicals on the other. Yet it started with such high ideals, the ecclesiological counterpart to the secular optimism of 1790. Though the non-jurors might mourn the demise of Gallicanism, the Constitutional clerics thought their Church was the fulfilment of that ideal, free at last from papal interference, a truly national body for a reinvigorated state with a structure inspired by the libertarian vision that had distinguished true Gallicanism from an inferior version – of service only to royal and episcopal absolutism. They hoped it would restore the Church to its primitive, unsullied state, and express a modern spiritual-ity inseparable from France's experience of the Enlightenment. It was a high calling, admirably summed up in its attachment as proclaimed by Pierre Pontard, Bishop of the Dordogne in March 1791 to 'Religion, *la patrie* and the Constitution', but one that seemed to sit well with the political regeneration of France in the early 1790s.

There was a serious attempt to reflect these ideals in the organisa-tion of the Church under the Civil Constitution. As Colin Jones has tellingly observed, it 'may in many respects be viewed as the charter of a professionalised secular clergy'[7] with rationalised procedures, and a definite career structure all making for an attempt at civic har-mony; the emphasis was less on the priest in the hierarchy than the citizen-priest in the heart of the lay community.[8] The Constitutional clergy accepted the logic of national sovereignty, which left them minimal corporate rights and a primary status as officials rather than priests. So there were resemblances to the urban bourgeoisie staffing local government, and mutual support was both expected and given in 1791 and 1792. The lay elite – many of whom had rushed to purchase Church lands as soon as they had come on the market – endorsed the view of the Constitutional Church's archi-tects that it should be the one lawful and established confession in France; whatever the reality of the situation on the ground, it extended across the entire nation with an absence of 'no-go' areas. Wherever there was a *département*, there would be a diocese. Such brand-new units, staffed and supported by the early beneficiaries of the Revolution, would inevitably attract disparagement from the towns and people who had lost in status. Thus even in potentially friendly areas, like much of Normandy, urban support was hazardous: Caen might at last have its cathedral, but smaller cities like Avranches and Sées resented the loss in official importance caused by the downgrading of their cathedral, the abolition of chapters, the decrease in business among tradesmen and craftsmen dependent on them and the deleterious consequences for the local economy that followed.[9] This was a very important aspect of opposition to the new system, one that influenced waverers to opt for the non-juring arm of the Church.

The bishops in the new Church had inherited an infrastructure that was quickly slimmed down. Numerous church buildings were simply abandoned or auctioned off, to be turned into barracks, hospitals, depots of every sort – or just left to the wind and rain; the land they stood on was sold to raise ready cash, and anything adjudged superfluous by way of vestments, furniture and fittings was disposed of. Parishes were fewer, cathedral chapters had been disbanded, and the dichotomy between higher and lower clergy that had characterised the pre-Revolutionary Church was absent. It all underscored a leaner Church with a pastoral priority, neatly symbolised by the spartan personal lifestyles of its hierarchy. Isaac-Etienne Robinet, the new Bishop of La Rochelle, attracted much favourable comment at the expense of one of his predecessors – a La Rochefoucauld had been Bishop of Saintes, a see abolished under the Civil Constitution – by appearing before the electoral assembly on 28 February dressed rustically in woollen leggings, then bringing just one servant and two vicars-general into the town with him.[10] Yet there were anomalies. Here was a Church intended to concentrate on the spiritual welfare of the nation but unable to free itself from temporal functions precisely because it had that national character. As Colin Lucas has pointed out, parish priests were explicitly called 'public officials' and 'the revolutionaries expected priests to preach virtues which were civic before they were Christian'.[11] Nothing better demonstrated it than the principle of electing clergy, and throwing that right open to members of the departmental assemblies irrespective of their faith. Equally, nothing more infuriated non-jurors who were aghast at the way this innovation opened the doors to pollution of the Church by lay, non-Catholic outsiders.

In fact, the procedure laid down for episcopal elections was scrupulously followed in the majority of cases during the first four months of 1791. Protestants and Jews took part in the Alsace and the Gard, some women cast votes in the first round in the Pas-de-Calais, but that was the extent of it. It could not stop the complainants for, of course, refractory Catholics had boycotted the assemblies.[12] That helps to explain the predictably poor turnout of 30 to 40 per cent in the Vendée (though not in Brittany) and the Massif Central. It was higher elsewhere (70 to 80 per cent in the south-east and also in the east in general), so there are important differences from the geography of the clerical oath. 'Never, since Charlemagne's time', protested the royalist journalist de Rozoi, 'has a decision about such a crucial matter been taken by sovereigns without the advice of at least a national council.'[13] But such criticisms were powerless to dislodge the new mechanisms.

That order, in essentials, was recognisably Catholic. There was no change in the liturgy and none in doctrine. The hierarchical descent of bishops, priests and deacons was retained unmodified; there was no obligation on the two old-regime bishops who remained in post (Viviers and Orléans) to be elected; notification to the Pope of consecration was required, and a Mass was celebrated before elections. The vows taken by each at ordination and consecration were identical to their pre-Revolutionary equivalents, with the notorious addition of the oath to the state required by the Civil Constitution.[14] That, in itself, was little different from the loyalty expected by the monarchy before 1789.

None of which stopped the opponents of the new bishops elected to the vacant sees in the first half of 1791 from losing any time in blackening their reputation. Edmund Burke, in his *Letter to a Member of the National Assembly*, lent a willing ear to preposterous claims that the sons of Jewish usurers had been made bishops, 'persons not to be suspected of any sort of Christian superstition, fit colleagues to the holy prelate of Autun [Talleyrand]', he observed with heavy irony.[15] The royalist press generally echoed this sort of polemical abusiveness: the new episcopate consisted of uneducated nobodies who could say Mass without understanding a word of it, who had cynically advanced themselves for the worst motives like the Bishop of Nîmes, depicted as a debauchee dancing on the day of his consecration with the prettiest women, or like Luc-François Lalande of Nancy (*département* of the Meurthe):

Mons. Lalande has in an orgy
lost his pastoral ring
pilfered by a pretty hand.
But this robbery isn't a bad thing
Because they say that the pilferer
Who doesn't want to be a thief
Is going to use it as their wedding ring![16]

At Vannes the election of Charles Le Masle as Bishop of the Morbihan provoked local wags to reformulate the last request of the
Lord's Prayer to read – '*Délivrez-nous du Masle*',[17] while the royalist
house-magazine, the *Acts of the Apostles*, from July 1790 attacked Fauchet of Calvados for his well-known liaison with Mme Calon.[18] Such
bitter burlesques were less than fair. Just to take Lalande's case, he
was a distinguished but timid intellectual who was so surprised and
frightened by his election that he twice refused and twice accepted
the see! But fundamental to his makeup was the confident belief that
Christianity, once severed from superstition and ignorance, was
more likely to benefit governments than any other religion.[19] Generalisations are as difficult about these men as about their pre-Revolutionary predecessors, though the words used by the departmental
directory of the Vosges to commend Mgr Maudru to its citizens as
one 'recommended by his intellect, his manners, and his civic quali-
ties [*civisme*]', might plausibly be applied to the new episcopate as a
whole.[20] Rare indeed were those like François-Auguste Rodrigue at
Luçon, who drew his salary but otherwise did nothing to announce
his presence in the diocese to his *curés*, not even by a pastoral letter.[21]

Four of the Constitutional bishops – Brienne, Talleyrand, Lafont
de Savine and the younger Jarente – had been diocesans before the
Revolution, and their decision to break ranks with former episcopal
colleagues attracted particular opprobrium. Brienne won plaudits as
a democrat from those who had formerly blamed him for ministerial
despotism, but his attempts to justify his conduct on grounds of expediency did not impress Pius VI; Brienne returned his cardinal's hat in
March 1791, and was declared a perjuror and an apostate in a papal
consistory the following September. Nevertheless, his church reforms
were popular in the Yonne *département*, with local supporters of the
new order gratified that their prelate had turned down the invitation
to return to his old diocese in Toulouse as metropolitan of the south.[22]
Talleyrand did not take a see. He limited his services to consecrating

the first new bishops, then became exclusively concerned with secular politics. His example ensured that over half the priests in the Saône-et-Loire *département* took the oath (345 of 658), but it made him the target of spectacular abuse from higher clergy. Jarente justified his decision to take the oath from the necessity of a reformation in ecclesiastical administration, and the old Gallican theses about the power of the Holy See, but said nothing publicly about the way his chronic indebtedness necessitated holding on to a salary.[23] Lafont de Savine was an idealistic maverick moving fast towards his own form of heresy; he voluntarily resigned his see and submitted to popular re-election. He later admitted to Jacques Emery in the Conciergerie prison during the Terror that his sense of Gallican principle had been too exalted.[24]

Many of the other new bishops were frustrated men of talent drawn from the parish clergy (55 out of the 80) and the ecclesiastical teaching orders who had been held back under the aristocratic monopoly of the episcopate that lasted down to 1788.[25] Often they had been among the most progressive members of the former First Estate in the National Assembly, like Lalande, the author of *Apologie des décrets de l'Assemblée nationale, sur la constitution civile du clergé* [*Apology for the Decrees of the National Assembly on the Civil Constitution of the Clergy*]. Deservedly best known is Henri-Baptiste Grégoire, Bishop of the Loir-et-Cher, 'one of the few men who lived through the Revolution without betraying a friend or abandoning a principle'.[26] He was unrelenting in working for the emanicipation of slaves in French colonies, was the architect of the decree removing the last legal restrictions on the Jews of France, and continued doggedly loyal to his Church against its detractors, whether dechristianisers or non-jurors. In 1792 he undertook a thorough pastoral visitation of his diocese (the first of three), insisting to his clergy on the overwhelming need to yoke together love of religion and one's country. He was not welcome everywhere: the nuns of one convent where he called told him bluntly he was not the bishop of Jesus Christ but the bishop of the town hall and the local popular society.[27] Other newly mitred talents included Claude Fauchet (Bishop of the Calvados *département* in Normandy), a smooth Parisian socialite and intellectual who had spent 14 July 1789 with the conquerors of the Bastille; like Grégoire, a member of the philanthropic society of the 'Amis des Noirs' dedicated to abolition of the slave trade, Fauchet was deeply committed to revolutionary progress and sponsor of one the leading

Parisian clubs devoted to its achievement – Le Cercle Social of the Friends of Truth founded in 1790 – a democratic debating club that resembled one of the Masonic lodges.[28]

Fauchet had no problem in identifying Christianity with democracy and fraternity and, in his *Vie de Jésus, homme du peuple* [*Life of Jesus, Man of the People*], blamed the Saviour's crucifixion on 'the aristocracy'.[29] Not all the new 'Fathers-in-God' had Fauchet's combative and ostentatious revolutionary zealotry, but they shared his sense that recent events in France were linked with Biblical apocalypse and the building of the New Jerusalem, that the times were coming when would befall 'the great evils foretold by the Prophets which would precede the total conversion of the nations and the reign of Jesus Christ on earth'.[30] There was a strong millenarian streak in the Constitutional Church as in so many other religious phenomena in Europe in the 1790s. Bishop Pontard of the Dordogne became a patron of the Périgourdine prophetess Suzette Labrousse. Pontard took up her cause, wrote her biography and founded in January 1792 the *Prophetic Journal*, entirely devoted to her predictions, among them the impending resurrection of the first Dauphin (d. 1789) and Mirabeau.[31] Other prelates had a more practical bent. Undeterred by the low turn-out of a dozen or so priests walking in procession when he took possession of his cathedral, Hugues Pelletier of the Maine-et-Loire had the character of a dedicated priest, and tried vainly to win sympathy from the estranged Catholics of Angers by such gestures as attending the funerals of all local clergy, whether jurors or otherwise.[32] So – unavailingly – did Joseph Pouchot, elected Bishop of the Isère at the age of seventy-two. He was one of several bishops called to his post from a mere curacy.[33] Others had canonries and more leisure to aspire to the ideal of a learned clergyman like J-B. Aubry, former Professor of Humanities and Philosophy at the Collège de Bar, elected Bishop of the Meuse *département*,[34] or Pacareau, Bishop of the Gironde, Canon of Saint-André (Bordeaux) down to 1790, fluent in Hebrew and Syriac as well as Greek and Latin.[35] Comparable colleagues, usually those who had held academic posts before the Revolution, often held similar broadly Jansenist sympathies.[36]

Diocesan organisation was an uphill task. Constant, Bishop of the Lot-et-Garonne and former Professor of Theology at the University of Bordeaux, produced a new edition of the catechism, but found much of his energy going into the defence of the new ecclesiastical

order: his numerous *Mandements* defending the constitutional oath
are among the best examples of their kind. His, like most other pastoral literature and sermons issued that spring, had an essentially
moderate character. The Constitutional clergy insisted that the
cause of religion was not lost, whatever the detractors of the oath
and its supporters maintained, and they called into question the
validity, sometimes the authenticity, of the recent papal briefs. Even
had they come from the Holy Father, wrote Mgr Delcher, Bishop of
the Haute-Loire:

> I would not consider myself obliged to defer to them. I am a
> Frenchman, and I have some knowledge of our liberties albeit
> that they are only the feeble remains of the discipline, of the
> maxims of the first, the best centuries of the Church. According to
> those principles, the Pope has no immediate jurisdiction over the
> people of France ...[37]

Clergy newly installed in post likewise insisted on the purity of their
motives. Pontard, Bishop of the Dordogne, rebuked his predecessor,
Mgr de Flammarens of Périgueux, for imagining that ambition lay
behind his acceptance of office: 'Who could wish to steer a ship in
such a frightful tempest? Ah! If you really wish to have this see, it's
certainly in my power to put it back in your hands!' Pontard knew
well enough the conditions were unacceptable. Elsewhere, he could
strike a note of menacing watchfulness towards the refractories. In
giving thanks for his election as bishop, Pontard warned he was
'going to be very vigilant in surveying all these fanatical and antisocial
efforts' and pleased his audience by saying that 'Your patriotism will
stop the secular aristocracy and my activity will do the same for the
religious aristocracy.'[38] Pontard was not alone in replying in kind to
the invective levelled at him by the former bishop and his supporters.
Gay-Vernon, newly elected to the episcopate in the Haute-Vienne,
rounded furiously on his libellors in May 1791: 'Before the Revolution, [Church] dignities were always the inheritance of the proud,
the price of silver, the reward for vice, the conquest of intrigue ...'[39]
This defence only brought down new attacks on his head. Some
of his colleagues were far more emollient towards the refractories.
Bishop Lalande briefly encouraged his *curés* to assist wherever possible at their services,[40] while François Bécherel, elected Bishop of the

Manche *département*, gained respect for leaving in peace those clergy who did not recognise his authority.

Pastoral work could be the most constructive form of counter-offensive against non-jurors. At Angers, Bishop Pelletier struggled to keep the seminary open (it was functioning as a prison by 1792) and filled with students, although for him, as for all the prelates, it was hard to find recruits. But such efforts were appreciated only by clergy and people who considered themselves to be 'patriots', like the priests who accompanied the Constitutional bishop, Deville, into the counter-revolutionary stronghold of Roussillon on the Spanish frontier, a showing dismissed by one royalist detractor as 'a little cortège of apostate monks and priests of bad repute'.[41] Otherwise, the prelates of 1791 depended crucially on official support and, at district and departmental level, it was usually forthcoming in 1791 and 1792. The arrival of a Constitutional bishop in his diocesan centre would commonly be accompanied by the drums and trumpets of the local National Guardsmen in a show of force – Pouderous at Béziers never lost his nickname as 'Bishop of the Bayonets' – drowning out the jeering of dissentients, and hoping that this official approval would – sometimes with a party,[42] or illuminations and fireworks[43] – offset at best the indifference, at worst the open hostility of the local townsfolk.

Bayonets were not much use against the taunting women who came to jeer, as at Nantes, where Bishop Minée entered his cathedral to cries of 'Minée, you're a mouse, you're a mouse!'[44] But demonstrations were not always verbal. Protection could well be needed, as Bishop Nogaret of the Lozère found when he was attacked with stones at Chirac in his new diocese.[45] Many of the new prelates belonged to the clubs, bastions of revolutionary affirmation and energy like Léonard Gay-Vernon, *curé* and Mayor of Compreignac, north of Limoges, before his election as Constitutional bishop.[46] Constant in the Lot-et-Garonne had his candidature pushed by the 'Society of the Friends of the Constitution': in a scenario that was common throughout France, fellow members helped organise the installation and then keep him steady at his post – a necessary gesture when the newly mitred needed all the backing they could get in most dioceses, especially as the law prohibited the Church any corporate identity. A national council would not meet until the era of the Directory.

Some permitted innovations worked well. Thus the newly instituted episcopal vicars soon proved invaluable assistants for the

Constitutional bishops in 1791–2, their presence in the Church a sign
that it was by definition both hierarchical and collegiate. There was
at that date little evidence that they would be among the leading
dechristianisers.[47] The bishops could also usually rely between 1791
and 1793 on the unstinting support of the new parish clergy. There
were numerous vacant benefices to fill, quite a temptation for those
who had struggled for years on the *portion congrue*. But it could mean a
move a long way from home, to take up a post in a parish unsympathetic to the new order, loyal to its old priest, its bishop and, in the last
analysis, to the Pope. For large numbers of the Constitutional *curés*
overcoming the virulent hostility of their parishoners was the first
priority, and that could apply where a priest already in post, like
the abbé Bernauer of Thannenkirch in Alsace, had decided to
take the oath. He lost most of his parishioners, who dubbed him
'impious, sacrilegious and heretical', and kept their children back
from his catechism classes.[48] To such people, Bernauer had overnight
become as much an alien as the 'priestly' strangers moving into other
parishes up and down France – outsiders, unwanted intruders in
their midst, whose physical presence contaminated the church.
Invariably, the National Guard would turn out to escort the new
curé to his presbytery, 'like Judas, accompanied by soldiers', as one
non-juror noted; at Montaut in the Landes, the *département* had
to declare martial law before the constitutional priest could be
installed.[49] This token display of state power was not always enough
to extract cooperation, and it was not unknown for the mayor of the
commune to offer no assistance to the intruded priest, or even to
resign in protest at his arrival.

Once the townsmen in their uniforms had left, the new *curé* was
often shunned and 'sent to Coventry' by villagers who ignored him,
jeered at him, and made him the subject of community derision. Parishioners could be very resourceful in expressing their disapproval: it
varied from banging and clattering home-made instruments outside
his front door (the so-called rough music), through having dead animals left on the doorsteps of the presbytery, to burning the intruder in
effigy. Non-cooperation often centred on the church itself. The keys
would be hidden, sacred objects stolen for 'better keeping', its clock
left unrepaired, a cat concealed inside the tabernacle on the altar,
or villagers would sing their own chants outside the church to drown
out the noise of the Mass the 'intruder' was celebrating inside. It was
never easy after such an inauspicious start for a well-meaning priest

to win over his people, though many juring clergy worked harder to do so than is commonly acknowledged.

A letter from Bishop Nogaret of the Lozère to the President of the National Assembly's Ecclesiastical Committee (26 August 1791) affords us a vivid sense of how difficult the work of the Constitutional Church could be:

> For 3 months, I have tried patiently to carry out a difficult ministry in the Lozère, where fanaticism has made and continues to make daily fearful ravages ... I stuggle almost alone against public opinion, seduced as it is by the troops of refractory priests, none of whom, despite the decrees, have been replaced [in their parishes]. All the authorities, who ought to sustain me, refuse me their support. I am booed and insulted publicly; the local administrators see it and offer me no help.[50]

Some families reacted to the confusion by not going to Church at all, and would be very reluctant returnees thereafter; their babies were not brought to the new *curé* for baptism, nor their parents for burial, as his polluting presence rekindled ancestral memories of Protestantism.[51] A vociferous minority of wives and mothers could not leave things at that. The hatred of many women for the 'intruders' could pass all limits, as at Caen in 1791, where two hundred drunken females hurled stones at the altar of one celebrant and nearly killed him.[52] It was against this background that juring priests began to complain about Woman usurping authority within the family, an Eve influenced by a sinister figure in the guise of a refractory clergyman.[53]

It is hardly surprising that some priests were reluctant to accept the parishes offered to them: the figure of those without a Constitutional incumbent went from about a quarter in the Sarthe to three-quarters in counter-revolutionary strongholds like the Ardèche, Maine-et-Loire and the Vendée.[54] In the early days of the Church, priests could be speedily consecrated, some of them either old men or under age for the ministry according to canon law (Porion in the Pas-de-Calais advanced many nineteen-year-olds into holy orders). In the Manche *département*, 44 men received the tonsure and were rushed through to priesthood in three months,[55] but moving those newly ordained into the parishes was another matter, and a vigorous demonstration from villagers might drive out a Constitutional clergyman before he could take up residence. From sheer necessity, the rules under the Civil Constitution stipulating the minimum experience needed before priests had their own benefice were either abandoned or never implemented. Ex-members of the religious orders were prevailed on to serve the parishes, and bishops nominated clergy to benefices without recourse to the electoral requirements. In the diocese of the Calvados, Bishop Fauchet's episcopal vicars had by 1792 also left Caen to do what they could in rural parishes to eke out numbers. That was one way out of the embarrassment. Another, still more drastic, was provisionally to leave in place a non-juring *curé* in order that public worship could continue.[56]

Faced with an unpromising situation in their dioceses, it was not long before many of the new Church leaders, like some of their pre-Revolutionary predecessors, succumbed to the temptation to seek a role in national politics. Adrien Lamourette, Bishop of the metropolitan diocese of Rhône-et-Loire (Lyon), used his membership of the Legislative Assembly to articulate his passionate belief in national brotherhood and reconciliation. With deputies divided over their response to the invasion of the Tuileries on 20 June 1792, he tried at the last hour to bring Left and Right together by asking for an 'oath of eternal fraternity' to be sealed by an embrace. If it was a brief – and mildly riduculous – moment of harmony before the *fédérés* began to reach the capital, the 'Kiss of Lamourette' was also brilliantly emblematic of Constitutional ideals.[57] Many other churchmen were spokesmen for the Revolution *before* they were advocates for Christianity, such as the Brissotin, Bishop Fauchet, a tireless pamphleteer over the two years from summer 1791 to summer 1793. Like his brother prelates (Grégoire among them), he was reluctant to abandon his political ambitions, and served as a deputy in both the Legislative Assembly and the Convention, as well as keeping an eye on local affairs around Caen; Bishop Gay-Vernon did much the same in Limoges.[58] It should not be assumed that relations between the Constitutional episcopate and local authorities were always harmonious. Pierre-Mathieu Joubert, Bishop of the Charente, encountered many problems in imposing his authority on priests who *had* taken the oath, but received little help from the *département* which, characteristically, refused to give him official permission to spend time in Paris on business. As a result, he resigned as Bishop in December 1792, and resumed life as a parish priest.[59] Many *curés* were, of course, themselves continuously active in local government and the political clubs behind the official apparatus.

Whatever the political involvement of its clergy, nothing more typified the Constitutional Church at parish level than its willingness to celebrate its place in the revolutionary scheme by drawing on 'patriotic' rhetoric and iconography as much as on the usual scriptural and ecclesiological tokens of legitimation. It expressed a fervent belief that Christian renewal in France was entirely compatible with the revolutionary polity. What undid these expectations was the disowning by the state of the creature it had called into life, and leaving it to its own devices. The definite cooling-off in official support for the state Constitutional Church actually predates the inauguration of the Republic in the autumn of 1792: the Legislative Assembly was drifting towards a conspicuously *laissez-faire* approach the previous spring. Though invited to join in the Corpus Christi Day procession on 7 June 1792 by the *curé* of Saint-Germain-l'Auxerrois, the Assembly decided that, though there would be no sittings on that day, individual deputies were at liberty to attend or not according to preference.[60] Once the monarchy was overthrown, the nominal support of 'patriots' for the Church evaporated still further.

Apart from those priests who took part in the Federalist revolt in the provinces against the Jacobin coup of 1 June 1793, the loyalty of the Constitutional clergy to the new republic held, despite the evidence that Jacobin politicians had come round to the view that the revolutionary loyalties of *all* priests were suspect. The state had certainly lost interest in the ecclesiastical bequest of the constitutional monarchy, beyond the bare formality of confirming in November 1792, then again in January and June 1793, that the state would continue to fund the stipends of the clergy, barring those compromised by their Federalist allegiance.[61] Many clerics had participated in the elections to the new National Convention – some were even candidates – and as many as 46 were actually returned, including 16 bishops.[62] As Catholics, they were increasingly on the defensive in both attitudes and actions. Jean-Baptiste Royer, Bishop of the Aisne, successfully elected, left behind a pastoral letter referring to God as the Father of the Enlightenment, who would answer people's prayers for the restoration of law and order.[63] Once at the Convention, Royer and other episcopal deputies found themselves rather isolated figures, for the current of republican politics had moved on from the religious settlement of 1790, which no longer had the fixed character the Constitutional churchmen badly wanted to believe it possessed. Despite losing the right of registering births, marriages and deaths from September 1792 to the municipalities, clerical deputies mostly attempted to play a constructive part in the Conventions's deliberations: the field of national public instruction was a key area in which they campaigned to retain a role for the Catholic religion in a republican constitution by working on the *Comité d'Instruction Publique*. Another area formerly the primary concern of the clergy – charity – also engaged them, through the *Comité des Secours Publics* of the Convention.[64]

Over the nine months from September 1792 to June 1793, most clerical deputies worked in loose alliance with the Brissotins, while remaining critical of their conduct on key issues like the fate of Louis XVI. Four Constitutional bishops voted for his death and six against, interesting evidence of political divisions within the Church. These efforts did nothing to attract reciprocal favours from republican politicians at either national or regional level. There was no reference in the (still-born) Constitution of 1793 of operating under the protection of the Supreme Being, and the evaporation of active support for the Constitutional clergy in the larger towns and cities continued unabated. Siren voices like Danton's inveighed against the 'duplicity' of the Constitutional clergy, and he told the Jacobin Club shortly before his assassination:

> You don't know who your mortal enemies actually are. It is the constitutional priests, those who shout the loudest in the countryside about anarchy, about disorganizers, about Dantonism, Robespierrianism, Jacobinism! They want to establish their priestly throne on the ruins of liberty![65]

His removal from the scene did not silence the critics, and the pace at which the State Church lost favour accelerated after the overthrow of the Brissotins in June 1793; its bishops and clergy became increasingly vulnerable to patriotic victimisation, like Fauchet, arrested after the murder of Marat, and one of the twenty-two deputies denounced by the Paris *sections* in October 1793.[66] The clergy had paid a high political price for their alignment with the Girondins. Grégoire was joined by colleagues in the Convention in a protest against the purge of the Girondins, for which, in October, Bishops Royer and Cazeneuve were imprisoned while Saurine went into hiding.[67] The protest had no effect. The new agents of the Republic moved faster towards open support for dechristianisation, and at diocesan level, episcopal power collapsed under pressure. In May 1793 Bishop Porion of Saint-Omer was rebuked for not having forbidden his priests to keep civil registers. He learnt his lesson. On 12 July he was claiming credit for having married off a former clergyman in Calais; on 2 September he spoke about the superiority of a republican regime compared with its rivals, and on 24 November he resigned his *lettres de prêtrise* entirely.[68]

During the First Republic, the awkward amalgam of Christian and revolutionary fervour was further loosened (sometimes involuntarily) by Constitutional clergy who were committed enemies of priestly 'fanaticism' in any manifestation. It led counter-revolutionary leaders like Burke in 1793 to claim that 'The Constitutional Clergy are not the Ministers of any religion: they are the agents and instruments of this horrible conspiracy against all morals,'[69] but such a diatribe conceals the extent to which anti-Christian policies were deplored by many leaders of the Constitutional Church. Audrein, an episcopal vicar, had produced a memorandum for the legislature that argued for maintaining the existing laws on the Catholic cult on the basis that, despite the efforts of Voltaire and his disciples, the nation's preference for Catholicism was incontestable.[70] In January 1793, the Constitutional Bishop of Clermont was complaining to his flock in a pastoral letter:

> Some deeply corrupted men have conspired against the Lord and His Christ. Under the false pretext of freedom of opinion, they are destroying all morality, undermining the foundations of all virtue, annihilating all principles of sociability . . . Extravagance is carried to the point of saying that no God is needed, no public worship, no religion . . .[71]

Grégoire likewise accused the dechristianisers of blaspheming in the name of Voltaire,[72] but could not deter thousands of clergy from – formally and informally – abandoning their ministry. Gradually, the marks of identifiable Catholicity became less distinguishable in the juring Church, so that its Christian character appeared imperilled. Nowhere was this more evident than among the so-called *curés rouges*, committed Revolutionaries in holy orders who, in due course, often married, abdicated or both. It was not just an urban phenomenon. Several rural *curés* questioned the idea that the law of property had absolute force, and wanted to see the fruits of the earth divided among their parishioners on an equal basis. Among them was Jacques-Michel-Marie Coupé, a *curé* near Noyon in the Oise, the son of a small farmer, who cultivated his own land, and won applause from Gracchus Babeuf, the egalitarian socialist, for his interest in the rural poor. He was elected to the Convention and was one of the foremost supporters of the Law of the Maximum on prices (29 September 1793).[73] For the most part, such *curés* were in charge of urban parishes. Before long, their pastoral preoccupations took them so far into street politics that their priesthood became redundant. The most famous was Jacques Roux, *vicaire* of Saint-Nicolas des Champs, Paris, in 1791 and, two years later, a power to be reckoned with in the Cordeliers club. He placed the Committee of Public Safety under unrelenting pressure until it conceded the Maximum, and acted as the enemy of profiteers of every hue and the friend of the very poor:

> Liberty is only a vain phantom when one class of men can starve another with impunity. Equality is only a vain phantom when the rich man, through monopoly, exercises the right of life and death over his fellow men.[74]

Interestingly enough, although the archetypal *curé rouge*, Roux never abdicated from his priesthood before he committed suicide in prison in February 1794. Roux was a social egalitarian, but former colleagues in holy orders turned against their old faith in its entirety, like the unfrocked Parisian priest, Charles-Alexandre de Moÿ, who in 1792 had published *Accord de la religion et des cultes chez une nation libre* [*Harmony of Religion and Worship in a Free Nation*]. It asked for the complete laicisation of the State, the abolition of ecclesiastical dress, and the final closure of all remaining religious orders. Moÿ was also an unashamed atheist, a forerunner of the better-known Fouché.[75]

Such radical sentiments vividly underlined the difficulty of yoking together 'primitive Christianity' with revolutionary fervour. Some, like the self-proclaimed Orator of the Human Race, Anacharsis Cloots, insisted a nation could exist without religion. He was denounced by Bishop Fauchet as a miserable cosmopolite at the Cercle Social,[76] but such sentiments were nevertheless becoming the fashion as Constitutional priests were singled out for anticlericalist intimidation. The pressure on them to adapt could take various forms. From early 1793, bishops and priests in the Constitutional Church were encouraged to marry, in flagrant breach of ecclesiastical discipline, and it aroused strong feelings on both sides of the question. Most bishops were firmly against it, including Gratien of the Seine-Inférieure and Fauchet, determined not to give their refractory opponents extra ammunition by condoning a breach of canonical law,[77] though the converse price was 'patriotic' displeasure that stoked up Jacobin intolerance. It was well expressed by François Chabot, an ex-Capuchin turned representative on mission, who, in passing through Toulouse *en route* to the Aveyron, used the occasion to inveigh against the metropolitan bishop, Sermet, and his clergy – from the cathedral pulpit! Chabot

> declaimed against the luxury of the clergy, reproached their embroidered slippers [*pantoufles*] and the expensive lodgings occupied by these successors of the sansculotte Jesus. And if they kept up their opposition to the law on divorce and the marriage of priests, we would soon see them with the refractories, breathing the air of Guiana.[78]

Most bishops resisted these pressures, but not all. Thomas Lindet, Bishop of the Eure, had led the way by taking a wife in November 1792, but episcopal example of this sort was not always persuasive – even Lindet's brother deplored his abandonment of celibacy. In Paris, four *curés* protested unavailingly in 1793 at Bishop Gobel's decision to appoint a married priest into the parish of Saint-Augustin:[79] Gobel was only too aware he had powerful backing inside the Convention, where deputies tried every inducement to persuade the lower clergy to imitate Thomas Lindet's example. The Convention declared in July 1793 that even if such priests were expelled from their parishes, they could keep their salary and pension, and that any bishop who tried to prevent a priest from marrying could be deported; in August that depriving them of a benefice on the grounds of wedlock was illegal; and in November it made communes who had persecuted married clergy responsible for their salaries. It is estimated that about 4500 to 6000 priests took wives, a phenomenon most marked in Paris, in the frontier regions of the north and east, and in the centre of France.[80]

For ardent revolutionaries, this was the fast-track approach to dechristianisation, and it gave the Constitutional Church a credibility gap that the best efforts of Grégoire after 1795 could not wholly repair. For the couples involved, the evidence suggests they were predominantly genuine love-matches; only a committed woman could withstand the ribald public amusement and abuse that surfaced whenever a former priest went through a civil marriage ceremony. Whether married or single, a still higher number of Constitutional clergy resigned their holy orders entirely in favour of 'natural religion' shorn of 'priestcraft' and 'superstition', often submitting to a mock service of renunciation. Of the 85 Constitutional bishops, 24 abdicated, 23 apostasised and renounced their faith, and the others stayed in post; of the 16 bishops with seats in the Convention, 7 departed into secular life.[81]

Where encouragement failed, threats of arrest, imprisonment, or just suspension of salary usually had the desired effect on priests who initially did nothing. In the Loiret, the representative on mission, Javogues, sent out agents or *commissaires* into the southern area of his *département* who either inspired priests to renounce their status or had them arrested as part of the process of '*déprêtrisation*';[82] a surge of abdications in the Hérault during *Frimaire* was largely due to the presence of a Revolutionary army and 139 eventually ceased their ministry in the 343 communes.[83] By January 1794 just to be a priest was enough to make one liable to immediate arrest. In the Loir-et-Cher diocese, Grégoire was horrified to find in the spring of 1794 that some of his own *vicaires épiscopaux* were assisting the representative on mission, Garnier de Saintes, to pressurise clergy into wedlock under pain of death. Intimidation worked: 'better to be on the side of the killers than the killed' admitted another of Grégoire's former colleagues.[84] The most recent estimate suggests the Constitutional Church lost more than half its ordained ministry (50 to 57 per cent). Few went cursing Jesus Christ (one who tried to curry favour that way was told abruptly, 'You are a wicked villain. Jesus Christ was the first one to preach Liberty and Equality'), but there were many ritualised denunciations of 'priestly despotism' and Christian prejudices and 'superstitions'. Others like Jean Radier, parish priest from Lansargues in Hérault, embraced a future with affirmations of faith: 'Now that the state of priesthood contravenes the happiness of the people, and hinders the progress of the Revolution, I abdicate from it and throw myself into the arms of society.'[85]

Death for celibacy was a relatively rare Revolutionary punishment;[86] it was more often the penalty for priests caught on the losing side in the vicious factional struggles wracking France. 8 bishops died on the scaffold, 5 retracting their 'errors' befor dying. There were some major casualities like Fauchet and Lindet, as well as Louis XVI's former minister, Loménie de Brienne, latterly Bishop of the Yonne *département*. He was arrested at Sens in November 1793, and poisoned himself in gaol the following February.[87] Several Constitutionalist clergy out of sympathy with Jacobin centralisation and dechristianisation associated themselves with the Federalist revolt of 1793, and the destruction of that cause led to clerical deaths, imprisonment and victimisation. In Lyon well over a hundred priests and nuns lost their lives in the mass executions ordered by Collot d'Herbois.

There was a suspicion that many Jacobins encouraged the notion that *all* Constitutional clergy were tainted by Federalist sympathies,[88] but there was little evidence for it, beyond the fact that, by contrast with the other southern cities in revolt, there was a religious revival in Toulon in 1793 under municipal auspices. The authorities had ceased to discriminate. Thus at Toulouse, while the Convention sat, of the 509 priests arrested, 125 were jurors; in Paris, 9 refractories were executed, but no fewer than 21 Constitutional clerics; out of the 484 ecclesiastics sent from all over France to appear before the revolutionary tribunal in Paris, at least 319 belonged to the Constitutional Church.

Faced with this unrelenting drive against Christianity across France, a total of approximately 20 000 clergy left holy orders and thousands more ceased to act as priests; in Paris, 410 of 1500 priests abdicated, a percentage total of 27. Michel Vovelle's study of 21 *départements* in the south-east suggests that about one-fifth of secular clergy in 1789 had abdicated four years later, but one should not lose sight of the local variations: in the Provins district (Seine-et-Marne), 81 of 116 members of the clergy (70 per cent) abdicated in November 1793; in Mont-Terrible, only 40 out of 247 (16 per cent).[89] Arguably, in France as a whole it was less the abdicators than the abstainers – those who just stopped exercising their ministry – who had the maximum impact on parish life. As churches were locked up or converted into 'temples of reason', the public practice of Catholicism ceased, to such an extent that by the spring of 1794, it has been estimated, only about 150 of the 40 000 pre-1789 parishes in the whole country were openly celebrating mass;[90] in Bayeux, the juring priest of Saint-Jean's church stated on 3 September 1793 that his congregation consisted of no more than the three priests resident in the parish.[91] Many juring congregations were forced to embrace the new revolutionary cults, to risk savage legal penalties by worshipping with a refractory clergyman, or to have services led by laymen.

With Christianity effectively abolished, and clergy referred to officially – with studied casualness – as the '*ci-devant prêtres*', the basic problem for the Constitutional Church's staff over the period 1793–5 was primarily one of survival. Even in adversity, a hard core of its leaders battled to keep its organisation basically intact at both diocesan and parish level. At *Nivôse* Year II, most churches were open and worship going forward in *départements* where the Constitutional Church had always had numerous adherents: the Dordogne, the Loiret, the Loir-et-Cher. At Louvigné-du-Désert, in that part of Brittany that remained aloof from the *Chouans*, the offices were recited and children catechised as part of an attempt by the 'blues' to keep the village loyal to the Republic.[92] It was all very precarious, claiming protection from the decree of 16 *Frimaire*. The slightest hint of political dissent and the local Jacobins would apply to the representative on mission to close places of worship again.[93] A patchy form of episcopal ministry was still in place by 1795, despite massive losses: 47 Constitutional bishops had renounced their functions in 1793 alone.[94] The last elected bishop was Rovère in the Vaucluse in August 1793, and that was by acclamation rather than by ballot – *à la mode* in 1793 where voting was concerned.[95] Some natural leaders like Grégoire stayed at their posts. He believed more deeply than most in the ideals of the 1791 Church, and attempted to live out that faith despite the state reneging on its side of the bargain. Ignoring fears for his life, he had told fellow members of the Convention on 7 November 1793 that he was not resigning as a bishop:

> A Catholic both out of sentiment and conviction, a priest from choice, I have been designated by the people as a bishop, but it's neither from you nor from them that I hold my mission. I've agreed to bear the burden of the office of bishop at a time when it bristles with thorns: having been castigated for accepting it, I am now tormented today to try to force an abdication that can never be torn from me! Acting on the basis of the sacred principles so dear to me, and which I defy you to tear from me, I have tried to do what good I can in my diocese: I shall remain bishop to do more.[96]

To Grégoire's enduring credit, he succeeded in preventing his Church folding up beyond the point of no return, though in the process any pretension that it could be meaningfully described as 'national' had to be discarded. Once state pressure to conform had gone, loyal lay followers turned out to be so thin in number that holding on to them became the first priority: squeezed from the Right by the non-jurors and the counter-revolutionaries and, from the Left by the dechristianisers and those who preferred an alternative public cult to Christianity, the Constitutional Church retained a precarious foothold in a few regions, especially the northern half of central France and in the south-east.

Its leading bishops had originally worked hard to exact financial assistance from the local authorities to keep their local seminary open, but the battle was never conclusively won. Ordinands had always been no more than a trickle, with revolutionary activists from the summer of 1792 flocking instead to the armies and local government; such candidates as there were found themselves rushed through training, but bishops were philosophical: 'When you don't

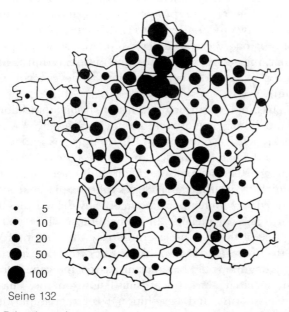

5
10
20
50
100
Seine 132

Map 3 Priests' marriages

have horses, you have to work with asses', one said sardonically.[97] So with most priests in post tempted or constrained either to desert to the refractories[98] or to abandon the Christian ministry altogether, that the Constitutional Church survived at all was a tribute to the minority of clergy who stayed with it continuously from the spring of 1791. They could build up their own following, as did Chaussy, priest at Bourg-sur-Rhône. When the local representative on mission, Châteauneuf-Randon, tried to arrest him early in 1794, he triggered a rising of women in the town.[99] It was early evidence of a groundswell of popular support for the Constitutional Church and its beleaguered clergy – a rising tide on which Grégoire was to launch his project to reconvert the nation to primitive Christianity as embodied in the Constitutional Church.[100]

Four months after Robespierre's overthrow, a handful of Constitutional clerics met secretly in Paris to plan the revival of their Church, and give it the centralised authority it had hitherto lacked. From these small beginnings originated the 'Society of the Friends of Religion' which would meet weekly until 1806 and introduce reforms in worship and organization that enabled the Constitutional Church successfully to take its chances alongside other religious groupings – without any realistic prospect of government favour.[101] By the time of the law of 3 *Ventôse* Year III (21 February 1795), with its promise of religious liberty and permission for small groups to worship together, the power base of the Constitutional Church had been sharply pared away, and as a political force it never recovered after the state disowned it.

Nevertheless, as revolutionary creations went, its life of eleven years was much longer than most and, even as a flawed attempt to marry the French Revolution and Christianity, its importance for the student of the period is undeniable. If the state could be remade in a new image, then so could the Church, in tune to a restorative myth to which most progressive clerics subscribed. That myth was given an added and contemporary dynamic by the writings of Rousseau, and it is no coincidence that many of those who took the oath (including one of the four prelates to do so, the Bishop of Viviers) imagined that Jean-Jacques would have approved of their actions, especially as dogma would be subordinate to expressions of benevolence from the 'citizen-*curé*' towards his fellow citizens. The trouble was that Christianity and Revolution went their separate ways. According to Colin Lucas,

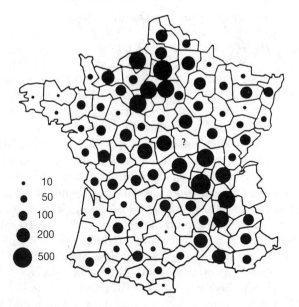

Map 4 Abdicating priests (numbers)

The French Revolution was quite incapable of supplying modern political culture with an established church in a liberal state, such as existed in the English model. Its contribution in this domain had to be the religion of republicanism.[102]

The debate will no doubt continue about this logic. But there is a related point to stress. Produced in a period when the regenerative hopes of 1789 were still high, the divisiveness that attended the creation of the Constitutional Church did more than any other event to shatter the illusion of national uninimity by obliging Frenchmen to make a factitious choice between the Revolution and the Roman Catholic Church. Indeed, the irony was that, in the end, faced with dechristianising pressures, Constitutional clerics found it hard to escape the same clear-cut choice between Christianity and the Revolution that the non-jurors had confronted in 1791.

9(ii)   The Survival of Religious Groups: The Refractory Church

Bishops and priests who either could not initially subscribe to the Civil Constitution, or subsequently retracted their oath, faced a constant struggle for survival over the four years from 1791. For them, more than most, it was a time when, as Bishop Bonal of Clermont believed, 'The vessel of the Church of France is more violently swept by the storm than it has been for fourteen centuries.'[1] Revolutionary sympathisers had badly miscalculated. Assuming that the ideal of the 'citizen-*curé*' would be definitive in this new era, they had not imagined that nearly half the clergy would become refractories, ready to abandon material comforts, or the assurance of a higher income than any available to them under the old régime, for a precarious future. The refractories' unexpectedly high numbers were thus an affront to those who had lulled themselves into giving the religious changes passed by the National Assembly an irresistible force, or supposing that Catholicism and Revolution could so readily be reconciled. The consequences of these false expectations were considerable. They helped turn active support for the Revolution from a national consensus to a minority option, plunged the State into intermittent civil war, and opened up religious fault lines that would endure for nearly two hundred years. As Bishop Duplessis d'Argentré plaintively expressed it, 'Schism, frightful schism has torn out the heart of the Church of France, that part of the universal Church that was formerly so precious and so brilliant.'[2]

Non-jurors tended to be predominantly either at the beginning or the end of their priestly ministry. Young, unbeneficed *vicaires* could proclaim their loyalty to principle without standing to lose much in material terms, while their colleagues in their sixties or older were often sufficiently well-off to make the prospect of a principled, if penny-pinching, old age far more attractive than, in the evening of life, losing the respect of their people. Whatever their age, in social terms, they were often of relatively humble origins from a rural parish, genuine sons of the *pays* like the priests of the Vendée, educated in their diocesan seminary. It was not uncommon for them to remain in their village with the blessing of the local mayor, using the parish church as long as practicable, and denouncing both the services and the presence of the 'usurper' who had taken possession of the presbytery. In time, the ex-*curé*'s hard core of supporters invariably became associated with the counter-revolutionary cause.

In identifying a large proportion of the former First Estate with opposition to the new order, the revolutionaries had given the Counter-Revolution a following unknown over the two years from May 1789 and created it as a popular movement. Many non-jurors may have felt uncomfortable with a dissident role but, as the Revolution turned against the monarchy and then Christianity, any initial unease was soon dissipated. Besides, there was from the beginning a pastoral demand for their services from laity affronted at the disruption inflicted by the Revolution on what mattered most in their lives – their religion. They knew at first hand the social implications of unwanted religious change: village schools where the *curé* taught the catechism and the rudiments of literacy had gone; nothing had replaced the almshouses and charitable foundations for the old and infirm. As Gwynne Lewis has well said, 'For the devotees of Voltaire and Diderot the modernisation of the Church meant coming to terms with reality and reason: for the poor, the beggars, the maimed and the blind it meant increased hardship'.[3]

The scale and impact of the changes attempted by the Assembly became dramatically evident in the first half of 1791, as battle for the hearts and minds of the people was joined. Local authorities wanted to know as early as possible how the local bishop stood as regards the oath, and it is interesting to see how keen several members of the episcopate were in offering olive branches. Mgr de Messey of Valence offered discussions about the possibility of a restrictive oath (spiritual authority apart), but commissioners insisted on all or nothing.[4] Gain-Montaignac, Bishop of Tarbes, refused to sign the Civil Constitution despite strong local pressure, and was soon charged with uncitizenly behaviour. At Auch, the Archbishop spent much of January accounting for himself to the municipal officers. Some of them claimed he had branded the Civil Constitution as the work of the devil. He explicitly repudiated the remark, and insisted that conscience only dictated his refusal of the oath, while Bishop Narbonne Lara, denying rumours in Evreux that he was poised to take the oath, was expressing hopes as late

as 10 January that the Pope would find some means, acceptable to the bishops, of conciliating and realigning Church and state
in France.[5]

Many non-juring prelates were in Paris, often on National Assembly duties, but that did not stop many writing promptly to warn their
flocks about what had happened, to set out their own attitude to the
oath, and declare as schismatic anyone who would defy their legitimate pastoral authority.[6] It was difficult for local government to
ignore these documents when they were printed and circulated, and
it frequently led, as at Meaux, to a counter-declaration that a prelate
was dismissed and the see vacant.[7] The more sensitive officials did
their best to coax prelates into accepting the new order. The former
Mayor of Bayeux, Mgr Cheylus, was given a lengthy period up to
26 February 1791 to take the oath, though it made no difference to
his decision to ignore it.[8] Defying the civil law was not an attitude
that most bishops and clergy were used to striking, as the Bishop of
Saintes told the electors of the *département* of the Charente-Inférieure
in February:

> Caught between the fear of making myself a criminal in the eyes of
> the sovereign judge, and of exposing myself to be regarded as an
> enemy of the laws, and perhaps of being a disturber of the public
> peace, I have had to experience every sort of violent inner
> combat.[9]

Yet the bishop could not in the end strain his conscience by taking the
oath to the Civil Constitution. He joined other like-minded prelates
and priests in resisting efforts to evict them from palaces and presbyteries, a form of intimidation that had started in late 1790 and lasted
into the following year.

Most were not going to leave quietly, and three prelates – Tulle,
Besançon and Troyes – were so bent on contesting the new arrangements they even stood for election into their old dioceses.[10] It was a
defiant, provocative gesture of no-surrender, and further raised the
political temperature. The upheavals could be protracted. In most
dioceses across France, paper warfare erupted in the first months of
1791 as former bishops tried direct appeals to the electors not to pre-
cipitate schism by choosing their replacement. Thus Bishop Bareau
de Girac told the electors of his *département* in Lower Brittany meeting
to dispose of his bishopric:

Canonical laws deny the possibility of granting any benefice that is not vacant. They prohibit men from giving two leaders, two pastors to the same church. In as much as I am your bishop, to name another would be as vain an undertaking as it would be sacriligious.

He appealed emotionally:

It depends on you, Messieurs, to prevent these fearful scouges; good and evil are in your hands. Weeping religion implores you not to despise her feelings.[11]

Where such remonstrations had no effect (as at Rennes, where Le Coz was chosen as constitutional bishop), non-juring prelates largely declared the election of their replacements null and void, and forbade the faithful from recognising the interloper. Machault of Amiens's Pastoral Letter of 4 March was typical:

We forbid every cleric from receiving from the aforesaid intruded bishops or *curés* any order, power, jurisdiction, title, office or ecclesiastical function, or from exercising them in their name and by their authority, under the same penalty of excommunication for adhering to intrusion and schism.[12]

These were unyielding words, announcing fearsome spiritual pains and penalties; such instructions had consequences for the laity too, as found in Bishop Duplessis d'Argentré of Limoges's letter of 3 April denouncing the election of Gay-Vernon in the Haute-Vienne and Huguet in the Creuse: 'The sinners they absolve will not be absolved ... the marriages they bless will not be blessed and will count as nothing in the eyes of religion'.[13]

Most bishops followed the path they considered duty dictated, and worked to ensure circular letters were distributed throughout the dioceses. The Pope's pastoral letter of 13 April condemning the Civil Constitution was both a salve to tender consciences worrying over disobedience to the laws of the state and an incentive to all their flock to stand firm; bishops took pains in their communiqués to make the papal brief known to their *curés*, and to ask them to pass on the news to the faithful, 'to ensure that it makes an impact on consciences and thus contributes to the peace of the Church and the

re-establishment of the laws'.[14] Such advice infuriated local revolutionaries: in April 1791, Cardinal La Rochefocauld's pastoral
instruction was torn up and burnt by the tribunal of Rouen as contrary to the laws of the National Assembly. Hounded by the authorities, some bishops, undeterred, developed flexibile tactics. Thus it
was from the relative safety of the prince-bishopric of Trier – on the
German side of the Moselle – that the Bishops of Metz, Verdun and
Nancy issued an ordinance on 10 May for their people enjoining
obedience to the previous month's brief.[15] Cardinal Rohan, openly
counter-revolutionary in his sympathies, condemned as a schismatic
anyone the Constitutional bishop chose to ordain; as a prince of the
Holy Roman Empire, and with a jurisdiction he still actively exercised on the east bank of the Rhine, Rohan was a constant irritant to
the revolutionaries throughout 1791.

For those still on French soil, each day's post brought to episcopal
residences anonymous letters full of censures and blunt menaces.
It did not stop with the post. At Vannes, a delegation preceded by
two cannons and including a Constitutional cleric dressed up with a
tricolour sash and cockade broke into the palace and threatened Mgr
Amelot with having his ears cut off and his skull turned into a snuff
box;[16] at Soissons, after weeks of defying officialdom, Bishop Bourdeilles left hastily in early March, pursued by a crowd hurling stones
at his coach.[17] He had in his time shown considerable charity to
those who now turned against him. So had Cheylus of Bayeux,
who had left 24 000 livres to the *bureau de charité* in the city to help
pay for bread. None of this counted with the municipality, which
ordered him out of town in April.[18]

Prelates could usually be arrested on a flimsy pretext. Many were
hauled up before the local criminal tribunals to explain pastoral letters that the authorities adjudged both inflammatory and treasonable. Mgr Cheylus had embarked at Cherbourg for the Channel
Islands on the day his arrest was ordered,[19] but Narbonne Lara,
Bishop of Evreux, was not so lucky. He claimed in self-defence against
charges of *lèse-nation* that he had just wanted to explain to the electors 'the inconveniences and certain disaster of proceeding to an uncanonical nomination'.[20] In response, the authorities in the Eure
ensured he left town promptly to follow the King's aunts to exile in
Rome (he was their chaplain),[21] but colleagues like Pierre Louis
de La Rochefoucauld of Saintes – who, admittedly, had been
denounced by the procurator-general of the *département* for his

anti-Civil Constitution writings as 'an enemy of the nation, the law and the King'[22] – was briefly locked up without any formal arrest simply because his brother, the Bishop of Beauvais, was regarded as a serious troublemaker by the authorities.

This kind of intimidation at local level coincided with the National Assembly's greater leniency towards dissidents, and resourceful non-jurors took full advantage. Thus, while his successor was being consecrated in Paris, Bishop Nicolaï of Béziers spent the spring of 1791 touring his diocese, confirmed infants in their cradles, gave eight-year-olds their first communion and indeed worked harder pastorally than since first arriving in it, knowing that his time among the faithful could be numbered in days.[23] He slipped away for Spain when summoned to the Hôtel de Ville as an 'incendiary'. Like his colleagues, he was aware that subterfuge had become a prerequisite of successful ministry. Since most bishops were on the point of leaving for exile, it was vital where possible to transfer some of their powers to others, to put in place arrangements that could allow for continuing contacts with the diocese from afar. Thus in the *département* of the Gers, Archbishop La Tour du Pin had asked his *aumônier*, the abbé Pison, and his secretary, the abbé Dupuy, to stay in Auch and distribute his pastoral letters. Most important of all, and to the fury of the authorities, he conducted a night-time ordination service despite an official ban.[24] The respected Bishop of Boulogne, Mgr Asseline, in his *Mandement* of May, gave his extensive powers of confession and dispensation to all priests exercising their holy ministry, having the foresight to see that their operations would be largely covert. He concluded:

> Let us not cease to hope for salvation, by praying to God with a simple heart and with a unanimous voice; let us join our groans and tears to our prayers, as we must when we are surrounded by ruins, destruction, lamentations and terrors.[25]

Asseline was writing from Paris, unable to return to his diocese, but in Mende, *after* the Constitutional Bishop Nogaret had been installed and returned to Paris, his predecessor came back to the town in the spring. He proceeded to appoint fourteen *grands vicaires* around the diocese to help restrain any priest still undecided about the oath and encourage those who had taken it to recant.[26]

Comparable pressures existed at the parish level as well as the diocesan centre. After following a policy of non-cooperation as long as possible, it commonly happened that many a refractory priest moved out of his presbytery to be sheltered elsewhere in the parish, often taking vestments, the church plate, and the bulk of his parishioners with him. However, there are innumerable instances, for example in the countryside around Paris, of a non-juror having found his congregation ranged against him, unwilling to hear his excuses, and ready to shout him down and drive him out of town.[27] If the parish church was barred to him, services could be held in redundant churches and, where they too were unavailable, barns, granaries and even kitchens were utilised for worship. Noblemen who had not emigrated did what they could. In Poitou the Baron de Vareilles walled up his proprietary chapel from the rest of the village church – 'profaned' by the arrival of an '*intrus*' – and made it available for use by the non-jurors.[28] In Paris and other cities, their priests made use of the chapels in convents, and ignored charges that these were the occasions for violent abuse of the Revolution. There was also the possibility – on paper anyway – of taking advantage of the law of 7 May 1791 permitting refractories conditionally to use the parish churches, but many bishops were reluctant to use it because of the unavoidable contact it would bring with their Constitutional rivals.

Adversity could have its consolations. In some areas like the west, the Pays Basque and parts of the south-east, where priest and people were united in opposition, the bond between them grew firmer during the summer of 1791. In the Angevin area, one former 'citizen-*curé*' of 1789, Rabin of Notre-Dame de Cholet, celebrated mass in the open air with two or three thousand people present. Such activities, especially when combined with priests issuing pamphlets stirring up the countryside, were bound to attract the unfavourable notice of administrators, who tried to believe that it was all a question of superstition and a people corrupted by false guides. Here is Pascot, *procureur* of the commune of Prats-de-Mollo in Roussillon, writing in May 1791 about the 'gullibility' of his fellow citizens:

> They even decided to hold an extraordinary procession of the very Holy Sacrament under the pretext of bringing peace and tranquillity to the realm. These good people are so fallen into the trap that I have seen women go so far in their idiotic devotions as following the procession bare-footed.[29]

Only in a few areas, where local authorities moved slowly and sometimes reluctantly, like the *département* of the Moselle, could non-jurors go publicly about their business much longer. Priests who continued their work undisturbed into the new year were few, but they included the cathedral chapter of Alet, which celebrated daily services until 25 January 1792, the last cathedral in France to do so,[30] and Yves-Michel Marché, *curé* of La Chapelle-du-Genêt in the Mauges. For him, in that highly traditionalist area, the arrival of a Constitutional replacement was a constant threat which might never happen. He went on conducting a full sacramental ministry until arrested and removed to Angers in May 1792, as part of a general policy of separating non-juring clergy from their people by moving the former into the towns where they could be supervised.[31] It was not unknown for their supporters to try to use the Revolutionaries' own weapons against them. In February 1792, a 'Petition of the Citizens of the *département* of the Nord' defended the monks, insisting that any further moves against them would breach the Declaration of the Rights of Man.[32]

To avoid this fate, refractories for the most part either left France or took to the fields and hedgerows; in the Cévennes they hid in the grottoes used by the Protestant Camisard rebels against Louis XIV ninety years previously. About the only group relatively unaffected were nuns who, for the most part, stayed in their communities and kept up, indeed increased, their charitable and educational work.[33] This scattering of its personnel was dramatic evidence of the rupture that had occurred with the pre-1789 Church, with its autonomous institutions and revenues. That had gone, and the clergy loyal to its leaders faced the task of creating something new from its ruins, of adjusting to the reality of life as a beleaguered sect utterly distanced from a hostile state while maintaining the pretension of constituting the one holy, Catholic Church, both apostolic and Roman.

It was natural that, confronted with this trauma of abrupt and massive change, most clergy were anxious for responsive episcopal leadership perhaps more than at any time in their ministry. With most prelates in exile, filling this pastoral vacuum was not straightforward. In Paris there was an *ad hoc* committee of eight bishops in existence by early 1792 doing its best to direct the orthodox, but itself looking to Archbishop Boisgelin (exiled in London) for inspiration, and thereby incurring the distrust of the papacy's representative, Salamon, for excessive moderation towards the government.[34]

This committee apart, non-juring leaders had not much choice but to act independently. Some of the pastoral letters they issued in 1791–2 struck a philosophical note about adversity, like the Bishop of Mende's:

If we are to be more useful, let us voluntarily renounce our titles and our old privileges; let us receive a pathetic pittance in exchange for those rich possessions of which, as so many monuments make plain, our predecessors as well as ourselves made unjust use . . .[35]

Other bishops were almost relieved that their ministry was to be supremely tested, and expressed the hope that they would not be found wanting. 'How glorious it is for me,' wrote Bishop de Ruffo-Bonneval, 'at the start of my episcopate, to be able like St Paul, to display the signs of my apostolic mission in the cross and the combat!'.[36] Others, older than the forty-four-year-old Bishop of Senez, were just bewildered. How to explain the cataclysm that had befallen them? The rhetoric of the dispossessed French Catholics tended rather to embrace suffering as a sign of sin and the consequent need for repentance. But the firier spirits among them, such as the abbé Maury, went to the other extreme and adopted a theology and rhetoric of apocalypse, seeing the mark of anti-Christ in events in France. Such views were echoed across Europe by the counter-revolutionaries as they tried to explain the events that had destroyed the monarchical order in France.

Maury was in Rome by the end of 1791, where he confirmed his standing as a militant Counter-Revolutionary by acting as unofficial spokesman for the *émigrés* of Koblentz. Pius VI tried to use his services – and propel him out of Rome at the same time – by naming him a cardinal, Archbishop of Nicea *in partibus infidelium*, and papal envoy to the Diet of Frankfurt for the coronation of the Emperor Francis II, where he was expected to ask Francis for his help in restoring the rights of the Holy See over Avignon.[37] But if this new prelate poured his considerable energies into working to rescue the monarchy, the majority of non-juring episcopal *émigrés* who left France during 1791 were too stressed by the experience of exile to commit themselves to the cause so prominently. The two notable exceptions were the *ci-devant* Bishops of Arras and Pamiers in the train of Louis XVI's youngest brother, the Comte d'Artois. Significantly, they had both left France in the first, miniature wave of emigration after the fall of the Bastille.

At a less exalted level, the majority of priests were concerned more with the practical ministry than with Counter-Revolution, and discountenanced efforts to become prominent as internal agitators in 1791–2. There were a few exceptions, including the final abortive Jalès encampment (*département* of the Gard) of spring 1792, perhaps the last sign of large-scale, right-wing, clerical participation in rebellion before the Terror.[38] Its failure forced non-jurors in the south underground. 'The black aristocrats' were easy scapegoats for the military setbacks France suffered in the summer of 1792. Charlotte Corday, the future killer of Marat, reported how in May 1792 National Guardsmen from Caen came to the village of Verson looking for non-jurors who had been celebrating Mass there. The priests, tipped off, had gone, but the troops sacked the chapel, cut off the hair of the *curé*'s sister, branded other women, and took fifty people prisoner and forced them to walk back to Caen bound by ropes. The National Guard knew only too well that widows and spinsters were playing a vital organisational role in keeping communities loyal to the refractories and their clandestine services.

Despite this kind of intimidation, Revolutionaries were embarrassed to find that in some areas during 1792 the numbers of nonjuring clergy actually grew; in rural parts of the Midi like the Cévennes, and *départements* like the Hérault and Haute-Garonne, there were numerous recantations by priests who had earlier signed the Civil Constitution.[39] These were often sent to right-wing journals like the *Ami du Roi* for maximum publicity. 'Happy it is,' wrote one repentant *curé*, 'if by a sincere if belated recognition, I can lead to truth all those people whom my example may have seduced and influenced'.[40] Royalist journalists like Royou, Fontenai, de Rozoi and Montjoye made the most of these 'deserters from the altar of the *patrie*'. Repression did little to stifle popular religiosity. Thus when the Blessed Virgin allegedly appeared in an oak tree at Saint-Laurent-de-la-Plaine in the Mauges in 1792 pilgrims flocked to the site from across Anjou and Haut-Poitou without any attempt by the clergy to impede them. Indeed, by comparison with pre-Revolutionary times, many refractories seem to have encouraged dubious popular religious practices and connived in the creation of new sacred spaces and the saints to go with them, particularly in areas like the Maine, Brittany and Anjou.[41] This clerical latitude is explicable in a time of repression and persecution, when martyrs – often children and women – were not hard to find. The honouring of their example was for the survivors a means both of reaffirming their religious commitment and of gaining supernatural assistance in preserving it. Moreover, refractory clergy were seldom in one place long enough either to discourage such practices or to have them dismantled, even if they were so inclined. They would become a characteristic of the early-nineteenth-century French Church. So would other devotional practices which repression encouraged, and especially the Sacred Heart. The ex-Jesuit, P.J. Picot de Clovière, even managed to found two congregations during the imposition of the Civil Constitution: the Daughters of the Heart of Mary (1790) and the Institute of the Heart of Jesus (1791).[42]

After the Revolution of 10 August 1792 in Paris, and the passing of a new law requiring another oath (the so-called 'little oath') of faithfulness to the nation and of maintaining Liberty and Equality, the position of refractory clergy became doubly perilous. Authoritative guidance on a response was hard to come by. The *ad hoc* steering committee of bishops in and around Paris had dispersed; Salamon, the Pope's representative, was arrested on 27 August before he could issue a response, and it would take a minimum of two months before there was word from the Vatican.[43] Though, eventually, the oath was not condemned outright by Pius VI, most refractory clergy could still not bring themselves to kow-tow to the new regime by taking it, and their stubbornness was applauded by hardline *émigré* prelates like Maury. An exception to this inflexibility were the fifteen or so bishops who remained in France, supported by influential opinion among academic clergy, especially the abbé Jacques Emery, formerly the superior-general of the seminary of Saint-Sulpice, and currently Archbishop Juigné's vicar-general in the archdiocese of Paris. Emery declared to priests who had come to consult him that the oath did not affect the spiritual sphere and was therefore lawful ('*licite*'); he feared the practical repercussions of refusal on the holding of services, in reducing still further the paltry living standards of non-juring priests and, above all, in linking the cause of the refractory clergy too closely with the monarchy and thereby the Counter-Revolution.

Most Parisian refractories followed Emery, including what remained of congregations of the Lazarist, Sulpician and Oratorian orders;[44] in other large dioceses, Lyon for instance, they did not. The 'jurors' made an effort to spread news of Emery's decision among the scattered refractories abroad. Opinion was divided on the new oath's legitimacy, with progressively minded bishops – Boisgelin and Champion de Cicé among those in London, and La Luzerne, one of six resident in Constance and author of a controversial *Mémoire* in their name[45] – broadly in favour, though agonising about how submission to the law could be combined with faithfulness to the King, but the main body of opinion was suspicious if not downright hostile: 'It contains in my view more poison than any of the oaths we have previously refused to swear', opined Bishop Mercy of Luçon, 'and the consequences of taking it will be still more deadly'.[46] The six bishops at Friburg – Sisteron, Gap, Poitiers, Chalon-sur-Saône, Riez and Meaux – convened in November 1792, condemned the oath, and circulated their decision widely;[47] the influential theologian Asseline, formerly Bishop of Boulogne, produced a treatise against compliance with the laws of the Republic, and accused those who had shown it of lacking in sincerity.[48] He was in exile, but in France submission was virtually a precondition of personal survival for non-juring bishops. Another warning of the risks they were courting by not taking it was delivered in Paris by the September Massacres, which were particularly directed towards the imprisoned clergy, as men suspected of being in treasonable contact with the Austrians. Significantly, many of those martyred on 2 and 3 September 1792 – including Dulau, Archbishop of Arles – had refused to compromise their principles in line with Emery's recommendation. Their sacrifice and the others that followed – the execution of Mgr de Castellane (former Bishop of Mende), and the priests massacred by crowds in southern cities like Marseille and Toulon, and bloodletting at Versailles, Meaux, Lyon and in Normandy – only had the effect of hardening resistance to the oath, and it made headway in no more than a few dioceses, among them Tours, Cambrai, Troyes, Nancy and Langres.

For most clergy, discussion of the merits or otherwise of the Liberty-Equality oath were not a priority. Their lives were in danger, and taking the oath did little to guarantee survival. The number of priests leaving France in the winter of 1792–3 after the September Massacres was on an unprecedented scale but, harried by the authorities, many felt they had no choice. A recent estimate suggests about 40 per cent of the clergy in total, or 30 000 to 40 000 priests and members of the religious orders left France at this juncture.[49] Even non-juring bishops who, against all odds, had stayed in their diocese, like Mgr Chanterac of Alet, were among them.[50] These destitute clergy commonly headed for the frontier nearest to their own diocese, or the states previously reached by their clerical neighbours or superiors: the Low Countries, Italy, Spain, Portugal, Germany, Britain, even Russia. There they re-established contact with dignitaries already in exile drawn from among canons, vicars-general, university professors, and bishops, often pathetically attempting to recreate their own diocesan circle. Forced, as they had been, from their home soil, the *émigré* clergy felt keenly about provincial loyalties. Thus when the English hostel for them at the King's House, Winchester, was shut down, Normans went on to Reading, Bretons to Thame in Oxfordshire.[51]

Those who either could not or would not leave were left to the small mercies of the new Republic's war on the refractories. The decree of 18 August 1792 had banned religious habits and abolished teaching and hospital congregations, confraternities and penitents, and all associations with pious or charitable aims. Across France municipalities ordered nuns to leave their houses. Most had no choice but to obey the law though, even if formally dispersed, many sisters kept up unofficial contact with each other and with their mother-superior. They proved surprisingly adaptable. In Troyes, the Carmelites who had been forced to seek shelter with families in the town put aside their rule of strict withdrawal from the world to give a Christian education to the poor of their quarter.[52] Only communities of sisters who cared for the sick were exempted from the 18 August decree. Thus the Sisters of Charity stayed on in Paris and continued their work on an individual basis at the request of republican section committees.[53] But could the legislation be applied to female orders like the *béates*, the *béguines* or the *congréganistes*? They wore no veil, had sworn no perpetual vows, and in practice tended to live on in small towns and villages. Most of these women defied the authorities to move against them and, in so doing, helping to give the survival of French Catholicism in the 1790s a more distinctively feminine identity than it had ever before possessed.[54] Many women from the religious orders were prepared to give their lives for their faith, most famously the Carmelite nuns of Compiègne, executed in July 1794 for obstructing measures of dechristianisation by staying together as one community after their convent had been suppressed.[55] Other sisters brought their rosaries to the place of death.

The Ursulines of Valenciennes even sang the *Te Deum* and prayed for their executioners.

In the most unpromising circumstances, the non-juring Church in 1793 clung on to life and the affections of its followers. Expedients became the norm, for instance using those chapels in Paris that, despite everything, remained open. Those of the Oratory, the religious order of the Conception and English religious orders were heavily used until they too were sealed off in February 1794. Otherwise, only a clandestine ministry was possible. With worship prohibited, the non-juring Church converted itself into an underground organisation, with the exception of those areas of the west in open rebellion against the Republic. There may have been as many as four hundred clergy operating in the Orne, but barely a hundred in the Sarthe, a dozen in the Aude, and even less than that in the Haute-Saône, Jura and Doubs. These numbers reflected the relative effectiveness of the Church's clandestine operations as well as local sympathies. While these varied, in most areas refractory priests tried to ensure that the faithful had the occasional service of an ordained minister, and that news circulated in the parishes about the time and place of the next (illegal) Mass.

It was not always possible. Clergy were isolated figures, usually disguised, never staying long in one place so as to avoid capture and aware of their vulnerability to greedy informers; Fr Coudrin was known across Poitou as 'Marche à Terre' because he was always on the move. Others took menial posts as clerks, water-carriers, woodworkers or national guardsmen, the better to undertake their furtive ministry. Others just hid, in cupboards, under stairs, in barns or, like the former nuncio, Salamon, underneath a kiosk in the Bois de Boulogne. A lynch mob could await those who had been arrested and sentenced to deportation. This was the fate of priests at La Rochelle on 21 and 22 March 1793, once the escorting National Guard had withdrawn.[56] The number of priestly deaths and exiles reached its peak in 1793–4.[57] More priests died in western France than anywhere else, but other areas produced their martyrs during the great Terror, with monks and friars as well as secular clergy among them. Gestures of humility and contempt were legion as death approached. Fr Imbert, a Dominican from Castres in the Midi, refused to board the tumbril. 'My Master, Jesus, walked', he protested, 'and I insist on walking'.

The suffering among all Catholics was as terrible as it was long-remembered. Just to harbour a priest was enough to merit the death

penalty irrespective of sex or age. Neither of those considerations prevented Mme de La Béraudière, born in Louis XIV's reign, from
going to the guillotine in Anjou.[58] The clergy, in their turn, did
what they could to minister and prepare their people for death.
Some acted as 'chaplains of the guillotine', like the abbé Carrichon,
dressed in red coat and blue shirt, who hung around Parisian street
corners during the Terror, and daringly accosted coaches with victims for the tumbrils, to absolve and bless those on their last earthly
journey.[59] In the Paris prisons, Emery used all his gifts of spiritual
comfort and human *savoir-faire* to reconcile many of the incarcerated
to the Church, despite the insults numerous clergy had received from
their fellow prisoners and the desperate scoffing – 'Don't go and tell
me I shall be dining with the angels', said General Miacinski, when
he was asked if he wanted to confess himself. It was the most delicate
sort of ministry, but one facilitated by Emery's winning the tacit connivance of the gaolers.[60]

Vicar-generals appointed by the refugee bishops did their best to
keep the prohibited Church in existence, none more so than the
abbé Linsolas in the Lyon diocese, who organised *chefs de paroisse* to
assemble the faithful for prayer and clerically led clandestine services; in Bordeaux the abbé Langoiran and Fr Martinien Pannetier,
respectively Canon of Saint-André and Professor of Theology at the
University, were among the four senior priests whom Champion de
Cicé left in charge of his see, and they inspired the clergy and their
people by their preaching and writings not to succumb to schism
before each in his turn was arrested and executed.[61] They were not
alone in their efforts in the Bordeaux diocese. The abbé Joseph
Boyer founded the Association for the Sacred Heart of Jesus, an elite
group of priests and former nuns who followed a life of prayer,
self-denial and mutual support for each other and the laity who
looked to them. Still more covert a secret religious association was
the 'Aa' (*Association des Amis* or *Associatio Amicorum*), dedicated to the
sanctification of its members and apostolic zeal. Its importance in
explaining how refractory priests somehow kept in contact should
not be underestimated. Founded at La Flèche (Sarthe) in 1630, it
quickly established itself in most French towns, and had links with
the dissolved Jesuit order. Strict equality was practised among its
members, both ordained and lay, with recruits gathered by cooption,
and rarely more than twenty members per branch. These were run
entirely independent of each other, with secrecy the watchword.

The identity of members was never disclosed beyond the group.[62] The Aa came into its own in the 1790s by helping to facilitate a clandestine priestly ministry[63] and bring sacramental comfort to those hundreds of thousands who, despite the risks, still looked to the refractories for pastoral comfort. At Toulouse – the best documented Aa branch – the faithful were in 1793 organised into a 'Holy Militia', an association of priests and laymen who would dedicate their prayers to bringing an end to the persecution.

The most serious counter-revolutionary challenges of 1792–5 possessed a religious inspiration that gave them purpose and justification and was alone capable of inducing countless hundreds of priests and thousands of ordinary French men and women to die for their beliefs. Nowhere was this more the case than in the first Vendée rising of 1793–4, which affected the *départements* immediately south of the River Loire, areas that had been much affected by the Montfortain missions earlier in the century. Admittedly, town–country rivalries and other socio-economic factors such as land tenure, social tensions and the impact of commercialisation on the rural economy have been emphasised by historians like Paul Bois and Charles Tilly, but it is questionable how far their investigations of localities can be applied to the west as a whole. Historians are endorsing again Michelet's classic formulation – 'Women and priests, that's all there is to the Vendée' – and Timothy Tackett, whose groundbreaking work has been fundamental, has discerned 'an independent cultural clash' in the Vendée rising between a revolution that drew its strength from the urban bourgeoisie and a predominantly rural opposition which brought together seigneurs and day-labourers in a defence of Church and King that was, at the same time, a defence of local culture.[64] Here deportation and internment of refractory priests started early, ordered by town-based administrators against a highly 'clericalised' countryside; even the law of 7 May 1791 briefly permitting relative religious freedom had been generally ignored.[65]

Not surprisingly, rebellion across the west won the allegiance of hundreds of thousands of country-dwellers. There were more of them in the west than elsewhere, and they spanned the social spectrum. On one side were farm labourers, owners of nothing more than the roof over their head and a tiny patch of ground. They had no hopes of benefiting from the sale of Church lands, and remained heavily taxed by comparison with their urban neighbours;

then there were the wealthier peasantry, more significant property-holders in their own right, who had also been outbid in the land market by the townsman with cash in his pockets. Neither group had gained materially from the Revolution and were ready to obey the orders of their parish priests, usually local men themselves, from elite peasant backgrounds, who detested the Revolution and all it stood for.

In many ways the insurrection of the west took on the character of a religious crusade, as the widespread wearing of popular symbols like the Sacred Heart and crosses, often with the royalist white cockade, displayed. The Sacred Heart, one Vendean *curé* explained in 1793, 'is the livery and distinctive mark of Catholicism, just as the tricolour ribbon and medal of the federation are for adherents of the new regime, like intruded priests and other constitutionalists.'[66]

These distinctive religious devotions of the far west were vital in motivating local people to take up arms, a devotion very far removed in intensity and practice from what one might have encountered in the Yonne recently studied by Desan. With a rosary in one hand and a musket in the other, Vendean rustics risked everything on victory for the King of France – and the Queen of Heaven. The missionary priests with their 'baroque' Catholicism had done their work in the area earlier in the century very well.

Leading the revolt was a 'Royal and Catholic Army', which sang hymn and canticles on the march, halted to pray, and bore standards decorated with the image of the Blessed Virgin Mary; in one battle near Fontenay-le-Comte, the leaders detailed a hundred troops to protect the holy sacrament and communion vessels carried by two chaplains in the centre of the army. These were the emblems of a holy war, a force that came to think of itself in Old Testament terms as the host of Israel. On being congratulated after Saumur fell into their hands, the Vendean leader, Jacques Cathelineau insisted 'it is God who has given us victory', and he meant it.[67] That success and the ones that followed led to the release of royalist prisoners, including clergy who usually returned to their old parishes if these were in a 'safe' area.[68] Other priests played a prominent leadership role in the army. Thus the force that took the town of Cholet was controlled as much by the abbé Barbotin as by Jean-Nicolas Stofflet. After the capture of Chemillé, Barbotin became 'Almoner of the Catholic Army' and gave mass absolution prior to battles. He was the author of an 'Address to the French' which expressed his dedication to the

Roman Catholic religion and the King. Most celebrated of all was the abbé Bernier, curé of Saint-Laud d'Angers, who in the summer of 1793 gave a firmer basis to the structure of the Vendean military and civil organisation, in conjunction with a returned *émigré*, the Marquis de Lescure, the 'saint of Poitou'.[69]

Not that these changes were enough to prevent the Royal and Catholic Army going down to catastrophic defeat, explained by one *curé* on the basis that God had wished to punish the 'Whites' for their unworthy conduct towards republican prisoners, which to his mind displayed a ruthlessness far removed from the Gospel spirit.[70] The clergy paid a high price for the failure of the rebellion. Their part in fomenting the insurrection removed any last restraints 'patriots' had in seeking them out for arrest and punishment, whether they had been part of the Royal and Catholic Army or not. All felt the repressive force of what one priest called 'these furious tigers' who had come into the west 'to fill it with blood and carnage', going about 'roaring like ferocious beasts, blaspheming even against demons', destroying and burning, 'and leaving under our eyes, to right and left, in fields and houses, heaps of corpses, dead bodies with no graves'.[71] Priests taking the sacraments around the countryside to the sick and the dying knew that recognition could only lead to execution; disguise was not always enough, as Canon Barat of Angers found when he was detected in Angers disguised as a miller, 'carrying on his person the instruments of fanaticism'.[72] At Nantes, clerics were among the principal victims of the *noyades*: priests joined laymen in boats where they were tied together and deliberately sunk on the river Loire, dechristianisation by immersion as Richard Cobb said with savage irony; hundreds more were left to rot in prison or, as in the port of Rochefort, in old slaving ships hastily converted into floating dungeons. In a field near Avrillé in Anjou, numerous priests joined the Daughters of Charity and over 2000 laity put to death by Revolutionary troops between January and April 1794 because of their adherence to the old Catholic order.[73]

The *Chouan* disturbances, north of the Loire in Upper Brittany, also had an important religious dimension, with the majority of villagers alienated from the Revolution, and refractory priests stirring up their people to resist the changes coming from outside. *Chouannerie* was generally plebeian in character, relying on farmhands and tenant farmers as its irregular troops, men with an intimate knowledge of the hedgerows and copses of territory east of Le Mans and from the river Loire northwards to Rouen. Working in bands with limited command structures, they had less recourse to priests for active leadership, but still depended on non-jurors to act as unofficial chaplains, offering spiritual comforts and blessings including, not uncommonly, the last rites. Church bells summoned the *Chouans* to war, pilgrimages and religious processions could be turned to new military purposes.[74]

The *Chouans*, like all other committed French Catholics, could no longer rely on the presence of a priest close at hand. From 1792 most lay people were necessarily organising themselves, and whether refractories or constitutionalists, they did not shy away from confrontation with a state that had turned into the foe of their faith. At Jouy-sur-Morin (Seine-et-Marne), a hundred men armed with pikes and muskets chanted menacingly before the representative on mission, Morisson, 'We want the Catholic religion and no more Jacobins.' Such a demonstration had its counterparts all over France. At Villequiers in the Cher they cried 'We want our religion! We'll die to uphold it! We want everything just as it was in the past, and then we'll go forward in good heart.'[75] Where priests were imprisoned, their followers often marched *en masse* to try and see them, bringing them food and necessities. In April 1793 the 120 clergy locked up at Amiens were still receiving visitors, often with the tacit connivance of the local authorities. As one woman told a foreign visitor: 'Yes, we still contrive to see them, because there are no guards found here who don't befriend them.'[76]

Guiding and directing these spontaneous feelings was not easy, either for the Republican authorities or the non-juring clergy. There were sometimes written tracts available. For a while, some of the wealthiest supporters of the Refractory Church had access to publications from the royalist press like *Le guide du catholique pendant le schisme*, and bought up as many copies as they could to distribute among the faithful and hope to win over followers from the jurors.[77] In one sense, such initiatives in self-help were much as refractory priests could have wished, knowing that pastoral provision could only be limited: no one loyal to them wanted to attend services led by a Constitutional priest, let alone be interred by one, and well-conducted lay burials were quite acceptable to the refractory leadership – in the Haute-Loire *département* by 1793, the women undertaking them at night.[78] In his last sermon before leaving Saint-Hilaire-de-Mortagne, *curé* Mathieu Paunaud had insisted that even without him his people should assemble for Sunday service at ten, confident that wherever he was, he would be joining his worship with theirs.[79] Yet clergy more senior than him were unclear and divided about how much authority to confer on a lay leadership, or how far the revival of popular religious practices should be condoned, like the spontaneous canonisation of victims of republican repression in the *départements* of the west. Verdier, vicar-general in the Autun diocese, encouraged lay assemblies in church for the recitation of prayers, but many such gatherings saw the recital of the Mass down to but excluding the consecration of the elements. These services, known as the *messes blanches*, caused much disquiet. François Viart, vicar-general of the Bishop of Auxerre in 1795, deplored what he called this 'mimicry of priests'.[80] On one level such unilateral resourcefulness was a sign of religious vitality, and was to be found among adherents of both the refractory and Constitutional Church in numerous *départements*, notably the Aisne, Marne, Yonne, Nièvre, Vienne and Ardennes, and across Normandy.[81] Although lay ministers generally tried to follow closely the liturgical rites of the Church, and guarded and handled the sacred books – where they were available – with care, their actions had a wider significance: they expressed a search for new expressions of faith, new forms of religious sociability when the traditional parish structures were no longer in place. In dangerous circumstances, a zealous laity won an entitlement to be given a much greater share in the running of the Church once 'normality' was restored at some far distant point.

The pronouncements of senior clergy like Verdier and Viart could sound no more than faint echoes if and when they reached the remote rural enclaves within which the refractory Church largely operated. They were certainly ignored by the women who, as Olwen Hufton and Suzanne Desan have shown, perhaps more than their men kept the flame alive in these crisis years for the Church. As Hufton writes:

> What the women wanted was a reversion to normality as they had known it and to the familiar rhythms of parish life. The Revolution had not shaken the bedrock of rural women's faith nor altered their perception of the intrinsic priorities of life, the family, the raising of children, the search for sufficiency, ways of doing.[82]

Their prominence in standing for the faith that they had lived out in their way – not always in line with what the clergy wanted – has led modern scholars to accept with some persuasive force the likelihood that the Revolution saw the feminisation of religious practice. These women wanted their old clergy back to lead them, but, given that such an aspiration was an impossibility in most places between 1792 and 1794, they were prepared to take the initiative. Some of them were former nuns like Mlle de Lamourous, once a Carmelite, who was sustaining refractories in the Bordeaux area, helping Joseph Boyer run the diocese during the archbishop's absence.[83] But most of the impetus came from ordinary Catholic laywomen, determined to stand up for their beliefs in every way imaginable, not least by catechising their own children in the absence of a priest.[84] In the Queyras area, missionary priests charged the most capable person in the family (and it was usually the mother) with reading from the Bible to her children and telling them about the lives of the saints. One of the missionaries, J.-E. Izoard, left behind a 'rule of life' from which mother could teach them their catechism as they started talking. The faith of the archetypal parish priest of the nineteenth century, the *curé* d'Ars (b. 1786), was nourished by his mother in these years when he discovered his priestly vocation in childhood.[85]

Women were proud to conceal in their houses those sacred images and objects to which they had been devoted when housed in the parish church; across the Limousin, the centre of the enammelling trade in France, there was massive reluctance in 1793 to sacrifice to the war effort the reliquaries, masterpieces of the goldsmith's art, which were personal to them in a way which the holy vessels used by priests were not. At Limoges there is a tradition that during the Terror the gardeners of the dissolved confraternity of Saint-Fiacre passed the reliquary of the saint from family to family in a continuing veneration.[86] Devotions before religious images went on despite the draconian penalties in most areas of France. A few risked death during the Terror by concealing non-jurors in their attics and cellars, while more than one refractory priest was freed by women forcibly pulling him away from his captors. Usually reliance on taunts and jeers against the hated Republican troops and officials was enough to secure what the women wanted.[87] The authorities were often uncertain about how to meet this unfamiliar challenge. One representative on mission, having heard that women had assembled in the local chapel to say the rosary, decided on no further action: 'They will soon weary of that ridiculous practice, and will renounce it quickly.'[88] That was far from the case, however. Another frustrated

representative in the *département* of the Gers taunted the women with
the charge that they were 'priests' prostitutes', but it only reinforced
their loyalties.

Women kept up the pressure for freedom of worship right through
this period, until the Convention granted the (limited) right to toleration under the law of *Ventôse* year III (February 1795). Once it
was conceded, they determined to take advantage of it. In the
Yonne and other *départements* in 1795 women rioted to get their
churches reopened, pulling out priests from hiding to have them say
Mass, and there are numerous instances of females ringing bells to
summon other women to join them in prayers and hymns.[89] It was
all as unseemly to the male leadership of the non-jurors as it was to
their Revolutionary adversaries, but it had played a decisive part in
keeping their Church in being over the previous four years, so that by
1795 it had grown significantly in strength at the expense of its Constitutional rival. The challenge was now to capitalise on that resilience, and it was not easy. Even pastors of the abbé Linsolas's
dedication and resourcefulness found it hard to limit the pastoral
damage caused by imprisonment, death or exile: the sacerdotal survivors of persecution were a ragged remnant.

Most bishops were either abroad or remained in private life, so
there was a shortage of senior figures in a position to offer guidance
to the faithful in an uncertain future. Bellescize, Bishop of Saint-
Brieuc, for instance, had converted the *philosophe* La Harpe while
imprisoned in the Terror but, though freed on 9 *Thermidor*, died in
1796 from the rigours endured during his captivity. Bellescize was
one of just a handful of non-juring prelates who did not emigrate at
any point – those of Alais, Angers, Lectoure, Mâcon, Marseille,
Saint-Papoul and Senlis were the others. Ill health had taken its toll.
A large proportion of their clergy, who had also stayed in France
in 1792–4, began to emerge cautiously from hiding in the months
after Robespierre's fall, including former canons of urban collegiate churches, the sort who could give the refractory Church much
needed leadership skills as it regrouped from 1795 onwards.[90] If they
had not obtained martyrdom, they commonly owed that delivery to
well-placed protectors, like Canon Cambacérès, future Cardinal
Archbishop of Rouen under Napoleon, who relied on the good standing of his brother in Montpellier to keep him unmolested in his
hiding-place. Most of these people were hostile in principle to a
republic, whether its character was more moderate or not. In the

west and in parts of the south, refractory priests returning from exile
in Spain took an active part in fomenting discontent against a republic they denounced as the Anti-Christ; in Lyon, they arrived in bands
from Switzerland and northern Italy and did little either to stem the
popular demand for revenge after the terrible repression of 1793 following the defeat of the Federalist revolt.

Every one of these returning clerics had his tale of cruelty, depriva-
tion and death. Few had any illusions that anything other than continued hardships were in prospect, like this *curé* who, unlike many of
his parishioners, had survived the Vendée:

> Such is our lot in the present circumstances: we must resolve to be
> martyrs, either in fact or by inclination. I mean by that either in
> dying in anguish or living in tribulation. Thus are all things
> ordered now, and after what it has pleased God to sanction against
> us, it is impossible that we can escape one or the other fate, and we
> must either shed our own blood or live on in destitution.[91]

This village priest, Marchais, was among those Vendean insurgents who distanced themselves from the shortlived peace treaty of
La Jaunaye signed by the Republic with the rebel leader Charette
in February 1795, even though it laid down freedom of worship
(in private) and an amnesty for all participants, including refractory
priests. It did not end the suffering of the clergy, especially in the
rebellious provinces. In June 1795 Charette took up arms again,
and in July numerous priests – and the former bishop of Dol, Mgr
de Hercé – landing with the *émigré* forces at Quiberon Bay, were
among the victims of the defeat inflicted by Hoche's 'Army of the
Ocean Coasts', which for months continued its mopping-up operations with trial by military commission in the Breton heartlands of
the Counter-Revolution.[92] Thus, even as the refractory clergy
emerged from hiding and began to resume open pastoral activity,
they had no good reason for condoning the 'moderate' republican
Constitution of the Year III. For the majority of them, attachment
to Church *and* Throne remained non-negotiable or, as the constitutional monarchist Mallet du Pan expressed it, 'In recreating Catholics, the Convention is recreating Royalists.'[93] The Declaration of
Verona, issued in June 1795, made it plain that the *de jure* monarch
Louis XVIII intended nothing less than the restoration of the
Church to its pre-Revolutionary splendour. Monarchists remained

wedded to the vision of a vanished Gallicanism whose retrieval they assumed to be a vital part of an overall restoration of the *status quo*. Yet as Year III of the Republic dawned, the first priority for refractory priests was not monarchy, but holding on to the loyalties of those who had maintained the faith since 1791 and winning back the active allegiance of those millions of men and women who had simply given up the public practice of Christianity. This formidable undertaking was one, moreover, to be undertaken with none of the material resources available to the Church before the Revolution, either in money or manpower. Its formal organisation, too, would have to be recreated. Since the abolition of religious orders and lay bodies like the confraternities, the Church had been kept alive by informal, often secretive modes of operating that lay men and women would not easily see given up in favour of the authoritarian and formal structures of the pre-Revolutionary era.

9(iii) The Survival of Religious Groups: Protestants and Jews, 1789–95

During the Revolution, Protestants and Jews tended, where they could plausibly do so, to exhibit a moderate patriotic citizenship. This attitude was in their best interests. As communities who were among the Revolution's foremost beneficiaries, they were unlikely to gain any increase in the rights of citizenship extended to them under the Constitution of 1791 from any subsequent royalist overthrow of the Republic. Indeed the reverse was more likely. Protestants and Jews tended to avoid participation in the power struggles going on in Paris and the major provincial cities and, on the whole, they did not suffer for their neutrality. No faction considered formal annulment of the full toleration conferred on them by the Revolution, even if they came under much official and unofficial pressure to abandon religious practice, pressure that amounted on occasion to blatant intimidation. In fact, they both came through the religious persecution of 1793–4 more successfully than their Catholic counterparts. Having coped with the often savage efforts of the Bourbon monarchy to prohibit their worship and punish as outlaws those who refused to acknowledge the confessional character of the state, Protestants and Jews alike were well placed to counter the antagonism of the Jacobins and the 'dechristianisers'. During the most savage periods of the 'religious' Terror here were two groups to whom the Republic exhibited a milder bearing than the one displayed towards Catholics, a reminder that to characterise the French state in 1792–4 as simply intolerant *tout court* is less than accurate.

I

Fifteen Protestant deputies were chosen for the Estates-General, among them their *de facto* leader, the pastor Rabaut de Saint-Etienne, and Antoine-Pierre Barnave, both of whom became prominent political figures during the Revolution, with Barnave one of the leading Feuillants in the second half of 1791. The Declaration of the Rights of Man with its general principle of religious liberty gave the Reformed every prospect of full participation in the life of the state. The complete legal emancipation of Protestants followed within months of the National Assembly's formation: a decree of Christmas Eve 1789 ended every legal distinction between Protestants and Catholics. Patriots rejoiced, like this deputy from the Morbihan:

> Today the nation itself recalls to its bosom those unfortunate children cast aside by fanaticism and intolerance . . . God alone has the right to judge men's conscience, and a simple error cannot be the basis for excluding someone from the constitution.[1]

The generosity of the constitutional state did not stop with this civic recognition: the descendants of families who had either fled abroad to preserve their faith or had lost property in the one hundred and four years since the Edict of Nantes had been repealed were awarded compensation by the state under laws of 10 July and 10 December 1790. Little wonder that the first eighteen months of the Revolution were greeted with such acclamation by the Huguenots, who generally rejoiced that they were no longer 'foreigners in their own homeland'. The Synod of Saintonge, Angoumois and the Bordelais was typical in its patriotic sentiments, declaring in 1791:

> Conscious of its gratitude towards the Supreme Being for the inestimable favour of unrestricted religious liberty that the Protestants of the kingdom enjoy under the Constitution, the Assembly exhorts them to make themselves worthy of it by redoubling their zeal for the faith of our fathers, especially by making their religious sentiments amply clear in their public and private conduct.[2]

Wherever there were Protestants, they were quick to take advantage of the unprecedented opportunities the Revolution had opened up. Thus in Bordeaux, the Protestant Pierre Sers was elected to the city council in 1790, and also took office as the first president of the local Jacobin club; at La Rochelle, nine of the eighteen purchasers of Church lands put on the market by the state were Protestants.[3] In Paris they used the newly vacant church of the Théatins, and it was here on 13 October 1791 that Pastor Marron was joined by a delegation from the municipality to celebrate the passing of the new constitution.[4] These new legal freedoms and civic prominence were, in some areas, not achieved without religious rivalries and resentments, spilling blood on the streets in some of the worst outbreaks of violence in the first two years of the Revolution.

The Protestants of Nîmes, as a tightly knit community wealthy from commerce and self-reliant in the face of persecution, had been quick to take advantage of the opportunities offered to them by the Revolution, and were bent on reducing the power of the Catholic clergy. These well-off merchants made up the majority of the officer corps of the town's citizen militia established in July 1789 (it was the same story in another Reformed stronghold in the south – Montauban),[5] and this gave them a supremacy in local politics that had come from nowhere in two years and disrupted a pattern that had endured in the area for a century. Suddenly, local Catholics found themselves pushed to the margin, with no choice but to develop their own organisation and, by the spring of 1790, had their own pressure groups in Toulouse, Montauban, Uzès and Nîmes itself. With their ascendancy in what would soon become the *département* of the Gard so quickly undermined, many among them began to wonder if the whole Revolution was nothing but an elaborate Protestant plot, as they heard with horror of the 'October Days' and pondered the likelihood of Calvinist plotting at national as well as regional level. As the royalist journalist Montjoye later insisted, 'Calvinism has from its birth displayed itself in a spirit of rebellion',[6] and the Revolution was just its latest work, a repudiation of divinely ordained authority that had precedents reaching back directly to the Fall of Man. For Catholics in the south, news of the failure of Dom Gerle's motion to declare Catholicism the state religion was the final goad into creating what amounted to an anti-Protestant crusade in a desperate, last-minute attempt to reimpose Catholic supremacy.[7] An article in the *Journal de Louis XVI* summed up the angry mood tersely: 'Your Kings, O people, refuse to the ministers of the State's religion the tolerance and relief accorded to Jews, Lutherans and Calvinists.'[8]

With the press thus inflaming local rumour beyond control, Catholics based their counter-response in Nîmes on wild tales about the impending massacre of their people by revolutionary Protestants, and it was enough to enable them to take control of the city in the municipal elections of the spring of 1790. The Protestants, however, would not relinquish their hold on the militia without coercion. As James N. Hood has noted, the National Guard, established to defuse tension, was the centre of it in Nîmes.[9] Riots in Montauban in May – 5 were killed and 50 wounded – ignited by attempts to draw up an inventory of confiscated monastic property, prefigured larger disturbances in Nîmes the next month as the voting day for the first departmental elections came closer. In four days of street fighting starting on 13 June (the so-called *bagarre* or brawl), order collapsed completely and the Protestants (whose control of the National Guard proved decisive) eventually gained the upperhand. It is estimated that about 20 among them died, but as many as 300 Catholics were slain in scenes reminiscent of the Wars of Religion in the same area two centuries earlier.[10] Thereafter Protestant control of the Gard *département* was unassailable, and they implemented the ecclesiastical legislation of the Revolution with a singlemindedness that had no counter-part elsewhere,[11] for they perhaps more than any other group in French society sensed the benefits and opportunities they stood to gain from the Revolution.

It was the sharpness of the religious question which led Protestants in Montauban and Nîmes to set up clubs in the aftermath of the bloody clashes with their Catholic neighbours. These became the cornerstone of their political control in the town which was consistently at the disposal of the moderate Left. The supremacy of this Protestant urban elite in the Gard secured by bloodletting had driven most Catholic electors out into the countryside and encouraged an interest in Counter-Revolution among them that took form in local plots, sectarian killings and above all the first *camp de Jalès*. To them, the Revolution was seen as exclusively designed to benefit wealthy Protestants, and it reopened the worst sort of sectarian bitterness, with democrats and Protestants viewed as interchangeable. The same tensions were also felt to the west of Nîmes, around Montauban and Alès; at Uzès in February 1791, Protestants were attacked twice, and Catholic and Protestant began mutually terrorising each other in the aftermath.[12] But this is only part of the picture. Once members of the reformed faith felt their dearly won legal status was secure, they were ready to look more kindly on their Catholic neighbours, especially after the Revolution began to turn away from supporting any version of Christianity at all. Thus in the Pays de Montbéliard and the Vivarais there was more than one instance of a Protestant family hiding a refractory priest, and saving him from death or deportation.[13] Significantly, there was a high proportion of Lutherans in the former area, and their adhesion to the Revolution was far less enthusiastic than that of their Reformed brethren: it had brought them little, and threatened to deprive them of much.

As one recent historian has well said, 'From Protestantism to patriotism there was only one step'.[14] Protestants had acquiesced in the creation of the Republic in 1792, and some had positively welcomed it, like the 41 of the 285 Rochelais signitaries who petitioned the Convention against a referendum on the fate of Louis XVI.[15] Most offered their general support to the Girondin faction in the National Convention, to which nine Protestants were elected. The overthrow and proscription in June 1793 of these politicians resulted in some dark days for the Protestants. Within weeks, Rabaut de Saint-Etienne had been executed,[16] while many other leaders were drawn into the Federalist revolt in the Gard, and 47 were condemned to death in the reprisals that followed its defeat, including the father of Louis-Philippe's premier in the 1840s, Guizot. For the most part, Protestant chapels were closed down a mere two years after opening or reopening, or were used as 'temples of reason' decorated, as at Marennes near Rochefort, with the Declaration of the Rights of Man and maxims of 'universal morality'. At Marennes the constitutional *curé* and the Protestant minister allowed the popular society to nominate them to the newly invented office of 'preachers of morality', and agreed to preach turn and turn about in each other's former church buildings in the hope that 'There will be only one religion, that of fraternity and equality.' During these early, moderate days of dechristianisation, the aim seemed to be to usher in a time when, in the words of J. Barre, the former pastor at Bordeaux, 'the Supreme Being could only be worshipped in the hearts of the faithful'.[17] His confident expectations were not fulfilled, as dechristianisation quickly developed an extremist character. Indeed, there is also much evidence of bourgeois Protestant involvement at La Rochelle in the drive against every form of Christian survival.[18]

Many pastors imitated that large proportion of the Constitutional clergy in 1793–4 which had abandoned both their ministry and their faith in favour of an undivided allegiance to the Revolution itself. Here the lead was given by Julien, a pastor from Toulouse, who followed Gobel at the Convention in November 1793 in renouncing his Christian allegiance, confident that 'the same destiny awaited every virtuous man whether he adores the God of Geneva, Rome,

Mahomet or Confucius'.[19] Julien wanted to serve the Revolution through a secular career. So did other ex-pastors, most famously Jeanbon Saint-André, who was given responsibility on the Committee of Public Safety for the navy. There was systematic pressure on pastors to resign in the Cévennes region (ironically the historic home of Huguenot resistance) from Jean Borie, the representative on mission in the Gard and Lozère; between January and March 1794, Borie and his colleague, Boisset, had secured the abdication of 51 pastors. Indeed, it has been calculated that of some 106 pastors in the synods of Languedoc, about 69 per cent abandoned their pastoral functions during the dechristianisation movement of 1793–4 with, at most, one pastor in five attempting to keep some form of ministry going.[20] What Borie was doing against the Reformed pastors of the Nîmes region, his fellow representative Monet was undertaking in the Bas-Rhin *département* against their Lutheran counterparts. He was furious at their unwillingness to participate in the cult of 'Reason' as celebrated in the ex-cathedral of Strasbourg from November 1793. Those who declined to sign a document of renunciation of their orders were summarily imprisoned. Throughout France, Protestant pastors who had no intention of resigning ceased their public ministry.

On the whole, it seems likely that only a minority of pastors felt genuinely comfortable about equating Revolutionary ideology with the morality of the Gospels. Among them were men like Jacques Molines, former pastor of the town of Ganges, who at the insistence of the local Jacobin club drew up the 'Prayer of the free man to the God of Nature and Liberty'. The leading authority on the pastors of Languedoc, J.D. Woodbridge, is in no doubt that abdications among them owed most to 'visceral fears'. The ingrained habit among them of obedience to the law also disposed the majority not to quarrel with the new dispensation. If the state called on them to abdicate, that is what they would do. The long familiarity of many with a covert form of ministry also made abdication less of a blow than might otherwise have been the case. Whatever the position, Woodbridge's conclusion is stark:

> During its [dechristianisation's] rather brief run, its instigators successfully brought about what the French monarchy had failed to achieve during the years, 1715–1787: the practical elimination of the pastoral corps of the 'Church of the Desert' in Languedoc.[21]

But if pastors put away their Genevan bands and black gowns to melt into private life causing the synodal and consistorial structures of the Reformed Church to collapse, the Protestant laity were seldom ready to give up their prized freedom of worship without a struggle, as recent research on La Rochelle has shown. There, paying lip-service to the republican cults, they went on clandestinely with their worship, and conducted marriages and baptisms.[22] Even in Monet's fiefdom of the Bas-Rhin beyond Strasbourg, Lutheran services continued wherever possible, indeed were often held in patriotic clubs specifically formed for the faithful to worship in on the days of the *décadi*.[23]

Here, as elsewhere, scattered congregations continued to worship throughout the Terror, though Calvinist and Lutheran Churches alike greeted the return to freedom of worship at the end of 1794 with no small relief.[24] This new position was confirmed by the law of 3 *Ventôse* Year III (21 February 1795), when Church and State were formally separated, and Protestants seized the opportunity to reopen some of their most hallowed 'temples', like Saint-Louis in Paris. However, confessional divisions were once again uppermost in the last months of the Convention in 1795,[25] and the authorities did little to protect hundreds of Calvinists from being hunted down by vengeful Catholics in the Gard and Lozère during the 'White Terror'.

II

To the majority of educated Frenchmen in 1789, the Jews in their country were still a people apart, whose distinctive identity required toleration and legal protection. For this constituency, still very much a minority one, the most practicable way forward was not integration but for Jewish communal rights to be preserved and guaranteed by the Estates-General, as several of the *cahiers* recommended. Less tolerant observers were more cautious, with many countervailing suggestions to limit the numbers of Jews and supervise their activities.[25] For reformers who thought in terms of Jewish integration within a unified political nation, it had been a hopeful sign when Necker invited the Jews to submit their own *cahiers*, but the whole exercise was a reminder of the divisions that endured. As Simon Swarzfuchs has noted, 'The regional Jewish "nations" of France did not wish to turn themselves into Jewish Frenchmen.'[26] In Bayonne, they preferred instead to participate on the fringes of Third Estate activity, but the Ashkenazim of Alsace, excluded (unlike the Sephardim of Bordeaux) from electoral activity, had their own *cahiers* drawn up by the most progressive members of the community, in which they asked for the end of special taxation, for the granting of fiscal equality and assimilation, and for the rights of free residence and travel. They wished to preserve their community organisations, their rabbis and their syndics. None of these proposals was popular with the Third Estate in Alsace, which voiced its continued dislike of Jewish commercial competition, and would not sanction their unrestricted admission into the province.[27] The disdain of the bourgeoisie had its counterpart in rural areas, and in July–August 1789 antisemitic riots erupted in seventy locations across Alsace, directed to destroying the records of moneylending. It was an outbreak of violence that coincided with the 'Great Fear' in other regions. Many Jews were forced to flee into Switzerland.[28]

Against this troubled background, the three groups of Jews in Paris – Portuguese, German and Comtadins – belatedly submitted their *cahiers*. What makes them so important is that here, for the first time, in response to the universal language of the Declaration of the Rights of Man and the sentiments of national unity expressed across the nation, they declared themselves ready to abandon their community autonomy and claim citizenship in the new constitutional monarchy, with unrestricted access to cities, an end to special taxes, and the possibility of pursuing careers in the professions.[29] It had an immediate effect, for the Jewish voters of Alsace–Lorraine followed suit with their own similar declaration, submitted in the name of the majority of Ashkenazim. Significantly, their claim to full legal recognition was *not* accompanied by expressed willingness to renounce their corporate identity: 'It is only to be better citizens that we ask for the conservation of our synagogue, our rabbis, and our syndics.'[30] Despite this qualification, the Jewish commitment to the new France was very acceptable to majority opinion in the National Assembly. As Stanislas Clermont-Tonnerre noted at the end of August:

> We should refuse the Jews any rights as a separate nation, but grant them the same as individuals. They must not make in the State either a distinctive corps or an order. They must become individual citizens.

The desired corollary of bestowing citizenship was that over time the Jewish communities of France would vanish along with their religion and their distinctive languages, Yiddish in Alsace and Judeo-Spanish in the south-west. It was a price progressive Jews might find acceptable, but it threatened to cause fresh divisions among them to run alongside Sephardim–Ashkenazim suspicions.

For the moment the threat to their property weighed most heavily on the latter group, and it was some reassurance to them when on 28 September the Assembly made the symbolic declaration that the Jews were under the safeguard of the laws. But, despite the erroneous assumption by the Sephardim that they were fully included within the terms of the Declaration of the Rights of Man, there was still no formal admittance to citizenship. On 14 October 1789 a Jewish delegation of six from the eastern provinces came to the bar of the Assembly and Berr Isaac Berr, the lay leader of the Jewish community in Nancy, spoke movingly on behalf of his people and begged deputies to look on the Jews as their brothers who cried out for change.

The cause of the Jews was not taken up again in debate until just before Christmas, when it was raised by the abbé Grégoire – the most indefatigable advocate of Jewish emancipation throughout the Assembly's lifetime and author of the influential *Motion en faveur des Juifs*, published in October 1789.[31] He was assisted by Clermont-Tonnerre, Robespierre, Custine and Adrien Duport, leading deputies who added their philosemite voice to other heavyweight backing from the likes of Talleyrand and Mirabeau. Active opposition tended to come from those who lived alongside the Jews of the eastern provinces, notably the future Director, Jean-François Reubell, deputy for Colmar, who insisted, against all the evidence, that the Jews were not even interested in winning citizenship;[32] La Fare, Bishop of Nancy, talked only in terms of guaranteeing the rights of person and property of individual Jews,[33] but, as with other members of the moderate Right in the Assembly, found that defending the rights and privileges of the Church involved maintaining the Jewish 'nation' generally in an inferior legal state. He opposed Clermont-Tonnerre's motion of 23 December for admittance to citizenship by warning the Assembly that any such concession could ignite 'a huge blaze' in Lorraine where 'the people have a horror of them'. The Bishop was actually trying to be pragmatic about the issue. He conceded that 'the Jews have given great services to Lorraine, and particularly to the town of Nancy', but Maury, the uncompromising clerical champion of the Right, was quite blunt in his refusal to concede citizenship. He reminded his colleagues how the Jews 'had passed seventeen centuries without ever mixing themselves in other nations'. They were not Frenchmen, but foreigners living in France, to be excluded from the nation.[34] Despite the Assembly's public commitment to religious toleration, and the recent award of full civic rights to Protestants, many otherwise progressive deputies had their doubts about a wholesale commitment to granting civic freedoms to the Jews. So the Assembly proceeded on a piecemeal basis, and a majority was particularly swayed by a letter from the Sephardim dated 31 January 1790. They insisted they had been naturalized and recognized Frenchmen for centuries, drew attention to previous acts of patriotism, and denied having separate laws, officers, or tribunals, insisting that they, unlike other French Jews, were not organised into corporations.[35] It was therefore the Sephardim of the Bordelais and Avignon who benefited from the first emancipation decree of 28 January 1790, agreed after an eleven-hour debate by a vote of 374 votes to 224, and a direct appeal to deputies not to omit them from active citizenship by a Jewish delegation from Bordeaux on 31 December.[36]

There, with emancipation granted to a mere 4 000 people, the process halted. Whereas the wealthy Sephardim were the obvious candidates for full citizens' rights, the same could not be said of the much more numerous, Yiddish-speaking Ashkenazim of Alsace, whose culture and language alike appeared distinctly 'foreign' and prima facie incompatible with French citizenship; their insistence on preserving their community rights had confirmed the doubts of deputies. Meanwhile, the Comtadin Jews were the gradual beneficiaries of the civil unrest existing between Avignon and the Comtat, especially after they had aligned themselves behind the pro-French annexation party. The distinctive yellow hat of local Jews was abolished by decree of the National Assembly in October 1790, at the price of some smallscale rioting in Carpentras.[37] In Paris, some Ashkenazi Jews did their best to exhibit their patriotic credentials in the hope that this would influence the constitutional committee of the Assembly. About a hundred had joined the capital's National Guard, and persuaded the *commune* to intervene with the Assembly on their behalf on 24 February 1790. It was not enough to change attitudes, and concessions were slow to come and small in substance. Indeed, in September 1790, the Ashkenazi Jews were excluded from new laws admitting non-Catholics to judicial office and from the law of naturalisation.[38]

The unwillingness of the local Christians to ease their distrust of the Jews worked in favour of the plea made by Reubell, himself a native Alsatian, in the Assembly. Drawing on his first-hand familiarity with the Ashkenazi community, he insisted that to empower such Jews would be an unnecessary restraint on the Revolution. The Right had its own objections, and menacingly correlated revolutionary change with Jewish influences. 'Who', asked *Le Journal de la Ville et de la Cour*, 'can assure us that we won't be required to have ourselves all circumcised before we're thirty?'[39] In the Assembly, clerical deputies largely eschewed this vulgar antisemitism, but could not in conscience go beyond permitting a minimal passive citizenship for the Ashkenazim (especially after the passage of the Civil Constitution into law raised the alarming possibility that Jews could act as electors of Christian bishops and *curés*). Even that concession stipulated a *quid pro quo* of Jewish corporate autonomy being abandoned.

It was only on 27 September 1791, three days before the Assembly was dissolved, that Clermont-Tonnerre and his supporters finally prevailed on it to grant all Jewish communities in France equality as citizens. It was a dramatic, last-minute finale to completing the constitution, one that had no counterpart anywhere in the world except in the United States.[40] Yet the decree in itself did little to lessen popular suspicions about the place of the Jews in the new France, while reformers remained to be persuaded that they would not act as a drag on change in the revolutionary state.

Nevertheless, the Legislative Assembly confirmed the Emancipatory decree of its predecessor on 13 November, and the Jews of France were finally admitted as full citizens when they took the civic oath in the months that followed, for the most part collectively rather than individually, as at Nancy where the rabbi took the oath for all his people on 2 January 1792, following a patriotic speech.[41] That oath obliged them to renounce all their 'privileges and exemptions', but the precise nature of what exactly they had renounced under the Emancipation decree remained open to dispute until Napoleon settled the matter after discussion with Jewish notables making up '*un Grand Sanhédrin*'. However, the rabbinate, like the Catholic clergy, had incurred a major diminution in their capacity to stand as intermediaries between their people and the Revolutionary state with its pretensions to unrestricted authority.[42] There were resemblances to the precarious situation of the Constitutional Church hierarchy after 1793, where, in an otherwise distinguished episcopate, few stood alongside Grégoire in not compromising their faith for the sake of the Revolution. They would also pay a high price in re-establishing their credibility beyond the ranks of their most devoted followers.

Unlike Catholics, Jews had an ethnic identity that made its own claims on them. Berr Isaac Berr had emphasised that, as far as he was concerned, emancipation did not entail assimilation. Elsewhere in Alsace and Lorraine, many municipalities reckoned that it did; hence the unachieved insistence by the town council of Bischheim-au-Saum, near Strasbourg, that any Jew taking the oath must cross himself. Such obstacles at town or village level did nothing initially to encourage Jews to take the oath. Besides this, many Ashkenazim possessed nothing like the amount of property required under the Constitution of 1791 for active citizenship and, seeing no advantage in the passive option available to them, continued to lead their traditional life as before the Revolution.[43] They joined many of their more prosperous brethren in detecting in the abolition of community autonomy a new form of persecution and humiliation. The tensions and misgivings reflected how little the Revolution had done to change attitudes on both sides, but nevertheless the emancipation decree merits recognition, in Jacques Godechot's words, as 'a unique event in contemporary Europe',[44] one of the finest fruits of the Revolution. Jewish communal rights survived emancipation, as did the Yiddish language, and the debts of former Jewish communities. Those Jewish communities in debt – the *nation juive* of Alsace and Metz – had to maintain an administrative structure to levy and collect taxes that clashed with Revolutionary dislike of sectional institutions, but those sentiments deferred still gave way to lingering antisemitism in eastern France and the unremitting appetite of a state at war for ready funds.[45]

Though the victory at Valmy in September 1792 had been celebrated at Thionville by a ceremony where a Hebrew canticle was sung to the tune of the Marseillaise,[46] only a few Jews participated in Revolutionary republican politics, such as the Parisian Salomon Hesse, and Jacob Pereira, the friend of Hébert. The Jewish attachment to the Federalist cause in cities like Bordeaux was another reason behind the Jacobin Republic's concern over their conduct, and led one prominent Terrorist, Baudot, to talk in terms

of 'a regeneration for the Jews guillotine style'.[47] Those implicated in
Federalism included Furtado, who fled Bordeaux in time to cheat
death, and Jean Mendès, who did not. But if Jews died during the
Terror, it was on account of their politics, not their Judaism. Since
the Jewish religion was not recognised by the state, though its practice was tolerated (the Jewish community of Bordeaux transformed
itself into a voluntary charitable society while continuing to direct
the religious affairs of the community), Jews were unusually advan-
taged when the Republic began to distance itself from Christianity in
1792. If there were no Constitutional rabbis, there could be no refractory ones. Jews could hardly be 'dechristianised' during the first
Terror, but a handful joined in the ceremonies ushering in the new
cult of the Revolution itself. Two rabbis, in Paris and Orange respectively, are known to have renounced their religion; Schweig,
the rabbi of Nancy, joined in a civic fête on 30 *Brumaire* Year II
(20 November 1793) where sacred objects were handed back to the
'nation' as part of a parody of the Hebrew cult. He also offered up his
patents of ordination for burning at the same moment as 62 Christian
priests. Other rabbis fled rather than submit to these indignities, for
the criticism made of their culture and religion during the Enlightenment continued to characterise the attitudes of watchful 'patriots',
and it became common to pressurise the men into shaving off their
beards, and the women to leave off wigs in favour of a more 'republican' form of hairstyle. Republicanism was in itself a feeble curb on
popular antisemitism. Indeed, its focus on a national will and a
common identity made Jews the more conspicuous as 'outsiders',
and added a fresh legitimacy to other prejudices.

On the eastern border, the Yiddish-speaking Ashkenazim (70 per
cent of whose vocabulary had words of German origin) were credited
with communicating with or spying for the Prussian and Austrian
enemy once hostilities began in April 1792. They were universally
suspect among their fellow citizens, as rumours flourished about
their money-laundering, printing of fake assignats, and profiteering
at the expense of other citizens from the sale of Church lands.
At Nancy, the revolutionary committee of surveillance decided that
the Jews in the city, despite their status as citizens, could not
be regarded as 'assimilated', and passports were refused them in
October 1793.[48] As a member of the municipal council argued the
following month, Jews not married to non-Jews were intrinsically
suspect. Punitive taxation was imposed on the whole city of Nancy

in November 1793, ordered by the representatives on mission, Saint-Just and Lebas, to pay a revolutionary levy of 5 million livres. This was later reduced to 2 million, but it still had to be divided up among the most prominent citizens.[49] The Nancy experiment was subsequently repeated in Strasbourg, Metz and other towns across Alsace-Lorraine. Synagogues and religious schools were closed almost everywhere, and ritual objects of silver and gold were confiscated; some Jewish cemeteries were profaned with the stones overturned, and in the Haut-Rhin, in *Brumaire* Year II, the municipalities were ordered to burn copies of the Talmud and 'other Jewish books'. That last decree coincided with demands from the Jacobins of Nancy and Colmar for revocation of the emancipatory decrees. Additionally, Jews were required to work on the Sabbath, were barred from lighting candles on the Sabbath,[50] and expelled from National Guard membership in several centres, including Nancy and Avignon.[51]

The Jews faced not merely political pressures and the loss of their unique community organisations over the period 1792–5; the depreciation of the paper currency made moneylenders acutely vulnerable to loss, and the merchants and traders among them also had to come to terms with the emigration and impoverishment of many of their noble clients, and the potential loss of income, even bankruptcy this represented. Most Ashkenazi Jews in this category were quick to identify new markets. Their loans went instead to wealthy farmers eager to purchase the church lands on sale, and the outbreak of the war in 1792 increased the demand for army purveyors. Antisemitic accusations took new forms as conditions changed. Local suspicions that Alsatian Jewry disposed of the best of the Church lands in the province or, after initial purchase, sold them on again to their own financial advantage, were greatly exaggerated; one recent estimate for the Bas-Rhin suggests that between 1791 and 1811 Jews purchased a mere 2 per cent of the national lands sold in the *département*, about 10 per cent if control through loans is included. But the resentments of the populace could not be stopped from boiling over into direct action. Peasant pogroms against them in 1793 and 1794 caused many Jews to flee across the frontier after confiscation; these included Benjamin Bernheim at Haguenau, whose field workers were in July 1793 forcibly taken away, probably with the complicity of the local mayor.[52] Jews could expect little sympathy from republican administrators. It was embarrassing for the Ashkenazim that the reduced power of the Church if anything increased their opportunities for usury, and after Thermidor new accusations were launched against financiers which the Directory countenanced.

Though the first Jewish lawyers and army officers date from this time, most Jews stayed in private life, and adjusted cautiously to the new climate. In Alsace their numbers continued their gradual increase begun in the early 1780s, so that by 1810 they constituted 3 per cent of the province's total population, resident more than ever in the large centres of Strasbourg and Colmar.[53] The Sephardim of the southwest had their own problems, notably the collapse of the Atlantic trade centred on the port of Bordeaux. Final recognition of their Frenchness was some compensation, but the revolutionaries found it hard to comprehend their tenacious attachment to a religion that seemed to be a relic of superstion with no place in a reformed, regenerate and unified nation. Not until the First Empire could any French régime comfortably accept the coexistance of Judaism and loyalty to the state,[54] while that concession did nothing in itself to eradicate or significantly reduce France's endemic antisemitism, which survived the Revolution intact at every social level.

10 Dechristianisation and the Alternatives to Christianity

Dechristianisation is a term that has long been central to the religious history of the Revolution and, like nuclear armaments, is probably incapable of being dismantled once invented. It is not a homogeneous entity, and drags along with it a considerable weight of ideological and religious baggage that makes understanding and using the concept rather problematic for the student. At risk of over-simplification, it may be said that there are basically two ways in which the term 'dechristianisation' can be deployed. The first is its use to describe the deliberate attempt by the First Republic from 1792 to 1794 to use the resources of the state to extirpate Christianity and replace it as the dominant cultural mode of French society with a new frame of references springing directly from the Revolution itself. The second meaning of the word characterises the longer-term trends that suggest the gradual detachment during the eighteenth century of a growing number of the French population from (Catholic) Christianity. Scholars who have taken up this second, more diffuse definition tend to argue that the official dismantling of Christian culture in 1792–4 was facilitated at grass-roots level by men and women who already stood at a remove to the historic faith. The convulsion may have lasted just two years, but that was long enough to reveal longer-term tendencies pointing towards secularisation. In this chapter, dechristianisation will be used specifically in the first sense.

Dechristianisation was a concept unknown in the 1790s, but it has attracted much interest among twentieth-century historians of the Revolution, especially from Frenchmen sympathetic to socialism and *laïcité* ('laicisation'). In the hey-day of the Third Republic, Alphonse Aulard and Albert Mathiez pioneered scholarly study of the subject, and in the postwar world the much respected Albert Soboul and Marcel Reinhard continued their work, ensuring that, through to the Fifth Republic, fascination with dechristianisation has not waned. Indeed, Serge Bianchi was even prepared to compare

259

the movement (if it can be called that) to the 'Cultural Revolution' undertaken in Maoist China during the 1960s.[1] Richard Cobb and Colin Lucas (neither of them known for their socialist credentials) led the way in involving British scholars in researching the phenomenon, while contemporary French work on dechristianisation is associated primarily with Michel Vovelle, the centre-left historian entrusted by President François Mitterrand with coordinating national commemoration of the Revolutionary bicentenary in 1989.

In 1976 Vovelle produced his *Réligion et Révolution: la déchristianization de l'an II*, and followed it up in 1988 with *The Revolution Against the Church. From Reason to the Supreme Being* (English translation by Alan José, 1991). Both works drew on local studies by Vovelle's pupils to advance our knowledge of the movement's incidence and impact. Vovelle's claims that these can be directly related to earlier signs of change such as declining priestly vocations and confraternity memberships have intrigued scholars, but have not always persuaded them,[2] and his argument for the long-term significance of Revolutionary dechristianisation has been even less compelling. As this book has argued, we should be cautious about interpreting the absence of religious fervour in one area or the slow growth of indifference in another (reflected, for example, in Easter communion figures) as tantamount to the abandonment of Christianity. Explaining the motives of those who responded to the new revolutionary creeds remains a problematic exercise, and scholars specialising in the dechristianisation of 1792–4 have not always been sensitive enough to the variants or patterns of religious observation earlier in the century.

How popular was dechristianisation, or specific aspects of it? There is evidence from some parts of Aquitaine and Provence that the closure of churches during the Terror was in tune with public sympathies, and the new republican ceremonies were initially given an enthusiastic response. Significantly, these were areas where Catholic fervour was already waning and, more crucially still, anticlericalism had long been established. Perhaps historians have been too willing to take for symptoms of full-blown dechristianisation what are really just heightened expressions of anticlericalism. And to suggest that French men and women were 'converted' away from Christianity in any number during 1793–4 is unwarranted, let alone the recent claim by Gwynne Lewis that there 'was an explosion of popular sentiment against the moralising wing of the post-Tridentine clergy' which led parishioners to embrace the revolutionary cults with zeal.[3] Admittedly, the habitual appeal of novelty and the fear of offending local political organisers were incentives enough to prompt the semblance of a positive response from a sizeable section of the population, especially where, as in those areas of Normandy bordering the disturbed Vendée, they were fearful of Counter-Revolutionary contagion. It seemed the right thing to do at a time of acute crisis, but once the state lost interest in sponsorship of religious observances acceptable to the Revolution, the absence of unconstrained popular interest in dechristianised alternatives soon became apparent.

The neutering of the Jacobin zealots at Thermidor (or even before the coup) was decisive in halting the dechristianisation offensive. No longer would peasant communities have to fear the coercive activities of the revolutionary army moving out across 'le plat pays' and intimidating their numbers in the central *départements* – the Aisne, Yonne, Nièvre and Cher – into abandoning Christianity. And with the departure of fervent dechristianising representatives like Georges Couthon in the Puy-de-Dôme, or Joseph Le Bon in the Pas-de-Calais, anti-Christian activity was largely abandoned and villagers could try to recover what remained of their communal life and Catholic practice. Much still depended on how soon after Thermidor particular representatives left, and the Directory, as will be seen, despite its policy of official state neutrality in religion, also continued a campaign to impose republican values that involved a whole series of *fêtes*, the best device to hand for the containment of an all-too resilient Christianity after 1795. It was a more temperate, less vicious form of dechristianisation, which could go hand in hand with a periodic crackdown on priests. Over the longer term, what essentially survived of dechristianisation after 1795 – and here the Vovelle thesis is hard to ignore – was a tepid attitude to the Catholic faith that thereafter made it marginal in some areas.

Chapter 8 considered the role of the Revolutionary authorities in launching and sustaining the violence and vandalism of dechristianisation. It argued that the dechristianisation of 1792–4 was essentially foisted on the majority by urban-based politicians relying on the energies of a minority of fervent revolutionaries to coerce their fellow citizens into abandoning whatever loyalty they had to the faith of their ancestors. But there was more to the phenomenon than the destruction of Christian buildings, the prohibition of the priesthood, and blasphemous mock ceremonies to celebrate them both. Here our main focus will be to look at what was on offer to French citizens during 1792–5 as religious alternatives to Christianity, acts that would complete the emergence of the Revolution as a religion.[4]

The great *Fête de la Fédération* of 14 July 1790 in Paris was sanctified by the rites of the Church, but it was the Revolution as an entity in itself that was really acclaimed on that wet summer afternoon. It proclaimed that the first good of every citizen was that of national regeneration and public well-being; it had its own symbols and its mystic character drawn from masonry, sentimental literature (notably Rousseau), and classical antiquity. Jacobins at the centre and the localities were inspired by the possibilities: the problem of transferring sacrality to the Revolution itself, from the religious sphere to the political, could be an inspirational project – 'an act of foundation, consecrated by its own symbolism, by its own rituals, by its own moral teaching'.[5] The attempt to marry it with Catholic Christianity had, as the response to the Constitutional Church indicated, been extremely divisive, and no better than nominally successful. Such an ambiguous response prompted republican zealots to go one step further and break the hold of Christianity over French men and women altogether.

Religious rebirth, like the Republic itself, was a new start, a Year Zero of optimism. Its proponents wanted to attach a sense of the sacred to objects associated with the Revolution – the tricolour flag, the red bonnet and the cocarde. At Abbeville, on 24 *Frimaire*, a bonfire of wooden and plaster saints produced tricoloured flames; at Caen, on 24 *Ventôse*, children released doves, a dragon was set on fire, and a hermit emerged from a grotto to place his rosary beads and crosses on one side, and take the oath of fidelity to the Constitution.[6] In place of Christianity, the dominant Jacobin grouping in the Convention wanted to sponsor new forms of religious practice celebrating the achievements and future of Revolutionary Man: women were almost completely peripheral to the practice and ideologies of dechristianised religion and the gendered presumptions on which it rested. The dechristianisers made no particular effort to endear what they were offering to half the population. If revolutionaries had trouble from women who were passionately attached to the Christian faith, it was ascribable largely to offering them in return nothing that was designed to appeal.

The widely shared initial hope in the summer of 1793 was that a natural religion would emerge spontaneously, one that was at once civic, domestic and patriotic, designed to construct the new Republican man. He would be habitually austere, impeccably moral, passionate only in his defence of the new cultural order and the politicians who served it. Yet the response to the new 'faith' was lukewarm; even well-intentioned, religiously minded dechristianisers met enormous resistance at grassroots level. What was on offer in 'doctrinal' terms – cool abstractions founded on virtue and benevolence looking to the sublime in Man and Nature alike – simply failed to correspond to the harsh, daily realities as most of their countrymen experienced them.

So the Jacobin state called on local municipal officers, members of the clubs, and popular societies to stir up enthusiasm. That could be by peaceful example and symbolic demonstration, as at interments where a club member carrying pike and red bonnet would take the place of a priest, or the body of the deceased be wrapped in a tricoloured mortuary cloth.[7] Too frequently, there was a resort to intimidation dressed up in patriotic guise, but there were also real converts to the cause. Civil sermons were preached around Lyon in Year II by an actor and a journalist; at Bourg, the local doctor, one Rollet, took the lead, while at L'Ouhans, on 12 *Pluvôise*, the popular society argued that every commune should nominate a worthy inhabitant, who could give instruction in republicanism and edify other citizens through his exemplary life.[8]

Architects of the republican order like Fouché believed that Christianity could not coexist in any form with the Revolution. Patriotism should be the new faith, the Declaration of the Rights of Man its Apostles' Creed, to be celebrated with compelling new symbolism and public spectacles. The influential Thomas Lindet advised replacing religious assemblies by civic festivals, and the momentum became unstoppable. The great national festivals were to be celebrations of the Republic. Songs were written and public festivals planned that would bring citizens together in spontaneous celebration of the non-Christian virtues prized in the new France;[9] the anniversary of Louis XVI's execution was to be an occasion for national rejoicing, a festival for the whole family to enjoy, one characterised in many places by the decapitation of a mannequin and the dancing of the Carmagnole.[10] The funerals of the 'martyrs' Lepelletier and Marat were marked by festivals acclaiming the Republic, but it was the *Fête de la Réunion* of 10 August 1793 commemorating the victims of the storming of the Tuileries Palace a year earlier that constituted the first national festival with an exclusively civil character.[11] It was presided over by the leading Jacobin, Hérault de Séchelles, and the statue of Nature was honoured by libations. A month later, the first anniversary of the fall of the throne was remembered. A procession moved from the site of the Bastille to the Champ de Mars to salute an enormous statue of Nature, from whose ample breasts poured a continuous flow of water – the 'Fountain of Regeneration'. But 'patriot' enthusiasm for a new religious order was not in itself enough to bring quick results. It was all very well for the Convention on 15 *Brumaire* Year II to order the printing of a discourse drawn up by Marie-Joseph Chénier in the name of its *Comité d'Instruction Publique* and his hopes for the founding of 'the single universal religion, which has neither secrets nor mysteries, whose single dogma is equality, whose orators are our laws, and our magistrates its priests',[12] but who would read it? The sheer passiveness of the masses, particularly the rural population, in the face of what the revolutionary elite wished to impose on them, was not the least effective weapon against dechristianisation.

Among the various phenomena making up dechristianisation, were the changes introduced to purge the calendar of associations with the historic faith. The Gregorian calendar was abandoned completely, to the joy of Jacobins like Joseph Chalier: 'Through this new calendar, you [the Convention] have shown how much you want to kill fanaticism.' In October 1793, the Convention adopted the new one proposed by the mathematician, Romme, and Danton's friend, the poet Fabre d'Eglantine, who had wrecked the old 'catalogue of charlatanism'. Once again, there were echoes of Rousseau. The agricultural cycle was emphasised; pagan Gods and botanical specimens replaced Christian martyrs, all suited to a republican cosmology; Christmas became dog day, Epiphany cod day and All Saints was dedicated to the goat's beard herb. Twelve months remained from the old Christian order, but the months were renamed and each one newly divided into three ten-day units, the *décades*, ending in a rest day, the *décadi*; five extra days in the year were called *sans-culottides* and consecrated to national festivals of Genius, Work, Virtue, Opinion and Recompense.[13] The removal of saints' days from the calendar was dislocation enough, along with the deletion of the great Christian festivals familiar to every man, woman and child in France. But it was the official disappearance of Sundays (caused by the replacement of the week by the *décade*) and the concomitant reduction in days off work that most affected the individual lives. The authorities were told to take steps against those who ignored the new measures. Thus in *Messidor* Year II (June/July 1794), harvesters at Plaisance in the Toulouse region who stopped work on a Sunday were arrested, and at Arras servants taking off any other day but the *décadi* were liable to the same fate; in the Haute-Garonne the deputy on mission decreed that those who did not observe the Tenth Day as the sole day of rest would receive no bread, flour or grain, and would have their names pinned up on a list of 'do-nothing citizens and suspects'.[14] Despite the risks of arrest and denunciation, some citizens tried to have the best of both worlds by staying home both on Sunday and on the *décadi*, causing a drop in farm production. From Thionville on the eastern frontier, the representative on mission Mallarmé in March 1794 indignantly snorted that 'the stupid scrap of papalism, the former Sunday, was religiously observed, and national repose degraded'.[15] The Revolutionary calendar never caught on outside official circles though it somehow survived until 1806, when it was finally adjudged incompatible with the dignity of an Imperial regime.

Several months before the new calendar was introduced, the Convention had embarked on a programme of renaming the streets of the capital so that all Christian references would be removed. Thus the Rue Saint-Jacques and the Quai Saint-Michel both lost their 'Saint'. Provincial centres frequently followed the Parisian example. In Toulouse, classical heroes with appropriate republican credentials – Cato and Brutus prominent among them – joined foreign revolutionaries like William Tell and Benjamin Franklin on street signs, together with recent native revolutionary martyrs such as Marat. Some local authorities might declare that 'the names of Brutus and others are sweeter to a republican ear than those of a hermit like St John',[16] but few people who lived or worked on the streets bothered to use the new nomenclature. In Bosher's words, it may have been 'a dictatorial minority' that renamed the villages to get rid of the saints' names,[17] but these people had a reserve authority that made defiance risky. At Ris, the popular society compelled the municipal council to change the name of the commune to Brutus on 30 October 1793 and, for good measure, insisted it be accompanied by ordering the suppression of Christian worship and the confiscation of precious metals from the church.[18]

In the *département* of the Gard, about a quarter of the communes changed their names to empty them of any Christian connotations, with another quarter replacing the word Saint in their name by Mont or Font. This process was known as *débaptisation*. Besides villages and streets, even people were renamed; it became briefly fashionable for the militantly non-Christian to display their convictions to the world by renaming their children after republican pagans or the new martyrs of the French Republic in a way deliberately intended to efface the Christian associations of family life. The popularity of the practice varied considerably. Over half the children born in Beauvais during the Year II were given revolutionary appellations, 40 per cent at Saint-Pol in the Pas-de-Calais.[19] On the other hand, only 62 out of 593 children born at Poitiers during the Year II received republican names, and in Toulouse no member of the revolutionary committee called himself anything different.[20] The mothers seem to have had the last word: it was by no means unknown for a boy called Lepeletier in 1794 to be baptised as Jacques two years later.[21]

The local variants among the alternatives to Christianity were considerable, a reflection of varying pressures and priorities, but sufficient to suggest that there was a chaotic element in the whole dechristianising process. In Toulouse, for instance, the underlying motive was local defence rather than national considerations. According to Martin Lyons:

> it derived its virulence from the confrontation between urban poor and superstitious peasantry, and within the city itself, between the urban sans-culotterie, and a strongly entrenched ecclesiastical establishment.[22]

If the various rites had one aspect in common, it was a commitment to 'Reason', as seen in quasi-religious festivities held in former cathedrals and parish churches (converted into 'temples of reason').

Such was the rationale for the most famous of all the dechristianising festivities, that held in Notre-Dame de Paris (now designated the 'Temple of Reason') on 10 November 1793. A temple of philosophy occupied the place of the high altar and before it paraded patriotic maidens dressed in white. At the climax of the ceremony, an actress from the Opéra representing Liberty in a white dress topped by a red Phrygian cap emerged from the temple and, to acclamation, bowed to the flame of Reason before leading the officials of the commune to the Convention. The hope was that Liberty would be like an ordinary woman, not a superstitious icon. As one journalist insisted:

> One wanted from the first moment to break the habit of every species of idolatry; we avoided putting in the place of a holy sacrament an inanimate image of liberty because vulgar minds might have misunderstood and substituted in place of the god of bread a god of stone ... and this living woman, despite all the charms that embellished her, could not be deified by the ignorant, as would a statue of stone.[23]

Most spectators were bemused by what they saw. Was she a blaspheming whore or a carnival queen? Just to confuse the picture, in the provinces where the cult of 'Reason' began to be celebrated later in the month, most but not all of the 'Goddesses' were young women of some character from decent families.[24] At Digne, Madelaine, a patriotic daughter of the popular society reclined in the temple of reason (a former church) beneath a canopy of red velvet, draped in a linen gown.[25] In the north-east, such occasions were initially an urban phenomenon, with cities like Nancy and Toul leading the way, impelled by their enthusiastic representative, Faure. His colleague, Baudot, was no less keen at Strasbourg, and by late 1793 Auch and Dijon were among the other major centres putting together a celebration. In the adjacent villages, the festivities were ritualised, commonly with a procession of a 'goddess' to the local Tree of Liberty, but there was little to suggest any genuine religious practice.[26]

Across France as a whole, the number of places holding a festival of Reason – usually in a consecrated building, including former cathedrals like Bayeux for, as Richard Wrigley has recently observed, 'it was hoped to redirect the respect and subjective sentiments such buildings commanded into new political channels'[27] – reached a climax in January–February 1794, with the Midi by that date having started to participate.[28] Historians have still much to discover about what went on inside these buildings – usually former churches – outside festival time. It was the official hope that such 'temples of reason' would become places, as representative Javogues in the Loiret département put it, 'where the people could read the official papers and laws, learn their rights and duties, and exercise the civic virtues'.[29] Javogues may have been optimistic about what

could be achieved, but so were colleagues elsewhere, like Lanot in
Limoges, who wrote ecstatically (13 *Frimaire*):

> The public spirit here is at a great height, and fanaticism this
> morning is in its last agony and will be dead by evening. I am
> going today to the temple of Reason where I shall proclaim the
> revolt of earth against heaven. I am convinced that after this cere-
> mony there will be in the Haute-Vienne neither a trace nor a ves-
> tige of ecclesiastical feudalism.[30]

Figures based primarily on addresses and petitions to the Convention from popular societies and local authorities suggest that just
under one-quarter of all communes in France opened a temple of
reason in 1793–4.[31] In Laon, Besançon, Toulouse and Bordeaux, one
time Constitutional clergymen consecrated ex-churches as such, and
at Reims the services of the former Bishop of the Oise, Massieu, were
enlisted for the occasion only two days before Christmas 1793 (3 *nivôse*
Year II).[32] By spring 1794 even some peripheral regions like Provence
and parts of the Languedoc around Béziers and Montpellier had
joined the Île de France, Berry, the Lyonnaise and a crescent-shaped
strip stretching from Normandy down to northern Burgundy in
experimenting with the new religious order.

It was not usually enough for the dechristianisers to commend the
alternatives to Christianity; the old religion had to submit to public
ridicule of 'priestcraft' and 'superstition', and the participation of
turncoat clerics was particularly sought. The climax of the ceremony
came with the burning of their *lettres de prêtrise* and the renouncing of
their vows in favour of a resolve to marry; then followed burlesque
ceremonies judged suitable for the occasion such as burning stuffed
straw images of the Pope. It was managed to perfection at Dol
(Ille-et-Vilaine):

> For this ceremony we had prepared a bonfire on Brutus Square and
> had dressed up two old effigies of religious fanaticism, one decked
> out as a tyrant crowned with a fleur-de-lys, and the other as the
> Pope, complete with papal tiara and slippers.[33]

The anticlerical sentiments exhibited on these patriotic occasions
disclosed the popular roots of the militant dechristianisation of the
autumn of 1793: predominantly urban, male, artisan and youthful.

In some areas of France, the burlesque procession, with its 'mitred donkey', quickly became ritualised, but whatever good humour the occasion generated was always limited, especially where a village cleric was dragged behind the donkey and revolutionaries were capering about in his sacred vestments. Priests of all allegiances were turned by the sansculottes into hate-figures, by definition non-patriots and likely to be conspiring against the Republic. 'Remember,' one army officer told his men, 'it is fanaticism and superstition we will be fighting against, lying priests whose dogma is falsehood ... whose empire is founded upon the credulity of women. These are the enemy.'[34]

In the Nièvre, representative Fouché ordered clerics who refused to marry to adopt and support orphans or aged citizens. Those who did comply and find a wife, like Jérôme-Balthazard Levée, former *vicaire* of a church in Le Havre and the bishop's financial broker turned blasphemous songster, or Pascal-Antoine Grimaud, Professor of Theology at the College of Clermont-Ferrand before the Revolution (one of the several ex-clergy who made up the Commission of dechristianisers operating from Moulins), seem to have done so out of a new-found religious zeal for the Revolution, a zeal frequently demonstrated by a willingness to lead the way in ransacking churches and ripping out their fittings.[35] Such destruction often included deliberate desecration of holy objects. A crowd that invaded Quimper cathedral in Brittany watched with approval as an agent of the *département* of the Finistère urinated into the chalice and other eucharistic vessels ransacked from the altar; in the Isère, horrified villagers looked on as one leading terrorist, Vauquoy, looted the communion vessels and defiantly drained the local wine from a chalice. 'If there is a God,' he taunted them, 'let him strike me down here on the spot in front of you'. At Moulins on 27 November, when 130 of the local revolutionary army left for Lyon to combat the Federalists, 'The two sappers were wearing the mitres of the former bishop of the Allier and his crozier served the drum-major as a staff.'[36]

The removal and profanation of Christian symbols was accompanied by the substitution of new ones in a gesture that was both imitation and creation.[37] It was operative at every level of artistic expression, from religious paintings to street culture. Christian subjects painted before 1789 were often lucky to survive, but some were adapted, like Pierre-François Dalauney's *An Offering to St Nicholas* altered into an *Offering to Liberty* by the careful erasure of the saint and the substitution of an allegorical figure.[38] The revolutionaries imposed such fresh visual reference points in the hope of capturing the interest of those who had not come to terms with the removal of Christian symbolism, and offered regular alternatives like the *cérémonies décadaires*, or occasional celebratory festivals in addition to the festivals of Reason, like that for the recapture of the naval base of Toulon from the British in late 1793.

Most popular societies soon had busts and images of the new pantheon of dead revolutionary celebrities in places of honour. Their statues were carried through the streets; their relics were treasured and invoked at public ceremonies with the objective of creating 'a religious atmosphere' in a manner reminiscent of the Corpus Christi Day processions.[39] Such celebrations and invocations were designed to elevate revolutionary martyrs to the status of deities- one former priest compared the heart of Marat – 'The People's Friend' – (it was contained in a vase suspended from an archway in the meeting hall of the Codeliers) to the Sacred Heart of Jesus. Other enthusiasts replaced the formula 'In the name of the Father, Son and Holy Ghost' with 'In the name of Marat, Lepeletier, liberty or death!'[40] Such acclamations were often regarded by less committed onlookers as both blasphemous and tastelessly triumphalist. Even a candlemaker's boy in Paris, a good sansculotte, preferred arrest to honouring Marat, saying 'he would prefer to die a thousand times rather than attend a celebration like that'.[41] But during the autumn of 1793 the new iconography appeared to carry all before it. It was clearly seen after the liberation of Lyon, a former Federalist stronghold where some kind of purgative, cleansing ceremonial was required to symbolise its restoration to the revolutionary cause. The leading Jacobin, Collot d'Herbois, masterminded ceremonies in Lyon, assisted by two real specialists, Couthon and Fouché. Events climaxed with the exposure to 'public veneration' on 10 November 1793 of the physical remains of Joseph Chalier, the Jacobin martyr of Lyon, before his head was packed up and sent to the Convention.[42]

These irreligious trends were not viewed with equanimity by all leading Jacobins. By the spring of 1794, Robespierre had persuaded the governing committees to abandon sponsorship of dechristianisation, and the cult of the martyrs was wound down with commemorations of Marat discouraged after Hébert's execution on 24 March. 'If Marat were still alive at this moment,' one police observer heard someone say, 'he'd have been indicted and probably guillotined.'[43]

As an alternative, on 7 May the cult of the Supreme Being was launched, for God, like the streets of Paris, had changed His name.[44] The cult was a form of warm-hearted deism inspired by Rousseau, intended to reconcile the divinity to the republic, and in so doing marry the immortality of the soul to the promotion of virtue. It grew out of the cult of Reason already established, and offered some recognition of the religious aspirations of the masses. It was designed to give the republic a more overt divine sanction than previously, and constitute a constant reminder of justice.[45] One could not govern, insisted Robespierre, without the idea of God,

> which makes up for the inadequacy of human authority; it is the religious sentiment that imprints on souls the idea of the sanction given to moral precepts by a power superior to man's. Thus I am totally unaware of any legislator who has ever been advised to nationalise atheism.[46]

Robespierre would have no truck with 'priestcraft', but if he was realistic in sensing the overwhelming desire of the French nation to recognise God (to which the flood of addresses to the Convention, thanking its membership for having proscribed atheism and offering citizens a new civic religion, bore testimony), there was an artificiality in the form he chose to give the French state's recognition of the religious impulse. Nevertheless, it should not be imagined that the cult was somehow personal to Robespierre, turning him into a revolutionary 'pope',[47] and adherence to it merely feigned by his opponents in the Convention while they plotted to remove him. Belief in the Supreme Being permitted enough variations to accommodate many tastes. Here is Carnot, for example, speaking in the Convention on 27 Floréal Year II, having first ennumerated all the best human values as friendship, filial piety and justice: 'These are things to be found in the Supreme Being; he is the seal of all those thoughts which make for the happiness of man.'[48]

20 Prairial Year II (8 June 1794, ironically, the feast of Pentecost) was set aside for national commemoration of the Supreme Being, but little guidance was given by the Convention to authorities outside the capital on how they should observe the day. David's artificial mountain in the Champ de Mars is well known; so too is Robespierre's solemn progress to its summit at the head of the Conventionnels (sniggering behind his back) after morning festivities had culminated in

the burning of the figure of Atheism from which the statue of Wisdom emerged, and the singing of the hymn:

Father of the universe,
Supreme intelligence
Benefactor unknown to mortals
You will reveal your existence
To those who alone raise altars in your name.[49]

Robespierre's colleagues from the Convention may not have treated the occasion with much solemnity, but the cannons sounded, young girls strewed the way of the procession with flowers, and some older citizens were appropriately glimpsed weeping. Yet there is no sign of standardized choreography for the occasion outside the capital.[50] *Départements* where the representatives were firm Robespierre supporters – as the Ariège and the Pyréneés-Orientales – were quick to acknowledge the Supreme Being, but it was commonly hard to discern much difference between the worship of Reason and the cult of the Supreme Being. It seems that some areas had a definite preference for the Supreme Being as opposed to 'Reason': Calvados, Manche, Orne, Ille-et-Vilaine in the west; the Côte d'Or, Haute-Marne, Meurthe in the north-east; the Hautes and Basses Alpes and the Var in the south-east.[51]

The uncertainty about the new Supreme Being decree was reflected in the behaviour of the crowds in most of the eighty-three *départements* that staged a ceremony, in some places even at village level. As usual, a large proportion of the onlookers turned up out of curiosity, just to stand and stare. As the parade was forming up at Auxerre on 30 June one soldier asked an old woman why she was not joining in – 'It's not your God I adore,' she replied. 'He is too young. It's the old one.'[52] The diverse festivals of the Supreme Being nevertheless encouraged some Catholics to view them as distinct from their faith only in theory and to imagine – wrongly – that their own religion might soon be rehabilitated sufficiently for them to resume public worship. In some places the faithful came along to the festivals with their rosaries, while in Lyon the likelihood that Catholics living on the procession route might honour the rites and processions they saw passing beneath their windows was so pronounced that the leaders of the refractory church advised them against any sort of participation. Republican enemies of Robespierre were clearly worried that his personal commitment to the Supreme Being might unintentionally allow Christianity to slip in through the back door. These developments coincided with the sudden prominence of the prophetess Catherine Théot, the 'Mère de Dieu' as she called herself, whose visionary identification of the Messiah with Robespierre himself further unsettled his gathering enemies.[53]

Robespierre's eventual overthrow at *Thermidor* Year II soon curtailed official interest in promulgating the cult of the Supreme Being. The subsequent purge of Jacobin zealots in the *départements* also reduced the incidence of militant dechristianisation, though in some centres, notably Lyon, it persisted well into 1795. Aggrieved revolutionaries even in Paris had not much choice except to trim their sails or put their lives at risk. On 30 *Thermidor* Year III (17 August 1795), in the Nord *section*, 'the statues established by terrorism and placed in the choir of the Church of Saint-Laurent' were destroyed.[54] The Thermidorian realists were cutting their losses, modifying the bloodier aspects of a policy that had done nothing to endear the Revolution to the majority of the nation. After news of the victory at Fleurus in June 1794 survival was no longer at risk, and the leaders of the French state lost interest in exclusively promulgating one cult rather than another. Even so, the campaign to impose republican values through festivals and their like went on after Robespierre's death.

The experiment had shown how relatively few were the rank-and-file supporters of dechristianisation, but subsequent historians have found it hard to concede as much. Thus the great Communist historian Albert Soboul (d. 1982) once argued that the masses adapted to the new republican forms fairly successfully while keeping the essential content of their religious (folk) beliefs intact, and cited the cult of Marat as an instance. But such an assessment only persuades if one follows Soboul and denies the Christian understanding of the rural masses, minimises their capacity to distinguish the old from the new, and disregards the force of passive resistance encountered by Jacobins in evangelising the countryside for the alternative religious forms offered by the Revolution. The peasants of 'la France profonde' instinctively doubted the revolutionary cults, at once blasphemous and anodyne, offering none of the inner consolation that (folk) Christianity gave them in their drab, laborious existence. As Olwen Hufton has memorably written:

A relationship with this deity [the Goddess of Reason] was like taking an ice-maiden for bedfellow. She added neither to the business of living or to the process of dying. She proffered no alternative on crop devastation by hail; she could not be called upon when labour pains came thick and fast or when a new-born infant took a few faltering breaths and expired and the mother who had laboured in vain needed solace.[55]

In most areas outside the war zones and the strongholds of republican politics, implementation of dechristianisation had incurred popular disapproval from the start. We should also not forget that in many places it arrived only just before Thermidor ran down the curtain of official disapproval and declared a truce in the battle for cultural supremacy between Christianity and republican values. After the initial curiosity had worn off, attitudes to dechristianisation ranged from indifference to the sort of contempt evidenced in recent local studies like that of the Limousin by Louis Pérouas and Paul d'Hollander.[56] There was in most localities a surprising willingness of people to make clear their disdain for the new cultural order, and women took the lead using every trick and ruse to display disdain. People were restless for the reopening of their churches and an end to the newfangled ceremonies.

Opposition to other aspects of the programme could be more pronounced. In the Doubs, at Fontaine, parents withdrew their children from the school when the teacher refused to show them how to make the sign of the cross and offered instead a lecture on the virtues of the Supreme Being; at Besançon, only club members turned up at the temple of reason in the city. Attacks on parish churches by Jacobins and their supporters could lead to popular violence in response; across France, villagers replaced crosses cut down by the authorities, and uprooted the tricolours and Trees of Liberty that had replaced them.[57] Local officials and municipalities, on whom so much depended, were often sluggards in promulgating dechristianisation, and found it hard to obtain workmen willing to undertake demolition work when it involved former church premises. When the contractors started on the job they were threatened and had their ladders stolen, and the objects they had come to confiscate were hidden away.

Women were among the leading opponents of dechristianisation, much as they had been earlier of the Civil Constitution, working to keep open the churches the men were attempting to close, and the clubs tried vainly to have husbands coerce their spouses. At Arles, the *société populaire* wanted the wives of male householders to join in a sacreligious ceremony that required collective spitting on the host.[58] Such actions did nothing for the popularity of the Revolution across a range of female opinion. The new Goddesses of Reason were no substitute for the Blessed Virgin Mary. These young women were scandalous fakes whose looks might interest the men, but 'commanded no hot line to the deity, no proven record in the alleviation of labour pains or the extermination of grain weevils'.[59] Instead, local women tried hard to keep religious rituals alive even during the Terror, and they used tactics that included collective obstinacy and sexist ridicule of officials trying to implement dechristianization. In the countryside of the Île de France, they urged their men to join them in opposing the enforced silence of the bells, and demanded the reopening of the churches. In the Haute-Loire, the *béates* (see Chapter 2) undertook burials of the dead at midnight, cajoling even threatening relatives to get hold of the body and give the deceased something like a Christian interment.

At Le Puy, local women showed their collective disdain for the representative on mission Albitte's insistence on taking a civic oath by showing their buttocks at a prearranged signal to the altar of liberty. The humiliated officiant might deplore 'these abnormal and obscene gestures', but he was powerless to stop their imitation elsewhere.[60] In the Rhône, a crowd of women surrounded the popular society at Condrieu, demanding the right to choose the place in which they would 'practice their customs', and were not impressed when the society read out to them a patriotic address claiming that the sans-culotte Jesus should be put in the pantheon.[61] Patriots often chose the easier course and ignored gatherings of women to say the rosary in former consecrated buildings. Such defiant actions leave historians in no doubt about the extent to which a new public sphere for robust, semi-independent action had suddenly opened up to women. It worried officialdom, vexed their husbands and disquieted the clandestine clergy, but no amount of insults like 'priests' prostitutes' – and worse – could weaken the strong Christian commitment of women of all ages across France.

Thermidor revealed both the isolation of the dechristianisers and their failure to make much impact on the majority population. The masses wearied of the Revolution, desperate as they were under the pressure of the hard winter of 1794–5, and found the only acceptable comfort in the historic faith. It was the 'terrible and universal reaction' that Robespierre had predicted when he warned against the excesses of dechristianisation at the close of 1793. But if passive and active resistance had forced the politicians to call off their campaign to impose new revolutionary faiths, Catholic Christianity paid a high price. In the medium term, dechristianisation achieved its maximum impact by massively reducing the clerical presence in the parishes. Routine, regular public worship stopped. Dechristianisation shattered the habits of open observance, and half a generation of young people missed out on formal religious teaching. The damage to a collective Catholic culture was soon there for all to see. Cardinal Consalvi, on his way to negotiate the Concordat, described the French as 'indifferent for the most part, entirely so in the towns, and to an appreciable degree in the countryside'.[62] Certainly, in 1801, a majority could hardly dare to believe a regime (then still republican) would not just permit Christians to worship openly, but was even encouraging them to organise publicly. As they did so, it became apparent how many clergy the dechristianisers had either degraded or driven out, so breaking the old network of pastoral contacts and worship centres that had until so recently covered the whole country. For the Catholic Church in France, recovery would be slow and confidence would take a long time to rebuild, and it would only really make headway when the First Empire had been finally overthrown in 1815.

Part IV Towards a New Religious Order: The Directory and the Consulate

11 Religion and the Directory, 1795–9

I

The passing of the Constitution of the Year III and the establishment of the Directory was an attempt to restore something like political normality to France after six years of revolutionary upheaval. The mood of the nation was ready for quieter times and, while prepared to preserve the Republic, it wanted to marginalise extremists – whether of the Left or of the Right – to achieve stability. That was one of the lessons of the immediate past. Another was that efforts to extirpate expression of the Christian faith were futile: any such policies merely created martyrs and confirmed the vast majority of Catholics in their loyalty. The moral was clear: if the Churches – both the Constitutional clergy and the non-jurors – could learn to live with the Republic, then the Republic might try to coexist with the Churches. This insight motivated the most constructive individuals among both politicians and clergy throughout the second half of the 1790s and culminated in Napoleon's attempt at final settlement of the religious problem in the Concordat of 1801/2. Yet precious few of the Directors or other ministers in central government (at local level the picture varied enormously) during the period 1795–9 were ready to admit as much: they could not envisage either the detachment of Catholicism from Counter-Revolution or the Bonapartist logic that eventually led to the Concordat.

So there were powerful influences working against stability based on religious toleration. The intransigent majority that could not accept compromise even cold-shouldered overtures for official accommodation from the rump of the Constitutional Church which, led by the resilient Grégoire, showed how much Catholicism and republicanism *could* be brought together. There was, then, a real sense in which the Directory in practice functioned as the latest revolutionary regime, predicated on an assumption that its best interests could not be harmonised with those of Christianity. Nevertheless, since the separation of the revolutionary Church from the state under the decree of 3 *Ventôse* Year III (21 February 1795) (confirmed

279

in article three hundred and fifty-four of the Year III Constitution), the Republic was legally committed to religious neutrality, and the law of 11 *Prairial* Year III (30 May 1795) required priests to submit to the laws of the state in order to minister in public. They would be left uncoerced by the state so long as their activities were deemed no threat to the republic. This remained the position when the first Directors took up post in the Luxembourg Palace the following October.

They inherited religious legislation which, in the words of one recent scholar, 'offered substantial encouragement both to anticlericalism and to advocates of toleration'.[1] The moment seemed ripe for experiment. Over the next few years some of the Directors would sponsor alternatives to Christianity, like theophilanthropy, the crankiest religious manifestation of the late 1790s, to be placed alongside other trends like the cult of the *décade* and resurgent Freemasonry. Yet these developments did not alter the fact that, as far as the French state was concerned, so long as Christians kept out of politics (other than to endorse the regime) and respected the many legal restrictions on their activities, they were free to worship privately and denounce each other if they so wished. Such constraints were acceptable enough to Protestants and Jews, but it was an open question in the Year III whether these concessions were either sufficient or could be made to work acceptably for Catholics.

All religious groups in France faced the new challenge of adjusting to a free market in faith, one that has been identified by religious sociologists as that of *voluntarism*, the norm for religious organisations in the modern world.[2] This policy went much further than the toleration endorsed by the 'Enlightened absolutists', or even by Louis XVI under the edict of 1787. For the first time in post-Reformation Europe, a state was declaring itself to be wholly disinterested towards the survival of the faith: if Christianity withered away, so be it. Meanwhile, refractories and Constitutionals, Protestants and Jews, would have to compete for popular support against each other. Could they deal with the practical implications of the concept of religious allegiance as an associational commitment to be entered into voluntarily?

Priests of all persuasions remained cautious and bewildered, slow to resume public worship because of the dangers until so recently associated with it, and with good reason; the Directory remained suspicious of Christianity to the extent that, as Martin Lyons has argued, 'Far from reconciling their differences, the Directory and the traditional Catholic Church became, if anything, more intransigent in their relations with one another.'[3] After the left-wing *coup* of 18 *Fructidor* (September 1797) all Christians were at the mercy of a volatile anticlerical régime. Signs of official reluctance to concede toleration were on early display. Unlike the Declaration of Rights that prefaced the Year I Constitution, that of the Year III made no reference to the free exercise of religion.[4] The new oaths imposed on Catholic clergy requiring the hatred of royalty (see below) were almost designed to provoke them into breaking the law and so facilitate their depiction as enemies of the regime. An edict of 29 September 1795 codifying previous measures prohibited all external manifestations of religion. Priests could not wear clerical dress in public; outdoor processions and worship were banned; bell-ringing, statues and crosses that could be seen by the general public were also forbidden; service times had to be registered at the town hall.

With such restrictive legislation, it was hard for Catholics to derive much benefit from the law of 3 *Ventôse*. Churches and presbyteries often remained state property (they were frequently kept locked deliberately), and communes could neither buy nor rent a building to be used for worship; only in exceptional circumstances were villagers able to reclaim churches for Christian practice. The repression that the Convention imposed after the royalist revival of 1795 (especially the Parisian revolt of 13 *Vendémiaire*) also worked against Catholics hoping for better times. The law of 3 *Brumaire* Year IV (25 October 1795) re-established the legislation of 1792–3 against refractory priests, denied an amnesty to all in that category, and gave émigré priests recently returned to France fifteen days to leave or risk execution.[5] It was no idle threat. Fr Pierre-René Rogues had carried on a clandestine ministry at Vannes in Brittany all through the Terror only to fall a victim of the Directory's tough new laws. He was discovered carrying the Eucharist through the streets of the town on Christmas Eve 1795, and died on the scaffold the following March. The uncompromising penalties did nothing to deflect popular support for the refractories in Brittany. It was hard for the authorities to uncover a priest's hiding place, all part of what one republican complainant in 1796 noted was 'fanaticism still exercising its sway' in the Ille-et-Vilaine *département*.[6]

The legal disincentives to religious revival were not enough to prevent the Catholic laity up and down the country petitioning the authorities for use of church premises or alternatively, especially in poorer areas, breaking into buildings or holding an illegal festival. These recalcitrants were liable to stiff penalties, if apprehended, from a regime that regarded their fervour as misplaced. Its indifference as early as 1795–6 to Catholics in custody furnished another salutary reminder of what the religious opponents of the Republic might expect. Refractory clergy newly released from the pestilential prison hulks off Rochefort on the Atlantic coast gained little benefit from their freedom. A ragged band of them converged on the fortified coastal town of Brouage, where they were joined by 143 nuns from different congregations. Imprisoned in the parish church, illness and malnutrition killed 80 of them before the Ministry of Marine consented in 1796 to the town authority's request to grant the prisoners permission to walk within the fortifications.

Such a harrowing example gives the flavour of the Directory's deep-seated anticlericalism, widely disseminated among deputies and junior office-holders, though the refractories were not without friends among state officials at every level, especially among judges in the south;[7] they were sometimes willing to permit the return of monks (such as the Christian Brothers) and *congréganistes* to take up work in schools and hospitals. The adminstrative chaos of the era could thus be exploited to the refractories' advantage. For the most part, the servants of the Directory – with some justification – found priestly loyalties suspect, especially after *Fructidor*, when the sense that Catholicism and the Revolution were incompatible effectively became official policy. As early as the winter of 1795–6 there were rumours that refractory priests in hiding in the hill country were allied to army deserters.[8] The clamours for renewed repression never died away, even in the royalists' 'good year' of 1796, when Drulhe, deputy of Toulouse, made his report on 4 *Floréal*, Year IV (23 April):

> Priests are the most dangerous enemies of the Republic: the heads of seditious movements, a rallying point for all malcontents, and correspondents of the *émigrés*. A blind indulgence and the immunity they enjoy has encouraged them to return to the country from which a salutary Terror had removed them.[9]

Drulhe's plan for deporting all the old refractory priests was – for the time being – unacceptable to moderate opinion in the Council of Ancients.

The Directory's religious policy miscalculated the popular mood. The groundswell of support for Roman Catholicism in France was consistently stronger than any for the Directory, as was indicated even before its formation with the general observance of Easter duties in 1795. During the preceding Lent, one journal reported that there were 'two sorts of queues: queues at Mass, queues at the baker's door'. Here was a public hungry for both.[10] With very few churches yet reopened, services were held in private oratories or hired rooms. Hard though it was for the executive to concede, the French people did not want a republic if the price was to be a continued assault on Catholic Christianity. On the other hand, if the Church and the Republic could be accommodated then most laymen – and an increasing number of clergy – were not going to hold out for a crowned Head of State. Royalism and Catholicism could be divorced. In the last instance, the Church's future was more important to Catholics than the Monarchy's, the cross a more appropriate emblem for this crisis of European civilisation than the crown.

For a brief period, in 1796–7, political exigencies made the régime more inclined to walk with the Right, in response to the challenge to government posed by Babeuf and his followers. The Minister for Police, Cochon de Lapparent, hitherto a stickler for enforcing the laws against the refractory clergy, advised loyal government officials not to disturb, at least for the time being, the 'quieter' sort of priest with oaths and declarations. The mood was soon caught by deputies. On 26 August 1796 Jean-Etienne-Marie Portalis (later architect of the Concordat and Napoleon's Minister for Religious Affairs) in the legislature had successfully and passionately argued for observation of the right to liberty of conscience: 'laws are only relative for citizens, but religion can really take hold of you [*saisit l'homme*]'. Most deputies applauded his courage, despite grumbling from one radical. '*Voilà les chouans*', he said, jabbing his finger at Portalis, a bourgeois lawyer of Clichyen views, '*les voilà!*' It was not enough to prevent other concessions, such as permitting nuns who had not sworn the 'Liberty-Equality' oath to claim their pensions.[11] More followed. On 14 *Frimaire* Year V (14 December 1796), the recent reinvigoration of the laws of 1792–3 was put aside. Moderate and right-wing candidates did well in the national elections of April 1797, often with counter-revolutionary-minded clergy on hand to encourage voters.

Those successfully elected pushed ahead with their plans for a more generous policy towards religion. Camille Jordan proposed the unfettered liberty of conscience and worship. There should be no more oaths, because 'they infringe on the domain of belief', and his plea for the church bells to ring out again brought him the nickname of 'Jordan-the-Bells' from his enemies. The voting figures on such contentious matters were close enough to indicate that the refractory clergy had highly placed friends in the Republic. Indeed, a measure to repeal laws imposing deportation or imprisonment for priests guilty only of refusing to swear submission to the laws of the Republic had by late August passed both the Councils of the Ancients and the Five Hundred.[12] Then came the coup of *Fructidor*, and the purge of right-wing politicians in both the chambers of the Five Hundred and the Ancients. A new wave of anti-Christian repression followed the coup, with existing laws more rigorously enforced and the overtures of the Constitutional Church – concurrently convened in its first National Council – disdained again.[13]

The religious revival of the later 1790s fuelled the regime's enduring antipathy towards priests and religious dogmas: it could not accept at face value numerous assertions of loyalty to the effect that, as petitioners from Chablis said in 1795, 'We wish to be Catholics and republicans and we can be both one and the other.'[14] The army remained the most powerful anti-Catholic force at the disposal of the regime, an agency of sacrilege and dechristianisation awaiting activation, and it was given its head by the so-called 'Second Directory' after *Fructidor* in a renewed clampdown on organised Christianity. Churches were sold off more quickly to prevent any resumption of worship in them; others, even the great abbey of Cluny, were demolished.[15] Beyond the frontier, French armies were advancing into the Low Countries and Italy, and the way the Directory discharged executive functions in these areas was instructive. French Catholics, ever tempted to imagine the possibility of a rapprochement between the regime and the Church, only had to notice anticlerical policies pursued in the occupied Rhineland, Switzerland and the Austrian Netherlands.

The Army of Italy contained innumerable soldiers with no respect for any Church or clergy, and Bonaparte found their prejudices hard to restrain after he occupied Milan in the spring of 1796. He soon learnt that Pius VI had rejected the French demand that he withdraw his condemnation of the Civil Constitution and the Revolution.

The Directory viewed the papacy as the symbol of resistance to French republican power, and advised Bonaparte in an instruction of 3 February 1796 to 'consider the idea of destroying Rome as a scourge in the hands of fanaticism'; the Director La Révellière-Lépeaux talked in terms of 'putting an end to the power of the divine Braschi [Pius VI's family name]'.[16] In fact there were signs of a new realism in Vatican circles. The papal Brief *Pastoralis sollicitudo* (5 July 1796) was actually drafted by Pius's entourage, its proclamation that subjects owed submission to established governments being one of the first signs that the Pope had learnt from recent events; it appeared to vindicate Emery and the moderate refractories who had recommended recognition of the *de facto* government at home, despite the subsequent oath of hatred to royalty.[17] Extremists on either side were actually rather embarrassed by the Brief. Royalist refractories, aware of the pressure on Pius after the fall of Bologna to the Army of Italy, claimed it was a forgery, diehard republicans no less so. As for the Directory, with French armies steadily advancing in the Italian peninsula, the diplomatic opportunity to exploit the Brief and meet the Pope halfway with an appeal to Catholics to obey the Republic was squandered; ministers instead concentrated on driving home their military advantage to the point of public humiliation for Pius. They made impossible demands of the papal representative, Pieracchi, sent to Paris to negotiate a peace, and a follow-up commission, despatched to Florence in September 1796, was treated half seriously. War was declared by Bonaparte on 21 January 1797, and an 'army' of 7000 commanded by monks with eight cannons had no more effect against his veterans than reports of a weeping Madonna.

When the Treaty of Tolentino in February 1797 confirmed the Cispadane Republic it was largely on the basis of land belonging to the papacy. Pius was compelled into accepting the confiscation, together with the cession of the papal provinces of Avignon, the Venaissin and the Legations of Bologna, Ferrara and Ravenna; France would be paid a 30 million livres fine and the Republic be 'given' a hundred works of art, selected by the French commissioners.[18] Bonaparte's treaty probably forestalled the outright destruction of the papacy and, for the next few months, Franco-papal relations continued to improve, with Pius going so far as to drop hints about negotiating a Concordatory settlement between Paris and Rome.[19] *Fructidor* changed all that as the Republic turned left, and talk of a rapprochement with the refractory clergy was shown up as premature. There were rumours of an imminent Jacobin coup in Rome itself, but they could not prevent Pius from condemning the new oaths imposed on the refractory clergy. In February 1798, the army of General Louis-Alexander Berthier (Bonaparte's replacement) invaded the Papal States, and allowed the proclamation of the Roman Republic on the anniversary of the Pope's accession in 1775: 'The people have recovered their rights', the General reported to Talleyrand, ex-bishop turned Foreign Minister. Pius VI was taken as a prisoner to Siena and then to Florence, and remained in French hands until he died at Valence in the Dauphiné on 29 August 1799. As General Masséna's destitute troops began to loot the city, and cardinals and bishops left hurriedly, it was assumed in Paris there would not be another Pope. As if to speed the papacy into extinction, the army of occupation in Rome during the winter of 1798–9 removed the papal arms from public buildings, introduced the republican calendar, and changed the place names so that, for instance, the Castel San Angelo was transmuted into the 'Castle of Genius'.[20]

That the Catholic hierarchy in France survived – and would indeed be recognised by First Consul Bonaparte – was not due only to luck or high policy. Popular Christian fervour was hard to restrain as feelings, so long internalised and concealed, demanded open expression: no matter that sacred structures and symbols across France had been violated as in Chartres, where half the churches were destroyed, calvaries and crosses smashed, streets 'debaptised' and convents transformed into prisons, schools or lawcourts.[21] This mass destruction of 'sacred spaces' could not prevent, irrespective of legal restrictions, country people taking matters into their own hands, rebuilding calvaries and re-erecting crosses at crossroads. Pilgrimages resumed, while Marian devotions and processions took place from one corner of France to the other: at Marseille for Corpus Christi Day in 1795, 6000 people climbed up the hill of Notre-Dame-de-la-Garde with tambourines jangling and banners flying.[22]

Yet the sociology of this revival remains problematic, despite the research of scholars like Desan and Hufton.[23] They and others have shown the vital role of women in securing the resumption of Catholic worship from 1795, equally capable of flouting government restraints and the age-old convention that leadership descended down from a male priesthood to a deferential laity. The extent of feminine involvement in the religious politics of 1795–7 was unprecedented, as women filled the gaps left by the collapse of the traditional ecclesiastical structures.[24] They took the lead in reclaiming church keys and in forcing the reopening of churches. The resourcefulness of these packs of women extended to intimidation. 'Stop there, you damned scoundrel', cried the formidable Marie-Anne Baillot, carrying a huge stick and leading rioters in Chablis against one hapless townsman trying to make an inventory of church goods. Officialdom found them hard to restrain because they relied on their special status as women to have their way. 'We are only women; they don't do anything to women,' those women accused of breaking the church doors at Toucy in 1795 insisted.[25]

Those who tried to obstruct them risked public humiliation, often by having ashes carried in the womens' aprons poured over them. They validated their claims through disposing of rival symbols and flaunting their own. Thus they were prominent in intimidating disgraced Jacobins into cutting down Trees of Liberty (female images of Liberty were a favourite object of laceration or dismemberment) and replacing them with crucifixes, with the peal of the church bells after years of disuse as the increasingly heard sound of their success.[26] Such irrepressible energy in the service of religion offered them 'virtually their only opportunity for autonomous activity during the Revolution' and they made the most of it.[27] It was resented by male opinion of all shades. As the Bishop of Mâcon wrote in 1801, outraged, about women trying to instruct their priests rather than vice versa:

> How does it come about ... that women, whom the Apostle has commanded to learn their duties in silence, dare to permit themselves ... to influence the doctrine and conduct of those given to them by the Lord to lead and teach them?[28]

The story is so often the new one of lay initiative and clerical response. For both Constitutional and refractory supporters, Church organization at parish level could not be repaired overnight. It was thus difficult for priests to direct or control the faithful, and leadership roles were readily reversed: at Blesle in the Haute-Loire in the Year V, two old and ailing refractories were rescued from house arrest and forced to say Mass by the locals.[29] Overburdened officials had neither the time nor the inclination (some made little effort to hide their royalist sympathies) to see that the laws on religion were being obeyed. It was virtually impossible to stop the locals from having some kind of *ad hoc* service. When police tried to arrest a refractory saying Mass in a hayloft to 200 people at Marie in the Haut-Rhin, they received no help from the municipal officer, while his wife expostulated, 'Yes, we want the Mass and we'll have it and . . . watch yourself for everybody detests you.' In the Lozère, by the time of the royalist electoral victories in the Year V, officials had compliantly allowed refractories to take over any church they wanted – including Mende Cathedral – in defiance of the law; it was the same tale at Rieux, while at Montesquieu-Volvestre in the Haute-Garonne, only weeks after 3 *Ventôse*, the government was told that the former *curé* had been restored 'with all possible pomp'.[30] Even when the government had swung to the left after *Fructidor*, its power in the localities was too weak to make much of an impact, except in key areas like Brittany where watchfulness against royalism was politically vital.

It may be that in some regions the refractory clergy were willing to accommodate themselves to manifestations of popular religious fervour many of them had denounced before the Revolution. The disappearance of the priest in most parishes had the effect of entrenching time-honoured lay observances, and the Revolution had added to them, as in the popular canonisation of victims of government repression in the Vendée and the respect accorded to the sites of their martyrdom. As well as externals, men and women had found a comfort in an inner religious life that would not submit easily to clerical ministrations. We should be wary of concluding that such believers were confined to ordinary society. One of the most important mystics in the late 1790s was on the fringes of the royal family: she was the Duchesse de Bourbon who, influenced by the mystic reveries of Swedenborg (by no means unusual among women of her rank), believed neither in the efficacy of the sacraments nor that the clergy held the keys to the kingdom of heaven.[31] With the men away at the front – or hiding from going to it – women took charge of what had become a private matter rather than a public observance. They practised their faith in devotions often based on the rosary inside the family circle, calling on a respected male villager when they wanted their child baptised.[32] It was hard for all age-groups to have access to reliable religious instruction in these years. Bayeux was one centre in 1797 where it was available: Mother Sainte-Rosalie, an old Ursuline, offered classes for children during daytime and for adults in the evening, with help from two sisters and a lay assistant.[33]

With pitifully few support networks available to uphold sheep who had wandered from the fold, the legacy of dechristianisation could be indifference quite as much as renewed fervour after Thermidor. Jean de Viguerie has argued persuasively that the Revolution had resulted in large sections of the population failing to practise regularly. Other scholars remain unclear about how many people belong to this category, or think this is the product of short-term revolutionary dechristianisation policies rather than an accelerated decline in religious observance predating 1789.[34] From recent work on religious practice in the Limousin, evidence points towards 1797–8 (at the height of the Directory's crackdown on Catholicism) as a key date for men ceasing to make their Easter communion, a pattern which persisted right down to the 1840s, helped by the abandonment of formal religious instruction after 1792.[35]

There was under the Directory a sizeable passive constituency, neither Catholic loyalist nor willing supporters of the *cultes décadaires*, and it is one about which much remains for historians to recover. Here is Gratien, jurist and Constitutional bishop of the Seine-Inférieure, writing to Grégoire in 1797 about his experience in the capital of Normandy:

> There are at Rouen numerous Catholics who make a point of preserving their neutrality between the two rival clergies. The party favouring laziness and devotional indifference makes progress. Meanwhile, the number of children without religious instruction, confession or first communion has increased; they marry without any church blessing. Yes, the churches are passably attended, but not for the sacraments they offer.[36]

In the Loir-et-Cher, the abbé Gallerand in 1797 reported a similar story, where habit rather than conviction still led a majority to church each Sunday, but this went with increasing unconcern about whether the priest followed Grégoire or the refractories as the cause of the quarrel became, for many families, distant and academic.[37] So the asperities were less, at least in *départements* where, like the Loir-et-Cher, the rivalries of the revolution had brought limited bloodshed. People by the late 1790s sensed the need for a common

Christian front, however loath the clergy were to acknowledge as much.

The interruption in public worship and instruction, together with the instability and confusion they saw around them, had arguably left numerous men and women with a preference for avoiding open religious commitment of any sort. The return to repression following the 'Second Terror' redoubled their caution. These people readily withdrew into private life as a means of security, and open attachment to one of the religious associations competing for their adherence was, despite the law of 3 *Ventôse* Year III, a form of political statement they were not prepared to risk so long as the Directory remained in power and Christianity remained as the most identifiable token of Counter-Revolutionary commitment. Grégoire summed it up thus: 'The Terror made more hypocrites than martyrs; a crowd of people conserved in their hearts the idea of God, but his name expired on their lips ...'[38]

Religious groups were thus confronted with a society that had hurriedly evolved voluntaristic attitudes towards religious behaviour. The good health and survival of the Churches depended on *persuading* enough members of the public to come over to them. But a positive response could not be taken for granted, and it would not necessarily be unconditional.

II

Despite the Christian revival that began before the regime was in place, the Directory remained committed to a public celebration of a republicanism that was essentially at odds with the historic faith. From the Year IV, it began to reinvigorate the *fêtes*. The planning of festivities was undertaken on a systematic basis, and was better concerted than anything attempted by the Jacobins. There were seven principal national *fêtes* (often visually spectacular) listed for celebration by the Convention on 4 *Brumaire* Year IV (26 October 1795): one for the foundation of the Republic (1st *Vendémaire*/21 September), and others for youth, married life, knowledge, agriculture, liberty and old people. Three further commemorative festivals were quickly added: the excution of the King (2 *Pluvoise*/21 January); the taking of the Bastille (26 *Messidor*/14 July); and the abolition of the monarchy and founding of the Republic (23 *Thermidor*/10 August), key dates in the revolutionary calendar and part of its rapidly accumulating heritage. There was additional provision for supplementary commemorative festivities, like those proclaimed for the funerals of military heroes like Hoche and Joubert, or the outbreak of continental peace on 20 *Nivôse* Year VI.[39]

Throughout its existence the Directory made steady if fitful efforts to encourage citizens to enjoy these highpoints in the republican calendar and acclaim their recent heritage as an alternative to conventional holy days in the Church's year. However, these exalted aims were alien to the majority of their fellow countrymen, who, as on their Christian festival days before 1789, were more concerned to enjoy a day off work (and, with luck, the day *after* the official holiday) than enter soberly into the official spirit of things. By and large, the masses were unimpressed by non-political celebrations of Youth, Old Age, Agriculture and Marriage, even if they were preferable to dates like 21 January or 10 August, which, for so many, remained anniversaries for private mourning rather than public celebration. In some cases, functionaries would be the only people celebrating, though they would try to boost their numbers with schoolchildren, musicians and, best of all, gendarmes and soldiers.

Zealous officials were still less successful in inducing the population to observe the *décadi* ('tenth day'), of the republican calendar in preference to Sundays. There were plenty of stories to act as disincentives to those minded to comply, like the woman at Saint-Chinian near Montpellier, who, paid to ring in the *décadi*, claimed 'she had been thrown to the earth by an invisible force which had cut the [bell] rope in her hands'.[40] Nevertheless, shops had to close – officially – and a series of national festivals were designed to complement it, forcefully publicised after 22 *Floréal* Year VI. François de Neufchateau, once again at the Interior Ministry in 1798 after serving briefly as a Director, relaunched the ceremonies to be observed in the *culte décadaire* in a circular issued on 13 *Fructidor* Year VI (30 August 1798), significantly after the *coup* of the Year V: new laws would be read by local officials to the assembled citizens, military successes would be announced, civil marriages would be celebrated and schoolchildren would sing patriotic hymns. All this was accompanied by the legal obligation to work on Sundays, and the compulsory use of the revolutionary calendar, thereby causing many fresh conflicts over the observance of Christian, republican and national festivals.

Several of the Directors might publicly attest that the *cultes décadaires* proclaimed the French nation at ease with its revolutionary

heritage, but the reality – a subdued, non-violent dechristianisation – was concealed in republican affirmations intended in large
part to shore up a regime embarrassingly lacking in active supporters. The French population would simply not countenance the loss
of its old Sabbath. Not just churchgoing but the other Sunday pas-
times of dancing in the afternoons, tilting at the ring, and handball,
were not to be given up lightly; a Tree of Liberty was removed at
Raismes, near Valenciennes, in the Year V to make way for the
resumption of the game of *longue paulme* – an early form of tennis.[41]
If Jansenist castigations had made no impact, neither would republican ones. Indeed, it has been argued that the Directorial restrictions
on Sunday observance had exactly the opposite effect, in *départements*
as widely separated as the Oise, Calvados and the Indre.

But if the significance of Sunday was reaffirmed whatever the government wanted, only a minority of men and women took any notice
of the *fête* of the 9 Thermidor, or the *fête* of the 10 August (the anniversary of the Republic's foundation in 1792), let alone played an
active part in them. This was not for want of obvious attractions,
or any meanness over funding. The 10 August commemorations in
Paris, for instance, included the burning of two statues symbolising
Despotism and Fanaticism, and there were gushing fountains, hot-
air balloons and horse racing to keep the whole family amused.[42]
Only in the dechristianised areas, Paris, parts of eastern France,
and some *départements* in the centre – the Yonne, Nièvre, Cher, and
Allier – was there much popular interest, and that principally confined to the towns. Research is at an early stage. On the whole, it was
men who were most attracted by republican festivals, perhaps
because of their more 'masculine' forms of sociability, while women
remained loyal to Christianity because it encapsulated the more
stable values of family and community. At any rate, by the Year
VII, observance of the *décadi* was once again faltering, and ministers
had turned most *fêtes* into little more than military parades in a bid
to save money. It was an implicit admission that that this attempt to
construct social morality on a republican foundation had not worked.

Festivals were visual affirmations of the regime and its values, but
other manifestations of the civic order's moral basis were to be
found, devised to appeal mainly but not exclusively to educated citizens. The writings of the 'Idéologue' philosophers in vogue in
the mid-1790s (those sometimes referred to as the Auteuil Circle)
were particularly favoured in government ranks. The 'Idéologues'

included Cabanis (1757–1808), Chénier (1764–1811), Destutt de Tracy (1754–1836), Dominique-Joseph de Garat (1749–1833) and, most notably, the Comte de Volney (1757–1820).[43] Though their individual emphases differed (Cabanis and Destutt de Tracy were materialists), their stress on 'natural laws' was largely compatible with recognition of the importance of a moral order. At least as importantly for the Directory, they took a firm anti-Catholic line (including theology) and, in their journal, the *Décade Philosophique*, articulated a moderate republicanism with echoes of Enlightenment anticlericalism.[44] Catholicism was depicted as a reactionary, obscurantist force and, while they deplored religious persecution, they fought hard for the consolidation of a lay republic. Typical of this school's views was a book like the ex-priest Charles François Dupuis's *Origines de tous les cultes, ou Religion universelle* of 1795, full of generalisations intended to persuade the public of the historical development of religion, and therefore the falseness of Christian claims to exclusive truths.

The Directory was always keen to sponsor non-dogmatic 'worship' that could proclaim the uses of benevolent republican values. The best-known cult to attract official patronage was Theophilanthropy.[45] It owed much to the response of a Normandy bookseller, Chemin-Dupontès, to a competition held in the Years V and VI based on the question 'What are the most suitable institutions on which to found the morality of a people?' Chemin-Dupontès's answer of September 1796, in the form of a manual (he was an ex-Freemason and supporter of Robespierre's Supreme Being, who hoped to rally Protestant support), was to recognise – on the basis of deduction from rational principles – the existence of God, and the soul's immortality. He wanted no hierarchy, no dogmas, no ceremonies, no visible Church.[46] It was a harmless form of deism that appealed to some sections of educated opinion and, when services began in January 1797, it took hold mostly in towns – those in the Yonne in upper Burgundy, for instance – which had responded to dechristianisation.[47] The cult attracted favourable notice at the highest level: La Révellière-Lépeaux was one of the most important patrons of Theophilanthropy in 1797, for he, like Robespierre before him, was worried about the absence of an official morality to guide the citizens of the Republic;[48] not that his concern and interest actually extended to attending the services of the new faith. Other politicians like Dupont de Nemours and Regnault de Saint-Jean d'Angely professed an interest, and there were writers like Marie-Joseph Chénier and Bernardin de Saint-Pierre who found it had something to offer them.[49]

The heyday of Theophilanthropy came in the six months after *Fructidor* Year V, when the government was more desperate than usual to reinforce its own foundations. Worship was held both on the *décadis* and on Sundays to maximise attendance. The cult was allocated former church buildings for its services – no less than eighteen in Paris, while it shared all but two of the other churches in use in the capital jointly with the Constitutional Church (including the choir of Notre-Dame cathedral) – in an accommodation that Grégoire's embarrassed supporters were powerless to prevent, despite the damage it did their credibility with the refractories.[50] Indeed, at the national council of 1797, a priest from Bayonne expressed concern at the way Theophilanthropy appealed to those who might otherwise attend Constitutional Church services: The simplicity of dogma, the popularity of the language, the conciseness of their observances, the melody of their chanting, flatter the self-regard and the senses [of the worshippers].'[51] An official in a tricoloured tunic would preside over readings from such diverse sources as the Koran, Socrates, Seneca, Confucius and Pascal, with some chants honouring the heroes of humanity as diverse as St Vincent de Paul, George Washington and Rousseau. No images or icons were permitted, only flowers or fruits on a simple 'altar'. Austerity was the watchword, 'neither statuettes of saints nor pictures of miracles, still less *ex votos*, or offerings for the people'.[52]

Like most invented republican ceremonies, it met with disdain and indifference outside the metropolitan areas. It was abstract, unemotional, calculated to appeal to a republican intelligentsia – and no one else. When La Révellière-Lépeaux complained of its slow progress, Talleyrand pointedly commented, 'Jesus Christ died for His religion: you must do something similar for yours.'[53] Catholics derided the observances. During the Year VI, in the aftermath of *Fructidor*, Catholics and Theophilanthropists jostled over shared church space. In one Paris church (Saint-Laurent) on Christmas Eve 1797, the *curé*, Fr Margarita (later deported to Guiana – the 'dry guillotine') was to be found blessing marriages in the sacristy, while various Theophilanthropic ceremonies were going on in the main part of the building.[54] The cult in the end constituted what Gwynne Lewis has dubbed an 'intellectual cul-de-sac',[55] and even the government backed away from its former open regard once the predominantly Jacobin sympathies of Theophilanthropists became evident after the elections of 1798. Ministerial patronage in the last year of the Directory was confined to emphasising the *décadi*; and the public rites of Theophilanthropists, choked off by denying access to church buildings, dwindled away into private, recreational use. Bonaparte's soldiers seem to have been keen on the movement, but he banned it all the same in 1801.

Ostentatiously parading its republican credentials in institutions and ideology alike, the Directory was incapable of admitting the obvious point, that national union would be achieved only when citizenship was married up with Christianity. There were signs that Grégoire's 'Church of France' would have responded to such overtures[56] and, as suggested earlier, some strands of moderate refractory opinion was beginning to face up to a possible parting of the ways for Catholicism and monarchism. All this is not to suggest that any reconciliation of citizenship and Christianity would have constituted a simple solution for the Directors, given the bitter legacy of 1792–4, and a settlement that excluded the non-jurors was no such thing. Contrariwise, neither before nor after *Fructidor* was there any indication that the non-juring clergy were yet disposed to accept a settlement that did not give Catholicism pride of place and in which they would be left to share the stage with Protestant ministers and Jewish rabbis. Nevertheless, a settlement with the Churches *was* a policy option whose desirability was not lost on Bonaparte when Consulate replaced Directory at the end of 1799. He inaugurated an era of *realpolitik* and genuine religious toleration that would end the Churches' constant struggle for survival over the previous four years, years which had been as difficult for Protestants and Jews as they had been for Catholics of the two main persuasions.

III

The religious life of French Protestants recovered slowly after 1795. The process was not helped by the disproportionate number among them attracted to Theophilanthropy,[57] while Article sixteen of the Law of 7 *Vendémiaire* Year IV (29 September 1795) – 'The ceremonies of every cult are prohibited except inside the building selected for that purpose' – made their traditional open-air worship difficult, a situation further exacerbated by the post-*Fructidor* drive against religion. In the circumstances, the possibility of using local Catholic churches was not ruled out, as the Synod of Haut-Languedoc made clear in November 1796, abjuring its pastorate 'to inculcate all their members as much as possible in sentiments of tolerance, and fraternal benevolence towards their fellow citizens of another communion'.[58] There were considerable regional variations in Protestant recovery. In Alsace, pastors were able to restart Church life quite promptly in 1795, but in Montbéliard, Uzès, the Vivarais and the Agennais, organisation needed substantial rebuilding; in La Rochelle worship resumed in 1798, in Marseille in 1801, and not in Toulouse before 1805.[59]

To survive financially some pastors had taken up other jobs; others had lapsed, or found their congregations had gone. Thus, excluding Alsace, there were only 120 pastors active in 1799, at least a third less than ten years previously; in the Hautes-Alpes, about 4000 isolated Protestants had, by the First Empire, to share one pastor among them.[60] Increasingly, in a manner that closely resembled the refractory experience, the reformed Churches in the later 1790s had to function without ordained ministers, for nowhere did dechristianisation have more success than among Protestant pastors. The leading expert on the Protestants of Languedoc, J.D. Woodbridge, estimates that only 50 to 60 members of the 1793 pastoral corps (106 in strength) were back in post by the time of the Concordat.[61] Such a trend hardly augured well for the future of Protestantism in France. Neither did the apparent loss to the Huguenots of their rich, middle-class members, the backbone of their consistories in the difficult days before 1787, men whose zeal had cooled enough after the Revolutionary years of political strife to distance themselves from their former brethren.[62] The decline in synodal meetings was a particular casualty of this lapse. Records survive of only one full assembly. This was held at Castres in November 1796, and was notable for the public reparation made by some of the pastors who had reneged on their faith and their people during the Terror.

It was the two-thirds of the Protestant population who lived in the countryside who had best stayed true to 'l'esprit du Désert' by holding onto their beliefs during the Terror. After it was over, they worked to ensure that the faith of their forefathers survived. At least the annexation of the great Calvinist centre of Geneva to France in

1798 could function as a boost to Protestant esteem, and there was never any question of the Directory ending toleration: the anti-royalist character of the oaths demanded by the laws of 1795 and 1797 was less unpalatable to them than to the Catholic majority. Relations between adherents of the two great religious traditions remained awkward, despite limited efforts at church-sharing.

As far as Jews were concerned, it was technically open to them to take advantage of the decree of February 1795. That duly took place – and fast – in many centres of the faith. Thus in Metz the synagogue (used as a barn for animals during the Terror) reopened on 17 *Fructidor* Year III (3 September 1795) with the rabbi's salary fixed by the municipality.[63] But the Jewish people were to some extent scattered, and it was not easy to rebuild community life quickly. Also, the end of the Terror had not marked an end to prejudices found on the streets or among republican officials who found the Hebraic faith and culture an embarrassing reminder of 'unenlightened' times. At Saverne in 1797 the *département* thus wanted to get rid of tombs in the Jewish cemetery as the exterior signs of a cult.[64] So the extent and nature of Jewish integration into the French state remained problematic. Indeed, the immigration of German Ashkenazi into Alsace in the late 1790s as a result of small-scale pogroms east of the Rhine exacerbated local tensions, especially as this remained the area where integration had hardly made any progress.[65] The principal concern of community leaders remained the state's settlement of their debts, and petitions were sent up to the legislature from their major centres of residence, notably Avignon and Metz. A commission was set up by the Council of the Five Hundred, which reported in August 1797 that not to pay off the debts would be unconstitutional, since it would imply that the Jews possessed a continuing legal right to corporate status. However, the Council postponed action, and nothing would be done until the First Empire. Despite this failure to resolve their financial grievances, the Jews enjoyed a basic toleration, and the leadership of the Constitutional Church under Grégoire continued to take an interest in their status: it may have wished to convert them, but it also respected their beliefs enough to deplore any systematic attempts at proselytism. True to this spirit of goodwill, when in 1801 the constitutionalists proposed an ecumenical church council, the Bishop of Versailles asked that representatives of the Jews be invited to attend.[67]

IV

The Directors had at no point evinced any interest in reviving the fortunes of the Constitutional Church, which by 1795 had lost whatever bourgeois support it had possessed to indifference, the revolutionary cults or the non-jurors. The surviving followers of Grégoire were on their own, for, as he said, 'You will no longer be tempted to rely on the arm of flesh. God alone will be your support.'[68] Such an injunction brought limited comfort to clergy looking for congregations. The steady revival of Catholicism in the aftermath of Thermidor did nothing of itself to win back a following for the Constitutional party; even juring priests who had not succumbed to the dechristianising campaign often retracted and reconciled themselves to Rome. It was much the same story with lay followers. Bishop Sermet of Toulouse reported to Grégoire that a quarter of his original adherents had left, and the remainder were apathetic: 'The anti-Constitutionals alone make up a crowd, and are singing at the top of their voices ... The abjurations [of Constitutional clergy] are well under way in the town and especially in the countryside.'[69] The picture was not quite so gloomy everywhere. Pockets of loyal lay followers existed, as in some cantons of the Breton *département* of Ille-et-Vilaine, for whom patriotism still corresponded to support of the Constitutional Church, and in towns as far apart apart as Béziers and Bourges, where parishioners stayed loyal to their *curés*.[70] They at least had priests to minister to them. Not everywhere else was so fortunate. Marriage, deaths and desertion had crippled the ranks of its ordained ministry: only 25 of the 83 bishops of 1792 remained in place by the Year III; 44 of the 85 dioceses remained vacant the following year, and 22 000 of 28 000 priests had abdicated during the Terror.[71] Dechristianisation in the centre and north had obliterated parochial structures, and the 6000 surviving priests still risked murder at the hands of laymen loyal to the refractories, especially in the west: in towns, they dared not go outside in daytime, so real was the threat. Thus Bishop Claude Le Coz, though freed from prison in December 1794, stayed in Rennes for eighteen months afterwards rather than imperil his life by venturing into the 'white' parishes that surrounded the town, and Dufraisse, Bishop of Bourges, who took possession of his cathedral only after Bonaparte's coup of 18 *Brumaire*, felt no less threatened.[72] Masses had to be held furtively, behind locked doors. This was a situation that endured in many areas: a royalist death-squad murdered Audrein, the regicide Constitutional Bishop of the Finistére, as late as November 1800.

Despite these unpropitious circumstances, the Constitutional Church not only survived; it revived beyond expectation between 1795 and 1799, leaving – much to the fury of the refractories – Napoleon with little alternative but to make it a significant part of the equation in the negotiations leading up to the Concordat. This recovery of health was thanks in no small part to the loyalty and organising genius of Bishop Henri Grégoire, who had stayed in his post throughout the Terror. The first concern for its leaders as they surveyed the wreckage after *Ventôse* was to restore a semblance of hierarchical order. Looking back from 1797, Eléonore-Maries Desbois de Rochefort, the bishop of the Somme, summed up the immensity of the problem confronting the bishops two years earlier:

> The most holy laws of ecclesiastical discipline were violated: one could well say that the Church had no government. The parishes believed they could enjoy Catholic worship while doing without *curés*; and if bishops were not strictly necessary for ordination and confirmation, their ministry was only called for by a small minority of priests; it might even be dangerous if they tried to exercise their personal ministry.[73]

As early as late 1794, Grégoire had gathered together other episcopal colleagues residing (or hiding) in or near the capital in a forum that became known as the 'United Bishops'. In March 1795 it issued the *Lettre Encylique à leurs Frères, les autres Évêques et aux Églises vacantes*, a manifesto designed both to canvas opinion about the work to go before a future national council and, more basically, to rally the scattered adherents of the Civil Constitution.[74] About thirty dioceses responded positively to this letter, but the United Bishops continued to convene and act as a steeering committee for the next few years. This committee was essentially responsive to Grégoire and the metropolitan Bishop of Rouen (Gratien), but the bishops of the *départements* of the Somme, Landes (Saurine) and Aisne (Royer) were also regular members.[75] Their participation is a reminder that revival was a collective effort – not just, as historians have too often presented it, the result of Bishop Grégoire's lone initiative. For all his gifts, he could have done very little without other Constitutional bishops doggedly getting on with their work in the localties. Men like Le Coz, the Catholic Girondin as he has been called, were indispensable. He never seems to have lost faith in Enlightenment possibilities, and his definition of the Church of Jesus Christ to his diocesan synod of 1799 has a wider application to the Constitutional Church as a whole: 'a religious society, in which citizens submissive to the laws of their government agree to offer to God worship both pure and sublime'.[76]

Although it gave the Constitutional Church a leadership dimension hitherto lacking, the United Bishops went unrecognised by both the Directory and the papacy. Undaunted, Grégoire and his colleagues invoked a Gallican-inspired sense of collegiality to justify their existence, and proceeded to issue further encyclical letters and generally supervise a slow pastoral and administrative rebirth. Grégoire also produced a periodical, the *Annales de la Religion*, intended primarily as another means for him to bond together his clergy and people, but it was also an opportunity to remind sceptics of the the Constitutionalists' unswervable commitment to Christianity when the abbé Caffardeau, one of the contributors, replied to attacks on the journal mounted by the Idéologues in their *Décade Philosophique*.[77] As in 1791, the Constitutionalist clergy, nothing daunted, still looked beyond the best Gallican practices to what they took to be the unsullied Christian idealism of the primitive Church. There was a concern to recover the Jansenist roots of the Church, to look for inspiration in these difficult times to the memory of Port-Royal.

Where discipline had lapsed in 1792–4, they battled to reimpose it and so deny their enemies on the Right the chance to stigmatise them as heretics. Thus married priests were not tolerated, and every effort was made to expel them from parishes. The rebuilding of Church government helped to that end, with the gradual creation under the bishops of a hierarchy of clerical assemblies to include both metropolitan and departmental synods. Where there were no bishops in place, emergency provisions established presbyteries or 'episcopal councils' to administer 'widowed' local churches (in other words, those dioceses deprived of their bishops), as an interim measure leading to the election of a prelate. Typical of this creativity was the institution of a new intermediate authority – the archpriest, 'the eye of the bishop', elected by a synod.[78] It was his job to institute and supervise revived rural synods in which priests could meet to share their concerns in a spirit of primitive collegiality. Admittedly, much of this synodal apparatus was no more than patchily effective with limited attendances,[79] but it was an attempt to give the Constitutional Church structures that might in the medium term help to achieve recovery, and one historian has even hailed its distinctive ecclesiology as anticipating the modern post-Vatican-II Roman Catholic Church.[80] Equally, the emphasis on elections by the members of the Church was what many of its original supporters had wanted back in 1790–1 only to find the National Assembly – still focused on the ideal of a state Church – preferred one based on the wider political nation and its local government framework.

At the apex of the new machinery, and central to the discipline and order that Grégoire wanted to establish, was episcopal and metropolitan authority, whether it concerned supervision of elections, appointments to office or pastoral oversight. There were enormous problems in achieving it, but it did not stop several bishops as early as 1795 making pastoral visits and baptising hundreds of children, often giving them the sacrament before their refractory rivals could do so! The majority of Constitutional bishops already in office visited the parishes of their dioceses with renewed zeal between 1796 and 1801, confirming, baptising and confessing, and the results could be startlingly encouraging. In 1796 and 1798 Le Coz of Rennes noted how 'the holy eagerness of our Catholic patriots' was very evident. In one Breton town, Plélan, he spent two days confessing 'a vast concourse of Catholic citizens'; everyone turned out to communicate.[81] Such oversight could not, however, easily be created in sees to which a new prelate had been named. Thus, in Besançon, the nomination of *curé* Demandre (a Freemason) in June 1798 to the bishopric was a paper removal, for he continued to act as a parish priest; in the Haut-Rhin, Bishop Berdolet could never take possession of his seat at Colmar and remained as *curé* of Pfaffhans. In the Vienne, the Creuse and the Indre-et-Loire, it proved impossible to make an appointment, and other important dioceses like Maine-et-Loire, Mayenne and Finistère stayed vacant.[82] But there were successes to record on the balance sheet, like the arrival of a second Constitutional bishop for the Pas-de-Calais following the reorganisation of the Church in the area by the abbé Warenghien at the Synod of Lestrem in late 1796.[83]

This Grégorién stress on episcopacy conflicted with the Richerist inheritance of the Constitutional Church. Respect for the rights and dignities of priests had played no small part in winning over a narrow majority of the *curés* in 1791 and, four years on, those who had not renounced their holy orders were reluctant to sacrifice their independence in the name of episcopal revival. Presbyterian impulses at ground level among the parish priests remained powerful throughout 1795–1802.[84] Although the law laid down that they were supposed to be elected by districts, it was increasingly the members of their own congregations who were motivated enough to take part, often along with embarrassingly high numbers of Theophilanthropists! Bishops had not much choice except to tread carefully. With scattered and independent-minded congregations, it was hard for an executive committee like the United Bishops to be effective as a disciplinary power. When congregations backed them, Constitutional priests (including those who stubbornly insisted on staying married) could just ignore Grégoire, his colleagues in Paris, and – where there was one – their local bishop.[85]

The United Bishops can be seen at their most creative in the worshipping life of their Church. They devised a uniform rite for services with the aim of encouraging a decent, dignified atmosphere, but it remains hard to gauge the impact their injunctions had on observances at parish level. Above all, the liturgy was translated into French, partly driven by a desire to counteract the popularity of Theophilanthropic rites in the vernacular and win over this constituency to the 'Church of France'. This move was approved by the national council of 1797, but it divided the bishops among themselves and prompted a flood of letters from provincial priests, who predicted that it would add credibility to attacks on them as schismatics. However, a pamphlet war was not enough to halt Grégoire's resolve. The Mass in French was used in the Versailles diocese from 1799, and was approved after extended debate by the national council of 1801; delegates were hesitant about the ammunition this break with Catholic tradition would hand to their rivals just when negotiations for the Concordat were at a delicate stage.[86] The ill-feeling the dispute engendered added to personality clashes and weakened the collective force of the United Bishops around the turn of the century.

Consistent with a Gallicanism coloured by Jansenist views on the importance of consultation and consent, the United Bishops (in principle) considered that their policy provisions were advisory until approved by their Church as a whole in a national council. In 1797 and 1801 two such councils ratified the proposals of the United

Bishops for electing prelates, disciplining apostate priests and, as mentioned above, agreeing to celebration of the Mass in the vernacular. The occasions generated much debate, but at the end of it the policy recommendations of the prelates were usually passed with few or no amendments. The council of 1797 also affirmed the principle of election for priests, but departed from the Civil Constitution in declaring that all electors had to be adult male Catholics, the 'priesthood of the baptised'. In all cases, a two-thirds majority was required for a result.[87] Such arrangements sat awkwardly within the context of a reaffirmed adherence to the orthodox Catholic faith, and the expression of a genuine if unrealistic wish for communion with the papacy, to whom the council accorded a primacy of 'honour'. However, in the end perhaps the most significant point was that the two national councils convened at all. The first lasted from August to November 1797 and its numbers increased as its sessions went on from 72 members at the beginning (including 27 bishops) to 101 by closure (including 31 bishops), despite the discomforts: four or five delegates sharing a room, dining on thin soup and using folding beds.[88]

The well-disposed leadership of the Constitutional clergy made a real effort to mend fences with the refractories, though a formal agreement was never a possibility. Rivalries at parish level between the two Christian communions remained endemic, with both concentrating their energies not just on survival but also on struggling against each other for dominance. Grégoire might urge reconciliation wherever possible, but the majority of his supporters were disinclined to go so far, or pay any attention to the peace feelers of the national council of 1797.[89] The refractory party was scornful. They had no incentive to take any notice of these overtures, at least before *Fructidor* Year V. Their priests were still returning from exile in significant numbers, while the defection of Constitutional clergy in some places to join them had not halted, so much so that organising the Constitutional Church remained very difficult for bishops like Sermet of Toulouse. He wrote despairingly on 16 May 1797: 'I expect only that this epidemic malady [defection] is going to increase and win over the whole area.'[90]

Then *Fructidor* intervened to give a new lease of life to the Constitutional Church by unleashing a fresh Terror against the refractories. But nothing the 'Church of France' could do won Directorial approval, despite the constant play it made of the slogan 'priests submissive to the laws'. The regime had initially prohibited the

Constitutional Church from electing its bishops on the votes of its clerical and lay adherents, though it rescinded its opposition enough for twenty-five elections to be held between 1797 and 1802.[91] It also criticised both the expulsion of married clergy from their benefices and the Constitutionalists' condemnation of obligatory observance of the *décadi* , forbade local synods like the one convoked in Toulouse in June 1798 and, for good measure, banned publication of the *Annales de la Religion* in 1798 as a vehicle for disseminating fanatical and retrograde ideas, although it somehow continued to appear.[92] Grégoire's men might trumpet their loyalty to 'God and the Nation' and annually celebrate the anniversary of Bastille Day every 14 July between 1796 and 1801, but it had no affect on their status.

The changes were not to the satisfaction of all Constitutionalist churchmen: they reduced the scope for involvement in decision-making of the wealthy urban elites; they offered nothing to the rural masses; and they marginalised women. Grégoire was worried that the Constitutional Church had failed to cater for the latter, and urged his colleagues to set up lay societies dedicated to pious works, but the suggestion was largely ignored at parish level and it proved fatal to survival.[93] As Olwen Hufton insists, 'it was the determined boycott by women of the schismatic constitutional church between 1796 and 1801 which determined its ultimate demise'.[94] The Constitutional bishops meant well, but they failed to grapple with the fundamental question facing any voluntary ecclesiastical society: how to create a mass following. And despite the election of new bishops and clergy, they had no answer to the haemorrhaging of lay support that persisted right down to the Concordat, with the most loyal congregations based, unsurprisingly, in regions also loyal to the republic. There remained numerous *départements* in which the Gregorien 'Church of France' had no visible presence and where the report of the departmental directory in July 1796 for the Maine-et-Loire could serve for them all: 'The refractory priests make up almost the entirety of ministers of religion.'[95]

Nevertheless, though any pretensions to a national network had been put aside, where Constitutional congregations had endured they showed no sign of withering away by the time the Directory was overthrown in 1799. Quite the opposite, for they had been able to take advantage of the new drive against the refractories in 1797–9 to consolidate their position. Their persistence was proof that a framework of existence could be rescued from the wreckage of the

Terror. They thought of themselves as good Catholics, and the Pope's condemnation of them as a fundamental error. These were Christians who consistently affirmed the possibility of Catholics holding an alternative political allegiance to royalism. It was a position whose possibilities would not be lost on Bonaparte after 1799, and he would find a use yet for the followers of Grégoire in achieving the religious settlement that he knew would more securely underpin his regime than anything else.

V

Émigré priests, who returned in considerable numbers from abroad during 1795–6, often found that other non-juring priests, those who had taken no notice of the 1792 deportation order, had already begun to lead worship openly in the very parishes the *émigrés* had once held.[96] Such situations gave rise to squabbles that hampered the essentially missionary work of the refractory Church in the later 1790s, though they did not prevent a serious measure of religious revival. For all the bickering, most clergy – *émigrés* or not – were eventually reintegrated into the life of the parishes, and a priestly presence was reimposed on a people who had often gone without one – and become used to it.

There were more than pastoral problems to preoccupy the refractory priests for, once again, the question of oath-taking threatened to divide them internally. Under a law of 11 *Prairial* Year III (28–9 September 1795) priests seeking to use church buildings had to swear, 'I recognise that the universality of French citizens is sovereign and I promise submission and obedience to the laws of the Republic', and another law of submission was passed on 7 *Vendémiaire* Year IV. Issued after the proclamation of the Bourbon pretender, Louis XVIII, as king on the death of his nephew, and the Counter-Revolutionaries' destruction at Quiberon Bay, these edicts were deliberately framed to make life slightly easier for the ex-Constitutional clergy to the detriment of their 'Roman' counterparts. Despite defeat, the Directory was aware that many of the latter remained dedicated to the Republic's destruction and, if they refused to take an oath promising obedience to its laws, could they be expected to encourage that same obedience in their parishioners?

From the beginning, the oath provoked divergent opinions in the refractory camp, and created a sizeable category of new non-jurors among those who could not bring themselves to betray their consciences by renouncing the Bourbon cause. As in 1791 and the imposition of the Civil Constitution, lay attitudes could be decisive in swaying a priest's decision. For those many priests who never bothered to take the new oaths, it often came down to the confidence derived from knowing they could rely on local support. By the Year V in the Nord and Pas-de-Calais, armed peasants were guarding refractories or missionaries from Belgium who said Mass in the open air, often to a congregation of thousands.[97] Attempts by local authorities to round up non-juring priests in such neighbourhoods could easily lead to outright insurrection. Therefore the pressure on such priests to swallow their scruples and take the oaths was less than overwhelming, even for the minority who knew that such conduct was approved by one of the most influential clerics of his generation, Jacques-André Emery, who had declared in June 1795 that 'Submission to laws does not entail approval of unjust laws; one can indeed submit to very unjust decrees.'[98]

For those refractories who thought like Emery, nothing should compromise the revival of Catholicism, not even compliance with republican laws. His recommendations (the so-called 'Parisian method') were influential in republican strongholds, especially the big cities where pressure on the non-jurors to either recognise the republic's authority or face arrest was most intense. In Paris most of the clergy subscribed and lay societies for Catholic worship were established in accordance with the law of Prairial Year III that led to limited lay participation in the election of their *curés*. This *de facto* accommodation with the regime has led some historians to speak of an influential *tiers parti* of moderate Gallicans, including Bausset, Bishop of Alais, a cardinal after the Concordat.[99] The jurors' reward before the coup of *Fructidor* was a degree of vocal support from right-wing pragmatist republicans, whose numbers extended as far as the Council of the Five Hundred.

This convergence with the Directory remained a minority sentiment among the higher clergy who stayed in exile after 1795. For the most part, they deprecated assent to the Directorial oaths as a betrayal both of Louis XVIII personally and of those clergy killed in the royalist cause over the previous three years. Of course, it was easy enough for twelve *émigré* bishops safely in London to denounce the oath-takers and to urge priests to prefer the pains of 'banishment, imprisonment and even of death',[100] but for priests on the spot the first imperative was often settling down to minister to those so long deprived of their presence. If taking an oath to the Republic was the price of that pastoral care then so be it, and even in royalist Brittany there was evidence of a new religious realism. Supporters included some of the most talented prelates of the 'generation of 1789'. Clermont-Tonnerre at Altona in north Germany actually ordered the clergy in his old diocese of Châlons-sur-Marne to take the oath,[101] while Mercy of Luçon's advice to militant priests in his portion of the Vendée was likewise to submit. The Archbishops of Aix and Bordeaux, and the Bishops of Digne and Saint-Pol-de-Léon, also indicated their endorsement of Emery's position, and the Bishop of Clermont condemned those who stood out against the oath required: 'The conduct of these gentlemen is absurd, insensitive, scandalous. The principles that they dare to put before us are truly schismatic ....'[102] These were the first important signs that some elements in the Gallican leadership were preparing for an accommodation with a non-Bourbon government in return for a guarantee of protection from the Directory,[103] and their numbers would increase.

Yet one should not overestimate the influence of academics like Emery and Bausset, or suggest that the divergent views on the oaths of 1795 created a new schism among the refractories, despite some bitter exchanges and mutual maledictions on each other's altars. If they could go about their pastoral work without taking them, most priests would do so, because the oaths revived painful memories of the schismatics of 1791 at a time (1796–7) when the hopes of restoring the monarchy were higher than at any previous point in the Republic. And there were some persuasive voices to warn off those who were tempted, like the abbé Bernier, agent-general of the Royal and Catholic armies. He entreated the priests of the Vendée: 'Don't let yourselves be fooled ... these people want to separate the cause of the altar from the throne, and the interests of the leaders [of the Counter-Revolution] from those of the ministers of God.'[104] Bernier and his ilk were very persuasive, so that, as has been well observed, 'the refractory church was for all intents and purposes a royalist church',[105] to the point where in Brittany some priests served on royalist councils and, in the Midi, others were chiefs of royalist brigand gangs. The Bishop of Bayeux, from his exile in Jersey, urged his priests to encourage *chouannerie*, and put his own purse at the disposal of the cause in 1795.

The hostility to the republic could be flagrantly displayed. As early as August 1795, in the village of Chevrières in the Loire valley, a white flag with the fleur-de-lis was shown after Sunday Mass, and white cockades handed out.[106] For such defiant men and women, there could be no compromise with a Godless republic, one that had murdered so many Catholics. No wonder it was said in the Côtes-du-Nord that priests 'inspired the greatest contempt for the patriots and promised heaven as a reward for those who assassinate them'.[107] In Paris, greater watchfulness was required. A future Archbishop of Aix, Cardinal Bernet, recalled how he had no idea of where he was to be ordained priest when he was stopped on the Pont-Neuf by a rough-looking revolutionary and verbally abused. To his astonishment, he recognised Mgr de Maillé, former Bishop of Saint-Papoul, who had ministered in the capital throughout the Terror and now whispered 'Tonight, at midnight, Rue des Rats.'[108]

Episcopal divisions precluded a firm, authoritative and collective statement about the line the refractories should adopt towards the Directory and its religious policies (those in Puisaye's Counter-Revolutionary circles wanted one badly). A lead from the papacy might have made a significant difference, the Bishop of Grenoble, Dulau d'Allemans, joined d'Aviau, Archbishop of Vienne, in begging for guidance 'in such a conflict of situations, and having regard to the very real peril which can result from individual opinions'.[109] But throughout 1795–6, Pius VI – who was increasingly forced into diplomatic contact with the Directory – stayed silent and the refractories had to make the best of things. The first priority was to confirm their people in the Catholic faith; the dissemination of royalist propaganda – despite Louis XVIII's hopes – came second. And to fulfil the first objective, refractories who would have no truck with any oath were running every sort of risk, like the priests operating on the Roussillon frontier with Spain in the Year IV, offering the sacraments to the faithful wherever they had an opportunity, but keeping on the road, always one step ahead of the forces sent to apprehend them.[110] In these circumstances, even hardline refractory bishops began to see attitudes to the oath as a distraction.

Overall, there was a new emphasis on concerted action rather than random, individual efforts. The expectation of Church reconstruction was never far away, although this turn to religion could contain – or conceal – a movement for revenge against every sort of patriot as the White Terror in the Midi showed that summer.[111] Even Louis XVIII's advisors were ready to admit that, as far as Church organisation was concerned, the pre-1789 arrangements would have to be adapted to changed conditions. In 1796 the abolition of traditional diocesan boundaries was proposed and, meanwhile, an ecclesiastical committee was established to administer the Church in France from a distance. Unfortunately for the Bourbons, the plan was unacceptable to the majority of exiled prelates, who would not see episcopal power compromised further; in particular, the London exiles endorsed Dillon's warnings that the '*libertas ecclesiae*' was sacred. Monarchists they might be, but the 'stubborn conservatism' of the majority of bishops ensured they were no more willing to see change imposed on the Church by the King than they had been by the National Assembly. There was a warning, too, that the King should not contemplate involving the papacy in any restructuring of the Gallican Church, one that anticipated the response of many bishops when faced with the Concordat 5 years later.[112]

Paradoxically, at grassroots level, away from the petty jealousies and point-scoring of the disempowered grandees, the refractory Church was capable of considerable adaptation. The sophistication of its organisation was constantly improving, usually helped by the generosity of its supporters in the provinces. In Avignon in August 1795, refractory clergy set up an Ecclesiastical Council to coordinate their efforts in the ex-papal diocese, and to determine their respective powers.[113] Episcopal involvement was also steadily increasing, if only from a distance as, under émigré legislation, they would have faced arrest. Though 41 of the non-juring bishops had died by 1795, those that remained were trying harder than ever to strengthen their ties with the local faithful and curb the independent-mindedness of the *curés*.

Across Europe, in towns like Brunswick and Ferrara, the exiled higher clergy were meeting semi-officially to re-establish ties with those left in the French dioceses, and concert what amounted to a missionary strategy.[114] It was the last flourish – in very reduced circumstances – of episcopal Gallicanism before the Concordat imposed new restrictions on its independent operation. In several dioceses, like Rouen, Le Mans, Le Puy and Lyon, itinerant vicars-general (*vicaires ambulants*) stood at the apex of a reviving organization, acting as head of the local Church with the backing of the bishop in exile. Archbishop Marbeuf of Lyon's deployment of the abbé Linsolas served as a model that was widely imitated, with the see of Lyon divided into 25 missions containing more than 600 priests responsible to Linsolas; in Toulouse, Archbishop Fontanges commissioned the abbé Dubourg to reconsecrate churches, and remarry and/or rebaptise those who had earlier used the services of a Constitutional priest.[115] In most sees, especially along the eastern frontier regions, vicars-general like Viart in Auxerre, Maugras in Langres and Verdier in Autun spearheaded successful campaigns both to rally the faithful and, in the name of the old diocesan bishops, encourage the Constitutional priests to retract and re-enter the fold. By 1797 there were missionary priests in the Le Mans diocese, next year in Tarbes. It was a successful, adaptable model. It was not unknown even for the diocesan to risk returning, in defiance of the legislation against émigrés, to join the fifteen who had never left. Thus, in June 1797, the Bishop of St Papoul ordained seventy new priests in Paris; Mgr de Prunières, Bishop of Grasse, came to Marseille in September 1797, and held occasional ordinations in town and country until his death in March 1799.[116] Neither should the work of the numerous former constitutional clergy who had abjured and made their peace with the refractories be overlooked.

It seems that a semblance of parochial organisation was best restored in parishes where the collaboration of the faithful was readily available, in other words those whose scope for independent action had been significantly increased by the Revolution. One of Archbishop Marbeuf's vicars-general might complain how 'these laymen, anxious to persuade, to charm by their talents, seem to forget about the need for the ministry',[117] yet the refractory priests, above all those returning from abroad, depended on lay support and involvement in the frequently precarious day-to-day running of the Church, especially where they had not taken the most recent oath. They could no longer rule over a laity willing to accept a clerical leadership uncritically. Few dioceses had the same success in reimposing deference as Lyon, where mission priests nominated a lay *chef de paroisse* who announced the festival days and on Sundays, when a clergyman was absent, recited some of the liturgy of the Mass.[118] Women continued to give time, money and practical help to the refractory clergy, so that the *Annales de la religion* claimed they had turned themselves into doctors of theology, and suggested they return home to mind their families properly.[119]

Once arrived, the priest would say Mass, and distribute the little brochures that told of the dangers facing the Gallican Church, aimed particularly at young people. They had a propagandist as well as a catechetical purpose: 'Question: Can the faithful take part in Masses held by juring priests? Reply: no, they cannot separate themselves from the society of the Catholic Church.' Indeed, young people who had been married by Constitutional priests frequently 'regularized' their unions through the good offices of a refractory after 1795, and took their infants to the font again.[120] The clergy were fortunate that there was often help on hand from the lay confraternities (like those of the Rosary and the Holy Sacrament) that had, although officially proscribed, continued to meet, however furtively and infrequently, especially in the south-east in a line running approximately from Colmar to Marseille. Such lay religious associations (including those for women only) were reappearing in appreciable numbers by 1797.[121] Particularly vital was the contribution of the Aa (see Chapter 9(ii)), a secret association of educated, devout laymen that was not strictly a confraternity at all, but helped to keep religious instruction and Marian devotions going, notably in Toulouse.

It was uphill work for the returning clergy to propose a Tridentine model of observance, and the republican bishops plausibly accused them of not trying, of distributing tickets at open-air Easter Masses guaranteed to heal the sick and give safe childbirth.[122] Refractory priests, with their more 'rational' beliefs, might feel affronted at the way many of the faithful – especially the women – were investing their rosaries and other outward signs of faith with almost 'pagan' meaning, but could they afford to alienate their most loyal supporters? The answer was usually no, as time for re-education was limited. It was also clear that the Revolution had confirmed that the popular appetite for formal religious instruction was much less than that for reassuring visual rituals that could function as an expression of community solidarity and sociability. Families were in no hurry to resume formal catechetical instruction even where it was on offer, and such classes were poorly attended. Children continued to learn most about Christianity – even after the end of the Terror – from their mother rather than from their parish priest.[123]

The challenges facing the leaders of the non-juring Church were at all times formidable, even before *Fructidor* Year V. In an article of January 1797 in the the *Annales Catholiques*, Bishop Asseline denounced 'an oppressive system in which violence and deception are combined'; the letter of the law might promise protection, but instructions to functionaries authorised persecution.[124] Even so, Catholic worship was resumed in as many as 30 000 parishes across France by the summer of 1797. In Paris alone, according to the abbé de Boulogne, worship was going on in about fifty churches and chapels by Easter of that year.[125] The number of refractory priests struggling in the parishes to regain the affection and attention of their people grew steadily between 1795 and 1797, and in some *départements*, like the Ariège, the Constitutional clergy were squeezed out almost completely.

Yet the stay of many clergy with welcoming congregations was brief, even for those who took the oath. When royalist sympathisers were purged from the legislature and government by the coup of 18 *Fructidor* (4 September 1797), many priests left France again, with the abrupt revival of Jacobin-style laws against *émigrés* and refractory priests, including the Law of 3 *Brumaire* year IV. It inaugurated a 'Second Terror' lasting for more than a year, one that remains much less explored than its famous predecessor of 1792–94, though recent scholarship indicates its severity. Suzanne Desan, for instance, in her study of the *département* of the Yonne (northern Burgundy) argues that this second dechristianisation was 'more penetrating than the first, particularly in its treatment of the clergy'.[126] The prohibitions included the celebration of midnight Mass at Christmas; forbidding the sale of fish on Fridays; and requiring priests to observe and sanctify not Sunday but the *décadi*. In one sense, these were pettifogging, irritating and spiteful acts of repression but, in another, they signified a continuing attempt to impose more secularised values on the population through a non-Christian set of cultural references. However interpreted, these actions flew in the face of the public demand for the free expression of faith, not its further curtailment. Typically, the gendarmes who went to prevent the celebration of a religious festival at Vézelay in the Year VI (1797–8) were met with the defiant cry: 'Where are your orders? Those are only departmental decrees. We don't give a damn. This won't last long. If we had a flute, we would dance despite you. We are no longer under the reign of Robespierre.'[127]

Yet a purged Directory ready to see some of the virtues of Jacobinism would not be diverted from inventing new weapons of repression against the Church. The principal one was yet another new oath demanded of all clergy, based on publicly expressing hatred for royalty, that immediately rendered the earlier squabbles among the refractories largely academic. Confronted with the latest challenge from the State, the refractory clergy again drew together, excoriating the minority of colleagues who felt they must submit, and forcing pastoral intervention from some of the exiled bishops to urge their clergy to show restraint and sympathy towards colleagues who had buckled under Directorial pressure. It was condemned by virtually all the bishops – Mercy of Luçon was a brave but unpopular exception for, of all places, the Vendée[128] – and even Emery drew back from subscription. Such a stipulation turned all but a tiny minority of priests into non-jurors, despite the penalty of summary deportation to Guiana.[129] Reliable figures remain hard to obtain, but Martin Lyons suggests that only one-third (a sizeable proportion of them based in or near Paris) of those who had taken the oath of submission in 1795 felt able to take this latest imposition, and only one-fifth of the refractories of 1791.[130]

Even Louis XVIII was imaginative enough to try and turn the post-*Fructidor* situation to his own advantage. In an address to the bishops of 10 October 1797, he took up the theme of a renewed throne and altar alliance originally articulated in his uncompromising Declaration of Verona (July 1795), urging the clergy 'to sustain among my subjects the monarchical spirit at the same time as religious feeling'. He selected the Archbishop of Reims and the Bishop of Boulogne to act as the 'apostles of royalty', to work on public opinion and drive home the message that the Catholic religion could not exist without monarchical protection.[131] The republic's behaviour seemed to bear out royalist polemic. It is estimated that no fewer than 10 000 to 11 000 priests were condemned under the new laws, their numbers swollen by the proscription of priests from the annexed *départements* of Belgium (formerly the Austrian Netherlands), especially the Flemish-speaking ones. In all, approximately 1500 nonjurors were sent to the west coast islands of Ré and Oléron *en route* to Guiana. Many old and infirm priests got no further, others were intercepted by the British navy in the Atlantic, and only about 240 reached their destination.[132] In the period 1797–9, in several *départments*, concerted efforts were made to purge refractories and arrest those who hosted clandestine Masses, those identified by 'patriots' in the royalist Ardèche as 'the returned *émigrés*, the refractory priests and the despots ... They are ferocious animals who wish to devour the Republic and annihilate its faithful supporters.'[133] The response of local authorities was often more dilatory than 'patriots' could have wished, even though the legislature had passed a law on 18 *Messidor* Year VI authorising the police to arrest both *émigrés* and priests without a warrant. Relatively few efforts were made to track down the younger, mobile clergy who took to their hiding places, and it was predominantly the old and infirm who were picked up. In the Sarthe, a mere 19 refractories were reported to the authorities, who arrested just 8 of them.[134]

The so-called *coup* of 22 *Floréal* against Jacobin sympathisers gave the non-juring clergy a respite: in the Ardèche, the crowds were out in procession again on Ascension Day and Corpus Christi 1798, while in the capital the churches were reported full, and priests were openly wearing their cassocks in the street. Slowly, as if synchronized with the public mood, the pace of persecution decreased, especially after the elections of the Year VII, and complaints in both the Council of Five Hundred and the Ancients arose against the measures in place. This was not before the state crackdown had disabled much of the reviving refractory organisation just as it was reasserting its presence in the parishes, leaving congregations deprived of their priest before they had become used to him. Once more they had to resort to 'White Masses' and other public rituals conducted by 'lay ministers', men – schoolteachers were a popular choice as literate members of the community with previous experience as priest's assistant – who had taken custody of the sacred books normally lodged in the sacristy and who performed the rites of the church without any hint of parody;[135] men like the roof thatcher and his fellow worshippers in Préhy in the Yonne, who 'sang mass, vespers, evening prayer, and the rosary, finally everything, and even more than the former priest sang'.[136]

It was thanks to unstinting support from such quarters, that the refractory Church was found to be too strong to be uprooted during the renewed state repression of 1797–8. It was also the beneficiary of a widespread mood of public sympathy, one tired of the anticlericalism of the Directory, anxious to make toleration general and genuine in France and, less welcome to the clergy, keen to adopt a more egalitarian basis of worship, one in which priestly authority might count for less. All of this contributed to the readiness of the nation to welcome Bonaparte's overthrow of the regime in November 1799, and the immediate concession he made to popular religious feeling at home by ending what remained of the persecution. There can be no doubt that the persistence of religious tension had been a cause of the failure to restore stability between 1795 and 1799, a major issue that brought the Directory down. It was left to Bonaparte to try and remedy the situation.

12 Religion and the Consulate, 1799–1804

The coup of 18 *Brumaire* (November 1799), which brought Napoleon Bonaparte to power, extinguished the Directory, and made him head of state as First Consul, had been a precarious affair, secured in the end only because of the army's personal loyalty to him. Bonaparte would have to lose no time in gathering allies, winning over the uncommitted and make the most of the public's weariness with the Directory. Devoid of personal faith except in his own destiny,[1] and contemptuous of the artificial cults encouraged by the Directory, Bonaparte wanted to be conciliatory towards Roman Catholics. In 1799–1800 his thoughts turned less to Grégoire's constitutional clergy (whose numbers he then probably underestimated) than to the more moderate among the refractories – those who were not die-hard monarchists. If he could win over this middle ground, and underpin the Consulate with this constituency, then royalism might be irrevocably enfeebled.[2] Once in power, he lost no time in publicly signifying his intentions with new laws on religion that can be seen as the counterpart to measures repatriating lay counter-revolutionary exiles.

Edicts of 28–30 December 1799 (7–9 *Nivôse*) returned church buildings not yet sold off to the communes and allowed the Churches to make use of buildings available for worship on any day except the *décadi*, thus removing any state obstacles to Sunday observance. The oath of hatred for monarchy was also replaced by a less controversial one simply requiring loyalty to the constitution, and an assurance from priests and ministers that they would not attack civil institutions, though even that relaxed requirement was enough to rekindle briefly the quarrel between hawks and doves among the clergy.[3] Bell-ringing and outdoor religious ceremonies were as yet illegal, but even the most cautious among the faithful were hard put to deny Bonaparte's underlying sensitivity to Catholic consciences – whatever his motivation – when he also abolished the date of Louis XVI's execution as an annual republican *fête*, and released priests still incarcerated on the islands of Ré and Oléron. Wherever they looked, the signs were encouraging. In December 1799 Pius VI was buried with full pontifical honours; the following month, the *chouans* received strong hints that their religious grievances would be met; meanwhile, any pretence that the *décadi* should be observed in preference to Sunday was in practice abandoned. With the First Consul's power base still fragile, only the revolutionary calendar temporarily survived as an expression of Bonaparte's lip-service to republicanism.

The response of the refractories to these hectic changes varied. It was widely felt that the new order was merely a stage on the way to either monarchical or republican consolidation. Why, the more cautious wondered, should it last longer than any of its predecessors? The coup of *Brumaire* was initially perceived by the refractory leaders as anti-Jacobin, one that would bring a reversion to approximately the conditions prevailing in 1795–7. Few of them had any illusions that Bonaparte would imitate the English Restoration precedent of 1660 and play the role of General Monck to Louis XVIII's Charles II, and restore him to the throne of Saint-Louis. Bonaparte was best known to the country as the architect of French military domination in Italy, which had been notorious for its militant anticlericalism. It was hard for non-jurors to see why he should want any sort of agreement with their Church. Despite taunts from Grégoire's followers that they were behaving like 'Jacobins of impiety', refractory bishops loyal to Louis XVIII were not minded to encourage clergy to submit as the new regime demanded. It was suspected that any accommodation would implicitly entail acceptance of previous laws not renounced by Bonaparte such as divorce, priestly marriage and the (continued) dissolution of the regular orders by the breaking of monastic vows.[4] Even more menacing was the likely prospect of Bonaparte seeking power to appoint bishops to office himself.

The refractory clergy would need reassurance on these questions before any deal could be finalised and, from Rome, Cardinal Maury encouraged them in this line of resistance, despite the absence of papal authorisation. Prelates meeting in Bavaria in February 1800 signalled their disapproval of the oath of loyalty, and circulated news of their decision, which was eventually endorsed by 3 archbishops and 11 bishops; about another 40 subscribed to a pastoral instruction of Bishop Asseline, which declared that the new Constitution was devised to prevent the re-establishment of legitimate power and the good of religion. The Bishop of Le Puy prohibited all priests from exercising their ministry if they had promised loyalty, 'whatever were their reserves and restrictions on the heart of the matter', while the Bishop of Lombez cancelled the authority of 3 of his 4 vicars-general to act in his name because they had authorised clergy to make their peace with the Consulate.[5] But the episcopate in exile was, once again, in no position to make much of an impact on the local situation. After experiencing the 'Second Terror' unleashed since Fructidor, it was only human for many refractory clergy to rejoice over the liquidation of the Directory. Bonaparte's terms towards them had to be a change for the better. Thus in Alsace and along the Pyrenees, priests actively encouraged their followers to vote in the affirmative in the plebiscite held on the Constitution of the Year VIII establishing the Consulate and, generally, return-ing exiles had no compunction about promising fidelity to the Year VIII settlement just so as to occupy the churches and recom-mence worship.[6]

Such was the relief among Catholics at the destruction of the Directory that it was commonly hard during the winter of 1799–1800 to restrict outbursts of religious zeal to the narrow limits that the state laws (still basically those of 7–9 *Ventôse*) stipulated: as in the Year III, great things were expected quickly, even the end of the Republic. At Caen, there were lavish funeral processions in the streets, while in the Yonne the statues of Liberty were covered with a cloth during Sunday worship. More priests came out of hiding, while thousands of them poured over the frontiers into France to resume the ministries most of them had necessarily abandoned during the repression initiated in 1797. They took advantage of the government's willingness to let exiles return but, for the most part, still ignored the oath making them technically liable to arrest by the regime. Thus defiance towards the republic – whoever presided over it – largely continued. Reports reaching Fouché, Minister of the Police and former representative on mission, in the first months of the Consulate from his 'spies' that the Catholic 'party' was essentially a front for royalist opposition were by no means inaccurate. Fouché, anxious to guard himself should Bonaparte's regime disintegrate, made it clear to prefects in a circular of 22 April 1800 that refractory priests were still required to submit to the laws of 1792 and 1793.[7] Enforcing this provision was quite another matter.

Indeed, the presence of growing numbers of the dissident clergy in the winter of 1799–1800 exacerbated religious tensions and did nothing to dampen down political ones: either way, the pressure was increased on the new regime to move without delay towards an inclusive religious settlement. The Constitution of the Year VIII had confirmed the *coup d'état* of the previous November, but its endorsement by plebiscite was predictable. Acceptance of the Consulate by the Roman Catholic Church and French Catholics was much more of a prize, one that would give the new order rock-solid underpinnings at the expense of the Bourbon monarchy. But the First Consul appreciated that any such deal would outrage many of his key supporters, for republican personnel and prejudices remained powerful. They dominated local government and had a tight grip on the police. In places like the great naval port of Toulon, where sailors mixed with administrators, there was thus no public worship taking place in 1800, and no sign of private Masses either.[8] But Toulon was not typical of France as a whole, and the window of opportunity slowly opened for Consulate and Catholics to do business.

For a start, there was a new Pope with whom to negotiate, Pius VII; he was elected in Venice in March 1800 by an *ad hoc* meeting of cardinals gathering in conclave under Austrian protection. Despite the unpropitious circumstances, 35 of the 46 living cardinals wrangled over the choice of a new pontiff for three and a half months, rejecting pressures from the Emperor Francis II's government to produce the candidate most acceptable to all the factions. Their preferred nominee as successor in St Peter's chair took governments across Europe by surprise. He was Cardinal Luigi Barnabà Chiaramonti, Bishop of Imola, only fifty-seven years old, a Benedictine monk with a reputation for adaptability in changed times, as calling himself Cardinal-Citizen Chiaramonti and preaching in support of the Cisalpine Republic in 1797 testified. Here was a cleric who had publicly declared that democracy and equality were reconcilable with Christianity, so that even Bonaparte was reputed to have remarked, 'The Citizen-Cardinal of Imola preaches like a Jacobin.'[9]

The Austrians might signal their disapproval of this intelligent, mild-mannered Pope by refusing permission for his coronation to take place at St Mark's in Venice, but the French Consulate glimpsed the best opportunity for constructive negotiations in a decade with the head of the Roman Catholic Church, despite the way in which he had notified his election to St Peter's throne to Louis XVIII in just the same way as to all the other crowned heads of Europe.[10] Bonaparte, however, knowing the value of the prize he stood to win, quickly demonstrated his goodwill. While on active service against the Austrians in June 1800, Bonaparte addressed an assembly of clergy in Milan Cathedral. He publicly criticised 'the cruel policy of the Directory' in interfering with religious expression, and expressed his hope of having 'the happiness of removing every obstacle that might hinder complete reconciliation between France and the head of the Church'.[11] Immediately after victory on the field of Marengo later in the month, Bonaparte began private conversations with Cardinal Martiana, the (Jansenist) Bishop of Vercelli, which in effect inaugurated discussions towards a new religious settlement for France in conjunction with the papacy.[12] It was a calculated policy decision in the interests of a new, Bonapartist France.

Official reports in the Year VIII/IX always refer to the problems caused by the refractory priests. Repression had not eradicated the problem; could conciliation work instead? The stakes were high, but Bonaparte was determined to resolve the matter in typically bold fashion. He was looking to smash the resilient alliance of religion and counter-revolution, to end by accommodation the murderous bloodletting in the western *départements* of France, and to appease citizens in the annexed territories of Belgium and the Rhineland. In a word, to prevent the draining away of support that successive republican regimes had incurred because of their antipathy to Roman Catholicism. As the First Consul told Thibaudeau, 'A religion is necessary for the people .... Fifty émigré bishops paid by England lead the French clergy today. It is necessary to destroy their influence. The authority of the Pope is necessary for that. ...' But there were numerous awkward questions to confront in the process. How far, if it all, would the Gallican liberties be restored? What would happen to the Constitutional Church, which in Paris by late 1800 was down to just six churches attended by a handful of worshippers?[13] Was the land settlement of 1789 threatened? In all of this, Bonaparte had no intention of recreating a wealthy ecclesiastical order that would be a partner rather than a subordinate entity in the state he was constructing around himself. From the Pope's angle, an end to the schism in France that would also enhance his authority was eminently desirable, not least because it might serve to end the wrangling and petty divisions that in 1800 were poisoning Church life in France as much as ever – France, said Emery, was 'full of minor schisms among Catholics'.[14] And a diplomatic agreement might incidentally forestall any plans of Austria and Naples to partition his own dominions in central Italy, or the nightmare of a second French occupation of those lands. Thus, with both sides sizing up each other with a view to a settlement, Pius sent Cardinals Spina and Caselli from Rome to Paris in September 1800.

Great secrecy was observed in the exchanges between the parties in the winter of 1800–1.[15] Bonaparte's regime was only a year old, and though he was justifiably confident about the backing of his soldiers, he had no wish to upset his republican supporters who could see in the Church only the forces of royalism and reaction. On the other hand, he was quite persuaded of the social necessity of religion. 'No worship, no government,' he told his brother Lucien in April 1801. 'Skilful conquerors have not got entangled with priests. They can both contain them and use them.' He was aware that refractory feeling towards him was slowly softening as the Consulate put down roots and the practitioners of *realpolitik* among the clergy were talking as bluntly to Louis XVIII as at any time since his 'accession' in 1795. 'It would be a grave error', wrote Archbishop Champion de Cicé in January 1801, 'to regard as identical the restoration of the monarch's authority in France and that of the Catholic religion'.[16] Through reports from the office of Fouché, Minister of Police, Bonaparte could gauge with some accuracy the change of direction in the religious wind blowing across France that winter. He knew that he could not pressurise the loyalties of his republican supporters like Laplace and Fouché too soon. Accordingly, the Consul made it clear to the papacy he had only limited scope for concessions, and so Cardinal Spina was informed by the abbé Étienne Bernier, Bonaparte's chief negotiator, when he reached Paris on 6 November 1800 that Pius must accept the loss of his confiscated lands and the resignation of all the loyalist bishops, including those who had never wavered in their resistance to the Revolution over the last decade. In return, Napoleon would treat with Pius on the basis of the Pope as monarch, having full authority over his 'subjects'. This was the antithesis of Gallicanism, but it suited Napoleon's purpose at the time.[7]

Discussions lasted eight months, and twenty-one different drafts were prepared before the Concordat was finally signed on 15 July 1801. The hectic exchanges several times appeared on the point of breakdown, with Bonaparte having to order into line his two other negotiators, the ex-bishop Talleyrand and the ex-priest Fouché, who were more ready than their master to call into play the entitlement of the Constitutional Church to consideration. It required all the Consul's prestige and power to ensure a successful outcome, and even Cardinal Consalvi, sent to Paris in June 1801 to avoid a rupture, admitted as much: 'I must in all truth say', he reported, 'all the energy of character and good will that the First Consul had was necessary to resist so many sources of opposition.'[18] But this drive to a conclusion went hand in hand with diplomatic intimidation born of the hard-nosed realisation that the papacy needed a settlement more than the Consulate did. Not that any price was acceptable to Pius VII, as he insisted to Cacault, Napoleon's agent who went to Rome in May to tighten the ratchet: 'We are prepared to go to the gates of Hell – but no further.[19] Pius did not approve of the Concordat *per se*, and would demonstrate as much to Napoleon later when, as Emperor, the latter extended it.

Bonaparte's brinkmanship during the negotiations pressurised the papacy relentlessly in the spring and early summer of 1801, with the threat to halt the talks – or worse: more fearsome possibilities included the military occupation of the Papal States and the alternative establishment in France of some form of 'natural religion'.[20] Pius had problems from another direction with the more conservative, royalist or pro-Austrian members of the sacred college, though their influence counted for a good deal less after France imposed peace on Austria by the Treaty of Lunéville in February 1801. Pius was well served in the final stage of discussions by one of the most formidable diplomatic talents of his generation, Cardinal Ercole Consalvi, the Papal Secretary of State, whose shrewd realism admirably complimented his master's spiritual vision and leadership.

The complicating factor in the last half of the discussions from March 1801 was Bonaparte's decision to insist that the place of the Constitutional Church in the settlement had to be acknowledged. Thus, suddenly the following spring, Grégoire's followers held the key to the outcome, their diplomatic clout increased beyond anything envisaged even a few months previously. In January 1801 Bonaparte told Cardinal Spina that Bonaparte was thinking of appointing Constitutional bishops to places in a newly united Church and, by March, 7 of their number were included on a confidential appointments list. What had made the difference? It owed nothing to any sense of obligation Bonaparte might have had to the Constitutional party and everything to his sense of the factional balance, and his emerging respect for Grégoire himself: he recognised in Grégoire –'Iron Head' as he called him – a kindred authoritarian spirit. The advice of old hands like Talleyrand was also not readily overlooked, with his recommendation that 'religious peace can only be effected by bringing together every tender conscience and all the classes of clergy under the benevolent and paternal authority of the holy see.'[21] And there was more objective evidence which indicated that Bonaparte would have to think in terms of satisfying a much wider religious constituency than the refractory clergy.

The First Consul had instituted two national surveys of religion through his newly established prefectoral corps in late 1800 and early 1801, and the returns were so surprising that they made an immediate impact on negotiations. Though in some regions, like the Côtes-du-Nord, it was the refractories who were in the ascendant, the survey also showed their return over the previous eighteen months had not been acceptable to all Catholics. Reports were coming in from many provincial areas during 1800-1 that public attendance at Constitutional Churches was actually increasing from people alarmed at the stern pastoral messages emanating from the returnees. These laymen and women were especially worried about attacks on their marriages not being valid if conducted by a Constitutional cleric and then about the legitimacy of their children. One prefect reported that the 'unsworn priests' were influencing the parents through the children: if it emerged from the child's confession that he or she had been to the service of the Constitutional priest, a long penance could be imposed, and the child's first communion postponed.[22] The social stigma of such a delay was strong, and it drove many of the 'guilty' parties back into the fold of the Constitutional Church (of course, it could also work the other way round). Those laymen who had purchased ecclesiastical lands and properties [biens nationaux] may have been a further factor in explaining renewed support for the Constitutional clergy.

Bonaparte was concerned only with the implications of these development. He had come to admire the obedience of the Constitutional clergy to the laws of the state, and appreciated the way their bishops had made favourable reference to his regime in the patriotic glow that followed victory at Marengo (Grégoire was a notable exception). It threw into heightened contrast the divisive, lawless behaviour of the refractory clergy, seen in events like the murder of the Bishop of the Finistère and the attempt on Bonaparte's own life on Christmas Eve 1800 by royalist fanatics with their 'infernal machine'. Such first-hand exposure to right-wing extremism played its part in hardening the First Consul's resolve to break the tie between refractory clergy and the Bourbon pretender. One way of stopping the trend would be to demonstrate his goodwill towards their religious rivals, who thus emerged as the beneficiaries of recent events. Refractory and Constitutional clergy might still loathe each other. The report, for instance, of the Prefect of the Seine *département* in early 1801, makes that clear enough. But Bonaparte was insistent that both sides must be involved in the final settlement however obnoxious the strategy was to the Vatican. If Pius and Consalvi were not prepared to make this last concession and offer some recognition of the followers of Grégoire then, the First Consul was adamant, there would be no final settlement.

The result was an end to the separation of Church and State brought about by the Revolution. The Concordat represented a hard-won compromise on both sides, especially the Pope's, for whom the prize of religious peace and the combatting of urban apathy and hostility to Catholicism was too precious to be easily abandoned. Yet the Concordat should not be presented as a one-sided triumph for Bonaparte without according Pius VII credit for grasping the opportunity presented to him. The turnround is stark: in 1798–9 the rulers of France had once again reinvigorated the campaign against Catholic culture and belief, while three years later the head of state was attending Mass in Notre-Dame Cathedral. Pius VII had at all times in the deliberations between the Vatican and the Tuileries played a cool and close hand. With talented servants like Consalvi interpreting his wishes, and refusing to be intimidated into an extremist response, he had the insight to notice the degree to which the Bonapartist regime had stabilised, and the courage to take the tremendous step of cutting the cable linking Church and Bourbons.

The detail of the Concordat made it clear that the confessional state was no more in France. The position of 1790 was essentially reaffirmed in the first article of the Concordat: Catholicism was acknowledged as 'the religion of the majority of the French' – but no more. Thus the legal right to existence of Protestants and Jews was safeguarded. The reconstituted Gallican Church would receive nothing back of the lands put at the nation's disposal in 1789. Unwillingly, Pius recognised the permanency of the tranfers and obtained nothing tangible by way of compensation.[23] With these key points enshrined, the Concordat set out the details of the French Church's organisation. It was to be governed by bishops, chosen, as before 1790, by the head of state (the First Consul), and invested with spiritual authority by the Holy Father. They would be responsible for dioceses whose frontiers had been redrawn to make them broadly compatible with local government boundaries;[24] the new bishops, and indeed the whole lower clergy, would take a declaration of loyalty to the government and, at the end of every Mass, would offer prayers for the well-being of the Consulate.

Bonaparte was adamant that clerics must permanently abandon their role as recruiting agents for the Bourbon monarchy, and the bishops were expected to support the regime in the provinces, the sacerdotal equivalent, as it were, of the newly instituted prefectoral corps. With the revolutionary land settlement deemed untouchable, there could be no going back to tithe. Henceforward, bishops and clergy would be paid out of the public purse (chapters and seminaries could be established, but the state was not obliged to pay them), and with parish priests exclusively nominated by the episcopate and subject also to the new oath, there was a twin-track approach towards ensuring good behaviour. Bonaparte had won for himself the two vital points of nominating prelates and leaving no place for the regular clergy in the arrangements. It was true that the electoral provisions of the Civil Constitution had been discarded by the Consulate in the name of effective oversight and man-management. But so, too, were the pastoral rights of the priesthood to independent power. A hierarchical structure suited the interests of the Napoleonic state well enough, and interest in versions of ecclesiology influenced by Jansenism or the Enlightenment were frowned upon.

All this left the vital question unanswered – would the interested parties in the Church accept what had been done, and the settlement that had been negotiated without their participation? The refractory bishops and priests could resume the trappings of office, but it would mean cutting loose from their royalist affiliations and, at least in theory, accepting the Constitutional clergy as their legal equals in a reunited Gallican order. No less drastically, the bishops were expected by Bonaparte to surrender their offices to Pius VII, who would then 'appoint' a new episcopate for France, drawn from Grégoire's followers as well as the refractories. There were two obvious points of controversy. First, the Pope was being required to admit the validity of the Constitutional Church's holy orders, and contradict the decision of his predecessor in the Brief *Tam Multa*. Second, the stipulation that he had the power to disinherit existing bishops flew in the face of Gallican claims of episcopal equality, which saw the Pope as no more than first among equals, and might set a precedent for his greater involvement in the day-to-day government of the French Church at the expense of diocesan officials, up to and including the bishop. In fact, when the idea was first broached, the curia – by no means yet an ultramontane body – was aghast at this affront to Gallican sensibilities; the majority of episcopal opponents, who for a decade had set their faces against the Civil Constitution and everything that followed, had hardly done so only to be disowned by Rome and constrained into abandoning principle when the Holy See commanded. No wonder that Louis XVIII thought his hour had come and that the settlement could be stopped.

Any such expectations were soon dispelled. The Pope appreciated that the interests of the Catholic religion could not be subordinate to the Bourbon monarchy, and that must necessitate mass episcopal resignations if Bonaparte insisted on the clause requiring episcopal submission to be inserted in the Concordat – as he did.[25] A high proportion of the refractory bishops were not prepared to compromise with the Concordat –which Bishop de Coucy of La Rochelle scorned as 'a derivative of the Civil Constitution', blameable on 'Emeryian influence' – and deplored Pius VII's betrayal of principles they had struggled to uphold for a decade. Of 93 surviving refractory prelates, 55 eventually obeyed; the remainder were deprived by the Pope, though their jurisdiction continued to be recognised by a large body of the faithful. Thus was initiated the minor schism of the *petite église*, especially strong in parts of the west, Poitou and the Lyonnais.[30]

Meanwhile, Bonaparte hardly needed to do much to prompt the Constitutional clergy into accepting the new arrangements, since, as explained above, he had made their inclusion a vital part of the package. Despite a reluctance to abandon their faithful followers, they resigned in compliance with the Concordat, a glaring contrast to the refractories. In June 1801, Bonaparte had deliberately allowed forty of their bishops to hold a second national council in Paris.[31] It would serve as a lever on Pius and Consalvi as the discussions neared their climax, especially when on 14 July the members proclaimed the duty of obedience to the established power in France and its laws. Otherwise, there was much internal business to be transacted at the council, as the previous chapter noted, like the contentious question of authorising a vernacular liturgy, and the unconcealed rivalries of the United Bishops with presbyterian clergy clinging to Richerist notions of the divine right of *curés*. If there was an air of unreality about it all, as the Constitutional Church faced official extinction anyway, such a gathering was provoking in itself to the refractory party. It was a reminder to the papacy that Bonaparte endorsed the right of Grégoire's followers to obtain recognition of their orders and a share of the spoils in the unified ecclesiastical order.

With the conclusion of the Concordat imminent, justification for the national council's continued sitting had really gone and the delegates were happy to accede to a polite request from Minister of the Police Fouché to close down their proceedings quickly to preserve the impression of an uncoerced agenda. Their compliance provides an interesting token of the national council manoeuvring to win official favour at a crucial juncture in France's religious history, with some of the government going out of their way to facilitate the business: Fouché even showed some of the bishops an advance draft text of the Concordat, and on 16 July had led Grégoire and the Bishop of Clermont (Périer) to meet the First Consul; he duly authorised the continuation of the council until the imminent signing of the Concordat. The process of closure was not completed until mid-August, but Bonaparte remained unconcerned with the Concordat safely concluded.[32] Bernier, the Consul's representative, had recourse to subterfuge to achieve his objective and, though his reputation never recovered, it did the trick. Cardinal Consalvi was told that the Constitutional bishops had accepted Pius VI's condemnation of the rupture of 1791. It was a diplomatic falsehood, but it played an important part in ensuring the Concordat was not wrecked at the last moment. The policy caused tensions within the Bonaparte family: Napoleon's brother Joseph remonstrated about possible charges of double-dealing with Consalvi, whereas his wife, Josephine, was emerging as a sponsor of the Constitutionalist cause.[33]

It was actually only *after* the Concordat had been signed that the position of the Constitutional clergy became central. In the period from August 1801 to April 1802 Bonaparte was under intensive pressure to accept Consalvi's demand that if the ordained followers of Grégoire were to have any future in the new Church then they must, as a precondition of taking office, retract their errors. He could so easily have done so. Key members of his negotiating team – Bernier, Portalis and the latter's nephew d'Astros – carried tremendous influence, and they urged him to abandon the Constitutional side; Cardinal Caprara had intimated to them that he was under instructions from His Holiness in Rome not to give any more ground. Instead,

Napoleon listened to ministers like Fouché, Talleyrand and the latter's protégé, d'Hauterive, who managed to confirm the First Consul in selecting a conciliatory approach to the Constitutionals. He also had the same advice from Josephine. When the national council was shut down, its leading members were invited to an official dinner at the Tuileries, and Josephine listened with interest to some of their sermons.

This unambiguous sign of official approval was underlined after a stormy meeting in November 1801 between Caprara and Bonaparte. The latter proclaimed his intention to appoint Constitutional prelates into new posts without any retractions and left the Cardinal to contain his anger. Some of the Consul's own councillors urged him to change course. Portalis in February 1802 implored him not to appoint Constitutional bishops; most prefects were against it because of the outrage it would provoke among the majority of Catholics. Such a policy was inherently destabilising rather than conciliatory. Bonaparte was not impressed. On 15 March he made a final declaration of his plan to appoint a minimum of 12 Constitutional bishops to the 10 archbishoprics and 60 bishoprics there would be in the reintegrated Church; Caprara met him on the 30th, when the Consul was no less inflexible. Retraction was out of the question, and the prefects would see to it that any priest who disobeyed such a bishop was expelled from his living.

For a time it seemed as if the fate of the Concordat was in jeopardy. The moment of truth came in April when 7 Constitutional bishops were nominated. Confronted with the threat of even more such candidates, Caprara in the end had swallowed his pride and instituted them, without officially giving up the papacy's reservations about those who had declined to retract their 'errors'. The controversy rumbled on until 1804, but Pius was obliged to concede defeat. Eventually, a total of 12 Constitutional prelates were appointed to the newly united bench of bishops, with Grégoire himself elected to the Senate in December 1801. Bonaparte contented himself with the nomination of his maternal uncle Joseph Fesch to the see of Lyon in 1802 as a means of achieving reconciliation between the refractories and the Constitutional party, but it was only a gesture in that direction. Integration was much more difficult than he expected.

If seeing some of their enemies preferred and resigning their offices into papal hands was agonising for Gallican-minded refractories, they soon found that Bonaparte had no intention of allowing the

Pope to assume a greater status in the post-Concordat order than he had possessed before 1790: the state would have the final word, even in a republican guise, leaving the clergy dependent on the government. So much was clear from the seventy-seven Organic Articles added unilaterally to the Concordat immediately before its promulgation in April 1802. The time-lag between signing and promulgating the Concordat owed much both to the Consul's insistence on providing for the Constitutional clergy and to the Pope's reluctance to accept the power Bonaparte was abrogating to himself. Delay also allowed the First Consul time to apprise himself of the opposition in republican circles to the Concordat and to guard against it, not least by securing public goodwill by the signing of peace with Britain.

And if the papal envoy, Cardinal Caprara, had known little about the contents of the Organic Articles, then that too suited Bonaparte's diplomacy. There was a rush to sign the Concordat; thereafter protraction suited his purpose. The Articles made it clear that the Brief *Tam multa* was, as far as Bonaparte was concerned, no more than an expedient. In matters of administration, the Church's rights to institutional freedom of action were severely limited: from the publication of papal bulls and the convocation of national councils down to the creation of new parishes, the clergy could not act independently of state sanction. Duties at every level in the hierarchy were apportioned in the Organic Articles; bishops (who must all be French) could not leave their dioceses or re-establish chapters without first obtaining permission from the government; at cantonal level would be one *curé*, whose responsibilities would include supervision of *desservants* in the communes. Four-fifths of the parish clergy would have no security of tenure, with all except those in the chief towns of a canton removable at will. And there would be far fewer bishops than before 1789. Dioceses would correspond exactly with the *départements*, a stipulation accepted a decade previously by the Constitutional clergy. The Organic Articles even revived the most extreme statement of Gallicanism – the Four Articles of 1682 – which were again to be taught in schools and seminaries. Bonaparte calculated that Pius would not imperil the whole settlement merely because of this imposition, and he was correct, though Pius still refused to recognise the Organic Articles.

The Concordat survived this demonstration of Bonapartist authority, and indeed it became a model for subsequent redefinitions of

Church–State relations after the Consulate was converted into the Empire in 1804. In France, Church and State were realigned if not reunited, and there was once again a single, legally recognised Catholic Church commanding majority support; the papacy had restored relations with the *de facto* government of France and found itself professing rights of deposition as well as investiture of bishops, while the vast body of the faithful could worship without obstruction from republican officialdom.[28] It spoke volumes that neither the Pope nor the Consul had invited French bishops and clergy – not even the numerically dominent refractories – to make their own submissions on the preparation of the Concordat. There was no serious possibility of a national council, the classic Gallican solution, to restore Church unity in 1801. In 1790–1 the French bishops had unavoidably relied on papal authority as a last-ditch means of holding the Church together; ten years later, the papacy had no intention of respecting the integrity of episcopal authority to the letter, as the terms of *Tam multa* revealed. The Organic Articles may have done something to reassure Gallican-minded clergy, but the settlement as a whole had, with the consent of the state, given the Pope a degree of supervisory involvement in its affairs that would not easily be displaced. Beyond that was the symbolic point that no Catholic could ignore: that in a world destabilised by Revolution, the Holy Father offered that unconditional support for the Catholic faith that could be no longer be relied on from the government with the monarchy gone.

Bonaparte, however, made it clear to all that toleration would be a lasting fruit of the Revolution, and the Concordat made every provision for it. Under that agreement and separate Organic Articles of April 1802, the 480 000 Calvinists and 200 000 Lutherans received better terms than those granted to the Catholics. It gave them an unprecedented degree of official recognition, with Protestant churches established on a parallel basis to the Catholics, including provision for regularising the formation of consistories (intended to ensure dominance by the social elite), and salaried pastors from 1804. But there was also continuing watchfulness by the new prefects in the provinces: Protestant synods could gather only with the express permission of the government. The new arrangement enabled Protestant groups to take up their worshipping and communal life again, and relations with the Catholic majority were seldom a problem thereafter, except in one or two areas like the Gard, the scene of renewed blood-letting during the Restoration of 1814–15.

There was also the question of the Jews. Bonaparte, for his part, wanted to include them in a general settlement of religion. It had been evident since 1797 on his first Italian campaign that he favoured their liberation, with his sense – corresponding to a typical Enlightenment position – that they constituted less a distinctive religious grouping than a people that considered God as its supreme legislator.[29] His expedition to Egypt and a French presence in the Middle East from 1798 had even awakened messianic expectations among some sections of the Jewish population. One administrator from the Nord told the Director Merlin de Douai of a conversation on the subject he had in the coach from Lille to Douai with a Jew who said he was no longer awaiting the Messiah since Bonaparte had conquered the Holy Land. The official tried to dampen down these high hopes: 'But what in common has the Messiah with our general who eats lard and black pudding?'[30] In the first months of the Consulate a high proportion of Jews seem to have given a cautious welcome to the new order. Bonaparte's Minister of Religion (initially head of a General Directory of Cults set up in October 1801 within the Ministry of the Interior to administer the Concordat), J-E-M. Portalis, consulted Parisian Jews in the run-up to the Concordat, and there was talk of government recognition involving reform on a Protestant model. In the end, the First Consul judged this scheme insufficient to make further negotiations worthwhile. For one thing, the internal bickering within the Jewish community in Alsace reported by the prefects made it hard to contemplate reaching an agreement satisfactory to all sides.[31] So by c. 1805 Portalis – who opined that the Jews formed less of a religion than a people – was moving towards a position of allowing the Jews the opportunity to regulate themselves. In fact, it was not until 1808, after Napoleon had been crowned Emperor, that the position of the Jews in the French state was recognised along lines similar to those accorded Christian denominations under the Concordat.[32]

Protestants had every reason to be grateful to Bonaparte, but they left it to Catholic churchmen who had once sanctified the monarchy to come forward and offer to do the same for the Consulate. On 18 April, Easter Sunday 1802, the bells of Notre-Dame rang out across the city for the first time in over a decade summoning the First Consul and other senior members of the regime from the Tuileries to attend a solemn Mass to confirm the new order of Church–State relations. They were greeted on the steps by the Archbishop-elect of

Paris, the ninety-year-old Mgr de Belloy; Cardinal Caprara celebrated Mass with twenty-seven bishops who, with hands on the
Gospel, affirmed their loyalty to the Consulate. The building was
packed with faithful Catholics, as well as the young and fashionable,
curious to sample the novelty of a state occasion sanctified by the
Church. There was a symbolic appropriateness that the sermon
should be delivered by one of the greatest *prélats politiques* of the age,
Cardinal Boisgelin, who had obeyed the Pope's injunction, resigned
the see of Aix-en-Provence he had held since the 1770s, and received
Tours as recompense.[33] Boisgelin had preached before Louis XVI
at his coronation in Reims in 1775. Twenty-seven years later he came
to inauguarate both the new respectability of the Church and a
new constitutional era, for Bonaparte, secure in power, was about to
declare himself First Consul for life. And Boisgelin was preaching not
to a hereditary monarch of twenty-one disposed to take his words
seriously, but to a thirty-three-year-old army officer, a modern
Machiavelli whose interest in Christianity as a system of belief was
minimal. At every point between 1799 and 1802, his conduct has
little more than a superficial resemblance to earlier Erastian traditions. This was a harsh new polity that rested on *force majeure*, in
which any sense of 'resacralisation' was a means not an end.

It was diehard republicans who actually posed more of a threat to
the Concordat and the Organic Articles than the clergy. As usual, the
First Consul anticipated problems by purging the Tribunate and
Legislative Body of his opponents in March 1802, on the pretext of
obtaining the renewal of one-fifth of the membership of the legislature that the Constitution strictly required.[34] That done, the new
ecclesiastical regime in France was inaugurated under the Law on
Cults of 18 *Germinal*, Year X (8 April 1802) without any legislative
problems. Several months previously, in August 1801, the head of
state had made it plain that he would not permit the parading
of militantly republican, anticlerical views when he ordered Fouché
to prevent journalists writing on religion or the clergy. It was a
risky strategy, possible only because of his unassailable military
power base. Even a Councillor of State close to Bonaparte like
Defermon noted the fragility of it all: 'All that will go very well
so long as the Consul lives. The day after his death, we will all have
to emigrate.'[35]

Bonaparte himself had achieved what no previous revolutionary
régime had really wanted to bring about – the acceptance by the

leadership of the Catholic Church of a government that was not led by a legitimate Bourbon prince. Under the Organic Articles, the clergy were required to denounce all crimes to the police – not least, subversion – and preach obedience to the state.[36] In one stroke, he ensured (at least on paper) that sacerdotal influence over the faithful majority of the 'Grande Nation' in the pulpit and the confessional would not be exercised against him. It was a statesmanlike if ruthless achievement, and he was unconcerned that his enemies on the Left might claim that he had betrayed the Revolution. If that was the cost of reconciliation with Catholic Christians, Bonaparte was ready to pay it. Those enemies were, anyway, a containable threat. High royalists and Gallican diehards on one side, disappointed constitutionals and dechristianisers on the other, none of them were able to stop the Concordat giving additional respectability to the Bonapartist regime and preparing the way for the Empire.

He sealed the new order in December 1804 when Pius VII, against the advice of many in the curia – Consalvi, significantly, was among those asking him to decline the 'honour' – came to Paris to take part in Bonaparte's coronation as Napoleon I. Hopes that the new Emperor would accept modifications in the Organic Articles or restore French-occupied papal territories came to nothing. And the coronation itself was a token symbol of legitimacy, with the Emperor essentially uninterested in sacred institutions. If the beleagured band of French royalist clergy around Louis XVIII, led by Cardinal Maury, felt the Pope's blessing on Bonaparte counted for nothing against the monarchy's sanctification over centuries, the new Emperor was not interested in disabusing them. The Concordat was securely in place, a protocol defining Church–State relations with a precision far removed from the elasticity still to be found in Louis XVI's time, one that could serve as a model for monarchs looking to legitimate state power through the Churches. Denomination was a secondary consideration. Thus the Protestant, Frederick William III of Prussia, for instance, was greatly influenced by it in the Church of the Prussian Union, founded in 1817, which brought together most Lutherans and Calvinists in his kingdom. Frederick, obsessively concerned with uniformity, even wrote the liturgy for the Prussian Union.[37] It was an initiative Napoleon might have applauded, for the Emperor inhabited a different world to his Bourbon predecessors, one that was, as John McManners has memorably written, 'imperial rather than French and Gallican, a world in which force was supreme, rather than privilege, [and] in which the sacraments had no relevance to politics'.[38]

Meanwhile, with the new laws laid down, a struggle for places ensued in the dioceses and parishes. The government wanted figures it judged as non-subversives in the most senior posts, and drew on the dossiers it had prepared on existing bishops to see who could be incorporated safely into the reintegrated Church.[39] Whatever their reservations about acceding publicly to the new political order, the ex-refractories could perceive that their ten years of resistance had not gone uncompensated under the Concordat, while Grégoire and his constitutionalist followers had less to show for their oft proclaimed attachment to the Revolution – though more, admittedly, than had seemed likely at one time. Grégoire himself received no bishopric (he continued to sign himself 'former Bishop of Blois' regardlessly), and it was Le Coz, named to the see of Besançon, who thereby assumed the unofficial leadership of the former Constitutional clergy. Their marginalised status was reflected less in a meagre share of episcopal appointments than at the parochial level. In the diocese of Rouen, for instance, they received only one in ten of the cures.[40] The picture overall is obscured by the lack of work on the role of the Constitutional clergy in the construction and organisation of the new Church.[41] It seems that parishes that tried to retain their Constitutional priests were relatively few and far between. Where bishops did try to impose them as parish priests the popular demonstrations to keep them out could be as strong as 1791, especially in the west.

In dioceses from Bordeaux to Nancy, and from Bayeux to Aix, many Constitutional priests had to undergo humiliating retractions, despite Bonaparte and Portalis doing their best to guard against it. Undoubtedly, others found the price of submission too high and their exclusion from the new Church may have prompted their supporters to stop going to services also. There are resemblances here to the oath conflict of 1791, but the topic has not yet been adequately researched.[42] Other ritual gestures of purgation included the cleansing from impurity of churches the Constitutional priests had used – with the local prefects often not intervening if the state of local politics indicated inaction as the most politic choice. Collective rebaptisms and remarriages were also not uncommon. Not that the refractories were able to return quickly to anything like the pre-1790 situation. In the Marne and the Isère, dechristianisation and other Revolutionary pressures meant that only one-third of priests could be restored to their former parishes and, as elsewhere, those who did return were ageing. In the *département* of the Vienne, nearly half the secular clergy had died or disappeared without trace by 1801; in the vicinity of Auxerre, only a quarter of the pre-revolutionary parish priests were reported as in residence about the same date, and the local Church relied on former canons and regular clergy to fill the gaps.[43]

Shortage of clergy often meant the new Catholic hierarchy had little hope of imposing clericalist ideas of orthodoxy on unwilling laity in rural areas, and they could certainly expect no help from the Bonapartist state in that task. Nevertheless, by the time the Empire was overthrown in 1814–15, the fruits of Catholic revival were becoming visible, a revival that had its origins in the Directorial period, and could not be blighted even by the Emperor's much disliked 'Concordat of Fontainbleau', unilaterally if briefly imposed on the Church in 1814–15. By *c.* 1810, Bonaparte had forgotten the lesson driving his policy at the time of the first Concordat – of never underestimating either the power of religion or the resilience of the Church.

Conclusion: The First Empire and Beyond

Napoleon's coronation had dramatically underlined the Roman Catholic Church's return to the public sphere and the chance for religious reconstruction in France, possibly even for religious revival. But, as far as the post-Concordat Church was concerned, no triumphalist note marked the new *modus vivendi* with the Imperial government. The reality was that, in terms of institutional capacity to take an independent line from the state, little had survived of the spirit of pre-1789 Gallicanism; that lived on, if anywhere, in the congregations of the *petite église*, the Catholic traditionalists who would not have the Concordat foisted on them. Another version was manufactured by the bureaucrats in the Ministry For Religious Affairs after relations with the papacy entered a new crisis period in *c.* 1810, but it had few backers among the clergy of Bonapartist France, for whom the Holy Father was far more of a friend than the Emperor.

The Concordat had endorsed authoritarian episcopal leadership in the dioceses. That was intended to provide a counterweight to the new prefects, but not to rival them: in any future Church–State dispute there would be no ambiguity about the legal supremacy of the Empire. From a Bonapartist perspective, the Church was primarily an organ of social utility, but a subordinate one. Bishops would be expected to toe the line, or leave office in ignominy. Henceforth, they were deprived of a leadership role in society. It was their job to inculcate loyalty to his person through the new imperial catechism[1] and other devices designed to remind priest and people of the first duty of obedience, such as fêting his victories on the battlefield and using the feast of the newly discovered 'Saint-Napoléon', which was to outshine Epiphany at the beginning of every year. (It was subsequently moved to the Feast of the Assumption on the basis that good summer weather would encourage more observants!) The Emperor was relying – rather too easily – on the Pope hauling dissident clergy into line. On the face of it, Pius VII had incentive enough. French bishops and clergy were subject to papal authority weighted in the latter's favour; it went well beyond the eighteenth-century conventions operative within the Paris–Rome axis.

The Church was emphatically no longer the First Estate with its corporate privileges and vast landed estates. There was not the remotest prospect that either would ever be restored. Similarly, the Catholic hierarchy could not expect a return to a religious monopoly. The right of Protestants and Jews to toleration and participation in such civic life as there was in Bonapartist France was built into the new settlement of the state, and those groups could organise and worship without hinderance. Consolations for Catholics were hard to come by. Talented clerics like Grégoire of the Constitutional Church and Lauzières de Thémines of the *petite église* (both former Bishops of Blois) remained unreconciled, a reminder that the Concordat had vexed many who called themselves Catholics. And any private expectation they might have entertained of a speedy delivery by the *de jure* Louis XVIII was scotched after Napoleon's great victories at Ulm and Austerlitz in 1805 consigned the Bourbon pretender to indefinite exile. Though deprived of their historic control of the registration of births, marriages and deaths, the clergy would have to make the best of it, for the decisive point of state control was that clerics depended on it for their livelihoods. Education, too, was opened up to lay influences, though teachers who were committed, anticlerical republicans only tended to make an impact much later in the century. And there would be no more opulence, with archbishops receiving only 15 000 francs per annum and bishops just 10 000.

Historians usually emphasise the government's indifference to the restored, technically reunited Catholic Church, an indifference that became overt hostility, manifesting itself in the breakdown of relations with the papacy after 1808–9. But there is another more positive perspective. Some bishops did their best to work with the new order in what Bernard Plongeron has described as the 'first *ralliement*' of the Church. He has singled out Davoisin, Bishop of Nantes after the Concordat, while there is the more celebrated example of Napoleon's uncle, Cardinal Fesch, Archbishop of Lyon and Primate of the Gauls, who used his considerable status to open several seminaries in the archdiocese and worked to ensure that obstacles to catechetical teaching were minimised.[2]

The renascent Church was exceptionally fortunate in having Jean Portalis as Minister for Religious Affairs, a loyal Catholic. He guarded the Church as much as he could from anticlerical prefects, allowing it to refuse the sacraments at will and to deny remarriage for divorcees. Thanks to him, the government provided scholarships for students at seminaries in 1807, from 1808 effectively made primary and female education a matter for the Catholic Church, and in 1809 even exempted theology students from the military draft.[3] Female religious orders like the Ursulines and the Visitandines were also provisionally re-established with government connivance in 1807. It was next to nothing beside the wholesale abolition of most of the orders, but it would subsequently be seen as marking the start of the extraordinary nineteenth-century growth in female vocations.

Such support in high quarters increased the pressure on royalists (and indeed republicans) to accept the new political reality, even if they could not endorse its legitimacy. That would mean putting aside their own distinctive political cultures in the interests of national unity and, if diehard Bourbon loyalists remained numerous among the clergy, activists were few. For most bishops and clergy – as for Pius VII himself – the resumption of Catholic worship had become the priority. That could be dangerous where republicans signalled their displeasure at a clerical presence. At Toulon, the *curé* Brun was apparently so apprehensive of assault that he kept a loaded pistol under his altar napkin.[4] Nothing daunted, Brun, like the vast majority of priests, got down to work in his parish after 1802, though few former Constitutionalist clergy had this opportunity. Their ecclesiological inheritance was derided by royalists and revolutionaries alike, and precious little of it found a home in the post-Concordat Church.

Napoleon had wanted at least one-third of benefices to go to Constitutional priests, but that quota was not uniformly imposed, often at the behest of civil servants. Prefects were worried about disorder in parishes if the presence of such a compromised incumbent was popularly viewed as a return to the days of the Civil Constitution. The Emperor had other concerns in the early 1800s and did not force the issue. So throughout his reign the accumulated hatred and mistrust of the rival clergies was still to be found. Brittany was not appeased by the Concordat. The Bishop of Saint-Brieuc used it to establish refractory, openly royalist priests throughout the diocese, while the Bishop of Rennes was in league with the *petite église*.[5] In such a hostile environment, those who had followed Grégoire and the United Bishops were bound to face discrimination. Unfair it may have been, but one side-effect of former jurors being the exception rather than the rule in the post-Concordat Curch was to ensure that invidious distinctions between themselves and former refractories were becoming redundant well before the end of the first Empire. In that restricted sense at least, a healing process was underway, though by no means everywhere.

Not every parish that wanted a priest could have one, even a former Constitutional one. Throughout the First Empire the Church suffered from a manpower crisis that threatened to disrupt pastoral work more purposefully than political constraints: there were only 36 000 secular priests in 1814 compared with 60 000 in 1789. The numbers of men in holy orders had been greatly depleted during the 1790s from resignations, deaths, the diminished number of ordinands and the opportunties for ordaining them. For every 100 *curés* in 1789 there were only 64 in 1815, for every 100 *vicaires*, the number had fallen to 27 by 1815, and for every 100 priests without parochial responsibilities, there were only 15 by the time of the Bourbon return to power.[6] Despite appeals to ex-monks and friars to take up posts, and even to apostate but repentant priests to do likewise, the recovery of the pre-revolutionary ratios between priests and parishioners was an objective that could not be fulfilled, especially as the total population grew. In Grenoble, for instance, there was a 15 per cent increase between 1801 and 1809, yet the number of priests fell by just over 18 per cent.[7] It was not the case everywhere. By 1816, the proportion of parishes vacant was 15 per cent for France as a whole, but it was only 5 per cent in the Tarn, 3 per cent in Aveyron, 1 per cent in the Ardèche, and zero in Lozère, a sign of vigorous local recruitment. But these were areas where resistance to dechchristianisation had been strongest; where the opposite was the case, recruitment levels were feeble.[8]

The age-profile of priests had climbed considerably as a consequence of revolutionary upheaval: in 1814, 42 per cent of active priests were sixty or over and, partly deterred by the small salaries on offer, younger men were not coming forward in sufficent numbers to make good the shortfall. Nor was it just a question of money. The lower clergy had received minimal consultative rights, their subordinate status had been confirmed by the Napoleonic settlement and it would not be reversed. Even so, there were about 6000 ordinations in France between 1802 and 1814, roughly the number ordained in one year in the late *ancien régime*.[9] It was a start, one that represented no small achievement for the newly reopened seminaries. The situation slightly improved after the Bourbon Restoration of 1814–15, but the diminished priestly presence became a feature of nineteenth-century

Catholic parish life and the network of pastoral care that existed before the 1790s would never be restored, especially in urban parishes.[10] And these new ordinands tended to have more lowly social origins than their eighteenth-century predecessors, to be predominantly rural in their backgrounds, and to be poorer.

For Protestants, the problem was not dissimilar. Their right to worship freely was not in question. Toleration was guaranteed to minorities in France by the Revolution, and not even the most conservative Bourbon, Charles X (1824–30), would dare to revoke that right. But Protestants had lost a lot of their most wealthy and influential lay supporters during the Revolution, and by no means all went back to the Reformed Church and active religious practice with the return of more settled times; where superintendent ministers found they were short of clergy in 1802–3, they reduced the number of parishes to minimise vacancies. The trend continued under the Restored monarchy after 1814–15.[11] Even though ministerial salaries were now paid by the state, Protestant structures were pared down to save money wherever possible. Generally, local consistories continued in existence, but there were no more synods or other mechanisms to bring ministers and laity officially together at a provincial level. Protestants also faced a ministerial recruiting crisis. Swiss pastors had to be brought into France to swell the ranks so long as the Empire lasted.

Those who discovered a vocation were sent out to meet their congregations with an education that compared very favourably with anything on offer to Catholic seminarians. A faculty of theology was opened for Protestants in their Nîmes heartland in 1813, but theological disputes undermined much of the work among the faithful, especially as they were superimposed upon political divisions. In the Midi, Protestant spirituality was rekindled by a pietistic fervour that came to be associated with royalist ardour and anti-Bonapartist sentiments; those who rejected this enthusiasm and opted for a cooler, more rational religion within the tradition associated with Rabaut de Saint-Étienne backed Napoleon during the Hundred Days of 1815. Those three months were marked in the Gard by the seizure of the most important administrative positions by Protestants, and many paid for it with their lives in the blood-letting that followed the second Restoration of the Bourbons. The echoes of the Calas affair were palpable. In the Gard, the resulting internal bitterness took many years to die down, a depressing sign of how hard it was for Protestant–Catholic relations to break out of the ancestral tradition of tribal antagonism that had characterised them at a popular level for two hundred and fifty years.

The Jews, particularly the Ashkenazim of eastern France, faced similar problems. The extent of assimilation brought about by the Revolution had been limited, and antisemitism remained an endemic characteristic of popular culture in areas with a strong Jewish presence on the streets. Emancipation had led to a weakening of Jewish structures as the wealthy social climbers assimilated further and faster, sometimes forgetting their roots in the process, one encouraged by Napoleon who prohibited usury and introduced a greater degree of supervising their commercial operations, as well as requiring Jewish landowners to cultivate their estates themselves and – most importantly – allowing them no exemption from military service.[12] It was harder for those who remained wedded to community life to support the indigent, and there was no let-up in legal disputes over collective debts.

The patterns of population and settlement were changing rapidly. German Jews headed to Paris, as did Portuguese and Comtadins. Some *départements* were well down on pre-1789 numbers. Thus there were only 631 Jews in the Vaucluse in 1831. Alsace, however, showed a steady increase. Out of a total number of 26 000 Alsatian Jews in 1814, more were to be found in Strasbourg (1286 in 1806 compared with 68 in 1784), and other emerging industrial centres like Colmar and Mulhouse. In Lorraine, Thionville and Nancy gained at the expense of Metz, where living conditions were poor. These Ashkenazi communities preserved their traditions the most successfully, but still found it hard to recruit rabbis, finding it necessary to engage ones of German origin. Improved educational opportunities in Talmudic learning were gradually set up in Metz and, after 1830, French-speaking rabbis once again appeared in some numbers.[13]

There were fewer Jews than Protestants. Napoleon was therefore under less pressure to include them under the religious umbrella provided by the Concordat, and the state did not take responsibility for paying the salaries of rabbis until the time of the July Monarchy in 1831. In other areas, the degree of official involvement rose slowly. In 1806 the newly formed Jewish consistories were placed under the supervision of the Ministry for Religious Affairs, and the following year saw the meeting of the *Grand Sanhédrin* of European rabbis and scholars,[14] in other words a controlling council for Jewish affairs that paid some respect to Hebrew tradition in a manner acceptable

to the modern Napoleonic Empire. The delegates expressed their dislike of mixed marriages (something the Emperor favoured), but were
otherwise keen on further civic integration. That was more feasible
for them during the first Empire than it subsequently became after
the Bourbons returned.

Jews may have wanted rabbis, Protestants ministers and Catholics
priests, but these shortages had not stopped believers from organising themselves for worship during the darkest days of the 1790s.
The Revolution had given the laity the confidence to assume a
prominence in the religious life that stayed with them throughout
the early nineteenth century. Religion had to a significant extent
in France been declericalised. In the Yonne, lay cults continued in
some parishes through to the 1820s, despite the best efforts of bishops
and prefects. Sometimes these were a response to the shortage of
priests after the Concordat, at other times they lasted because parishioners preferred their lay minister to the priest.[15] In religious
terms, the Revolution may have loosened for good the hold of the
Catholic Church in some areas, but it had not really created a 'new
man' and certainly not a 'new woman'. It was the old observances
they wanted, not the ones that reforming priests and dechristianising
Revolutionaries had attempted to foist on them. The vast majority of
these people, both Catholic and Protestant, regular and occasional
attenders at services, were, in the last analysis, attached to revealed
religion for its proven capacity to offer more comfort than any of the
alternatives on offer in a harsh world that the Revolution had made
no more endurable.

The hard, slow recovery of the 1800s seemed to bear out the
gloomier voices, like the writer in the *Courrier de Londres* who in 1801
wondered bleakly about 'the religious state of communes which for
ten years have not had the Gospel preached, or seen any first communions . . . in a word, communes without both the scriptures and the
sacraments.' He complained about what would become a commonplace as the century wore on, of country folk 'who came to church
every Sunday, sang in the choir morning and evening, but never
come near the confessional'.[16] The loss of the confessional habit had
its roots in pre-1789 religious practice.[17] It became more pronounced
during the Consulate and Empire, and was both symptom and product of the relentless spread of birth control, and the consequent
rapid fall in the birth rate during the Revolution.[18] Regular confession acted as a litmus test that separated practising Catholics who

wanted to communicate regularly from those who just wanted their services and buildings back. Sacramental indifference was highlighted by continuing falls in the total number of Easter communicants, a further confirmation that the Revolution had devalued the authority of the priest from its pre-1789 standing.

That was particularly the case for nominal male Catholics. During the First Empire the majority of men were conscripted into the army at one time or another, shouldering arms in this most militant of anti-Christian organisations which never appointed field chaplains: the soldiers of the *Grande Armée* died in their tens of thousands on distant battlefields without any priestly ministrations, whether they wanted them or not. Most did not return to regular worship after the wars were over and Napoleon was consigned to exile on St Helena. Differences in religious practice according to sex soon became very apparent. Reports from the Limousin from the early nineteenth century that the once universal Easter duty had become predominantly a female observance can be paralleled from many other areas of France.[19] Most households were expected to attend Mass as a body down to the July Revolution of 1830, but well before then men were staying away or going to the alehouse. For millions of men, tavern sociability became an acceptable alternative to religious ritual, and the republican connotations of the tavern as the meeting place of the popular societies during the 1790s persisted.[20] This trend lay behind the figures furnished by the prefect of the Seine-Inférieure for his *département*: a paltry 2 per cent of males in Rouen took the sacrament as opposed to 90 per cent of women in the more rural pays de Caux.[21]

Of course, local variations abounded. Some men were just more selective about their church attendance, but there remain undeniable tokens of male disaffection for the Church. The men limited their presence to ceremonies that marked the major rites of passage or the cycle of the year, thus intensifying a trend already apparent in some areas during the later eighteenth century.[22] Where men did stay loyal to Church they often expressed their faith through membership of confraternities, some of which had displayed a remarkable capacity for adaptation and survival throughout the Revolution – not just the Aa but also the Company of the Holy Sacrament, with laymen rapidly adapting to the displacement of a clerical presence. After *c*.1802, the confraternities re-emerged into society and recruited heavily among the faithful. Compared with the late eighteenth century, they were far less particular about social origins. Down through eastern France, from the Vosges to Provence, from *c.* 1800 the parish church would become the centre of confraternal practice rather than their own chapel and the assembly of their lay members.

The confraternal revival was nevertheless patchy and conditional where it existed at all. Penitent fraternities, for instance, helped revive devotional observances, but not always to the satisfaction of the clergy.[23] Napoleon, ever anxious that confraternities might elude imperial controls, abolished most of them in the last years of his reign, retaining only a few open to all and under the explicit control of the *curé*. Private associations were banned at the same time, and their chapels and chattels were distributed among the parishes. *Curé* and bishop were now beyond doubt the equivalents of the mayor and the prefect, whether they liked it or not. The fact that most resented this equivalence played its part in causing the collapse of Church–State relations between *c.* 1810–14, and the introduction of a new Concordat.

Catholicism was predominantly driven back into the home more than ever in the period 1800–30, with women as its primary supporters. Napoleon's decision to return female education to the religious orders was decisive in keeping women in Church.[24] To coincide with the full reappearance of Catholic worship, new congregations sprang up (like the Presentation of Mary at Thueyts in the Vivarais, founded by Marie Piver), which were dedicated to instructing the young.[25] Their influence on the girls they taught lasted a lifetime, and it was a faith based on the rosary and Marian religiosity. The Blessed Virgin came to dominate popular devotion, and the clergy were happy to go along with the trend if it curtailed the cult of dubious local saints. Pilgrimages, as we have seen, had continued throughout the Revolution and had a new lease of life from the first years of the new century. The Church tried to control them, guarding against superstitious observances through liturgical inventiveness, sacramental emphasis and devotional exercises. The syncretic political and cultural associations of pilgrimages were as noticeable as ever, as exampled by the resumption of the cult of Notre-Dame-de-la-Garde at Marseille in 1807. Yet the elements of revival and triumphalism were hard to separate. The cult drew on a medley of Provençal folklore, the pre-revolutionary traditions of the penitential confraternities and manifestations of support for the Bourbon monarchy.

There, as at other Marian shrines, there were signs of a rekindled popular fervour in the form of alleged miracles, regular gifts of crucifixes,
and other *ex-voto* offerings.[26] It was clear that, in the early 1800s, lay
Catholics, for the most part, wanted a traditional, localised religiosity. Priests had to accept these popular religious tendencies after the
Revolution more than they would have wished as the price of having
their influence accepted at all. Catholicism, as preached in the nineteenth century in rural France had to exist alongside complementary
expressions of popular belief, a religion which 'brought health and
even wealth; a religion which could transform life, alleviate its suffering and monotony, and whose marvellous powers were not confined to
the next world but counted in the present one also'.[27]

The religious solidarity that pilgrimages generated could not disguise the fact that there was no return to the quasi-universal religious
practice of the *ancien régime*. As Timothy Tackett has argued, there
are strong continuities between patterns of response to the oath of
1790 and the religious geography of France ever since that date.
Practice remained solid on the peripheries – in Alsace and Lorraine
to the east, and in western France, above all Brittany. Parts of the
Massif Central, too, never wavered in their commitment to Catholicism. But in areas where response to the Civil Constitution had been
favourable, like south-eastern France, the Limousin, parts of the
Loire valley and the Orléannais, there would at best be a lukewarm
return to Catholic practices after the Concordat.[28]

Town–country divisions counted as much as they had always done.
Early-nineteenth-century religious revival was limited to rural areas,
with only towns in the west re-embracing the faith to any significant
degree. Municipalities tended to remain centres of anticlericalism as
well as republicanism. To an appreciable extent, Catholicism became
primarily a rural phenomenon, staffed by priests from the countryside.[29] As always, the variants within a small geographical zone
could be pronounced and the supposedly unanimous rural Christianity of *c*. 1815 rarely corresponds to the reality, as research on the
Tarbes, Metz and Strasbourg dioceses has indicated.[30] Henceforth,
there would be two Frances, divided by terrible memories. This was
to be nowhere more so than in the west, where Vendéan and *Chouan*
resistance left an indelible print on the character of Catholicism. Religion became the ideological enemy of any and every manifestation
of republicanism in a more intensive form than anywhere else in
France.[31] Memories of the suffering inflicted by fellow Frenchmen

in the name of national unity on those who simply wanted to worship their God in peace lingered on well into the twentieth century, to poison relations with republican régimes still working against clerical influence in the State.

Napoleon never ceased to be aware of the way in which Catholic fervour could intensify discontent with his regime but, with the clergy signed up to the Concordat and himself possessed of unequalled military resources, he was willing to risk upsetting his Catholic subjects by his insensitive treatment of the papacy and the clergy living in countries subject to French occupation. He expected obedience from everyone in a position of Church authority, and this was the impetus for extending and enforcing the Concordat with disruptive effect into Italy and Germany beyond the Rhineland after 1804.[32] It was made very clear to Pius that Napoleon expected the papacy to sanction and recommend the French imperial reordering of Europe rather than adopting the Emperor's preferred position of neutrality. Despite the growth of Napoleonic power in Italy, the symbolically important resignation of Francis II as Holy Roman Emperor in 1806, and the pleas of the French hierarchy, Pius would not make this humiliating accommodation with the French Emperor.[33] In 1809 Napoleon annexed the Papal States, and provoked papal excommunication. Pius was then forcibly abducted from Rome and removed to Savona, where he remained for the next three years. Nothing could more dramatically demonstrate the extent to which the Concordat had not worked.

This was, on the surface, a far cry from Napoleon's earlier exercise in consultation with Rome to end schism, which produced the 1801 Concordat. Yet even in that process, the pressure on Pius VII had come close to intimidation and the Franco-papal crisis of 1809 merely put that defining aspect of the relationship on open show. It had, as its counterpart, a deepening rift between Church and State in France, with officials who wanted more power over the clergy and priests who felt that the regime was essentially inimical to the interests of the faith. Napoleon was, predictably, more sympathetic to the complaints of officials. The 1801 Concordat had not provided a lasting solution to Church–State relations. A new, hardline replacement was being drawn up in the late 1800s, and was being pushed on the dioceses by the Ministry for Religious Affairs from 1810.

The issue was then further complicated by the Emperor's desire for papal recognition of his divorce from Josephine and remarriage to

Marie-Louise of Austria. Weary of the problem, and after years of progressive deterioration in Franco-papal relations, Napoleon at last told Pius VII in late 1812 that he considered the Concordat void, and his Ministry for Religious Affairs unveiled a new one – the Concordat of Fontainbleau (where the Pope was imprisoned between 1812 and 1814). In January 1813 Pius was compelled to sign this new Concordat on distinctly unfavourable terms. Here was Napoleon casting himself as a much more extreme version of Louis XIV in the 1680s, but running into the same problems as the Sun King over the Pope's canonical authority. Unlike Louis, Napoleon had the chance to browbeat the Pope at first hand into 'accepting' this unilateral Concordat. Negotiation was not a possibility. It was a radical, anticlerical, even Voltairean document. In Michael Broers's words, 'It was an assault on the traditional character of Catholic belief and the role of the Church in society of at least the same magnitude as the Civil Constitution of the Clergy.'[34] Fortunately, as far as the clergy were concerned, implementation was limited. There were sporadic efforts to apply it from 1810–11. However, France's military situation was weakening, and with the abdication of the Emperor in April 1814 the new Concordat was rendered a dead letter.[35]

Despite his sufferings, the Pope gained in power and prestige from the Revolution. With nineteenth-century regimes that were frequently hostile or indifferent to the Roman Catholic Church, the faithful had to look beyond France for protection in a manner that was unnecessary when throne and altar were allies. Pius VII was widely admired for his courage in standing up to Napoleon, and it generated popular ultramontanist sentiment beyond anything previously experienced. The Gallican tradition may have lingered, but it was much more the preserve of the episcopate than of the parish clergy. The papacy was deemed an essential bastion of order after the Congress of Vienna had restored a legitimate, monarchist order to Europe in 1814–15. The ringing, prophetic proclamation of Joseph de Maistre's *Du Pape* of 1817 that the Pope was the centre of unity of all local churches found many echoes in France, where the Concordat was renegotiated in 1817.

The Napoleonic ruptures with the Church assisted the politicisation of Catholicism, which the Restoration encouraged still further. It was a time of Indian summer for the Catholic Church in France as, for the last time, it received unconditional endorsement for its work from the regime. Not surprisingly, the bishops became upholders of the monarchical order and the sumptuous coronation of Charles X at Reims in 1825 testified to the resurgence of clericalist authority. They found their work fostered by the government far more than during the Empire. The Concordatory system of having only one parish per canton (about 3000 in total) was abandoned, much to the pleasure of most Catholics, and the creation of new dioceses from 1822 onwards also helped. Ordinations doubled from 1185 in 1816 to 2357 in 1830.[36] The parish clergy recovered much of their power in the village schools, there were fresh laws on sacrilege, and the Jesuits (restored with the monarchy in 1814) undertook new missions.[37] Missionary work in the parishes had been possible between 1804 and 1809, where manpower resources permitted it, but it was not something the Napoleonic regime liked and was not approved unless undertaken by local clergy.

It was only after 1814 that serious work of this kind went forward in the towns under the sympathetic eye of the restored Bourbon monarchy and helped by the Jesuits and the female religious orders. Though divorce remained a civil matter, and Church lands were not to be returned, the clergy's aspirations to restoring France and themselves to an imagined pre-1789 order of things were for a time unbounded. It was an unrealistic dream; the laity were beyond their control, and society could not be rechristianised on the scale they envisaged. Moreover, another French Revolution in 1830 rudely disabused the Church of its pretensions to power in the State. It confirmed both the influence of anticlericalism as an abiding force in French politics, and the commitment of the Church hierarchy to right-wing politics, usually in a monarchical form. For most of the period down to the Great War, Church and state were rival forces in French society, whose uneasy coexistence often broke down into open hostilities.

However, the 1830 Revolution could no more quench the power of Christianity and Judaism in France than 1789 had done. A frenzied pace of political and social upheaval redoubled the appeal of religion rather than dampened it. Faith endured. Organised religion might struggle to maintain its structures, but lay men and women went on making Christian observances that their ancestors would have recognised. The mission priests of the eighteenth century had done their work well: they had intensified the religious life of countless numbers, especially women. The experience of Revolution confirmed that the existence of feminine support for the Church on a scale that would ensure the survival of Catholicism in France, though not necessarily on the clergy's preferred terms. If politicians offered women no scope for life outside the home, the early-nineteenth-century Church depended on their participation and could not fail to admit their influence.

Religion remained a consoling force for the rigours and calamities of ordinary life much as it has always done. It had helped thousands deal with unexpected, often unprovoked and violent death in the 1790s; after 1804 it was there for a new generation to sample whose parents had preferred the more amorphous spirituality of Rousseau. A religion resting on the irrational was attractive for many repentant supporters of Revolution, and for younger people like Chateaubriand, wanting to bring about a reconciliation between the modern world and the faith, and help prevent future revolutionary upheavals. His *Génie du christianisme* of 1802 is often interpreted as a rejection of the rationalist spirit of the Enlightenment, a sign that the monied and the blue-blooded saw the link between irreligion and Revolution clearly enough, especially after the Restoration. It is certainly a milestone in the rediscovery of religiosity by the more imaginative members of the elite; it was far from the only book to show a haunted appreciation of mysticism and medievalism in a way that thousands of readers found compelling, and was altogether more serious than the Gothic escapism of earlier texts.

Yet the *Génie* was not an identifiably counter-revolutionary text: it had a strongly aesthetic dimension as its subtitle – *The Moral and Poetic Beauties of the Christian Religion made Plain*. Its fascination with the individual's sentimentalised self-awareness would have resonated to an audience familiar with Rousseau; it expressed its author's belief that most Frenchmen would welcome a Napoleonic regime founded on the unlikely combination of sentiment and *étatisme* (Chateaubriand was appointed by the First Consul secretary to to the French Embassy in Rome in 1803). All these factors took it out of that genre.[38] That it romanticised Catholicism was, in an important sense, incidental to its purpose.

Measuring the extent of religious commitment and the practice of personal piety at any social level is fraught with difficulty, but the balance of the evidence suggests that talk of the 'dechristianisation' of French notables or the 'secularisation' of society is misleading. There were too many spectacular conversions of former *philosophes* like La Harpe and Joubert in the 1790s for that to be so. The Churches

and royalty became a rallying point for those who had, when youthful, flirted with Revolution and lived to regret the experience. It was
not exclusively a Christian reaction. The lapsed Bordelais Jew, Abra-
ham Furtado, (whom rabbinical gossip accused of having learnt
about the Bible from Voltaire) had been a Girondin during the
early Republic, but by 1815 was receiving the *Légion d'Honneur* from
the Duc d'Angoulême, and was confirmed as Mayor of Bordeaux by
the King.

Yet inside the elites, for every Joseph de Maistre arguing in *Consid-
érations sur la France* (1797) that the evil of the Revolution can only be
undone by returning to the traditional wisdom proclaimed by the
Church or the monarchy, or Louis de Bonald (in his *Théorie du pouvoir
politique et religion dans la société civile* of 1793),[39] insisting that the principles of Catholicism must be the base of social structures, there was a
clear majority living at a remove from the Church's influence. There
was also a continuing taste among middle-class readers for popular
fictions with anticlerical themes as an essential part of their enjoyment. It reflected the sense in which the doubts of the *philosophes*
about revelation, originally confined to the salons and polite society,
had put down deep roots, and become common intellectual property.

Like or loathe them, from whatever perspective they were viewed,
the bishops and clergy, ministers and rabbis were fixtures in French
society. The relationship Christianity and Judaism enjoyed with the
state had undergone massive alteration during the Revolution, but it
had survived even Napoleon. Indeed, he had acknowledged its force
early in his regime, but wanted it based on his terms, just like the
revolutionary governments before him in the 1790s. Those terms, in
effect, insisted that religious loyalties must be subordinated to the
good of the nation state, whether embodied in empire or republic.
And if churchmen could not always accept this imperative, the
experience of the Revolution made very plain that large sections of
the laity would not do so. The 1790s had made lay men and women
vital to the survival of organised religion: the ordained ministry
might have shrunk or disappeared completely, but Christian worship
went on (often at great personal risk) in gatherings that found comfort and relief in staging these rituals notwithstanding the absence
of priest or minister. Women, in particular, took the lead in preserving the Christian faith, taking advantage of republican uncertainty about how to deter or punish them, unwilling to respect
either chauvinist, atheist officials or priests who wanted them to

resume a passive, subordinate position in their communities. This assertion of their religious rights by women across France (by no means all of whom could be adjudged dedicated counter-revolutionaries) gave their sex its greatest opportunity to affect the course of the Revolution. What Timothy Tackett has said about the oath demanded by the National Assembly to the Civil Constitution really has a much wider application to the whole period:

> In the end, it was perhaps the humble women of provincial and rural France, protesting with their whole beings [at] this 'change in religion' thrust upon them by the men in Paris, who delivered the single most influential political statement by any women of the revolutionary decade.[40]

Whether in attending church, taking up a religious vocation or simply insisting on their preferences in worship, women would make a key contribution to early-nineteenth-century French Catholicism.

But this should not be exaggerated.[41] Simply because models of male lay piety for the period *c.* 1775–1840 have been insufficiently studied does not entitle historians to claim that religion no longer held much attraction for men. To accept that proposition is to rely too uncritically on the predictable commonplaces of generation after generation of republican anticlericals whose views became establishment orthodoxy in Third Republic France. In fact, Christian and Jewish belief would act as a key element in the political philosophies of most non-radical republican groups for many decades after 1815. For Catholics, as indeed for Protestants and Jews, religion had an appeal that transcended the gender divide well into the nineteenth century, and comfortably rivalled that of revolution.

Notes

Chapter 1.   The Gallican Church – Structures and Personnel

1. Quoted in Christian Taillard, 'Bible et architecture en France', in Yvon Belaval and Dominique Bourel (eds), *Le Siècle des Lumières et la Bible* (Paris, 1986), 365–96, at 386.
2. Wolfgang Herrmann, *Laugier and Eighteenth Century French Theory* (London, 1985), 102–30; Philippe Loupès, *La Vie religieuse en France au XVIIIe siècle* (Paris, 1993), 25; William Weber, 'Learned and General Musical Taste in Eighteenth-Century France', *Past and Present*, 89 (1980), 58–85.
3. Devon Record Office, Buller MS, 2065M/C1/1, Diary of James Buller, 24 Apr. 1788.
4. Philip Conisbee, *Painting in Eighteenth Century France* (London, 1981); R. Wrigley, *The Origins of French Art Criticism: From the Ancien Régime to the Restoration* (Oxford, 1993).
5. J.R. Mongrédien, *Jean-François Le Sueur, contribution à l'étude d'un demi-siècle de musique française (1780–1830)* (Berne, 1980), 52–9, 121–56; *Le Grand Motet français (1663–1792)* (Paris, 1986); C. Pierre, *Histoire du Concert Spirituel, 1725–1790* (Paris, 1975); Weber, 'Learned and General Music Taste', 58–85.
6. Olwen Hufton, *Bayeux in the Late Eighteenth Century. A Social Study* (Oxford, 1967), 5.
7. C. Langlois and T. Tackett, 'L'Épreuve de la Révolution', in François Lebrun (ed.), *Histoire des Catholiques en France du XVe siècle à nos jours* (Toulouse, 1980), 216; cf. J. Dupâquier (ed.), *Histoire de la population française* (2 vols, Paris, 1988), II, 70–71.
8. The different streams in Gallicanism are discussed in E. Laboulaye, 'Les Libertés de l'église gallicane', *Revue Historique de Droit Français et Etranger*, 4 (1858), 477–500; F.J. Moulart, *L'Église et l'etat ou les deux puissances* (2nd edn, Louvain, 1879), 32–8; A-G. Martimort, *Le Gallicanisme* (Paris, 1973).
9. Quoted in Philip Mansel, *The Court of France 1789–1830* (Cambridge, 1988), 36.
10. Dale K. Van Kley, *The Damiens Affair and the Unraveling of the Ancien Régime, 1750–1770* (Princeton, NJ, 1984); Jeffrey W. Merrick, *The Desacralization of the French Monarchy in the Eighteenth Century* (Baton Rouge, LA, 1990).
11. Cf. Lynn Hunt, *The Family Romance of the French Revolution* (Berkeley, CA, 1992), 49–52.
12. M. Péronnet, 'Police et religion à la fin du XVIIIe siècle', *Annales historiques de la Révolution Française* [hereafter *A.H.R.F.*], 42 (1970), 375–97, at 397.
13. M. Valensise, 'Le Sacre du roi: stratégie symbolique et doctrine politique de la monarchie française', *Annales: economies, sociétés, civilisations* [hereafter *Annales E.S.C.*], 41 (1986), 543–77; John McManners, 'Authority in Church and State. Reflections on the Coronation of Louis XVI', in *Christian Authority. Essays in Honour of Henry Chadwick* (Oxford, 1988); Hermann Weber, 'Das Sacre Ludwigs XVI vom Juni 1775 und die Krise des Anciens Régime', in Ernst Hinrichs, Eberhard Schmitt and Rudolf Vierhaus (eds), *Vom Ancien Régime zur Französischen Revolution: Forschungen und Perspektiven* (Göttingen, 1978), 539–69.

14. Charles Robert, *Urban de Hercé, dernier évêque de Dol* (Paris, 1900), 162–3, 183; A. Lods, 'L'Attitude du clergé catholique à l'égard des Protestants en 1789', *La Révolution française*, 33 (1897), 128–30.

15. See his *The Jansenists and the Expulsion of the Jesuits from France: 1757–1765* (New Haven, CT/London, 1975), and, most recently, *The Religious Origins of the French Revolution. From Calvin to the Civil Constitution, 1560–1791* (New Haven, CT, 1996). His studies should now be set against the authoritative summary of Cathérine Maire, *De la Cause de Dieu à la Cause de la Nation. Le jansénisme au XVIIIe siècle* (Paris, 1998). This replaces E. Préclin, *Les Jansénistes du XVIIIe siècle et la Constitution civile du Clergé* (Paris, 1928). See also Cathérine Maire, 'Minorités religieuses. Port-Royal', in Pierre Nora (ed.), *Les Lieux de Mémoire*, pt 3, *La France* (vol. 1, *Conflit et Partages*, Paris, 1992), 470–529, at 504–5. For midcentury politics and Jansenism, see J. Swann, *Politics and the Parlement of Paris under Louis XV, 1754–1774* (Cambridge, 1995), esp. 98–100.

16. Discussed in Van Kley, *The Damiens Affair*. The link between Jansenist political ideology and constitutionalism is problematic. See Cathérine Maire, 'L'Église et la nation. Du dépôt de la vérité au dépôt des lois: la trajectoire janséniste au XVIIIe siècle', *Annales E.S.C.*, 46 (1991), 1177–1205. For the pluralist nature of late Jansenism see William H. Williams, 'The Significance of Jansenism in the History of the French Catholic Clergy in the Pre-Revolutionary Era', *Studies in XVIIIth century Culture*, Roseann Puntz (ed.), vol. 7 (Wisconsin, 1978), 289–306, at 291. Historians have tended to exaggerate the unity of the so-called *parti janséniste*, as Julian Swann perceptively notes in *Politics and the Parlement of Paris*, 100–1.

17. Dale K. Van Kley, 'The Estates General as Ecumenical Council: The Constitutionalism of Corporate Consensus and the *Parlement*'s Ruling of September 25, 1788', *Journal of Modern History* [hereafter *J.M.H.*], 61 (1989), 1–52; 'The Religious Origins of the Patriot and Ministerial Parties in Pre-Revolutionary France', in Thomas Kselman (ed.), *Belief in History: Innovative Approaches to European and American Religion* (Indianapolis, 1991), 237–66, esp. 185–6; Bailey Stone, *The Genesis of the French Revolution: A Global Historical Interpretation* (Cambridge, 1994), 82–3; Peter R. Campbell, *Power and Politics in Old Régime France, 1720–1745* (London, 1996), 218–19.

18. D. Julia, 'Les Deux Puissances, chronique d'une séparation de corps', in Baker, *The Political Culture*, 293–310; Van Kley, *The Religious Origins*, 222.

19. G. Lefebvre, *Les Paysans du Nord pendant la Révolution française* (Paris, 1972).

20. Harangue faite au Roy, 29 Mai 1785, Archives Nationales [hereafter A.N.] G8 704, p. 51.

21. This involved a claim by ministers that Church lands were not allodial, and were therefore held directly from the Crown, whose feudal superiority should be admitted. See A.N. G8* 791c, *Rapport de l'Agence, contenant les Principales Affaires du clergé, depuis 1780 jusqu'en 1785* (Paris, 1788), 61–74.

22. Charles C. Noel, 'Charles III of Spain', in H.M. Scott (ed.), *Enlightened Absolutism. Reform and Reformers in Later Eighteenth-Century Europe* (Basingstoke, 1990), 131–2; M.S. Anderson, 'The Italian Reformers', in ibid., 58–60; Charles Ingrao, 'The Smaller German States', in ibid., 240–1.

23. Quoted in Raymond Darricau, 'Les Préoccupations pastorales des Assemblées du Clergé de France à la veille de la Révolution (1775–1789)' [*Actes du Colloque de Sorèze, 1976: Le Règne de Louis XVI et la Guerre d'Indépendance américaine*, Sorèze, 1977], 249–97, at 250.

24. L.S. Greenbaum, *Talleyrand, Statesman Priest: The Agent General of the Clergy of the Church of France and the end of the Old Régime* (Washington, DC, 1970), and 'Talleyrand and the Temporal Problems of the French Church, 1780–85', *French Historical Studies* [hereafter *F.H.S.*] (1963), 41–71 have full details of Talleyrand's

skilful defence of the Church's fiscal privileges and immunities against government encroachment see also E. Besnier, *Les Agents généraux du Clergé spécialement de 1780 à 1785* (Paris, 1939).

25. Langlois and Tackett, 'L'Épreuve de la Révolution', 222.

26. Stone, *The Genesis of the French Revolution*, 85–99.

27. For instance, the links between Bishop Bareau de Girac of Rennes and the ministry of Calonne are fascinatingly presented in Munro Price, *Preserving the Monarchy. The Comte de Vergennes, 1774–1787* (Cambridge, 1995), 139ff.

28. Greenbaum, *Talleyrand*, 11.

29. For Austria and the Netherlands see the essays in W.J. Callahan and D. Higgs (eds), *Church and Society in Catholic Europe of the Eighteenth Century* (Cambridge, 1979). For England see Geoffrey Holmes, *Augustan England: Professions, State and Society, 1680–1830* (London, 1982); Norman Ravitch, *Sword and Mitre: Government and Épiscopate in France and England in the Age of Aristocracy* (The Hague/Paris, 1966).

30. Ravitch, *ibid.*; Joseph Bergin, *Cardinal de la Rochefoucauld* (Yale, 1987); *The Making of the French Episcopate, 1589–1661* (Yale, 1996); M. Péronnet, *Les Evêques de l'ancienne France* (2 vols, Lille/Paris, 1977).

31. Jean-Pierre Brancourt, 'Les Evêques de Louis XVI et la défense de la foi', [*Actes du Colloque de Sorèze, 1976*], 228–48.

32. Bernard Plongeron, *La Vie quotidienne du clergé français au 18e siècle* (Paris, 1974), 61–5. The experience of one future bishop and contemporary of Talleyrand's at Saint-Sulpice is helpfully followed in Bernard de Braye, *Un Evêque d'Ancien Régime à l'épreuve de la Révolution. Le Cardinal A.L.H. de la Fare (1752–1829)* (Paris, 1985), 42–50.

33. Nigel Aston, 'The Abbé Sieyes before 1789: The Progress of a Clerical Careerist', *Journal of Renaissance & Modern Studies*, 33 (1989), 41–52.

34. For non-noble appointments to the sees of Vienne and Boulogne in 1789–90, see Nigel Aston, *The End of an Elite. The French Bishops and the Coming of the Revolution 1786–1790* (Oxford, 1992), 220–1.

35. Dominique Julia and Jacques Revel (eds), *Les Universités européennes du XVI au XVIIIe siècle. Histoire sociale des populations étudiantes* (vol. 2, Paris, 1989), 203. The best general work on the seminaries remains A. Degert, *Histoire des séminaires français jusqu'à la Révolution* (2 vols, Paris, 1912).

36. M. Carré, *Parallele du gouvernement civil et du gouvernement Ecclésiastique* (Paris, 1789), 8. British Library [hereafter B.L.] F.1102 (2).

37. Daniel Ligou, *Montauban à la fin de l'ancien régime et aux débuts de la Révolution, 1787–1794* (Paris, 1958), 55; Abbé Entraygues, *Mgr de Royère, évêque de Tréguier, dernier évêque de Castres, 1727–1802* (Paris, 1912), 146–7.

38. Abbé Boz, *Histoire de l'Eglise d'Apt* (Apt, 1820), 391, 392.

39. L. Lévy-Schneider, *L'Application du Concordat par un prélat d'Ancien Régime: Mgr Champion de Cicé Archêveque d'Aix et d'Arles* (Paris, 1921),13; Compte de Montbrison (ed.), *Mémoires de la Baronne d'Oberkirch* (2 vols, Paris, 1853), contains abundant information on Cardinal Rohan.

40. J-M. Trichaud, *Histoire de la Sainte Eglise d'Arles* (4 vols, Paris, 1859–64), IV, 258.

41. Quoted in Abbé Durengues, *Pouillé historique du diocèse d'Agen pour l'année 1789* (Agen, 1894), 87n.

42. When famine devastated the Limousin in 1770 he helped Turgot to establish *bureaux de charité*. R. Lamothe-Limouzin, *Le diocèse de Limoges du XVIe siècle à nos jours* (Paris, 1953), 72.

43. Their numbers tended to increase. Champion de Cicé, Archbishop of Bordeaux in the 1780s, had twelve, by no means all of whom resided. E. Allain, *Organisation administrative et financière du diocèse de Bordeaux avant la Révolution* (Paris, 1894), 15.

44. As one critic put it: 'Their arrogance is not only ridiculous, which one can happily mock, but it is also unsupportable for all those under their cane.' *Essai sur la Reforme du Clergé, par un vicaire de campagne, Docteur de Sorbonne* (Paris, 1789), 131.

45. See Ch. Bertelot du Chesnay, 'Le Clergé diocésain français au XVIIIe siècle et les registres d'insinuations ecclésiastiques', *Revue d'histoire moderne et contemporain* [hereafter *R.H.M.C.*] 10 (1963), 241–69.

46. Timothy Tackett, *Priest and People in 18th Century France: A Social and Political Study of the Curés in a Diocese of Dauphiné* (Princeton, NJ, 1977); Michel Bernard, 'Revendications et aspirations du bas clergé dauphinois à la veille de la Révolution', *Cahiers d'Histoire* 1 (1956), 327–47.

47. A. Nicolaï, *Essai statistique sur la Population à Bordeaux au 18e siècle (1700–1800)* (Paris/Bordeaux, 1909), 12.

48. Quoted in Alan Forrest, *The Revolution in Provincial France. Acquitaine, 1789–1799* (Oxford, 1996), 154.

49. Plongeron, *La Vie quotidienne du clergé*, 121–4; Philippe Loupès, *Chapitres et chanoines de Guyenne aux XVIIe et XVIIIe siècles* (Paris, 1985).

50. eds. Gabriel Le Bras and Jean Gaudemet (eds), *Le Monde des Religieux. L'Époque moderne 1563–1789* (Paris, 1976) [Histoire du Droit et des Institutions de l'Eglise en Occident], 394, summarises the *Commission des reguliers's ad hoc* successors 1780–90.

51. See P. Chevallier, *Loménie de Brienne et l'ordre monastique, 1766–1789* (2 vols, Paris, 1959). 458 establishments shut but they had only 509 members between them!

52. Patrice Cousin, *Précis d'histoire monastique* (Louvain, 1956), 453–4.

53. Loupès, *La Vie religieuse*, 160.

54. B. Longeron, *Les Reguliers de Paris devant le serment constitutionnel. Sens et conséquences d'une option, 1789–1801* (Paris, 1964), 69. Cf. eds. Le Bras and Gaudemet, *Le Monde des Religieux*, 410–12.

55. Yves Chaussy, *Les Bénédictines de Saint-Maur. Aperçu Historique* (Paris, 1989); René Taton (ed.), *Enseignement et diffusion des sciences en France au XVIIIe siècle* (Histoire de la Pensé, XI) (Paris, 1964), 103–23; Cousin, *Précis d'histoire monastique*, 451.

56. Ibid., 480. Cajot's book was *Recherches historiques sur l'esprit primitif et les collèges dans l'ordre de saint Benoît* (2 vols, Paris, 1787).

57. David Garrioch, *Neighbourhood and community in Paris, 1740–1790* (Paris, 1986), 158.

58. Quoted in Jean Dumont, *La Révolution française ou les prodiges du sacrilége* (Paris, 1984), 26.

59. B.L. Add. MS. 26716, 'Établissement d'un Corps de Chanoinenesses en France'; Malcolm Cook, *Toulon in war and revolution. From the ancien régime to the Restoration, 1750–1820* (Manchester, 1991), 71.

60. John McManners, *Death and the Enlightenment. Changing attitudes to death in eighteenth-century France* (Oxford, 1985 edn), 30–1; Colin Jones, *The Charitable Imperative. Hospitals and Nursing in Ancien Régime and Revolutionary France* (London, 1989), 122–205.

61. For the female Religious orders Olwen Hufton, *The Prospect Before Her. A History of Women in Western Europe, I. 1500–1800* (London, 1995), 382–96, is the best starting point. See also O. Hufton and F. Tallett, 'Communities of Women, the Religious Life, and Public Service in Eighteenth-Century France', in M.J. Boxer and J.H. Quataert (eds), *Connecting Spheres: Women in the Western World, 1500 to the Present* (Oxford, 1987), 75–85; C. Jones, 'Sisters of Charity and the Ailing Poor', *Social History of Medicine*, 19 (1989), 339–48; M. de Chantal Gueudré, *Histoire de l'ordre des Ursulines en France* (2 vols, Paris, 1957–60); Geneviève Reynes, *Couvent de femmes. La vie des religieuses cloîtrées dans la France des XVIIe et XVIIIe siècles* (Paris, 1987); R. Devos, *Vie religieuse féminine et société. Les Visitandines d'Annecy aux XVIIe et XVIIIe siècles* (Annecy, 1973).

62 Elizabeth Rapley, 'The Shaping of Things to come: the Commission des Secours, 1727–1788', *French History* 8 (1994), 420–41; Le Bras and Gaudemet, *Le Monde des Religieux*, 374–7.

63. A.N. G9 158 (13), quoted in ibid., 435.

64. Van Kley has argued that her presence made Saint-Denis one of the main headquarters of the *parti dévot* in the Paris area, and helped underpin the religious dimension he finds in the Maupeou coup of 1771. *The Religious Origins of the French Revolution*, 278, 280.

65. This simplifies a complicated picture with numerous regional variations. See the breakdown in Lebrun, *Histoire des Catholiques en France*, 217.

66. See Robert Triger, *L'Année 1789 au Mans et dans le Haut–Maine* (Mamers, 1889), 11, for a discussion of the *vicaires* in the Maine region; Hufton, *Bayeux*, 32; Joseph Bergin, 'The Catholic parish clergy of early modern western Europe', in M.L. Bush (ed.), *Social Orders and Social Classes in Europe since 1500: Studies in Social Stratification* (London, 1992), 66–85, at 74–5.

67. For Voltaire, see William H. Williams, 'Voltaire and the utility of the Lower Clergy', *Studies on Voltaire and the Eighteenth Century*, 58 (1967), 1869–74. The classic work on the image of the *curés* is Pierre Sage, *Le Bon Prêtre dans la littérature française* (Geneva/Lille, 1951).

68. Letter of the *curé* Mollevant, 11 Feb. 1788, in Leicestershire Record Office, DG 39/1229 who noted 'libertine conduct has slid into the sanctuary'.

69. Quoted by Dominique Julia, in Jean Ehrard (ed.), *Le Collége de Riom et l'enseignement oratorien en France au XVIIIe siècle* (Paris/Oxford, 1993), 276. Laurence Brockliss, *French Higher Education in the Seventeenth and Eighteenth Centuries* (Oxford, 1987), 231–5; Plongeron, *La Vie quotidienne du Clergé*, 69–70; It was a model increasingly copied in other Catholic states. Bergin, 'The Catholic Parish Clergy', 84–5. Cf. T. Tackett, *Religion, Revolution and Regional Culture in Eighteenth-Century France: The Ecclesiastical Oath of 1791* (Princeton, 1986), 102–3.

70. Michel Mallévre in Nadine-Josette Chaline (ed.), *Histoire du diocèse de Rouen-Le Havre* (Paris, 1976), 180.

71. Jean Delumeau, *Un chemin d'histoire. Chrétieneté et christianisation* (Paris, 1981), 237; also 133.

72. Quoted in Daniel Roche, *The Culture of Clothing. Dress and fashion in the Ancien Régime*, trans. Jean Birrell (Cambridge, 1994), 202–3.

73. J-P. Fleury, *Mémoires sur la Révolution et le premier Empire* (Le Mans, 1874), 54.

74. Raymond Darricau, 'Les Préoccupations pastorales des Assemblées du Clergé de France à la veille de la Révolution (1775–1789)', [*Actes du Colloque de Sorèze, 1976*], 249–97, at 260–1 for archbishop Brienne's report on the subject at the General Assembly of 1775; Loupès, *La Vie religieuse*, 158–62.

75. Plongeron, *La Vie quotidienne du clergé*, 70.

76. See particularly T. Tackett, 'The Social History of the Diocesan Clergy in Eighteenth-Century France', in R.M. Golden (ed.), *Church, State and Society under the Bourbon Kings of France* (Lawrence, Kan., 1982), 327–79, esp. 333–6.

77. Pierre Pierrard, *Histoire des curés de campagne de 1789 à nos jours* (Paris, 1986), 13.

78. Philippe Loupès, *La Vie religieuse en France au XVIIIe siècle* (Paris, 1993), 78; Timothy Tackett, 'Le Clergé de l'archidiocèse d'Embrun à la fin de l'Ancien Régime', *Annales du Midi* 88 (1976), 177–97, at 182–4.

79. Louis Châtellier, *Tradition chrétienne et renouveau Catholique dans le cadre de l'ancien diocèse de Strasbourg (1650–1770)* (Paris, 1981). In Vannes, noble parish priest numbers fell by more than half between 1710 and 1780. T.J.A. Le Goff, *Vannes in the Eighteenth Century* (Oxford, 1981), 248–51.

80. Jean Quéniart, *Les Hommes, l'église et Dieu dans la France du XVIIIe siècle* (Paris, 1978), 78–80.

81. *Essai sur la Reforme du Clergé*, 21.
82. Ravitch, *Sword and Mitre*, 180. The best guides to benefice values are contemporary diocesan surveys. For a helpful modern edition of a survey of the diocese of Comminges in 1786 see Armand Sarramon (ed.), *Les paroisses du diocèse de Comminges en 1786* (Paris, 1968). Similar questionnaires were issued at Toulouse (1763), Rodez (1771), Bordeaux (1772), Reims (1772), Tarbes (1783). Plongeron, *La Vie quotidienne du clergé*, 106–7.
83. A. Deramecourt, *Le Clergé du diocèses d'Arras, de Boulogne et de Saint-Omer pendant la Révolution (1789–1802)* (4 vols, Arras, 1884), I, 317.
84. John McManners, 'Tithe in Eighteenth-Century France: A Focus for Rural Anticlericalism', in Derek Beales and Geoffrey Best (eds), *History, Society and the Churches. Essays in honour of Owen Chadwick* (Cambridge, 1985), 147–68, at 161–2.
85. Gilles Deregnaucourt, *De Fénelon à la Révolution. Le clergé paroissial de l'archevêché de Cambrai* (Lille, 1991), 42.
86. Quoted in Pierrard, *Histoire des curés de campagne*, 18.
87. Cf. J. Rives, *Dîme et société dans l'archevêché d'Auch au xviiie siècle* (Paris, 1976).
88. Quéniart, *Les Hommes, L'église et Dieu*, 23–4; P. Loupès, 'Le casuel dans le diocèse de Bordeaux au XVII et XVIIIe siècles', *Revue d'histoire de l'Eglise de France* (1972), 19–52; McManners, *Death and the Enlightenment*, 282.
89. A.N. G8 188, 'Mémoire sur les Congruistes du Diocèse de Poitiers, 1785'.
90. Quoted in Pierrard, *Histoire des Curés de campagne*, 20.
91. The different kinds of tithes and their owners are discussed in McManners, 'Tithe in eighteenth-century France', 148–9. See generally P. Gagnol, *La dîme écclésiastique au XVIIIe siècle* (Paris, 1910).
92. Pierrard, *Histoire des curés de campagne*, 19.
93. Abbé P. Tavernier, *Le diocèse du Puy pendant la Révolution (1789–1801)* (Le Puy, 1938), 11.
94. Plongeron, *La Vie quotidienne du clergé*, 43. Archbishops Dulau of Arles and Le Franc de Pompignan of Vienne wanted the king to sanction provincial councils. There were encouraging replies in 1775 and 1780, but no action. However, de Conzié convened one for the province of Tours in 1780. A.N. G8 701, f. 393; *Procés verbal de l'assemblée générale du clergé tenue à Paris en 1780* (Paris, 1782), pp. 35 ff.
95. François-Yves Besnard, *Souvenirs d'un nonagénaire*, Celestin Port (ed.) (2 vols, Paris, 1880), I, 568. In 1788 the well-meaning bishop summoned a Diocesan Synod so that he could present new statutes on clerical organisation and discipline, only to provoke open criticism. François Dornic (ed.), *Histoire du Mans* (Paris, 1975), 197; Abbé F. Pichon, *Vie de M. Marquis-Ducastel* (Le Mans, 1873), 163–4. Jouffroy de Gonsans's pastoral concern was unflagging in a diocese where confirmation had not taken place on a regular basis since 1740. ibid., 188. See also J-P. Fleury, *Mémoires sur la Révolution*, 14. Cf. the energetic diocesan tours of Duplessis d'Argentré, bishop of Limoges. L. Pérouas, 'L'activité pastorale des évêques de Limoges', *Bull. de la Soc. arch. et hist. du Limousin*, XCVIII (1971), 207–22, at 220–1.
96. Abel Poitrineau (ed.), *Le diocèse de Clermont* (Paris, 1979), 138. For Bonal's tendency to heavy-handedness, see R. Crégut, *Le diocèse de Clermont pendant la Révolution* (Clermont, 1914), 11.
97. Pierre Ordioni, *La survivance des idées gallicanes et jansénistes en Auxerrois de 1760 à nos jours* (Auxerre, 1933); D. Dinet, 'Une Déchristianisation provinciale au XVIIIe siècle: le diocèse d'Auxerre', *Histoire, Économie, Société*, 10 (1991), 476; Charles Monternot, *L'Église de Lyon pendant la Révolution: Yves-Alexandre de Marbeuf* (Lyon, 1911), 40, calculated that there were approximately 60 Jansenist curés in the Lyon diocese on Archbishop Montazet's death in 1787.

98. Marquis de Roux, *La Révolution à Poitiers et dans la Vienne* (Paris, 1914), 54.
99. A. Challe, *Histoire de l'Auxerrois* (Auxerre/Paris, 1878), 595.
100. Arlette Farge, *Subversive Words. Public Opinion in Eighteenth-Century France*, trans. Rosemary Morris (Oxford, 1994), 36–53; B. Plongeron, 'Les Nouvelles écclésiastiques', *Revue historique de l'église de France* (1977); 'Les Nouvelles écclésiastiques', *Mémoires de la Fédération des sociétés historiques et archéologiques de Paris et de Île de France*, 7 (1955); J. C. Havinga, *Les Nouvelles Écclésiastiques* (Paris, 1925).
101. Moulart, *L'Église et l'etat*, 28–30. In due course, the system named after him was often associated with Protestantism. J.J. Bonnaud wrote that 'richerism is only a system which combines the maxims of the [16th-century Catholic] Leaguers, the Calvinists, and the Jansenists'. *Découverte importante sur le vrai système de la constitution du clergé* (Paris, 1791), 11. The argument about the descent from the 12 and the 72 dates from Nicolas Le Gros, *Du Renversement des libertez de l'église gallicane, dans l'affaire de la constitution Unigenitus* (Paris, 1717). I am grateful to John McManners for clarification on this point.
102. Jacques Bernet, 'Les Serments à la Constitution civile du clergé en Picardie', in Alain Lottin (ed.), *Église, vie religieuse et révolution dans la France du Nord* (Lille, 1990), 25–39, at 34; Préclin, *Les Jansénistes du XVIIIe siècle*, 397; A.N. G8* 2533, fos. 21/22; G8 30, fos. 60–6.
103. The phrase actually appears in a subsequent publication of 1788.
104. *Essai sur la Reforme du Clergé*, 75.
105. Tackett, *Priest and People in 18th Century France*, 240–2; P.M. Jones, *Reform and Revolution in France. The Politics of Transition, 1774–1791* (Cambridge, 1995), 132–3; Bernard, 'Revendications et aspirations du bas clergé dauphinois', 336; Préclin, *Les Jansénistes du XVIIIe siècle*, 402.
106. Dominique Julia, 'Le Prêtre au 18e siècle', *Recherches de science religieuse*, 58 (1970), 521–34, at 533.
107. Robert Darnton, 'A Pamphleteer on the Run', in *The Literary Underground of the Old Regime* (Cambridge, MA, 1982), 72–121.
108. Alfred Leroux, *Étude critique sur le XVIIIe siècle à Bordeaux* (Bordeaux, 1921), 211n., 267.
109. Jean-Claude Meyer, 'Les Diverses tendances de l'Église reflétées en pays Toulousain à la veille de la Révolution', in Pierre Léon Féral (ed.), *La France Pré-Révolutionnaire* (Paris, 1991), 83–95, at 89–92.

Chapter 2.   Catholicism in Eighteenth-Century France Varieties of Practice and Belief

1. Alan Forrest's reduction of Catholic traditions to an emphasis on 'inequality and order, obedience and hierarchy' goes too far. *The French Revolution* (Oxford, 1995), 88.
2. J.B. Lebrun des Marettes, *Voyages liturgiques de France* (Paris, 1718).
3. Jean de Viguerie, 'Quelques aspects du catholicisme des Français au XVIIIe siècle, *Revue historique*, CCLXV (1981), 337–9. Preaching styles generally are discussed in Chapter 4 *infra*.
4. Most *curés* complained about the reluctance of some families to send children to their classes. Philippe Loupès, *La Vie religieuse en France au XVIIIe siècle* (Paris, 1993), 91.
5. Jean Quéniart, *Le Clergé déchiré. Fidéle ou rebelle?* (Paris, 1988), 17.

6. Jacques-Louis Ménétra, *Journal of My Life*, trans. Arthur Goldhammer (New York, 1986), 130, 348.
7. ibid., 342. Many ex-priests would be among the leading dechristianisers of the first Terror. *See infra*, Chapters 8, 10.
8. Jean Bart, 'Encore un mot sur les curés de campagne', in Robert Chagny (ed.), *Aux Origines provinciales de la Révolution* (Grenoble, 1990), 157–68, at 160.
9. For efforts by the clergy to reduce their unofficial, autonomous authority see Jean Pierre Gutton, 'Confraternities, *Curés* and Communities in rural areas of the Diocese of Lyons under the Ancien Régime', in Kaspar Von Greyerz (ed.), *Religion and Society in Early Modern Europe 1500–1800* (London, 1984), 202–11.
10. Quéniart, *Le Clergé déchiré*, 17; J. Salvini, 'Le Clergé rural en Haut-Poitou', *Bull. Soc. antiquaires de l'Ouest*, 4th ser. (1957–8), 238.
11. Quoted in Pierrard, *Histoire des curés de campagne*, 21.
12. Cf. Tackett, *Priest and People in 18th Century France*, 166–9.
13. See letter of the *curé* Mollevant, 11 Feb. 1788, in Leicestershire Record Office, DG 39/1229.
14. ibid.
15. Timothy Tackett, 'The West in France in 1789', *Journal of Modern History*, 54 (1982), 715–45, at 728.
16. H. Platelle, *Journal d'un curé de campagne* (Paris, 1965), 35.
17. P.M. Jones, 'Parish, Seigneurie, and the Community of Inhabitants in Southern Central France during the Eighteenth and Nineteenth Centuries', *Past and Present*, 91 (1981), 74–108, at 104; Y-M. Bercé, *Fête et révolte* (Paris, 1976), 127–36.
18. Suzanne Desan, *Reclaiming the Sacred. Lay religion and popular politics in Revolutionary France* (Cornell, 1990), 96. See generally Gabriel Le Bras, *L'Église et le Village* (Paris, 1976).
19. Jean-Louis Flandrin, *L'Église et le controle des naissances* (Paris, 1970).
20. The British ambassador's wife, the Countess of Sutherland, wrote to her mother-in-law in 1792 after having had her third child: 'The French ladies are all astonished at how anybody can be si béte as to have trois enfants. They are perfectly right and I shall mind what they say another time.' Quoted in Judith Schneid Lewis, *In the Family Way: Childbearing in the British aristocracy, 1760–1860* (New Brunswick, NJ, 1986), 228–9.
21. Ralph Gibson, *A Social History of French Catholicism 1789–1914*, 7–8.
22. Jean Quéniart, *Les Hommes, l'église et Dieu*, 136, 230–33; Jean-Louis Flandrin, *Families in Former Times: Kinship, Household and Sexuality*, trans. Richard Southern (Cambridge, 1979), 236–9. See also Jacques Dupâquier, *La Population française au XVIIe et XVIIIe siècles* (Paris, 1979), 85–94 for the background to reductions in births after 1740 and, generally, Angus McLaren, *A History of Contraception. From Antiquity to the Present Day* (Oxford, 1990).
23. Joseph Pochard, *Méthode pour la direction des âmes dans le tribunal de la pénitence. et pour le bon gouvernement des paroisses* (2 vols, Besançon, 1783), I, 143, quoted in Hazel Mills, 'Negotiating the Divide: Women, Philanthrophy and the "Public Sphere" in Nineteenth-Century France', in Frank Tallett and Nicholas Atkin (eds), *Religion, Society and Politics in France since 1789* (London, 1991), 28–54, at 36.
24. M. Albistur and D. Armogathe, *Histoire du féminisme français* (2 vols, Paris, 1972).
25. John McManners, *Reflections on the death bed of Voltaire: the art of dying in eighteenth-century France*, (Oxford, 1975).
26. See letter of the *curé* Mollevant, 11 Feb. 1788, in Leicestershire Record Office, DG 39/1229.
27. Drinking hours were restricted on Sundays and great festivals, though there were numerous complaints at the way the law was flouted. 'The abuse', pronounced

the Bishop of Le Mans in 1789, 'has grown to such a point that one can view it as one of the most blatant signs of the depraved morals of this kingdom'. Quoted in A. Aulard, *Le Christianisme et la Révolution française* (Paris, 1910), 28. See also Olwen H. Hufton, 'Attitudes Towards Authority in Eighteenth-Century Languedoc', *Social History*, 3 (1978), 281–302.

28. M. Tyson and H. Guppy, (eds.), *The French journals of Mrs. Thrale and Dr. Johnson*, (Manchester, 1932), 84. Cf. [J.C. Villiers], *A Tour through Part of France* (London, 1789), 118: '... between the intervals of Mass, the vacancy is most frequently filled with cards. Devotion is here of so portable and so accommodating a nature, that it may with equal ease, and at any time, be laid down or resumed.'

29. Dr Thomas Campbell, *Diary of a Visit to England, 1775* (Sydney, 1854), 100–1.

30. See O. Hufton, 'The French Church', in Callahan and Higgs (eds.), *Church and Society in Catholic Europe*, 13–33.

31. Gérard Cholvy and Yves-Marie Hilaire, *Histoire religieuse de la France contemporaine*, (3 vols, Toulouse, 1985–8), I.24.

32. Olwen H. Hufton, *Women and the Limits of Citizenship in the French Revolution* [The Donald G. Creighton Lectures, 1989] (Toronto, 1992), 102.

33. In B. Plongeron and R. Pannet (eds), *Le Christianisme populaire* (Paris, 1976). See also M-H. Froeschlé-Chopard, *La Religion populaire en Provence orientale au XVIIIe siecle* (Paris, 1980); Loupès, *La Vie religieuse*, 111–17. For some of the conceptual and methodological problems associated with the study of popular culture see Bob Scribner, 'Is a History of Popular Culture Possible?', *History of European Ideas*, 10 (1989), 175–91; Tim Harris (ed.), *Popular Culture in England, c. 1500–1850* (Basingstoke, 1994), 1–27. Judith Devlin, *The Superstitious Mind. French Peasants and the Supernatural in the Nineteenth Century* (New Haven, 1987), is the indispensable guide for a slightly later period.

34. See John McManners, '*Popular Religion' in Seventeenth and Eighteenth-Century France. A New Theme in French Historiography* [John Coffin Memorial Lecture, 1982] (London, 1982), 8, which talks of ' "traditional innovation" through the alliance of clergy and people'.

35. See Anne-Marie Foynat, 'Jansénisme et Aufklarüng Catholique devant la fête chrétienne à la fin de l'ancien régime', 99–113, at 100–11 in Jean Ehrard and Paul Viallaneix (eds), *Les Fêtes de la Révolution. Colloque de Clermont-Ferrand (juin, 1974)* (Paris, 1977).

36. There briefly existed in the 1720s and 1730s a popular Jansenism that held some appeal for the common people of Paris, but this vein was worked out well before Louis XVI's accession. See Peter R. Campbell, *Power and Politics in Old Regime France, 1720–1745* (London, 1996).

37. Alphone Dupront, *Du sacré: Croisade et pèlerinages, images et language* (Paris, 1987), 422–4; Roger Chartier, *The Cultural Origins of the French Revolution* (trans. Lydia G. Cochrane) (Durham, NC, 1991), 104–5.

38. Jean-Pierre Sironneau, *Sécularisation et religions politiques* (The Hague, 1982), 142–3. See generally on popular religion and Tridentine Catholicism, Jean Delumeau, *Le Catholicisme entre Luther et Voltaire* (Paris, 1971); Robert Muchembled, *Culture populaire et culture des élites dans la France moderne, XVe-XVIIIe siècles* (Paris, 1978).

39. Devlin, *The Superstitious Mind*, 51; McManners, *Death and the Enlightenment*, 29–30.

40. Chartier, *Cultural Origins*, 104.

41. See Maurice Gontard, *L'Enseignement primaire en France de la Révolution à la Loi Guizot (1789–1833)* (Paris, 1959), pt. 1.

42. P. Hoffman, *Church and Community in the Diocese of Lyon, 1500–1789* (Yale, 1984).

43. Harvey Mitchell, 'Resistance to the Revolution in Western France', *Past and Present*, 63 (1974), 94–131, at 123.

44. See the discussion of this possibility in Daniel Roche, *La France des lumières* (Paris, 1993), 527–8.

45. Hufton, *The Prospect Before Her*, 383–6; Hufton and Tallett, 'Communities of Women', 79–84.

46. Marcel Bernos, 'La Catéchèse des filles par les femmes aux XVII et XVIIIe siècles', in J. Delumeau (ed.), *La Religion de ma mère. Le Rôle des femmes dans la transmission de la foi* (Paris, 1992), 269–86, at 272.

47. Yves Durand, *Vivre au pays au XVIIIe siècle* (Paris, 1984), 213–15.

48. Louis Châtellier, *The Religion of the Poor: Rural Missions in Europe and the Formation of Modern Catholicism c. 1500–c. 1800*, trans. Brian Pearce (Cambridge, 1997).

49. Mitchell, 'Resistance to the Revolution in Western France', 123.

50. F.A. Weyland, *Une Ame d'apôtre, le vénérable Jean-Marton Moyë* (Metz, 1901).

51. Letter of the *curé* Mollevant, 11 Feb. 1788, in Leicestershire Record Office, DG 39/1229.

52. Raymond Darricau and Bernard Peyrous, *Histoire de la Spiritualité* (Paris, 1991), 107–8.

53. Albert Mathiez, *Contributions à l'Histoire Religieuse de la Révolution française* (Paris, 1907), 213. He was also an important eighteenth-century patron of the cult of Notre Dame of Loretto.

54. Quéniart, *Les Hommes, l'Église et Dieu*, 258–9; McManners, *Death and the Enlightenment*, 197–8.

55. Viguerie, 'Quelques aspects du catholicisme', 347–50.

56. Jean Quéniart, *Culture et société urbaines dans la France de l'Ouest au XVIIIe siècle* (Paris, 1978), pt 2 (esp. III. 708–9) suggests that in nine towns of the West, the proportion of books in private libraries fell from 44 per cent *c.* 1680 to 30 per cent *c.* 1780. See also articles by Furet and Bollême in G. Bollême (ed.), *Livre et société dans la France du XVIIIe siècle* (Paris/The Hague, 1965); helpful discussion in Bernard Cousin, Monique Cubells, René Moulinas, *La Pique et la croix. Histoire religieuse de la Révolution française* (Paris, 1989), 43–5. Loupès, *La Vie religieuse*, 162–6, suggests that decreasing interest in the theological aspects of Jansenism speeded the decline of this market.

57. J. Brancolini and M-T. Bouyssy, 'La Vie provinciale du livre à la fin de l'Ancien Régime', in F. Furet, *Livre et société* (Paris, 1970), II. 9–15.

58. McManners, *Death and the Enlightenment*, 222. See also 242.

59. Mills, 'Negotiating the Divide', 34.

60. Annick and Louis Châtellier, 'Les Premiers Catéchistes des temps modernes: Confrères et consoeurs de la Doctrine Chrétienne au XVI–XVIIIe siècles', in Delumeau, *La Religion de ma mère* (ed.), 287–300, at 299.

61. For the early development of the cult see Foynat, 'Jansénisme et Aufklarüng Catholique', 109–11; M. Péronnet, 'Monseigneur Fumel et le sacre-coeur', *Etudes sur l'Hérault* (1985); Henri-Félix Fumel, *Culte de l'amour divin ou dévotion au Sacre Coueur de Jésus; Instruction pastorale de Mgr l'évêque de Lodève sur les sources de l'incredulité du siècle* (Paris, 1765). He also published the popular *Amour de Dieu* of 1770.

62. Quoted in *Nouvelles Ecclésiastiques*, 30 Jan. 1768.

63. Jean de Viguerie, *Le Catholicisme des français dans l'ancienne France* (Paris, 1988), 249–53, 324.

64. Vovelle, *La mentalité révolutionnaire*, 46, notes that the Provençal elites were moving from the confraternities to the masonic lodges. This should not necessarily be seen as an anti-Christian move. Cf. P. Chevallier, *Histoire de la Franc-Maçonnerie en France: I. La Maçonnerie: école de l'égalité 1725–1799* (Paris, 1974). The work of Maurice Agulhon on the 'laicisation' of confraternities in the region is important, esp. *Pénitents et Franc-Maçons de l'ancienne Provence* (Paris, 1968). M-H. Froeschlé-Chopard, *La Religion populaire en Provence orientale au XVIIIe siècle* (Paris, 1980),

contrasts the confraternities – those supported by the clergy under episcopal direction (especially those of the Holy Sacrament, the Rosary and Saint Joseph) – as against the Penitents, which drew support directly from the layfolk.

65. Chartier, *Cultural Origins*, 101.
66. Châtellier, *The Europe of the Devout*, 197–8; Viguerie, *Le Catholicisme des français*, 162–3.
67. Hoffman, *Church and Community*, 126–28, 144–46.
68. J.N. Vuarnet, *Le Dieu des femmes* (Paris, 1989).
69. E. Le Roy-Ladurie, *Histoire de la France urbaine* (Paris, 1981), vol. 3, *La Ville classique*, 100.
70. See most recently Sophie Hasquenoph, 'Faire retraite au couvent dans le Paris des Lumières', *Revue Historique*, 598 (1996), 353–65.
71. Robert A. Schneider, *Public Life in Toulouse, 1463–1789: From Municipal Republic to Cosmopolitan City* (Cornell, 1984).
72. B. Plongeron, *Histoire du diocèse de Paris* (Paris, 1987); Garrioch, *Neighbourhood and Community in Eighteenth Century Paris* (Cambridge, 1986); 'Parish Politics', op. cit.; Jeffrey Kaplow, *The Parisian Laboring Poor in the Eighteenth Century* (New York, 1972).
73. Abbé Expilly, *Almanach spirituel pour l'année M.DCC.LXXIII* (Paris, 1773), V. 480, 515.
74. Garrioch, *Neighbourhood and Community*, 151–3; Kaplow, *The Parisian Laboring Poor*, 113.
75. Hugh McLeod, *Religion and the People of Western Europe 1789–1970* (Oxford, 1981), 7.
76. There is no essay on this important topic in Peter Clark (ed.), *Small Towns in Early Modern Europe* (Cambridge, 1995). Michael Reed's excellent essay, 'The Cultural Role of Small Towns in England 1600–1800', 121–47, needs a counterpart for France.
77. J. Berthélé (ed.), *Montpellier en 1768 et en 1836 d'après deux manuscrits inédits* (Montpellier, 1909), 27.
78. D. Dinet, 'La Déchristianisation des pays du sud-est du Bassin Parissien au XVIIIe siècle', *Christianisation et déchristianisation* (Angers, 1986), 122; M. Crubellier, *Histoire de la Champagne* (Toulouse, 1975).
79. Garrioch, *Neighbourhood and Community*, 156, 59–60.
80. See, generally, Viguerie, 'Quelques aspects du catholicisme', 344–5.
81. Robert A. Schneider, *The Ceremonial City. Toulouse Observed 1738–1780* (Princeton, 1995), 118–22, 125–9.
82. 'R.W.C.', *Letters from France*, 8, quoted in John Lough, *France on the Eve of Revolution. British Travellers' Observations 1763–1788* (London, 1987), 153.
83. Loupés, *La Vie Religianse*, 20.
84. F. Boulard, *Premiers Itinéraires en Sociologie Religieuse* (Paris, 1966), 49; idem, *La Pratique Religieuse Urbaine* (Paris, 1968), 107.
85. Cousin et al., *La Pique et la croix*, 37; Chartier, *Cultural Origins*, 105.
86. Louis-Sébastien Mercier, *Le Tableau de Paris*, in Jeffrey Kaplow (ed.) (Paris, 1985), art. Liberté religieuse, 257.
87. Cholvy, *Le diocèse de Montpellier*, 185.
88. David Garrioch, 'Parish Politics, Jansenism and the Paris Middle Classes in the Eighteenth Century', *French History* 8 (1994), 403–19.
89. Pierre Chaunu, *La Mort à Paris aux XVIe, XVIIe, et XVIIIe siècles* (Paris, 1978).
90. M. Vovelle, *Piété baroque et déchristianisation en Provence au XVIIIe siècle* (Paris, 1973). See also his essay in *Mourir autrefois*. Cf. the observations of McManners, *Death and the Enlightenment*, 519. J. Quéniart, *Culture et société urbaine dans la France de l'Ouest au XVIIIe siècle* (Paris, 1978) deals with the secularisation of bourgeois elites in the eighteenth century.

91. Gibson, *Social History*, 6; Loupès, *La Vie religieuse*, 166–71.
92. Jacques Solé, *La Révolution en Questions* (Paris, 1988), 23.
93. Schneider, *The Ceremonial City*, 117, 135–6.
94. Mercier, *Le Tableau de Paris*, art. Liberté religieuse, 259.
95. John St. John, *Letters from France to a Gentleman in the south of Ireland* (2 vols, Dublin, 1787), II, 233; [John Villiers], *A Tour Through Part of France* (London, 1789), 118.
96. See the interesting comparisons made in Guy Chaussinand-Nogaret, *The French Nobility in the eighteenth century. From feudalism to enlightenment* (trans. William Doyle) (Cambridge, 1985), 74–8.
97. D. Roche, 'La diffusion des lumières. Un exemple: l'Académie de Châlons-sur-Marne', *Annales E.S.C.*, 19 (1964), 887–922, esp. 911, 918–22.
98. *Mandement de Mgr l'archevêque et comte de Lyon, portant permission de manger du Beurre, du Lait, du Fromage & des Oeufs pendant le Carême de l'année 1789* (Paris, 1789), 7; R. Po-Chia Hsia, *The World of Catholic Renewal 1540–1770* (Cambridge, 1998), 206.
99. Harry C. Payne, *The Philosophes and the People* (New Haven, 1976), 75–6.
100. F.P. Bowman, 'Necker et l'apologétique', *Cahiers staëliens*, 36 (1985), 30–52; Agnes Marcetteau-Paul and Sabine Juratic, 'Les Bibliothèques de quelques acteurs de la Révolution', in Frédéric Barbier, Claude Jolly and Sabine Juratic (eds), *Mélanges de la Bibliothèque de la Sorbonne*, 9 (1989), 189–207.
101. Munro Price, *Preserving the Monarchy*, 19, 240; Darrin M. McMahon, 'The Counter-Enlightenment and the Low-Life of Literature in Pre-Revolutionary France', *Past and Present*, 159 (1998), 77–112, at 94, 98n. The quotation is from D.G. Levy, *The ideas and career of Simon-Nicolas-Henri Linguet* (Urbana, Illinois, 1980), 264 n.28.
102. See Duc de Lévis, *Souvenirs et portraits, 1780–1789* (Paris, 1813), 103; Jean-François Labourdette, 'Vergennes ou la tentation du ministériat', *Revue historique*, 557 (1986), 73–108, at 84–5.
103. D. Roche, *Les Républicains des lettres. Gens de culture et lumiéres aux XVIIIe siècle* (Paris, 1988), 98.
104. Loupès, *La Vie religieuse*, 219–20.
105. Jean-Pierre Bardet, *Rouen au XVIIe et XVIIIe siècles* (Paris, 1983), 307.
106. *Anecdotes piquantes de Bachaumont et Mairobert, etc., pour servir à l'histoire de la société française, à la fin du règne de Louis XV* (1762–1774) (Bruxelles, 1881).
107. *Espion Anglais*, quoted in Van Kley, *The Religious Origins of the French Revolution*, 293.
108. Roche, *Les Républicains des lettres*, 98.
109. Robert Darnton, *Mesmerism and the End of the Enlightenment in France* (Cambridge, Mass., 1968); Eloïse Mozzani, *Magie et superstitions: De la Fin de l'ancien régime à la restauration* (Paris, 1988).
110. Cf. Cholvy, *La Religion en France*, 5; Loupès, *La Vie religieuse*, 194.
111. Speech of 22 Aug. 1789, cited by Octave Teissier, *Les Députés de la Provence à l'Assemblé nationale de 1789* (Draguignan, 1898), 106–7.

Chapter 3. Other Denominations

1. There is an excellent introduction to eighteenth-century French Protestantism by Philippe Joutard, in eds. Jacques Le Goff and Réné Rémond (eds), *Histoire de la France religieuse* vol. 3, *Du Roi très Chrétien à la laïcité républicaine* (Paris, 1991), 50–61.
2. Raymond Birn, 'Religious Toleration and Freedom of Expression', in Dale Van Kley (ed.), *The French Idea of Freedom. The Old Regime and the Declaration of Rights of 1789* (Stanford, 1994), 265–99, at 284.

3. McManners, *Death and the Enlightenment*, 321–2.
4. Laura Maslow Amand, 'La bourgeoisie protestante. La Révolution et le mouvement de Déchristianisation à La Rochelle', *R.H.M.C.*, 31 (1986), 489–500, at 489–92.
5. D. Ligou, 'Le Protestantisme français dans la seconde moitié du XVIIIe siècle', *Information historique* 25 (1963), 8–14, at 10. For economic life in Nîmes on the eve of the Revolution see Gwynne Lewis, *The Second Vendée. The Continuity of Counter-revolution in the Department of the Gard 1789–1815* (Oxford, 1978), 5–10, 14–16.
6. James N. Hood, 'Revival and Mutation of Old Rivalries in Revolutionary France', *Past and Present*, 82 (1979), 82–115 at 88.
7. Lévy–Schneider, *L'Application du Concordat par un Prélat d'Ancien Régime*, 15.
8. Henry Lyte to Lord Dartmouth, 9 Dec. 1754, *H.M.C., 20th Report* (1887), MSS of the Earl of Dartmouth, 331.
9. John D. Woodbridge, *Revolt in Prerevolutionary France: The Prince de Conti's Conspiracy Against Louis XV, 1755–1757* (Baltimore, 1995).
10. John Pappas, 'La Représsion contre les protestants dans la séconde moitié du siècle d'aprés les régistres de l'Ancien régime', *Dix-huitiéme Siècle* 17 (1985), 111–28, at 122–4.
11. David D. Bien, *The Calas Affair. Persecution, Toleration, and Heresy in Eighteenth-Century Toulouse* (Princeton, 1960); J. van den Heuvel (ed.), *L'Affaire Calas* (Paris, 1975); Cousin, Cubells, Moulinas, *La Pique et la croix*, 47–8; Geoffrey Adams, *The Huguenots and French Opinion 1685–1787. The Enlightenment Debate on Toleration* (Waterloo, Ont., 1991), 211–27.
12. Ligou, 'Les Protestants Français', 128; Samuel Mours et Daniel Robert, *Le Protestantisme en France du XVIIIe siècle à nos jours (1685–1970)* (Paris, 1972), 160; D. Robert, *Les Églises réformés en France (1800–30)* (Paris, 1961), 6–7.
13. See the reports of La Rochelle, Saintonge and Poitiers in 1767, in L. Delmas, *L'Eglise Reformée de La Rochelle* (Toulouse, 1870), 343–4.
14. James N. Hood, 'Protestant-Catholic Relations and the Roots of the First Popular Counterrevolutionary Movement in France', *J.M.H.*, 43 (1971), 245–75, at 258; Mours et Robert, *Le Protestantisme en France*, 161.
15. Humphrey Smollett, *Travels through France and Italy*, Frank Felsenstein (ed.), (Oxford, 1979), 105.
16. M. Péronnet, 'Les Assemblées du clergé de France sous le règne de Louis XVI', *A.H.R.F.*, 34 (1962), 15.
17. See Geoffrey Adams, 'Monarchistes ou Républicaines?', in *Dix-huitième Siècle*, 17 (1985), 83–95.
18. Yves Krumenacker, 'L'Élaboration d'un "modèle Protestant": Les Synodes du Désert', *R.H.M.C.*, 42 (1995), 46–70.
19. M. Sonenscher, 'Note sur la famille de Rabaut Saint-Etienne', *Bull. de la Soc. hist. du Prot. Fr.*, [hereafter *B.S.H.P.F.*], 121 (1975), 370–4.
20. Birn, 'Religious Toleration and Freedom of Expression', 289–90, 414; Adams, *The Huguenots and French Opinion*, 147–93; Derek Beales, 'Social Forces and Enlightened Policies', 42–53, at 42–3, in H.M. Scott (ed.), *Enlightened Absolutism. Reform and Reformers in Later Eighteenth-Century Europe* (Basingstoke, 1990).
21. Graham Gargett, *Voltaire and Protestantism* [Studies on Voltaire and the Eighteenth Century, 188] (Oxford, 1980); D'Alembert quoted in Adams, *The Huguenots and French Opinion*, 139. See also 103–117.
22. Hélène Kern, 'Le Séminaire de Lausanne et le Comité Français', *B.S.H.P.F.*, 108 (1962), 192–218.
23. Mours et Robert, *Le Protestantisme en France*, 170.
24. Philippe Joutard, 'Une Mentalité du 16e siècle au temps des lumières: Les Protestants du Vivarais', *Dix-huitième siècle*, 17 (1985), 67–73.

25. Daniel Ligou, 'Les Protestants Français à la veille de la Révolution', in Pierre Léon Féral (ed.), *La France Pré-Révolutionnaire* (Paris, 1991), 125–35, at 127.
26. Philip Thicknesse, *A Year's Journey Through France and Part of Spain* (2 vols, Bath, 1777), I, 86–7.
27. Paul Rabaut, *Ses Lettres à Divers (1744–1794)*, Charles Dardier (ed.) (2 vols, Paris, 1892), I. xix.
28. Bodleian Library (henceforth BODL.), MS. Eng. Misc. f. 55, pp. 86–7.
29. Cf. Louis Mazoyer, 'The monarchy had not the force to continue Louis XIV's work, but it had neither the courage nor the intention of disavowing it.' 'Essai critique sur l'histoire du Protestantisme à la fin du xviiie siècle', *B.S.H.P.F.*, 79 (1930), 33–56, at 39.
30. Bernard Plongeron, *La Vie quotidienne du clergé*, 148.
31. T. Tackett, *Priest and Parish in Eighteenth-Century France*, 21; Burdette C. Poland, *French Protestantism and the French Revolution. A Study in Church and State, Thought and Religion, 1685–1815* (Princeton, NJ, 1957), 62.
32. Quoted in Joseph Dedieu, *Histoire politique des Protestants français (1715–94)* (2 vols, Paris, 1925), II, 190.
33. Pappas, 'La Répréssion contre les protestants', 126.
34. Norman Ravitch, *The Catholic Church and the French Nation 1589–1989* (London, 1990), 35.
35. Birn, 'Religious Toleration and Freedom of Expression', 290–2.
36. For a summary of growing contacts between government circles and the Huguenots see Ligou, 'Les Protestants français', 129; Rabaut, *Ses Lettres à Divers*, I, xix.
37. A.N., O1 480, fos. 33, 34, letters between the Bishop of Chartres and Breteuil; Adams, *The Huguenots and French Opinion*, 257.
38. Jean–Pierre Brancourt, 'Les Evêques de Louis XVI et la défense de la foi', [*Actes du Colloque de Sorèze, 1976*], 228–48, at 241–2; Michel Péronnet, 'Les Assemblées du Clergé et les protestants', *Dix-huitième siècle*, 17 (1985), 141–50.
39. Lafayette, *Mémoires, correspondances et manuscrits* (6 vols, Paris, 1837), letter to George Washington, 11 May 1785, II, 121–2.
40. See the vital discussion in Adams, *The Huguenots and French Opinion*, 265–83, and Dedieu, *Histoire politique des Protestants*, II, 249.
41. Aston, *The End of an Élite*, 92.
42. Adams, *The Huguenots and French Opinion 1685–1787*, 285–93.
43. H. de Peyster, *Les Troubles de Hollande à la veille de la Révolution française (1780–1795)* (Paris, 1905), 230.
44. The text of the edict and the remonstrances of the Paris parlement are in Cathérine Bergeal, *Protestantisme et tolérance en France au XVIIIe siècle. De la Révocation à la Révolution (1685–1789)* (La Cause, 1988), 176–93, 198–205.
45. Dedieu, *Histoire politique des Protestants*, II, 263–5; H.M. Scott, 'Reform in the Habsburg Monarchy, 1740–90', in id., *Enlightened Absolutism*, 145–87, at 168–9.
46. Bergeal, *Protestantisme et tolérance en France*, 222–4.
47. Ravitch, *The Catholic Church and the French Nation*, 37. The Edict is discussed in Jean Egret, *The French Pre-Revolution*, 77–84. See also Elisabeth Labrousse, 'L'Édit de Tolérance de 1787', in Féral, *La France Pré-Révolutionnaire*, 117–23; Michel Richard, *La Vie quotidienne des protestants sous l'ancien régime* (Paris, 1966), 305–6; Aston, *The End of an Élite*, 92–7.
48. Quoted in Dedieu, *Histoire politique des Protestants*, II, 275–6.
49. A.N., G8 94, Provincial assembly of Bordeaux, 9 Apr. 1788, p. 7; Leroux, *Étude critique sur le XVIIIe siècle à Bordeaux*, 211n.
50. 'Protestation de l'Evêque de La Rochelle contre l'édit de Louis XVI accordant l'Etat Civil aux non-Catholiques', *B.S.H.P.F.*, 7 (1858), 157–69; A. Lods,

'L'Attitude du clergé catholique à l'égard des Protestants en 1789', *B.S.H.P.F.*, 33 (1897), 128–9.

51. V.H. Dubief, 'La Réception de l'Edit du 17 novembre par les Parlements', *B.S.H.P.F.*, 134 (1968), 281–95; Egret, *The French Pre-Revolution*, 83.

52. Dedieu, *Histoire politique des Protestants*, II, 281.

53. Quoted in D.I. Wright, *The French Revolution: Introductory Documents* (Queensland, Australia, 1974), 15. I am grateful to Malcolm Crook for advice on this point.

54. Quoted in Dedieu, *Histoire politique des Protestants*, II. 282.

55. Ligou, 'Les Protestants français', 132–3.

56. Daniel Ligou, 'Sur la Contre-Révolution à Montauban', in Jean Sentou (ed.), *Révolution et Contre-Révolution dans la France du Midi (1789–1799)* (Toulouse, 1991), 91–105.

57. Hood, 'Protestant–Catholic Relations', 267–8.

58. Well discussed in Gary Kates, 'Jews into Frenchmen: Nationality and Representation in Revolutionary France', in Ferenc Fehér (ed.), *The French Revolution and the Birth of Modernity* (Berkeley, CA, 1990), 103–116, at 105–8.

59. Pierre Pluchon, *Nègres et Juifs au XVIIIe siècle. Le Racisme au siècle des lumières* (Paris, 1984), 75–6.

60. Bernard Blumenkranz et Albert Soboul (eds), *Les Juifs et la Révolution française* (2nd edn, Paris, 1989), 49; Nicolas Weill, 'Les Juifs et la Révolution: nouvelles questions sur l'émancipation', in M. Vovelle (ed.), *Recherches sur la Révolution* (Paris, 1991), 212–18.

61. Zosa Szajkowski, 'Relations among Sephardim, Ashkenazim and Avignonese Jews in France', in id., *Jews and the French Revolutions of 1789, 1830 and 1848* (New York, 1970), 235–66.

62. Szajkowski, 'Relations Among Sephardim etc.', 255.

63. Richard Menkis, 'Patriarchs and Patricians: the Gradis Family of eighteenth-century Bordeaux', in Frances Malino and David Sorkin (eds), *From East and West. Jews in a Changing Europe, 1750–1870* (Oxford, 1990), 11–45.

64. Cousin, Cubells, Moulinas, *La Pique et la croix*, 51.

65. Shanti Marie Singham, 'Betwixt Cattle and Men: Jews, Blacks, and Women, and the Declaration of the Rights of Man', in Van Kley, *The French Idea of Freedom*, 114–53, at 119.

66. Robert Badinter, *Libres et égaux. L'Émancipation des Juifs (1789–1791)* (Paris, 1989), 35.

67. Szajkowski, 'The Jewish Status in Eighteenth Century France and the 'Droit d'Aubaine', *Jews and the French Revolutions*, 227–8.

68. cf. Cousin, Cubells, Moulinas, *La Pique et la croix*, 52.

69. Quoted in Badinter, *L'Émancipation des Juifs*, 35.

70. ibid., 58, 34.

71. Cousin, Cubells, Moulinas, *La Pique et la croix*, 52–3.

72. R. Badinter, *Libres et égaux*, 95; Forrest, *The Revolution in Provincial France*, 160.

73. See Soboul et Blumenkranz, *Les Juifs et la Révolution française*, 213–14.

74. Patrick Girard, *Les Juifs de France de 1789 à 1860. De l'Émancipation à l'égalité* (Paris, 1976), 44–5.

75. See Chapter 9(iii) below.

Chapter 4. The Church and the Enlightenment

1. Chartier, *The Cultural Origins of the French Revolution*, 5.

2. The three most useful and up-to-date introductory texts are Roy Porter and Norman Hampson, *The Enlightenment* (Harmondsworth, 1968); 'The Enlightenment

in France', in Roy Porter and Mikulás (eds), *The Enlightenment in National Context* (Cambridge, 1981), 41–53; Dorinda Outram, *The Enlightenment* (Cambridge, 1995).

3. Chapters by Joachim Whaley, T.C.W. Blanning and Ernst Wangermann in Porter and Mikuls̆, *The Enlightenment in National Context*, 106–40; Thomas E. Kaiser, 'This Strange Offspring of *Philosophie*: Recent Historiographical Problems in Relating the Enlightenment to the French Revolution', *French Historical Studies*, 15 (1987–8), 549–62.

4. Bernard Plongeron, 'Recherches sur l'"Aufklärung" Catholique en Europe occidentale (1770–1830)', *R.H.M.C.*, 16 (1969), 555–605.

5. Paul Hazard, *The European Mind (1680–1715)*, trans. J.L. May (London, 1953), remains a classic guide; R. Pomereau, *La Religion de Voltaire* (2nd edn, Paris, 1969), is also unsurpassed.

6. See Alec Mellor, *Histoire de l'anticléricalisme français* (Paris, 1966). Van Kley, *The Religious Origins*, 176, mentions the rash of physical attacks on priests in Paris in the late 1750s.

7. Robert Darnton, *The Forbidden Best-Sellers of Pre-Revolutionary France* (London, 1996), 66–7, 70; 'A Clandestine Bookseller in the Provinces', in *The Literary Underground of the Old Regime* (Cambridge, MA, 1982), 122–47, at 141–2.

8. Mellor, *L'Anticléricalisme français*, 150.

9. Charles La Font de Savine, Bishop of Viviers from 1778 (and one of the four pre-revolutionary diocesan prelates to take the oath to the Civil Constitution) was actually called by his friends 'the Jean-Jacques Rousseau of the clergy'. Simon Brugal, *Le Schisme constitutionnel dans l'Ardèche* (2nd edn, Toulouse, 1977).

10. Aston, *The End of an Elite*, 12, 221.

11. Dom Aidan Bellenger, 'Benedictine Responses to the Enlightenment', in Nigel Aston (ed.), *Religious Change in Europe, 1650–1914. Essays for John McManners* (Oxford, 1997), 149–60, at 153–4.

12. Marquis de Roux, *La Révolution à Poitiers et dans la Vienne* (Paris, 1912), 50–1.

13. Bergier was also a strong anti-Jansenist and an enemy to extreme Augustinian views in theology. See A. Jobert, *N. Bergier, un théolgien du siècle des Lumières* (Lyon, 1984).

14. Jacques Godechot, *The Counter-Revolution. Doctrine and Action 1789–1804*, trans. Salvator Attanasio (Princeton, 1971), 41–8. The full background is in R.R. Palmer, *Catholics and Unbelievers in Eighteenth-Century France* (Princeton, 1939). See also Jean-Christian Petitfils, 'Les Origines de la pensé contre-Révolution', in ed. J. Tulard, *La Contre-Révolution. Origines, histoire, postérité* (Paris, 1990), 15–35, at 20–1; Daniel Roche, *La France des lumières* (Paris, 1995), 348–9; Quéniart, *Les Hommes, l'Église et Dieu*, 289–91.

15. Jean Balcou, *Fréron contre les philosophes* (Geneva, 1975); Jack Censer, *The French Press in the Age of Enlightenment* (London, 1994), 102–10.

16. McMahon, 'The Counter-Enlightenment', 77–112.

17. Marc Fumaroli, 'Voltaire', *Proceedings of the British Academy. Lectures and Memoirs*, 87 (1994), 19–34.

18. Langlois and Tackett, 'L'Épreuve de la Révolution', 225. For Montesquieu and social utility see Payne, *The Philosophes and the People*, esp. 67–75.

19. Ronald Grimsley, *Rousseau and the Religious Quest* (London, 1968).

20. Jones, *Reform and Revolution in France*, 129.

21. Thomas O'Connor, *An Irish Theologian in Enlightenment France: Luke Joseph Hooke, 1714–96* (Dublin, 1995).

22. Quoted in A. Artaud, 'Gay-Vernon: Evêque constitutionnel et député de la Haute-Vienne (1748–1822)', *La Révolution française*, 27 (1894), 314–34, 447–67, 502–31.

23. Pierre Pierrard (ed.), *Les Diocèses de Cambrai et de Lille* (Paris, 1978), 176.
24. Fauchet, *Éloge civique de Benjamin Franklin, prononcé le 21 juillet 1790 etc.* (Paris, 1790), 28; H. Cros, *Claude Fauchet, 1744–1793; ses idés politiques, économiques et sociales* (Paris, 1912); Chapter 9(i), *infra*.
25. Fauchet, *De la Religion nationale* (Paris, 1789), 108.
26. Charles Aimond, *Histoire des Lorraines* (Bar-le-Duc, 1960), 352.
27. Daniel Roche, *Le Siècle des lumiéres en province: Académies et académiciens provinciaux, 1680–1789* (2 vols, The Hague, 1978).
28. François-Georges Pariset (ed.), *Bordeaux au XVIIIe Siécle* (Bordeaux, 1968), 139–40; Abbé Brun, *L'Abbé J.-P. Lapauze, curé de Bonzac et Galgon, archiprêtre de Fronsac, au diocèse de Bordeaux, 1750–92* (Bordeaux, 1903), 100 ff.
29. Cousin, *Précis d'histoire monastique*, 452, 57.
30. Graham, 'Enlightened and Revolutionary Oratorians', 171–83; Gusdorf, *Dieu, la nature, l'homme*, 56; Chapter 9(i), *infra*.
31. Plongeron, *La Vie quotidienne du clergé*, 228; Lavaquery, *Le Cardinal de Boisgelin*, I, 297–304, who conjectures that that the manuscript may have been completed in 1785.
32. J. Gog, *A Reims, le Sacre des Rois de France* (Paris, 1980), 95; McManners, 'Authority in Church and State', 278–9. There is an invaluable overview in Keith Michael Baker, 'French Political Thought at the Accession of Louis XVI', *Journal of Modern History* 50 (1978), 281–303.
33. Quoted in Bernard Plongeron, *L'Abbé Grégoire (1750–1831), ou l'Arche de la Fraternité* (Paris, 1989), 54.
34. A.N., 198 AP 1, cited in Bernard de Braye, *Un Evêque d'Ancien Régime à l'épreuve de la Révolution. Le Cardinal A.L.H. de la Fare (1752–1829)* (Paris, 1985), 53.
35. *Requéte des fidèles à Nosseigneurs les Evêques de l'Assemblée générale du Clergé de France* (Paris, 1781?), 3, 4.
36. Charles-Louis Richard, *Exposition de la doctrine des philosophes modernes* (Malines, 1785), vii, quoted in McMahon, 'The Counter-Enlightenment and the Low-Life of Literature', 106.
37. Petitfils, 'Les Origines de la pensé contre-Révolution', 20.
38. Quoted in Darricau, 'Les Préoccupations pastorales des Assemblées du Clergé de France', 255. See also, for instance, the Bishop of Le Mans's pastoral letter for Lent, 15 Jan. 1789, against 'a proud philosophy', and Archbishop Rohan of Bordeaux's equivalent of 1772 recommending the General Assembly's publication. Triger, *L'Année 1789 au Mans*, 128; Leroux, *Étude critique sur le XVIIIe siècle à Bordeaux*, 266.
39. Quoted in John Lough, *The Philosophes and Post-Revolutionary France* (Oxford, 1982), 59, 65. The last extract is from a memorandum of 20 July 1780.
40. Darnton, *The Forbidden Best-Sellers*, 222–3.
41. J.M. Thompson, *Robespierre* (2 vols, London, 1935), I, 9.
42. Darnton, *The Forbidden Best-Sellers*, 68; Mahon, 'The Counter-Enlightenment and the Low-Life of Literature', *passim*.
43. Robert Darnton, 'The High Enlightenment and the Low-Life of Literature in Pre-Revolutionary France', *Past and Present* 51 (1971), 81–115.
44. Darnton, *The Forbidden Best-Sellers*, 71.
45. Diderot, *The Nun*, trans. Leonard Tancock (Harmondsworth, 1974), 24.
46. Darnton, *The Forbidden Best-Sellers*, 85–113, 249–99. Darnton argues that its prescription of coitus interruptus may even had made an impact on eighteenth-century French demography.
47. ibid., 72–3, 87. It was probably written by J.-C. Gervaise de Latouche.
48. Laurence Brockliss, *French Higher Education in the Seventeenth and Eighteenth Centuries* (Oxford, 1987), 241.

49. Deregnaucourt, *De Fenelon à la Révolution*, 272.
50. Merrick, *The Desacralization of the French Monarchy*; Van Kley, *The Damiens Affair*.
51. Quoted in Lough, *The Philosophes and Post-Revolutionary France*, 181. See also W.H. Williams, 'Voltaire and the utility of the Lower Clergy', *Studies on Voltaire and the Eighteenth-Century*, 58 (1967), 1869–91; A. Playoust–Chaussis, *La Vie Religieuse dans la diocèse de Boulogne au XVIIIe siècle* (Arras, 1976), 177–8; M-L. Fracard, 'Le Recrutement du clergé seculier dans la région Niortaise au XVIIIe siècle', *Revue d'histoire de l'Eglise de France*, 57 (1971), 262–4.
52. Ian Green, '"Reformed Pastors" and Bons Curés', in *The Ministry: Clerical and Lay*, W.J. Sheils and Diana Wood (eds) [Studies in Church History] (Oxford, 1989) 259.
53. Mansel, *The Court of France 1789–1830*, 22.
54. Plongeron, *La Vie quotidienne du clergé*, 228.
55. ibid., 230; Abbé de Beauvais, *Sermon sur la Parole de Dieu*, col. 38.
56. Cf. A. Bernard, *Le Sermon au XVIIIe siècle. Étude historique et critique sur la Prédication en France de 1715 à 1789* (Paris, 1900), 364–5, 522.
57. Nicolas Charles Joseph Trublet, *Panégyriques des saints* (2 pts, 2nd edn, 1755), I, art. 39.
58. Quoted in Plongeron, *La Vie quotidienne du clergé*, 230.
59. Brockliss, *French Higher Education*, 245.
60. For the two prophetesses see Albert Mathiez, *Contributions à l'histoire religieuse de la Révolution française* (Paris, 1907), 98 ff. See generally Gusdorf, *Dieu, la nature, l'homme*, esp. 22–3.
61. J. Godel and B. Plongeron, '1945–1970, un quart de siècle d'histoire religieuse', *A.H.R.F.*, 44 (1972), 181–203.
63. Robert Darnton, *The Great Cat Massacre and other episodes in French Cultural History* (New York, 1984); Claude Labrosse, *Lire au XVIIIe siècle. La Nouvelle Héloïse et ses lecteurs* (Lyon, 1985).
64. J.P. Bertaud, *Camille et Lucile Desmoulins, un couple dans la tourmente* (Paris, 1989), 26–7.
65. Langlois and Tackett, 'L'Épreuve de la Révolution', 225.
66. Anna Ridehalgh, 'Preromantic attitudes and the birth of a legend: French pilgrimages to Ermenonville, 1778–1789', *Studies on Voltaire and the eighteenth-century*, 215 (1982), 231–52, at 235; McManners, *Death and the Enlightenment*, 350.
67. A.H. Wandelaincourt, *Plan d'éducation publique* (Paris, 1777).
68. Joan McDonald, *Rousseau and the French Revolution 1762–91* (London, 1961); Norman Hampson, *Will and Circumstance: Montesquieu, Rousseau and the French Revolution* (London, 1983), *passim*; Châtellier, *The Religion of the Poor*, 220.
69. Quoted in *Nouvelles Ecclésiastiques*, 30 Jan. 1768.

Chapter 5. The Gallican Church and the Crisis of the Monarchy, 1786–9

1. Few general accounts offer more than a glance at the role of the First Estate in the heated politics of the monarchy's last years. William Doyle, *Origins of the French Revolution* (Oxford, 1980), is indispensable, but Julian Swann's 'The French Revolution', in Pamela M. Pilbeam (ed.), *Themes in Modern European History 1780–1830* (London, 1995), 12–39, is also an excellent starting point to the subject for students. And see Campbell, *Power and Politics in Old Regime France*, 314–18.

2. Keith Michael Baker, 'Politics and Public Opinion under the Old Regime: Some Reflections', in Jack Censer and Jeremy Popkin (eds), *Press and Politics in Pre-Revolutionary France* (Berkeley, 1987), 204–46; articles by Daniel Gordon, Dena Goodman and Bernadette Fort in 'The French Revolution in Culture', *Eighteenth-Century Studies*, 22 (1989); Chartier, *The Cultural Origins of the French Revolution*, 27; Farge, *Subversive Words, passim*. Cf. the cautionary comments of Campbell, *Power and Politics in Old Regime France*, 302–4, 316–17.

3. Aston, *The End of an Elite*, 51; Jones, *Reform and Revolution*, 113, 150; John Hardman, *French Politics 1774–1789. From the Accession of Louis XVI to the Fall of the Bastille* (London, 1995), 136.

4. Quoted in ibid.

5. A.N., K. 689.

6. Dale Van Kley, 'Church, State, and the Ideological Origins of the French Revolution: The Debate over the General Assembly of the Gallican Clergy', *Journal of Modern History*, 51 (1979), 649–52.

7. Quoted in Van Kley, *The Religious Origins of the French Revolution*, 339.

8. P. Goubert, *Beauvais et le Beauvaisis de 1600 à 1730* (2 vols, Paris, 1960), I, 180.

9. McManners, 'Tithe in Eighteenth-Century France', 166–7.

10. Ch-L. Chassin, *Les Cahiers des curés* (Paris, 1882); Charles Ledré, *L'Église de France sous la Révolution* (Paris, 1949), 14.

11. Darnton, 'A Pamphleteer on the Run', 72–121, at 111.

12. The writings of Vivian Gruder on the first Assembly of Notables are essential. Among the most important are 'Class and Politics in the Pre-Revolution: The Assembly of Notables of 1787', in Hinrichs, Schmitt, Vierhaus (eds), *Vom Ancien Régime*, 207–32; 'Paths to Political Consciousness: The Assembly of Notables of 1787 and the "Pre-Revolution" in France', *F.H.S.*, 13 (1984), 323–55; 'The Society of Orders at its Demise: The Vision of the elite at the end of the Ancien Régime', *French History*, 1 (1987), 210–37.

13. Target, *Journal*, 23 Feb. 1787, in *Un Avocat du 18e siècle* (Paris, 1893), 48.

14. There is no modern biography of Archbishop Brienne. His ministry of 1787–88 is discussed in John Hardman, *Louis XVI* (New Haven, 1993), 128–36.

15. Jean Egret, 'La Dernière Assemblée du clergé de France (5 Mai–5 Août 1788)', *Revue Historique*, 219 (1958), 1–15; Péronnet, 'Les Assemblées du clergé de France sous le règne de Louis XVI', 8–35; 'L'Assemblé du Clergé de France tenue en 1788', *A.H.R.F.*, 60 (1988), 227–46.

16. A.N. G8 706, p. 159.

17. Jeremy D. Popkin, 'The *Gazette de Leyde* and French Politics Under Louis XVI', in Censer and Popkin (eds), *Press and Politics in Pre-Revolutionary France*, 75–132 at 112; Van Kley, *The Religious Origins of the French Revolution*, 344–5.

18. Quoted in Albert Babeau, *Le Parlement de Paris à Troyes en 1787* (Paris, 1871), 100.

19. Egret, *The French PreRevolution*, 176–7, 181–2.

20. J. Egret, 'La Seconde Assemblée des Notables', *A.H.R.F.*, 21 (1948), 193–228.

21. See, for instance, that of the *curés* of Poitiers to Villedeuil, 18 Jan. 1789, A.N., Ba, 68.

22. Cf. Gibson, *A Social History of French Catholicism*, 33: 'The *curés* wanted not simply a disinterested reform of the Church: they wanted power for themselves ... Their vision of a reformed Church was thus one in which they were all-powerful.' Such a claim too readily projects unrest in the Dauphiné on to the rest of France. Cf. Jones, *Reform and Revolution*, 133.

23. Jacques Cadart, *Le Régime électoral des Etats-Généreux de 1789 et ses origines (1302–1614)* (Paris, 1952), 121–5; Pierrard, *Histoire des Curés de campagne*, 28, 29.

24. *Représentations et protestations, que fait à Sa Majesté le Chapitre de l'Eglise Primatiale et metropolitaine d'Auch, contre le règlement du 24 janvier 1789* (Paris, 1789), 5. B.L. F.R.

23 (4). Cf. the Auxerre chapter. Abbé Lebeuf, *Mémoires concernant l'histoire d'Auxerre* (3 vols, Paris, 1854), II. 369.

25. Bishop of Rieux to Necker, 22 Feb. 1789, A.N., AA. 62.

26. M. Péronnet, *Les Evêques de l'Ancienne France* (Paris/Lille, 1978), 1150; André Mathieu, *La Convocation des Etats-Généreux de 1789 en Languedoc* (Montpellier, 1917), 94.

27. Anon., *Les Curés du Dauphiné à leurs confrères les Recteurs de Bretagne*. See generally Bernard, 'Revendications et aspirations du bas clergé dauphinois'.

28. Marcel Bruneau, *Les Débuts de la Révolution dans les départements du Cher et de l'Indre (1789–91)* (Paris, 1902), 12, 13.

29. Triger, *L'Année 1789 au Mans*, 130.

30. Quoted in M. Hutt, 'The Curés and the Third Estate: the ideas of Reform in the pamphlets of the French Lower Clergy in the period 1787–89', *Journal of Ecclesiastical History*, 8 (1957), 74–92, at 80.

31. René Taveneaux, 'L'Abbé Grégoire et la démocratie cléricale', in *Jansénisme et Réforme catholique*, (Nancy, 1992) 137–57, at 138–44; M. Parisse, *Histoire de la Lorraine* (Toulouse, 1978), 353.

32. [Henri Grégoire], *A MM. les Curés lorrains et autres écclésiastiques séculiers du diocèse de Metz* (Nancy, 1789).

33. F.D. Mathieu, *L'Ancien Régime en Lorraine et Barrois* (3rd edn, Paris, 1907), 428–9; *Les Curés du Dauphiné à leurs confrères*, 8.

34. Triger, *L'Année 1789 au Mans*, 144.

35. For an example of inept tactical planning at Poitiers see Marquis de Roux, *La Révolution à Poitiers et dans la Vienne* (Paris, 1912), 163.

36. Triger, *L'Année 1789 au Mans*, 150.

37. Quoted in Pierrard, *Histoire des curés de campagne*, 29.

38. Nigel Aston, 'Survival Against the Odds?', The French Bishops Elected to the Estates-General, 1789', *Historical Journal* 32 (1989), 607–26. 49 of the 51 were full diocesan bishops. Péronnet points out that they tended to control the larger dioceses and estimates that the 49 had canonical authority over three-quarters of French parishes; M. Péronnet, 'Nos Seigneurs du Clergé de France en 1789', *Dix-huitième siècle* 20 (1988), 119–31, at 123.

39. Aston, 'Survival Against the Odds?', *passim*; Peronnet, 'Nos Seigneurs', 122–3; Sutherland, *The Chouans: The Social Origins of Popular Counterrevolution in Upper Brittany, 1770–1796* (Oxford, 1982), 225–6.

40. Quoted in A. Kwanten, 'A.-A.-J. de Clermont-Tonnerre, évêque de Châlons (1782–1801),' *Mémoires de la Société d'Agriculture, Commerce, Sciences et Arts de la Marne*, 89 (1974), 267–89 at 281. See also 282.

41. Lebeuf, *Mémoires concernant Auxerre*, II. 369, 389n.

42. Sub-delegate's letter (16 Mar.), quoted in Mathieu, *La Convocation des Etats-Généreux de 1789*, 83–4.

43. Sub-delegate's letter (28 Mar.), quoted in ibid., 95; J. Viguier, 'La lutte électorale de 1789 en Languedoc', *La Révolution française*, 20 (1891), 5–25, at 15–16.

44. Péronnet, *Les Evêques de l'Ancienne France*, 1127. Two general articles on the *Cahiers* that incidentally deal with religious issues are B. Hyslop, 'Les Cahiers de doléances de 1789', *A.H.R.F.*, 27 (1955), 115–25; George V. Taylor, 'Revolutionary and non-Revolutionary Content in the Cahiers of 1789: An Interim Report', *F.H.S.*, 7 (1971–2), 479–502.

45. Only 21 *cahiers* of the Third Estate, and 1 of the Second wanted the abolition of tithe; ibid., 1129. Gagnol, *La dîme écclésiastique au XVIIIe siècle*, 170, 184–433 for extensive local inventory of the tithe, and its appearance in the *cahiers* listed on departmental basis.

46. See, for instance, the clergy of Bourges. Bruneau, *Les Débuts de la Révolution*, 32.

47. See, for instance, Triger, *L'Année 1789 au Mans*, 161.
48. Péronnet, *Les Evêques de l'Ancienne France*, 1147.
49. Ibid.
50. Limouzin-Lamothe, *Le diocèse de Limoges*, 158.
51. See, for instance, articles 7 and 12 of the Toul Cahier. Albert Denis, *Toul pendant la Révolution* (vol. I, Toul, 1892), 61, 62; Gibson, *A Social History of French Catholicism*, 31.
52. Péronnet, *Les Evêques de l'Ancienne France*, 1142–3.
53. As at Toul. See Mathieu, *L'Ancien Régime en Lorraine*, 484.
54. Viguier, 'La lutte electorale', 13.
55. Mentioned outright by only 14 *cahiers*. See the comments of Péronnet, *Les Evêques de l'Ancienne France*, 1144–5.
56. Ibid., 1141, 1142.
57. Quoted F. Saurel, *Raymond de Durfort, archevêque de Besançon* (Montpellier/Paris, 1898), 123.
58. Letter of 9 May 1789 from Versailles, in Louis Audiat, *Deux victimes des Septembriseurs: Pierre-Louis de La Rochefoucauld, dernier évêque de Saintes et son frère, évêque de Beauvais* (Lille/Paris, 1897), 132.
59. *Mandement de Mgr l'archevêque de Paris qui ordonne des prieres publiques dans tout son Diocese pour les Etats-Genereux du Royaume* (Paris, 1789), 6. B.L. F.62* (19).
60. *Mandement de Mgr l'archevêque et comte de Lyon, portant permission de manger du Beurre, etc.*, 10.
61. *Le Gouvernement sénati-clerico-aristocratique* (Paris, 1788), B.N. Lb767, p. 29.
62. B.C. Schafer, 'Quelques jugements de pamphlétaires sur le clergé à la veille de la Révolution', *A.H.R.F.*, 16 (1939), 110–22.
63. Timothy Tackett, *Becoming a Revolutionary. The Deputies of the French National Assembly and the emergence of a revolutionary culture (1789–1790)* (Princeton, NJ, 1996), 25, and 24–7 for a general discussion of clerical deputies' backgrounds.

Chapter 6. The Collapse of the Historic Ecclesiastical Order, 1789–90

1. Edna Hindie Lemay, *La Vie quotidienne des députés aux etats généraux* (Paris, 1989), 29–30; C. Constantin, *L'Evéché du Département de la Meurthe de 1791 à 1802* (vol. I, Nancy, 1935), 17.
2. A. Houtin (ed.), *Les Séances des députés du clergé aux états généraux, journaux du curé Thibault et du chanoine Coster* (Paris, 1916), letter of 9 May, p. 85; Timothy Tackett, *Becoming a Revolutionary*, 129–32; Lemay, *La Vie quotidienne des députés*, 168.
3. E. Barbotin, *Lettres de l'abbé Barbotin, député de l'Assemblée constituante* (Paris, 1910), 9.
4. *Journal inédit de Jallet*, ed. J-J. Brethé (Fontenay-le-Comte, 1871) 86–8; Pierrard, *Histoire des curés de campagne*, 32.
5. Ibid., 32–3.
6. *Mémoires de Madame de Chastenay, 1771–1815*, ed. Alphone Roderot (2 vols, Paris, 1896), I, 100.
7. Munro Price, 'The "Ministry of the Hundred Hours: a reappraisal', *French History*, 4 (1990), 317–39.
8. *Mémoires du Comte de Paroy (1789–1797)*, ed. Etienne Charavay (Paris, 1895), 22.
9. Quoted in Pierrard, *Histoire des curés de campagne*, 36.

10. M.L.D.L.S., 'Le Curé Pous: Correspondence inédite d'un membre de l'Assemblée Constituante', *Revue de l'Anjou* 22 (1879), 268–89, at 274. See generally Tackett, *Becoming a Revolutionary*, 180–1.

11. *Lettres de l'abbé Barbotin*, 9.

12. There is an excellent summary in M. Péronnet, 'Nos Seigneurs du Clergé de France en 1789', 119–31, at 127–8.

13. Ibid., 128; Michel Vovelle, 'La politique religieuse de la Révolution française', in Jacques Le Goff and Réné Rémond (eds), *Histoire de la France religieuse*, vol. 3, 74–108, at 82.

14. Malouet, *Mémoires* (2nd edn, 2 vols, Paris, 1874), II, 258–9.

15. Yvonne Crewouw, 'Le Débat sur le veto et la fonction royale dans la Constitution de 1791', in Roger Bourderon (ed.), *Saint-Denis ou le jugement dernier des Rois* (Saint-Denis, 1993), 49–65.

16. Letter of 27 Sept. 1789, *BODL.*, Bowood MSS (microfilm).

17. Audiat, *Deux Victimes des Septembriseurs*, 141.

18. Pierrard, *Histoire des curés de campagne*, 34; R. Dupuy, *De la Révolution à la chouannerie. Paysans en Bretagne, 1788–1794* (Paris, 1988), 94; Saurel, *Raymond de Durfort*, 126.

19. Malouet, *Mémoires*, II, 29–32, for the articles of the club. See also Pascal Simonetti, 'Les Monarchiens: La Révolution à contretemps' in Jean Tulard (ed.), *La Contre-Révolution. Origines, Histoire, Postérité* (Paris, 1990), 62–84; François Furet and Mona Ozouf (eds), *Terminer la Révolution. Mounier et Barnave dans la Révolution française* (Grenoble, 1990), 11.

20. Jean-Nicolas Moreau, *Mes Souvenirs* (2 vols, Paris, 1898–1901), C. Hermelin (ed.) I, 446–7.

21. Quoted in Vicomte de Brimont, *M. de Puységur et l'Eglise de Bourges pendant la Révolution, 1789–1802* (Paris, 1897), 55–6.

22. Bishop Le Mintier was also alleged to be encouraging desertion among his local National Guard. M. Marion, *La Justice en France Pendant la Revolution (1789–1792)* (2 vols, Paris, 1901), I, 216; Péronnet, 'Nos Seigneurs du Clergé de France', 119–31; Léon Dubreuil, 'Les Origines de la Chouannerie dans les Côtes-du-Nord', *La Révolution française*, 68 (1915), 128–55, especially 138, 141–2.

23. Philip Mayow to his mother, 13 Nov. 1789, Cornwall Record Office, DD. WM.592.

24. See, for instance, the plan of campaign decided on by the *Impartiaux* in Jan. 1790, with their letter to the *Amis de la paix*. Malouet, *Mémoires*, II, 43, 48–55.

25. Quoted in Tackett, *Becoming a Revolutionary*, 203.

26. Contemporary description quoted in A.V. Arnault, *Souvenirs d'un Sexagénaire* (2 vols, Paris, 1833), I, 223; Triger, *L'Année 1789 au Mans*, 151; Malouet, *Mémoires*, I, 272.

27. A.C. Duquesnoy, *Journal ... sur l'Assemblé Constituante 3 mai 1789–3 avril 1790*, ed. R. de Crevécour (2 vols, Paris, 1894), II, 179.

28. Patrice Cousin, *Précis d'histoire monastique* (Brussels, 1956), 474; A. Aulard, *Le Christianisme et la Révolution française* (Paris, 1910), 83. On 20 Mar. 1790 municipal officers were ordered to draw up an inventory of monastic properties and to find out what the plans were of the communities affected by the Assembly's decrees.

29. Quoted in Jean Dumont, *La Révolution française*, 45.

30. Duquesnoy, *Journal*, II, 382; André Latreille, *L'Église Catholique et la Révolution française. Le Pontificat de Pie VI et la crise française* (2 vols, Paris, 1946), I, 81.

31. *Moniteur*, III, 345.

32. Ibid., 356.

33. Fréderic Masson, *Le Cardinal de Bernis depuis son ministère 1758–94* (Paris, 1884), 477–8.

34. Cousin, *Précis d'histoire monastique*, 474–5; Chaline, *Histoire des diocèses de France. Rouen et Le Havre*, 191–2.

35. Quoted in H.M. Leclercq, *L'Église constitutionelle, juillet 1790–avril 1791* (Paris, 1934), 176.

36. Michel Lhéritier, *Liberté (1789–90): Les Girondins, Bordeaux et la Révolution française* (Paris, 1947), 231; quotation is in Forrest, *The Revolution in Provincial France*, 162.

37. P. de la Gorce, *Histoire religieuse de la Révolution française* (5 vols, 1909–23), I, 184; N.-D. Chaline et al., *L'église de France et la Révolution* (Paris, 1983), 22.

38. Pierrard (ed.), *Les Diocèses de Cambrai et de Lille*, 187.

39. Cousin, *Précis d'histoire monastique*, 475–6.

40. Elizabeth and Robert Rapley, 'An Image of Religious Women in the Ancien Régime: The États des Religieuses of 1790–1791', *F.H.*, 11 (1997), 387–410, at 409.

41. Quoted in H. Daniel-Rops, *The Church in an Age of Revolution, 1789–1870*, trans. John Warrington (London, 1965), 7.

42. Duquesnoy, *Journal*, II, 509, 3 Apr. 1790.

43. Tackett, *Religion, Revolution, and Regional Culture*, 19.

44. As at Toul on 23 Feb. 1790. See Denis, *Toul pendant la Révolution*, I. 144. Only two bishops declined to submit to it. McManners, *The French Revolution and the Church*, 50.

45. Charles Aimond, *Histoire religieuse de la Révolution dans le département de la Meuse 1789–1802)* (Paris/Bar-le-Duc, 1949), 71.

46. Lhéritier, *Liberté (1789–90)*, 224–5.

47. *Le Désespoir du Haut Clergé ou Réponse du Peuple au Discours de M. l'Evêque de Nancy* (Paris, 1790), 2. B.L. FR 131 (17).

Chapter 7.   The Civil Constitution

1. Michael P. Fitzsimmons, *The Remaking of France. The National Assembly and the Constitution of 1791* (Cambridge, 1994).

2. A. Gazier, *Histoire générale du mouvement janséniste* (Paris, 1924), II, 142; Norman Hampson, *Prelude to Terror. The Constituent Assembly and the Failure of Consensus* (Oxford, 1988), 145.

3. Bernard Plongeron, 'Permanence d'une idéologie de "civilisation chrétienne" dans le clergé constitutionnel', *Studies in Eighteenth-Century Culture*, 7 (1978), 271 ff.

4. Treilhard, 30 May 1790, quoted in *Moniteur*, IV, 500. See also Roland G. Bonnel, 'Ecclesiological Insights at the 1790 National Assembly. An Assessment of the Contribution of Catholic Thought to the French Revolution', in David G. Troyansky, Alfred Cismari and Norwood Andrews, Jr (eds), *The French Revolution in Culture and Society* (New York, 1991), 45–56, at 47–8.

5. Aulard, *Le Christianisme et la Révolution*, 48–9; Préclin, *Les Jansénistes du XVIIIe siècle*, 466, 535.

6. Details in ibid., 473–90. The debates are summarised in Tackett, *Becoming a Revolutionary*, 288–91.

7. There was much apprehension in towns designated to lose their bishopric that it would result in economic depression for them and many lobbyied the National Assembly to try and retain that status at the the expense of neighbouring centres. See Ted W. Margadant, *Urban Rivalries in the French Revolution* (Princeton, NJ, 1992), 122–5, 224–5.

8. See Françoise Hildesheimer, *Le Jansénisme* (Paris, 1992), 102; Cathérine Maire, 'Minorités religieuses. Port-Royal', 480, 505–7; Yann Fauchois, 'Les Jansénistes

et la constitution civile du clergé: Aux marges du débat, débats dans le débat', ed.
Maire, *Jansénisme et Révolution*, 195–207; Van Kley, *The Religious Origins of the French Revolution*, 353–6; Préclin, *Les Jansénistes du XVIIIe siècle*, 479–80, 535. In Poitiers Jansenist canon lawyers joined their old adversary, Bishop Sainte-Aulaire, in rejecting the Civil Constitution. Roux, *La Révolution à Poitiers et dans la Vienne*, 375.

9. Régine Pernoud, *Histoire de la bourgeoisie en France*, vol. II, *Les Temps modernes* (Paris, 1962), 358–62.
10. Ledré, *L'Eglise de France sous la Révolution*, 75.
11. Joseph Lacouture, *La Politique religieuse de la Révolution*, (Paris, 1940), 29; Marquis de Ferrières, *Correspondance inédite*, H. Carré (ed.) (Paris, 1932), II, 56.
12. David C. Miller, 'A-G. Camus and the Civil Constitution of the Clergy', *Catholic Historical Review*, 76 (1990), 481–505. Camus was said to keep a life-sized crucifix in his office, and wrote in 1793 that 'nothing in the world is more precious to me than religion'. Pierre Préteux, *Armand-Gaston Camus, 1740–1804* (Paris, 1932), 13.
13. William Doyle, *The Oxford History of the French Revolution* (Oxford, 1989), 129.
14. Deramecourt, *Le Clergé du diocèse d'Arras, etc.*, II, 31.
15. Quoted in Simon Brugal, *Le Schisme Constituionnel dans l'Ardèche. Lafont-Savine, evêque-jureur de Viviers* (2nd edn, Toulouse, 1977), 14–15.
16. Joseph Perrin, *Le Cardinal de Loménie de Brienne, archevêque de Sens* (Sens, 1896), 54–5; Fréderic Bitton, *Histoire de la ville de Sens* (Paris, 1943), 82; Jean Mortier, *Martial de Loménie, dernier abbé de Jumièges et son oncle Loménie de Brienne, ministre de Louis XVI* (Paris, 1967), 17–18.
17. See C. Rougane (*ancien curé d'Auvergne*), *Plaintes à M. Burke sur la lettre de M. l'archevêque d'Aix* (Paris, 1790), B.L.F.R. 142 (10).
18. Audiat, *Deux victimes des Septembriseurs*, 156.
19. 1 July 1790. Quoted in A. Barruel, *Collection ecclésiastique* (14 vols, Paris, 1791–3), I, 446ff.
20. H. de Formeville, *Histoire de l'évêché-comté de Lisieux* (Lisieux, 1873), 292; Bruneau, *Les Débuts de la Révolution*, 346.
21. To Comtesse de Gramont, late June 1790, quoted in Tackett, *Becoming a Revolutionary*, 291.
22. Quoted in Ledré, *L'Eglise de France sous la Révolution*, 74.
23. Maurice Vaussard, 'Eclaircissements sur la Constitution civile du clergé', *AHRF* 42 (1970), 286–93, at 287–8.
24. René Vaillot, *Le Cardinal de Bernis. La Vie extraordinaire d'un honnête homme* (Paris, 1985), 309–10. He had told the French Foreign Minister, Montmorin, on 30 June, that the Civil Constitution was 'the overthrow of the discipline and general organisation of the Catholic Church, founded on the canons and councils'. Quoted in Masson, *Le Cardinal de Bernis*, 479.
25. Vaussard, 'Eclaircissements sur la Constitution civile du clergé', 292.
26. 7 Aug. 1790. A. Theiner (ed.), *Documents inédits relatifs aux affaires religieuses de la France, 1790 à 1800* (2 vols, Paris, 1857), I, 285.
27. ibid., I, 264–5; Ludovic Sciout, *Histoire de la Constitution civile du clergé (1790–1801)* (4 vols, Paris, 1872), I, 272.
28. Jean-Paul Bertaud, *Les Amis du Roi. Journaux et journalistes royalistes en France de 1789 à 1792* (Paris, 1984),155; Harvey Chiswick, *The Production, Distribution and Readership of a Conservative Journal of the Early French Revolution: the Ami du Roi of the Abbé Royou* (Philadelphia, 1992).
29. Quoted in McManners, *French Ecclesiastical Society Under the Ancien Regime*, 261–2.
30. F.M. Tresvaux, *Histoire de la Persécution Révolutionnaire en Bretagne à la fin du XVIIIe siècle* (2 vols, Paris/Vannes, 1845), I, 97–102.

31. Quoted in ed. Theiner, *Documents inédits*, I, 296.

32. *Lettre du Roi du 3 Septembre, et Mandement de Mgr l'évêque de Tréguier* (Morlaix, 1789), B.N. Lb39 2350; R. Kerviler, *La Bretagne pendant la Révolution* (Rennes, 1912), 42; H. Pommeret, *L'Esprit public dans le département des Côtes-du-Nord pendant la Révolution*) (Saint-Brieuc, 1921), 77–9.

33. *Exposition des Principes sur la Constitution du Clergé* (Paris, 1790), 25.

34. ibid., 53.

35. ibid., 49 ff.

36. *Lettre de MM. les Curés et Vicaires de la ville et faubourgs de Saintes, et du Supérieur de Seminaire à M. l'évêque de Saintes* (Paris, 1790), 2, B.L. F.151(3).

37. Quoted in Leclercq, *L'Église constitutionnelle*, 51.

38. Joseph-Marie Téphany, *Histoire de la Persécution Religieuse dans les diocèses de Quimper et de Léon de 1790 à 1801* (Quimper, 1879), 137–9; Lévy-Schneider, *L'Application du Concordat par un Prélat d'Ancien Régime*, 56–7.

40. *Declaration de M. l'évêque de Rennes sur la Nouvelle organisation du Clergé* (Paris, 10 Dec. 1790), 5. BODL., 237. f. 211 (13).

41. McManners, *French Revolution and the Church*, 45.

42. Leclercq, *L'Église constitutionnelle*, 48; D. Lottin, *Recherches historiques sur la ville d'Orléans* (2e partie, vol. I, Orléans, 1838), 228; Perrin, *Le Cardinal de Loménie de Brienne*, 56.

43. Letter to the *conseil général du département*, 9 Dec. 1790, quoted in Y.-G. Paillard, 'Fanatiques et patriotes dans le Puy-de-Dôme', *A.H.R.F.*, 42 (1970), 294–328, at 298.

44. *Réponse de M. l'archevéque d'Auch, à M. le Procureur-Général-Syndic du département du Gers* (Paris, 1790), 2–3, B.L. R.348 (8).

45. Quoted in Kwanten, 'A.-A.-J. de Clermont-Tonnerre', 285; *Lettre de M. l'évêque d'Angoulême à M. le procureur général de département de la Charente* (24 Dec. 1790).

46. de la Gorce, *Histoire religieuse de la Révolution française*, I, 337–48.

47. Auguste Allou, *Chronique des Evêques de Meaux* (Meaux, 1875), 132; Tresvaux, *Histoire de la Persécution révolutionnaire en Bretagne*, I, 287.

48. Many of the cardinals were unofficially encouraging the most intransigent prelates like Cardinal Rohan of Strasbourg. Leclercq, *L'Église constitutionnelle*, 48.

49. The quotation is from Louis-Joseph-Amour de Bouillé, *Souvenirs et Fragments (1769–1812)*, (2 vols, Paris, 1821), I, 185.

50. *Discours de l'évêque de Clermont, relativement au serment exigé par l'assemblée nationale, et qu'il a prononcé en partie dans la séance du dimanche matin, 2 janv. 1791*, BODL., 237 f.211(15), p. 9; M. Picot, *Mémoires pour servir à l'histoire ecclésiastique pendant le dix-huitième siècle* (7 vols, Paris, 1855), VI. 52; *Mercure de France*, 8 Jan. 1791.

51. Hampson seems unconvincing with his claim that the Right in January 1791 was looking for a grievance. He quotes Maury: 'Let the decree pass [the oath]; we need it. Two or three more like that and it will all be over.' This insistence on the popularity of the *politique du pire* overlooks the constructive contribution of clerical deputies to debate for the remainder of the National Assembly's life. *Prelude to Terror*, 153.

52. Quoted in Leclerq, *L'Église constitutionnelle*, 106. St Laurence was a Roman Deadon martyred in A.D. 258 who was believed –incorrectly – to have been killed on a gridiron.

53. Quoted in Leflon, *Monsieur Emery*, 187.

54. Sagnac, *Histoire de France contemporaine*, I, 248.

55. Lindet to the municipal officers of Bernay, 5 Jan. 1791, quoted in *Le Correspondent* (1899), 255, n. 150.

56. Hampson, *Prelude to Terror*, 153.

57. *A Diary of the French Revolution by Gouverneur Morris*, ed. Beatrix Cary Devenport (2 vols, London), II, 124; Lacourt-Gayet, *Vie de Talleyrand*, I, 131–2. There were unfounded rumours he would be translated to the see of Paris in Feb. 1791 – ibid., 110; J.M. Thompson, *The French Revolution* (Oxford, 1943), 152, 15; J. Leflon, *Monsieur Emery. L'Église d'Ancien Régime et la Révolution* (2nd ed., Paris, 1944), 204–5.

58. Owen Chadwick, *The Popes and European Revolution* (Oxford, 1981), 447.

59. Daniel-Rops, *The Church in an Age of Revolution*, 11; *Ami du Roi*, 6 Jan. 1791, quoted in William James Murray, *The Right-Wing Press in the French Revolution: 1788–92* (Woodbridge, 1986), 109.

60. Quoted in R. Mirabaud, *Rabaut Saint-Etienne* (Paris, 1930), 183.

61. Jones, *Reform and Revolution*, 245.

62. See the provocative essay by Claude Langlois, 'La rupture entre l'Église catholique et la Révolution', in François Furet and Mona Ozouf (eds), *The French Revolution and the Creation of Modern Political Culture*, vol. 3. *The Transformation of Political Culture 1789–1848* (Oxford, 1989), 375–90.

63. Fitzsimmons, *The Remaking of France*. As Peter Jones has sardonically noted, it 'was no mean achievement for legislators who had enjoyed the overwhelming support of rank-and-file clerics at the start of the Revolution' – *Reform and Revolution*, 212.

64. C. Langlois, 'Le serment révolutionnaire archaïsme et modernité', in ed. J. Martin, *Religion et Revolution* (Paris, 1994), 25–39, at 36.

Chapter 8.   Church, State and Revolution, 1791–5

1. Doyle, *The Oxford History*, 144. This view echoes an overlaid seam of earlier French historiography. Cf. A. Debidour, *Histoire des rapports de l'Église et de l'État en France de 1789 à 1870* (Paris, 1898), 68, 'the capital error of the Revolution'.

2. Gwynne Lewis, *The French Revolution. Rethinking the Debate* (London, 1993), 61; cf. Jones, *Reform and Revolution*, 212.

3 Quoted in Émile Lafont, *La Politique religieuse de la Révolution Française* (Paris, 1909), 30.

4. The Declaration of the Rights of Man was specifically condemned in the Encyclical *Adeo nota* of 23 Apr. 1791. These rights, wrote Pius, were those 'of a being without a father or mother', they showed 'man amputated from God'.

5. Quoted in Cousin, Cubells, Moulinas, *La pique et la croix*, 142; Aulard, *Le Christianisme et la Révolution française*, 61–2. See also Bernard Plongeron, 'L'Église et les Déclarations des droits de l'homme au XVIIIe siècle', *Nouvelle Revue théologique*, 101 (Louvain, 1979), 363. The Brief received only a tepid endorsement from the bishops left in Paris, still piqued that they should need recourse to the Pope in the first place. See M. de Richemont (ed.), *Correspondance secrète de l'abbé de Salamon, chargé des affaires du Saint-Siège pendant la Révolution avec le cardinal Zelada (1791–1792)* (Paris, 1898), xi, n.2.

6. Daniel-Rops, *The Church in an Age of Revolution*, 12.

7. Aulard, *Le Christianisme et la Révolution française*, 52–3; C.S. Phillips, *The Church in France 1789–1848: A Study in Revival* (New York, 1966), 16.

8. Quoted in Guillon, *Brefs*, I. 352–3. There are slight variants in the wording in some other summaries. See also J. Chaunu, *Pie VI et les Evêques français. Droits de l'Église et de l'Homme. Le bref Quod aliquantum et autres textes* (Limoges, 1989);

Picot, *Mémoires pour servir à l'histoire ecclésiastique*, VI, 90–1; Leclercq, *L'Église constitutionnelle*, 371–2; Julien Loth, *Histoire du Cardinal de La Rochefoucauld et du diocèse de Rouen pendant la Révolution* (Evreux, 1893), 205–31.

9. J. Lacouture, *La Politique religieuse de la Révolution* (Paris, 1940), 49; A. Mathiez, 'Les Divisions du Clergé Refractaire', *La Révolution française*, 39 (1900), 44–73, at 49–50. Cf. Charles Ledré, *L'Abbé de Salamon: Correspondent et Agent du Saint-Siège pendant la Révolution* (Paris, 1965), 104 ff. 26. Episcopal deputies were among the signatories of the *Compte-rendu par une partie des députés à leurs commetants* which defended their qualified resistance to recent legislative measures (10 Sept. 1791). The prelates in the Assembly continued to act as an unofficial steering committee for the non-juring Church until August 1792.

10. Ledré, *L'Église de France sous la Révolution*, 107.

11. Hampson, *Prelude to Terror*, 154.

12. Letter of 29 Mar. 1791 from Paris, in Achille Bardon (ed.), *Lettres du Cardinal de Bausset (1790–1820)* (Nîmes, 1886), 32.

13. E. Pionnier, *La Révolution à Verdun (1789–95)* (Nancy, 1905), 93.

14. A.N. D XXIX, f. 1, 10 Aug. 1791; L. Viguier, *Les Débuts de la Révolution en Provence* (Paris, 1894), 292–3.

15. Hampson, *Prelude to Terror*, 153–4; D.M.G. Sutherland, *France 1789–1815. Revolution and Counterrevolution* (London, 1985), 117.

16. M. Picot, *Mémoires pour servir à l'histoire ecclesiastique*, VI, 113.

17. Aulard, *Le Christianisme et la Révolution française*, 65.

18. ed. F. Mirouse, *Franéois Ménard de la Groye, député de Maine aux Etats-généraux. Correspondance, 1789–1791* (Le Mans, 1989), 379, quoted in Jones, *Reform and Revolution in France*, 202.

19. P. Caron, *Rapport des Agents du Ministre de l'Intérieur dans les Départements* (2 vols, Paris, 1913, 1951), II, 423.

20. Jacques Bernet, 'Les Serments à la Constitution civile du clergé en Picardie', in Alain Lottin (ed.), *Eglise, Vie religieuse et révolution dans la France du Nord* (Lille, 1990), 25–39, at 33.

21. In Normandy as a whole, 52 per cent of the clergy refused the oath. E. Sévestre, *Le Personnel de l'Eglise constitutionnelle en Normandie, 1791–1795* (Paris, 1925), 297.

22. There is a helpful chart in Michel Vovelle, *Religion et révolution: la déchristianisation de l'an II*, 63. See also the excellent maps and graphs throughout Tackett, *Religion, Revolution, and Regional Culture*.

23. Vovelle, *Religion et révolution*, 50–2.

24. Quoted in ibid., 65.

25. Quoted in S. Gruget, *Histoire de la Constitution civile du clergé en Anjou* (Paris, 1905), 71.

26. Quoted in Tackett, *Religion, Revolution, and Regional Culture*, 64.

27. 'The base of this constitution, the fundamental principle from which all the articles arise, is that all powers come from the people and should be conferred by them. On the contrary, the constitutive power of the Church is that all it possesses, all its powers have been given to it by Jesus Christ, and that it's from God Himself that it holds its government.' Quoted in Leclercq, *L'Église constitutionnelle*, 151. La Luzerne's *Letter* went into 6 editions and was widely adopted and used by other prelates. See, for instance, Polignac of Meaux's Address of 5 Apr. 1791. Allou, *Chronique des Evêques de Meaux*, 133.

28. Hufton, *Women and the Limits of Citizenship in the French Revolution*, 104–5.

29. T. Tackett, 'Women and Men in Sommières and the Ecclesiastical Oath of 1791', in B. Plongeron (ed.), *Pratiques religieuses dans l'Europe révolutionnaire*

(Turnhout, 1988), 351–60; Claude Le Foll, 'La Crise religieuse à Rouen pendant la Révolution française: gestes, attitudes et comportements féminins', in ibid., 331–5.

30. Tackett, *Religion, Revolution and Regional Culture*, 40–3, based on a survey of 51 000 priests in post. Tackett has been criticised for overestimating the number of jurors. See J. de Viguerie, *Christianisme et Révolution. Cinq leçons d'histoire de la Révolution française* (Paris, 1986), 92–3, and, generally, Dominique Julia, 'La Révolution, L'Église et la France', *Annales ESC* (1988), 761–9.
31. P. Lesprand, 'Louis-Joseph de Montmorency-Laval, évêque de Metz', *Les Cahiers Lorrains*, 7 (1928), 33–9, at 37–8. The cardinal resigned soon after the events of 18 Apr. Mansel, *The Court of France*, 26.
32. Girault de Coursacs, *Sur la Route de Varennes* (Paris, 1984); Hardman, *Louis XVI*, 185–207.
33. Mellor, *Histoire de l'anticléricalisme français*, 164.
34. L. de Cardenal, *La Province pendant la Révolution. Histoire des Clubs Jacobins (1789–1795)* (Paris, 1929), 285–8.
35. Quoted in Mellor, *Histoire de l'anticlericalisme français*, 163.
36. *Archives parlementaires*, vol. 34, p. 724.
37. Marcel Reinhard, *La chute de la royauté, 10 août 1792* (Paris, 1969), 232; Aulard, *Le Christianisme et la Révolution française*, 78.
38. Quoted in Cardenal, *La Province pendant la Révolution*, 288.
39. W.D. Edmonds, *Jacobinism and the Revolt in Lyon 1789–1793* (Oxford, 1990), 92–3; Gwynn Lewis, *Life in Revolutionary France* (London, 1972), 43. See generally on the persecution of non-jurors in 1792, de la Gorce, *Histoire religieuse de la Révolution française*, chapters 9–12.
40. Ibid.; McLeod, *Religion and the People of Western Europe*, 2–3; Forrest, *The Revolution in Provincial France*, 178–9.
41. *A Residence in France During the Years 1792, 1793, 1794, and 1795; Described in a Series of Letters from an English Lady* (2nd edn, 2 vols, London, 1797), I, 210–16.
42. Frank Paul Bowman, *L'Abbé Grégoire. Evêque des Lumières* (Paris, 1988), 12.
43. Frédéric Bluche, *Septembre 1792. Logiques d'un massacre* (Paris, 1986), is the most recent work on the topic.
44. As early as 16 May in the Legislative Assembly, the abbé de Moy had unsuccessfully requested the abrogation of the Civil Constitution, the gradual suppression of priests' salaries, and religious liberty for all who supported the Constitution of 1791. Lafont, *La Politique religieuse*, 61; Aulard, *Le Christianisme et la Révolution française*, 79.
45. Frank Tallett, 'Dechristianizing France: The Year II and the Revolutionary Experience', in Frank Tallett and Nicholas Atkin (eds), *Religion, Society and Politics in France since 1789* (London, 1991), 1–28, at 1.
46. M-J. Chénier, Nov. 1793, quoted in F-V. Alphone Aulard, *Le Culte de la raison et de l'Etre suprême* (2nd edn, Paris, 1904), 35.
47. Quoted in Sutherland, *France 1789–1815*, 211.
48. Emmet Kennedy, 'The French Revolutionary Catechisms: Ruptures and Continuities with Classical, Christian, and Enlightenment Moralities', *Studies on Voltaire and the Eighteenth Century* 199 (1981), 353–62; B. Plongeron, *Théologie et politique au siècle des Lumières 1770–1820*, vol. 3, 'Combats révolutionnaires pour une théologie de sécularisation 1790–1804' (Geneva, 1973), 121–83; Isser Woloch, *The New Régime. Transformations of the French Civic Order, 1789–1820* (New York, 1994), 180–207.
49. Richard Cobb, 'Les débuts de la déchristianisation à Dieppe', *A.H.R.F.*, 28 (1956), 191–209, at 200, who points out that the local patriots blamed

the clergy for encouraging farmers not to take their produce into the market towns.

50. Quoted in Cardenal, *La Province pendant la Révolution*, 296. On 23 July 1793 the Convention decreed that only one church bell per parish should be left. The rest were to be melted down for canons. Aulard, *Le Christianisme et la Révolution française*, 92.

51. Richard Cobb, *The People's Armies. The armées révolutionnaires, instruments of the Terror in the departments. April 1793 to Floréal Year II*, trans. Marianne Elliott (New Haven, 1987), 645; Viguerie, *Christianisme et Révolution*, 171–2.

52. J. Bernet, 'La Déchristianisation dans le District de Compiègne (1789–1795)', *A.H.R.F.*, 50 (1978), 299–305, at 301. Michel Vovelle, *The Revolution Against the Church. From Reason to the Supreme Being*, trans. Alan José (Oxford, 1991), 126–33, discusses the variety of tactics and practices among the representatives.

53. Discussed in Viguerie, *Cinq Leçons d'histoire*, 169; Lucas, 'The Revolution and Christianity' 348–9, and Claude Lefort, 'La Révolution comme religion nouvelle', in Furet and Ozouf, *The French Revolution and the Creation of Modern Political Culture*, vol. 3, 391–9.

54. For other ex-Oratorians involved in dechristianisation, see Ruth Graham, 'The Enlightened and Revolutionary Oratorians in France', *Journal of the British Society for Eighteenth Century Studies*, 4 (1981), 171–83, at 178–81.

55. Bernet, 'La Déchristianisation dans le District de Compiègne', 301; Cousin, Cubells, Moulinas, *La Pique et la croix*, 173.

56. Ruth Graham, 'The Secularization of the Ecclesiastical Deputies', *The Consortium on Revolutionary Europe*, 65–79 at 69.

57. G. Cholvy, *Religion et Société au XIXe siècle: Le diocèse de Montpellier* (2 vols, Lille, 1973), I, 86.

58. The latest estimate suggests the figure in Donald Greer should be increased to the 3000 mark. See Michel Vovelle, 'La Politique religieuse de la Révolution française', in Jacques Le Goff and Réné Rémond (eds), *Histoire de la France religieuse*, vol. 3, *Du Roi très Chrétien à la laïcité républicaine* (Paris, 1991), 74–108, at 100.

59. Plongeron, *La Vie quotidienne du clergé*, 190.

60. Jean-Claude Meyer, 'L'Opinion publique et l'Eglise en Haut-Garonne (1790–1799)', in Jean Sentou (ed.), *Révolution et Contre-Révolution dans la France du Midi (1789–1799)* (Toulouse, 1991), 107–43, at 111; Norman Hampson, *A Social History of the French Revolution* (London, 1963), 199.

61. Lynn Hunt, *Politics, Culture and Class in the French Revolution* (London, 1984), 62–6, 98. For a festival of Reason held in Angers see McManners, *French Ecclesiastical Society*, 287–8.

62. Vovelle, *The Revolution Against the Church*, 46–8; Aulard, *Le Christianisme et la Révolution française*, 100–1.

63. Robespierre, *Oeuvres* (10 vols, Paris, 1912–67), V, 117.

64. As in the Compiègne district. Jacques Bernet, 'Les origines de la déchristianisation dans le district de Compiègne (Septembre–Decembre 1793)', *A.H.R.F.*, 48 (1978), 405–32.

65. M. Bée, 'Pétition et défense de la religion catholique dans le Perche en 1792', in Plongeron (ed.), *Pratiques religieuses dans l'Europe révolutionnaire*, 281–92.

66. See eds. Simone Bernard-Griffiths, Marie-Claude Chemin and Jean Ehrard, *Révolution française et "vandalisme révolutionnaire"*, Actes du Colloque international de Clermont-Ferrand, 15–17 Dec. 1988 (Paris, 1992); S.J. Idzerda, 'Iconoclasm During the French Revolution', *American Historical Review*, [hereafter *A.H.R.*], 60 (1954), 13–26; Gabriele Sprigath, 'Sur le Vandalisme révolutionnaire (1792–1794)', *A.H.R.F.*, 52 (1980) 510–35.

67. Tallett, 'Dechristianizing France' 6–7.

68. André Vauchez, 'La Cathédrale', in Pierre Nora (ed.), *Les Lieux de Mémoire*, vol. 2, *Traditions* (Paris, 1993), 90–127, at 111.
69. Warren Roberts, *Jacques-Louis David, Revolutionary Artist. Art, Politics, and the French Revolution* (Chapel Hill, NC, 1989), 72.
70. McManners, *Death and the Enlightenment*, 353–4; Blordier-Langlois, *Angers et le Département de Maine-et-Loire* (2 vols, Angers, 1837), I, 324.
71. Viguerie, *Christianisme et Révolution*, 164.
72. Mary Lee Nolan and Sidney Nolan, *Christian Pilgrimage in Modern Western Europe* (Chapel Hill, NC, 1989), 211.
73. Quoted in Daniel-Rops, *The Church in an Age of Revolution*, 29.
74. K.A. Roider, *Baron Thugut and Austria's Response to the French Revolution* (Princeton, NJ, 1987).
75. Peter Jupp, *Lord Grenville, 1759–1834* (Oxford, 1985); John Ehrman, *The Younger Pitt, vol. 2, The Years of Transition* (London, 1983).

Chapter 9(i).   The Survival of Religious Groups: The Constitutional Church

1. Claude Fauchet, *De la Religion nationale* (Paris, 1789), 4. For Montesquieu's popularity with the Constitutional bishops, see Ruth Graham, 'The Revolutionary Bishops and the *Philosophes*', *Eighteenth Century Studies*, 16 (1982–3), 117–40, at 130.
2. Bernard Plongeron, 'Le Fait religieuse dans l'histoire de la Révolution. Objet, Méthodes, Voies nouvelles', in *Colloque Albert Mathiez-Georges Lefebvre. Voies nouvelles pour l'Histoire de la Révolution française* (Paris, 1978), 237–64, at 259; 'Permanence d'une idéologie de "civilisation chrétienne" dans le clergé constitutionnel', *Studies in XVIIIth century Culture* (vol. 7, Wisconsin, 1978), ed. Roseann Punte, 262–87; P-M. Masson, *La Religion de Jean-Jacques Rousseau* (3 vols, Paris, 1916), III, 230–4.
3. Fauchet, *De la Religion nationale*, 274.
4. Bishop A.J.C. Clément to Scipione de Ricci, Bishop of Pistoia and Prato, 17 Apr. 1791, quoted in John Rogister, 'A Quest for Peace in the Church: The Abbé A.J.C. Clément's Journey to Rome of 1758', in Aston, *Religious Change in Europe, 1650–1914*, 103–33, at 132.
5. Quoted in Bertaud, *Les Amis du Roi*, 157.
6. McManners, *French Ecclesiastical Society under the Ancien Régime*, 267, 268.
7. Colin Jones, 'Bourgeois Revolution Revivified: 1789 and Social Change', in Colin Lucas (ed.), *Rewriting the French Revolution* (Oxford, 1991), 69–118, at 115.
8. Julia, 'La Révolution, l'Eglise et la France', 764.
9. For a discussion of the implications of administrative reorganisation see the illuminating essay by Alan Forrest, 'Regionalism and Counter-Revolution in France', in Lucas, *Rewriting the French Revolution*, 151–82, at 162–6.
10. Audiat, *Deux victimes des Septembriseurs*, 252, 279.
11. Lucas, 'The Revolution and Christianity', 348.
12. Latreille, *L'Église Catholique et la Révolution française*, I, 96–7.
13. Quoted in Bertaud, *Les Amis du Roi*, 155.
14. In fact, most elections were 'one-off' affairs. While *curé* elections occurred quite frequently in 1791 and 1792, replacements for prelates were limited. They are

found in the Seine-Inférieure and the Isère, early and late 1792, and there were elections for bishops in two newly created departments in 1793: Savoie and Vaucluse. I am grateful to Malcolm Crook for allowing me access to his recent research on the clerical elections.

15. Edmund Burke, 'Letter to a Member of a National Assembly', in *The Writings and Speeches of Edmund Burke*, vol. 8, *The French Revolution*, ed. L.G. Mitchell (Oxford, 1989), 304.

16. Quoted in Bertaud, *Les Amis du Roi*, 159–60.

17. Geoffroy de Grandmaison, *Un Curé d'autrefois: L'abbé de Talhouët, 1737–1802* (Paris, 1894), 135. For other examples of mocking ditties see Leclerqc, *L'Église constitutionnel*, 190.

18. Fauchet was always a favourite for royalist caricaturists. See Claude Langlois, *La Caricature contre-Révolutionnaire* (Paris, 1988), 56, 57.

19. Marie-Louise Massonie-Wehrung, 'Le Jeu de la Constitution civile du Clergé en Lorraine', *Annales de l'Est*, 5th sér., 12 (1961), 181–211, at 198; Graham, 'The Revolutionary Bishops', 121.

20. 8 Apr. 1791, quoted in Félix Bouvier, *Les Vosges pendant la Révolution, 1789–1795–1800* (Paris, 1885), 94.

21. Paul Pisani, *Répertoire biographique de l'Episcopat constitutionnel (1791–1802)* (Paris, 1907), 448–9.

22. Joseph Perrin, *Le Cardinal de Loménie de Brienne, Archevêque de Sens* (Sens, 1896), 57–84; Bitton, *Histoire de la ville de Sens*, 82.

23. Louis d'Illiers, *Deux Prélats d'Ancien Régime: Les Jarente* (Monaco, 1948), 84–95. He renounced his functions as a bishop in November 1792 in protest at the bloody events of that autumn; ibid., 101.

24. Brugal, *Le Schisme Constitutionnel dans l'Ardèche*, 17–29; B. Plongeron, 'Théologie et Applications de la collégialité dans l'église constitutionnelle de France (1790–1801)', *A.H.R.F.*, 45 (1973), 70–84, at 78; ed. Theiner, *Documents inédits*, I, 442.

25. Graham, 'The Revolutionary Bishops', 117–40; Latreille, *L'Église catholique et la Révolution française*, I, 107.

26. McManners, *The French Revolution and the Church*, 123.

27. Plongeron, *L'Abbé Grégoire*, 24; Ruth Graham, 'Women versus Clergy, Women pro Clergy', in ed. Samia I. Spencer, *French Women and the Age of Enlightenment* (Bloomington, IN, 1984) 128–40, at 136.

28. Gary Kates, *The Cercle Social, the Girondins, and the French Revolution* (Princeton, NJ, 1985); Hans Maier, *Revolution und Kirche –Studien zur Frühgeschichte der christlichen Demokratie (1789–1901)* (Freiburg in Breisgau, 1979), 130–7; Ravitch, *The Catholic Church and the French Nation*, 55.

29. N. Ravitch, 'The Abbé Fauchet: Romantic Religion during the French Revolution', *Journal of the American Academy of Religion*, 13 (1974), 247–62.

30. Fauchet, *De la Religion nationale*, 31.

31. Clarke Garrett, *Respectable Folly: Millenarians and the French Revolution in France and England* (Baltimore, 1975), 36–53; Albert Mathiez, *Contributions à l'histoire religieuse de la Révolution française* (Paris, 1907), 100–6.

32. Quéniart, *Le Clergé déchiré*, 54; McManners, *French Ecclesiastical Society*, 275–6, 278, 284–5. Little notice was taken of his pastoral letter of 1791 insisting the faithful take Easter communion only in their parish churches.

33. V. Chomel, *Histoire de Grenoble* (Toulouse, 1976), 229.

34. E. Pionnier, *La Révolution à Verdun (1789–1795)* (Nancy, 1905), 97.

35. Bernard Guillemain (ed.), *Le Diocèse de Bordeaux* (Paris, 1974), 167, 176; Pisani, *Répertoire biographique*, 409–10.

36. Hildesheimer, *Le Jansénisme*, 102.
37. Quoted in Latreille, *L'Église Catholique et la Révolution française*, I, 99.
38. Quoted in P.-J. Crédot, *Pierre Pontard. Evêque constitutionnel de la Dordogne* (Paris, 1893), 16.
39. Quoted in in Artaud, 'Gay-Vernon: Evêque Constitutionnel et député, 328.
40. Massonie-Wehrung, 'Le Jeu de la Constitution civile du Clergé', 202.
41. Abbé Thomas Tolra, quoted in M. Brunet, *Le Roussillon 1780–1820: une société contre l'état* (Toulouse, 1986), 448.
42. At Nîmes, Bishop Dumouchel presided over dancing until 3 a.m.; E. de Beaufond, 'L'Épiscopat constitutionnel 1791–1801', in *Revue des questions historiques*, 51 (1892), 161.
43. As at Evreux for Bishop Thomas Lindet; Huntly Dupre, *Two Brothers in the French Revolution. Robert and Thomas Lindet* (Hamden, 1967), 44.
44. Fleury, *Mémoires sur la Révolution*, 46n.
45. Pierre J-B. Delon, *La Révolution en Lozère* (Mende, 1922), 76–7.
46. Paul R. Hanson, *Provincial Politics in the French Revolution. Caen and Limoges, 1789–1794* (Baton Rouge, LA, 1991), 62.
47. Plongeron, 'Théologie et applications de la collégialité', 78–9.
48. Tackett, *Religion, Revolution, and Regional Culture*, 167.
49. Alan Forrest, *The Revolution in Provincial France. Aquitaine, 1789–1799* (Oxford, 1996), 172.
50. Quoted in Delon, *La Révolution en Lozère*, 89.
51. Mitchell, 'Resistance to the Revolution in Western France', 126–7.
52. Graham, 'Women versus Clergy, Women pro Clergy', 135.
53. Hufton, *Women and the limits of Citizenship*, 105; Tackett, *Religion, Revolution, and Regional Culture*, 172–7.
54. J. Leflon, *La Crise révolutionnaire 1789–1846*, vol. 20 of *Histoire de l'Église*, ed. A. Fliche and V. Martin (Paris, 1949), 76.
55. Pisani, *Répertoire biographique*, 190–91n.; Ledré, *L'Eglise de France sous la Révolution*, 87, 101. It is estimated that a total of 500 to 600 new priests were consecrated by the Constitutional bishops of Normandy in a two-year period.
56. Cousin, Cubells, Moulinas, *La Pique et la croix*, 146; Hufton, *Bayeux*, 195.
57. Robert Darnton, *The Kiss of Lamourette. Reflections in Cultural History* (New York, 1990).
58. Hufton, *Bayeux*, 197; Artaud, 'Gay-Vernon: Evêque constitutionnel et député', 314–34, 447–67, 502–31.
59. Pisani, *Répertoire biographique*, 415.
60. Aulard, *Le Christianisme et la Révolution*, 82.
61. Ibid., 86.
62. Alison Patrick, *The Men of the First French Republic. Political Alignments in the National Convention of 1792* (Baltimore, 1792), 274. They also participated heavily in the vote on the Constitution of 1793 in July/August of that year. The Clergy were among the broader issues treated by the electoral assemblies (*ex info.* Malcolm Crook).
63. Graham, 'The Revolutionary Bishops', 123.
64. Ibid., 131; Graham, 'The Secularization of the Ecclesiastical Deputies', 70.
65. Quoted in Latreille, *L'Église Catholique et la Révolution*, I, 147.
66. Hufton, *Bayeux*, 196; Hanson, *Provincial Politics*, 39. Fauchet kept his Christian faith to the end. Pisani, *Répertoire biographique*, 171.
67. Graham, 'The Revolutionary Bishops', 136.
68. Michel Lancelin, 'La lutte contre le clergé à Saint-Omer entre avril 1793 et juillet 1794', in Lottin, *Église, Vie religieuse et révolution dans la France du Nord*, 56–7.

69. Edmund Burke, 'Remarks on the Policy of the Allies (1793)', in *The Writings and Speeches*, vol. 8, 485. 70. Audrein, *Mémoire à l'Assemblé nationale sur l'importance de maintenir les loix qui organisent le culte catholique en France* . . . (Paris, 1792), 6.
71. Quoted in Paillard, 'Fanatiques et patriotes dans le Puy-de-Dôme', 377.
72. Graham, 'The Revolutionary Bishops', 126.
73. A. Espenas, *La Philosophie sociale au xviiie siècle et la Révolution* (Paris, 1893), 403–12; Cousin, Cubells, Moulinas, *La Pique et la croix*, 208–10.
74. Quoted in P. Christophe, *1789, Les Prêtres dans la Révolution* (Paris, 1986), 162.
75. Mellor, *Histoire de l'anticléricalisme français*, 164.
76. For Fauchet's disapproval of other republican policies in 1793, see Hufton, *Bayeux*, 195–6.
77. Latreille, *L'Église Catholique et la Révolution*, I, 139–40; Phillips, *The Church in France 1789–1848*, 28.
78. Delivered 19 March 1793, quoted in Meyer, 'L'Opinion publique et l'Église en Haut-Garonne', 111.
79. Plongeron, 'Théologie et applications de la collégialité', 79.
80. François Lebrun (ed.), *Histoire des Catholiques en France du XVe siècle à nos jours* (Toulouse, 1980), 261; Hufton, 'The reconstruction of a church 1796–1801', 27; Vovelle, *The Revolution Against the Church*, 84.
81. Ruth Graham, 'The Secularization of the Ecclesiastical Deputies', 67. For more details about the geography of abdication see Vovelle, *The Revolution Against the Church*, 33–6, 62–82.
82. Colin Lucas, *The Structure of the Terror* (Oxford, 1973), 288.
83. The comparable figure for the adjacent Gard was 163 abdications for the 355 communes. Vovelle, 'Essai de cartographie de la déchristianisation sous la Révolution Française', *Annales du Midi*, 76 (1964), 529–42, at 531.
84. Ravitch, 'The Abbé Fauchet', *passim*.
85. Vovelle, *The Revolution Against the Church*, 67, 76–7, 80.
86. Incarceration could be. 'I was forced to take a wife', reported the *curé* Romieu from Gers in the Alps, 'after twenty-two months in prison'. Quoted in ibid., 90.
87. Morellet, *Mémoires inédits* (2 vols, Paris, 1823), II, 15–16, 467–8.
88. Graham, 'The Revolutionary Bishops', 119–20; Latreille, *L'Église Catholique et la Révolution*, I, 146–7; Cousin, Cubells, Moulinas, *La Pique et la croix*, 167–8.
89. Cousin, Cubells, Moulinas, *La Pique et la croix*, 176–7.
90. Gibson, *A Social History of French Catholicism*, 44.
91. Hufton, *Bayeux*, 201–2.
92. Chaline et al., *L'Église de France et la Révolution*, 36.
93. Aulard, *Le Christianisme et la Révolution*, 108–9.
94. Gérard Cholvy, *La Religion en France de la fin du XVIIIe siècle à nos jours* (Paris, 1991), p. 11.
95. *Ex info*. Malcolm Crook.
96. Grégoire, *Mémoires* (Paris, 1837), II, 37 ff.
97. Plongeron, *La Vie quotidienne du clergé*, 71–3; Cousin, Cubells, Moulinas, *La Pique et la croix*, 146. For the situation in Angers see McManners, *French Ecclesiastical Society*, 282, and in Bayeux, Hufton, *Bayeux*, 194–5.
98. The royalist press gave honourable individual mention to any of the 'evil priests' who renounced their oath and changed sides. Bertaud, *Les Amis du Roi*, 160.
99. Gérard Cholvy (ed.), *Histoire du Vivarais* (Toulouse, 1988), 174.
100. Suzanne Desan, 'Redefining Revolutionary Liberty. The Rhetoric of Religious Revival during the French Revolution', *J.M.H.*, 60 (1988), 1–27, at 12–13.

101. R.F. Necheles, 'The Constitutional Church, 1794–1802: An Essay in Voluntarism', *Proceedings of the Consortium on Revolutionary Europe* (1974), 80.
102. Lucas, 'The Revolution and Christianity', 347.

Chapter 9(ii). The Survival of Religious Groups: The Refractory Church

1. *Lettre de M. l'Évêque de Clermont à MM. les Electeurs du Département du Puy-de-Dôme* (Paris, 1791), 4–5. BODL. 237 f.211(17).
2. See his ordonnance of 3 Apr. 1791 in L. Jouhaud, *La Révolution française en Limousin; pages d'histoire vécue, 1789–92* (Limousin, 1947), 124.
3. Lewis, *Life in Revolutionary France*, 43.
4. F. Baboin, 'L'Application de la Constitution Civile du clergé dans la Drôme', *La Révolution française*, 37 (1899), 222–51, esp. 229.
5. J.B. Laffon, *Le Diocèse de Tarbes et Lourdes* (Paris, 1971), 115; A. Tarbouriech, *Curiosités Révolutionnaires du Gers* (Auch, 1892), 39–44; Robert Anchel, 'Cinq Procès de religion dans l'Eure (1791–99)', *La Révolution française*, 43 (1912), 513–39, at 514–15.
6. See, for instance, the letter of Archbishop Fontanges of Toulouse, 16 Jan. 1791, Abbé Cayre, *Histoire des Évêques et Archevêques de Toulouse* (Toulouse, 1873), 460–1.
7. Th. Lhuillier, *Pierre Thuin, évêque constitutionnel de Seine-et-Marne* (Paris, 1885), 3.
8. A. Dédouit, *Bayeux sous la Révolution* (Bellême, 1892), 11.
9. *Lettre de M. l'Évêque de Saintes à MM. les électeurs du département de la Charente-Inférieure* (Paris, 18 Feb. 1791).
10. Joseph Lacouture, *La Politique Religieuse de la Révolution* (Paris, 1940), 46.
11. *Lettre de M. l'Évêque de Rennes à MM. les Electeurs du Département d'Isle et Vilaine* (Paris, 18 Feb. 1791), 11, 15. B.L. R.348(20).
12. Quoted in J-M. Mioland, *Actes de l'Eglise d'Amiens* (2 vols, Amiens, 1848–9), II, 559.
13. Quoted in Lamothe-Limouzin, *Le Diocèse de Limoges*, 163.
14. Bishop of Saintes's pastoral letter, 3 June 1791, quoted in Joseph Briand, *Histoire de L'Eglise Santone et Aunisienne depuis son origine jusqu'à nos jours* (3 vols., La Rochelle, 1843), III, 30; Audiat, *Deux Victimes des Septembriseurs*, 354.
15. Abbé Guillaume, *Histoire du diocèse de Toul et celui de Nancy* (5 vols, Nancy, 1866–7), III, 409. The bishop of Toul subsequently adhered to the ordonnance.
16. The bishop had his supporters. There were 1500 peasants on the outskirts of Vannes 'to deliver their bishop from imprisonment and to fight for the king'. Quoted in quoted in Pierre Caillet, *Les Français en 1789 d'après les papiers du Comité des Recherches de l'Assemblée Constituante (1789–1791)* (Paris, 1991), 231.
17. M. Picot, *Mémoires pour servir à l'Histoire ecclésiastique*, VI. 91n.; L. Métais, 'H.J.C. de Bourdeilles, évêque de Soissons (1720–1802)', *Bulletin de la société archéologique et scientifique du Vendômois*, 22 (1883), 127.
18. Dédouit, *Bayeux sous la Révolution*, 11.
19. P. du Guilhermier, 'Un Prélat Comtadin d'Ancien Régime: Mgr de Cheylus', *Mémoires de l'Académie de Vaucluse*, 5th sér., 6–7 (1957–60), 87.
20. Robert Anchel, 'Cinq Procés de Religion dans l'Eure (1791–1799)', *La Révolution française*, 63 (1912), 513–39, at 524; Dupre, *Two Brothers in the French Revolution*, 44–6.

21. M.A. Chassant and M.G-E. Sauvage, *Histoire des Evéques d'Evreux* (Evreux, 1846), iii–iv, 177–9.
22. M.D. Massiou, *Histoire politique, civile et religieuse de la Saintonge et de l'Aunis* (6 vols, Saintes, 1846), VI, 110.
23. A.N. F 1 c III, Hérault, f. 6.
24. Tarbouriech, *Curosités révolutionnaires du Gers*, 47, 49. For arrangements in Bordeaux see Guillemain (ed.), *Le Diocèse de Bordeaux*, 177.
25. Deramacourt, *Le Clergé du diocèse d'Arras, etc.*, II, 213, 14.
26. Delon, *La Révolution en Lozère*, 79.
27. Tackett, *Religion, Revolution, and Regional Culture*, 170.
28. Marquis de Roux, *La Révolution à Poitiers et dans la Vienne*, 405.
29. Quoted in Brunet, *Le Roussillon 1780–1820*, 457.
30. J-T. Lasserre, *Vie Abrégé de Mgr Charles La Cropte de Chantérac* (Carcassonne, 1877), 19.
31. François Lebrun (ed.), *Parole de dieu et révolution. Les Sermons d'un curé angevin avant et pendant la guerre de Vendée* (Angers, 1979), 31, 7; McManners, *French Ecclesiastical Society*, 279.
32. Pierrard (ed.), *Les Diocèses de Cambrai et de Lille*, 187.
33. Graham, 'Women versus Clergy, Women pro Clergy', 135.
34. André Latreille, *L'Église Catholique et la Révolution française. Le Pontificat de Pie VI et la crise française* (2 vols, Paris, 1946), I, 112. The committee formally condemned in May 1792 a publication on the liquidation of ecclesiastical goods.
35. Pastoral letter of 27 Jan. 1791, quoted in Delon, *La Révolution en Lozère*, 79.
36. Pastoral letter of 21 Mar. 1791, quoted in T. Berengier, *Vie de Mgr. J.-M.-M. Scipion de Ruffo-Bonneval, évêque de Senez (1747–1837)* (Marseilles, 1885), 13.
37. Latreille, *L'Église Catholique et la Révolution française*, I, 116–17; Vaillot, *Le Cardinal de Bernis*, 318–19.
38. Hubert C. Johnson, *The Midi in Revolution. A Study of Regional Political Diversity (1789–1793)* (Princeton, 1986), 142; Lewis, *The Second Vendée*, 27–8, 37–8; Godechot, *The Counter-Revolution*, 231–5. The first 'Camp of Jalès' had been held in August 1790, with another the following summer. The Bishop of Mende had been a prominent member of the organising committee.
39. Johnson, *The Midi in Revolution*. 138. Retraction often caused more anguish than royalist propagandists cared to admit, as the comments of the *vicaire* of Chablis in June 1791 suggest: 'Seen as an enemy of the Nation, ... I will be forced to go far away ... reduced to poverty and misery ... But I had no choice. So loud was the cry of my conscience.' Quoted in Desan, *Reclaiming the Sacred*, 81.
40. Letter of the *curé* Aldiéres to the *Ami du Roi*, Paris, 26 Oct. 1791, in O. Delarc, *L'Église de Paris pendant la Révolution Francaise, 1789–1801* (3 vols, Paris, 1896) I, 302–3.
41. Vovelle, *Recherches sur la Révolution*, 187–8.
42. Nicholas Perry and Loreto Echeverría, *Under the Heel of Mary* (London, 1988), 66.
43. Salamon, *Correspondance*, xxxvii.
44. Albert Mathiez, *Contributions à l'histoire religieuse de la Révolution française* (Paris, 1907), 217.
45. For its reception see J. Charonnot, *Mgr de La Luzerne et les serments* (Paris, 1918), 150–4.
46. Letter of 27 Nov. 1792, quoted in Sicard, *L'Ancien Clergé de France*, III, 278n.
47. Ibid., III, 290.
48. Asseline, *Avertissement concernant l'acte de soumission aux lois de la République* (Paris, 1792).
49. Lebrun, *Histoire des Catholiques*, 253.
50. Lasserre, *Vie Abrégé de Mgr Charles La Cropte de Chantérac*, 19.

51. Dominic Bellenger, *The French Exiled Clergy in the British Isles after 1789* (Bath, 1986), 9.

52. Geneviève Gadbois, 'La Foi des femmes face à la déchristianisation de 1789 à 1880', in Delumeau, *La Religion de ma mère*, 301–25, at 303.

53. Jean Boussoulade, 'Soeurs de charité et comités de bienfaisance des faubourgs Saint-Marcel et Saint-Antoine (septembre 1793–mai 1794)', *A.H.R.F.*, 42 (1970), 350–6.

54. Tallett, 'Dechristianizing France', 25.

55. Daniel-Rops, *The Church in an Age of Revolution, 1789–1870*, 36. They were beatified by Pius X in 1906.

56. Forrest, *The Revolution in Provincial France*, 176–7, has details.

57. Ivan Gobry, *Les Martyrs de la Révolution française* (Paris, 1989), 282–320.

58. Luc Boisnard, *La Noblesse dans la tourmente 1774–1802* (Paris, 1992), 296.

59. Ibid., 319.

60. Leflon, *Monsieur Emery*, 334–5.

61. Susan Desan, *The Revival of Religion during the French Revolution* (Michigan, 1988), 257–8; Dumont, *La Révolution française ou les Prodiges du Sacrilège*, 303–4; Guillemain, *Le Diocèse de Bordeaux*, 177; Abbé E. Pioneau, *Un Martyr Bordelais ou Éloge historique de M. l'abbé Langoiran* (Bordeaux, 1861); Charles Chauliac, *Un Martyr Bordelais sous la Terreur. Vie et Mort de R.P. Pannetier* (Paris/Bordeaux, 1877).

62. See P. Lesourd and Claude Paillat, *Dossier secret de France* (2 vols, 1967–8), I, 564–7.

63. Godechot, *The Counter-Revolution*, 203; *Regards sur l'époque révolutionnaire* (Toulouse, 1980), 85–94; Darricau and Peyrous, *Histoire de la Spiritualité*, 108 and n.; B. Fay, *La Grande Révolution* (Paris, 1959).

64. 'The West in France in 1789: the religious factor in the origins of counterrevolution', *Journal of Modern History*, 54 (1982), 715–45.

65. Charles Tilly, *The Vendée* (London, 1964). Two important articles question the universality of the town-country divide in the West. T.J.A. Le Goff and D.M.G. Sutherland, 'The Revolution and the Rural Community in Eighteenth-Century Brittany', *Past and Present*, 62 (1974), 96–119, and T.J.A. Le Goff and D.M.G. Sutherland, 'The Social Origins of Counter-Revolution in Western France', *Past and Present*, 99 (1983), 65–87. There is a helpful discussion of the Mauges in McLeod, *Religion and the People of Western Europe*, 4–5; Julia, 'La Révolution, l'Église et la France', 767. See also J-L. Ormières, 'Politique et religion dans l'Ouest', *Annales E.S.C.*, 40 (1985), 1041–66.

66. Quoted in Lebrun, *Histoire des Catholiques*, 255.

67. Schama, *Citizens*, 702–5; Jean Tulard and Patrick Buisson, *Vendée. Le Livre de la Mémoire, 1793–1993* (Paris, 1993), 111.

68. That also briefly happened in Roussillon in 1793–4, when refractory priests returned to their old cures in the wake of the invading Spanish army. Brunet, *Le Roussillon 1780–1820*, 459.

69. Godechot, *The Counter-Revolution*, 219.

70. Lebrun, *Parole de dieu*, 34, 110.

71. Ibid., 115, sermon of 30 Nov. 1794.

72. McManners, *French Ecclesiastical Society*, 288–9.

73. Serge Chassagne, *Histoire du diocèse d'Angers* (Paris, 1981), 168; André Merlaud, *Les Martyrs d'Angers* (Paris, 1983). Pope John-Paul II beatified the '99 martyrs of Angers' in 1984. Estimates of casualties in the Vendée vary. The most reliable is offered by François Lebrun who suggests 150,000 for local people only in 'La Guerre de Vendée: massacre ou génocide?', *L'Histoire*, 78 (1985), 93–9.

74. Dupuy, *De la Révolution à la Chouannerie*, 730–2.

75. Aulard, *Le Christianisme et la Révolution française* 108.
76. *A Residence in France*, I, 253–4.
77. Bertaud, *Les Amis du Roi*, 160.
78. Hufton, *Women and the Limits of Citizenship*, 119.
79. Schama, *Citizens*, 699.
80. Tallett, 'Dechristianizing France', 20–1; Desan, *Reclaiming the Sacred*, 76–7, 92–121.
81. Vovelle, *Recherches sur la Révolution*, 186.
82. Hufton, *The Prospect Before Her*, 485. See also Desan, *Reclaiming the Sacred*, 197–216.
83. Raymond Darricau, 'Le rôle de mademoiselle de Lamourous pendant la Révolution', in *Pratiques Religieuses. Mentalités et Spiritualités dans l'Europe Révolutionnaire (1770–1820). Actes du Colloque de Chantilly Nov. 1986* (Paris, 1988), 200–9.
84. See the brilliant picture of the Counter-Revolutionary woman in Hufton, *Women and the limits of Citizenship*, 114–15.
85. Geneviéve Gadbois, ' "Vous étes la seule consolation de l'église", La foi des femmes face à la déchristianisation de 1789 à 1880', in Delumeau, *La Religion de ma mère*, 301–25 at 306, 7.
86. Louis Pérouas, *Une Religion des Limousins? Approches historiques* (Paris, 1993), 33–4, 99; *Les Limousins, leurs saints, leurs prêtres* (Paris, 1988), 126–7, 130, 133.
87. Julia, 'La Révolution, l'Église et la France', 765.
88. Quoted in Hufton, *Women and the Limits of Citizenship*, 109.
89. Desan, *Revival*, 257–8, 295–8. Olwen Hufton, 'Women in Revolution, 1789–1796', *Past and Present*, 53 (1971), 90–108, at 107–8.
90. Desan, *Reclaiming the Sacred*, 73.
91. Lebrun, *Parole de dieu*, 112–13, sermon of 30 Nov. 1794.
92. For Quiberon Bay, see ibid., 254–60; Doyle, *Oxford History*, 312–15. It must be said that in his dealings with the Breton laity, Hoche was more restrained. 'Speak of God with reverence', he told his officers. Maurice Hutt, *Chouannerie and Counter-Revolution. Puisaye, the Princes and the British Government in the 1790s* (2 vols, Cambridge, 1983), II, 430–60.
93. G. Lefebvre, *The Thermidorians*, trans. Robert Baldick (London, 1964), 69.

Chapter 9(iii).   The Survival of Religious Groups: Protestants and Jews

1. Quoted in Tackett, *Becoming a Revolutionary*, 262.
2. Quoted in Mours and Robert, *Le Protestantisme en France du XVIII siècle à nos jours*, 194.
3. Alan Forrest, *Society and Politics in Revolutionary Bordeaux* (Oxford, 1975), 243–5; Armand, 'La Bourgeoisie Protestante à La Rochelle', at 494.
4. Cousin, Cubells, Moulinas, *La Pique et la croix*, 153.
5. Hood, 'Revival and Mutation of Old Rivalries in Revolutionary France', 105.
6. From his *L'Histoire de la Révolution de France*, quoted in Bertaud, *Les Amis du Roi*, 66. See also J.M. Roberts, 'The Origins of a Mythology: Freemasons, Protestants and the French Revolution', *Bulletin of the Institute of Historical Research*, XLIV (1971), 78–97. The *locus classicus* for the Revolution as a Protestant plot is the Abbé Barruel's *Collection ecclésiastique* (14 vols, Paris, 1791–3).
7. Tackett, *Religion, Revolution, and Regional Culture*, 210–18; Sutherland, *France 1789–1815*, 109; Johnson, *The Midi in Revolution*, 139.
8. Quoted in Léon Kahn, *Les Juifs de Paris pendant la Révolution* (Paris, 1898). 48.

9. James N. Hood, 'Enduring Redefinition of the Established Hostilities, Autumn 1789', in Donald D. Horwood and John C. Horgan, eds., *The Consortium on Revolutionary Europe 1750–1850. Proceedings, 1989, to commemorate the Bicentennial of the French Revolution* (Tallahassee, Florida, 1990), 797.

10. Lewis, *The Second Vendée*, 1–40, has full details. Daniel Ligou has argued that the motivations were more political than religious in his review of B.C. Poland. See his 'Sur le Protestantisme révolutionnaire. À propos d'un ouvrage récent', *B.S.H.P.F.*, 103 (1958), 25–6.

11. The defeated Protestants were prominent in one of the first manifestations of counter-revolution, the 20 000 who gathered at the Jalès camp in the northern Gard in Aug. 1790. See Lewis, *The Second Vendée*, 28.

12. Johnson, *The Midi in Revolution*, 140.

13. A. Lods, 'Elie Thomas. Un Protestant défenseur de prêtres persécutés', *B.S.H.P.F.*, 38 (1889), 74–85, for Protestant help granted to priests imprisoned in the port of Rochefort.

14. Jacques Poujol, 'Le Changement de l'image des protestants pendant la Révolution', *B.S.H.P.F.*, 135 (1989), 501–41, at 504.

15. Armand, 'La Bourgeoisie Protestante à La Rochelle', 496.

16. Two other pastors in the Gard were executed for their political activities. Pierre Soulier and Pierre Ribes were both guillotined at Nîmes in April 1794. A. Lods, 'Les Pasteurs et l'echafaud révolutionnaire. Pierre Soulier de Sauve (1743–1794), *B.S.H.P.F.*, 40 (1891), 97–104; D. Benoit, 'Encore un pasteur du désert mort sur l'echafaud révolutionnaire. Pierre Ribes (1754–1794)', *B.S.H.P.F.*, 43 (1894), 561–94.

17. Cobb, 'Les débuts de la déchristianisation à Dieppe', 202.

18. Armand, 'La Bourgeoisie Protestante à La Rochelle', 496–7.

19. Quoted in Schama, *Citizens*, 778.

20. J.D. Woodbridge, 'The Reformed Pastors of Languedoc face the Movement of Dechristianization (1793–1794)', in Michèle Max (ed.), *Sécularisation: Problèmes d'Histoire du Christianisme*, 13 (1984), 77–89, at 85–6; Henri Dubrief et Daniel Robert, 'Les protestants et la Révolution: esquisse de vue générale', *B.S.H.P.F.*, 135 (1989), 488–90; Ligou, 'Sur le Protestantisme révolutionnaire', 43. Regional variations were marked. There was one abdication in the pays de Castres, two in Haut-Languedoc, none in the Montalbanais, Ariège, or pays de Montbéliard. Cousin, Cubells, Moulinas, *La Pique et la croix*, 178.

21. Woodbridge, 'Reformed Pastors of Languedoc', 88.

22. Armand, 'La Bourgeoisie Protestante à La Rochelle', 498–500.

23. Two Lutheran pastors in Alsace were executed. An eye-witness account of the worship meetings masquerading as Revolutionary Clubs is given in C. Leenhardt, *La Vie de J-F. Oberlin, 1740–1826* (Paris, 1911), 317–19.

24. In Paris, Lutherans worshipped throughout the Terror in the chapel of the Swedish embassy, whose chaplain had expediently transferred services from Sunday to the *décadi*. Aulard, *Le Christianisme et la Révolution française*, 100.

25. J. Godechot, 'La Révolution française et les Juifs (1789–1799)', *A.H.R.F.*, 48 (1976), 47–70, at 56.

26. Simon Schwarzfuchs, 'Les Nations juives de France', in *Dix-huitième Siécle*, 13 (1981), 127–36, at 135.

27. Roland Marx, 'De la Pré-Révolution à la Restauration', in *Histoire de l'Alsace*, ed. Phillipe Dollinger (Toulouse, 1970), 364. For details on the elections of 1789, J. Godechot, 'Comment les Juifs élurent leurs députés en 1789', *Revue des Etudes juives*, 81 (1925), 48–54, remains useful.

28. Zosa Szajkowski, 'Anti-Jewish Riots during the Revolution of 1789, 1830, and 1848' [Hebrew], *Zion*, 20 (1955), 83–6, cited in Paula E. Hyman, *The Emancipation*

of the Jews of Alsace. Acculturation and tradition in the nineteenth century (New Haven, CT, 1991), 14; Blumenkranz & Soboul, *Les Juifs et la Révolution française*, 10.

29. Badinter, *Libres et égaux*, 119–20; Girard, *Les Juifs de France*, 47.
30. Joseph de Lataulade, *Les Juifs sous l'ancien régime* (Bordeaux, 1906) 254–5; Girard, *Les Juifs de France*, 48; Hertzberg, *French Enlightenment*, 348–9, 354–9; Singham, 'Between Cattle and Men', 123–4.
31. Singham, ibid., 118.
32. G-D. Homan, 'Jean-François Reubell à l'Assemblé nationale constituante', *A.H.R.F.*, 44 (1972), 28–42.
33. *Opinion de M. l'évêque de Nancy, député de Lorraine, sur l'admissibilité des Juifs à la plénitude de l'état civil, et des droits de citoyens actifs* (Paris, 1789).
34. Extracts from the debates are taken from Badinter, *Libres et égaux*, 149–54.
35. Singham, 'Between Cattle and Men', 120–1.
36. Girard, *Les Juifs de France*, 52; R. Necheles, 'L'Emancipation des Juifs 1787–1795. Aspects intellectuels et politiques', *A.H.R.F.*, 48 (1976), 71–86, at 80–1. Grégoire attacked the Sephardic request of 31 Dec. as selfish, one that could only lead to the further isolation of the Ashkenazim. Singham, 'Between Cattle and Men', 121.
37. Girard, *Les Juifs de France*, 53; Badinter, *Libres et égaux*, 168–83. Emancipation was not finally granted in all the towns of the Comtat until July 1791.
38. Blumenkranz and Soboul, *Les Juifs et la Révolution française*; 10; Godechot, 'La Révolution française et les Juifs', 58–9; Necheles, 'L'Émancipation des Juifs', 82.
39. Issue of 3 Apr. 1791, quoted in Girard, *Les Juifs de France*, 56.
40. Arthur Hertzberg, *The French Enlightenment and the Jews* (New York, 1968), p. 353; François Delpech, 'L'Histoire des Juifs en France de 1780 1840', *A.H.R.F.*, 48 (1976), 3–46; Necheles, 'L'emancipation des Juifs', 83. The Assembly simultaneously extended citizenship to coloured men, mulattos and blacks, resident in France.
41. Kates, 'Jews into Frenchmen', 103. This essay contains an important critique of Hertzberg's assertion that for French Jews, emancipation was the first step on the road to Auschwitz.
42. This illuminating insight is developed in Bertrand Eugene Schwarzbach's important article, 'Une nation reniée – une nation adoptée: la politicisation du judaisme en France', *Studies on Voltaire and the Eighteenth-Century*, 302 (1992), 321–78, at 338.
43. Necheles, 'L'Émancipation des Juïfs', 83.
44. P. Leuilliot, 'L'Usure judaïque en Alsace sous l'Empire et sous la Restauration', *A.H.R.F.*, 7 (1930), 231–51; Annie Perchenet, *Histoire des Juifs de France* (Paris, 1988), 142.
45. Hyman, *The Emancipation of the Jews of Alsace*, 15.
46. Robert Anchel, *Les Juifs de France* (Paris, 1946), 236.
47. Cited in Cobb, *The People's Armies*, 652.
48. Girardin, *Les Juifs de France*, 65.
49. Godechot, 'La Révolution française et les Juifs', 60–1, 62–3.
50. Girardin, *Les Juifs de France*, 64; Viguerie, *Cinq Leçons d'histoire*, 168.
51. Blumenkranz and Soboul, *Les Juifs et la Révolution française*, 11; Szajkowski, *Jews and the French Revolutions of 1789, 1830, and 1848*, 785–825.
52. Roland Marx, *La Révolution et les classes sociales en Basse-Alsace. Structures agraires et ventes des biens nationaux* (Paris, 1974); 'La Régénération économique des Juïfs d'Alsace à l'époque révolutionnaire', *A.H.R.F.*, 48 (1976), 105–20, at 114–15; Singham, 'Between Cattle and Men', 126.
53. S. Posener, 'The Immediate Economic and Social Effects of the Emancipation of the Jews in France', *Jewish Social Studies*, 1 (1939), 271.

54. See below, Chapter 11. Until recently, historians were equally committed to a narrow, assimilationist model, but recent writing on French Jewry has widened the perspectives in the most creative way. See Nicolas Weill, 'Les Juifs et la Révolution: nouvelles questions sur l'émancipation', in Vovelle, *Recherches sur la Révolution*, 212–18.

Chapter 10. Dechristianisation and the Alternatives to Christianity

1. Serge Bianchi, *La Révolution culturelle de l'an II* (Paris, 1982). See also his 'La Déchristianisation de l'an II. Essai d'interprétation', *A.H.R.F.*, 50 (1978), 341–78.
2. D.M.G. Sutherland's objections in *France 1789–1815*, are particularly worth studying. Cf. Forrest, *The French Revolution*, 146- 7.
3. Lewis, *The French Revolution*, 96.
4. The essay by Albert Soboul, 'Religious Sentiment and Popular Cults during the Revolution. Patriot Saints and Martyrs of Liberty', in J. Kaplow (ed.), *New Perspectives on the French Revolution. Readings in Historical Sociology* (New York, 1965), remains essential. It first appeared in French in *A.H.R.F.*, 29 (1957), 195–213. See Lefort, 'La Révolution comme religion nouvelle', 391–99.
5. Lucas, 'The Revolution and Christianity', 348.
6. Vovelle, *The Revolution Against the Church*, 59.
7. Cardenal, *La Province pendant la Révolution*, 296.
8. Vovelle, *The Revolution Against the Church*, 145–6.
9. Stendhal emphasised the constant pressure on the adolescents of 1794 to respect this sentiment. See his *Mémoires sur Napoléon* (written 1836–7), 31, in *Oeuvres*, ed. H. Martineau (79 vols, Paris, 1927–37).
10. Viguerie, *Cinq Leçons d'histoire*, 170–1.
11. Roberts, *Jacques-Louis David*, 73.
12. Quoted in Aulard, *Le Christianisme et la Révolution française*, 95.
13. Bronislaw Baczko, 'Le Calendrier Républicain. Décréter l'éternité', in Pierre Nora (ed.), *Les Lieux de Mémoire*, vol. 1, *La République* (Paris, 1986), 37–83; Godechot, *Les institutions de la France*, 363–6; Serge Bianchi, *La Révolution culturelle de l'an II*, 198–203; Hampson, *A Social History of the French Revolution*, 200.
14. Lyons, *Revolution in Toulouse*, 162; James Friguglietti, 'Creating a Revolutionary Culture. Gilbert Romme and the making of the French Republican Calendar', in David G. Troyansky, Alfred Cismari and Norwood Andrews, Jr (eds), *The French Revolution in Culture and Society* (New York, 1991), 13–22, at 20.
15. Quoted in Tallett, 'Dechristianizing France', 4.
16. Quoted in Daniel-Rops, *The Church in an Age of Revolution*, 28.
17. J.F. Bosher, *The French Revolution, A New Interpretation* (London, 1989), 207. Cf. Vovelle, *The Revolution Against the Church*, 40–2.
18. Bianchi, *La Révolution culturelle*, 349.
19. G. Sangnier, *La Terreur dans le District de Saint-Pol* (Blangermont, 1938), II, 186.
20. Lyons, *Revolution in Toulouse*, 160.
21. Bernard Cousin, 'Prêtres et laics: les sacrements dans la clandestinité (Avignon 1793–1801)', in *Pratiques Religieuses*, 191–200, at 196–7.
22. Martyn Lyons, *Revolution in Toulouse. An Essay on Provincial Terrorism* (Bern, 1978), 148.

23. *Les Revolutions de Paris*, no. 215 (25–30 *brumaire* an II), vol. 17, quoted in Hunt, *Politics, Culture, and Class*, 64–5.
24. Hunt, *Politics, Culture, and Class*, 63–5.
25. Vovelle, *From Reason to the Supreme Being*, 116.
26. Viguerie, *Cinq Leçons d'histoire*, 166.
27. Richard Wrigley, 'Breaking the Code: Interpreting French Revolutionary Iconoclasm', in Alison Yarrington and Kelvin Everest (eds), *Reflections of Revolution. Images of Romanticism* (London, 1993), 189.
28. Vovelle, *Combats Pour la Révolution*, 288.
29. Lucas, *The Structure of the Terror*, 288.
30. Quoted in Cardenal, *La Province pendant la Révolution*, 297.
31. Much work remains to be done on assessing numbers who attended the temples of Reason, especially women. For some early suggestions see Soboul, 'Religious Sentiments and Popular Cults', 348.
32. Graham, 'The Secularization of the Ecclesiastical Deputies', 77.
33. Vovelle, *The Revolution Against the Church*, 106.
34. Cited in Cobb, *Revolutionary Armies*, II, 450.
35. Cobb, 'Les débuts de la déchristianisation à Dieppe', 200; Sutherland, *France 1789–1815*, 212–13.
36. P. Caron, *Rapport des Agents du Ministre de l'Intérieur dans les Départements* (2 vols, Paris, 1913, 1951), I, 463. Cf. the incident involving mock hosts dipped in a chamber-pot cited in Cobb, 'Les Débuts de la déchristianisation à Dieppe', 201.
37. Discussed in Soboul, 'Religious Sentiment and Popular Cults', 342–8. For a recent work which emphasises continuity rather than rupture with popular Christian observances, see Louis Trenard, 'Les fêtes révolutionnaire dans une région frontiére Nord-Pas-de-Calais', in eds. Ehrard and Viallaneix, *Les Fêtes de la Révolution*, 191–221.
38. Richard Wrigley, 'Pierre-François Dalauney, Liberty and Saint Nicholas', *Burlington Magazine*, 122 (1980), 745–7.
39. Viguerie, *Cinq leçons d'histoire*, 175–7; A. Soboul, *Paysans, sans–culottes et jacobins* (Paris, 1966), 183–98; Soboul, 'Religious Sentiment and Popular Cults', 345–6; McLeod, *Religion and the People of Western Europe*, 12.
40. F-P. Bowman, 'Le "Sacre-Coeur" de Marat', in Ehrard and Viallaneix (eds), *Les Fêtes de la Révolution*, 155–79; ed. J-C. Bonnet, *La Mort de Marat* (Paris, 1986); Cardenal, *La Province pendant la Révolution*, 321.
41. 26 *Brumaire* An II (16 Nov. 1793). Quoted in Soboul, 'Religious Sentiment and Popular Cults', 347.
42. Edmonds, *Jacobinism and the Revolt of Lyon*, 227–8, 291; P. Mansfield, 'Collot d'Herbois and the Dechristianisers', *Journal of Religious History* 14 (1986–7), 406–18, at 408–9.
43. Quoted in Soboul, 'Religious Sentiment and Popular Cults', 349.
44. Albert Mathiez, 'Robespierre et le culte de l'Etre Suprême', in *Autour de Robespierre* (Paris, 1957), 93–135; Josiane Boulad-Ayoub, *Contre Nous de la tyrannie ... des relations idéologiques entre lumières et Révolution* (Quebec, 1989), 215–302, Aulard, *Le Culte de la raison*, 273.
45. Norman Hampson, *The Life and Opinions of Maximilien Robespierre* (London, 1974), 273; Michel Vovelle, *Combats pour la Révolution* (Paris, 1993), 298–9. For an explicitly 'holistic' account of the cult see Ferenc Fehér, 'The Cult of the Supreme Being and the Limits of the Secularization of the Political', in id. (ed.), *The French Revolution and the Birth of Modernity* (Berkeley, CA, 1990), 174–97.
46. Speech in Robespierre, *Oeuvres*, ed. Poperen, quoted in Viguerie, *Cinq Leçons d'histoire*, 174.

47. A view held by the nineteenth-century French historian Edgar Quinet. See Colin Lucas, 'The Revolution and Christianity', 345, and Simone Bernard-Griffiths, 'Quinet: Mythification et Démythification de la Révolution', in Christian Croisille and Jean Ehrard (eds), *La Légende de la Révolution: Actes du colloque internationale de Clermont-Ferrand* (June 1986) (Clermont-Ferrand, 1988), 431–62.
48. Robespierre, *Rapport du 18 floréal etc.* (Paris, 1794), 42.
49. Viguerie, *Cinq Leçons d'histoire*, 175.
50. Schama, *Citizens*, 831–6; Tiersot, *Les Fêtes*, 122–68; De la Gorce, *Histoire religieuse*, III, 503.
51. Daniel-Rops, *The Church in an Age of Revolution*, 31; Vovelle, *Combats pour la Révolution*, 297.
52. Abbé Fortin, *Souvenirs* (2 vols, Auxerre, 1865), I, 18, quoted in Suzanne Desan, 'The Role of Women in Religious Riots during the French Revolution', *Eighteenth Century Studies*, 22 (1988–9), 451–68, at 451.
53. Sutherland, *France 1789–1815*, 242–3.
54. Quoted in Soboul, 'Religious Sentiment and Popular Cults', 351.
55. Hufton, 'The Reconstruction of a Church 1796–1801', 31.
56. Louis Pérouas and Paul d'Hollander, *La Révolution française: une rupture dans le Christianisme? Le Cas du Limousin, 1775–1822* (Treignac, 1988). See generally Cholvy, *La Religion en France*, 13.
57. Mona Ozouf, *Festivals and the French Revolution* (London, 1988), 226–7.
58. M. Vovelle, *Les Métamorphoses de la fête en Provence 1750–1820* (Paris, 1976), 251.
59. Hufton, *Women and the Limits of Citizenship*, 109. Two girls who had been goddesses at Marseille were murdered during the 1795 White Terror. McLeod, *Religion and the People of Western Europe*, 4.
60. A.D. Haute Loire L376 ancien côte, quoted in Hufton, *Women and the Limits of Citizenship*, 118.
61. Vovelle, *The Revolution Against the Church*, 155.
62. Quoted in Cholvy and Hilaire, *Histoire Religieuse de la France contemporaine*, I, 44.

Chapter 11. Religion and the Directory, 1795–9

1. Marcus Lowell Ackroyd, 'Constitution and Revolution: Political Debate in France, 1795–1800' (unpublished D.Phil. dissertation, Oxford 1995), 81.
2. Peter L. Berger, *The Social Reality of Religion* (London, 1969), 137 ff. See generally W.J. Sheils and Diana Wood (eds), *Voluntary Religion*, Studies in Church History, 23 (Oxford, 1986).
3. Martin Lyons, *France under the Directory* (Cambridge, 1975), 108.
4. Cf. J. McManners, *Lectures on European History 1789–1814. Men, Machines and Freedom* (Oxford, 1966), 67.
5. Jean-René Suratteau, 'Le Directoire. Avait-il une politique religieuse?', *A.H.R.F.* 63 (1991), 79–92, at 82.
6. A.D. F19 1009, Ille-et-Vilaine. Observations générales, unfoliated, cited in Bellenger, *French Exiled Clergy*, 22.
7. Charles Doyle, 'Internal Counter-Revolution: the judicial reaction in southern France 1794–1800', *Journal of Renaissance and Modern Studies*, 33 (1989), 106–25, at 119.
8. Colin Lucas, 'The First Directory and the Rule of Law', *French Historical Studies*, 10 (1977), 231–60, at 238.

9. Quoted in Emile Lafont, *La Politique Religieuse de la Révolution française* (Paris, 1909), 121–2.
10. Claude Langlois and Timothy Tackett, 'A l'Épreuve de la Révolution, 1770–1830', in ed. François Lebrun, *Histoire des Catholiques en France du XVe siècle nos jours* (Toulouse, 1980), 266.
11. Latreille, *L'Église catholique et la Révolution française*, I, 221; Ackroyd, 'Constitution and Revolution', 125–37.
12. Lyons, *France under the Directory*, 106; Phillips, *The Church in France, 1789–1848*, 35; Suratteau, 'Le Directoire', 84–5.
13. About 100 Constitutional clergy were imprisoned between 1797 and 1799. Lyons, *The First French Republic*, 154.
14. Quoted in Desan, *Reclaiming the Sacred*, 146.
15. It has been estimated that 425 parish churches and 60 chapels were sold off in the one department of the Nord. G. Lefebvre, *Les Paysans du Nord* (Lille, 1924).
16. Angus Heriot, *The French in Italy 1796–1799* (London, 1957), 109; Suratteau, 'Le Directoire', 85.
17. C. Latreille, *L'Opposition religieuse au Concordat de 1792 à 1803* (Paris, 1910), 25–6. As Asseline, Bishop of Boulogne, expressed it in Sept. 1797: 'The Catholic religion can co-exist with any form of legitimate government.' Quoted in Ledré, *L'Église de France sous la Révolution*, 250, n.16.
18. Stuart Woolf, *A History of Italy, 1700–1860. The Social Constraints of Political Change* (London, 1979), 157, 163–4; Chadwick, *The Popes and European Revolution*, 462; Heriot, *The French in Italy*, 114–5. The handover of works of art had begun after the fall of Bologna the previous summer. ibid., 96.
19. Heriot, *The French in Italy*, 156–7; Suratteau, 'Le Directoire', 86.
20. Sydenham, *The First French Republic*, 385; Chadwick, *The Popes and the European Revolution*, 467–70; E.E.Y. Hales, *Napoleon and the Pope* (London, 1962), 13; *Revolution and the Papacy* (London, 1960), 113–15.
21. Vovelle, ed., *Recherches sur la Révolution*, 185.
22. Cousin, Cubells, Moulinas, *Le Pique et le croix*, 251; Gérard Cholvy, 'La Révolution française et la question religieuse', *L'Histoire* (Nov. 1984), 50–9; Cholvy, *La religion en France*, 13.
23. Desan, *Reclaiming the Sacred*; O. Hufton, 'The Reconstruction of a Church, 1796–1801', in G. Lewis and C. Lucas (eds), *Beyond the Terror: Essays in French Regional and Social History, 1794–1815* (Cambridge, 1983), 21–52.
24. ibid.
25. Quoted in Desan, *Reclaiming the Sacred*, 200, 204.
26. Hufton, 'The Reconstruction of a Church', 23–6; Sutherland, *France 1789–1815*, 282; Hufton, *Women and the Limits of Citizenship*, 125; ibid., *The Prospect Before Her*, 482–3; Desan, *Reclaiming the Sacred*, 145–6, 184.
27. Quoted in ibid., 27.
28. Bishop of Mâcon to the archpriest de Charlieu, 14 Jan. 1801, in Abbé Chaumont, *Recherches historiques sur la persécution religieuse dans le département de Saône-et-Loire, diocèse de Mâcon*, 152ff.
29. Sutherland, *France 1789–1815*, 280–1.
30. Meyer, 'L'Opinion publique et l'Eglise en Haut-Garonne, 107–43, at 131. Hufton, *The Limits of Citizenship*, 124, points out that two women were rivals for the honour of restoring Mende cathedral for use.
31. Graham, 'Women Versus Clergy, Women Pro Clergy', 132; Mathiez, *Contributions à l'histoire religieuse*, 97–8.
32. Hufton, 'The Reconstruction of a Church 1796–1801', 50.
33. Gadbois, ' "Vous êtes la seule consolation de l'église" ', 303.
34. Viguerie, *Cinq Leçons d'histoire*, esp. 256–60.

35. Vovelle, *Recherches sur la Révolution*, 184, who calls for more work on religious activities in the later 1790s. *La découverte de la politique: géopolitique de la révolution Français* (Paris, 1993), 180.
36. Quoted in Cholvy and Hilaire, *Historie religieuse de la France contemporaine*, 22. Grégoire reported that there were 400 Constitutional priests in the Rouen diocese in 1802; *ex info*. Rodney Dean.
37. Gallerand, *Les Cultes sous la Terreur en Loir-et-Cher*, 136, 742.
38. Quoted in Latreille, *L'Eglise Catholique et la Révolution Française*, I, 175.
39. Details are set out in Ozouf, *Festivals and the French Revolution*, 118–25, esp. 119–20; Suratteau, 'Le Directoire', 88.
40. Quoted in G. Cholvy, *Histoire du diocèse de Montpellier* (Paris, 1976), 186.
41. Richard Wrigley, 'Breaking the code: interpreting French Revolutionary iconoclasm', 187.
42. Lyons, *France under the Directory*, 112–13.
43. See F. Picaret, *Les Idéologues* (Paris, 1891); Mac Regaldo, 'Luminères, élite démocratie: la difficile position des Idéologues', *Dix-huitième Siècle*, 6 (1974), 193–207; G. Gusdorf, *La Conscience révolutionnaire. Les Idéologues* (Paris, 1978); M.S. Staum, *Cabanis: Enlightenment and Medical Philosophy in the French Revolution* (Princeton, 1980).
44. Discussed in Lyons, *France under the Directory*, 116–22; Charles Hunter Van Duzer, *Contribution of the Ideologues to French Revolutionary Thought*, Johns Hopkins University Studies in Historical and Political Science, vol. 5 (Baltimore, MD, 1935), 67.
45. Discussed most recently by James Livesey, 'The Sovereign as God? Theophilanthropy and the Politics of the Directory 1795–99', in Judith Devlin and Ronan Fleming (eds), *Religion and Rebellion*, Historical Studies, 20 (Dublin, 1997), 95–96, esp. 91–3.
46. Albert Mathiez, *Contributions à l'histoire-religieuse de la Révolution français* (Paris, 1907), 174–7; Lyons, *France under the Directory*, 110–11; Suratteau, 'Le Directoire', 88–9.
47. Desan, *Reclaiming the Sacred*, 69–70; A. Mathiez, *La Théophilanthropie et le Culte décadaire (1796–1801)* (Paris, 1904).
48. H. Grange, 'La Révellière-Lépeaux, théoricien de la fête', in Jean Ehrard and Paul Viallaneix (eds), *Les Fêtes de la Révolution. Colloque de Clermont-Ferrand (juin 1974)* (Paris, 1977), 493–501.
49. G. Robison, *Révellière-Lépeaux, Citizen Director* (New York, 1938), 161 ff.
50. Sydenham, *The First French Republic*, 154–5.
51. Bernard Plongeron, 'La Fête devant la critique Chrétienne', in eds. Ehrard and Viallaneix, *Les Fêtes de la Révolution*, 543–4.
52. Amaury Duval, *La décade*, 30 Floréal, Year V, quoted in Ozouf, *Festivals and the French Revolution*, 271; A. Aulard, *Le Christianisme et la Révolution française*, 148–9.
53. Quoted in Phillips, *The Church in France, 1789–1848*, 34.
54. J. Boussoulade, *L'Église de Paris du 9 Thermidor au Concordat* (Paris, 1950), 139.
55. Lewis, *The French Revolution*, 103.
56. In 1796, for instance, he recommended to the bishops meeting in Paris that they publish references from the philosophe Mably's writings on the need for religion and an officially recognised public worship. Ruth Graham, 'The Revolutionary Bishops and the Philosophes', *Eighteenth-Century Studies*, 16 (1982–3), 117–40, at 138.
57. The resemblances are well discussed in Mathiez, *Contributions à l'histoire religieuse de la Révolution française*, 176–7; 186–7 citing Mme de Stäel, Necker's daughter.
58. Mours and Robert, *Le Protestantisme en France*, 200–1.
59. Lyons, *France under the Directory*, 110.

60. F. Laugier, *Le Schisme constitutionnel et la persécution du Clergé dans le Var* (Dra-guignan, 1897), 163; Gérard Cholvy and Yves-Marie Hilaire, *Histoire religieuse de la France contemporaine 1800/1880* (Toulouse, 1985), 29.

61. Woodbridge, 'Reformed pastors of Languedoc', 88.

62. Cholvy and Hilaire, *Histoire religieuse de la France contemporaine*, 17; D. Robert, 'Note provisoire sur la situation des Eglises Réformés à la fin de la période révo-lutionnaire', *B.S.H.P.F.*, 105 (1959).

63. H. Tribout de Morembert, 'Les Juifs de Metz et de Lorraine (1791–1794)', *A.H.R.F.*, 48 (1976), 87–104, at 100–2.

64. Robert Anchel, *Napoléon et les Juifs* (Paris, 1928), 26–7, 17.

65. Perchenet, *Histoire des Juifs de France*, 142.

66. Girard, *Les Juifs de France*, 68; Zosa Szajkowski, *Autonomy and Jewish Communal Debts during the French Revolution of 1789* (New York, 1959).

67. Blumenkranz and Soboul, *Les Juifs et la Révolution française*, 11–12.

68. Quoted in Phillips, *The Church in France, 1789–1848*, 39.

69. J. Adher, 'Lettres de Sermet', in *Revue des Pyrénées* (1894), 101–4.

70. R.F. Necheles, 'The Constitutional Church, 1794–1802': An Essay in Voluntar-ism', in *Proceedings of the Consortium on Revolutionary Europe* (1974), 80–90, at 82–3; Lyons, *France under the Directory*, 109; Lebrun, *Histoire des Catholiques*, 268; Cholvy and Hilaire, *Histoire religieuse de la France contemporaine*, 25.

71. Necheles, 'The Constitutional Church', 87n.; Cholvy, *La Religion en France*, 11.

72. Dumont, *La Révolution française ou les Prodiges du Sacrilège*, 416.

73. *Lettre pastorale de l'évêque d'Amiens pour la convocation du Synode diocésain* (Paris, Mai 1797), quoted in Bernard Plongeron, 'Théologie et applications de la collé-gialité dans l'église constitutionelle de France (1790–1801)', *A.H.R.F.*, 45 (1973), 70–84, at 81.

74. ibid., 82.

75. Discussed in Necheles, 'The Constitutional Church', 83–4. See also J. Leflon, 'La reconstruction de l'épiscopat constitutionnel aprés Thermidor', *Actes du 81e Con-grès des sociétés savantes, Rouen-Caen* (Paris, 1956), 475–81.

76. Quoted in Chaline et al., *L'Église de France et la Révolution*, 54.

77. Van Duzer, *Contribution of the Ideologues to French Revolutionary Thought*, 68–9.

78. Plongeron, *Grégoire*, 74–5.

79. Between 1799 and 1800, 53 dioceses formed their first synodal assembly. Plon-geron, 'La Collegialité dans l'église constitutionelle', 84; Quéniart, *Le Clergé déchiré*, 120.

80. Details are set out in Plongeron, *Grégoire*, 75–8; 'L'Exercice de la démocratie dans l'Eglise constitutionnelle de France (1790–1801)', *Concilium*, 77 (1972), 125–32; Necheles, 'The Constitutional Church', 86. Cf. Dumont, *La Révolution française ou les Prodiges du Sacrilège*, 418–19.

81. Plongeron, 'Théologie et Applications de la Collégialité dans l'église constitutio-nelle de France', 81n; Le Coz's tour cited in Chaline et al., *L'Église de France et la Révolution*, 50.

82. Dumont, *La Révolution française ou les Prodiges du Sacrilège*, 416.

83. Michel Lancelin, 'La lutte contre le clergé à Saint-Omer entre avril 1793 et juillet 1794', in ed. Alain Lottin, *Eglise, Vie religieuse et révolution dans la France du Nord* (Lille, 1990), 53–64, at 61.

84. Plongeron, 'La Collégialité dans l'Eglise constitutionelle', 86–7; Lyons, *France under the Directory*, 108.

85. Abbé Boussoulade, 'Le Presbytérianisme dans les Conciles de 1797 et de 1801', *A.H.R.F.*, 23 (1951), 17–38.

86. Necheles, 'The Constitutional Church', 88.

87. Plongeron, 'La Collégialité dans l'Eglise constitutionelle', 83.
88. Plongeron, *Grégoire*, 30, 74; *La Vie quotidienne du clergé français*, 111.
89. Some priests in the west were ready to consider reunion. Boutouillic, former vicar-general of the Bishop of Vannes, on their behalf requested Pius VI to admit the jurors to the Church as coadjutors.
90. Meyer, 'Opinion publique et Eglise en Haute-Garonne', 137–8.
91. Necheles, 'The Constitutional Church', 87n. The Church subsequently moved itself to ban the laity from electing bishops.
92. Lyons, *France under the Directory*, 109; Meyer, 'Opinion publique et Eglise en Haute-Garonne', 140; Boussoulade, *L'Eglise de Paris*, 140–1.
93. Necheles, 'The Constitutional Church', 88.
94. Hufton, 'The reconstruction of a church', 23.
95. Quoted in Dumont, *La Révolution française ou les Prodiges du Sacrilège*, 415.
96. Colin Lucas, 'The First Directory and the Rule of Law', *French Historical Studies* 10 (1977), 231–60, at 238. Lucas notes that most deportees and missionaries had not come back to the Loire before the Years IV and V. Those in hiding were often aged and infirm, and lacked the physical resources to resume an active parish ministry in 1795–6. See F. Tallett, 'Religion and Revolution. The rural clergy and parishioners of the Doubs, 1780–1797' (Ph.D. dissertation, University of Reading, 1981), 366.
97. Sutherland, *France 1789–1815*, 281, 285, 288.
98. See Emery's 'Question sur la soumission aux lois de la République', 23 June 1795, B.N. MSS. Nouv. acq. fr., 4525; Leflon, *Monsieur Emery*, 376–80.
99. Langlois and Tackett, 'A l'Épreuve de la Révolution', 270.
100. B.L., Puisaye Papers, Add. MS. 8012, f. 81, quoted in Mitchell, 'Resistance to the Revolution in Western France', 120.
101. McManners, *Lectures on European History*, 68–9; Sicard, *Annales*, III, 479–80, 577. The Bishops of Agen, Grenoble, Luçon and Perpignan also inclined to the Emery view.
102. Quoted in Leflon, *Monsieur Emery*, 44.
103. "Must religion perish because the government has changed?', demanded Boisgelin of Aix. Quoted in Lyons, *France under the Directory*, 105.
104. Quoted in Mathiez, *Contributions à l'histoire religieuse de la Révolution français*, 235–6; see also 218 ff.
105. Sutherland, *France 1789–1815*, 283.
106. Lucas, 'The First Directory and the Rule of Law', 238.
107. Quoted in Sutherland, *France 1789–1815*, 283.
108. See Boussoulade, *L'Église de Paris*, 146.
109. Letter to Pius VI, 22 Aug. 1795, quoted Theiner, *Documents inédits*, I, 436.
110. Brunet, *Le Roussillon 1780–1820*, 459.
111. Hufton, 'The reconstruction of a church 1796–1801', 36.
112. Full details in Bellenger, *The French Exiled Clergy*, 113.
113. Bernard Cousin, 'Prêtres et laïcs: les sacrements dans la clandestinité (Avignon 1793–1801)', in *Pratiques Religieuses*, 191–200, at 191.
114. Langlois and Tackett, 'A l'Épreuve de la Révolution', 270; Quéniart, *Le Clergé déchiré*, 121.
115. Lyons, *France under the Directory*, 104.
116. Phillips, *The Church in France, 1789–1848*, 35; D. Robert, 'Note provisoire sur la situation des Eglises Réformées à la fin de la période révolutionnaire', *B.S.H.P.F.* 105 (1959), 154–73, at 161.
117. Letter of vicar-general Ruivet, *c.* 1798, quoted in Charles Ledré, *Le Culte caché sous la révolution. Les missions de l'abbé Linsolas* (Paris, 1949), 229.

118. ibid., 88–9.
119. Graham, 'Women versus Clergy', 136.
120. Mitchell, 'Resistance to the Revolution', 127.
121. Mills, 'Negotiating the Divide', 47.
122. Graham, 'Women versus Clergy', 136–7.
123. Hufton, 'The Reconstruction of a Church 1796–1801', 29.
124. Quoted in Latreille, *L'Église catholique et la Révolution*, I, 221.
125. Aulard, *Le Christianisme et la Révolution française*, 142.
126. Howard G. Brown, of the State University of New York, has recently questioned this assessment. See his 'Myths and Massacres: Reconsidering the Fructidorian Terror', unpublished paper given at the eleventh annual conference for the Study of French History, University of Birmingham, 25–26 March 1997.
127. Quoted in Desan, 'Redefining Revolutionary Liberty', 13.
128. Mathiez, *Contributions à l'histoire religieuse de la Révolution Française*, 250. For Mercy's evolving position see Yann Fauchois, 'Les Evêques émigrés et le royalisme pendant la Révolution française', in *Les Résistances à la Révolution*, 386–93, at 391.
129. Victor Pierre, *La Déportation écclésiastique sous le Directoire. Documents inédits* (Paris, 1896).
130. Lyons, *France under the Directory*, 106.
131. Quoted in Gerard Gengembre, *La Contre-Révolution ou l'histoire désespérante* (Paris, 1989), 130; Fauchois, 'Les Evéques émigrés', 389. Asseline, however, insisted to the pretender that the interests of the Church and monarchy could be divergent, and that coexistence, in the final analysis, was not essential. Archbishop Champion de Cicé told Louis XVIII that 'Religion has always remained afloat amid the débris of human politics'. Quoted in ibid., 393.
132. Chadwick, *The Popes and the European Revolution*, 479.
133. Quoted in Sutherland, *France 1789–1815*, 310–11.
134. Lyons, *France under the Directory*, 107.
135. Desan, *Reclaiming the Sacred*, 92–5, 103–6; Tallet, 'Dechristianising France', 17–19.
136. Quoted in Desan, *Reclaiming the Sacred*, 99.

Chapter 12.   Religion and the Consulate, 1799–1804

1. The definitive discussion is now Geoffrey Ellis, 'Religion according to Napoleon: The Limitations of Pragmatism', in Aston, *Religious Change in Europe 1650–1914*, 235–55.
2. The development of Bonaparte's thinking on the religious question is inimitably depicted in McManners, *Lectures on European History 1789–1814*, 69–70. See also the discussion in Chadwick, *The Popes and European Revolution*, 467–9.
3. Albert Mathiez, *Contributions à l'histoire religieuse de la Révolution Française* (Paris, 1907), 253–4. The oath still had to be taken by those who wanted to draw a state pension, like the 'secularized' regular clergy; *Ex info*. Michael Broers.
4. Latreille, *L'Opposition religieuse au Concordat*, 46–8.
5. Mathiez, *Contributions à l'histoire religieuse*, 258–9; Latreille, *L'Opposition religieuse au Concordat*, 60–2.
6. Sutherland, *France 1789–1815*, 340; Boussoulade, *L'Église de Paris*, 163.
7. Boussoulade, ibid., 150, 154.

8. Crook, *Toulon in war and revolution*, 199.
9. Robinson, *Cardinal Consalvi*, 49–52; Chadwick, *The Popes and European Revolution*, 455–6.
10. Mathiez, *Contributions à l'histoire religieuse*, 259. By contrast, Pius VI never formally recognised the rights of the comte de Provence (the *de jure* Louis XVIII) to the French throne.
11. Markham, *Napoleon*, 79; M. Hutt, *Napoleon: Great Lives Observed* (New Jersey, 1972), 28.
12. H.H. Walsh, *The Concordat of 1801* (New York, 1967), 249; Robinson, *Cardinal Consalvi*, 64. For Martiana see C. Zaghi, *Posere, Chiesa e Soliefà* (Naples, 1984), 524 ff.
13. Boussoulade, *L'Église de Paris*, 164–5.
14. Letter of 15 May 1800, quoted in Sicard, *Le clergé de France* III, 356. See, generally, Latreille, *L'Opposition religieuse au Concordat*, 72–5.
15. The major guide remains Cte Boulay de la Meurthe, *Documents sur la négociation du Concordat et sur les autres rapports de la France avec le Saint-Siége en 1800 et 1801* (5 vols, Paris, 1891–7). The most accurate account of the negotiations may be found in J. Leflon, *Étienne-Alexandre Bernier, évêque d'orleáns, 1762–1806* (2 vols, Paris, 1938) (vol. 1).
16. Quoted in Sicard, *Le clergé de France* III, 377–80.
17. Cf. S. Delacroix, *La réorganisation de l'Église de France après la Révolution 1801–9* (Paris, 1962), I, 16.
18. Quoted in Ilario Rinieri, *La Diplomazia Pontificia nel Secolo XIX* (5 vols, Rome and Turin, 1901–6), I, 245.
19. The principles governing relations between Bonaparte and Pius are well discussed in Geoffrey Ellis, *Napoleon* (Harlow, 1996), 112–14.
20. J. Thiry, *Le Concordat et le Consulat* (Paris, 1956), 63–8, 78, 81–2; Walsh, *The Concordat*, 52.
21. Quoted in ed. Boulay de la Meurthe, *Documents sur la négociation du Concordat*, I, 267.
22. F. Rocquain, *L'Etat de la France au 18 Brumaire* (Paris, 1874), 278.
23. Martyn Lyons, *Napoleon Bonaparte and the Legacy of the French Revolution* (Basingstoke, 1994), 85–6; Sydenham, *The First French Republic*, 270–1.
24. There were actually fewer dioceses than *départements* in 1802, ex info. Malcolm Crook.
25. Sutherland, *France 1789–1815*, 355–6; Lyons, *Napoleon Bonaparte*, 86–7.
26. See P. Lesourd and Claude Paillat, *Dossier secret de France* (2 vols, 1967–8), II, 154–73.
27. Boussoulade, *L'Eglise de Paris*, 183–99.
28. Chadwick, *The Popes and European Revolution*, 388–9; Sydenham, *The First French Republic*, 271.
29. Perchenet, *Histoire des Juifs de France*, 142.
30. Godechot, 'La Révolution française et les Juifs', 68–9.
31. Blumenkranz and Soboul, *Les Juifs et la Révolution*, 214, 222; Anchel, *Napoléon et les Juifs*, 45–7.
32. Ibid., 58; Franéois Delpech, 'Les Juifs en France et dans l'Empire et la genèse du Grand Sanhedrin', *A.H.R.F.*, 51 (1979), 1–26; Perchenet, *Histoire des Juifs de France*, 143–6.
33. For criticisms of Boisgelin's pliability see Latreille, *L'Opposition religieuse au Concordat*, 156–8.
34. For details see Ellis, *Napoleon*, 58.
35. Quoted in Sutherland, *France 1789–1815*, 362.

36. Ibid., 370. This was not how it worked in practice over the period 1802–14 as Catholic disenchantment with the Napoleonic regime grew intense.
37. See Christopher Clark, 'Prussia and the Church after Napoleon', unpublished paper given at 'Napoleon's legacy: Problems of government in restoration Europe', Institute of Historical Research (London), April 1997.
38. McManners, *Lectures on European History*, 72.
39. A.N., AF IV. 1044. 'Rapports du ministère de l'intérieur, ans VII–XII. Dossier 1', cited in Bellenger, *The French Exiled Clergy*, 126.
40. Sutherland, *France 1789–1815*, 370–1; Hufton, *Bayeux*, 280–1.
41. Delacroix, *La réorganisation de l'Eglise*, v.
42. G. Cholvy, 'Les Peuples de France entre religion et révolution', *Religion et Révolution*, ed. J. Martin, 11–24, at 21.
43. Cousin, Cubells, Moulinas, *La Pique et la croix*. 275–6; Desan, *Reclaiming the Sacred*, 221.

Conclusion.   The First Empire and Beyond

1. André Latreille. *Le Catéchisme Impériale de 1806. Etude et documents pour servir à l'histoire des rapports de Napoléon et du clergé concordataire* (Paris, 1935).
2. B. Plongeron, 'Vers un Premier Ralliement: Jean-Baptiste Duvoisin (1744–1813), théologian de la Sorbonne et premier évêque concordataire de Nantes', in B. Plongeron (ed.), *Catholiques entre Monarchie et République: Monsieur Freffel et son Temps* [Colloque de l'Université de l'Ouest] (1995), 147–65; Hélène Colombani, *Le Cardinal Fesch* (Paris, 1979).
3. C. Langlois, 'Portalis', *Dictionnaire Napoléon* (Paris, 1987), ed. Jean Tulard, 1365.
4. Crook, *Toulon in War and Revolution*, 201.
5. R. Durand, *Le Départment des Côtes-du-Nord sous le Consulat et l'Empire (1800–1815)* (2 vols, Paris, 1926), I, 365–486, quoted in Michael Broers, *Europe under Napoleon 1799–1815* (London 1996), 185.
6. M. Vovelle, 'C'est la faute à la Révolution', in (eds) Le Goff and Rémond, *Histoire de la France religieuse*, III.266.
7. Jean Godel, *La Reconstruction concordataire dans le diocèse de Grenoble après la Révolution (1802–1809)* (Grenoble, 1968), 246–80. In Angers in 1802, 10 per cent of priests were under forty whereas 20 to 25 per cent were over sixty. Quéniart, *Le Clergé déchiré*, 127.
8. Cholvy and Hilaire (eds), *Histoire religieuse de la France contemporaine*, I, 27; Langlois, 'Le Serment de 1791', 172.
9. On age structures see P. Genevray, *L'Administration et la vie ecclésiastique dans le grand diocèse de Toulouse pendant les dernières années de l'Empire et sous la Restauration* (Paris, 1941), 35; A. Poitrineau, *Histoire du diocèse de Clermont* (Paris, 1979), 221.
10. Pierre Pierrard, *La Vie quotidienne du prêtre fraçais aux XIXe siècle 1801–1905* (Paris, 1986); vital for clerical ministry after the Concordat.
11. Cholvy and Hilaire, *Histoire religieuse de la France contemporaine*, 17, 36–7.
12. Godechot, 'La Révolution française et les Juifs', 70.
13. Cholvy and Hilaire, *Histoire religieuse de la France contemporaine*, 17, 36.
14. Simon Schwarzfuchs, *Napoleon, the Jews and the Great Sanhedrin* (London, 1979); Bernhard Blumenkranz (ed.), *Le Grand Sanhédrin de Napoléon* (Paris, 1979); Charles Touati, 'Le Grand Sanhédrin de 1807 et la droit rabbinique', *A.H.R.F.*, 51 (1979), 27–48.

15. Desan, *Reclaiming the Sacred*, 102.
16. Quoted in Lebrun (ed.), *Histoire des Catholiques en France*, 265.
17. Pérouas, *Les Limousins*, 185–9.
18. Parents were willing to wait longer between the births of their children and families of 10 and more offspring became a rarity. J. Dupâquier and M. Lachiver, 'Sur les débuts de la contraception en France', *Ann. E.S.C.*, 24 (1969); E. Le Roy Ladurie, 'Démographie et "funestes secrets": le Languedoc, fin 18e-début 19e siècle', *A.H.R.F.*, 37 (1965) 385–400; J. Flandrin, *Les Amours paysannes, XVIe-XIXe siècles* (Paris, 1975). See Chapters 2 and 4 above.
19. Pérouas and Hollander, *La Revolution française: une rupture dans le Christianisme?*
20. Hufton, *Women and the Limits of Citizenship*, 103, 108, 126.
21. ed. Lebrun, *Histoire des Catholiques en France*, 285.
22. Martine Segalen, *Love and Power in the Peasant Family. Rural France in the Nineteenth Century*, trans. Sarah Matthews, (Oxford, 1983), 148–9.
23. See Crook, *Toulon in war and revolution*, 201.
24. Hufton, *The Reconstruction of a Church 1796–1801*, 25.
25. Cholvy, *Histoire du Vivarais*, 181.
26. Vovelle, *Recherches sur la Révolution*, 188–9.
27. Judith Devlin, *The Superstitious Mind*, 181.
28. Tackett, *Religion, Revolution, and Regional Culture*, 299. For the longer term impact of the Civil Constitution see also Claude Langlois, 'Le Serment de 1791 et la pratique religieuse des catholiques aux dix-neuvième et vingtième siècles', in *Proceedings of the eleventh annual meeting of the Western Society for French History* (Lawrence, KA, 1984), 166–76; 'Le serment révolutionnaire; archaisme et modernité', *Religion et Révolution*, ed. J. Martin (Paris, 1994).
29. Graphically shown in Claude Langlois, *Le Diocèse de Vannes au XIXe siècle, 1800–1830* (Paris, 1974).
30. *Matériaux pour l'Histoire religieuse du peuple française* (2 vols, Paris, 1982–6); Roger Magraw, 'Popular anticlericalism in nineteenth-century rural France', in Jim Obelkevich, Lyndal Roper, Raphael Samuel (eds), *Disciplines of Faith. Studies in Religion, Politics and Patriarchy* (London, 1987), 351–70.
31. Chaline, Lagrée and Chassagne, *L'Église de France et la Révolution*, 13, 41, 50–2, 59–60, 86.
32. Details in Broers, *Europe Under Napoleon*, 56, 109–14, who argues that 'the reforms of the Concordat ran counter to the deepest values of the common popular culture of Catholic Europe', 113.
33. For details see André Latreille, *Napoléon et le Saint-Siège 1801–8; l'ambassade du Cardinal Fesch à Rome* (Paris, 1935).
34. Broers, *Europe Under Napoleon*, 222.
35. Franco-papal relations from 1804–14 are still best traced in E.E.Y. Hales, *Napoleon and the Pope: The Story of Napoleon and Pius VII* (London, 1962).
36. Cholvy and Hilaire, *Histoire religieuse de la France contemporaine*, 17, 39.
37. E. Sevrin, *Les Missions religieuses en France sous la Restauration* (2 vols, Paris, 1959).
38. Gerard Gengembre, *La Contre-Révolution ou l'histoire déséspérante* (Paris, 1989), 122. See also Richard Fargher, 'Religious Reactions in Post-Revolutionary French Literature: Chateaubriand, Constant, Mme de Staël, Joseph de Maistre', in Aston, *Religious Change in Europe 1650–1914*, 258–64.
39. The best modern introduction to de Maistre is Richard A. Lebrun, *Joseph de Maistre, an intellectual militant* (Kingston, Ont., 1988), to Bonald, David Klinck, *The French Counter-Revolutionary Theorist Louis de Bonald (1754–1840)* (New York, 1996). The essay by P. Davies, 'Providence, Saviour Figures and Would-be Gods: Prophecy and the French Extreme Right', in Bertrand Taithe and Tim

Thornton (eds), *Prophecy. The Power of Inspired Language in History 1300–2000* (Stroud, 1997), 181–202, opens up the perspective.

40. Quoted in Tackett, *Religion, Revolution, and Regional Culture*, 177.
41. Cf. James F. McMillan, 'Religion and Gender in Modern France: Some Reflections', in Frank Tallett and Nicholas Atkin (eds), *Religion, Society and Politics in France Since 1789* (London, 1991), 55–66 at 58–9.

Bibliography

This is a selection of some leading books and articles written in English dealing with aspects of French religious history and culture in the period 1780–1804. It is intended merely to furnish readers of this book with a starting point for further study. A more comprehensive range of materials is referred to in the chapter notes.

————

Adams, Geoffrey, *The Huguenots and French Opinion 1685–1787. The Enlightenment Debate on Toleration* (Waterloo, Ontario, 1991).

Aston, Nigel, 'Survival Against the Odds? The French Bishops Elected to the Estates-General, 1789', *Historical Journal* 32 (1989), 607–26.

Aston, Nigel, *The End of an Élite. The French Bishops and the Coming of the Revolution 1786–1790* (Oxford, 1992).

Baker, Keith Michael, *Inventing the French Revolution* (Cambridge, 1990).

Bien, David D., *The Calas Affair. Persecution. Toleration, and Heresy in Eighteenth-Century Toulouse* (Princeton, 1960).

Bonnel, Roland G., 'Ecclesiological Insights at the 1790 National Assembly. An Assessment of the Contribution of Catholic Thought to the French Revolution', in Troyansky, David G., Cismari, Alfred, and Andrews, Jr., Norwood (eds), *The French Revolution in Culture and Society* (New York, 1991), 45–56.

Brockliss, Laurence, *French Higher Education in the Seventeenth and Eighteenth Centuries* (Oxford, 1987).

Chadwick, Owen, *The Popes and European Revolution* (Oxford, 1981).

Chartier, Roger, *The Cultural Origins of the French Revolution* (trans. Lydia Cochrane) (Durham, NC, 1991).

Conisbee, Philip, *Painting in Eighteenth Century France* (London, 1981).

Crook, Malcolm, *Toulon in War and Revolution. From the ancien régime to the Restoration, 1750–1820* (Manchester, 1991).

Daniel-Rops, H., *The Church in an Age of Revolution, 1789–1870*, trans. John Warrington (London, 1965).

Darnton, Robert, *The Great Cat Massacre and other episodes in French Cultural History* (New York, 1984).

Darnton, Robert, *The Forbidden Best-Sellers of Pre-Revolutionary France* (London, 1996).

Desan, Suzanne, 'Redefining Revolutionary Liberty. The Rhetoric of Religious Revival during the French Revolution', *Journal of Modern History*, 60 (1988), 1–27, at 12–13.

Desan, Suzanne, *Reclaiming the Sacred. Lay religion and popular politics in Revolutionary France* (Cornell, 1990).

Egret, Jean, *The French Pre-Revolution. 1787–1788*, trans. Camp, Wesley D. (Chicago, 1977).

Farge, Arlette, *Subversive Words. Public Opinion in Eighteenth-Century France*, trans. Rosemary Morris (Oxford, 1994).

Forrest, Alan, *The Revolution in Provincial France. Aquitaine, 1789–1799* (Oxford, 1996).

Garrioch, David, *Neighbourhood and community in Paris. 1740–1790* (Paris, 1986).

Gibson, Ralph, *A Social History of French Catholicism 1789–1914* (London, 1989).

Graham, Ruth, 'The Revolutionary Bishops and the *Philosophes*', *Eighteenth Century Studies*, 16 (1982–3), 117–40.

Graham, Ruth, 'Women versus Clergy, Women pro Clergy', in Spencer, Samia I. (ed.), *French Women and the Age of Enlightenment* (Bloomington, Ind., 1984) 128–40.

Greenbaum, L.S., *Tallevrand, Statesman Priest: The Agent General of the Clergy of the Church of France and the end of the Old Regime* (Washington, DC, 1970).

Grimsley, Ronald, *Rousseau and the Religious Quest* (London, 1968).

Hales, E.E.Y., *Revolution and the Papacy* (1960).

Hales, E.E.Y., *Napoleon and the Pope* (London, 1962).

Hampson, Norman, 'The Enlightenment in France', in Porter, Roy and Teich, M. (eds), *The Enlightenment in National Context* (Cambridge, 1981), 41–53.

Hampson, Norman, *Prelude to Terror. The Constituent Assembly and the Failure of Consensus* (Oxford, 1988).

Hufton, Olwen, *Bayeux in the late eighteenth century. A Social Study* (Oxford, 1967).

Hufton, Olwen, 'The French Church', in Callahan, W.J., and Higgs, D. (eds), *Church and Society in Catholic Europe of the Eighteenth Century* (Cambridge, 1979), 13–33.

Hufton, Olwen, 'The Reconstruction of a Church, 1796–1801', in G. Lewis and C. Lucas (eds), *Beyond the Terror: Essays in French Regional and Social History. 1794–1815* (Cambridge, 1983), 21–52.

Hufton, Olwen, *Women and the Limits of Citizenship in the French Revolution* [The Donald G. Creighton Lectures, 1989] (Toronto, 1992).

Hufton, Olwen and Tallett, F., 'Communities of Women, the Religious Life, and Public Service in Eighteenth-Century France', in Boxer, M.J., and Quaetaert, J.H. (eds) *Connecting Spheres: Women in the Western World. 1500 to the Present* (Oxford, 1987), 75–85.

Hutt, M., 'The Curés and the Third Estate: the ideas of Reform in the pamphlets of the French Lower Clergy in the period 1787–89', *Journal of Ecclesiastical History*, 8 (1957), 74–92.

Jones, P.M., *Reform and Revolution in France. The Politics of Transition. 1774–1791* (Cambridge, 1995).

Kates, Gary, 'Jews into Frenchmen: Nationality and Representation in Revolutionary France', in Fehér, Ferenc (ed.), *The French Revolution and the Birth of Modernity* (Berkeley, 1990), 103–16.

Le Goff, T.J.A., and Sutherland, D.M.G., 'Religion and Rural Revolt in the French Revolution: An Overview', in Bak, János M., and Benecke, Gerhard (eds), *Religion and Rural Revolt* (Manchester, 1984).

Lewis, G., *The Second Vendée: The Continuity of Counter-Revolution in the Department of the Gard 1789–1815* (Oxford, 1978).

Livesey, James, 'The Sovereign as God? Theophilanthropy and the Politics of the Directory 1795–99', in Devlin, Judith and Fleming, Ronan (eds) 'Religion and Rebellion', *Historical Studies*, 20 (Dublin, 1997), 75–96.

Lucas, Colin, Presentation on 'The Revolution and Christianity', in Furet, François, and Ozouf, Mona (eds) *The French Revolution and the Creation of Modern Political Culture. Vol. 3. The Transformation of Political Culture 1789–1848* (Oxford, 1989), 343–50.

McDonald, Joan, *Rousseau and the French Revolution 1762–91* (London, 1961).

McMahon, Darrin M., 'The Counter-Enlightenment and the Low-Life of Literature in Pre-Revolutionary France', *Past and Present*, 159 (1998), 77–112.

McManners, John, *French Ecclesiastical Society under the Ancien Regime. A Study of Angers in the Eighteenth Century* (Manchester, 1960).

McManners, John, *'Popular Religion' in seventeenth and eighteenth-century France. A New Theme in French Historiography* [John Coffin Memorial Lecture, 1982] (London, 1982).

McManners, John, 'Tithe in Eighteenth-Century France: a Focus for Rural Anticlericalism', in Beales, Derek, and Best, Geoffrey (eds), *History, Society and the Churches. Essays in Honour of Owen Chadwick* (Cambridge, 1985), 147–68.

McManners, John, *Death and the Enlightenment. Changing Attitudes to Death in Eighteenth-Century France* (Oxford, 1985 ed.).

McManners, John, 'Authority in Church and State. Reflections on the Coronation of Louis XVI', in *Christian Authority. Essays in Honour of Henry Chadwick* (Oxford, 1988).

Malino, Frances, *The Sephardic Jews of Bordeaux: Assimilation and Emancipation in Revolutionary and Napoleonic France* (Alabama, 1978).

Merrick, Jeffrey W., *The Desacralization of the French Monarchy in the Eighteenth Century* (Baton Rouge, 1990).

Miller, David C., 'A.-G. Camus and the Civil Constitution of the Clergy', *Catholic Historical Review*, 76 (1990), 481–505.

Necheles, R.F., 'The Constitutional Church, 1794–1802: An Essay in Voluntarism', in *Proceedings of the Consortium on Revolutionary Europe* (1974), 80–90.

Palmer, R.R., *Catholics and Unbelievers in Eighteenth-Century France* (Princeton, 1939).

Po-Chia Hsia, R., *The World of Catholic Renewal 1540–1770* (Cambridge, 1998).

Poland, Burdette C., *French Protestantism and the French Revolution. A Study in Church and State Thought and Religion, 1685–1815* (Princeton, 1957).

Ravitch, Norman, *Sword and Mitre: Government and Episcopate in France and England in the Age of Aristocracy* (The Hague/Paris, 1966).

Roberts, J.M., 'The Origins of a Mythology: Freemasons, Protestants and the French Revolution', *Bulletin of the Institute of Historical Research*, xliv (1971), 78–97.

Singham, Shanti Marie, 'Between Cattle and Men', in Van Kley, Dale (ed.), *The French Idea of Freedom. The Old Regime and the Declaration of Rights of 1789* (Stanford, 1994), 114–53.

Szajkowski, Zosa, *Jews and the French Revolutions of 1789, 1830 and 1848* (New York, 1970).

Tackett, Timothy, *Priest and People in Eighteenth-Century France: A Social and Political Study of the Curés in a Diocese of Dauphiné* (Princeton, 1977).

Tackett, Timothy, 'The Social History of the Diocesan Clergy in Eighteenth-Century France', in Golden, R.M. (ed.), *Church, State and Society under the Bourbon Kings of France* (Lawrence, Kan., 1982), 327–79.

Tackett, Timothy, 'The West in France in 1789', *Journal of Modern History*, 54 (1982), 715–45.

Tackett, Timothy, *Religion, Revolution and Regional Culture in Eighteenth-Century France: The Ecclesiastical Oath of 1791* (Princeton, 1986).

Tackett, Timothy, *Becoming a Revolutionary. The Deputies of the French National Assemby and the Emergence of a Revolutionary Culture (1789–1790)*, (Princeton, 1996).

Van Kley, Dale K., *The Jansenists and the Expulsion of the Jesuits from France: 1757–1765* (New Haven/London, 1975).

Van Kley, Dale K., *The Damiens Affair and the Unraveling of the Ancien Regime, 1750–1770* (Princeton, 1984).

Van Kley, Dale K., 'The Estates General as Ecumenical Council: The Constitutionalism of Corporate Consensus and the *Parlement's* Ruling of September 25, 1788', *Journal of Modern History*, 61 (1989), 1–52.

Van Kley, Dale K., 'The Religious Origins of the Patriot and Ministerial Parties in Pre-Revolutionary France', in Kselman, Thomas (ed.), *Belief in History: Innovative Approaches to European and American Religion* (Ind., 1991), 237–66.

Van Kley, Dale K., *The Religious Origins of the French Revolution. From Calvin to the Civil Constituition, 1560–1791* (New Haven, 1996).

Vovelle, Michel, *The Revolution Against the Church. From Reason to the Supreme Being*, trans. José, Alan, (Oxford, 1991).

Weber, William, 'Learned and General Musical Taste in Eighteenth-Century France', *Past and Present*, 89 (1980), 58–85.

Williams, William H., 'The Significance of Jansenism in the History (of the French Catholic Clergy in the Pre-Revolutionary Era', *Studies in XVIIIth century Culture*, ed. Roseann Puntz, vol. 7 (Wisconsin, 1978), 289–306.

Index